FOURIER SERIES AND BOUNDARY VALUE PROBLEMS

Brown and Churchill Series

Complex Variables and Applications, 8th Edition
Fourier Series and Boundary Value Problems, 8th Edition

The Walter Rudin Student Series in Advanced Mathematics

Bóna, Miklós: *Introduction to Enumerative Combinatorics*
Chartrand, Gary and Ping Zhang: *Introduction to Graph Theory*
Davis, Sheldon: *Topology*
Rudin, Walter: *Principles of Mathematical Analysis*
Rudin, Walter: *Real and Complex Analysis*

Other McGraw-Hill Titles in Higher Mathematics

Ahlfors, Lars: *Complex Analysis*
Burton, David M.: *Elementary Number Theory*
Burton, David M.: *The History of Mathematics: An Introduction*
Hvidsten, Michael: *Geometry with Geometry Explorer*

FOURIER SERIES AND BOUNDARY VALUE PROBLEMS

Eighth Edition

James Ward Brown

Professor of Mathematics
The University of Michigan–Dearborn

Ruel V. Churchill

Late Professor of Mathematics
The University of Michigan

The McGraw·Hill Companies

FOURIER SERIES AND BOUNDARY VALUE PROBLEMS, EIGHT EDITION
International Edition 2012

10   09   08   07   06   05   04   03   02   01
20   15   14   13   12   11
CTF   SEP

When ordering this title, use ISBN: 978-007-108615-8 or MHID: 007-108615-3
100646 9654
Printed in Singapore

www.mhhe.com

ABOUT THE AUTHORS

JAMES WARD BROWN is Professor of Mathematics at The University of Michigan–Dearborn. He earned his A.B. in physics from Harvard University and his A.M. and Ph.D. in mathematics from The University of Michigan in Ann Arbor, where he was an Institute of Science and Technology Predoctoral Fellow. He is coauthor with Dr. Churchill of *Complex Variables and Applications,* now in its eighth edition. He has received a research grant from the National Science Foundation as well as a Distinguished Faculty Award from the Michigan Association of Governing Boards of Colleges and Universities. Dr. Brown is listed in *Who's Who in the World*.

RUEL V. CHURCHILL was, at the time of his death in 1987, Professor Emeritus of Mathematics at The University of Michigan, where he began teaching in 1922. He received his B.S. in physics from the University of Chicago and his M.S. in physics and Ph.D. in mathematics from The University of Michigan. He was coauthor with Dr. Brown of *Complex Variables and Applications,* a classic text that he first wrote over 60 years ago. He was also the author of *Operational Mathematics*. Dr. Churchill held various offices in the Mathematical Association of America and in other mathematical societies and councils.

ABOUT THE AUTHORS

JAMES WARD BROWN is Professor of Mathematics at The University of Michigan–Dearborn. He earned his A.B. in physics from Harvard University and his A.M. and Ph.D. in mathematics from The University of Michigan in Ann Arbor, where he was an Institute of Science and Technology Predoctoral Fellow. He is coauthor with Dr. Churchill of Complex Variables and Applications, now in its eighth edition. He has received a research grant from the National Science Foundation as well as a Distinguished Faculty Award from the Michigan Association of Governing Boards of Colleges and Universities. Dr. Brown is listed in Who's Who in the World.

RUEL V. CHURCHILL was, at the time of his death in 1987, Professor Emeritus of Mathematics at The University of Michigan, where he began teaching in 1922. He received his B.S. in physics from the University of Chicago and his M.S. in physics and Ph.D. in mathematics from The University of Michigan. He was coauthor with Dr. Brown of Complex Variables and Applications, a classic text that he first wrote over fifty years ago. He was also the author of Operational Mathematics. Dr. Churchill held various offices in the Mathematical Association of America and in other mathematical societies and councils.

To the Memory of My Father,
George H. Brown,

and of My Long-Time Friend and Coauthor,
Ruel V. Churchill.

These Distinguished Men of Science for Years Influenced
The Careers of Many People, Including Mine.
J.W.B.

Joseph Fourier

JOSEPH FOURIER

JEAN BAPTISTE JOSEPH FOURIER   was born in Auxerre, about 100 miles south of Paris, on March 21, 1768. His fame is based on his mathematical theory of heat conduction, a theory involving expansions of arbitrary functions in certain types of trigonometric series. Although such expansions had been investigated earlier, they bear his name because of his major contributions. Fourier series are now fundamental tools in science, and this book is an introduction to their theory and applications.

Fourier's life was varied and difficult at times. Orphaned by the age of 9, he became interested in mathematics at a military school run by the Benedictines in Auxerre. He was an active supporter of the Revolution and narrowly escaped imprisonment and execution on more than one occasion. After the Revolution, Fourier accompanied Napoleon to Egypt in order to set up an educational institution in the newly conquered territory. Shortly after the French withdrew in 1801, Napoleon appointed Fourier prefect of a department in southern France with headquarters in Grenoble.

It was in Grenoble that Fourier did his most important scientific work. Since his professional life was almost equally divided between politics and science and since it was intimately geared to the Revolution and Napoleon, his advancement of the frontiers of mathematical science is quite remarkable.

The final years of Fourier's life were spent in Paris, where he was Secretary of the Académie des Sciences and succeeded Laplace as President of the Council of the Ecole Polytechnique. He died at the age of 62 on May 16, 1830.

CONTENTS

Appendixes   377

Index   389

PREFACE

This is an introductory treatment of Fourier series and their applications to boundary value problems in partial differential equations of engineering and physics. It is designed for students who have completed a first course in ordinary differential equations. In order that the book be accessible to as great a variety of readers as possible, there are footnotes to texts which give proofs of the more delicate results in advanced calculus that are occasionally needed. The physical applications, explained in some detail, are kept on a fairly elementary level.

The *first objective* of the book is to introduce the concept of orthonormal sets of functions and representations of arbitrary functions by series of functions from such sets. Representations of functions by Fourier series, involving sine and cosine functions, are given special attention. Fourier integral representations and expansions in series of Bessel functions and Legendre polynomials are also treated.

The *second objective* is a clear presentation of the classical method of separation of variables used in solving boundary value problems with the aid of those representations. In the final chapter, some attention is given to the verification of solutions and to their uniqueness, since the method cannot be presented properly without such considerations.

This book is a revision of its seventh edition, the first two of which were written by Professor Churchill alone. While improvements appearing in earlier revisions have been retained here, the entire book has been thoroughly rewritten. Some of the changes in this edition are mentioned below.

The regular Sturm-Liouville problems leading to Fourier cosine and sine series are treated by themselves in a separate section, and the same is true of the singular problems leading to Fourier cosine and sine integrals. It seemed that there were too many distractions when the solutions of those eigenvalue problems were obtained in the sections devoted mainly to illustrations of the method of separation of variables. A number of topics have been brought out of the problem sets and presented in their own sections, because of their special interest and importance. Examples of this are the Gibbs' phenomenon and the Poisson integral formula, together with the Sturm-Liouville problem involving periodic boundary conditions needed to obtain that formula. Another example is the derivation of a reduction formula to be used in evaluating integrals appearing in the coefficients of various Fourier-Bessel series.

Many other changes in this edition were suggested by readers who have spoken or written to me. Duhamel's principle, for instance, is discussed more thoroughly, and there are more physical problems using it later on. The chapter on Bessel functions now begins with a separate section on the gamma function in order to make the presentation of Bessel functions more efficient. Also, the Fourier-Bessel series found in this book are now listed in an appendix. While notation can vary from author to author, I have chosen to follow the classic text by Bartle that is listed in the Bibliography by changing to his notation for one-sided derivatives but keeping our notation in defining one-sided limits. Finally, it should be mentioned that problem sets appear even more frequently than in the last edition, in order to focus more directly on the material just introduced.

A *Student's Solutions Manual* (ISBN: 978-007-745415-9; MHID 007-745415-4) is available. It contains solutions to selected problems throughout the book.

This and earlier editions have benefited from the continued interest of friends, including current and former students. The late Ralph P. Boas, Jr., furnished the reference to Kronecker's extension of the method of integration by parts, and the derivation of the laplacian in cylindrical and spherical coordinates was suggested by a note of R. P. Agnew's in the *American Mathematical Monthly*, vol. 60, 1953. Finally, the most important source of support and encouragement was the staff at McGraw-Hill and my wife, Jacqueline Read Brown.

James Ward Brown

CHAPTER

1

FOURIER SERIES

This book is concerned with two general topics:

(*i*) one is the representation of a given function by an infinite series involving a prescribed set of functions;

(*ii*) the other is a method of solving boundary value problems in partial differential equations, with emphasis on equations that are prominent in physics and engineering.

Representations by series are encountered in solving such boundary value problems. The theories of those representations can be presented independently. They have such attractive features as the extension of concepts of geometry, vector analysis, and algebra into the field of mathematical analysis. Their mathematical precision is also pleasing. But they gain in unity and interest when presented in connection with boundary value problems.

The set of functions that make up the terms in the series representation is determined by the boundary value problem. Representations by Fourier series, which are certain types of series of sine and cosine functions, are associated with a large and important class of boundary value problems. We shall give special attention to the theory and application of Fourier series and their generalizations. But we shall also consider various related representations, concentrating on those involving so-called Fourier integrals and what are known as Fourier-Bessel and Legendre series.

In this chapter, we begin our discussion of Fourier series. Once the convergence of such series has been established (Chap. 2) and a variety of partial differential equations have been derived (Chap. 3), we shall see (Chaps. 4 and 5) how such series are used in what is often referred to as the Fourier method for solving boundary value problems.

The first section here is devoted to a description of a class of functions that is central to the theory of Fourier series.

1. PIECEWISE CONTINUOUS FUNCTIONS

If the values $f(x)$ of a function f approach some finite number as x approaches x_0 from the right, the *right-hand limit* of f is said to exist at x_0 and is denoted by $f(x_0+)$. Thus

$$\lim_{\substack{x \to x_0 \\ x > x_0}} f(x) = f(x_0+).$$

The *left-hand limit* is similarly defined, so that

$$\lim_{\substack{x \to x_0 \\ x < x_0}} f(x) = f(x_0-).$$

EXAMPLE 1. Let the function f be defined for all nonzero x by means of the equations (see Fig. 1)

$$f(x) = \begin{cases} -x & \text{when } x < 0, \\ x + 1 & \text{when } x > 0. \end{cases}$$

Observe that the usual limit as x tends to zero does not exist. But

$$\lim_{\substack{x \to 0 \\ x > 0}} f(x) = f(0+) = 1$$

and

$$\lim_{\substack{x \to 0 \\ x < 0}} f(x) = f(0-) = 0.$$

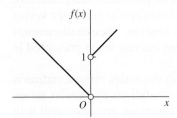

FIGURE 1

Let a function f be continuous at all points of a bounded open interval $a < x < b$ except possibly for a finite set of points $x_1, x_2, \ldots, x_{n-1}$, where

$$a < x_1 < x_2 < \cdots < x_{n-1} < b.$$

If we write $x_0 = a$ and $x_n = b$, then f is continuous on each of the n open subintervals

(1) $$x_0 < x < x_1, \quad x_1 < x < x_2, \quad \ldots, \quad x_{n-1} < x < x_n.$$

It is not necessarily continuous, or even defined, at their endpoints. But if in each of those subintervals, f has finite limits as x approaches the endpoints from the interior, f is said to be *piecewise continuous* on the interval $a < x < b$. More precisely, the one-sided limits

$$(2) \quad f(x_{k-1} +) = \lim_{\substack{x \to x_{k-1} \\ x > x_{k-1}}} f(x) \quad \text{and} \quad f(x_k -) = \lim_{\substack{x \to x_k \\ x < x_k}} f(x) \qquad (k = 1, 2, \ldots, n)$$

are required to exist.

Note that if the limiting values from the interior of a subinterval are assigned to f at the endpoints, then f is continuous on the *closed* subinterval. Since any function that is continuous on a closed bounded interval is bounded, it follows that f is bounded on the entire interval $a \leq x \leq b$. That is, there exists a nonnegative number M such that $|f(x)| \leq M$ for all points x $(a \leq x \leq b)$ at which f is defined.

EXAMPLE 2. Consider the function f that has the values

$$f(x) = \begin{cases} x & \text{when } 0 < x < 1, \\ -1 & \text{when } 1 \leq x < 2, \\ 1 & \text{when } 2 < x < 3, \end{cases}$$

and $f(3) = 0$. (See Fig. 2.) Although f is discontinuous at the points $x = 1$ and $x = 2$ in the interval $0 < x < 3$, it is nevertheless piecewise continuous on that interval. This is because the one-sided limits from the interior exist at the endpoints of each of the three open subintervals on which f is continuous. Note, for instance, that the right-hand limit at $x = 0$ is $f(0 +) = 0$ and that the left-hand limit at $x = 1$ is $f(1 -) = 1$.

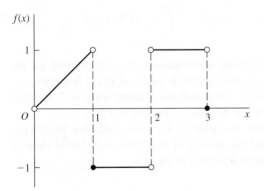

FIGURE 2

A function is piecewise continuous on an interval $a < x < b$ if it is continuous on the *closed* interval $a \leq x \leq b$. Continuity on the *open* interval $a < x < b$ does not, however, imply piecewise continuity there, as Example 3 illustrates.

EXAMPLE 3. The function $f(x) = 1/x$ is continuous on the interval $0 < x < 1$, but it is not piecewise continuous there since $f(0 +)$ fails to exist.

When a function f is piecewise continuous on an interval $a < x < b$, the integral of $f(x)$ from $x = a$ to $x = b$ always exists. It is the sum of the integrals of $f(x)$ over the open subintervals (1) on which f is continuous:

$$(3) \qquad \int_a^b f(x)\,dx = \int_a^{x_1} f(x)\,dx + \int_{x_1}^{x_2} f(x)\,dx + \cdots + \int_{x_{n-1}}^b f(x)\,dx.$$

The first integral on the right exists since it is defined as the integral over the interval $a \le x \le x_1$ of the continuous function whose values are $f(x)$ when $a < x < x_1$ and whose values at the endpoints $x = a$ and $x = x_1$ are $f(a+)$ and $f(x_1 -)$, respectively. The remaining integrals on the right in equation (3) are similarly defined and therefore exist.

EXAMPLE 4. If f is the function in Example 2 and Fig. 2, then

$$\int_0^3 f(x)\,dx = \int_0^1 x\,dx + \int_1^2 (-1)\,dx + \int_2^3 1\,dx = \frac{1}{2} - 1 + 1 = \frac{1}{2}.$$

Observe that the value of the integral of $f(x)$ over each subinterval is unaffected by the values of f at the endpoints. The function is, in fact, not even defined at $x = 0$ and $x = 2$.

If two functions f_1 and f_2 are each piecewise continuous on an interval $a < x < b$, then there is a finite subdivision of the interval such that *both* functions are continuous on each closed subinterval when the functions are given their limiting values from the interior at the endpoints. Hence linear combinations $c_1 f_1 + c_2 f_2$ and products $f_1 f_2$ have that continuity on each subinterval and are themselves piecewise continuous on the interval $a < x < b$. The integrals

$$\int_a^b [c_1 f_1(x) + c_2 f_2(x)]\,dx \qquad \text{and} \qquad \int_a^b f_1(x) f_2(x)\,dx$$

must then exist.

We refer to the class of all piecewise continuous functions defined on an interval $a < x < b$ as a *function space* and denote it by $C_p(a, b)$. It is analogous to three-dimensional space, where linear combinations of vectors are well defined vectors in that space. The analogy will be developed further in Chap. 7.

In this book we shall restrict our attention to functions that are piecewise continuous on bounded intervals; and the notion of piecewise continuity clearly applies regardless of whether the interval is open or closed.

2. FOURIER COSINE SERIES

Let f be any function in $C_p(0, \pi)$ and assume for the moment that $f(x)$ has a *Fourier cosine series* representation

$$(1) \qquad f(x) = \frac{a_0}{2} + \sum_{n=1}^{\infty} a_n \cos nx \qquad\qquad (0 < x < \pi),$$

where a_0 and a_n ($n = 1, 2, \ldots$) are constants. To find these constants, we also assume that series (1) and any related series that arises can be integrated term by term.

The constant a_0 is easily found by integrating each side of equation (1) from 0 to π and writing

$$\int_0^\pi f(x)\,dx = \frac{a_0}{2}\int_0^\pi dx + \sum_{n=1}^\infty a_n \int_0^\pi \cos nx\,dx,$$

or

$$\int_0^\pi f(x)\,dx = \frac{a_0}{2}[x]_0^\pi + \sum_{n=1}^\infty a_n \left[\frac{\sin nx}{n}\right]_0^\pi.$$

Inasmuch as $\sin n\pi = 0$ when n is an integer, this shows that

(2)
$$a_0 = \frac{2}{\pi}\int_0^\pi f(x)\,dx.$$

To find a_n ($n = 1, 2, \ldots$), we write equation (1) as

$$f(x) = \frac{a_0}{2} + \sum_{m=1}^\infty a_m \cos mx \qquad\qquad (0 < x < \pi),$$

with a new index of summation, and then multiply each side by $\cos nx$, where n is any fixed positive integer. Integration of the resulting equation from 0 to π yields

$$\int_0^\pi f(x)\cos nx\,dx = \frac{a_0}{2}\int_0^\pi \cos nx\,dx + \sum_{m=1}^\infty a_m \int_0^\pi \cos mx \cos nx\,dx.$$

But

$$\int_0^\pi \cos nx\,dx = 0$$

and (Problem 8, Sec. 5)

$$\int_0^\pi \cos mx \cos nx\,dx = \begin{cases} 0 & \text{when } m \neq n, \\ \pi/2 & \text{when } m = n. \end{cases}$$

Hence

$$\int_0^\pi f(x)\cos nx\,dx = a_n \frac{\pi}{2},$$

or

(3)
$$a_n = \frac{2}{\pi}\int_0^\pi f(x)\cos nx\,dx \qquad\qquad (n = 1, 2, \ldots).$$

Note that expression (2) for a_0 can be included with expression (3) when the integer n is allowed to run from $n = 0$, rather than from $n = 1$. This is the reason that $a_0/2$ was used instead of a_0 in series (1). Note, too, that $a_0/2$ is the mean, or average, value of $f(x)$ over the interval $0 < x < \pi$.

Because we cannot be certain at this time that representation (1) is actually valid for a specific f, we write

(4)
$$f(x) \sim \frac{a_0}{2} + \sum_{n=1}^\infty a_n \cos nx \qquad\qquad (0 < x < \pi),$$

where the tilde symbol $\sim$ merely denotes correspondence. Observe that correspondence (4), with coefficients (2) and (3), can be written more compactly as

$$(5) \qquad f(x) \sim \frac{1}{\pi} \int_0^\pi f(s)\, ds + \frac{2}{\pi} \sum_{n=1}^\infty \cos nx \int_0^\pi f(s) \cos ns\, ds,$$

where s is used for the variable of integration in order to distinguish it from the free variable x.

The fact that f is piecewise continuous on the interval $0 < x < \pi$ ensures the existence of the integrals in expressions (2) and (3) for the coefficients in a cosine series. We shall, in Chap. 2, establish further conditions on f under which series (4) converges to $f(x)$ when $0 < x < \pi$, in which case correspondence (4) becomes an equality.

A Fourier cosine series that represents a function $f(x)$ on the closed interval $0 \le x \le \pi$ also represents a function outside that interval, as described just below.

(*i*) If series (4) converges to $f(x)$ for all x in the interval $0 \le x \le \pi$, it also converges to the *even periodic extension, with period* 2π, of f on the entire x axis. That is, it converges to a function $F(x)$ having the properties

$$F(x) = f(x) \qquad\qquad\qquad \text{when } 0 \le x \le \pi$$

and

$$F(-x) = F(x), \qquad F(x + 2\pi) = F(x) \qquad\qquad \text{for all } x.$$

The reason for this is that each term in series (4) is itself even and periodic with period 2π. The graph of the extension $y = F(x)$ is obtained by reflecting the graph of $y = f(x)$ in the y axis, to give a graph for the interval $-\pi \le x \le \pi$, and then repeating that graph on the intervals $\pi \le x \le 3\pi$, $3\pi \le x \le 5\pi$, etc., as well as on the intervals $-3\pi \le x \le -\pi$, $-5\pi \le x \le -3\pi$, etc.

(*ii*) It follows from the observations in (*i*) that if one is given a function f that is both even and periodic with period 2π, then the cosine series corresponding to $f(x)$ on the interval $0 < x < \pi$ represents $f(x)$ for all x when that series converges to it on the interval $0 \le x \le \pi$. Clearly, a cosine series cannot represent a function $f(x)$ for all x if $f(x)$ is not both even and periodic with period 2π.

3. EXAMPLES

Examples 1 and 2 here illustrate the material in Sec. 2.

EXAMPLE 1. Let us find the coefficients in the Fourier cosine series correspondence

$$(1) \qquad\qquad\qquad f(x) \sim \frac{a_0}{2} + \sum_{n=1}^\infty a_n \cos nx \qquad\qquad (0 < x < \pi)$$

when $f(x) = x$ $(0 < x < \pi)$. It is easy to see that

$$a_0 = \frac{2}{\pi} \int_0^\pi x \, dx = \pi;$$

and, using integration by parts, we find that

$$a_n = \frac{2}{\pi} \int_0^\pi x \cos nx \, dx = \frac{2}{\pi} \left\{ \left[\frac{x \sin nx}{n} \right]_0^\pi - \frac{1}{n} \int_0^\pi \sin nx \, dx \right\} \quad (n = 1, 2, \ldots).$$

Since

$$\sin n\pi = 0 \quad \text{and} \quad \cos n\pi = (-1)^n$$

when n is an integer, this reduces to

$$a_n = \frac{2}{\pi} \cdot \frac{(-1)^n - 1}{n^2} \quad\quad (n = 1, 2, \ldots).$$

Note that a_0 needed to be found separately in order to avoid division by zero.

For the function $f(x)$ here, correspondence (1) evidently becomes

(2) $$x \sim \frac{\pi}{2} + \frac{2}{\pi} \sum_{n=1}^\infty \frac{(-1)^n - 1}{n^2} \cos nx \quad\quad (0 < x < \pi).$$

Since $(-1)^n - 1 = 0$ when n is even, series (2) can be written more efficiently by summing only the terms that occur when n is odd. This is accomplished by replacing n by $2n - 1$ wherever it appears after the summation symbol and noting that $(-1)^{2n-1} = -1$. The result is

(3) $$x \sim \frac{\pi}{2} - \frac{4}{\pi} \sum_{n=1}^\infty \frac{\cos(2n - 1)x}{(2n - 1)^2} \quad\quad (0 < x < \pi).$$

Conditions in Chap. 2 will ensure that correspondence (3) is actually an equality when $0 \le x \le \pi$. The even periodic extension to which the series converges is shown in Fig. 3, which tells us that

(4) $$|x| = \frac{\pi}{2} - \frac{4}{\pi} \sum_{n=1}^\infty \frac{\cos(2n - 1)x}{(2n - 1)^2} \quad\quad (-\pi \le x \le \pi).$$

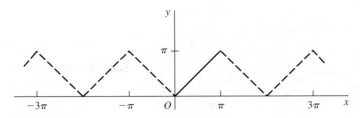

FIGURE 3

EXAMPLE 2. In this example, we shall find the Fourier cosine series for the function $f(x) = \sin x$ on the interval $0 < x < \pi$. The trigonometric identity

$$2\sin A \cos B = \sin(A + B) + \sin(A - B)$$

enables us to write

$$a_n = \frac{2}{\pi} \int_0^\pi \sin x \cos nx \, dx$$

$$= \frac{1}{\pi} \int_0^\pi [\sin(1 + n)x + \sin(1 - n)x] \, dx \qquad (n = 0, 1, 2, \ldots).$$

Hence, when $n \neq 1$,

$$a_n = \frac{1}{\pi}\left[-\frac{\cos(1 + n)x}{1 + n} - \frac{\cos(1 - n)x}{1 - n}\right]_0^\pi = \frac{2}{\pi} \cdot \frac{1 + (-1)^n}{1 - n^2};$$

and when $n = 1$, the coefficient is

$$a_1 = \frac{1}{\pi} \int_0^\pi \sin 2x \, dx = \left[-\frac{\cos 2x}{2}\right]_0^\pi = 0.$$

The desired cosine series correspondence is, then,

$$(5) \qquad \sin x \sim \frac{2}{\pi} + \frac{2}{\pi} \sum_{n=2}^\infty \frac{1 + (-1)^n}{1 - n^2} \cos nx \qquad (0 < x < \pi).$$

Note that $1 + (-1)^n = 0$ when n is *odd* (compare with Example 1). To sum the terms occurring when n is even, we replace n by $2n$ in this correspondence, observe that $1 + (-1)^{2n} = 2$, and write

$$(6) \qquad \sin x \sim \frac{2}{\pi} - \frac{4}{\pi} \sum_{n=1}^\infty \frac{\cos 2nx}{4n^2 - 1} \qquad (0 < x < \pi).$$

The function $\sin x$ will, in fact, satisfy conditions in Chap. 2 ensuring that the correspondence here is an equality for each value of x in the interval $0 \leq x \leq \pi$. Thus, at each point on the x axis, the series converges to the even periodic extension, with period 2π, of $\sin x$ ($0 \leq x \leq \pi$). That extension, shown in Fig. 4, is the function $y = |\sin x|$.

FIGURE 4

4. FOURIER SINE SERIES

We assume here that when f is in $C_p(0, \pi)$, there is a *Fourier sine series* representation

$$(1) \qquad\qquad f(x) = \sum_{n=1}^{\infty} b_n \sin nx \qquad\qquad (0 < x < \pi),$$

where the coefficients b_n ($n = 1, 2, \ldots$) are constants. The b_n can be found in a way similar to that used in Sec. 2 to find the coefficients in a cosine series. This time we write

$$f(x) = \sum_{m=1}^{\infty} b_m \sin mx \qquad\qquad (0 < x < \pi)$$

and multiply each side by $\sin nx$, where n is any fixed positive integer. Assuming that term-by-term integration is valid, we find that

$$(2) \qquad\qquad \int_0^{\pi} f(x) \sin nx \, dx = \sum_{m=1}^{\infty} b_m \int_0^{\pi} \sin mx \sin nx \, dx.$$

Then, because (Problem 9, Sec. 5)

$$\int_0^{\pi} \sin mx \sin nx \, dx = \begin{cases} 0 & \text{when } m \neq n, \\ \pi/2 & \text{when } m = n, \end{cases}$$

equation (2) reduces to

$$\int_0^{\pi} f(x) \sin nx \, dx = b_n \frac{\pi}{2}.$$

That is,

$$(3) \qquad\qquad b_n = \frac{2}{\pi} \int_0^{\pi} f(x) \sin nx \, dx \qquad\qquad (n = 1, 2, \ldots).$$

Inasmuch as we have only *assumed* the validity of representation (1), we use the tilde symbol $\sim$, as we did in Sec. 2, to denote correspondence:

$$(4) \qquad\qquad f(x) \sim \sum_{n=1}^{\infty} b_n \sin nx \qquad\qquad (0 < x < \pi).$$

Expression (3) can, of course, be used to put this correspondence in the form

$$(5) \qquad\qquad f(x) \sim \frac{2}{\pi} \sum_{n=1}^{\infty} \sin nx \int_0^{\pi} f(s) \sin ns \, ds.$$

The piecewise continuity of f ensures the existence of integrals (3). Further conditions that are given in Chap. 2 will also ensure that correspondence (4) is, in fact, an equality when $0 < x < \pi$.

The following remarks, similar to ones in Sec. 2 regarding the convergence of cosine series, can be made here.

(*i*) Suppose that f is defined on the open interval $0 < x < \pi$ and that series (4) converges to $f(x)$ there. Since series (4) clearly converges to zero when $x = 0$

and when $x = \pi$, it converges to $f(x)$ for all x in the closed interval $0 \le x \le \pi$ if f is assigned the values $f(0) = 0$ and $f(\pi) = 0$. It then converges to the *odd periodic extension, with period* 2π, of f for all values of x. This time, the extension is the function $F(x)$ defined by means of the equations

$$F(x) = f(x) \qquad\qquad \text{when } 0 \le x \le \pi$$

and

$$F(-x) = -F(x), \qquad F(x + 2\pi) = F(x) \qquad\qquad \text{for all } x.$$

The extension F is odd and periodic with period 2π since each term in series (4) has those properties. The graph of $y = F(x)$ is symmetric with respect to the origin and can be obtained by first reflecting the graph of $y = f(x)$ in the y axis, then reflecting the result in the x axis, and finally repeating the graph found for the interval $-\pi \le x \le \pi$ every 2π units along the entire x axis.

(*ii*) A Fourier sine series on the interval $0 < x < \pi$ can also be used to represent a given function that is defined for all x and is both odd and periodic with period 2π, provided that the representation is valid when $0 \le x \le \pi$.

5.   EXAMPLES

We now illustrate some methods for finding Fourier sine series.

EXAMPLE 1. For the sine series corresponding to the function $f(x) = x$ on the interval $0 < x < \pi$ (Fig. 5), we refer to expression (3), Sec. 4, and use integration by parts to write

$$b_n = \frac{2}{\pi} \int_0^\pi x \sin nx \, dx = \frac{2}{\pi} \left\{ \left[-\frac{x \cos nx}{n} \right]_0^\pi + \frac{1}{n} \int_0^\pi \cos nx \, dx \right\} = 2 \frac{(-1)^{n+1}}{n}$$

$$(n = 1, 2, \ldots).$$

Thus

$$(1) \qquad\qquad x \sim 2 \sum_{n=1}^{\infty} \frac{(-1)^{n+1}}{n} \sin nx \qquad\qquad (0 < x < \pi).$$

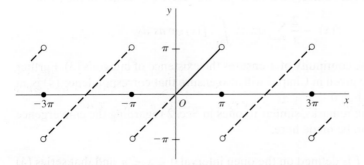

FIGURE 5

Our theory will show that this series converges to $f(x)$ when $0 < x < \pi$. Hence it converges to the odd periodic function $y = F(x)$ that is graphed in Fig. 5. The fact that the series converges to zero when $x = 0, \pm\pi, \pm3\pi, \pm5\pi, \ldots$ is in agreement with the theory in Chap. 2, which will tell us that it must converge to the mean value of the one-sided limits (Sec. 1) of $F(x)$ at each of those points.

In the evaluation of integrals representing Fourier coefficients, it is sometimes necessary to apply integration by parts more than once. We now give an example in which this can be accomplished by means of a single formula due to L. Kronecker (1823–1891). We preface the example with a statement of that formula.[†]

Let $p(x)$ be a polynomial of degree m, and suppose that $f(x)$ is continuous. Then, except for an arbitrary additive constant,

$$(2) \qquad \int p(x) f(x) \, dx = pF_1 - p'F_2 + p''F_3 - \cdots + (-1)^m p^{(m)} F_{m+1}$$

where p is successively differentiated until it becomes zero, where F_1 denotes an indefinite integral of f, where F_2 is an indefinite integral of F_1, etc., and where alternating signs are affixed to the terms. Note that the differentiation of p begins with the *second* term, whereas the integration of f begins with the *first* term. The formula, which is readily verified (Problem 7) by differentiating its right-hand side to obtain $p(x) f(x)$, could even have been used to evaluate the integral in Example 1, where only one integration by parts was needed.

EXAMPLE 2. To illustrate the advantage of formula (2) when successive integration by parts is required, let us find the Fourier sine series for the function $f(x) = x^3$ on the interval $0 < x < \pi$. With the aid of that formula, we may write

$$b_n = \frac{2}{\pi} \int_0^\pi x^3 \sin nx \, dx$$

$$= \frac{2}{\pi} \left[(x^3) \left(-\frac{\cos nx}{n} \right) - (3x^2) \left(-\frac{\sin nx}{n^2} \right) + (6x) \left(\frac{\cos nx}{n^3} \right) - (6) \left(\frac{\sin nx}{n^4} \right) \right]_0^\pi$$

$$= 2 (-1)^{n+1} \frac{(n\pi)^2 - 6}{n^3} \qquad\qquad (n = 1, 2, \ldots).$$

Hence

$$(3) \qquad\qquad x^3 \sim 2 \sum_{n=1}^{\infty} (-1)^{n+1} \frac{(n\pi)^2 - 6}{n^3} \sin nx \qquad\qquad (0 < x < \pi).$$

As was the case in Example 1, the series converges to the given function on the interval $0 < x < \pi$. Since x^3 is an odd function whose value is zero when $x = 0$, this series represents x^3 on the larger interval $-\pi < x < \pi$ too.

[†]Kronecker actually treated the problem more extensively in papers that originally appeared in the *Berlin Sitzungsberichte* (1885, 1889).

We conclude this section by pointing out a computational aid that is useful in finding the coefficients b_n $(n = 1, 2, \ldots)$ in the Fourier sine series for a linear combination $c_1 f_1(x) + c_2 f_2(x)$ of two functions $f_1(x)$ and $f_2(x)$ whose sine series are already known. Namely, since the expression

$$b_n = \frac{2}{\pi} \int_0^\pi [c_1 f_1(x) + c_2 f_2(x)] \sin nx \, dx$$

can be written

$$b_n = c_1 \left[\frac{2}{\pi} \int_0^\pi f_1(x) \sin nx \, dx \right] + c_2 \left[\frac{2}{\pi} \int_0^\pi f_2(x) \sin nx \, dx \right],$$

it is clear that each b_n is simply the same linear combination of the nth coefficients in the sine series for the individual functions $f_1(x)$ and $f_2(x)$. Such an observation applies as well in finding coefficients in cosine and other types of series encountered in this and later chapters.

EXAMPLE 3. In view of the sine series for x and x^3 found in Examples 1 and 2, respectively, the coefficients b_n in the sine series corresponding to the function

$$f(x) = x(\pi^2 - x^2) = \pi^2 x - x^3 \qquad (0 < x < \pi)$$

are

$$b_n = \pi^2 \left[2 \frac{(-1)^{n+1}}{n} \right] - \left[2(-1)^{n+1} \frac{(n\pi)^2 - 6}{n^3} \right] = 12 \frac{(-1)^{n+1}}{n^3} \qquad (n = 1, 2, \ldots).$$

Thus

$$(4) \qquad\qquad x(\pi^2 - x^2) \sim 12 \sum_{n=1}^{\infty} \frac{(-1)^{n+1}}{n^3} \sin nx \qquad (0 < x < \pi).$$

PROBLEMS

For each of the functions f in Problems 1 through 3, find (a) the Fourier cosine series; (b) the Fourier sine series on the interval $0 < x < \pi$.

1. $f(x) = 1$ $\quad (0 < x < \pi)$.

   Answers: (a) 1; (b) $\displaystyle\sum_{n=1}^{\infty} \frac{2[1 - (-1)^n]}{n\pi} \sin nx = \frac{4}{\pi} \sum_{n=1}^{\infty} \frac{\sin(2n - 1)x}{2n - 1}$.

2. $f(x) = \pi - x$ $\quad (0 < x < \pi)$.

   Answers: (a) $\displaystyle\frac{\pi}{2} + \frac{4}{\pi} \sum_{n=1}^{\infty} \frac{\cos(2n - 1)x}{(2n - 1)^2}$; (b) $\displaystyle 2 \sum_{n=1}^{\infty} \frac{\sin nx}{n}$.

3. $f(x) = x^2$ $\quad (0 < x < \pi)$.

   Answers: (a) $\displaystyle\frac{\pi^2}{3} + 4 \sum_{n=1}^{\infty} \frac{(-1)^n}{n^2} \cos nx$;

   (b) $\displaystyle 2\pi^2 \sum_{n=1}^{\infty} \left[\frac{(-1)^{n+1}}{n\pi} - 2 \frac{1 - (-1)^n}{(n\pi)^3} \right] \sin nx$.

4. Find the Fourier cosine series on the interval $0 < x < \pi$ that corresponds to the function f defined by means of the equations

$$f(x) = \begin{cases} 1 & \text{when} \quad 0 < x < \dfrac{\pi}{2}, \\ 0 & \text{when} \quad \dfrac{\pi}{2} < x < \pi. \end{cases}$$

Suggestion: Note that

$$a_n = \frac{2}{\pi} \int_0^{\pi/2} \cos nx \, dx \qquad\qquad (n = 0, 1, 2, \ldots)$$

and that

$$\sin \frac{(2n-1)\pi}{2} = \sin n\pi \cos \frac{\pi}{2} - \cos n\pi \sin \frac{\pi}{2} = (-1)^{n+1} \qquad (n = 1, 2, \ldots).$$

Answer: $\dfrac{1}{2} + \dfrac{2}{\pi} \displaystyle\sum_{n=1}^{\infty} \frac{(-1)^{n+1}}{2n-1} \cos(2n-1)x.$

5. By referring to the sine series for x in Example 1, Sec. 5, and the one found for x^2 in Problem 3(*b*) above, show that

$$x(\pi - x) \sim \frac{8}{\pi} \sum_{n=1}^{\infty} \frac{\sin(2n-1)x}{(2n-1)^3} \qquad (0 < x < \pi).$$

6. Show that

$$x^4 \sim \frac{\pi^4}{5} + 8 \sum_{n=1}^{\infty} (-1)^n \frac{(n\pi)^2 - 6}{n^4} \cos nx \qquad (0 < x < \pi).$$

Given that this correspondence is actually an equality when $0 \le x \le \pi$, sketch the function represented by the series for all x.

7. Verify Kronecker's formula (2), Sec. 5, by differentiating its right-hand side and using the product rule to obtain

$$(pF_1' + p'F_1) - (p'F_2' + p''F_2) + (p''F_3' + p'''F_3) - \cdots + (-1)^m \left(p^{(m)} F_{m+1}' + p^{(m+1)} F_{m+1} \right),$$

which telescopes to pf.

8. Use the trigonometric identity

$$2 \cos A \cos B = \cos(A - B) + \cos(A + B)$$

to show that

$$\int_0^{\pi} \cos mx \cos nx \, dx = \begin{cases} 0 & \text{when} \;\; m \neq n, \\ \pi/2 & \text{when} \;\; m = n, \end{cases}$$

where m and n are positive integers.

9. Use the trigonometric identity

$$2 \sin A \sin B = \cos(A - B) - \cos(A + B)$$

to show that

$$\int_0^{\pi} \sin mx \sin nx \, dx = \begin{cases} 0 & \text{when} \;\; m \neq n, \\ \pi/2 & \text{when} \;\; m = n, \end{cases}$$

where m and n are positive integers.

10. With the aid of the integration formula obtained in Problem 9, find the Fourier sine series corresponding to the function $f(x) = \sin x$ on the interval $0 < x < \pi$.

Answer: $\sin x$.

6. FOURIER SERIES

Consider a function f in $C_p(-\pi, \pi)$ and write

$$(1) \qquad f(x) = g(x) + h(x),$$

where

$$(2) \qquad g(x) = \frac{f(x) + f(-x)}{2} \quad \text{and} \quad h(x) = \frac{f(x) - f(-x)}{2}.$$

The function $g(x)$ is evidently *even*, and $h(x)$ is odd. That is,

$$g(-x) = g(x) \quad \text{and} \quad h(-x) = -h(x)$$

for each point x in the interval $-\pi < x < \pi$ at which these functions are defined. According to Secs. 2 and 4,

$$(3) \qquad g(x) \sim \frac{a_0}{2} + \sum_{n=1}^{\infty} a_n \cos nx \qquad (0 < x < \pi),$$

where

$$(4) \qquad a_n = \frac{2}{\pi} \int_0^{\pi} g(x) \cos nx \, dx \qquad (n = 0, 1, 2, \ldots),$$

and

$$(5) \qquad h(x) \sim \sum_{n=1}^{\infty} b_n \sin nx \qquad (0 < x < \pi),$$

where

$$(6) \qquad b_n = \frac{2}{\pi} \int_0^{\pi} h(x) \sin nx \, dx \qquad (n = 1, 2, \ldots).$$

When correspondence (3) is an equality that is valid for $0 < x < \pi$, it is also an equality on the interval $-\pi < x < 0$ since each side of the correspondence is an even function. A similar remark applies to correspondence (5) since each side there is an odd function. Because $f(x)$ is the sum of $g(x)$ and $h(x)$, this suggests that the correspondence

$$(7) \qquad f(x) \sim \frac{a_0}{2} + \sum_{n=1}^{\infty} (a_n \cos nx + b_n \sin nx) \qquad (-\pi < x < \pi)$$

may be an equality under certain circumstances.

In view of the first of equations (2), expression (4) for the coefficients a_n can be written

$$a_n = \frac{1}{\pi} \left[\int_0^{\pi} f(x) \cos nx \, dx + \int_0^{\pi} f(-s) \cos ns \, ds \right].$$

By making the substitution $x = -s$ in the second of these two integrals, we find that

$$a_n = \frac{1}{\pi} \left[\int_0^\pi f(x) \cos nx \, dx + \int_{-\pi}^0 f(x) \cos nx \, dx \right],$$

or

(8) $$a_n = \frac{1}{\pi} \int_{-\pi}^\pi f(x) \cos nx \, dx \qquad\qquad (n = 0, 1, 2, \ldots).$$

Likewise, the second of equations (2) enables us to write expression (6) for the b_n as

$$b_n = \frac{1}{\pi} \left[\int_0^\pi f(x) \sin nx \, dx - \int_0^\pi f(-s) \sin ns \, ds \right];$$

and the substitution $x = -s$ in the second integral here leads to

$$b_n = \frac{1}{\pi} \left[\int_0^\pi f(x) \sin nx \, dx + \int_{-\pi}^0 f(x) \sin nx \, dx \right].$$

Thus

(9) $$b_n = \frac{1}{\pi} \int_{-\pi}^\pi f(x) \sin nx \, dx \qquad\qquad (n = 1, 2, \ldots).$$

Correspondence (7), when combined with expressions (8) and (9) for the constants a_n and b_n, becomes

$$f(x) \sim \frac{1}{2\pi} \int_{-\pi}^\pi f(s) \, ds$$
$$+ \frac{1}{\pi} \sum_{n=1}^\infty \left[\cos nx \int_{-\pi}^\pi f(s) \cos ns \, ds + \sin nx \int_{-\pi}^\pi f(s) \sin ns \, ds \right].$$

The trigonometric identity

$$\cos(A - B) = \cos A \cos B + \sin A \sin B$$

then enables us to write this correspondence in the form

(10) $$f(x) \sim \frac{1}{2\pi} \int_{-\pi}^\pi f(s) \, ds + \frac{1}{\pi} \sum_{n=1}^\infty \int_{-\pi}^\pi f(s) \cos n(s - x) \, ds.$$

Note that the term

$$\frac{1}{2\pi} \int_{-\pi}^\pi f(s) \, ds$$

here, which is the same as the term $a_0/2$ in series (7), is the mean, or average, value of $f(x)$ over the interval $-\pi < x < \pi$.

The form (10) of correspondence (7) will be the starting point of the proof in Sec. 12 of a theorem ensuring the convergence of such a series to $f(x)$ on the interval $-\pi < x < \pi$.

Series (7), with coefficients (8) and (9), is the *Fourier series* corresponding to $f(x)$ on the interval $-\pi < x < \pi$. Suppose that the series converges to $f(x)$ when $-\pi < x < \pi$. Then, in view of the periodicity of its terms, it converges to a function $y = F(x)$ that coincides with $y = f(x)$ on $-\pi < x < \pi$ and whose graph there is repeated every 2π units along the x axis. The function F is, therefore, the *periodic extension, with period* 2π, of f. If, on the other hand, f is a given periodic function, with period 2π, series (7) represents $f(x)$ everywhere when it converges to $f(x)$ on the interval $-\pi \leq x \leq \pi$.

Finally, we note below how the Fourier series (7) is actually a Fourier cosine or sine series when $f(x)$ is even or odd, respectively.

(i) $f(x)$ is even: $f(-x) = f(x)$

If the given function f in $C_p(-\pi, \pi)$ is even on the interval $-\pi < x < \pi$, then

$$f(-x)\cos(-nx) = f(x)\cos nx \qquad\qquad\qquad (n = 0, 1, 2, \ldots)$$

and

$$f(-x)\sin(-nx) = -f(x)\sin nx \qquad\qquad\qquad (n = 1, 2, \ldots)$$

when $-\pi < x < \pi$; and we see that $f(x)\cos nx$ and $f(x)\sin nx$ are even and odd, respectively. Because the graph of $y = f(x)\cos nx$ is symmetric with respect to the y axis and the graph of $y = f(x)\sin nx$ is symmetric with respect to the origin, it follows that expressions (8) and (9) reduce to

$$a_n = \frac{2}{\pi} \int_0^\pi f(x)\cos nx\,dx \qquad\qquad\qquad (n = 0, 1, 2, \ldots)$$

and $b_n = 0\ (n = 1, 2, \ldots)$. Series (7) thus becomes a Fourier cosine series (Sec. 2) for $f(x)$ on the interval $0 < x < \pi$.

(ii) $f(x)$ is odd: $f(-x) = -f(x)$

If f is a function in $C_p(-\pi, \pi)$ that is odd on the interval $-\pi < x < \pi$, then

$$f(-x)\cos(-nx) = -f(x)\cos nx \qquad\qquad\qquad (n = 0, 1, 2, \ldots)$$

and

$$f(-x)\sin(-nx) = f(x)\sin nx \qquad\qquad\qquad (n = 1, 2, \ldots)$$

when $-\pi < x < \pi$. So the products $f(x)\cos nx$ and $f(x)\sin nx$ are odd and even, respectively. That is, the graph of $y = f(x)\cos nx$ is symmetric with respect to the origin and the graph of $y = f(x)\sin nx$ is symmetric with respect to the y axis. Consequently, expressions (8) and (9) reduce to $a_n = 0\ (n = 0, 1, 2, \ldots)$ and

$$b_n = \frac{2}{\pi} \int_0^\pi f(x)\sin nx\,dx \qquad\qquad\qquad (n = 1, 2, \ldots).$$

Hence series (7) is the same as the Fourier sine series (Sec. 4) for $f(x)$ on $0 < x < \pi$.

7. EXAMPLES

We include here some examples of Fourier series on the interval $-\pi < x < \pi$ that illustrate points made in Sec. 6.

EXAMPLE 1. Let us find the Fourier series corresponding to the function $f(x)$ that is defined on the fundamental interval $-\pi < x < \pi$ as follows:

$$(1) \qquad f(x) = \begin{cases} 0 & \text{when } -\pi < x \le 0, \\ x & \text{when } 0 < x < \pi. \end{cases}$$

The graph of $y = f(x)$ is indicated by the bold line segments in Fig. 6 that are solid.

FIGURE 6

According to expression (8), Sec. 6,

$$a_n = \frac{1}{\pi} \left(\int_{-\pi}^{0} 0 \cos nx \, dx + \int_{0}^{\pi} x \cos nx \, dx \right) = \frac{1}{\pi} \int_{0}^{\pi} x \cos nx \, dx$$

$$(n = 0, 1, 2, \ldots).$$

By applying integration by parts, or Kronecker's method (Sec. 5), one can show that

$$a_n = \frac{(-1)^n - 1}{\pi n^2}$$

when $n = 1, 2, \ldots$. In order to avoid division by zero, we must evaluate the integral for a_0 separately:

$$a_0 = \frac{1}{\pi} \int_{0}^{\pi} x \, dx = \frac{\pi}{2}.$$

Expression (9), Sec. 6, tells us that

$$b_n = \frac{1}{\pi} \left(\int_{-\pi}^{0} 0 \sin nx \, dx + \int_{0}^{\pi} x \sin nx \, dx \right) = \frac{1}{\pi} \int_{0}^{\pi} x \sin nx \, dx = \frac{(-1)^{n+1}}{n}$$

for all positive integers $n = 1, 2, \ldots$. Hence, on the interval $-\pi < x < \pi$,

$$(2) \qquad f(x) \sim \frac{\pi}{4} + \sum_{n=1}^{\infty} \left[\frac{(-1)^n - 1}{\pi n^2} \cos nx + \frac{(-1)^{n+1}}{n} \sin nx \right].$$

This series will be shown (Sec. 14) to converge to $f(x)$ on the fundamental interval, as well as to the periodic extension $F(x)$ that is indicated in Fig. 6, where the graph of $y = F(x)$ is sketched. As in Example 1, Sec. 5, the series must converge to the mean value of the one-sided limits of the periodic extension at each of the discontinuities $x = \pm\pi, \pm 3\pi, \pm 5\pi, \ldots$. Here those mean values are all $\pi/2$.

EXAMPLE 2. Since the function

$$f_1(x) = |x| \qquad\qquad (-\pi < x < \pi)$$

is even and since $|x| = x$ when $0 < x < \pi$, the Fourier series for $f_1(x)$ on $-\pi < x < \pi$ is the same as the Fourier cosine series (2), Sec. 3, for x:

(3) $\qquad f_1(x) = |x| \sim \dfrac{\pi}{2} + \dfrac{2}{\pi} \displaystyle\sum_{n=1}^{\infty} \dfrac{(-1)^n - 1}{n^2} \cos nx \qquad (-\pi < x < \pi).$

[See also equation (4) in Sec. 3.] On the other hand, the function

$$f_2(x) = x \qquad\qquad (-\pi < x < \pi)$$

is odd, and so its Fourier series on $-\pi < x < \pi$ is the Fourier sine series (1) in Sec. 5:

(4) $\qquad f_2(x) = x \sim 2 \displaystyle\sum_{n=1}^{\infty} \dfrac{(-1)^{n+1}}{n} \sin nx \qquad (-\pi < x < \pi).$

Note how the sum of series (3) and (4) provides us with the Fourier series corresponding to this function:

$$f(x) = \frac{f_1(x) + f_2(x)}{2} = \frac{|x| + x}{2} = \begin{cases} 0 & \text{when } -\pi < x \le 0, \\ x & \text{when } 0 < x < \pi. \end{cases}$$

That is,

$$f(x) \sim \frac{\pi}{4} + \sum_{n=1}^{\infty} \left[\frac{(-1)^n - 1}{\pi n^2} \cos nx + \frac{(-1)^{n+1}}{n} \sin nx \right] \qquad (-\pi < x < \pi).$$

This is, of course, the correspondence just found in Example 1.

EXAMPLE 3. The function $f(x) = |\sin x| \, (-\pi < x < \pi)$ is even. Hence the Fourier series corresponding to $f(x)$ on the interval $-\pi < x < \pi$ is actually the cosine series for the function

$$f(x) = |\sin x| = \sin x \qquad\qquad (0 < x < \pi).$$

That series has already been found in Example 2, Sec. 3; and, by referring to correspondence (6) there, we see that

(5) $\qquad |\sin x| \sim \dfrac{2}{\pi} - \dfrac{4}{\pi} \displaystyle\sum_{n=1}^{\infty} \dfrac{\cos 2nx}{4n^2 - 1} \qquad (-\pi < x < \pi).$

PROBLEMS

Find the Fourier series on the interval $-\pi < x < \pi$ that corresponds to each of the functions in Problems 1 through 6.

1. $f(x) = \begin{cases} -\pi/2 & \text{when } -\pi < x < 0, \\ \pi/2 & \text{when } 0 < x < \pi. \end{cases}$

$\qquad$ *Answer:* $2 \displaystyle\sum_{n=1}^{\infty} \dfrac{\sin(2n-1)x}{2n-1}.$

2. $f(x)$ is the function whose graph consists of the two bold line segments shown in Fig. 7.

$$\textit{Answer: } \frac{3}{2} + 2\sum_{n=1}^{\infty}\left[\frac{1-(-1)^n}{(n\pi)^2}\cos nx + \frac{(-1)^{n+1}}{n\pi}\sin nx\right].$$

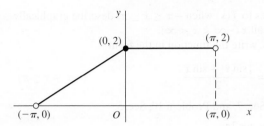

FIGURE 7

3. $f(x) = x + \frac{1}{4}x^2 \ (-\pi < x < \pi)$.

   Suggestion: Use the series for x in Example 2, Sec. 7, and the one for x^2 in Problem 3(a), Sec. 5.

$$\textit{Answer: } \frac{\pi^2}{12} + \sum_{n=1}^{\infty}(-1)^n\left(\frac{\cos nx}{n^2} - \frac{2\sin nx}{n}\right).$$

4. $f(x) = e^{ax} \ (-\pi < x < \pi)$, where $a \neq 0$.

   Suggestion: Use Euler's formula $e^{i\theta} = \cos\theta + i\sin\theta$, where $i = \sqrt{-1}$, to write

$$a_n + ib_n = \frac{1}{\pi}\int_{-\pi}^{\pi} f(x)e^{inx}\,dx \qquad (n = 1, 2, \ldots).$$

After evaluating this single integral, equate real parts and then imaginary parts.[†]

$$\textit{Answer: } \frac{\sinh a\pi}{a\pi} + \frac{2\sinh a\pi}{\pi}\sum_{n=1}^{\infty}\frac{(-1)^n}{a^2+n^2}(a\cos nx - n\sin nx).$$

5. $f(x) = \cosh ax \ (-\pi < x < \pi)$, where $a \neq 0$.

   Suggestion: Use the series found in Problem 4.

$$\textit{Answer: } \frac{\sinh a\pi}{a\pi}\left[1 + 2a^2\sum_{n=1}^{\infty}\frac{(-1)^n}{a^2+n^2}\cos nx\right].$$

6. $f(x) = \cos ax \ (-\pi < x < \pi)$, where $a \neq 0, \pm1, \pm2, \ldots$.

   Suggestion: With the aid of Euler's formula, stated in the suggestion with Problem 4, write

$$\cos ax = \frac{e^{iax} + e^{-iax}}{2}.$$

Then use the series already obtained in that earlier problem.

$$\textit{Answer: } \frac{2a\sin a\pi}{\pi}\left[\frac{1}{2a^2} + \sum_{n=1}^{\infty}\frac{(-1)^{n+1}}{n^2-a^2}\cos nx\right].$$

[†]For a justification of Euler's formula and background on complex variable methods, see the authors' book (2009), which is listed in the Bibliography.

7. Find the Fourier series on the interval $-\pi < x < \pi$ for the function f defined by means of the equations

$$f(x) = \begin{cases} 0 & \text{when } -\pi \leq x \leq 0, \\ \sin x & \text{when } 0 < x \leq \pi. \end{cases}$$

Then, given that the series converges to $f(x)$ when $-\pi \leq x \leq \pi$, describe graphically the function that is represented for all x $(-\infty < x < \infty)$.

Suggestion: To find the series, write the function in the form

$$f(x) = \frac{|\sin x| + \sin x}{2} \qquad (-\pi \leq x \leq \pi).$$

Then use the results in Example 3, Sec. 7, and Problem 10, Sec. 5.

Answer: $\dfrac{1}{\pi} + \dfrac{1}{2} \sin x - \dfrac{2}{\pi} \displaystyle\sum_{n=1}^{\infty} \dfrac{\cos 2nx}{4n^2 - 1}.$

8.   ADAPTATIONS TO OTHER INTERVALS

Let f denote a piecewise continuous function of x on an interval $-c < x < c$ of the x axis, and define the related function

$$(1) \qquad\qquad g(s) = f\left(\frac{cs}{\pi}\right) \qquad\qquad (-\pi < s < \pi)$$

of s. The Fourier series corresponding to this new function on the interval $-\pi < s < \pi$ is, according to Sec. 6,

$$(2) \qquad f\left(\frac{cs}{\pi}\right) \sim \frac{a_0}{2} + \sum_{n=1}^{\infty}(a_n \cos ns + b_n \sin ns) \qquad (-\pi < s < \pi)$$

where

$$(3) \qquad\qquad a_n = \frac{1}{\pi}\int_{-\pi}^{\pi} f\left(\frac{cs}{\pi}\right)\cos ns\, ds \qquad (n = 0, 1, 2, \ldots)$$

and

$$(4) \qquad\qquad b_n = \frac{1}{\pi}\int_{-\pi}^{\pi} f\left(\frac{cs}{\pi}\right)\sin ns\, ds \qquad (n = 1, 2, \ldots).$$

The function (1) is evidently also piecewise continuous, and we anticipate that correspondence (2) will become an equality when certain further conditions are imposed on f. Thus if we put

$$s = \frac{\pi x}{c}$$

in correspondence (2) and its conditions of validity, we arrive at the series

$$(5) \qquad f(x) \sim \frac{a_0}{2} + \sum_{n=1}^{\infty}\left(a_n \cos\frac{n\pi x}{c} + b_n \sin\frac{n\pi x}{c}\right) \qquad (-c < x < c).$$

The same substitution in expressions (3) and (4), moreover, enables us to write

$$(6) \qquad a_n = \frac{1}{c} \int_{-c}^{c} f(x) \cos \frac{n\pi x}{c} \, dx \qquad (n = 0, 1, 2, \ldots)$$

and

$$(7) \qquad b_n = \frac{1}{c} \int_{-c}^{c} f(x) \sin \frac{n\pi x}{c} \, dx \qquad (n = 1, 2, \ldots).$$

Series (5) is a Fourier series on the fundamental interval $-c < x < c$ and becomes series (7) in Sec. 6 when $c = \pi$. Conditions on f ensuring that correspondence (5) is, in fact, an equality at points where f is continuous will be given in Chap. 2. Note that if the series does converge to $f(x)$ when $-c < x < c$, the graph of $y = f(x)$ is repeated every $2c$ units along the x axis.

Arguments similar to those used above lead to Fourier cosine and sine series on $0 < x < c$:

$$(8) \qquad f(x) \sim \frac{a_0}{2} + \sum_{n=1}^{\infty} a_n \cos \frac{n\pi x}{c} \qquad (0 < x < c),$$

where

$$(9) \qquad a_n = \frac{2}{c} \int_{0}^{c} f(x) \cos \frac{n\pi x}{c} \, dx \qquad (n = 0, 1, 2, \ldots),$$

and

$$(10) \qquad f(x) \sim \sum_{n=1}^{\infty} b_n \sin \frac{n\pi x}{c} \qquad (0 < x < c),$$

where

$$(11) \qquad b_n = \frac{2}{c} \int_{0}^{c} f(x) \sin \frac{n\pi x}{c} \, dx \qquad (n = 1, 2, \ldots).$$

The convergence of series (8) and (10) is also treated in Chap. 2.

The following examples illustrate how Fourier series on intervals $-c < x < c$, as well as cosine and sine series on $0 < x < c$, can be obtained from known series on $-\pi < x < \pi$ and $0 < x < \pi$. Since we do not yet have theorems ensuring the convergence of Fourier series to the functions in question, we shall continue to use the tilde symbol $\sim$ to denote mere correspondence and not necessarily equality. Also, anticipating that the correspondences obtained will actually be equalities, we shall continue to include conditions of validity.

EXAMPLE 1. It is a simple matter to obtain the correspondence

$$(12) \qquad x^2 \sim \frac{c^2}{3} + \frac{4c^2}{\pi^2} \sum_{n=1}^{\infty} \frac{(-1)^n}{n^2} \cos \frac{n\pi x}{c} \qquad (0 < x < c)$$

from [Problem 3(a), Sec. 5]

$$(13) \qquad x^2 \sim \frac{\pi^2}{3} + 4 \sum_{n=1}^{\infty} \frac{(-1)^n}{n^2} \cos nx \qquad (0 < x < \pi).$$

We let x be any number in the interval $0 < x < c$ and note how it follows that

$$0 < \frac{\pi x}{c} < \pi.$$

Hence it is legitimate to replace x by $\pi x/c$ in correspondence (13) and its condition of validity:

$$(14) \qquad \frac{\pi^2 x^2}{c^2} \sim \frac{\pi^2}{3} + 4 \sum_{n=1}^{\infty} \frac{(-1)^n}{n^2} \cos \frac{n\pi x}{c} \qquad \left(0 < \frac{\pi x}{c} < \pi\right).$$

Then, multiplying each side by c^2/π^2 and multiplying through the new condition of validity by c/π, we arrive at correspondence (12).

Expression (9) could, of course, have been used to find the desired coefficients if correspondence (13) had not been available.

EXAMPLE 2. Let us find the Fourier series for e^x on the interval $-1 < x < 1$ using the known correspondence (Problem 4, Sec. 7)

$$(15) \quad e^{ax} \sim \frac{\sinh a\pi}{a\pi} + \frac{2 \sinh a\pi}{\pi} \sum_{n=1}^{\infty} \frac{(-1)^n}{a^2 + n^2} (a \cos nx - n \sin nx) \quad (-\pi < x < \pi),$$

where $a \neq 0$. Since

$$-\pi < \pi x < \pi \quad \text{when} \quad -1 < x < 1,$$

we can replace x by πx in correspondence (15) and write

$$e^{a\pi x} \sim \frac{\sinh a\pi}{a\pi} + \frac{2 \sinh a\pi}{\pi} \sum_{n=1}^{\infty} \frac{(-1)^n}{a^2 + n^2} (a \cos n\pi x - n \sin n\pi x),$$

which is valid when $-1 < x < 1$. Finally, by setting $a = 1/\pi$, we have the desired result:

$$(16) \quad e^x \sim \sinh 1 + 2 \sinh 1 \sum_{n=1}^{\infty} \frac{(-1)^n}{1 + (n\pi)^2} (\cos n\pi x - n\pi \sin n\pi x) \quad (-1 < x < 1).$$

As was the case with the series that was found in Example 1, this series could have been obtained using integral expressions that we have (Sec. 8) for the needed coefficients.

PROBLEMS

1. (*a*) Use the Fourier sine series in Example 1, Sec. 5, for

$$f(x) = x \qquad\qquad (0 < x < \pi)$$

to show that

$$x \sim \frac{2}{\pi} \sum_{n=1}^{\infty} \frac{(-1)^{n+1}}{n} \sin n\pi x \qquad\qquad (0 < x < 1).$$

(b) Obtain the correspondence in part (a) by using expression (11), Sec. 8, for the coefficients in a Fourier sine series on $0 < x < c$.

2. Show how it follows from the expansions obtained in Problem 1 and Example 1 in Sec. 8 that

$$x(1+x) \sim \frac{1}{3} + \frac{2}{\pi} \sum_{n=1}^{\infty} (-1)^n \left(\frac{2}{n^2 \pi} \cos n\pi x - \frac{1}{n} \sin n\pi x \right) \qquad (0 < x < 1).$$

3. Use the Fourier sine series found in Problem 3(b), Sec. 5, for

$$f(x) = x^2 \qquad (0 < x < \pi)$$

to obtain the correspondence

$$x^2 \sim 2c^2 \sum_{n=1}^{\infty} \left[\frac{(-1)^{n+1}}{n\pi} - 2 \frac{1 - (-1)^n}{(n\pi)^3} \right] \sin \frac{n\pi x}{c} \qquad (0 < x < c).$$

4. (a) Use the Fourier sine series correspondence found in Example 3, Sec. 5, for the function

$$f(x) = x(\pi^2 - x^2) \qquad (0 < x < \pi)$$

to establish the correspondence

$$x(1 - x^2) \sim \frac{12}{\pi^3} \sum_{n=1}^{\infty} \frac{(-1)^{n+1}}{n^3} \sin n\pi x \qquad (0 < x < 1).$$

(b) Replace x by $1 - x$ on each side of the correspondence in part (a) to show that

$$x(x - 1)(x - 2) \sim \frac{12}{\pi^3} \sum_{n=1}^{\infty} \frac{\sin n\pi x}{n^3} \qquad (0 < x < 1).$$

5. Show how it follows from the Fourier sine series obtained for

$$f(x) = x(\pi - x) \qquad (0 < x < \pi)$$

in Problem 5, Sec. 5, that

$$x(2c - x) \sim \frac{32c^2}{\pi^3} \sum_{n=1}^{\infty} \frac{1}{(2n-1)^3} \sin \frac{(2n-1)\pi x}{2c} \qquad (0 < x < 2c).$$

6. Use the method in Example 2, Sec. 8, to show that

$$e^x \sim \frac{\sinh c}{c} + 2 \sinh c \sum_{n=1}^{\infty} \frac{(-1)^n}{c^2 + (n\pi)^2} \left(c \cos \frac{n\pi x}{c} - n\pi \sin \frac{n\pi x}{c} \right) \qquad (-c < x < c).$$

7. By starting with the Fourier cosine series correspondence obtained for the function

$$f(x) = \pi - x \qquad (0 < x < \pi)$$

in Problem 2(a), Sec. 5, show that

$$\frac{c}{4} - x \sim \frac{2c}{\pi^2} \sum_{n=1}^{\infty} \frac{1}{(2n-1)^2} \cos \frac{(4n-2)\pi x}{c} \qquad \left(0 < x < \frac{c}{2} \right).$$

8. Use expression (11), Sec. 8, for the coefficients in a Fourier sine series on $0 < x < c$ to obtain the correspondence

$$\cos \pi x \sim \frac{8}{\pi} \sum_{n=1}^{\infty} \frac{n}{4n^2 - 1} \sin 2n\pi x \qquad (0 < x < 1).$$

Suggestion: To evaluate the integrals that arise, recall the trigonometric identity

$$2 \sin A \cos B = \sin(A + B) + \sin(A - B).$$

9. Show that in Sec. 8 the Fourier series (5), with coefficients (6) and (7), can be written in the compact form

$$\frac{1}{2c} \int_{-c}^{c} f(s)\, ds + \frac{1}{c} \sum_{n=1}^{\infty} \int_{-c}^{c} f(s) \cos\left[\frac{n\pi}{c}(s - x)\right] ds.$$

(See Sec. 6, where this form was obtained when $c = \pi$.)

CHAPTER
2

CONVERGENCE OF FOURIER SERIES

In this chapter, we shall establish conditions on a function $f(x)$, defined on the interval $-\pi < x < \pi$, that ensure a valid Fourier series representation. Corresponding results for Fourier cosine and sine series representations will follow readily. It will be a simple matter to extend the theory to Fourier series on arbitrary intervals $-c < x < c$, as well as to Fourier cosine and sine series on intervals $0 < x < c$. Some further aspects of the theory of convergence of Fourier series will be touched on later in the chapter.

9. ONE-SIDED DERIVATIVES

In developing sufficient conditions on a function f such that its Fourier series on the interval $-\pi < x < \pi$ converges to $f(x)$ there, we need to generalize the concept of the derivative

$$(1) \qquad f'(x_0) = \lim_{x \to x_0} \frac{f(x) - f(x_0)}{x - x_0}$$

of f at a point $x = x_0$.

Suppose that the right-hand limit $f(x_0 +)$ exists at x_0 (see Sec. 1). The *right-hand derivative* of f at x_0 is defined as follows:

$$(2) \qquad f'_+(x_0) = \lim_{\substack{x \to x_0 \\ x > x_0}} \frac{f(x) - f(x_0 +)}{x - x_0},$$

provided that the limit here exists. Note that although $f(x_0)$ need not exist, $f(x_0 +)$ must exist if $f'_+(x_0)$ does. When the ordinary, or two-sided, derivative $f'(x_0)$ exists, f is continuous at x_0 and $f'_+(x_0) = f'(x_0)$.

25

Similarly, if $f(x_0 -)$ exists, the *left-hand derivative* of f at x_0 is given by the equation

$$(3) \qquad f'_-(x_0) = \lim_{\substack{x \to x_0 \\ x < x_0}} \frac{f(x) - f(x_0 -)}{x - x_0}$$

when this limit exists; and if $f'(x_0)$ exists, $f'_-(x_0) = f'(x_0)$.

EXAMPLE 1. Let f denote the continuous function defined by means of the equations

$$f(x) = \begin{cases} x^2 & \text{when } x \leq 0, \\ \sin x & \text{when } x > 0. \end{cases}$$

With the aid of l'Hôpital's rule, we see that

$$f'_+(0) = \lim_{\substack{x \to 0 \\ x > 0}} \frac{\sin x}{x} = 1;$$

furthermore,

$$f'_-(0) = \lim_{\substack{x \to 0 \\ x < 0}} \frac{x^2}{x} = \lim_{\substack{x \to 0 \\ x < 0}} x = 0.$$

Since these one-sided derivatives have different values, the ordinary derivative $f'(0)$ cannot exist.

The ordinary derivative $f'(x_0)$ can fail to exist even when $f(x_0)$ is defined and $f'_+(x_0)$ and $f'_-(x_0)$ have a common value.

EXAMPLE 2. If f is the step function

$$f(x) = \begin{cases} 0 & \text{when } x < 0, \\ 1 & \text{when } x \geq 0, \end{cases}$$

then $f'_+(0) = f'_-(0) = 0$. But the derivative $f'(0)$ does not exist since f is not continuous at $x = 0$.

As is the case with ordinary derivatives, the mere continuity of f at a point x_0 does not ensure the existence of either *one-sided* derivative there.

EXAMPLE 3. The function $f(x) = \sqrt{x}\,(x \geq 0)$ has no right-hand derivative at the point $x = 0$, although it is continuous there.

A number of properties of ordinary derivatives remain valid for one-sided derivatives. Suppose, for instance, that the right-hand derivatives of two functions f and g exist at a point x_0. Let us find the right-hand derivative of the product

$$(fg)(x) = f(x)g(x)$$

at x_0. Since the difference quotient

$$\frac{(fg)(x) - (fg)(x_0 +)}{x - x_0} = \frac{f(x)g(x) - f(x_0 +)g(x_0 +)}{x - x_0}$$

can be written

$$f(x)\frac{g(x) - g(x_0 +)}{x - x_0} + \frac{f(x) - f(x_0 +)}{x - x_0}g(x_0 +),$$

it follows that

$$(fg)'_+(x_0) = f(x_0 +)g'_+(x_0) + f'_+(x_0)g(x_0 +).$$

Likewise, if $f'_-(x_0)$ and $g'_-(x_0)$ exist, the left-hand derivative of the product $(fg)(x)$ exists at x_0.

Finally, we turn to a property of one-sided derivatives that is particularly important in the theory of convergence of Fourier series. It concerns the subspace $C'_p(a, b)$ of $C_p(a, b)$ consisting of all piecewise continuous functions f on an interval $a < x < b$ whose derivatives f' are also piecewise continuous on that interval. Such a function is said to be *piecewise smooth* because, over the subintervals on which both f and f' are continuous, any tangents to the graph of $y = f(x)$ that turn do so continuously.

Theorem. *If a function f is piecewise smooth on an interval $a < x < b$, then at each point x_0 in the closed interval $a \leq x \leq b$ the one-sided derivatives of f, from the interior at the endpoints, exist and are the same as the corresponding one-sided limits of f':*

(4) $f'_+(x_0) = f'(x_0 +),$ $f'_-(x_0) = f'(x_0 -).$

To prove this, we assume for the moment that f and f' are actually continuous on the interval $a < x < b$ and that the one-sided limits of f and f' from the interior exist at the endpoints $x = a$ and $x = b$. If x_0 is a point in that open interval, $f'(x_0)$ exists. Hence $f'_+(x_0)$ and $f'_-(x_0)$ exist, and both are equal to $f'(x_0)$. Because f' is continuous at x_0, then, equations (4) hold.

The following argument shows how it is also true that $f'_+(a)$ exists and is equal to $f'(a +)$. If we let s denote any number in the interval $a < x < b$ and define $f(a)$ to be $f(a +)$, then f is continuous on the closed interval $a \leq x \leq s$ (Fig. 8). Since f' exists in the open interval $a < x < s$, the mean value theorem

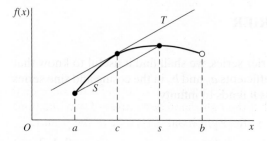

FIGURE 8

for derivatives applies. That is, there is a number c, where $a < c < s$, such that

$$(5) \qquad \frac{f(s) - f(a+)}{s - a} = f'(c).$$

This is shown geometrically in Fig. 8, where the slopes of the secant line S and the tangent line T are the same. Letting s, and therefore c, tend to a in equation (5), we see that since $f'(a+)$ exists, the limit of $f'(c)$ exists and has that value. Consequently, the limit of the difference quotient on the left in equation (5) exists, its value being $f'_+(a)$. Thus $f'_+(a) = f'(a+)$. Similarly, $f'_-(b) = f'(b-)$.

Now any piecewise smooth function f is continuous, along with its derivative f', on a finite number of subintervals at whose endpoints the one-sided limits of f and f' from the interior exist. If the results of the two preceding paragraphs are applied to each of those subintervals, the theorem is established.

Example 4 illustrates the distinction between one-sided derivatives and one-sided limits of derivatives.

EXAMPLE 4. Consider the function f whose values are

$$f(x) = \begin{cases} x^2 \sin(1/x) & \text{when } x \neq 0, \\ 0 & \text{when } x = 0. \end{cases}$$

Since $0 \leq |x^2 \sin(1/x)| \leq x^2$ when $x \neq 0$, both one-sided limits $f(0+)$ and $f(0-)$ exist and have value zero. Moreover, since $0 \leq |x \sin(1/x)| \leq |x|$ when $x \neq 0$,

$$f'_+(0) = \lim_{\substack{x \to 0 \\ x > 0}} \left(x \sin \frac{1}{x} \right) = 0 \quad \text{and} \quad f'_-(0) = \lim_{\substack{x \to 0 \\ x < 0}} \left(x \sin \frac{1}{x} \right) = 0.$$

But, from the expression

$$f'(x) = 2x \sin \frac{1}{x} - \cos \frac{1}{x} \qquad (x \neq 0),$$

we see that the one-sided limits $f'(0+)$ and $f'(0-)$ do not exist.

Note that although its one-sided derivatives exist everywhere, the function f is not piecewise smooth on any bounded interval containing the origin. Hence the above theorem is not applicable to this function on such an interval.

10.   A PROPERTY OF FOURIER COEFFICIENTS

In treating the convergence of Fourier series, we shall find it useful to know that for a function f in $C_p(0, \pi)$, the coefficients a_n and b_n in the cosine and sine series on $0 < x < \pi$ always tend to zero as n tends to infinity.

To show that the coefficients

$$(1) \qquad a_n = \frac{2}{\pi} \int_0^\pi f(x) \cos nx \, dx \qquad (n = 0, 1, 2, \ldots)$$

in a cosine series have this property, let $s_N(x)$ denote the partial sum consisting of the first $N + 1$ $(N \geq 1)$ terms in such a series:

$$(2) \qquad s_N(x) = \frac{a_0}{2} + \sum_{n=1}^{N} a_n \cos nx.$$

Then, by squaring the integrand, we have

$$(3) \qquad \int_0^\pi [f(x) - s_N(x)]^2 \, dx = \int_0^\pi [f(x)]^2 \, dx - 2 I_N + J_N$$

where

$$I_N = \int_0^\pi f(x) s_N(x) \, dx \quad \text{and} \quad J_N = \int_0^\pi [s_N(x)]^2 \, dx.$$

We need to evaluate these last two integrals. In order to evaluate I_N, we start by multiplying through equation (2) by $f(x)$ and then integrating each side of the result from 0 to π:

$$(4) \qquad \int_0^\pi f(x) s_N(x) \, dx = \frac{a_0}{2} \int_0^\pi f(x) \, dx + \sum_{n=1}^{N} a_n \int_0^\pi f(x) \cos nx \, dx.$$

The left-hand side here is I_N, and we know from expression (1) that

$$\int_0^\pi f(x) \cos nx \, dx = \frac{\pi}{2} a_n \qquad\qquad (n = 0, 1, 2, \dots, N).$$

Hence equation (4) tells us that

$$(5) \qquad I_N = \frac{a_0}{2} \cdot \frac{\pi}{2} a_0 + \sum_{n=1}^{N} a_n \cdot \frac{\pi}{2} a_n = \frac{\pi}{2} \left(\frac{a_0^2}{2} + \sum_{n=1}^{N} a_n^2 \right).$$

As for the integral J_N, we multiply through equation (2) by $s_N(x)$ and then integrate from 0 to π:

$$(6) \qquad \int_0^\pi [s_N(x)]^2 \, dx = \frac{a_0}{2} \int_0^\pi s_N(x) \, dx + \sum_{n=1}^{N} a_n \int_0^\pi s_N(x) \cos nx \, dx.$$

Also, integration from 0 to π on each side of equation (2) reveals that

$$(7) \qquad \int_0^\pi s_N(x) \, dx = \frac{a_0}{2} \int_0^\pi dx + \sum_{n=1}^{N} a_n \int_0^\pi \cos nx \, dx = \frac{\pi}{2} a_0.$$

Using m as the index of summation in expression (2) and multiplying through the result by $\cos nx$, where n has one of the values $n = 1, 2, \dots, N$, we have

$$s_N(x) \cos nx = \frac{a_0}{2} \cos nx + \sum_{m=1}^{N} a_m \cos mx \cos nx.$$

Thus

$$(8) \qquad \int_0^\pi s_N(x) \cos nx \, dx = \frac{a_0}{2} \int_0^\pi \cos nx \, dx + \sum_{m=1}^{N} a_m \int_0^\pi \cos mx \cos nx \, dx;$$

and since (see Sec. 2)

$$\int_0^{\pi} \cos mx \cos nx \, dx = \begin{cases} 0 & \text{when } m \neq n, \\ \pi/2 & \text{when } m = n, \end{cases}$$

equation (8) reduces to

$$(9) \qquad \int_0^{\pi} s_N(x) \cos nx \, dx = \frac{\pi}{2} a_n \qquad (n = 1, 2, \ldots, N).$$

By substituting expressions (7) and (9) into the right-hand side of equation (6) and recalling that the integral on the left-hand side of that equation is J_N, we arrive at

$$(10) \qquad J_N = \frac{a_0}{2} \cdot \frac{\pi}{2} a_0 + \sum_{n=1}^N a_n \cdot \frac{\pi}{2} a_n = \frac{\pi}{2} \left(\frac{a_0^2}{2} + \sum_{n=1}^N a_n^2 \right).$$

It now follows from equations (3), (5), and (10) that

$$\int_0^{\pi} [f(x) - s_N(x)]^2 \, dx = \int_0^{\pi} [f(x)]^2 \, dx - \frac{\pi}{2} \left(\frac{a_0^2}{2} + \sum_{n=1}^N a_n^2 \right).$$

Since the value of the integral on the left here is nonnegative, we thus arrive at *Bessel's inequality* for the coefficients (1):

$$(11) \qquad \frac{a_0^2}{2} + \sum_{n=1}^N a_n^2 \leq \frac{2}{\pi} \int_0^{\pi} [f(x)]^2 \, dx \qquad (N = 1, 2, \ldots).$$

The desired result,

$$(12) \qquad \lim_{n \to \infty} a_n = 0,$$

is an easy consequence of Bessel's inequality (11), as the following argument shows. We observe that the right-hand side of the inequality is independent of the positive integer N; and as N increases on the left-hand side, the sums of the squares there form a sequence that is bounded and nondecreasing. Since such a sequence must converge and since this particular sequence is the sequence of the partial sums of the series whose terms are $a_0^2/2$ and a_n^2 $(n = 1, 2, \ldots)$, that series must converge. Limit (12) then follows from the fact that the nth term of a convergent series always tends to zero as n tends to infinity.

A similar procedure can be used (Problem 3, Sec. 11) to show that the coefficients

$$(13) \qquad b_n = \frac{2}{\pi} \int_0^{\pi} f(x) \sin nx \, dx \qquad (n = 1, 2, \ldots)$$

in the Fourier sine series for f on $0 < x < \pi$ satisfy the Bessel inequality

$$(14) \qquad \sum_{n=1}^N b_n^2 \leq \frac{2}{\pi} \int_0^{\pi} [f(x)]^2 \, dx \qquad (N = 1, 2, \ldots)$$

and that

$$(15) \qquad \lim_{n \to \infty} b_n = 0.$$

Finally, we recall from Sec. 6 that the coefficients a_n and b_n in the Fourier series involving both cosines and sines for a piecewise continuous function f in $C_p(-\pi, \pi)$ are the same as the coefficients in the Fourier cosine and sine series, respectively, for certain related functions on $0 < x < \pi$. Hence those coefficients themselves tend to zero as n tends to infinity. (See also Problem 5, Sec. 11.)

11. TWO LEMMAS

We preface our theorems on the convergence of Fourier series with two lemmas, or preliminary theorems. The first is a special case of what is known as the *Riemann-Lebesgue lemma*. That lemma appears later on in Chap. 6 (Sec. 52), where it is needed in full generality.

Lemma 1. *If a function $G(u)$ is piecewise continuous on the interval $0 < u < \pi$, then*

$$(1) \qquad \lim_{N \to \infty} \int_0^{\pi} G(u) \sin\left(\frac{u}{2} + Nu\right) du = 0,$$

where N denotes positive integers.

Our proof starts with the trigonometric identity

$$\sin(A + B) = \sin A \cos B + \cos A \sin B,$$

which tells us that

$$\sin\left(\frac{u}{2} + Nu\right) = \sin\frac{u}{2}\cos Nu + \cos\frac{u}{2}\sin Nu.$$

Assuming that $G(u)$ is piecewise continuous, we are able to write

$$(2) \qquad \int_0^{\pi} G(u) \sin\left(\frac{u}{2} + Nu\right) du = \frac{\pi}{2}(a_N + b_N),$$

where

$$a_N = \frac{2}{\pi} \int_0^{\pi} \left[G(u) \sin\frac{u}{2}\right] \cos Nu \, du$$

and

$$b_N = \frac{2}{\pi} \int_0^{\pi} \left[G(u) \cos\frac{u}{2}\right] \sin Nu \, du.$$

Now the a_N are coefficients in a Fourier cosine series on the interval $0 < u < \pi$, and the b_N are coefficients in a Fourier sine series on that interval. Thus, by limits (12) and (15) in Sec. 10,

$$(3) \qquad \lim_{N \to \infty} a_N = 0 \qquad \text{and} \qquad \lim_{N \to \infty} b_N = 0.$$

With limits (3), we need only let N tend to infinity in equation (2) to see that Lemma 1 is true.

Our second lemma involves the *Dirichlet kernel*

(4)
$$D_N(u) = \frac{1}{2} + \sum_{n=1}^{N} \cos nu,$$

where N is any positive integer. Note that $D_N(u)$ is continuous, even, and periodic with period 2π. The Dirichlet kernel plays a central role in our theory, and two other properties will be useful:

(5)
$$\int_0^\pi D_N(u)\, du = \frac{\pi}{2},$$

(6)
$$D_N(u) = \frac{\sin\left(\frac{u}{2} + Nu\right)}{2 \sin \frac{u}{2}} \qquad (u \neq 0, \pm 2\pi, \pm 4\pi, \ldots).$$

Property (5) is obvious upon integrating each side of equation (4). Expression (6) can be derived with the aid of a certain trigonometric identity (Problem 6).

Lemma 2. *Suppose that a function $g(u)$ is piecewise continuous on the interval $0 < u < \pi$ and that the right-hand derivative $g'_+(0)$ exists. Then*

(7)
$$\lim_{N\to\infty} \int_0^\pi g(u) D_N(u)\, du = \frac{\pi}{2} g(0+),$$

where $D_N(u)$ is the Dirichlet kernel (4).

To prove this, we write

(8)
$$\int_0^\pi g(u) D_N(u)\, du = I_N + J_N,$$

where

(9)
$$I_N = \int_0^\pi [g(u) - g(0+)] D_N(u)\, du$$

and

(10)
$$J_N = \int_0^\pi g(0+) D_N(u)\, du.$$

In view of expression (6) for $D_N(u)$, integral (9) can be put in the form

$$I_N = \int_0^\pi \frac{g(u) - g(0+)}{2 \sin \frac{u}{2}} \sin\left(\frac{u}{2} + Nu\right) du.$$

Thus

(11)
$$I_N = \int_0^\pi G(u) \sin\left(\frac{u}{2} + Nu\right) du,$$

where the function

(12)
$$G(u) = \frac{g(u) - g(0+)}{2 \sin \frac{u}{2}}$$

is a quotient of two functions that are piecewise continuous on the interval $0 < u < \pi$. Even though the denominator vanishes at the point $u = 0$, one can show that $G(u)$ is itself piecewise continuous on $0 < u < \pi$ by establishing the existence of the right-hand limit $G(0+)$. This is done by referring to expression (12) and writing

$$G(0+) = G(u) = \lim_{\substack{u \to 0 \\ u > 0}} \left[\frac{g(u) - g(0+)}{u - 0} \cdot \frac{u}{2 \sin \dfrac{u}{2}} \right] = \lim_{\substack{u \to 0 \\ u > 0}} \frac{g(u) - g(0+)}{u - 0} \lim_{\substack{u \to 0 \\ u > 0}} \frac{u}{2 \sin \dfrac{u}{2}}.$$

These last two limits exist, and so $G(0+)$ exists. The first of those limits is, of course, the right-hand derivative $g'_+(0)$; and an application of l'Hôpital's rule reveals that

$$\lim_{\substack{u \to 0 \\ u > 0}} \frac{u}{2 \sin \dfrac{u}{2}} = \lim_{\substack{u \to 0 \\ u > 0}} \frac{1}{\cos \dfrac{u}{2}} = 1.$$

We have now established that $G(u)$ is piecewise continuous on the interval $0 < x < \pi$. According to Lemma 1, then, the limit of the right-hand side of equation (11) is zero as N tends to infinity. That is,

(13)
$$\lim_{N \to \infty} I_N = 0.$$

With property (5) of the Dirichlet kernel, one can see from expression (10) for J_N that

$$J_N = g(0+) \int_0^\pi D_N(u) \, du = \frac{\pi}{2} g(0+).$$

Hence

(14)
$$\lim_{N \to \infty} J_N = \frac{\pi}{2} g(0+).$$

The desired result (7) now follows from equation (8) together with limits (13) and (14).

PROBLEMS

1. With the aid of l'Hôpital's rule, find $f(0+)$ and $f'_+(0)$ when

$$f(x) = \frac{e^x - 1}{x} \qquad\qquad (x \neq 0).$$

Answers: $f(0+) = 1$, $f'_+(0) = 1/2$.

2. Show that the function defined by means of the equations

$$f(x) = \begin{cases} x \sin(1/x) & \text{when } x \neq 0, \\ 0 & \text{when } x = 0 \end{cases}$$

is continuous at $x = 0$ but that neither $f'_+(0)$ nor $f'_-(0)$ exists. This provides another illustration (see Example 3, Sec. 9) of the fact that the continuity of a function f at a point x_0 is *not* a sufficient condition for the existence of one-sided derivatives of f at x_0.

3. By following the steps used in Sec. 10 to find Bessel's inequality for the coefficients a_n in the Fourier cosine series on $0 < x < \pi$ for a function f in $C_p(0, \pi)$, derive the

Bessel inequality

$$\sum_{n=1}^{N} b_n^2 \leq \frac{2}{\pi} \int_0^{\pi} [f(x)]^2 \, dx \qquad (N = 1, 2, \dots)$$

for the coefficients b_n in the sine series on $0 < x < \pi$ for f. Then use this result to show that

$$\lim_{n \to \infty} b_n = 0.$$

4. In Chap. 1 (Sec. 6) we expressed a function $f(x)$ in $C_p(-\pi, \pi)$ as a sum

$$f(x) = g(x) + h(x)$$

where

$$g(x) = \frac{f(x) + f(-x)}{2} \quad \text{and} \quad h(x) = \frac{f(x) - f(-x)}{2}.$$

We then saw that the coefficients a_n and b_n in the Fourier series

$$\frac{a_0}{2} + \sum_{n=1}^{\infty} (a_n \cos nx + b_n \sin nx)$$

for $f(x)$ on $-\pi < x < \pi$ are the same as the coefficients in the Fourier cosine and sine series for $g(x)$ and $h(x)$, respectively, on $0 < x < \pi$.

(a) By referring to the Bessel inequalities (11) and (14) in Sec. 10, write

$$\frac{a_0^2}{2} + \sum_{n=1}^{N} a_n^2 \leq \frac{2}{\pi} \int_0^{\pi} [g(x)]^2 \, dx \qquad (N = 1, 2, \dots)$$

and

$$\sum_{n=1}^{N} b_n^2 \leq \frac{2}{\pi} \int_0^{\pi} [h(x)]^2 \, dx \qquad (N = 1, 2, \dots).$$

Then point out how it follows that

$$\frac{a_0^2}{2} + \sum_{n=1}^{N} (a_n^2 + b_n^2) \leq \frac{1}{\pi} \left\{ \int_0^{\pi} [f(x)]^2 \, dx + \int_0^{\pi} [f(-s)]^2 \, ds \right\} \qquad (N = 1, 2, \dots).$$

(b) By making the substitution $x = -s$ in the last integral in part (a), obtain the Bessel inequality

$$\frac{a_0^2}{2} + \sum_{n=1}^{N} (a_n^2 + b_n^2) \leq \frac{1}{\pi} \int_{-\pi}^{\pi} [f(x)]^2 \, dx \qquad (N = 1, 2, \dots).$$

5. Show how it follows from the Bessel inequality in Problem 4(b) that

$$\lim_{n \to \infty} a_n = 0 \quad \text{and} \quad \lim_{n \to \infty} b_n = 0,$$

where a_n and b_n are the coefficients in the Fourier series

$$\frac{a_0}{2} + \sum_{n=1}^{\infty} (a_n \cos nx + b_n \sin nx)$$

for a piecewise continuous function in $C_p(-\pi, \pi)$.

6. Derive the expression

$$D_N(u) = \frac{\sin\left(\dfrac{u}{2} + Nu\right)}{2\sin\dfrac{u}{2}} \qquad\qquad (u \neq 0, \pm 2\pi, \pm 4\pi, \dots)$$

for the Dirichlet kernel (Sec. 11)

$$D_N(u) = \frac{1}{2} + \sum_{n=1}^{N} \cos nu$$

by writing

$$A = \frac{u}{2} \qquad \text{and} \qquad B = nu$$

in the trigonometric identity

$$2\sin A \cos B = \sin(A + B) + \sin(A - B)$$

and then summing each side of the resulting equation from $n = 1$ to $n = N$.

Suggestion: Note that

$$\sum_{n=1}^{N} \sin\left(\frac{u}{2} - nu\right) = -\sum_{n=0}^{N-1} \sin\left(\frac{u}{2} + nu\right).$$

12.   A FOURIER THEOREM

A theorem that gives conditions under which a Fourier series

$$(1) \qquad\qquad \frac{a_0}{2} + \sum_{n=1}^{\infty} (a_n \cos nx + b_n \sin nx),$$

with coefficients

$$(2) \qquad\qquad a_n = \frac{1}{\pi} \int_{-\pi}^{\pi} f(x) \cos nx \, dx \qquad\qquad (n = 0, 1, 2, \dots)$$

and

$$(3) \qquad\qquad b_n = \frac{1}{\pi} \int_{-\pi}^{\pi} f(x) \sin nx \, dx \qquad\qquad (n = 1, 2, \dots),$$

converges to $f(x)$ is called a *Fourier theorem.* Such a theorem will now be established. A related one that is especially useful appears in Sec. 13, and both theorems are illustrated in Sec. 14.

Theorem. *Suppose that*

(*i*)   *f is piecewise continuous on the interval $-\pi < x < \pi$;*

(*ii*)   *f is periodic, with period 2π, on the entire x axis;*

(*iii*)   *$x(-\infty < x < \infty)$ is a point at which the one-sided derivatives $f'_+(x)$ and $f'_-(x)$ both exist.*

The Fourier series (1), *with coefficients* (2) *and* (3), *then converges to the mean value*

$$(4) \qquad \frac{f(x+) + f(x-)}{2}$$

of the one-sided limits of f at x.

Note that if f is actually continuous at x, the quotient (4) becomes $f(x)$. Hence

$$f(x) = \frac{a_0}{2} + \sum_{n=1}^{\infty} (a_n \cos nx + b_n \sin nx)$$

at such a point.

The fact that f is piecewise continuous on $-\pi < x < \pi$ ensures that integrals (2) and (3) always exist; and we begin our proof of the theorem by writing series (1) as (see Sec. 6)

$$\frac{1}{2\pi} \int_{-\pi}^{\pi} f(s)\, ds + \frac{1}{\pi} \sum_{n=1}^{\infty} \int_{-\pi}^{\pi} f(s) \cos n(s-x)\, ds,$$

with those coefficients incorporated into it. Then, if $S_N(x)$ denotes the partial sum consisting of the sum of the first $N+1$ $(N \geq 1)$ terms of the series,

$$(5) \qquad S_N(x) = \frac{1}{2\pi} \int_{-\pi}^{\pi} f(s)\, ds + \frac{1}{\pi} \sum_{n=1}^{N} \int_{-\pi}^{\pi} f(s) \cos n(s-x)\, ds.$$

Using the Dirichlet kernel (Sec. 11)

$$D_N(u) = \frac{1}{2} + \sum_{n=1}^{N} \cos nu,$$

we can put equation (5) in the form

$$S_N(x) = \frac{1}{\pi} \int_{-\pi}^{\pi} f(s) D_N(s-x)\, ds.$$

The periodicity of the integrand here allows us to change the interval of integration to any interval of length 2π without altering the value of the integral (see Problem 9, Sec. 14). Thus

$$(6) \qquad S_N(x) = \frac{1}{\pi} \int_{x-\pi}^{x+\pi} f(s) D_N(s-x)\, ds,$$

where the point x is at the center of the interval we have chosen. It now follows from equation (6) that

$$(7) \qquad S_N(x) = \frac{1}{\pi} [I_N(x) + J_N(x)],$$

where

$$(8) \qquad I_N(x) = \int_{x}^{x+\pi} f(s) D_N(s-x)\, ds$$

and

$$(9) \qquad J_N(x) = \int_{x-\pi}^{x} f(s) D_N(s-x) \, ds.$$

If we replace the variable of integration s in integral (8) by the new variable $u = s - x$, that integral becomes

$$(10) \qquad I_N(x) = \int_{0}^{\pi} f(x+u) D_N(u) \, du.$$

Since f is piecewise continuous on the fundamental interval $-\pi < x < \pi$ and also periodic, it is piecewise continuous on any bounded interval of the x axis. So, for a fixed value of x, the function $g(u) = f(x+u)$ in expression (10) is piecewise continuous on any bounded interval of the u axis and, in particular, on the interval $0 < u < \pi$. Recall now that the right-hand derivative $f'_+(x)$ exists. After observing that

$$g(0+) = \lim_{\substack{u \to 0 \\ u > 0}} g(u) = \lim_{\substack{u \to 0 \\ u > 0}} f(x+u) = \lim_{\substack{v \to x \\ v > x}} f(v) = f(x+),$$

one can show that the right-hand derivative of g at $u = 0$ exists:

$$g'_+(0) = \lim_{\substack{u \to 0 \\ u > 0}} \frac{g(u) - g(0+)}{u - 0} = \lim_{\substack{u \to 0 \\ u > 0}} \frac{f(x+u) - f(x+)}{u}$$

$$= \lim_{\substack{v \to x \\ v > x}} \frac{f(v) - f(x+)}{v - x} = f'_+(x).$$

According to Lemma 2 in Sec. 11, then,

$$(11) \qquad \lim_{N \to \infty} I_N(x) = \frac{\pi}{2} g(0+) = \frac{\pi}{2} f(x+).$$

If, on the other hand, we make the substitution $u = x - s$ in integral (9) and use the fact that $D_N(u)$ is an even function of u, we find that

$$(12) \qquad J_N(x) = \int_{0}^{\pi} f(x-u) D_N(u) \, du.$$

This time, we recall that the left-hand derivative $f'_-(x)$ exists; and we note that the function $g(u) = f(x-u)$ in expression (12) is piecewise continuous on the interval $0 < u < \pi$. Furthermore,

$$g(0+) = \lim_{\substack{u \to 0 \\ u > 0}} g(x) = \lim_{\substack{u \to 0 \\ u > 0}} f(x-u) = \lim_{\substack{v \to x \\ v < x}} f(v) = f(x-)$$

and

$$g'_+(0) = \lim_{\substack{u \to 0 \\ u > 0}} \frac{g(u) - g(0+)}{u - 0} = \lim_{\substack{u \to 0 \\ u > 0}} \frac{f(x-u) - f(x-)}{u}$$

$$= -\lim_{\substack{v \to x \\ v < x}} \frac{f(v) - f(x-)}{v - x} = -f'_-(x).$$

So once again by Lemma 2 in Sec. 11,

$$(13) \qquad \lim_{N\to\infty} J_N(x) = \frac{\pi}{2}\, g(0+) = \frac{\pi}{2} f(x-).$$

Finally, we may conclude from equation (7) and limits (11) and (13) that

$$\lim_{N\to\infty} S_N(x) = \frac{f(x+) + f(x-)}{2},$$

and the theorem is proved.

13.   A RELATED FOURIER THEOREM

The Fourier theorem in Sec. 12 is readily adapted to functions that are piecewise smooth on the fundamental interval $-\pi < x < \pi$. We recall from Sec. 9 that f is piecewise smooth if *both* f and f' are piecewise continuous.

   Theorem. *Suppose that*

   (i)   *f is piecewise smooth on the interval $-\pi < x < \pi$;*

   (ii) *F is the periodic extension, with period 2π, of f.*

Then, at each point $x(-\infty < x < \infty)$, the Fourier series for f on $-\pi < x < \pi$ converges to the mean value

$$\frac{F(x +) + F(x -)}{2}$$

of the one-sided limits $F(x +)$ and $F(x -)$.

   The proof relies on the theorem in Sec. 9, which tells us that when f is piecewise smooth on $-\pi < x < \pi$, its one-sided derivatives, from the interior at the endpoints $x = \pm\pi$, exist everywhere in the closed interval $-\pi \le x \le \pi$. Hence, because F is the periodic extension of f, with period 2π, its one-sided derivatives exist at each point $x\ (-\infty < x < \infty)$. According to the theorem in Sec. 12, then, the Fourier series for f on $-\pi < x < \pi$ converges everywhere to the mean value of the one-sided limits of F, and the theorem here is established.

   It should be emphasized that the conditions in this theorem, as well as the ones in the theorem in Sec. 12, are only sufficient, and there is no claim that they are *necessary* conditions. More general conditions are given in a number of the references listed in the Bibliography. Indeed, there are functions that even become unbounded at certain points but nevertheless have valid Fourier series representations.[†]

   The theorem here will be adequate for most of the applications in this book, where the functions are generally piecewise smooth. We note that if f and F denote the functions in the theorem, then

$$F(x +) = f(x +) \qquad \text{and} \qquad F(x -) = f(x -) \qquad \text{when } -\pi < x < \pi.$$

[†]See, for instance, the book by Tolstov (1976, pp. 91–94), which is listed in the Bibliography.

Consequently, when $-\pi < x < \pi$, the theorem tells us that the Fourier series for f on the interval $-\pi < x < \pi$ converges to the number

(1)
$$\frac{f(x+) + f(x-)}{2},$$

which becomes $f(x)$ if x is a point of continuity of f.

At the endpoints $x = \pm\pi$, however, the series converges to

(2)
$$\frac{f(-\pi +) + f(\pi -)}{2}.$$

To see this, consider first the point $x = \pi$. Since

$$F(\pi +) = f(-\pi +) \qquad \text{and} \qquad F(\pi -) = f(\pi -),$$

as is evident from Fig. 9, the quotient

$$\frac{F(x+) + F(x-)}{2}$$

in our theorem becomes the quotient (2) when $x = \pi$. Because of the periodicity of the series, it also converges to the quotient (2) when $x = -\pi$.

FIGURE 9

14. EXAMPLES

The following examples illustrate how the Fourier theorems in the last two sections can be used.

EXAMPLE 1. In Example 1, Sec. 7, we obtained the Fourier series

(1)
$$\frac{\pi}{4} + \sum_{n=1}^{\infty} \left[\frac{(-1)^n - 1}{\pi n^2} \cos nx + \frac{(-1)^{n+1}}{n} \sin nx \right]$$

on the interval $-\pi < x < \pi$ for the function f defined by means of the equations

$$f(x) = \begin{cases} 0 & \text{when } -\pi < x \leq 0, \\ x & \text{when } \quad 0 < x < \pi. \end{cases}$$

Since

$$f'(x) = \begin{cases} 0 & \text{when } -\pi < x < 0, \\ 1 & \text{when } \quad 0 < x < \pi, \end{cases}$$

f is clearly piecewise smooth on the fundamental interval $-\pi < x < \pi$.

Hence we may use the theorem in Sec. 13. In view of the continuity of f when $-\pi < x < \pi$, the series converges to $f(x)$ at each point in that open interval. Since

$$f(-\pi+) = 0 \quad \text{and} \quad f(\pi-) = \pi,$$

it converges to $\pi/2$ at the endpoints $x = \pm\pi$. The series, in fact, converges to $\pi/2$ at each of the points $x = \pm\pi, \pm3\pi, \pm5\pi, \ldots$, as indicated in Fig. 6 (Sec. 7), where the sum of the series for all x is described graphically.

In particular, since series (1) converges to $\pi/2$ when $x = \pi$, we have the identity

$$\frac{\pi}{4} + \sum_{n=1}^{\infty} \frac{(-1)^n - 1}{\pi n^2} (-1)^n = \frac{\pi}{2},$$

which can be written

$$\sum_{n=1}^{\infty} \frac{1}{(2n-1)^2} = \frac{\pi^2}{8}.$$

This illustrates how Fourier series can sometimes be used to find the sums of convergent series encountered in calculus. Setting $x = 0$ in series (1) also yields this particular summation formula.

The theorem in Sec. 13 tells us that a function f in the space $C'_p(-\pi, \pi)$ of piecewise smooth functions on the interval $-\pi < x < \pi$ has a valid Fourier series representation on that interval, or one that is equal to $f(x)$ at all but possibly a finite number of points there. It also ensures that a function f in the space $C'_p(0, \pi)$ has valid Fourier cosine and sine series representations on the interval $0 < x < \pi$. This is because, according to Sec. 6, the cosine series for a function f on the interval $0 < x < \pi$ is the same as the Fourier series corresponding to the *even* extension of f on the interval $-\pi < x < \pi$ and the sine series for f on the interval $0 < x < \pi$ is the Fourier series for the *odd* extension of f. In view of the even periodic function represented by the cosine series, that series converges to $f(0+)$ at the point $x = 0$ and to $f(\pi-)$ at $x = \pi$. The sum of the sine series is, of course, zero when $x = 0$ and when $x = \pi$.

EXAMPLE 2. In Example 2, Sec. 3, we found the Fourier cosine series corresponding to the function $f(x) = \sin x$ on the interval $0 < x < \pi$:

$$(2) \qquad\qquad \sin x \sim \frac{2}{\pi} - \frac{4}{\pi} \sum_{n=1}^{\infty} \frac{\cos 2nx}{4n^2 - 1}.$$

Since $\sin x$ is piecewise smooth on $0 < x < \pi$ and continuous on the closed interval $0 \leq x \leq \pi$, correspondence (2) is evidently an equality when $0 \leq x \leq \pi$.

Our final example here illustrates how the theorem in Sec. 12 can be useful when the one in Sec. 13 fails to apply.

EXAMPLE 3. The odd function

$$(3) \qquad\qquad\qquad f(x) = \sqrt[3]{x} \qquad\qquad\qquad (-\pi < x < \pi)$$

is piecewise continuous on the interval $-\pi < x < \pi$. But since

$$f'(x) = \frac{1}{3\sqrt[3]{x^2}}$$

when $x \neq 0$, it is clear that the one-sided limits $f'(0+)$ and $f'(0-)$ do not exist. Hence f is *not* piecewise smooth on $-\pi < x < \pi$, and the theorem in Sec. 13 does not apply.

If, however, F denotes the periodic extension, with period 2π, of the piecewise continuous function (3), the theorem in Sec. 12 can be applied to that extension. To be precise, since the one-sided derivatives of F exist everywhere in the interval $-\pi < x < \pi$ except at $x = 0$, we find that the Fourier series for F on $-\pi < x < \pi$ converges to $F(x)$ when $-\pi < x < 0$ and when $0 < x < \pi$. That series representation is also valid at $x = 0$ since F is odd and the series is actually a Fourier sine series on $0 < x < \pi$, which converges to zero when $x = 0$. Since $f(x) = F(x)$ when $-\pi < x < \pi$, we may conclude that the Fourier series for f on that interval is valid for all such x.

PROBLEMS

1. State why the Fourier sine series in Example 1, Sec. 5, for the function

$$f(x) = x \qquad\qquad\qquad (0 < x < \pi)$$

   is a valid representation for x on the interval $-\pi < x < \pi$. Thus verify fully that the series converges for all x $(-\infty < x < \infty)$ to the function whose graph is shown in Fig. 5 (Sec. 5).

2. For each of the following functions, point out why its Fourier series on the interval $-\pi < x < \pi$ is convergent when $-\pi \leq x \leq \pi$, and state the sum of the series when $x = \pi$:

   (a) the function

   $$f(x) = \begin{cases} -\pi/2 & \text{when } -\pi < x < 0, \\ \pi/2 & \text{when } \quad 0 < x < \pi, \end{cases}$$

   whose series was found in Problem 1, Sec. 7;

   (b) the function

   $$f(x) = e^{ax} \qquad\qquad\qquad (a \neq 0),$$

   whose series was found in Problem 4, Sec. 7.
   Answers: (a) sum $= 0$; (b) sum $= \cosh a\pi$.

3. By writing $x = 0$ and $x = \pi/2$ in the representation

   $$\sin x = \frac{2}{\pi} - \frac{4}{\pi} \sum_{n=1}^{\infty} \frac{\cos 2nx}{4n^2 - 1} \qquad\qquad (0 \leq x \leq \pi),$$

   established in Example 2, Sec. 14, obtain the following summations:

   $$\sum_{n=1}^{\infty} \frac{1}{4n^2 - 1} = \frac{1}{2}, \qquad \sum_{n=1}^{\infty} \frac{(-1)^n}{4n^2 - 1} = \frac{1}{2} - \frac{\pi}{4}.$$

4. Point out why the Fourier series in Problem 7, Sec. 7, for the function

$$f(x) = \begin{cases} 0 & \text{when } -\pi \le x \le 0, \\ \sin x & \text{when } \ \ 0 < x \le \pi \end{cases}$$

converges to $f(x)$ everywhere in the interval $-\pi \le x \le \pi$.

5. State why the correspondence

$$x \sim \frac{\pi}{2} - \frac{4}{\pi} \sum_{n=1}^{\infty} \frac{\cos(2n-1)x}{(2n-1)^2} \qquad (0 < x < \pi),$$

obtained in Example 1, Sec. 3, is actually an equality on the closed interval $0 \le x \le \pi$. Thus show that

$$\sum_{n=1}^{\infty} \frac{1}{(2n-1)^2} = \frac{\pi^2}{8}.$$

(Compare with Example 1, Sec. 14.)

6. (a) Use the correspondence

$$x^2 \sim \frac{\pi^2}{3} + 4 \sum_{n=1}^{\infty} \frac{(-1)^n}{n^2} \cos nx \qquad (0 < x < \pi),$$

found in Problem 3(a), Sec. 5, to show that

$$\sum_{n=1}^{\infty} \frac{(-1)^{n+1}}{n^2} = \frac{\pi^2}{12} \quad \text{and} \quad \sum_{n=1}^{\infty} \frac{1}{n^2} = \frac{\pi^2}{6}.$$

(b) Use the correspondence (Problem 6, Sec. 5)

$$x^4 \sim \frac{\pi^4}{5} + 8 \sum_{n=1}^{\infty} (-1)^n \frac{(n\pi)^2 - 6}{n^4} \cos nx \qquad (0 < x < \pi)$$

and the summations found in part (a) to show that

$$\sum_{n=1}^{\infty} \frac{(-1)^{n+1}}{n^4} = \frac{7\pi^4}{720} \quad \text{and} \quad \sum_{n=1}^{\infty} \frac{1}{n^4} = \frac{\pi^4}{90}.$$

7. With the aid of the correspondence (Problem 6, Sec. 7)

$$\cos ax \sim \frac{2a \sin a\pi}{\pi} \left[\frac{1}{2a^2} + \sum_{n=1}^{\infty} \frac{(-1)^{n+1}}{n^2 - a^2} \cos nx \right] \qquad (-\pi < x < \pi),$$

where $a \ne 0, \pm 1, \pm 2, \ldots$, show that

$$\frac{a\pi}{\sin a\pi} = 1 + 2a^2 \sum_{n=1}^{\infty} \frac{(-1)^{n+1}}{n^2 - a^2} \qquad (a \ne 0, \pm 1, \pm 2, \ldots).$$

8. Without actually finding the Fourier series for the even function $f(x) = \sqrt[3]{x^2}$ on $-\pi < x < \pi$, point out how the theorem in Sec. 12 ensures the convergence of that series to $f(x)$ when $-\pi \le x < 0$ and when $0 < x \le \pi$ but not when $x = 0$.

9. Let f denote a function that is piecewise continuous on an interval $-c < x < c$ and periodic with period $2c$. Show that for any number a,

$$\int_{-c}^{c} f(x)\,dx = \int_{a-c}^{a+c} f(x)\,dx.$$

Suggestion: Write

$$\int_{-c}^{c} f(x)\,dx = \int_{-c}^{a+c} f(x)\,dx + \int_{a+c}^{c} f(s)\,ds$$

and then make the substitution $x = s - 2c$ in the second integral on the right-hand side of this equation.

15. CONVERGENCE ON OTHER INTERVALS

In Sec. 8 we introduced Fourier series corresponding to piecewise continuous functions f on arbitrary intervals $-c < x < c$. To treat the convergence of such series, we include here a few remarks about the function

(1) $$g(s) = f\left(\frac{cs}{\pi}\right) \qquad\qquad (-\pi < s < \pi)$$

that was used in Sec. 8.

Let us write the function (1) as

(2) $$g(s) = f(x) \qquad \text{where} \qquad x = \frac{cs}{\pi} \qquad\qquad (-\pi < s < \pi).$$

It is clear that the equation $x = cs/\pi$, or $s = \pi x/c$, establishes a one-to-one correspondence between points in the interval $-\pi < s < \pi$ and points in the interval $-c < x < c$. Suppose now that f is piecewise smooth on the interval $-c < x < c$ and that $f(x)$ at each point x where f is discontinuous is the mean value of the one-sided limits $f(x+)$ and $f(x-)$, as is the case when f is continuous at x.

One can see from equations (2) that if a specific point s_0 corresponds to a specific point x_0, then

$$g(s_0 +) = f(x_0 +) \qquad \text{and} \qquad g(s_0 -) = f(x_0 -).$$

Since $f(x)$ is always the mean value of $f(x+)$ and $f(x-)$, it follows from these relations between one-sided limits that the number $g(s) = f(x)$ is always the mean value of $g(s +)$ and $g(s -)$. In particular, g is continuous at s when f is continuous at x. Since f is piecewise continuous on the interval $-c < x < c$, then, g is piecewise continuous on the interval $-\pi < s < \pi$. The derivative f' is also piecewise continuous, and a similar argument shows that g' is piecewise continuous. So g is piecewise smooth on the interval $-\pi < s < \pi$. According to the theorem in Sec. 13, the Fourier series for g on the interval $-\pi < s < \pi$ converges to $g(s)$ for each s in that interval. Moreover, since it was relation (1) that gave us the new correspondence for f on $-c < x < c$ in Sec. 8, the correspondence is, in fact, an equality. That is,

(3) $$f(x) = \frac{a_0}{2} + \sum_{n=1}^{\infty} \left(a_n \cos\frac{n\pi x}{c} + b_n \sin\frac{n\pi x}{c}\right),$$

where

(4) $$a_n = \frac{1}{c}\int_{-c}^{c} f(x)\cos\frac{n\pi x}{c}\,dx \qquad\qquad (n = 0, 1, 2, \ldots)$$

and

$$(5) \qquad b_n = \frac{1}{c} \int_{-c}^{c} f(x) \sin \frac{n\pi x}{c} \, dx \qquad\qquad (n = 1, 2, \ldots).$$

We state this result as a theorem that is sufficient for our applications. The theorem and the one that follows it apply to any function f that has the following properties:

(i) the function f is piecewise smooth on the stated interval;

(ii) the value $f(x)$ at each point of discontinuity of f in that interval is the mean value of the one-sided limits $f(x+)$ and $f(x-)$.

Theorem 1. Let f denote a function that has properties (i) and (ii) on an interval $-c < x < c$. The Fourier series representation (3), with coefficients (4) and (5), is valid for each x in that interval.

Note that series (3) also represents the *periodic extension, with period $2c$,* of the function f. That is, it converges to a function $F(x)$ whose graph coincides with the graph of $f(x)$ on $-c < x < c$ and is repeated every $2c$ units along the x axis. The series has the expected sums at the endpoints $x = \pm c$. The sum at $x = c$ is, for instance, the mean value of $F(c+)$ and $F(c-)$.

If we restrict function (1) to the interval $0 < s < \pi$, Fourier cosine and sine series representations on $0 < x < c$ follow from representations on $0 < s < \pi$ that involve only cosines and sines, respectively.

Theorem 2. Let f denote a function that has properties (i) and (ii) on an interval $0 < x < c$. The Fourier cosine series representation

$$(6) \qquad f(x) = \frac{a_0}{2} + \sum_{n=1}^{\infty} a_n \cos \frac{n\pi x}{c},$$

with coefficients

$$(7) \qquad a_n = \frac{2}{c} \int_{0}^{c} f(x) \cos \frac{n\pi x}{c} \, dx \qquad\qquad (n = 0, 1, 2, \ldots),$$

is valid for all x in that interval. The same is true of the Fourier sine series representation

$$(8) \qquad f(x) = \sum_{n=1}^{\infty} b_n \sin \frac{n\pi x}{c},$$

with coefficients

$$(9) \qquad b_n = \frac{2}{c} \int_{0}^{c} f(x) \sin \frac{n\pi x}{c} \, dx \qquad\qquad (n = 1, 2, \ldots).$$

Series (6) represents, of course, the *even* periodic extension, with period $2c$, of f; and series (8) represents the *odd* periodic extension, with period $2c$, of f.

PROBLEMS

1. Use formulas (4) and (5), Sec. 15, as well as Theorem 1 in that section, to show that if

$$f(x) = \begin{cases} 0 & \text{when } -3 < x < 0, \\ 1 & \text{when } 0 < x < 3 \end{cases}$$

and if $f(0) = \dfrac{1}{2}$, then

$$f(x) = \frac{1}{2} + \frac{2}{\pi} \sum_{n=1}^{\infty} \frac{1}{2n-1} \sin \frac{(2n-1)\pi x}{3} \qquad (-3 < x < 3).$$

Describe graphically the function that is represented by this series for all values of x $(-\infty < x < \infty)$.

2. Let f denote the function whose values are

$$f(x) = \begin{cases} 0 & \text{when } -2 < x < 1, \\ 1 & \text{when } 1 < x < 2, \end{cases}$$

and

$$f(-2) = f(1) = f(2) = \frac{1}{2}.$$

Use formulas (4) and (5) in Sec. 15, together with Theorem 1 there, to show that

$$f(x) = \frac{1}{4} - \frac{1}{\pi} \sum_{n=1}^{\infty} \frac{1}{n} \left[\sin \frac{n\pi}{2} \cos \frac{n\pi x}{2} + \left(\cos n\pi - \cos \frac{n\pi}{2} \right) \sin \frac{n\pi x}{2} \right]$$

for each x in the closed interval $-2 \le x \le 2$.

3. Let $M(c, t)$ denote the square wave (Fig. 10) defined by means of the equations

$$M(c, t) = \begin{cases} 1 & \text{when } 0 < t < c, \\ -1 & \text{when } c < t < 2c, \end{cases}$$

and $M(c, t + 2c) = M(c, t)$ when $t > 0$. Show that

$$M(c, t) = \frac{4}{\pi} \sum_{n=1}^{\infty} \frac{1}{2n-1} \sin \frac{(2n-1)\pi t}{c} \qquad (t \ne c, 2c, 3c, \ldots).$$

FIGURE 10

4. Let F denote the periodic function, of period c, where

$$F(x) = \begin{cases} \dfrac{c}{4} - x & \text{when } 0 \le x \le \dfrac{c}{2}, \\ x - \dfrac{3c}{4} & \text{when } \dfrac{c}{2} < x \le c. \end{cases}$$

(a) Describe the function $F(x)$ graphically, and show that it is, in fact, the even periodic extension, with period c, of the function

$$f(x) = \frac{c}{4} - x \qquad \left(0 \leq x \leq \frac{c}{2}\right).$$

(b) Use the result in part (a) and the Fourier cosine series correspondence found in Problem 7, Sec. 8, to show that

$$F(x) = \frac{2c}{\pi^2} \sum_{n=1}^{\infty} \frac{1}{(2n-1)^2} \cos \frac{(4n-2)\pi x}{c} \qquad (-\infty < x < \infty).$$

5. Let f denote the periodic function, of period 2, where

$$f(x) = \begin{cases} \cos \pi x & \text{when } 0 < x < 1, \\ 0 & \text{when } 1 < x < 2 \end{cases}$$

and where

$$f(0) = \frac{1}{2} \quad \text{and} \quad f(1) = -\frac{1}{2}.$$

By referring to the correspondence

$$\cos \pi x \sim \frac{8}{\pi} \sum_{n=1}^{\infty} \frac{n}{4n^2 - 1} \sin 2n\pi x \qquad (0 < x < 1),$$

obtained in Problem 8, Sec. 8, show that

$$f(x) = \frac{1}{2} \cos \pi x + \frac{4}{\pi} \sum_{n=1}^{\infty} \frac{n}{4n^2 - 1} \sin 2n\pi x \qquad (-\infty < x < \infty).$$

6. Suppose that a function f is piecewise smooth on an interval $0 < x < c$, and let F denote this extension of f on the interval $0 < x < 2c$:

$$F(x) = \begin{cases} f(x) & \text{when } 0 < x < c, \\ f(2c - x) & \text{when } c < x < 2c. \end{cases}$$

[The graph of $y = F(x)$ is evidently symmetric with respect to the line $x = c$.] Show that the coefficients B_n in the Fourier sine series for F on the interval $0 < x < 2c$ can be written

$$B_n = \frac{1 - (-1)^n}{c} \int_0^c f(x) \sin \frac{n\pi x}{2c} \, dx \qquad (n = 1, 2, \ldots).$$

Thus show that

$$f(x) = \sum_{n=1}^{\infty} b_n \sin \frac{(2n-1)\pi x}{2c},$$

where

$$b_n = \frac{2}{c} \int_0^c f(x) \sin \frac{(2n-1)\pi x}{2c} \, dx \qquad (n = 1, 2, \ldots),$$

for each point $x \ (0 < x < c)$ at which f is continuous.

Suggestion: Write

$$B_n = \frac{1}{c} \left[\int_0^c f(x) \sin \frac{n\pi x}{2c} \, dx + \int_c^{2c} f(2c - s) \sin \frac{n\pi s}{2c} \, ds \right]$$

and make the substitution $x = 2c - s$ in the second of these integrals.

7. Use the result in Problem 6 to establish the representation

$$x = \frac{8c}{\pi^2} \sum_{n=1}^{\infty} \frac{(-1)^{n+1}}{(2n-1)^2} \sin \frac{(2n-1)\pi x}{2c} \qquad (-c \leq x \leq c).$$

8. After writing the Fourier series representation (3), Sec. 15, as

$$f(x) = \frac{a_0}{2} + \lim_{N \to \infty} \sum_{n=1}^{N} \left(a_n \cos \frac{n\pi x}{c} + b_n \sin \frac{n\pi x}{c} \right),$$

use the exponential forms[†]

$$\cos \theta = \frac{e^{i\theta} + e^{-i\theta}}{2}, \qquad \sin \theta = \frac{e^{i\theta} - e^{-i\theta}}{2i}$$

of the cosine and sine functions to put that representation in exponential form:

$$f(x) = \lim_{N \to \infty} \sum_{n=-N}^{N} A_n \exp\left(i \frac{n\pi x}{c} \right),$$

where

$$A_0 = \frac{a_0}{2}, \qquad A_n = \frac{a_n - i b_n}{2}, \qquad A_{-n} = \frac{a_n + i b_n}{2} \qquad (n = 1, 2, \ldots).$$

Then use expressions (4) and (5), Sec. 15, for the coefficients a_n and b_n to obtain the single formula

$$A_n = \frac{1}{2c} \int_{-c}^{c} f(x) \exp\left(-i \frac{n\pi x}{c} \right) dx \qquad (n = 0, \pm 1, \pm 2, \ldots).$$

16. A LEMMA

We prove here an important lemma to be used in Sec. 17. Sections 17 and 18, regarding the absolute and uniform convergence of Fourier series, and Secs. 19 and 20, dealing with differentiation and integration of such series, will be used only occasionally later on and will be specifically cited as needed. Hence the reader may at this time pass directly to Chap. 3 without serious disruption.

For convenience, we treat only Fourier series for which the fundamental interval is $-\pi < x < \pi$. Adaptations to series on any interval $-c < x < c$ can be made by the method used in Sec. 8.

Lemma. *Let f denote a function such that*

(i)   *f is continuous on the interval $-\pi \leq x \leq \pi$;*

(ii)   *$f(-\pi) = f(\pi)$;*

(iii) *its derivative f' is piecewise continuous on the interval $-\pi < x < \pi$.*

[†]For background on these forms and an introduction to series and integrals involving complex-valued functions, see the authors' book (2009), listed in the Bibliography.

If a_n and b_n are the Fourier coefficients

(1) $$a_n = \frac{1}{\pi} \int_{-\pi}^{\pi} f(x) \cos nx \, dx, \qquad b_n = \frac{1}{\pi} \int_{-\pi}^{\pi} f(x) \sin nx \, dx$$

for f on $-\pi < x < \pi$, the series

(2) $$\sum_{n=1}^{\infty} \sqrt{a_n^2 + b_n^2}$$

converges.

The class of functions satisfying conditions (i) through (iii) here is, of course, a subspace of the space of piecewise smooth functions on the interval $-\pi < x < \pi$.

We begin the proof of the lemma with the observation that the Fourier coefficients

(3) $$\alpha_n = \frac{1}{\pi} \int_{-\pi}^{\pi} f'(x) \cos nx \, dx, \qquad \beta_n = \frac{1}{\pi} \int_{-\pi}^{\pi} f'(x) \sin nx \, dx$$

for f' exist because of the piecewise continuity of f'. Note that

$$\alpha_0 = \frac{1}{\pi} \int_{-\pi}^{\pi} f'(x) \, dx = \frac{1}{\pi}[f(\pi) - f(-\pi)] = 0.$$

Also, since f is continuous and $f(-\pi) = f(\pi)$, integration by parts reveals that when $n = 1, 2, \ldots,$

$$\alpha_n = \frac{1}{\pi} \int_{-\pi}^{\pi} (\cos nx) f'(x) \, dx$$

$$= \frac{1}{\pi} \left\{ [(\cos nx) f(x)]_{-\pi}^{\pi} + n \int_{-\pi}^{\pi} f(x) \sin nx \, dx \right\} = nb_n.$$

Likewise,

$$\beta_n = \frac{1}{\pi} \int_{-\pi}^{\pi} (\sin nx) f'(x) \, dx$$

$$= \frac{1}{\pi} \left\{ [(\sin nx) f(x)]_{-\pi}^{\pi} - n \int_{-\pi}^{\pi} f(x) \cos nx \, dx \right\} = -na_n;$$

and we find that

(4) $$a_n = -\frac{\beta_n}{n}, \qquad b_n = \frac{\alpha_n}{n} \qquad\qquad (n = 1, 2, \ldots).$$

In view of relations (4), the sum s_N of the first N terms of the infinite series (2) becomes

(5) $$s_N = \sum_{n=1}^{N} \sqrt{a_n^2 + b_n^2} = \sum_{n=1}^{N} \frac{1}{n} \sqrt{\alpha_n^2 + \beta_n^2}.$$

Cauchy's inequality

$$\left(\sum_{n=1}^{N} p_n q_n \right)^2 \leq \left(\sum_{n=1}^{N} p_n^2 \right) \left(\sum_{n=1}^{N} q_n^2 \right),$$

which applies to any two sets of real numbers

$$p_n \ (n = 1, 2, \ldots, N) \qquad \text{and} \qquad q_n \ (n = 1, 2, \ldots, N)$$

(see Problem 6, Sec. 20, for a derivation), can now be used to write

$$
(6) \qquad s_N^2 \leq \left(\sum_{n=1}^{N} \frac{1}{n^2} \right) \left[\sum_{n=1}^{N} (\alpha_n^2 + \beta_n^2) \right] \qquad (N = 1, 2, \ldots).
$$

The sequence of sums

$$
(7) \qquad \sum_{n=1}^{N} \frac{1}{n^2} \qquad (N = 1, 2, \ldots)
$$

here is clearly bounded since each sum is a partial sum of the convergent series whose terms are $1/n^2$ [see Problem 6(a), Sec. 14]. The sequence

$$
(8) \qquad \sum_{n=1}^{N} (\alpha_n^2 + \beta_n^2) \qquad (N = 1, 2, \ldots)
$$

is also bounded since $\alpha_n \ (n = 0, 1, 2, \ldots)$ and $\beta_n \ (n = 1, 2, \ldots)$ are the Fourier coefficients for f' on the interval $-\pi < x < \pi$ and must, therefore, satisfy Bessel's inequality:

$$
\sum_{n=1}^{N} (\alpha_n^2 + \beta_n^2) \leq \frac{1}{\pi} \int_{-\pi}^{\pi} [f'(x)]^2 \, dx \qquad (N = 1, 2, \ldots).
$$

[See Problem 4(b), Sec. 11.] In view of the boundedness of sequences (7) and (8), it now follows from inequality (6) that the sequence $s_N^2 (N = 1, 2, \ldots)$ of squares is bounded, in addition to being nondecreasing. Hence it converges, and this means that the sequence $s_N (N = 1, 2, \ldots)$ converges. Thus series (2) converges.

17. ABSOLUTE AND UNIFORM CONVERGENCE OF FOURIER SERIES

We turn now to the absolute and uniform convergence of Fourier series. We begin by recalling some facts about uniformly convergent series of functions.[†]

Let $s(x)$ denote the sum of an infinite series of functions $f_n(x)$, where the series is convergent for all x in some subset E of the real axis. Thus

$$
(1) \qquad s(x) = \sum_{n=1}^{\infty} f_n(x) = \lim_{N \to \infty} s_N(x)
$$

for all x in E, where each $s_N(x)$ denotes the partial sum of the first N terms of the series. The series converges *uniformly* with respect to x if the absolute value of the difference $s(x) - s_N(x)$ can be made arbitrarily small for all x in the set E

[†] See, for instance, the book by Kaplan (2003, Chap. 6) or the one by Taylor and Mann (1983, Chap. 20), both listed in the Bibliography.

by taking N sufficiently large. That is, for each positive number ε, there exists a positive integer N_ε, *independent of x*, such that, for each x in E,

$$(2) \qquad\qquad |s(x) - s_N(x)| < \varepsilon \qquad \text{whenever} \qquad N > N_\varepsilon.$$

For us, the set E will be some closed interval $a \leq x \leq b$, or possibly an open one $a < x < b$. Geometrically, statement (2) then tells us that for each fixed x in E, the distance between $s_N(x)$ and $s(x)$ is less than ε. Thus the graph of $y = s_N(x)$ lies entirely inside a band of width 2ε centered along the graph of $y = s(x)$, as shown in Fig. 11.

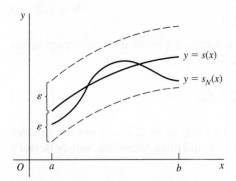

FIGURE 11

We include here a few properties of uniformly convergent series that are often useful. If the functions f_n are continuous and if series (1) is uniformly convergent, then the sum $s(x)$ of that series is a continuous function. Also, the series can be integrated term by term over the interval $a \leq x \leq b$ to give the integral of $s(x)$ from $x = a$ to $x = b$. If the functions f_n and their derivatives f_n' are continuous, if series (1) converges, and if the series whose terms are $f_n'(x)$ is uniformly convergent, then $s'(x)$ is found by differentiating series (1) term by term.

A sufficient condition for uniform convergence is given by the Weierstrass *M*-test. Namely, if there is a convergent series

$$(3) \qquad\qquad \sum_{n=1}^{\infty} M_n$$

of positive constants such that

$$(4) \qquad\qquad |f_n(x)| \leq M_n \qquad\qquad (a \leq x \leq b)$$

for each n, then series (1) is uniformly convergent on the stated interval.

Theorem. *Let f denote a function such that*

(i)   *f is continuous on the interval $-\pi \leq x \leq \pi$;*
(ii) *$f(-\pi) = f(\pi)$;*
(iii) *its derivative f' is piecewise continuous on the interval $-\pi < x < \pi$.*

The Fourier series

(5) $$\frac{a_0}{2} + \sum_{n=1}^{\infty}(a_n \cos nx + b_n \sin nx)$$

for f, with coefficients

(6) $$a_n = \frac{1}{\pi} \int_{-\pi}^{\pi} f(x) \cos nx\, dx, \qquad b_n = \frac{1}{\pi} \int_{-\pi}^{\pi} f(x) \sin nx\, dx,$$

converges absolutely and uniformly to $f(x)$ on the interval $-\pi \le x \le \pi$.

To prove this, we first note that the conditions on f ensure the continuity of the periodic extension of f for all x. Hence it follows from the theorem in Sec. 13 that series (5) converges to $f(x)$ everywhere in the interval $-\pi \le x \le \pi$. Observe how it follows from the inequalities

$$|a_n| \le \sqrt{a_n^2 + b_n^2} \qquad \text{and} \qquad |b_n| \le \sqrt{a_n^2 + b_n^2}$$

that

$$|a_n \cos nx + b_n \sin nx| \le |a_n| + |b_n| \le 2\sqrt{a_n^2 + b_n^2} \qquad (n = 1, 2, \ldots).$$

Since the series

$$\sum_{n=1}^{\infty} \sqrt{a_n^2 + b_n^2}$$

converges, according to the lemma in Sec. 16, the comparison test and the Weierstrass M-test thus apply to show that the convergence of series (5) is absolute and uniform on the interval $-\pi \le x \le \pi$, as stated.

Modifications of the statements in both the lemma in Sec. 16 and the above theorem are apparent. For instance, it follows from the theorem that the Fourier cosine series on $0 < x < \pi$ for a function f that is continuous on the closed interval $0 \le x \le \pi$ converges absolutely and uniformly to $f(x)$ when $0 \le x \le \pi$ if f' is piecewise continuous on $0 < x < \pi$. For the sine series, however, the additional conditions $f(0) = f(\pi) = 0$ are needed.

Since a uniformly convergent series of continuous functions always converges to a continuous function, a Fourier series for a function f cannot converge uniformly on an interval that contains a point at which f is discontinuous. Hence the continuity of f, assumed in the theorem, is necessary for the series there to converge uniformly. The lack of uniformity of the convergence of a Fourier series is illustrated in the next section.

18.   THE GIBBS PHENOMENON

Suppose that x_0 is a point at which a piecewise smooth function is discontinuous. The nature of the deviation near x_0 of the values of the partial sums of a Fourier series for f is commonly referred to as the *Gibbs phenomenon*.[†] We illustrate it here using the piecewise smooth function defined on the interval $-\pi < x < \pi$ by means of the equations

$$f(x) = \begin{cases} -\pi/2 & \text{when} \quad -\pi < x < 0, \\ \pi/2 & \text{when} \quad 0 < x < \pi, \end{cases}$$

and $f(0) = 0$.

According to Problem 1, Sec. 5, and the Fourier theorem in Sec. 13, the Fourier (sine) series

$$2\sum_{n=1}^{\infty} \frac{\sin(2n-1)x}{2n-1} \qquad (-\pi < x < \pi)$$

for f converges to $f(x)$ everywhere in the interval $-\pi < x < \pi$. Let $S_N(x)$ denote the sum of the first N terms of this series when $0 < x < \pi$. Thus

$$(1) \qquad S_N(x) = 2\sum_{n=1}^{N} \frac{\sin(2n-1)x}{2n-1} \qquad (0 < x < \pi),$$

and we know that the sequence $S_N(x)(N = 1, 2, \ldots)$ converges to $\pi/2 = 1.57 \cdots$ when $0 < x < \pi$. Differentiating expression (1), we have

$$(2) \qquad S_N'(x) = 2\sum_{n=1}^{N} \cos(2n-1)x.$$

This can be put in closed form with the aid of the trigonometric identity

$$2\sin A \cos B = \sin(A+B) + \sin(A-B).$$

More precisely, by writing $A = x$ and $B = (2n-1)x$ and then summing each side of the result from $n = 1$ to $n = N$, we have

$$2\sin x \sum_{n=1}^{N} \cos(2n-1)x = \sum_{n=1}^{N} \sin 2nx - \sum_{n=1}^{N} \sin 2(n-1)x.$$

The two summations on the right here telescope to give us

$$2\sin x \sum_{n=1}^{N} \cos(2n-1)x = \sin 2Nx,$$

and expression (2) becomes

$$(3) \qquad S_N'(x) = \frac{\sin 2Nx}{\sin x} \qquad (0 < x < \pi).$$

We find from expression (3) that this derivative is zero in the interval $0 < x < \pi$ when

$$x = \frac{k\pi}{2N} \qquad (k = 1, 2, \ldots, 2N - 1).$$

[†]For a detailed analysis of this phenomenon, see the book by Carslaw (1952, Chap. 9), which is listed in the Bibliography.

Hence $x = \pi/(2N)$ is the smallest positive number at which $S_N(x)$ has a critical point. By differentiating expression (3) and then substituting $x = \pi/(2N)$, we see that

$$S_n''\left(\frac{\pi}{2N}\right) = -\frac{2N}{\sin(\pi/2N)} < 0,$$

and this tells us that a relative maximum occurs at $x = \pi/(2N)$, as shown in Fig. 12.

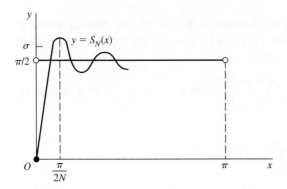

FIGURE 12

Next, we integrate each side of equation (3) from $x = 0$ to $x = \pi/(2N)$ in order to see that

$$(4) \qquad S_N\left(\frac{\pi}{2N}\right) = \int_0^{\pi/(2N)} \frac{\sin 2Nx}{\sin x}\,dx.$$

It is left to Problem 7, Sec. 20, to show how it follows from expression (4) that

$$\lim_{N\to\infty} S_N\left(\frac{\pi}{2N}\right) = \int_0^\pi \frac{\sin t}{t}\,dt.$$

The value of this integral is the number $\sigma = 1.85\cdots$ that is shown in Fig. 12, which indicates how "spikes" in the graphs of the partial sums $y = S_N(x)$, moving to the left as N increases, are formed, their tips tending to the point σ on the y axis.[†] The behavior of the partial sums is similar on the interval $-\pi < x < 0$.

The convergence of series (1) to $f(x)$ on $-\pi < x < \pi$ is not uniform, of course, because f is not continuous on that interval. It is, moreover, not uniform on $0 < x < \pi$ even though f is continuous there, because of the Gibbs phenomenon. To be specific, let ε denote any positive number smaller than the difference

$$\sigma - \frac{\pi}{2} \doteq 0.28,$$

where $\doteq$ denotes approximate equality. It is evident from Fig. 12 that because the tip of the "spike" occurring when $x = \pi/(2N)$ tends to σ, the graph of $y = S_N(x)$

[†]The integral occurs as a particular value of the *sine integral function* Si(x), which is tabulated in, for See also the more recent handbook edited by Olver, Logier, Boisvert, and Clark (2010) that is listed.

when N is large is not completely contained in a strip of width 2ε centered along the horizontal line segment $y = \pi/2$ on the interval $0 < x < \pi$.

19. DIFFERENTIATION OF FOURIER SERIES

Not all Fourier series are differentiable, as Example 1 illustrates.

EXAMPLE 1. According to Theorem 1 in Sec. 15, the Fourier series in Example 2, Sec. 7, for the function $f(x) = x \ (-\pi < x < \pi)$ converges to $f(x)$ at each point in the interval $-\pi < x < \pi$:

$$(1) \qquad\qquad x = 2 \sum_{n=1}^{\infty} \frac{(-1)^{n+1}}{n} \sin nx \qquad\qquad (-\pi < x < \pi).$$

But the differentiated series

$$2 \sum_{n=1}^{\infty} (-1)^{n+1} \cos nx$$

does not converge since its nth term fails to approach zero as n tends to infinity.

Sufficient conditions for differentiability can be stated as follows, where the conditions on f are the same as those in the theorem in Sec. 17, as well as in the lemma in Sec. 16.

Theorem. *Let f denote a function such that*

(*i*)   *f is continuous on the interval $-\pi \leq x \leq \pi$;*
(*ii*) *$f(-\pi) = f(\pi)$;*
(*iii*) *its derivative f' is piecewise continuous on the interval $-\pi < x < \pi$.*

The Fourier series representation

$$(2) \qquad\qquad f(x) = \frac{a_0}{2} + \sum_{n=1}^{\infty} (a_n \cos nx + b_n \sin nx) \qquad (-\pi \leq x \leq \pi),$$

where

$$a_n = \frac{1}{\pi} \int_{-\pi}^{\pi} f(x) \cos nx \, dx, \qquad b_n = \frac{1}{\pi} \int_{-\pi}^{\pi} f(x) \sin nx \, dx,$$

is differentiable at each point x in the interval $-\pi < x < \pi$ at which the second-order derivative f'' exists:

$$(3) \qquad\qquad f'(x) = \sum_{n=1}^{\infty} n(-a_n \sin nx + b_n \cos nx). \qquad\qquad (-\pi < x < \pi).$$

Our proof of this theorem is especially brief. To start, we consider a point x $(-\pi < x < \pi)$ at which f'' exists; and we note that f' is therefore continuous at x. Hence an application of the Fourier theorem in Sec. 12 to the function f'

shows that

$$f'(x) = \frac{\alpha_0}{2} + \sum_{n=1}^{\infty} (\alpha_n \cos nx + \beta_n \sin nx) \qquad (-\pi < x < \pi),$$

(4)

where

$$\alpha_n = \frac{1}{\pi} \int_{-\pi}^{\pi} f'(x) \cos nx \, dx, \qquad \beta_n = \frac{1}{\pi} \int_{-\pi}^{\pi} f'(x) \sin nx \, dx.$$

But since f and f' satisfy all the conditions stated in the lemma in Sec. 16, we know from the proof there that

(5) $$\alpha_0 = 0, \qquad \alpha_n = nb_n, \qquad \beta_n = -na_n \qquad (n = 1, 2, \ldots).$$

When these substitutions are made, equation (4) takes the form (3); and the proof is complete.

At a point x where $f''(x)$ does not exist, but where f' has one-sided derivatives, differentiation is still valid in the sense that the series in equation (3) converges to the mean of the values $f'(x+)$ and $f'(x-)$. This is also true for the periodic extension of f.

The theorem applies, with obvious changes, to other Fourier series. For instance, if f is continuous when $0 \le x \le \pi$ and f' is piecewise continuous on the interval $0 < x < \pi$, then the Fourier cosine series for f on $0 < x < \pi$ is differentiable at each point x $(0 < x < \pi)$ where $f''(x)$ exists.

EXAMPLE 2. We know from Problem 5, Sec. 7, and the theorem in Sec. 13 that when $a \ne 0$,

$$\cosh ax = \frac{\sinh a\pi}{a\pi} \left[1 + 2a^2 \sum_{n=1}^{\infty} \frac{(-1)^n}{a^2 + n^2} \cos nx \right]$$

on the closed interval $-\pi \le x \le \pi$. Inasmuch as the hypothesis in the theorem here is satisfied when $f(x) = \cosh ax$, it follows that

$$a \sinh ax = \frac{2a \sinh a\pi}{\pi} \sum_{n=1}^{\infty} \frac{(-1)^n}{a^2 + n^2} (-n \sin nx)$$

on the interval $-\pi < x < \pi$. That is, when $a \ne 0$,

(6) $$\sinh ax = \frac{2 \sinh a\pi}{\pi} \sum_{n=1}^{\infty} (-1)^{n+1} \frac{n}{a^2 + n^2} \sin nx \qquad (-\pi < x < \pi).$$

Note that equation (6) is, in fact, valid when the condition $a \ne 0$ is dropped.

20. INTEGRATION OF FOURIER SERIES

Integration of a Fourier series is possible under much more general conditions than those for differentiation. Suppose that f is piecewise continuous and that

(1) $$f(x) \sim \frac{a_0}{2} + \sum_{n=1}^{\infty} (a_n \cos nx + b_n \sin nx) \qquad (-\pi < x < \pi)$$

where

(2) $\qquad a_n = \dfrac{1}{\pi}\displaystyle\int_{-\pi}^{\pi} f(x)\cos nx\,dx, \qquad b_n = \dfrac{1}{\pi}\displaystyle\int_{-\pi}^{\pi} f(x)\sin nx\,dx.$

In the following theorem it is not even essential that series (1) converge in order that the integrated series converge to the integral of the function.

> **Theorem.** *Let f be a function that is piecewise continuous on the interval $-\pi < x < \pi$. Regardless of whether series (1) converges or not, the equation*

(3) $\qquad \displaystyle\int_{-\pi}^{x} f(s)\,ds = \dfrac{a_0}{2}(x+\pi) + \sum_{n=1}^{\infty} \dfrac{1}{n}\{a_n \sin nx - b_n[\cos nx + (-1)^{n+1}]\}$

is valid when $-\pi \le x \le \pi$.

Series (3) is, of course, obtained by replacing x by s in series (1) and then integrating term by term from $s = -\pi$ to $s = x$. Observe that if $a_0 \ne 0$, the first term on the right in equation (3) is not of the type encountered in a Fourier series. Hence integrating a Fourier series does not always yield an actual Fourier series.

Our proof starts with the fact that since f is piecewise continuous, the function

(4) $\qquad\qquad\qquad F(x) = \displaystyle\int_{-\pi}^{x} f(s)\,ds - \dfrac{a_0}{2}x \qquad\qquad (-\pi \le x \le \pi)$

is continuous; moreover,

(5) $\qquad\qquad\qquad F'(x) = f(x) - \dfrac{a_0}{2} \qquad\qquad\qquad (-\pi < x < \pi),$

except at points where f is discontinuous. Hence F' is piecewise continuous on the interval $-\pi < x < \pi$. Since F is piecewise smooth, then, it follows from Theorem 1 in Sec. 15 that

(6) $\qquad\qquad\qquad F(x) = \dfrac{A_0}{2} + \displaystyle\sum_{n=1}^{\infty}(A_n \cos nx + B_n \sin nx) \qquad (-\pi < x < \pi),$

where

(7) $\qquad A_n = \dfrac{1}{\pi}\displaystyle\int_{-\pi}^{\pi} F(x)\cos nx\,dx, \qquad B_n = \dfrac{1}{\pi}\displaystyle\int_{-\pi}^{\pi} F(x)\sin nx\,dx.$

We note from expression (4) and the first of expressions (2) when $n = 0$ that

(8) $\quad F(-\pi) = \dfrac{a_0}{2}\pi \quad$ and $\quad F(\pi) = \displaystyle\int_{-\pi}^{\pi} f(s)\,ds - \dfrac{a_0}{2}\pi = a_0\pi - \dfrac{a_0}{2}\pi = \dfrac{a_0}{2}\pi;$

hence

(9) $\qquad\qquad\qquad\qquad F(-\pi) = F(\pi).$

This shows that representation (6) is also valid at the endpoints of the open interval $-\pi < x < \pi$ and, therefore, at each point of the closed interval $-\pi \le x \le \pi$.

Let us now write the coefficients A_n and B_n in terms of a_n and b_n. When $n \ge 1$, we may integrate integrals (7) by parts, using the fact that F is continuous and F' is piecewise continuous. Thus

$$A_n = \frac{1}{\pi} \left\{ \left[F(x) \frac{\sin nx}{n} \right]_{-\pi}^{\pi} - \int_{-\pi}^{\pi} \frac{\sin nx}{n} F'(x) \, dx \right\}$$

$$= -\frac{1}{n\pi} \int_{-\pi}^{\pi} F'(x) \sin nx \, dx;$$

and, in view of expression (5) for $F'(x)$, we have

$$A_n = -\frac{1}{n\pi} \int_{-\pi}^{\pi} \left[f(x) - \frac{a_0}{2} \right] \sin nx \, dx$$

$$= -\frac{1}{n} \cdot \frac{1}{\pi} \int_{-\pi}^{\pi} f(x) \sin nx \, dx + \frac{a_0}{2n\pi} \int_{-\pi}^{\pi} \sin nx \, dx = -\frac{b_n}{n}.$$

Likewise, keeping relation (9) in mind, we find that

$$B_n = \frac{1}{\pi} \left\{ \left[-F(x) \frac{\cos nx}{n} \right]_{-\pi}^{\pi} + \int_{-\pi}^{\pi} \frac{\cos nx}{n} F'(x) \, dx \right\}$$

$$= \frac{1}{n\pi} \int_{-\pi}^{\pi} F'(x) \cos nx \, dx;$$

and, using expression (5) once again, we can see that

$$B_n = \frac{1}{n\pi} \int_{-\pi}^{\pi} \left[f(x) - \frac{a_0}{2} \right] \cos nx \, dx$$

$$= \frac{1}{n} \cdot \frac{1}{\pi} \int_{-\pi}^{\pi} f(x) \cos nx \, dx - \frac{a_0}{2n\pi} \int_{-\pi}^{\pi} \cos nx \, dx = \frac{a_n}{n}.$$

As for A_0, from the final value for $F(\pi)$ shown in the second of relations (8) and the fact that representation (6) is valid when $x = \pi$, we know that

$$\frac{a_0}{2} \pi = \frac{A_0}{2} + \sum_{n=1}^{\infty} A_n(-1)^n.$$

So, by solving for A_0 here and then using the relation $A_n = -b_n/n$ that we have found, we arrive at

$$A_0 = a_0 \pi - 2 \sum_{n=1}^{\infty} A_n(-1)^n = a_0 \pi - 2 \sum_{n=1}^{\infty} \frac{(-1)^{n+1}}{n} b_n.$$

With these expressions for A_n and B_n, including A_0, representation (6) takes the form

$$F(x) = \frac{a_0}{2} \pi + \sum_{n=1}^{\infty} \frac{1}{n} \{ a_n \sin nx - b_n [\cos nx + (-1)^{n+1}] \}.$$

Finally, if we use expression (4) to substitute for $F(x)$ here, we arrive at the desired result (3).

The theorem can be written for the integral from x_0 to x, where $-\pi \le x_0 \le \pi$ and $-\pi \le x \le \pi$, by noting that

$$\int_{x_0}^{x} f(s)\, ds = \int_{-\pi}^{x} f(s)\, ds - \int_{-\pi}^{x_0} f(s)\, ds.$$

PROBLEMS

1. Show that the function

$$f(x) = \begin{cases} 0 & \text{when } -\pi \le x \le 0, \\ \sin x & \text{when } \quad 0 < x \le \pi \end{cases}$$

satisfies all the conditions in the theorem in Sec. 17. Then, with the aid of the Weierstrass M-test in Sec. 17, verify that the Fourier series

$$\frac{1}{\pi} + \frac{1}{2}\sin x - \frac{2}{\pi}\sum_{n=1}^{\infty} \frac{\cos 2nx}{4n^2 - 1} \qquad (-\pi < x < \pi)$$

for f, found in Problem 7, Sec. 7, converges uniformly on the interval $-\pi \le x \le \pi$, as the theorem in Sec. 17 tells us. Also, state why this series is differentiable in the interval $-\pi < x < \pi$, except at the point $x = 0$, and describe graphically the function that is represented by the differentiated series for all x.

2. We know from Example 1, Sec. 3, that the series

$$\frac{\pi}{2} - \frac{4}{\pi}\sum_{n=1}^{\infty} \frac{\cos(2n-1)x}{(2n-1)^2}$$

is the Fourier cosine series for the function $f(x) = x$ on the interval $0 < x < \pi$. Differentiate this series term by term to obtain a representation for the derivative $f'(x) = 1$ on that interval. State why the procedure is reliable here.

3. State the theorem in Sec. 19 as it applies to Fourier sine series. Point out, in particular, why the conditions $f(0) = f(\pi) = 0$ are present in this case.

4. Let a_n and b_n denote the Fourier coefficients in the lemma in Sec. 16. Using the fact that the coefficients in the Fourier series for a function in $C_p(-\pi, \pi)$ always tend to zero as n tends to infinity (Problem 5, Sec. 11), show why

$$\lim_{n\to\infty} na_n = 0 \qquad \text{and} \qquad \lim_{n\to\infty} nb_n = 0.$$

5. Integrate from $s = 0$ to $s = x$ $(-\pi \le x \le \pi)$ the Fourier series

$$2\sum_{n=1}^{\infty} \frac{(-1)^{n+1}}{n}\sin ns$$

in Example 1, Sec. 19, and the one

$$2\sum_{n=1}^{\infty} \frac{\sin(2n-1)s}{2n-1}$$

appearing in Sec. 18. In each case, describe graphically the function that is represented by the new series.

6. Let p_n $(n = 1, 2, \ldots, N)$ and q_n $(n = 1, 2, \ldots, N)$ denote real numbers, where at least one of the numbers p_n, say p_m, is nonzero. By writing the quadratic equation

$$x^2 \sum_{n=1}^{N} p_n^2 + 2x \sum_{n=1}^{N} p_n q_n + \sum_{n=1}^{N} q_n^2 = 0$$

in the form

$$\sum_{n=1}^{N} (p_n x + q_n)^2 = 0,$$

show that the number $x_0 = -q_m/p_m$ is the only possible real root. Conclude that since *there cannot be two distinct real roots,* the discriminant

$$\left(2 \sum_{n=1}^{N} p_n q_n \right)^2 - 4 \left(\sum_{n=1}^{N} p_n^2 \right) \left(\sum_{n=1}^{N} q_n^2 \right)$$

of this quadratic equation is negative or zero. Thus derive Cauchy's inequality (Sec. 16)

$$\left(\sum_{n=1}^{N} p_n q_n \right)^2 \leq \left(\sum_{n=1}^{N} p_n^2 \right) \left(\sum_{n=1}^{N} q_n^2 \right),$$

which is clearly valid even if all the numbers p_n are zero.

7. Rewrite expression (4), Sec. 18, as

$$S_N \left(\frac{\pi}{2N} \right) = I + J$$

where

$$I = \int_0^{\pi/(2N)} \frac{x - \sin x}{x \sin x} \sin 2Nx \, dx \quad \text{and} \quad J = \int_0^{\pi/(2N)} \frac{\sin 2Nx}{x} dx.$$

(a) With the aid of l'Hôpital's rule, show that the one-sided limits

$$\lim_{\substack{x \to 0 \\ x > 0}} \frac{x - \sin x}{x \sin x} \quad \text{and} \quad \lim_{\substack{x \to 0 \\ x > 0}} \frac{\sin 2Nx}{x}$$

exist and hence, that the integrands in these two integrals are piecewise continuous on the interval $0 < x < \pi/(2N)$. This establishes the existence of the integrals.

(b) Use the fact (Sec. 1) that a piecewise continuous function defined on a finite interval is bounded on that interval to show that

$$|I| \leq \int_0^{\pi/(2N)} \left| \frac{x - \sin x}{x \sin x} \sin 2Nx \right| dx \to 0$$

as N tends to infinity.

(c) By making the substitution $t = 2Nx$ in the integral J, show that

$$J = \int_0^{\pi} \frac{\sin t}{t} dt.$$

(d) Conclude from the results obtained in parts (b) and (c) that

$$\lim_{N \to \infty} S_N \left(\frac{\pi}{2N} \right) = \int_0^{\pi} \frac{\sin t}{t} dt.$$

as stated in Sec. 18.

CHAPTER

3

PARTIAL
DIFFERENTIAL
EQUATIONS
OF PHYSICS

This chapter is devoted mainly to the derivation of certain partial differential equations arising in studies of heat conduction, electrostatics, and mechanical vibrations. Solutions of these equations, to be obtained in subsequent chapters, will involve not only Fourier series of the type treated in Chaps. 1 and 2 but also other kinds of series to be developed in the later chapters.

21. LINEAR BOUNDARY VALUE PROBLEMS

In the theory and application of partial differential equations, the dependent variable, denoted here by u, is usually required to satisfy some conditions on the boundary of the domain on which the differential equation is defined. The equations that represent those boundary conditions may involve values of derivatives of u, as well as values of u itself, at points on the boundary. In addition, some conditions on the continuity of u and its derivatives within the domain and on the boundary may be required. Such a set of requirements constitutes a *boundary value problem* in the function u. We use that terminology whenever the differential equation is accompanied by boundary conditions.

A boundary value problem is correctly set if it has one and only one solution within a given class of functions. Physical interpretations often suggest boundary conditions under which a problem may be correctly set. In fact, it is sometimes helpful to interpret a problem physically in order to judge whether the boundary conditions may be adequate. This is a prominent reason for associating such problems with their physical applications, aside from the opportunity to illustrate connections between mathematical analysis and the physical sciences.

The theory of partial differential equations gives results on the existence and uniqueness of solutions of boundary value problems. But such results are necessarily limited by the great variety of types of differential equations and domains on which they are defined, as well as types of boundary conditions. Instead of appealing to general theory in treating a specific problem, our approach will be to actually find a solution, which can often be verified and shown to be the only one possible.

Frequently, it is convenient to indicate partial differentiation by writing independent variables as subscripts. If, for instance, u is a function of x and y, we may write

$$u_x \text{ or } u_x(x, y) \text{ for } \frac{\partial u}{\partial x}, \qquad u_{xx} \text{ for } \frac{\partial^2 u}{\partial x^2}, \qquad u_{xy} \text{ for } \frac{\partial^2 u}{\partial y\, \partial x},$$

etc. We shall always assume that the partial derivatives of u satisfy continuity conditions allowing us to write $u_{yx} = u_{xy}.$[†] Also, we shall be free to use the symbol $u_x(c, y)$, for example, to denote values of the function $\partial u / \partial x$ on the line $x = c$.

EXAMPLE. The problem consisting of the differential equation

$$(1) \qquad\qquad u_{xx}(x, y) + u_{yy}(x, y) = 0 \qquad\qquad (x > 0, y > 0)$$

and the two boundary conditions

$$(2) \qquad\qquad u(0, y) = u_x(0, y) \qquad\qquad (y > 0),$$

$$(3) \qquad\qquad u(x, 0) = \sin x + \cos x \qquad\qquad (x > 0)$$

is a boundary value problem in partial differential equations. The differential equation is defined in the first quadrant of the xy plane (see Fig. 13). As the reader can readily verify, the function

$$(4) \qquad\qquad u(x, y) = e^{-y}(\sin x + \cos x)$$

is a solution of this problem. The function (4) and its partial derivatives of the first and second order are continuous in the region $x \geq 0, y \geq 0$.

FIGURE 13

[†] See, for instance, the book by Taylor and Mann (1983, pp. 200–201) that is listed in the Bibliography.

A differential equation in a function u, or a boundary condition on u, is *linear* if it is an equation of the first degree in u and derivatives of u. Thus, the terms of the equation are either prescribed functions of the independent variables alone, including constants, or such functions multiplied by u or a derivative of u. Note that the general linear partial differential equation of the second order in $u = u(x, y)$ has the form

$$(5) \qquad Au_{xx} + Bu_{xy} + Cu_{yy} + Du_x + Eu_y + Fu = G,$$

where the letters A through G denote either constants or functions of the independent variables x and y only. The differential equation and the boundary conditions in the example above are all linear. The differential equation

$$(6) \qquad zu_{xx} + xy^2u_{yy} - e^xu_z = f(y, z)$$

is linear in $u = u(x, y, z)$; but the equation $u_{xx} + uu_y = x$ is nonlinear in $u = u(x, y)$ because the term uu_y is not of the first degree as an algebraic expression in the two variables u and u_y, in accordance with equation (5).

As expected, a boundary value problem is said to be linear if its differential equation and all of its boundary conditions are linear. The boundary value problem in our example is, therefore, linear. The method of solution presented in this book does not apply to nonlinear problems.

A linear differential equation or boundary condition in u is *homogeneous* if each of its terms, other than zero itself, is of the first degree in the function u and its derivatives. Homogeneity will play a central role in our treatment of linear boundary value problems. Observe that equation (1) and condition (2) are homogeneous, but that condition (3) is not. Equation (5) is homogeneous in a domain of the xy plane only when the function G is identically equal to zero ($G \equiv 0$) throughout that domain; and equation (6) is nonhomogeneous unless $f(y, z) \equiv 0$ for all values of y and z being considered.

22. ONE-DIMENSIONAL HEAT EQUATION

Thermal energy is transferred from warmer to cooler regions interior to a solid body by means of conduction. It is convenient to refer to that transfer as a *flow of heat*, as if heat were a fluid or gas that diffused through the body from regions of high concentration into regions of low concentration. We shall now find a partial differential equation that is satisfied by temperatures in the solid. In order to do this, we need to consider some terminology that occurs in physics.

(i) Flux and Thermal Conductivity

Let P_0 denote a point (x_0, y_0, z_0) interior to the body and S a smooth surface through P_0. Also, let $\mathbf{n}$ be a unit vector that is normal to S at the point P_0 (Fig. 14). At time t, the *flux of heat* $\Phi(x_0, y_0, z_0, t)$ across S at P_0 in the direction of $\mathbf{n}$ is the quantity of heat per unit area per unit time that is being conducted across S at P_0 in that direction. Flux is, therefore, measured in such units as calories per square centimeter per second.

FIGURE 14

If $u(x, y, z, t)$ denotes temperatures at points (x, y, z) of the body at time t and if n is a coordinate that represents distance in the direction of **n**, the flux $\Phi(x_0, y_0, z_0, t)$ is positive when the directional derivative du/dn is negative at P_0 and negative when du/dn is positive there. A fundamental postulate, known as *Fourier's law,* in the mathematical theory of heat conduction states that the magnitude of the flux $\Phi(x_0, y_0, z_0, t)$ is proportional to the magnitude of the directional derivative du/dn at P_0 at time t. That is, there is a coefficient K, known as the *thermal conductivity* of the material, such that

$$(1) \qquad\qquad\qquad \Phi = -K\frac{du}{dn} \qquad\qquad (K > 0)$$

at P_0 and time t.

(ii) Specific Heat

Another thermal coefficient of the material is its *specific heat σ.* This is the quantity of heat required to raise the temperature of a unit of mass of the material one unit on the temperature scale. Unless otherwise stated, we shall always assume that the coefficients K and σ are constant throughout the solid body and that the same is true of density δ, which is the mass per unit volume of the material. With these assumptions, a second postulate in the mathematical theory is that conduction leads to a temperature function u which, together with its derivative u_t and those of the first and second order with respect to x, y, and z, is continuous throughout each domain interior to a solid body in which no heat is generated or lost.

Suppose now that heat flows only parallel to the x axis in the body, so that flux Φ and temperatures u depend on only x and t. Thus $\Phi = \Phi(x, t)$ and $u = u(x, t)$. We assume at present that heat is neither generated nor lost within the body and hence that heat enters or leaves only through its surface. We then construct a small rectangular parallelepiped, lying in the interior of the body, with one vertex at a point (x, y, z) and with faces parallel to the coordinate planes. The lengths of the edges are Δx, Δy, and Δz, as shown in Fig. 15. Observe that since the parallelepiped is small, the continuous function u_t varies little in that region and has approximately the value $u_t(x, t)$ throughout it. This approximation improves, of course, as Δx tends to zero.

The mass of the element of material occupying the parallelepiped is $\delta\,\Delta x \Delta y\,\Delta z$. So, in view of the definition of specific heat σ stated above, we know that one measure of the quantity of heat entering that element per unit time at

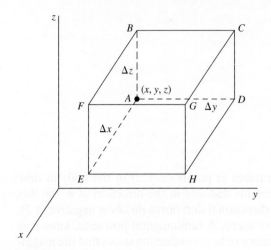

FIGURE 15

time t is approximately

(2) $$\sigma\delta\,\Delta x\,\Delta y\,\Delta z\,u_t(x,t).$$

Another way to measure that quantity is to observe that since the flow of heat is parallel to the x axis, heat crosses only the surfaces $ABCD$ and $EFGH$ of the element, which are parallel to the yz plane. If the direction of the flux $\Phi(x,t)$ is in the *positive* direction of the x axis, it follows that the quantity of heat per unit time crossing the surface $ABCD$ into the element at time t is $\Phi(x,t)\Delta y\,\Delta z$. Because of the heat leaving the element through the face $EFGH$, the net quantity of heat entering the element per unit time is, then,

$$\Phi(x,t)\,\Delta y\,\Delta z - \Phi(x+\Delta x,t)\,\Delta y\,\Delta z.$$

In view of Fourier's law (1), this expression can be written

(3) $$K\left[u_x(x+\Delta x,t) - u_x(x,t)\right]\Delta y\,\Delta z.$$

Equating expressions (2) and (3) for the quantity of heat entering the element per unit time and then dividing by $\sigma\delta\,\Delta x\,\Delta y\,\Delta z$, we have, approximately,

$$u_t(x,t) = \frac{K}{\sigma\delta}\cdot\frac{u_x(x+\Delta x,t) - u_x(x,t)}{\Delta x}.$$

Letting Δx tend to zero here, we find that temperatures in a solid body, when heat flows only parallel to the x axis, satisfy the one-dimensional *heat equation*

(4) $$u_t(x,\,t) = k u_{xx}(x,\,t),$$

where

$$k = \frac{K}{\sigma\delta}.$$

The positive constant k here is called the *thermal diffusivity* of the material.

In the derivation of equation (4), we assumed that there is no source (or sink) of heat within the solid body, only heat transfer by conduction. If there is a uniform source throughout the body that generates heat at a constant rate Q per unit volume, it is easy to modify the derivation to obtain the nonhomogeneous heat equation

(5) $$u_t(x, t) = ku_{xx}(x, t) + q_0,$$

where

$$q_0 = \frac{Q}{\sigma\delta}.$$

This is accomplished by simply adding the term $Q \, \Delta x \, \Delta y \, \Delta z$ to expression (3) and proceeding in the same way as before. The rate Q per unit volume at which heat is generated may, in fact, be any continuous function of x and t, in which case the term q_0 in equation (5) is replaced by a function $q(x, t)$.

The heat equation describing flow in two and three dimensions is discussed in Sec. 23.

23. RELATED EQUATIONS

When the direction of heat flow in a solid body is not restricted to be simply parallel to the x axis, temperatures u in the body depend, in general, on all of the space variables, as well as t. By considering the rate of heat passing through each of the six faces of the element in Fig. 15 (Sec. 22), one can derive (see Problem 1) the *three-dimensional* heat equation, satisfied by $u = u(x, y, z, t)$:

(1) $$u_t = k(u_{xx} + u_{yy} + u_{zz}).$$

The constant k is the thermal diffusivity of the material, appearing in equation (4), Sec. 22. When the *laplacian*

(2) $$\nabla^2 u = u_{xx} + u_{yy} + u_{zz}$$

is used, equation (1) takes the compact form

(3) $$u_t = k\nabla^2 u.$$

Note that when there is no flow of heat parallel to the z axis, so that $u_{zz} = 0$ and $u = u(x, y, t)$, equation (1) reduces to the heat equation for *two-dimensional* flow parallel to the xy plane:

(4) $$u_t = k(u_{xx} + u_{yy}).$$

The *one-dimensional* heat equation $u_t = ku_{xx}$ that was obtained in Sec. 22 for temperatures $u = u(x, t)$ follows, of course, from this when there is, in addition, no flow parallel to the y axis. If temperatures are in a *steady state*, in which case u does not vary with time, equation (1) becomes *Laplace's equation*

(5) $$u_{xx} + u_{yy} + u_{zz} = 0.$$

Equation (5) is often written $\nabla^2 u = 0$.

The derivation of equation (1) in Problem 1 takes into account the possibility that heat may be generated in the solid body at a constant rate Q per unit volume, and the generalization

$$(6) \qquad\qquad u_t = k\nabla^2 u + q_0$$

of equation (5), Sec. 22, is obtained. If the rate Q is a continuous function of the space variables x, y, and z and if temperatures are in a steady state, equation (6) becomes *Poisson's equation*

$$(7) \qquad\qquad \nabla^2 u = f(x, y, z),$$

where $f(x, y, z) = -q(x, y, z)/k$.

It should be emphasized that the various partial differential equations in this section are important in other areas of applied mathematics. In simple diffusion problems, for example, Fourier's law $\Phi = -K\,du/dn$ applies to the flux Φ of a substance that is diffusing within a porous solid. In that case, Φ represents the mass of the substance that is diffused per unit area per unit time through a surface, u denotes *concentration* (the mass of the diffusing substance per unit volume of the solid), and K is the *coefficient of diffusion*. Since the mass of the substance entering the element of volume in Fig. 15 per unit time is $\Delta x\,\Delta y\,\Delta z\,u_t$, one can write $Q = 0$ in the derivation of equation (6) and replace the product $\sigma\delta$ in that derivation by unity to see that the concentration u satisfies the *diffusion equation*

$$(8) \qquad\qquad u_t = K\nabla^2 u.$$

A function $u = u(x, y, z)$ that is continuous, together with its partial derivatives of the first and second order, and satisfies Laplace's equation (5) is called a *harmonic function*. We have seen in this section that the steady-state temperatures at points interior to a solid body in which no heat is generated are represented by a harmonic function. The steady-state concentration of a diffusing substance is also represented by such a function.

Among the many physical examples of harmonic functions, the velocity potential for the steady-state irrotational motion of an incompressible fluid is prominent in hydrodynamics and aerodynamics. An important harmonic function in electric field theory is the electrostatic potential $V(x, y, z)$ in a region of space that is free of electric charges. The potential may be caused by a static distribution of electric charges outside that region. The fact that V is harmonic is a consequence of the inverse-square law of attraction or repulsion between charges. Likewise, gravitational potential is a harmonic function in regions of space not occupied by matter.

In this book, the physical problems involving the laplacian, and Laplace's equation in particular, are limited mostly to those for which the differential equations are derived in this chapter. Derivations of such differential equations in other areas of applied mathematics can be found in books on hydrodynamics, elasticity, vibrations and sound, electric field theory, potential theory, and other branches of continuum mechanics. A number of such books are listed in the Bibliography.

PROBLEMS

1. Let $u = u(x, y, z, t)$ denote temperatures in a solid body throughout which there is a uniform heat source. Derive the heat equation

$$u_t = k\nabla^2 u + q_0$$

for those temperatures, where the constants k and q_0 are the same ones as in equation (5), Sec. 22.

    Suggestion: Modify the derivation of equation (5), Sec. 22, by also considering the net rate of heat entering the element in Fig. 15 (Sec. 22) through the faces parallel to the xz and xy planes. Since the faces are small, one may consider the needed flux at points on a given face to be constant over that face. Thus, for instance, the net rate of heat entering the element through the faces parallel to the xz plane is to be taken as

$$K\left[u_y(x, y + \Delta y, z, t) - u_y(x, y, z, t)\right]\Delta x\, \Delta z.$$

2. Suppose that the thermal coefficients K and σ (Sec. 22) are functions of x, y, and z. Modify the derivation in Problem 1 to show that the heat equation takes the form

$$\sigma\delta u_t = (Ku_x)_x + (Ku_y)_y + (Ku_z)_z$$

in a domain where all functions and derivatives involved are continuous and where there is no heat generated.

3. Show that the substitution $\tau = kt$ can be used to write the two-dimensional heat equation

$$u_t = k(u_{xx} + u_{yy})$$

in the form

$$u_\tau = u_{xx} + u_{yy},$$

where the thermal diffusivity is unity.

    Suggestion: Note that

$$\frac{\partial u}{\partial t} = \frac{\partial u}{\partial \tau}\frac{d\tau}{dt}.$$

4. Show that the physical dimensions of thermal diffusivity k (Sec. 22) are L^2T^{-1}, where L denotes length and T time.

    Suggestion: Observe first that the dimensions of thermal conductivity K and specific heat σ are $AL^{-1}T^{-1}B^{-1}$ and $AM^{-1}B^{-1}$, respectively, where M denotes mass, A is quantity of heat, and B is temperature. Then recall that $k = K/(\sigma\delta)$, where δ is density (ML^{-3}).

24. LAPLACIAN IN CYLINDRICAL AND SPHERICAL COORDINATES

We recall (Sec. 23) that the heat equation, and also Laplace's equation, can be written in terms of the laplacian

$$(1) \qquad\qquad \nabla^2 u = u_{xx} + u_{yy} + u_{zz}.$$

Often, because of the geometric configuration of the physical problem, it is more convenient to use the laplacian in other than the rectangular coordinates x, y, and z. In this section, we give expressions for $\nabla^2 u$ in two different coordinate systems already encountered in calculus. These alternative forms of $\nabla^2 u$ will then be derived in Sec. 25, where it is assumed that u possesses continuous partial derivatives of the first and second orders with respect to the independent variables.

(i) Cylindrical Coordinates

The *cylindrical coordinates* ρ, ϕ, and z determine a point $P(\rho, \phi, z)$, shown in Fig. 16. Cylindrical and rectangular coordinates evidently share the coordinate z. Also, ρ and ϕ are the polar coordinates in the xy plane of the projection Q of P onto that plane.[†]

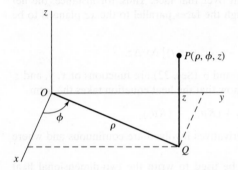

FIGURE 16

We shall show in Sec. 25 that *the laplacian of u in cylindrical coordinates* is

$$(2) \qquad \nabla^2 u = u_{\rho\rho} + \frac{1}{\rho} u_\rho + \frac{1}{\rho^2} u_{\phi\phi} + u_{zz}.$$

Note how one can group the first two terms in this expression to write

$$(3) \qquad \nabla^2 u = \frac{1}{\rho} (\rho u_\rho)_\rho + \frac{1}{\rho^2} u_{\phi\phi} + u_{zz}.$$

When u is independent of z, so that $u = u(\rho, \phi)$, expression (2) becomes the two-dimensional *laplacian of u in polar coordinates*:

$$(4) \qquad \nabla^2 u = u_{\rho\rho} + \frac{1}{\rho} u_\rho + \frac{1}{\rho^2} u_{\phi\phi}.$$

Laplace's equation $\nabla^2 u = 0$ in polar coordinates can, therefore, be written in the form

$$(5) \qquad \rho^2 u_{\rho\rho} + \rho u_\rho + u_{\phi\phi} = 0.$$

Also, it follows from expression (2) that when temperatures u in a solid body vary only with ρ and time t, and not with the space variables ϕ and z, the heat equation

---

[†]In calculus, the symbols r and θ are often used instead of ρ and ϕ, but the notation used here is common in physics and engineering. The notation for spherical coordinates, appearing later in this section, may also differ somewhat from that learned in calculus.

$u_t = k\nabla^2 u$ becomes

(6) $$u_t = k\left(u_{\rho\rho} + \frac{1}{\rho}u_\rho\right).$$

Equations (5) and (6) will be of particular interest in the applications. Another special case that will be used later on occurs when the function u in the laplacian (2) is independent of ϕ, in which case the term containing $u_{\phi\phi}$ vanishes.

(ii) Spherical Coordinates

The *spherical coordinates* r, ϕ, and θ of a point $P(r, \phi, \theta)$ are shown in Fig. 17. Note that the coordinate ϕ is common to spherical and cylindrical coordinates.

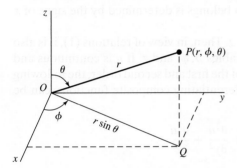

FIGURE 17

It will be shown in Sec. 25 that *the laplacian of u in spherical coordinates* is

(7) $$\nabla^2 u = u_{rr} + \frac{2}{r}u_r + \frac{1}{r^2 \sin^2\theta}u_{\phi\phi} + \frac{1}{r^2}u_{\theta\theta} + \frac{\cot\theta}{r^2}u_\theta.$$

Other forms of this expression are

(8) $$\nabla^2 u = \frac{1}{r}(ru)_{rr} + \frac{1}{r^2 \sin^2\theta}u_{\phi\phi} + \frac{1}{r^2 \sin\theta}(\sin\theta\, u_\theta)_\theta$$

and

(9) $$\nabla^2 u = \frac{1}{r^2}(r^2 u_r)_r + \frac{1}{r^2 \sin^2\theta}u_{\phi\phi} + \frac{1}{r^2 \sin\theta}(\sin\theta\, u_\theta)_\theta.$$

Some of our applications later on will involve Laplace's equation $\nabla^2 u = 0$ in spherical coordinates when u is independent of ϕ. According to expression (8), that equation can then be written

(10) $$r(ru)_{rr} + \frac{1}{\sin\theta}(\sin\theta\, u_\theta)_\theta = 0.$$

The reader who wishes to accept expressions (2) and (7) without derivation can at this time pass directly to Sec. 26.

25. DERIVATIONS

In deriving expressions for the laplacian in cylindrical and spherical coordinates that were stated in Sec. 24, we consider first the cylindrical coordinates ρ, ϕ, and z.

(i) Cylindrical Coordinates

One can see from Fig. 16 in Sec. 24 that the cylindrical coordinates ρ, ϕ, and z are related to the rectangular coordinates x, y, and z by the equations

$$(1) \qquad x = \rho \cos \phi, \qquad y = \rho \sin \phi, \qquad z = z,$$

as well as the ones

$$(2) \qquad \rho = \sqrt{x^2 + y^2}, \qquad \phi = \tan^{-1} \frac{y}{x}, \qquad z = z,$$

where the quadrant to which the angle ϕ belongs is determined by the signs of x and y, not by the ratio y/x alone.

Let u denote a function of x, y, and z. Then, in view of relations (1), it is also a function of the three independent variables ρ, ϕ, and z. If u is continuous and possesses continuous partial derivatives of the first and second order, the following method, based on the chain rule for differentiating composite functions, can be used to express the laplacian

$$(3) \qquad \nabla^2 u = \frac{\partial^2 u}{\partial x^2} + \frac{\partial^2 u}{\partial y^2} + \frac{\partial^2 u}{\partial z^2}$$

in terms of ρ, ϕ, and z.

Since

$$\frac{\partial u}{\partial x} = \frac{\partial u}{\partial \rho} \frac{\partial \rho}{\partial x} + \frac{\partial u}{\partial \phi} \frac{\partial \phi}{\partial x} + \frac{\partial u}{\partial z} \frac{\partial z}{\partial x},$$

it follows from relations (2) that

$$\begin{aligned}
\frac{\partial u}{\partial x} &= \frac{\partial u}{\partial \rho} \frac{x}{\sqrt{x^2 + y^2}} - \frac{\partial u}{\partial \phi} \frac{y}{x^2 + y^2} + \frac{\partial u}{\partial z} \cdot 0 \\
&= \frac{x}{\rho} \frac{\partial u}{\partial \rho} - \frac{y}{\rho^2} \frac{\partial u}{\partial \phi}.
\end{aligned}$$

Hence, by relations (1),

$$(4) \qquad \frac{\partial u}{\partial x} = \cos \phi \frac{\partial u}{\partial \rho} - \frac{\sin \phi}{\rho} \frac{\partial u}{\partial \phi}.$$

Replacing the function u in equation (4) by $\partial u/\partial x$, we see that

$$(5) \qquad \frac{\partial^2 u}{\partial x^2} = \cos \phi \frac{\partial}{\partial \rho} \left(\frac{\partial u}{\partial x} \right) - \frac{\sin \phi}{\rho} \frac{\partial}{\partial \phi} \left(\frac{\partial u}{\partial x} \right).$$

We may now use expression (4) to substitute for the derivative $\partial u/\partial x$ appearing on the right-hand side of equation (5):

$$\frac{\partial^2 u}{\partial x^2} = \cos \phi \frac{\partial}{\partial \rho} \left(\cos \phi \frac{\partial u}{\partial \rho} - \frac{\sin \phi}{\rho} \frac{\partial u}{\partial \phi} \right) - \frac{\sin \phi}{\rho} \frac{\partial}{\partial \phi} \left(\cos \phi \frac{\partial u}{\partial \rho} - \frac{\sin \phi}{\rho} \frac{\partial u}{\partial \phi} \right).$$

By applying rules for differentiating differences and products of functions and using the relation

$$\frac{\partial^2 u}{\partial \rho \partial \phi} = \frac{\partial^2 u}{\partial \phi \partial \rho},$$

which is ensured by the continuity of the partial derivatives, we find that

(6) $$\frac{\partial^2 u}{\partial x^2} = \cos^2 \phi \frac{\partial^2 u}{\partial \rho^2} - \frac{2 \sin \phi \cos \phi}{\rho} \frac{\partial^2 u}{\partial \phi \partial \rho} + \frac{\sin^2 \phi}{\rho^2} \frac{\partial^2 u}{\partial \phi^2}$$

$$+ \frac{\sin^2 \phi}{\rho} \frac{\partial u}{\partial \rho} + \frac{2 \sin \phi \cos \phi}{\rho^2} \frac{\partial u}{\partial \phi}.$$

In the same way, one can show that

(7) $$\frac{\partial u}{\partial y} = \frac{y}{\rho} \frac{\partial u}{\partial \rho} + \frac{x}{\rho^2} \frac{\partial u}{\partial \phi},$$

or

(8) $$\frac{\partial u}{\partial y} = \sin \phi \frac{\partial u}{\partial \rho} + \frac{\cos \phi}{\rho} \frac{\partial u}{\partial \phi},$$

and also that

(9) $$\frac{\partial^2 u}{\partial y^2} = \sin^2 \phi \frac{\partial^2 u}{\partial \rho^2} + \frac{2 \sin \phi \cos \phi}{\rho} \frac{\partial^2 u}{\partial \phi \partial \rho} + \frac{\cos^2 \phi}{\rho^2} \frac{\partial^2 u}{\partial \phi^2}$$

$$+ \frac{\cos^2 \phi}{\rho} \frac{\partial u}{\partial \rho} - \frac{2 \sin \phi \cos \phi}{\rho^2} \frac{\partial u}{\partial \phi}.$$

By adding corresponding sides of equations (6) and (9), we arrive at

(10) $$\frac{\partial^2 u}{\partial x^2} + \frac{\partial^2 u}{\partial y^2} = \frac{\partial^2 u}{\partial \rho^2} + \frac{1}{\rho} \frac{\partial u}{\partial \rho} + \frac{1}{\rho^2} \frac{\partial^2 u}{\partial \phi^2}.$$

Since cylindrical and rectangular coordinates share the coordinate z, it follows that equation (3) becomes

(11) $$\nabla^2 u = \frac{\partial^2 u}{\partial \rho^2} + \frac{1}{\rho} \frac{\partial u}{\partial \rho} + \frac{1}{\rho^2} \frac{\partial^2 u}{\partial \phi^2} + \frac{\partial^2 u}{\partial z^2}$$

in cylindrical coordinates. This is, of course, the same as expression (2) in Sec. 24.

(ii) Spherical Coordinates

As for the spherical coordinates r, ϕ, and θ, Fig. 17 in Sec. 24 shows that they are related to the rectangular coordinates x, y, and z as follows:

(12) $$x = r \sin \theta \cos \phi, \qquad y = r \sin \theta \sin \phi, \qquad z = r \cos \theta.$$

Spherical and cylindrical coordinates are, moreover, related by the equations

(13) $$z = r \cos \theta, \qquad \rho = r \sin \theta, \qquad \phi = \phi.$$

Expression (11) for $\nabla^2 u$ in cylindrical coordinates can be transformed into spherical coordinates quite readily by means of the proper interchange of letters, *without any further application of the chain rule.* This is accomplished in three steps, described below.

First, we observe that except for the names of the variables involved, relations (13) are the same as relations (1) connecting cylindrical and rectangular coordinates. Since relations (1) gave us expressions (8) and (10), it follows immediately, then, that

$$(14) \qquad \frac{\partial u}{\partial \rho} = \sin\theta \, \frac{\partial u}{\partial r} + \frac{\cos\theta}{r} \frac{\partial u}{\partial \theta}$$

and

$$(15) \qquad \frac{\partial^2 u}{\partial z^2} + \frac{\partial^2 u}{\partial \rho^2} = \frac{\partial^2 u}{\partial r^2} + \frac{1}{r} \frac{\partial u}{\partial r} + \frac{1}{r^2} \frac{\partial^2 u}{\partial \theta^2}.$$

Next, we note how the second of relations (13) and equation (14) enable us to write

$$(16) \qquad \frac{1}{\rho} \frac{\partial u}{\partial \rho} + \frac{1}{\rho^2} \frac{\partial^2 u}{\partial \phi^2} = \frac{1}{r} \frac{\partial u}{\partial r} + \frac{\cot\theta}{r^2} \frac{\partial u}{\partial \theta} + \frac{1}{r^2 \sin^2\theta} \frac{\partial^2 u}{\partial \phi^2}.$$

Finally, we rearrange terms in expression (11) for $\nabla^2 u$ in cylindrical coordinates and write

$$(17) \qquad \nabla^2 u = \left(\frac{\partial^2 u}{\partial z^2} + \frac{\partial^2 u}{\partial \rho^2} \right) + \left(\frac{1}{\rho} \frac{\partial u}{\partial \rho} + \frac{1}{\rho^2} \frac{\partial^2 u}{\partial \phi^2} \right).$$

Using equations (15) and (16) to substitute for the sums in parentheses here, we arrive at the expression

$$(18) \qquad \nabla^2 u = \frac{\partial^2 u}{\partial r^2} + \frac{2}{r} \frac{\partial u}{\partial r} + \frac{1}{r^2 \sin^2\theta} \frac{\partial^2 u}{\partial \phi^2} + \frac{1}{r^2} \frac{\partial^2 u}{\partial \theta^2} + \frac{\cot\theta}{r^2} \frac{\partial u}{\partial \theta},$$

which is the same as expression (7), Sec. 24, for $\nabla^2 u$ in spherical coordinates.

PROBLEMS

1. In Sec. 24, show how expressions (8) and (9) for $\nabla^2 u$ in spherical coordinates follow from expression (7).

2. Derive expressions (8) and (9) in Sec. 25 for

$$\frac{\partial u}{\partial y} \quad \text{and} \quad \frac{\partial^2 u}{\partial y^2}$$

in cylindrical coordinates.

3. We saw in Sec. 24 how the laplacian in cylindrical coordinates reduces to the two-dimensional laplacian

$$\nabla^2 u = u_{\rho\rho} + \frac{1}{\rho} u_\rho + \frac{1}{\rho^2} u_{\phi\phi}$$

in polar coordinates when $u = u(\rho, \phi)$ is independent of z. Follow the steps below to show how that two-dimensional laplacian also follows from the laplacian

$$\nabla^2 u = u_{rr} + \frac{2}{r} u_r + \frac{1}{r^2 \sin^2\theta} u_{\phi\phi} + \frac{1}{r^2} u_{\theta\theta} + \frac{\cot\theta}{r^2} u_\theta$$

in *spherical* coordinates that was stated in Sec. 24.[†]

[†]The method used here is from a note, using slightly different notation, by the first author and F. Farris in *Math. Mag.*, vol. 59, no. 4, pp. 227–229, 1986.

(*a*) Recall equations (13), Sec. 25, which relate spherical and cylindrical coordinates:

$$z = r \cos\theta, \quad \rho = r \sin\theta, \quad \phi = \phi.$$

Then, assuming that $\partial u/\partial z = 0$, use the chain rule to show that

$$\frac{\partial u}{\partial \theta} = \frac{\partial u}{\partial z}\frac{\partial z}{\partial \theta} + \frac{\partial u}{\partial \rho}\frac{\partial \rho}{\partial \theta} + \frac{\partial u}{\partial \phi}\frac{\partial \phi}{\partial \theta} = \frac{\partial u}{\partial \rho} r \cos\theta.$$

(*b*) Use the final result in part (*a*) to show that

$$\frac{\partial^2 u}{\partial \theta^2} = r\frac{\partial}{\partial \theta}\left(\frac{\partial u}{\partial \rho}\cos\theta\right) = \frac{\partial^2 u}{\partial \rho^2} r^2 \cos^2\theta - \frac{\partial u}{\partial \rho} r \sin\theta.$$

Then set $\theta = \pi/2$ and $r = \rho$ to express the derivative $\partial^2 u/\partial\theta^2$ in cylindrical coordinates:

$$\frac{\partial^2 u}{\partial \theta^2} = -\rho\frac{\partial u}{\partial \rho}.$$

(*c*) With the aid of the final result in part (*b*) and continuing to set $\theta = \pi/2$ and $r = \rho$, finish this derivation of the two-dimensional laplacian in polar coordinates that is stated at the beginning of the problem.

26. BOUNDARY CONDITIONS

Equations that describe thermal conditions on the surfaces of a solid body must accompany the heat or Laplace's equation if we are to determine the temperature function u within the body. Three types of such boundary conditions are described and illustrated below. It should be emphasized that when a surface S is mentioned, S is often only one of the surfaces of the solid; but it is possible that there is only one surface, as in the case of a solid sphere.

(i) Prescribed Temperatures
Temperatures on a surface may be prescribed. They are often constant temperatures but can be time-dependent, as will be the case in the next section. Stated initial temperatures throughout the body are also considered to be boundary conditions.

(ii) Constant Flux, Insulation
Conditions on surfaces may be other than just prescribed temperatures. Suppose, for example, that the flux Φ into the solid at points on a surface S is some constant Φ_0. That is, at each point P on S, we know that Φ_0 units of heat per unit area per unit time flow across S in the direction *opposite to* an outward unit normal vector $\mathbf{n}$ at P. From Fourier's law (1) in Sec. 22, we know that if du/dn is the directional derivative of u at P in the direction of $\mathbf{n}$, the flux into the solid across S at P is the value of $K\,du/dn$ there. Hence

$$(1) \qquad\qquad K\frac{du}{dn} = \Phi_0$$

on the surface S. Observe that if S is perfectly insulated, $\Phi_0 = 0$ at points on S and condition (1) becomes

$$(2) \qquad\qquad \frac{du}{dn} = 0.$$

(iii) Newton's Law of Cooling

There may be surface heat transfer between a boundary surface S and a medium whose temperature is a constant T. The inward flux Φ, which can be negative, may then vary from point to point on S; and we assume that at each point P, the flux is proportional to the difference between the temperature of the medium and the temperature at P. Under this assumption, which is sometimes called *Newton's law of cooling,* there is a positive constant H, known as the *surface conductance* of the material, such that $\Phi = H(T - u)$ at points on S. Condition (1) is then replaced by the condition

$$K \frac{du}{dn} = H(T - u),$$

or

$$(3) \qquad\qquad \frac{du}{dn} = h(T - u) \qquad\qquad \left(h = \frac{H}{K}\right).$$

The constant h is, of course, positive.

EXAMPLE 1. Consider a semi-infinite slab occupying the region $0 \le x \le c$, $y \ge 0$ of three-dimensional space. Figure 18 shows the cross section of the slab in the xy plane. Suppose that there is a constant flux Φ_0 into the slab at points on the face in the plane $x = 0$ and that there is surface heat transfer (possibly inward) between the face in the plane $x = c$ and a medium at temperature zero. Also, the surface in the plane $y = 0$ is insulated. Since

$$\frac{du}{dn} = -\frac{\partial u}{\partial x} \qquad \text{and} \qquad \frac{du}{dn} = \frac{\partial u}{\partial x}$$

on the faces in the planes $x = 0$ and $x = c$, respectively, a temperature function $u = u(x, y, z, t)$ evidently satisfies the boundary conditions

$$-Ku_x(0, y, z, t) = \Phi_0, \qquad u_x(c, y, z, t) = -hu(c, y, z, t).$$

The insulated surface gives rise to the boundary condition $u_y(x, 0, z, t) = 0$.

FIGURE 18

EXAMPLE 2. Let u denote temperatures in a long rod, parallel to the z axis, whose cross section in the xy plane is the sector $0 \le \rho \le 1, 0 \le \phi \le \pi/2$ of a disk (Fig. 19). We assume that u is independent of the cylindrical coordinate z, so that $u = u(\rho, \phi)$, and that the rod is insulated on its planar surfaces, where $\phi = 0$ and $\phi = \pi/2$. Evidently,

$$\frac{\partial u}{\partial y} = 0 \quad \text{when } y = 0 \quad \text{and} \quad \frac{\partial u}{\partial x} = 0 \quad \text{when } x = 0.$$

Also, in view of the transformation equations $x = \rho \cos \phi$ and $y = \rho \sin \phi$ (Sec. 25), the chain rule tells us that

$$\frac{\partial u}{\partial \phi} = \frac{\partial u}{\partial x}\frac{\partial x}{\partial \phi} + \frac{\partial u}{\partial y}\frac{\partial y}{\partial \phi} = -y\frac{\partial u}{\partial x} + x\frac{\partial u}{\partial y}.$$

Consequently, u must satisfy the boundary conditions

$$u_\phi(\rho, 0) = 0, \qquad u_\phi\left(\rho, \frac{\pi}{2}\right) = 0 \qquad (0 < \rho < 1).$$

FIGURE 19

27. DUHAMEL'S PRINCIPLE

Boundary value problems in heat conduction can have boundary conditions that are time-dependent. We present here a special case of a result, known as *Duhamel's principle*, that is often useful in solving boundary value problems involving such conditions. Suppose that a function $= u(P, t)$ satisfies the heat equation $u_t = k\nabla^2 u$ at each point P in the interior of a region throughout which the initial temperature is zero. Also, suppose that $u = F(t)$ on a portion S of the boundary of the region and that $u = 0$ on the remaining part S' (see Fig. 20). The boundary value problem for $u = u(P, t)$ is then

(1) $u_t = k\nabla^2 u, \qquad u(P, 0) = 0,$

(2) $u(P, t) = F(t) \quad \text{on} \quad S, \qquad u(P, t) = 0 \quad \text{on} \quad S'.$

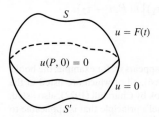

FIGURE 20

For simplicity here, we assume that $F(t)$ is continuous and differentiable when $t \geq 0$ and that $F(0) = 0$. Our special case of Duhamel's principle tells us that if $v = v(P, t)$ satisfies the related boundary value problem

$$(3) \qquad\qquad v_t = k\nabla^2 v, \qquad v(P, 0) = 0,$$

$$(4) \qquad v(P, t) = 1 \quad \text{on} \quad S, \qquad v(P, t) = 0 \quad \text{on} \quad S',$$

then

$$(5) \qquad\qquad u(P, t) = \int_0^t F(\tau)\, v_t(P, t - \tau)\, d\tau.$$

Note that the boundary value problem for $v(P, t)$ is obtained from the one for $u(P, t)$ by replacing $F(t)$ by unity.[†]

To obtain expression (5), we assume that $t > 0$ and consider a subdivision (see Fig. 21)

$$0 = \tau_0 < \tau_1 < \tau_2 < \tau_3 < \cdots < \tau_{n-1} < \tau_n = t$$

of the interval from 0 to t. We then approximate the function $F(t)$ by the step function described by means of the dashed line segments and solid dots in Fig. 21.

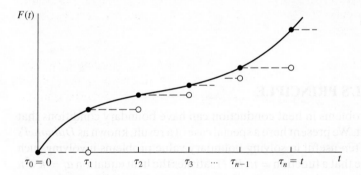

FIGURE 21

Keeping in mind that $F(\tau_0) = 0$, we observe that just after time $t = \tau_1$, the temperature $u(P, t)$ is approximately

$$[F(\tau_1) - F(\tau_0)]\, v(P, t - \tau_1).$$

Just after the time t has passed $t = \tau_2$, the approximation of $u(P, t)$ becomes

$$[F(\tau_1) - F(\tau_0)]\, v(P, t - \tau_1) + [F(\tau_2) - F(\tau_1)]\, v(P, t - \tau_2).$$

[†]The derivation that we shall give here is essentially Duhamel's and appears in, for example, the books by Carslaw and Jaeger (1986), Hildebrand (1976), and Arpaci (1966), all of which are listed in the Bibliography. The paper by Bartels and Churchill (1942) and the book by Churchill (1972), also listed, use Laplace transforms to establish a more general form of Duhamel's principle that is applicable to other types of time-dependent boundary conditions. The book by Churchill also adapts Duhamel's principle to boundary value problems in mechanical vibrations.

The sum here is a reasonable approximation because of the linearity of the problem in $u(P, t)$. Continuing in this way, we arrive at the approximation

$$(6) \qquad u(P, t) \doteq \sum_{k=1}^{n} [F(\tau_k) - F(\tau_{k-1})] v(P, t - \tau_k).$$

Now, according to the mean value theorem for derivatives in calculus, there exists a point τ_k^* in each subinterval $\tau_{k-1} < \tau_k^* < \tau_k$ such that

$$F(\tau_k) - F(\tau_{k-1}) = F'(\tau_k^*)\Delta\tau_k,$$

where $\Delta\tau_k = \tau_k - \tau_{k-1} (k = 1, 2, \ldots, n)$. Hence approximation (6) can be written

$$(7) \qquad u(P, t) \doteq \sum_{k=1}^{n} F'(\tau_k^*)v(P, t - \tau_k)\Delta\tau_k.$$

According to the definition of definite integral, then, approximation (7) becomes

$$(8) \qquad u(P, t) = \int_{0}^{t} F'(\tau)v(P, t - \tau)\, d\tau$$

as the $\Delta\tau_k$ tend to zero. Even though the two points τ_k and τ_k^* appearing in approximation (7) may not be the same, thinking of them as the same can be justified.[†]

Finally, it is straightforward (Problem 9) to use integration by parts to obtain expression (5) from expression (8).

EXAMPLE. In order to illustrate the use of Duhamel's principle, we turn now to a temperature problem involving an infinite slab occupying the region $0 \le x \le \pi$ in three-dimensional space. The problem consists of the heat equation

$$(9) \qquad u_t(x, t) = k u_{xx}(x, t) \qquad\qquad (0 < x < \pi, t > 0)$$

and the boundary conditions

$$(10) \qquad u(0, t) = 0, \qquad u(\pi, t) = F(t), \qquad \text{and} \qquad u(x, 0) = 0,$$

where $F(t)$ is as stated just after conditions (2).

Inasmuch as the second of conditions (10) is time-dependent, we consider the related boundary value problem

$$(11) \qquad v_t(x, t) = k v_{xx}(x, t) \qquad\qquad (0 < x < \pi, t > 0),$$

$$(12) \qquad v(0, t) = 0, \qquad v(\pi, t) = 1, \qquad \text{and} \qquad v(x, 0) = 0.$$

Anticipating a solution of a problem to be solved in Example 2, Sec. 39, namely solution (15) there, we know that

$$v(x, t) = \frac{1}{\pi} \left[x + 2\sum_{n=1}^{\infty} \frac{(-1)^n}{n} e^{-n^2 k t} \sin nx \right].$$

[†]See, for instance, p. 546 of the book by Taylor and Mann (1983) or pp. 984–985 of the one by Kaplan and Lewis (1971), both of which are listed in the Bibliography.

Hence, in view of Duhamel's principle,

$$u(x,t) = \int_0^t F(\tau) v_t(x, t-\tau) d\tau = \int_0^t F(\tau) \left[\frac{2}{\pi} \sum_{n=1}^{\infty} (-1)^{n+1} n k e^{-n^2 k(t-\tau)} \sin nx \right] d\tau.$$

That is,

$$(13) \qquad u(x,t) = \frac{2k}{\pi} \sum_{n=1}^{\infty} (-1)^{n+1} n \sin nx \int_0^t F(\tau) e^{-n^2 k(t-\tau)} d\tau.$$

PROBLEMS

1. Let $u(x)$ denote the steady-state temperatures in a slab bounded by the planes $x = 0$ and $x = c$ when those faces are kept at fixed temperatures $u = 0$ and $u = u_0$, respectively. Set up the boundary value problem for $u(x)$ and solve it to show that

$$u(x) = \frac{u_0}{c} x \qquad \text{and} \qquad \Phi_0 = K \frac{u_0}{c},$$

where Φ_0 is the flux of heat to the left across each plane $x = x_0$ $(0 \le x_0 \le c)$.

2. A slab occupies the region $0 \le x \le c$. There is a constant flux of heat Φ_0 into the slab through the face $x = 0$. The face $x = c$ is kept at temperature $u = 0$. Set up and solve the boundary value problem for the steady-state temperatures $u(x)$ in the slab.

$$\text{Answer: } u(x) = \frac{\Phi_0}{K} (c - x).$$

3. Let a slab $0 \le x \le c$ be subjected to surface heat transfer, according to Newton's law of cooling, at its faces $x = 0$ and $x = c$, the surface conductance H being the same on each face. Show that if the medium $x < 0$ has temperature zero and the medium $x > c$ has the constant temperature T, then the boundary value problem for steady-state temperatures $u(x)$ in the slab is

$$u''(x) = 0 \qquad\qquad (0 < x < c),$$

$$Ku'(0) = Hu(0), \qquad Ku'(c) = H[T - u(c)],$$

where K is the thermal conductivity of the material in the slab. Write $h = H/K$ and derive the expression

$$u(x) = \frac{T}{hc + 2} (hx + 1)$$

for those temperatures.

4. Let $u(r)$ denote the steady-state temperatures in a solid bounded by two concentric spheres $r = a$ and $r = b$ $(a < b)$ when the inner surface $r = a$ is kept at temperature zero and the outer surface $r = b$ is maintained at a constant temperature u_0. Show why Laplace's equation for $u = u(r)$ reduces to

$$\frac{d^2}{dr^2}(ru) = 0,$$

and then derive the expression

$$u(r) = \frac{bu_0}{b - a}\left(1 - \frac{a}{r}\right) \qquad\qquad (a \le r \le b).$$

Sketch the graph of $u(r)$ versus r.

5. In Problem 4, replace the condition on the outer surface $r = b$ with the condition that there be surface heat transfer into a medium at constant temperature T according to

Newton's law of cooling. Then obtain the expression

$$u(r) = \frac{hb^2 T}{a + hb(b - a)}\left(1 - \frac{a}{r}\right) \qquad (a \le r \le b)$$

for the steady-state temperatures, where h is the ratio of the surface conductance H to the thermal conductivity K of the material.

6. A slender wire lies along the x axis, and surface heat transfer takes place along the wire into the surrounding medium at a fixed temperature T. Modify the procedure in Sec. 22 to show that if $u = u(x, t)$ denotes temperatures in the wire, then

$$u_t = ku_{xx} + b(T - u),$$

where b is a positive constant.

Suggestion: Let r denote the radius of the wire, and apply Newton's law of cooling to see that the quantity of heat entering the element in Fig. 22 through its cylindrical surface per unit time is approximately $H\,[T - u(x,t)]\,2\pi r\,\Delta x$.

FIGURE 22

7. Show that the special case

$$u_t = ku_{xx} - bu$$

of the differential equation derived in Problem 6 can be transformed into the one-dimensional heat equation (Sec. 22)

$$v_t = kv_{xx}$$

with the substitution $u(x, t) = e^{-bt}v(x, t)$.

8. Suppose that temperatures u in a solid hemisphere $r \le 1, 0 \le \theta \le \pi/2$ are independent of the spherical coordinate ϕ, so that $u = u(r, \theta)$, and that the base of the hemisphere is insulated (Fig. 23). Use transformation (13), Sec. 25, which relates spherical and cylindrical coordinates, to show that

$$\frac{\partial u}{\partial \theta} = -\rho\,\frac{\partial u}{\partial z} + z\,\frac{\partial u}{\partial \rho}.$$

FIGURE 23

Thus show that u must satisfy the boundary condition

$$u_\theta\left(r, \frac{\pi}{2}\right) = 0.$$

9. Use integration by parts to obtain expression (5) in Sec. 27 from expression (8) in that section.

   Suggestion: Write

$$U = v(P, t - \tau), \qquad dV = F'(\tau)d\tau$$

   and

$$dU = -v_t(P, t - \tau)d\tau, \qquad V = F(\tau).$$

28. A VIBRATING STRING

A tightly stretched string, whose position of equilibrium is some interval on the x axis, is vibrating in the xy plane. Each point of the string, with coordinates $(x, 0)$ in the equilibrium position, has a transverse displacement $y = y(x, t)$ at time t. We assume that the displacements y are small relative to the length of the string, that slopes are small, and that other conditions are such that the movement of each point is parallel to the y axis. Then, at time t, a point on the string has coordinates (x, y), where $y = y(x, t)$.

Let the tension of the string be great enough that the string behaves as if it were perfectly flexible. That is, at a point (x, y) on the string, the part of the string to the left of that point exerts a force **T**, in the tangential direction, on the part to the right (see Fig. 24); and any resistance to bending at the point is to be neglected. The magnitude of the x component of the tensile force **T** is denoted by H. Our final assumption here is that H is constant. That is, the variation of H with respect to x and t can be neglected.

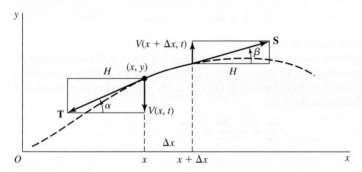

FIGURE 24

These idealizing assumptions are severe, but they are justified in many applications. They are adequately satisfied, for instance, by strings of musical instruments under ordinary conditions of operation. Mathematically, the assumptions will lead us to a partial differential equation in $y(x, t)$ that is linear.

Now let $V(x, t)$ denote the y component of the tensile force **T** exerted by the left-hand portion of the string on the right-hand portion at the point (x, y).

We see from Fig. 24 that V is negative when **T** is downward. It is, on the other hand, positive when **T** is upward. In the next paragraph we shall show that *the y component V(x, t) of the force exerted at time t by the part of the string to the left of a point (x, y) on the part to the right is given by the equation*

$$(1) \qquad\qquad V(x, t) = -Hy_x(x, t) \qquad\qquad (H > 0),$$

which is basic for deriving the equation of motion of the string. Equation (1) is also used in setting up certain types of boundary conditions.

To establish expression (1), we note that if α is the angle of inclination of the string at the point (x, y) at time t, then

$$\frac{-V(x, t)}{H} = \tan \alpha = y_x(x, t).$$

This is indicated in Fig. 24, where $V(x, t) < 0$ and $y_x(x, t) > 0$. If $V(x, t) > 0$, then $\pi/2 < \alpha < \pi$ and $y_x(x, t) < 0$; and a similar sketch shows that

$$\frac{V(x, t)}{H} = \tan(\pi - \alpha) = -\tan \alpha = -y_x(x, t).$$

Hence expression (1) continues to hold. Note, too, that $V(x, t) = 0$ when $y_x(x, t) = 0$.

Suppose that all external forces such as the weight of the string and resistance forces, other than forces at the endpoints, can be neglected. Consider a segment of the string not containing an endpoint and whose projection onto the x axis has length Δx. Since x components of displacements are negligible, the mass of the segment is $\delta \Delta x$, where the constant δ is the mass per unit length of the string. At time t, the y component of the force exerted by the string on the segment at the left-hand end (x, y) is $V(x, t)$, given by equation (1). The tangential force **S** exerted on the other end of the segment by the part of the string to the right is also indicated in Fig. 24. Its y component $V(x + \Delta x, t)$ evidently satisfies the relation

$$\frac{V(x + \Delta x, t)}{H} = \tan \beta,$$

where β is the angle of inclination of the string at that other end. That is,

$$(2) \qquad\qquad V(x + \Delta x, t) = Hy_x(x + \Delta x, t) \qquad\qquad (H > 0).$$

Note that except for a minus sign, this is equation (1) when the argument x there is replaced by $x + \Delta x$.

Now the acceleration of the end (x, y) in the y direction is $y_{tt}(x, t)$. Consequently, by Newton's second law of motion (mass times acceleration equals force), it follows from equations (1) and (2) that

$$(3) \qquad\qquad \delta \Delta x\, y_{tt}(x, t) = -Hy_x(x, t) + Hy_x(x + \Delta x, t),$$

approximately, when Δx is small. This suggests that we write

$$y_{tt}(x, t) = \frac{H}{\delta} \cdot \frac{y_x(x + \Delta x, t) - y_x(x, t)}{\Delta x};$$

and as Δx tends to zero,

$$(4) \qquad y_{tt}(x, t) = a^2 y_{xx}(x, t) \qquad \left(a^2 = \frac{H}{\delta}\right)$$

whenever these partial derivatives exist. This is the one-dimensional *wave equation*, satisfied by the transverse displacements $y(x, t)$ in a stretched string under the conditions stated above. The constant a has the physical dimensions of velocity.

One can choose units for the time variable so that $a = 1$ in the wave equation. More precisely, if we make the substitution $\tau = at$, the chain rule shows that

$$\frac{\partial y}{\partial t} = a \frac{\partial y}{\partial \tau} \qquad \text{and} \qquad \frac{\partial^2 y}{\partial t^2} = a \frac{\partial}{\partial \tau}\left(a \frac{\partial y}{\partial \tau}\right) = a^2 \frac{\partial^2 y}{\partial \tau^2}.$$

Equation (4) then becomes $y_{\tau\tau} = y_{xx}$. (A similar observation was made in Problem 3, Sec. 23, with regard to the heat equation.)

When external forces parallel to the y axis act along the string, we let F denote the force per unit length of the string, the positive sense of F being that of the y axis. Then a term $F \Delta x$ must be added on the right-hand side of equation (3), and the equation of motion is

$$(5) \qquad y_{tt}(x, t) = a^2 y_{xx}(x, t) + \frac{F}{\delta}.$$

In particular, with the y axis vertical and its positive sense upward, suppose that the external force consists of the weight of the string. Then $F\Delta x = -\delta \Delta x\, g$, where the positive constant g is acceleration due to gravity; and equation (5) becomes the linear nonhomogeneous equation

$$(6) \qquad y_{tt}(x, t) = a^2 y_{xx}(x, t) - g.$$

In equation (5), F may be a function of x, t, y, or derivatives of y. If the external force per unit length is a damping force proportional to the velocity in the y direction, for example, F is replaced by $-By_t$, where the positive constant B is a damping coefficient. Then the equation of motion is linear and homogeneous:

$$(7) \qquad y_{tt}(x, t) = a^2 y_{xx}(x, t) - by_t(x, t) \qquad \left(b = \frac{B}{\delta}\right).$$

If an end $x = 0$ of the string is kept fixed at the origin at all times $t \geq 0$, the boundary condition there is clearly

$$(8) \qquad y(0, t) = 0 \qquad (t \geq 0).$$

But if the end is permitted to slide along the y axis and is moved along that axis with a displacement $f(t)$, the boundary condition is the linear nonhomogeneous one

$$(9) \qquad y(0, t) = f(t) \qquad (t \geq 0).$$

Suppose that the left-hand end is attached to a ring which can slide along the y axis. When a force $F(t)$ $(t > 0)$ in the y direction is applied to that end, $F(t)$ is the limit, as x tends to zero through positive values, of the force $V(x, t)$ described earlier in this section. According to equation (1), the boundary condition at $x = 0$

is then

$$-Hy_x(0, t) = F(t) \qquad\qquad (t > 0).$$

The minus sign disappears, however, if $x = 0$ is the *right-hand* end, in view of equation (2).

PROBLEMS

1. A stretched string, with its ends fixed at the points 0 and $2c$ on the x axis, hangs at rest under its own weight. The y axis is directed vertically upward. Point out how it follows from the nonhomogeneous wave equation (6), Sec. 28, that the static displacements $y(x)$ of points on the string must satisfy the differential equation

$$a^2 y''(x) = g \qquad\qquad \left(a^2 = \frac{H}{\delta}\right)$$

on the interval $0 < x < 2c$, in addition to the boundary conditions

$$y(0) = 0, \qquad y(2c) = 0.$$

By solving this boundary value problem, show that the string hangs in the parabolic arc

$$(x - c)^2 = \frac{2a^2}{g}\left(y + \frac{gc^2}{2a^2}\right) \qquad\qquad (0 \le x \le 2c)$$

and that the depth of the vertex of the arc varies directly with c^2 and δ and inversely with H.

2. Use expression (1), Sec. 28, for the vertical force V and the equation of the arc in which the string in Problem 1 lies to show that the vertical force exerted on that string by each support is δcg, one-half the weight of the string.

3. Give the needed details in the derivation of equation (5), Sec. 28, for the forced vibrations of a stretched string.

4. The physical dimensions of the magnitude H of the x component of the tensile force in a string are those of mass times acceleration: MLT^{-2}, where M denotes mass, L length, and T time. Show that since $a^2 = H/\delta$, the constant a has the dimensions of velocity: LT^{-1}.

5. A strand of wire 1 ft long, stretched between the origin and the point 1 on the x axis, weighs 0.032 lb ($\delta g = 0.032, g = 32$ ft/s^2) and $H = 10$ lb. At the instant $t = 0$, the strand lies along the x axis but has a velocity of 1 ft/s in the direction of the y axis, perhaps because the supports were in motion and were brought to rest at that instant. Assuming that no external forces act along the wire, state why the displacements $y(x, t)$ should satisfy this boundary value problem:

$$y_{tt}(x, t) = 10^4 y_{xx}(x, t) \qquad\qquad (0 < x < 1, t > 0),$$

$$y(0, t) = y(1, t) = 0, \qquad y(x, 0) = 0, \qquad y_t(x, 0) = 1.$$

29. VIBRATIONS OF BARS AND MEMBRANES

We describe here two other types of vibrations for which the displacements satisfy wave equations. We continue to limit our attention to fairly simple phenomena.

(i) Vibrations of Elastic Bars

Let the coordinate x denote distances from one end of an elastic bar, in the shape of a cylinder or prism, to other cross sections when the bar is unstrained. Displacements of the ends, initial displacements, and velocities in the bar, all directed lengthwise along it and uniform over each cross section involved, cause the sections to move parallel to the x axis. At time t, the longitudinal displacement of the section at a point x is denoted by $y(x, t)$. Thus the origin of the displacement y of the section at x is in a fixed coordinate system outside of the bar, in the plane of the unstrained position of that section (Fig. 25).

FIGURE 25

At the same time, a neighboring section, labeled $x + \Delta x$ in Fig. 25 and to the right of the section at x, has a displacement $y(x + \Delta x, t)$. The element of the bar with natural length Δx is, then, stretched or compressed by the amount $y(x + \Delta x, t) - y(x, t)$. We assume that such an extension or compression of the element satisfies Hooke's law and that the effect of the inertia of the moving element is negligible. Hence the force exerted on the section at x by the part of the bar to the left of that section is

$$-AE\frac{y(x + \Delta x, t) - y(x, t)}{\Delta x},$$

where A is the area of each cross section, the positive constant E is *Young's modulus of elasticity,* and the ratio shown represents the relative change in the length of the element. As Δx tends to zero, it follows that the longitudinal force $F(x, t)$ exerted on the element at its left-hand end is given by the basic equation

$$(1) \qquad\qquad F(x, t) = -AEy_x(x, t).$$

Similarly, the force on the right-hand end is

$$(2) \qquad\qquad F(x + \Delta x, t) = AEy_x(x + \Delta x, t).$$

Let the constant δ denote the mass per unit volume of the material. Then, applying Newton's second law to the motion of an element of the bar of length Δx, we may write

$$(3) \qquad\qquad \delta A \, \Delta x \, y_{tt}(x, t) = -AEy_x(x, t) + AEy_x(x + \Delta x, t).$$

We find, after dividing by $\delta A \, \Delta x$ and letting Δx tend to zero, that

$$(4) \qquad\qquad y_{tt}(x, t) = a^2 y_{xx}(x, t) \qquad\qquad \left(a^2 = \frac{E}{\delta} \right).$$

Thus the longitudinal displacements $y(x, t)$ in an elastic bar satisfy the wave equation (4) when no external longitudinal forces act on the bar, other than at the ends. We have assumed that displacements are small enough that Hooke's law applies and that sections remain planar after being displaced. The elastic bar here may be replaced by a column of air, in which case equation (4) has applications in the theory of sound.

The boundary condition $y(0, t) = 0$ signifies that the end $x = 0$ of the bar is held fixed. If, instead, the end $x = 0$ is free when $t > 0$, then no force acts at that end; that is, $F(0, t) = 0$ and, in view of equation (1),

$$(5) \qquad\qquad\qquad\qquad y_x(0, t) = 0 \qquad\qquad\qquad\qquad (t > 0).$$

(ii) Vibrations of Membranes

Turning to another type of vibration, we let $z(x, y, t)$ denote small displacements in the z direction, at time t, of points on a flexible membrane that is tightly stretched over a horizontal frame. In the equilibrium position, a point on the membrane has coordinates (x, y) in the xy plane. The plane through that point and parallel to the xz plane intersects the displaced membrane in a curve containing the points labeled A and B in Fig. 26. By making similar constructions, we can form the element $ABCD$ of the membrane that is also shown in Fig. 26. The projection of the element onto the xy plane is a small rectangle with edges of lengths Δx and Δy.

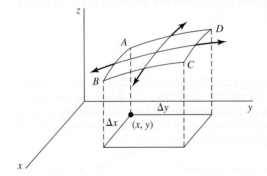

FIGURE 26

We now examine the internal tensile forces that are exerted on the element at points of the curve AB, those forces being tangent to the element and normal to AB. In analyzing such a force, we let H denote the magnitude *per unit length* along AB of the component parallel to the xy plane. We assume that H is constant, regardless of what point or curve on the membrane is being discussed. In view of expressions (1) and (2) in Sec. 28 for the forces V on the ends of a segment of a vibrating string, we know that the force in the z direction exerted over the curve AB is approximately $-Hz_y(x, y, t)\Delta x$ and that the corresponding force over the curve DC is approximately $Hz_y(x, y + \Delta y, t)\Delta x$. Similar expressions are found for the vertical forces exerted over AD and BC when the tensile forces on those curves are considered. It then follows that the sum of the vertical forces exerted over the entire boundary of the element is approximately

$$(6) \qquad \begin{aligned} &-Hz_y(x, y, t)\,\Delta x + Hz_y(x, y + \Delta y, t)\,\Delta x \\ &-Hz_x(x, y, t)\,\Delta y + Hz_x(x + \Delta x, y, t)\,\Delta y. \end{aligned}$$

If Newton's second law is applied to the motion of the element in the z direction and if δ denotes the mass per unit area of the membrane, it follows from expression (6) for the total force on the element that $z(x, y, t)$ satisfies the *two-dimensional* wave equation

$$(7) \qquad z_{tt} = a^2(z_{xx} + z_{yy}) \qquad\qquad \left(a^2 = \frac{H}{\delta}\right).$$

Details of these final steps are left to the problems, where it is also shown that if an external transverse force $F(x, y, t)$ per unit area acts over the membrane, the equation of motion takes the form

$$(8) \qquad z_{tt} = a^2(z_{xx} + z_{yy}) + \frac{F}{\delta}.$$

Equation (8) arises, for example, when the z axis is directed vertically upward and the weight of the membrane is taken into account in the derivation of equation (7). Then $F/\delta = -g$, where g is acceleration due to gravity.

From equation (7), one can see that the *static* transverse displacements $z(x, y)$ of a stretched membrane satisfy Laplace's equation (Sec. 23) in two dimensions. Here the displacements are the result of displacements, perpendicular to the xy plane, of parts of the frame that support the membrane when no external forces are exerted except at the boundary.

PROBLEMS

1. The end $x = 0$ of a cylindrical elastic bar is kept fixed, and a constant compressive force of magnitude F_0 units per unit area is exerted at all times $t > 0$ over the end $x = c$. The bar is initially unstrained and at rest, with no external forces acting along it. State why the function $y(x, t)$ representing the longitudinal displacements of cross sections should satisfy this boundary value problem, where $a^2 = E/\delta$:

$$y_{tt}(x, t) = a^2 y_{xx}(x, t) \qquad\qquad (0 < x < c, t > 0),$$

$$y(0, t) = 0, \qquad E y_x(c, t) = -F_0, \qquad y(x, 0) = y_t(x, 0) = 0.$$

2. The left-hand end $x = 0$ of a horizontal elastic bar is elastically supported in such a way that the longitudinal force per unit area exerted on the bar at that end is proportional to the displacement of the end, but opposite in sign. State why the end condition there has the form

$$y_x(0, t) = by(0, t) \qquad\qquad (b > 0).$$

3. Modify the derivation of equation (4), Sec. 29, to show that

$$y_{tt}(x, t) = a^2 y_{xx}(x, t) + g,$$

where g is acceleration due to gravity, when the bar is hung vertically and vibrates because of its own weight.

4. Let $z(\rho)$ represent static transverse displacements in a membrane, stretched between the two circles $\rho = 1$ and $\rho = \rho_0$ ($\rho_0 > 1$) in the plane $z = 0$, after the outer support $\rho = \rho_0$ is displaced by a distance $z = z_0$. State why the boundary value problem in $z(\rho)$

can be written

$$\frac{d}{d\rho}\left(\rho\frac{dz}{d\rho}\right) = 0 \qquad\qquad (1 < \rho < \rho_0),$$

$$z(1) = 0, \qquad z(\rho_0) = z_0,$$

and obtain the solution

$$z(\rho) = z_0 \frac{\ln\rho}{\ln\rho_0} \qquad\qquad (1 \le \rho \le \rho_0).$$

5. Show that the steady-state temperatures $u(\rho)$ in an infinitely long hollow cylinder $1 \le \rho \le \rho_0, -\infty < z < \infty$ also satisfy the boundary value problem written in Problem 4 if $u = 0$ on the inner cylindrical surface and $u = z_0$ on the outer one. Thus, show that Problem 4 is a *membrane analogy* for this temperature problem. Soap films have been used to display such analogies.

6. Use expression (6), Sec. 29, to derive the nonhomogeneous wave equation (8), Sec. 29, for a membrane when there is an external transverse force $F(x, y, t)$ per unit area acting on it. [Note that if this force is zero $(F \equiv 0)$, the equation reduces to equation (7), Sec. 29.]

7. Let $z(x, y)$ denote the static transverse displacements in a membrane over which an external transverse force $F(x, y)$ per unit area acts. Show how it follows from the nonhomogeneous wave equation (8), Sec. 29, that $z(x, y)$ satisfies *Poisson's equation*:

$$z_{xx} + z_{yy} + f = 0 \qquad\qquad \left(f = \frac{F}{H}\right).$$

[Compare with equation (7), Sec. 23.]

8. A uniform transverse force of F_0 units per unit area acts over a membrane, stretched between the two circles $\rho = 1$ and $\rho = \rho_0$ $(\rho_0 > 1)$ in the plane $z = 0$. From Problem 7, show that the static transverse displacements $z(\rho)$ satisfy the equation

$$(\rho z')' + f_0\rho = 0 \qquad\qquad \left(f_0 = \frac{F_0}{H}\right),$$

and derive the expression

$$z(\rho) = \frac{f_0}{4}\left(\rho_0^2 - 1\right)\left(\frac{\ln\rho}{\ln\rho_0} - \frac{\rho^2 - 1}{\rho_0^2 - 1}\right) \qquad\qquad (1 \le \rho \le \rho_0).$$

30. GENERAL SOLUTION OF A WAVE EQUATION

In this section, we shall find the general solution of the *one-dimensional* wave equation (Secs. 28 and 29)

(1) $$\qquad\qquad y_{tt}(x, t) = a^2 y_{xx}(x, t) \qquad\qquad (-\infty < x < \infty, t > 0)$$

that can be useful in special cases.

The differential equation (1) can be simplified as follows by introducing the new independent variables

(2) $$\qquad\qquad u = x + at, \qquad v = x - at.$$

According to the chain rule for differentiating composite functions,

$$\frac{\partial y}{\partial t} = \frac{\partial y}{\partial u}\frac{\partial u}{\partial t} + \frac{\partial y}{\partial v}\frac{\partial v}{\partial t}.$$

That is,

(3)
$$\frac{\partial y}{\partial t} = a\frac{\partial y}{\partial u} - a\frac{\partial y}{\partial v}.$$

Replacing the function y by $\partial y/\partial t$ in equation (3) yields the expression

$$\frac{\partial^2 y}{\partial t^2} = a\frac{\partial}{\partial u}\left(\frac{\partial y}{\partial t}\right) - a\frac{\partial}{\partial v}\left(\frac{\partial y}{\partial t}\right);$$

and using equation (3) again, this time to substitute for $\partial y/\partial t$ on the right here, we see that

$$\frac{\partial^2 y}{\partial t^2} = a\frac{\partial}{\partial u}\left(a\frac{\partial y}{\partial u} - a\frac{\partial y}{\partial v}\right) - a\frac{\partial}{\partial v}\left(a\frac{\partial y}{\partial u} - a\frac{\partial y}{\partial v}\right),$$

or

(4)
$$\frac{\partial^2 y}{\partial t^2} = a^2\left(\frac{\partial^2 y}{\partial u^2} - 2\frac{\partial^2 y}{\partial v\,\partial u} + \frac{\partial^2 y}{\partial v^2}\right).$$

We have, of course, assumed that

$$\frac{\partial^2 y}{\partial u\,\partial v} = \frac{\partial^2 y}{\partial v\,\partial u}.$$

In like manner, one can show that (Problem 1)

(5)
$$\frac{\partial^2 y}{\partial x^2} = \frac{\partial^2 y}{\partial u^2} + 2\frac{\partial^2 y}{\partial v\,\partial u} + \frac{\partial^2 y}{\partial v^2}.$$

In view of expressions (4) and (5), then, equation (1) becomes

(6) $y_{uv} = 0$

with the change of variables (2).

Equation (6) can be solved by successive integrations to give $y_u = \phi'(u)$ and

$$y = \phi(u) + \psi(v),$$

where the arbitrary functions ϕ and ψ are twice differentiable. The *general solution* of the wave equation (1) is, therefore,

(7) $y(x, t) = \phi(x + at) + \psi(x - at).$

EXAMPLE 1. Suppose that the function $y(x, t)$ in the wave equation (1) is subject to the boundary conditions

(8) $y(x, 0) = f(x),$ $y_t(x, 0) = 0$ $(-\infty < x < \infty).$

Physically, $y(x, t)$ represents transverse displacements in a stretched string of infinite length, initially released at rest from the position $y = f(x)$.

The boundary conditions here are simple enough that we can actually determine the functions ϕ and ψ in expression (7), that satisfies conditions (8) when

$$\phi(x) + \psi(x) = f(x) \qquad \text{and} \qquad a\phi'(x) - a\psi'(x) = 0.$$

The second of these equations tells us that $\psi(x) = \phi(x) + C$, where C is some constant. It then follows from the first equation that

$$\phi(x) = \frac{1}{2}[f(x) - C] \qquad \text{and} \qquad \psi(x) = \frac{1}{2}[f(x) + C].$$

Hence expression (7) becomes

$$(9) \qquad\qquad y(x,t) = \frac{1}{2}[f(x+at) + f(x-at)].$$

The solution (9) of the boundary value problem consisting of equations (1) and (8) is known as *d'Alembert's solution*. It is easily verified under the assumption that $f'(x)$ and $f''(x)$ exist for all x.

Note how solution (9) can be used to display the instantaneous position of the string at time t graphically by adding ordinates of two curves, one obtained by translating the curve

$$(10) \qquad\qquad y = \frac{1}{2}f(x)$$

to the right through the distance at and the other by translating it to the left through the same distance. As t varies, the curve (10) moves in each direction as a wave, with velocity a, that is often called a *traveling wave*.

EXAMPLE 2. In this example, we replace conditions (8) by

$$(11) \qquad\qquad y(x,0) = 0, \qquad y_t(x,0) = g(x) \qquad\qquad (-\infty < x < \infty),$$

where $g(x)$ is integrable over any finite interval. With these conditions, the displacements are initially zero and the initial velocities of points on the string are $g(x)$.

As in Example 1, it is easy to find the functions ϕ and ψ in expression (7). To do this, we first note how it follows from conditions (11) that

$$(12) \qquad\qquad \phi(x) + \psi(x) = 0, \qquad a\phi'(x) - a\psi'(x) = g(x).$$

Since $\psi(x) = -\phi(x)$ and

$$\frac{d}{dx}\int_0^x g(s)\,ds = g(x),$$

integration of each side of the second of equations (12) yields

$$(13) \qquad\qquad 2a\phi(x) = \int_0^x g(s)\,ds + C,$$

where C is an arbitrary constant. Because $\psi(x) = -\phi(x)$, expression (7) now becomes

$$y(x,t) = \frac{1}{2a}\left[\int_0^{x+at} g(s)\,ds + C\right] - \frac{1}{2a}\left[\int_0^{x-at} g(s)\,ds + C\right].$$

That is,

$$(14) \qquad y(x, t) = \frac{1}{2a} \int_{x-at}^{x+at} g(s)\, ds.$$

The solutions (9) and (14) in the two examples just above can be combined (Problem 2) to show that if

$$(15) \qquad y_{tt}(x, t) = a^2 y_{xx}(x, t) \qquad\qquad (-\infty < x < \infty, t > 0),$$

$$(16) \qquad y(x, 0) = f(x), \qquad y_t(x, 0) = g(x) \qquad\qquad (-\infty < x < \infty),$$

then

$$(17) \qquad y(x, t) = \frac{1}{2}[f(x + at) + f(x - at)] + \frac{1}{2a} \int_{x-at}^{x+at} g(s)\, ds.$$

PROBLEMS

1. Show that if $u = x + at$ and $v = x - at$, where a is the constant in the wave equation (1), Sec. 30, and $y(x, t)$ is the displacement of the string there, then

$$\frac{\partial y}{\partial x} = \frac{\partial y}{\partial u} + \frac{\partial y}{\partial v}.$$

Use this expression for $\partial y/\partial x$ to obtain expression (5) in Sec. 30:

$$\frac{\partial^2 y}{\partial x^2} = \frac{\partial^2 y}{\partial u^2} + 2\frac{\partial^2 y}{\partial v \partial u} + \frac{\partial^2 y}{\partial v^2}.$$

2. Let $Y(x, t)$ denote d'Alembert's solution (9), Sec. 30, of the boundary value problem solved in Example 1 in that section, and let $Z(x, t)$ denote the solution (14) of the related problem in Example 2 there. Verify that the sum

$$y(x, t) = Y(x, t) + Z(x, t)$$

is a solution of the boundary value problem

$$y_{tt}(x, t) = a^2 y_{xx}(x, t) \qquad\qquad (-\infty < x < \infty, t > 0),$$

$$y(x, 0) = f(x), \qquad y_t(x, 0) = g(x) \qquad\qquad (-\infty < x < \infty).$$

Thus, show that

$$y(x, t) = \frac{1}{2}[f(x + at) + f(x - at)] + \frac{1}{2a} \int_{x-at}^{x+at} g(s)\, ds$$

is a solution of the problem here.

3. Let $y(x, t)$ represent transverse displacements in a long stretched string one end of which is attached to a ring that can slide along the y axis. The other end is so far out on the positive x axis that it may be considered to be infinitely far from the origin. The ring is initially at the origin and is then moved along the y axis (Fig. 27) so that $y = f(t)$ when $x = 0$ and $t \geq 0$, where f is a prescribed continuous function and $f(0) = 0$. We assume that the string is initially at rest on the x axis; thus $y(x, t) \rightarrow 0$ as $x \rightarrow \infty$. The

boundary value problem for $y(x, t)$ is

$$y_{tt}(x, t) = a^2 y_{xx}(x, t) \qquad\qquad (x > 0, t > 0),$$

$$y(x, 0) = 0, \qquad y_t(x, 0) = 0 \qquad\qquad (x \geq 0),$$

$$y(0, t) = f(t) \qquad\qquad (t \geq 0).$$

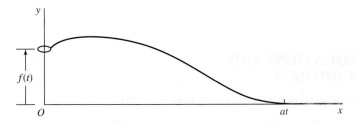

FIGURE 27

(a) Apply the first two of these boundary conditions to the general solution (Sec. 30)

$$y(x, t) = \phi(x + at) + \psi(x - at)$$

of the one-dimensional wave equation to show that there is a constant C such that

$$\phi(x) = C \qquad \text{and} \qquad \psi(x) = -C \qquad\qquad (x \geq 0).$$

Then apply the third boundary condition $y(0, t) = f(t)$ to show that

$$\psi(-x) = f\left(\frac{x}{a}\right) - C \qquad\qquad (x \geq 0),$$

where C is the same constant.

(b) With the aid of the results in part (a), derive the solution

$$y(x, t) = \begin{cases} 0 & \text{when } x \geq at, \\ f\left(t - \dfrac{x}{a}\right) & \text{when } x < at. \end{cases}$$

Note that the part of the string to the right of the point $x = at$ on the x axis is unaffected by the movement of the ring prior to time t, as shown in Fig. 27.

4. Use the solution obtained in Problem 3 to show that if the ring at the left-hand end of the string in that problem is moved according to the function

$$f(t) = \begin{cases} \sin \pi t & \text{when } 0 \leq t \leq 1, \\ 0 & \text{when } \quad\;\; t > 1, \end{cases}$$

then

$$y(x, t) = \begin{cases} 0 & \text{when } x \leq a(t - 1) \text{ or } x \geq at, \\ \sin\left[\pi\left(t - \dfrac{x}{a}\right)\right] & \text{when } \quad\;\; a(t - 1) < x < at. \end{cases}$$

Observe that the ring is lifted up 1 unit and then returned to the origin, where it remains after time $t = 1$. The expression for $y(x, t)$ here shows that when $t > 1$, the string coincides with the x axis except on an interval of length a, where it forms one arch of a sine curve (Fig. 28). Furthermore, as t increases, the arch moves to the right with speed a.

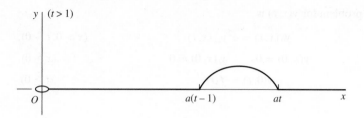

FIGURE 28

31. TYPES OF EQUATIONS AND BOUNDARY CONDITIONS

The second-order linear partial differential equation (Sec. 21)

$$(1) \qquad Au_{xx} + Bu_{xy} + Cu_{yy} + Du_x + Eu_y + Fu = G$$

in $u = u(x, y)$, where $A, B, \ldots, G$ are constants or functions of x and y, is classified in any given region of the xy plane according to whether $B^2 - 4AC$ is positive, negative, or zero throughout that region. Specifically, equation (1) is

(i) *hyperbolic* if $B^2 - 4AC > 0$;
(ii) *elliptic* if $B^2 - 4AC < 0$;
(iii) *parabolic* if $B^2 - 4AC = 0$.

For each of these categories, equation (1) and its solutions have distinct features. Some indication of this is given in Problems 2 and 3. The terminology here is suggested by the equation

$$(2) \qquad Ax^2 + Bxy + Cy^2 + Dx + Ey + F = 0,$$

where $A, B, \ldots, F$ are constants. From analytic geometry, we recall that equation (2) represents a conic section in the xy plane and that the different types of conic sections arising are similarly determined by $B^2 - 4AC$.

EXAMPLE 1. Laplace's equation

$$u_{xx} + u_{yy} = 0$$

is a special case of equation (1) in which $A = C = 1$ and $B = 0$. Hence it is elliptic throughout the xy plane. Poisson's equation (Sec. 23)

$$u_{xx} + u_{yy} = f(x, y)$$

in two dimensions is elliptic in any region of the xy plane where $f(x, y)$ is defined. The one-dimensional heat equation

$$-ku_{xx} + u_t = 0$$

in $u = u(x, t)$ is parabolic in the xt plane, and the one-dimensional wave equation

$$-a^2 y_{xx} + y_{tt} = 0$$

in $y = y(x, t)$ is hyperbolic there.

When some of the coefficients in equation (1) actually vary with x and y, the type of the equation can vary in the xy plane.

EXAMPLE 2. Consider the equation

$$u_{xx} - 2xu_{xy} + (1 - y^2)u_{yy} = 0.$$

Here

$$B^2 - 4AC = (-2x)^2 - 4(1)(1 - y^2) = 4(x^2 + y^2 - 1),$$

and we find that the equation is parabolic on the circle $x^2 + y^2 = 1$, elliptic inside it, and hyperbolic exterior to it.

As indicated below, the three types of second-order linear equations just described require, in general, different types of boundary conditions in order to determine a solution.

Let u denote the dependent variable in a boundary value problem. A condition that prescribes the values of u itself along a portion of the boundary is known as a *Dirichlet condition*. The problem of determining a harmonic function on a domain such that the function assumes prescribed values over the entire boundary of that domain is called a *Dirichlet problem*. In that case, the values of the function can be interpreted as steady-state temperatures. Such a physical interpretation leads us to expect that a Dirichlet problem may have a unique solution if the functions considered satisfy certain requirements as to their regularity.

A *Neumann condition* prescribes the values of normal derivatives du/dn on a part of the boundary. Another type of boundary condition is a *Robin condition*.[†] It prescribes values of $hu + du/dn$ at boundary points, where h is either a constant or a function of the independent variables.[‡]

If a partial differential equation in y is of the second order with respect to one of the independent variables t and if the values of both y and y_t are prescribed when $t = 0$, the boundary condition is one of *Cauchy type* with respect to t. In the case of the wave equation $y_{tt} = a^2 y_{xx}$, such a condition corresponds physically to that of prescribing the initial values of the transverse displacements y and velocities y_t in a stretched string. Initial values for both y and y_t appear to be needed if the displacements $y(x, t)$ are to be determined.

PROBLEMS

1. Classify each of the following differential equations in various regions and sketch those regions:

    (*a*) $yu_{xx} + u_{yy} = 0$;   (*b*) $u_{xx} + 2x^2u_{xy} + yu_{yy} = 0$;   (*c*) $xu_{xx} + yu_{yy} - 3u_y = 2$.

        Answers: (*a*) Parabolic on the x axis, elliptic above it, and hyperbolic below it; (*b*) parabolic on the curve $y = x^4$, elliptic above it, and hyperbolic below it.

[†]Victor Gustave Robin (pronounced *row-ban'*) (1855–1897), French mathematical physicist.

[‡]When such a condition is prescribed on the entire boundary of a region throughout which u is harmonic, the boundary value problem is sometimes referred to as a *Churchill problem*. See pp. 154–156 of the book by Sneddon (2006) that is listed in the Bibliography.

2. Consider the partial differential equation

$$Ay_{xx} + By_{xt} + Cy_{tt} = 0 \qquad (A \neq 0, C \neq 0),$$

where A, B, and C are constants, and assume that it is *hyperbolic*, so that $B^2 - 4AC > 0$.

(*a*) Use the transformation

$$u = x + \alpha t, \qquad v = x + \beta t \qquad (\alpha \neq \beta)$$

to obtain the new differential equation

$$(A + B\alpha + C\alpha^2)y_{uu} + [2A + B(\alpha + \beta) + 2C\alpha\beta]y_{uv} + (A + B\beta + C\beta^2)y_{vv} = 0.$$

(*b*) Show that when α and β have the values

$$\alpha_0 = \frac{-B + \sqrt{B^2 - 4AC}}{2C} \qquad \text{and} \qquad \beta_0 = \frac{-B - \sqrt{B^2 - 4AC}}{2C},$$

respectively, the differential equation in part (*a*) reduces to $y_{uv} = 0$.

(*c*) Conclude from the result in part (*b*) that the general solution of the original differential equation is

$$y = \phi(x + \alpha_0 t) + \psi(x + \beta_0 t),$$

where ϕ and ψ are arbitrary functions that are twice differentiable. Then show how the general solution (7), Sec. 30, of the wave equation

$$-a^2 y_{xx} + y_{tt} = 0$$

follows as a special case.

3. Show that under the transformation

$$u = x, \qquad v = \alpha x + \beta t \qquad (\beta \neq 0),$$

the given differential equation in Problem 2 becomes

$$Ay_{uu} + (2A\alpha + B\beta)y_{uv} + (A\alpha^2 + B\alpha\beta + C\beta^2)y_{vv} = 0.$$

Then show that this new equation reduces to

(*a*) $y_{uu} + y_{vv} = 0$ when the original equation is *elliptic* ($B^2 - 4AC < 0$) and

$$\alpha = \frac{-B}{\sqrt{4AC - B^2}}, \qquad \beta = \frac{2A}{\sqrt{4AC - B^2}};$$

(*b*) $y_{uu} = 0$ when the original equation is *parabolic* ($B^2 - 4AC = 0$) and

$$\alpha = -B, \qquad \beta = 2A.$$

CHAPTER
4

THE
FOURIER
METHOD

We turn now to a careful presentation of the Fourier method for solving boundary value problems involving partial differential equations. Once the basics of the method have been developed, we shall, in Chap. 5, use it to solve a variety of boundary value problems whose solutions entail Fourier series. Then, in subsequent chapters, we shall apply the method to problems whose solutions involve other, but closely related, types of representations.

32. LINEAR OPERATORS

If u_1 and u_2 are functions and c_1 and c_2 are constants, the function $c_1u_1 + c_2u_2$ is called a *linear combination* of u_1 and u_2. Note that $u_1 + u_2$ and c_1u_1, as well as the constant function 0, are special cases. A linear space of functions, or *function space,* is a class of functions, all with a common domain of definition, such that each linear combination of any two functions in that class remains in it; that is, if u_1 and u_2 are in the class, then so is $c_1u_1 + c_2u_2$. An example is the function space $C_p(a, b)$, introduced in Sec. 1.

A *linear operator* L on a given function space transforms each function u of that space into a function Lu, which need not be in the space, and has the property that for each pair of functions u_1 and u_2,

(1) $$L(c_1u_1 + c_2u_2) = c_1 Lu_1 + c_2 Lu_2$$

whenever c_1 and c_2 are constants. In particular,

(2) $$L(u_1 + u_2) = Lu_1 + Lu_2 \quad \text{and} \quad L(c_1u_1) = c_1 Lu_1.$$

The function Lu may be a constant function; in particular,

$$L(0) = L(0 \cdot 0) = 0L(0) = 0.$$

If u_3 is a third function in the space, then

$$L(c_1u_1 + c_2u_2 + c_3u_3) = L(c_1u_1 + c_2u_2) + L(c_3u_3)$$
$$= c_1 Lu_1 + c_2 Lu_2 + c_3 Lu_3.$$

Proceeding by mathematical induction, we find (Problem 7, Sec. 34) that L transforms linear combinations of N functions in this manner:

$$(3) \qquad L\left(\sum_{n=1}^{N} c_n u_n\right) = \sum_{n=1}^{N} c_n Lu_n.$$

EXAMPLE 1. Suppose that both u_1 and u_2 are functions of the independent variables x and y. According to elementary properties of derivatives, a derivative of any linear combination of the two functions can be written as the same linear combination of the individual derivatives. Thus,

$$(4) \qquad \frac{\partial}{\partial x}(c_1u_1 + c_2u_2) = c_1\frac{\partial u_1}{\partial x} + c_2\frac{\partial u_2}{\partial x},$$

provided that $\partial u_1/\partial x$ and $\partial u_2/\partial x$ exist. In view of property (4), the class of functions of x and y that have partial derivatives of the first order with respect to x in the xy plane is a function space. The operator $\partial/\partial x$ is a linear operator on that space. It is naturally classified as a linear *differential operator*.

EXAMPLE 2. Consider a space of functions $u(x, y)$ defined on the xy plane. If $f(x, y)$ is a fixed function, also defined on the xy plane, then the operator L that multiplies each function $u(x, y)$ by $f(x, y)$ is a linear operator, where $Lu = fu$.

If linear operators L and M, distinct or not, are such that M transforms each function u of some function space into a function Mu to which L applies, and if u_1 and u_2 are functions in that space, it follows from equation (1) that

$$(5) \qquad LM(c_1u_1 + c_2u_2) = L(c_1 Mu_1 + c_2 Mu_2) = c_1 LMu_1 + c_2 LMu_2.$$

That is, the *product LM* of linear operators is itself a linear operator.

The *sum* of two linear operators L and M is defined by means of the equation

$$(6) \qquad (L + M)u = Lu + Mu$$

and is found to be linear by writing

$$(L + M)(c_1u_1 + c_2u_2) = L(c_1u_1 + c_2u_2) + M(c_1u_1 + c_2u_2)$$
$$= c_1 Lu_1 + c_2 Lu_2 + c_1 Mu_1 + c_2 Mu_2$$
$$= c_1(Lu_1 + Mu_1) + c_2(Lu_2 + Mu_2)$$
$$= c_1(L + M)u_1 + c_2(L + M)u_2.$$

The sum of any finite number of linear operators is, in fact, linear.

EXAMPLE 3. Let L denote the linear operator $\partial^2/\partial x^2$ defined on the space of functions $u(x, y)$ whose derivatives of the first and second order with respect to x exist in a given domain of the xy plane. The product $M = f \, \partial/\partial x$ of the linear operators in Examples 1 and 2 is linear on the same space, and the sum

$$L + M = \frac{\partial^2}{\partial x^2} + f \frac{\partial}{\partial x}$$

is therefore linear.

33. PRINCIPLE OF SUPERPOSITION

Each nonzero term of a linear homogeneous differential equation in u consists of a function of the independent variables only, which may be a constant function, times a derivative of u or u itself. Hence every linear homogeneous differential equation has the form

$$(1) \qquad\qquad Lu = 0,$$

where L is a linear differential operator.

In particular, we recall from Sec. 21 that

$$(2) \qquad Au_{xx} + Bu_{xy} + Cu_{yy} + Du_x + Eu_y + Fu = 0,$$

where the letters A through F denote constants or functions of x and y only, is the general second-order linear homogeneous partial differential equation in $u(x, y)$. It can be written in the form (1) when

$$(3) \qquad L = A \frac{\partial^2}{\partial x^2} + B \frac{\partial^2}{\partial y \, \partial x} + C \frac{\partial^2}{\partial y^2} + D \frac{\partial}{\partial x} + E \frac{\partial}{\partial y} + F.$$

Linear homogeneous boundary conditions also have the form (1). Then the variables appearing as arguments of u and as arguments of functions that serve as coefficients in the linear operator L are restricted so that they represent points on the boundary of the domain.

We now state a *principle of superposition,* which is fundamental to the Fourier method for solving linear boundary value problems. It involves infinite series of the type

$$(4) \qquad\qquad u = \sum_{n=1}^{\infty} c_n u_n,$$

where c_n are constants and u_n are specified functions.

Theorem. *Suppose that each function of an infinite set $u_1, u_2, \ldots$ satisfies a linear homogeneous differential equation or boundary condition $Lu = 0$. Then the infinite series (4) also satisfies $Lu = 0$, provided that*

 (*i*) *the series converges and is differentiable for all derivatives involved in L;*
 (*ii*) *any required continuity condition at the boundary is satisfied by Lu when $Lu = 0$ is a boundary condition.*

Superposition is also useful in the theory of ordinary differential equations. For example, from the two solutions $y = e^x$ and $y = e^{-x}$ of the linear homogeneous equation $y'' - y = 0$, we know that $y = c_1 e^x + c_2 e^{-x}$ is also a solution. In this book, we shall be concerned mainly with applying the principle of superposition to solutions of *partial* differential equations.

To prove the theorem, we must deal with the convergence and differentiability of infinite series. Suppose that the functions u_n and constants c_n are such that series (4) converges to u throughout some domain of the independent variables, and let x represent one of those variables. The series is *differentiable,* or termwise differentiable, with respect to x if the derivatives $\partial u_n / \partial x$ and $\partial u / \partial x$ exist and if the series of functions $c_n \partial u_n / \partial x$ converges to $\partial u / \partial x$:

$$(5) \qquad \frac{\partial u}{\partial x} = \sum_{n=1}^{\infty} c_n \frac{\partial u_n}{\partial x}.$$

Note that a series must be convergent if it is to be differentiable. If, in addition, series (5) is differentiable with respect to x, then series (4) is differentiable twice with respect to x.

Let L be a linear operator where Lu is a product of a function f of the independent variables by u or by a derivative of u, or where Lu is a sum of a finite number of such terms. We now show that if series (4) is differentiable for all the derivatives involved in L and if each of the functions u_n in series (4) satisfies the linear homogeneous differential equation $Lu = 0$, then series (4) satisfies it.

To accomplish this, we first note that according to the definition of the sum of an infinite series,

$$f \frac{\partial u}{\partial x} = f \lim_{N \to \infty} \sum_{n=1}^{N} c_n \frac{\partial u_n}{\partial x}$$

when series (4) is differentiable with respect to x. Thus,

$$(6) \qquad f \frac{\partial u}{\partial x} = \lim_{N \to \infty} f \frac{\partial}{\partial x} \sum_{n=1}^{N} c_n u_n.$$

Here the operator $\partial / \partial x$ can be replaced by other derivatives if the series involved are differentiable. Then, by adding corresponding sides of equations similar to equation (6), including one that may not have any derivative at all, we find that

$$(7) \qquad Lu = \lim_{N \to \infty} L \left(\sum_{n=1}^{N} c_n u_n \right).$$

The sum on the right-hand side of equation (7) is a linear combination of the functions $u_1, u_2, \ldots, u_N$; and if $Lu_n = 0$ $(n = 1, 2, \ldots)$, it follows, with the aid of property (3), Sec. 32, that

$$Lu = \lim_{N \to \infty} \sum_{n=1}^{N} c_n L u_n = \lim_{N \to \infty} 0 = 0.$$

This is, of course, the desired result.

The above discussion applies as well to linear homogeneous boundary conditions $Lu = 0$. In that case, we may require the function Lu to satisfy a condition of continuity at points on the boundary so that its values there will represent limiting values as those points are approached from the interior of the domain. This completes the proof of the theorem.

34. EXAMPLES

We now illustrate how the superposition theorem in Sec. 33 is to be used in solving boundary value problems. In our discussion, we shall assume that needed conditions for convergence and differentiability of series are satisfied. We assume, moreover, that any continuity requirements involving boundary conditions are satisfied. The examples here will be used in sections immediately following this one, where two boundary value problems will be completely solved by means of the Fourier method.

EXAMPLE 1. Consider the linear homogeneous heat equation (Sec. 22)

$$(1) \qquad\qquad u_t(x, t) = k u_{xx}(x, t) \qquad\qquad (0 < x < c, t > 0),$$

together with the linear homogeneous boundary conditions

$$(2) \qquad\qquad u_x(0, t) = 0, \qquad u_x(c, t) = 0 \qquad\qquad (t > 0).$$

Equation (1) takes the form $Lu = 0$ when

$$L = k\frac{\partial^2}{\partial x^2} - \frac{\partial}{\partial t};$$

and it is straightforward to verify that if

$$(3) \qquad u_0 = 1, \qquad u_n = \exp\left(-\frac{n^2\pi^2 k}{c^2}t\right)\cos\frac{n\pi x}{c} \qquad\qquad (n = 1, 2, \ldots),$$

then

$$Lu_0 = \left(k\frac{\partial^2}{\partial x^2} - \frac{\partial}{\partial t}\right)u_0 = k\frac{\partial^2 u_0}{\partial x^2} - \frac{\partial u_0}{\partial t} = 0$$

and

$$Lu_n = \left(k\frac{\partial^2}{\partial x^2} - \frac{\partial}{\partial t}\right)u_n = k\frac{\partial^2 u_n}{\partial x^2} - \frac{\partial u_n}{\partial t} = -k\left(\frac{n\pi}{c}\right)^2 u_n + \frac{n^2\pi^2 k}{c^2}u_n = 0$$

$$(n = 1, 2, \ldots).$$

Thus, by the superposition theorem, $Lu = 0$ if u denotes the infinite series

$$(4) \qquad\qquad u = A_0 u_0 + \sum_{n=1}^{\infty} A_n u_n,$$

where A_n $(n = 0, 1, 2, \ldots)$ are constants. In view of expressions (3), then, the series

$$(5) \qquad\qquad u(x, t) = A_0 + \sum_{n=1}^{\infty} A_n \exp\left(-\frac{n^2\pi^2 k}{c^2}t\right)\cos\frac{n\pi x}{c}$$

satisfies the heat equation (1).

Conditions (2) can, moreover, be written in terms of the operator $L = \partial/\partial x$ as $Lu = 0$, where Lu is to be evaluated at $x = 0$ and at $x = c$.

Inasmuch as

$$(Lu_0)_{x=0} = \left(\frac{\partial u_0}{\partial x} \right)_{x=0} = 0$$

and

$$(Lu_n)_{x=0} = \left(\frac{\partial u_n}{\partial x} \right)_{x=0} = \left[-\frac{n\pi}{c} \exp \left(-\frac{n^2\pi^2 k}{c^2} t \right) \sin \frac{n\pi x}{c} \right]_{x=0} = 0$$

$$(n = 1, 2, \ldots)$$

when this operator is used, the first of conditions (2) is satisfied by the functions (3). Likewise, $(Lu_0)_{x=c} = 0$ and $(Lu_n)_{x=c} = 0$ $(n = 1, 2, \ldots)$. Hence, by the superposition theorem, series (5) satisfied both of the conditions (2).

This example will be used in Sec. 36, where the functions (3) are discovered and where it is shown how the results here can be used to complete the solution of a certain boundary value problem for temperatures in a slab.

EXAMPLE 2. It is easy to verify that if L is the linear operator

$$L = a^2 \frac{\partial^2}{\partial x^2} - \frac{\partial^2}{\partial t^2}$$

and

(6)
$$y_n = \sin \frac{n\pi x}{c} \cos \frac{n\pi a t}{c} \qquad (n = 1, 2, \ldots),$$

where a and c are positive constants, then

$$Ly_n = \left(a^2 \frac{\partial^2}{\partial x^2} - \frac{\partial^2}{\partial t^2} \right) y_n = a^2 \frac{\partial^2 y_n}{\partial x^2} - \frac{\partial^2 y_n}{\partial t^2}$$

$$= -a^2 \left(\frac{n\pi}{c} \right)^2 y_n + \left(\frac{n\pi a}{c} \right)^2 y_n = 0 \qquad (n = 1, 2, \ldots).$$

Hence it follows from our superposition theorem that $Ly = 0$ when y is the infinite series

(7)
$$y = \sum_{n=1}^{\infty} B_n y_n,$$

where B_n $(n = 1, 2, \ldots)$ are constants. That is, the series

(8)
$$y(x, t) = \sum_{n=1}^{\infty} B_n \sin \frac{n\pi x}{c} \cos \frac{n\pi a t}{c}$$

satisfies the wave equation (Sec. 28)

(9)
$$y_{tt}(x, t) = a^2 y_{xx}(x, t) \qquad (0 < x < c, t > 0).$$

Now write $L = 1$ and observe that

$$(Ly_n)_{x=0} = \left(\sin \frac{n\pi x}{c} \cos \frac{n\pi a t}{c} \right)_{x=0} = 0$$

and

$$(Ly_n)_{x=c} = \left(\sin \frac{n\pi x}{c} \cos \frac{n\pi at}{c} \right)_{x=c} = 0.$$

In view of our superposition theorem, this shows that series (8) also satisfies the boundary conditions

(10) $y(0, t) = 0,$ $y(c, t) = 0$ (t > 0).

On the other hand, if $L = \partial/\partial t$, we find that

$$(Ly_n)_{t=0} = \left(\frac{\partial y_n}{\partial t} \right)_{t=0} = \left(-\frac{n\pi a}{c} \sin \frac{n\pi x}{c} \sin \frac{n\pi at}{c} \right)_{t=0} = 0 \quad (n = 1, 2, \ldots).$$

So, again by the superposition principle, series (8) satisfies the condition

(11) $y_t(x, 0) = 0$ (0 < x < c).

The differential equation (9) and boundary conditions (10) and (11) are part of a boundary value problem for a vibrating string that will be fully stated and solved in Sec. 37, where it is also shown how the functions (6) arise.

PROBLEMS

1. Show that if an operator L has the two properties

$$L(u_1 + u_2) = Lu_1 + Lu_2, \qquad L(c_1 u_1) = c_1 Lu_1$$

for any functions u_1, u_2 in some space and for every constant c_1, then L is linear; that is, show that it has property (1), Sec. 32.

2. Use the linear operators $L = x$ and $M = \partial/\partial x$ to illustrate the fact that products LM and ML are not always the same.

3. Verify that each of the functions

$$u_0 = y, \qquad u_n = \sinh ny \cos nx \qquad (n = 1, 2, \ldots)$$

satisfies Laplace's equation (Sec. 23)

$$u_{xx}(x, y) + u_{yy}(x, y) = 0 \qquad (0 < x < \pi, \, 0 < y < 2)$$

and the boundary conditions

$$u_x(0, y) = u_x(\pi, y) = 0, \qquad u(x, 0) = 0.$$

Then use the superposition principle in Sec. 33 to show formally, without considering questions of convergence, differentiability, or continuity, that the series

$$u(x, y) = A_0 y + \sum_{n=1}^{\infty} A_n \sinh ny \cos nx$$

satisfies the same differential equation and boundary conditions.

4. Show that each of the functions

$$y_1 = \frac{1}{x} \qquad \text{and} \qquad y_2 = \frac{1}{1+x}$$

satisfies the *nonlinear* differential equation

$$y' + y^2 = 0.$$

Then show that the sum $y_1 + y_2$ fails to satisfy that equation. Also show that if c is a constant, where $c \neq 0$ and $c \neq 1$, neither cy_1 nor cy_2 satisfies the equation.

5. Let u_1 and u_2 satisfy a linear *nonhomogeneous* differential equation $Lu = f$, where f is a nonzero function of the independent variables only. Prove that the linear combination $c_1 u_1 + c_2 u_2$ fails to satisfy that equation when $c_1 + c_2 \neq 1$.

6. Let L denote a linear differential operator, and suppose that f is a function of the independent variables. Show that the solutions u of the equation $Lu = f$ are of the form $u = u_1 + u_2$, where the u_1 are the solutions of the equation $Lu_1 = 0$ and u_2 is any particular solution of $Lu_2 = f$. (This is a principle of superposition of solutions for *nonhomogeneous* differential equations.)

7. Use mathematical induction on the integer N to verify property (3), Sec. 32, of a linear operator:

$$L\left(\sum_{n=1}^{N} c_n u_n\right) = \sum_{n=1}^{N} c_n L u_n.$$

Suggestion: Point out that the property is true when $N = 1$ and then show that if it is true when N is any positive integer M, it must be true for $N = M + 1$.

35.   EIGENVALUES AND EIGENFUNCTIONS

In Secs. 36 and 37, where two boundary value problems involving partial differential equations are solved, we shall encounter two related problems involving a certain *ordinary* differential equation. We treat those related problems here in order to obtain solutions of the problems in Secs. 36 and 37 more efficiently.

We consider first the problem of finding values of λ and nontrivial functions $X(x)$, or functions that are not identically equal to zero, such that

$$(1) \qquad\qquad X''(x) + \lambda X(x) = 0, \qquad X'(0) = 0, \qquad X'(c) = 0,$$

where the differential equation is defined on the interval $0 < x < c$. All of the conditions in this problem are linear and homogeneous, and so any nonzero constant times a nontrivial solution $X(x)$ is essentially the same as $X(x)$. Problem (1) is called a *Sturm-Liouville problem*. The general theory of such problems is developed in considerable detail in Chap. 8, where it is shown that λ *must be a real number*.

Turning now to finding solutions of problem (1), we examine three cases.

(i) The case $\lambda = 0$
If $\lambda = 0$, the differential equation in problem (1) becomes $X''(x) = 0$. Its general solution is $X(x) = Ax + B$, where A and B are constants. Since $X'(x) = A$, the boundary conditions $X'(0) = 0$ and $X'(c) = 0$ require that $A = 0$. So $X(x) = B$; and, except for a constant factor, problem (1) has the solution $X(x) = 1$ if $\lambda = 0$. Note that any nonzero value of B might have been selected here.

(ii) The case $\lambda > 0$

If $\lambda > 0$, we can write $\lambda = \alpha^2$ $(\alpha > 0)$. The differential equation in problem (1) then takes the form $X''(x) + \alpha^2 X(x) = 0$, its general solution being

$$X(x) = C_1 \cos \alpha x + C_2 \sin \alpha x.$$

Writing

$$X'(x) = -C_1 \alpha \sin \alpha x + C_2 \alpha \cos \alpha x$$

and keeping in mind that α is positive and, in particular, nonzero, we see that the condition $X'(0) = 0$ implies that $C_2 = 0$. Also, from the condition $X'(c) = 0$, it follows that $C_1 \alpha \sin \alpha c = 0$. Now if $X(x)$ is to be a nontrivial solution of problem (1), $C_1 \neq 0$. Hence α must be a positive root of the equation $\sin \alpha c = 0$. That is,

$$\alpha = \frac{n\pi}{c} \qquad\qquad (n = 1, 2, \ldots).$$

So, except for the constant factor C_1,

$$X(x) = \cos \frac{n\pi x}{c} \qquad\qquad (n = 1, 2, \ldots),$$

and the corresponding values of λ are

$$\lambda = \alpha^2 = \left(\frac{n\pi}{c}\right)^2 \qquad\qquad (n = 1, 2, \ldots).$$

(iii) The case $\lambda < 0$

If $\lambda < 0$, we write $\lambda = -\alpha^2$ $(\alpha > 0)$. This time, the differential equation in problem (1) has the general solution

$$X(x) = C_1 e^{\alpha x} + C_2 e^{-\alpha x}.$$

Since

$$X'(x) = C_1 \alpha e^{\alpha x} - C_2 \alpha e^{-\alpha x},$$

the condition $X'(0) = 0$ implies that $C_2 = C_1$. Hence

$$X(x) = C_1(e^{\alpha x} + e^{-\alpha x}),$$

or

$$X(x) = 2C_1 \cosh \alpha x.$$

But the condition $X'(c) = 0$ requires that $C_1 \sinh \alpha c = 0$; and, since $\sinh \alpha c \neq 0$, it follows that $C_1 = 0$. So problem (1) has only the trivial solution $X(x) \equiv 0$ if $\lambda < 0$.

The values

$$(2) \qquad\qquad \lambda_0 = 0, \qquad \lambda_n = \left(\frac{n\pi}{c}\right)^2 \qquad\qquad (n = 1, 2, \ldots)$$

of λ for which problem (1) has nontrivial solutions are called *eigenvalues* of that problem, and the solutions

$$(3) \qquad\qquad X_0(x) = 1, \qquad X_n(x) = \cos \frac{n\pi x}{c} \qquad\qquad (n = 1, 2, \ldots)$$

are the corresponding *eigenfunctions*.

The second Sturm-Liouville problem that we shall encounter is

(4) $\qquad\qquad X''(x) + \lambda X(x) = 0, \qquad X(0) = 0, \qquad X(c) = 0,$

where the differential equation is the same as in problem (1) and is again defined on the interval $0 < x < c$. The method of solving this problem is similar to the one used to solve problem (1); and finding the solutions is left to Problem 5, Sec. 37, where the cases $\lambda = 0$ and $\lambda < 0$ both yield only trivial solutions $X(x) \equiv 0$. It turns out that the eigenvalues are

(5) $\qquad\qquad\qquad\qquad \lambda_n = \left(\dfrac{n\pi}{c}\right)^2 \qquad\qquad\qquad (n = 1, 2, \ldots)$

and that the corresponding eigenfunctions are

(6) $\qquad\qquad\qquad\qquad X_n(x) = \sin\dfrac{n\pi x}{c} \qquad\qquad\qquad (n = 1, 2, \ldots).$

36. A TEMPERATURE PROBLEM

The linear boundary value problem

(1) $\qquad\qquad\qquad u_t(x, t) = k u_{xx}(x, t) \qquad\qquad\qquad (0 < x < c,\ t > 0),$

(2) $\qquad\qquad u_x(0, t) = 0, \qquad u_x(c, t) = 0 \qquad\qquad\qquad (t > 0),$

(3) $\qquad\qquad\qquad\qquad u(x, 0) = f(x) \qquad\qquad\qquad\qquad (0 < x < c)$

is a problem for the temperatures $u(x, t)$ in an infinite slab of material, bounded by the planes $x = 0$ and $x = c$, if its faces are insulated and the initial temperature distribution is a prescribed function $f(x)$ of the distance from the face $x = 0$. (See Fig. 29.) We assume that the thermal conductivity k of the material is constant throughout the slab and that no heat is generated within it.

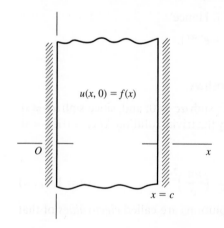

$u(x, 0) = f(x)$

O

x

$x = c$

FIGURE 29

In this section, we illustrate the Fourier method for solving linear boundary value problems by solving the temperature problem just stated. A number of the steps to be taken here are only *formal,* or manipulative. Verification of the final solution can be found in Chap. 11 (Sec. 110).

To determine nontrivial ($u \not\equiv 0$) functions that satisfy the homogeneous conditions (1) and (2), we seek *separated solutions* of those conditions,[†] or functions of the form

$$(4) \qquad\qquad u = X(x)T(t)$$

that satisfy them. Note that X is a function of x alone and T is a function of t alone. Note, too, that X and T must be nontrivial ($X \not\equiv 0$, $T \not\equiv 0$).

If $u = XT$ satisfies equation (1), then

$$X(x)T'(t) = kX''(x)T(t);$$

and, for values of x and t such that the product $X(x)T(t)$ is nonzero, one can divide each side of this equation by $kX(x)T(t)$ to separate the variables:

$$\frac{T'(t)}{kT(t)} = \frac{X''(x)}{X(x)}.$$

Since the left-hand side here is a function of t alone, it does not vary with x. However, it is equal to a function of x alone, and so it cannot vary with t. Hence the two sides must have some constant value $-\lambda$ in common. That is,

$$\frac{T'(t)}{kT(t)} = -\lambda, \qquad \frac{X''(x)}{X(x)} = -\lambda.$$

Our choice of $-\lambda$, rather than λ, for the *separation constant* is, of course, a minor matter of notation. It is only for convenience later on (Chap. 8) that we have written $-\lambda$.

If $u = XT$ is to satisfy the first of conditions (2), then $X'(0)T(t)$ must vanish for all t ($t > 0$). With our requirement that $T \not\equiv 0$, it follows that $X'(0) = 0$. Likewise, the second of conditions (2) is satisfied by $u = XT$ if $X'(c) = 0$.

Thus $u = XT$ satisfies conditions (1) and (2) when X and T satisfy these two homogeneous problems:

$$(5) \qquad X''(x) + \lambda X(x) = 0, \qquad X'(0) = 0, \qquad X'(c) = 0,$$

$$(6) \qquad\qquad T'(t) + \lambda kT(t) = 0,$$

where the parameter λ is the *same* in each problem. We recall from Sec. 35 that equations (5) make up a Sturm-Liouville problem whose eigenvalues

$$(7) \qquad\qquad \lambda_0 = 0, \qquad \lambda_n = \left(\frac{n\pi}{c}\right)^2 \qquad\qquad (n = 1, 2, \ldots)$$

correspond to the eigenfunctions

$$(8) \qquad\qquad X_0(x) = 1, \qquad X_n(x) = \cos\frac{n\pi x}{c} \qquad\qquad (n = 1, 2, \ldots).$$

[†]This terminology is borrowed from the book by Pinsky (2003), which is listed in the Bibliography.

Turning to the differential equation (6), we need to determine its solutions $T_0(t)$ and $T_n(t)$ $(n = 1, 2, \ldots)$ corresponding to each of the eigenvalues λ_0 and λ_n $(n = 1, 2, \ldots)$. Those solutions are found to be constant multiples of

$$(9) \qquad T_0(t) = 1, \quad T_n(t) = \exp\left(-\frac{n^2\pi^2 k}{c^2}t\right) \qquad (n = 1, 2, \ldots).$$

Hence each of the products

$$(10) \qquad u_0 = X_0(x)\,T_0(t) = 1$$

and

$$(11) \qquad u_n = X_n(x)\,T_n(t) = \exp\left(-\frac{n^2\pi^2 k}{c^2}t\right) \cos\frac{n\pi x}{c} \qquad (n = 1, 2, \ldots)$$

satisfies the homogeneous conditions (1) and (2). The procedure just used to obtain them is called the *method of separation of variables*.

Now, as already shown in Example 1, Sec. 34, the superposition principle in Sec. 33 tells us that the generalized linear combination

$$(12) \qquad u(x, t) = A_0 + \sum_{n=1}^{\infty} A_n \exp\left(-\frac{n^2\pi^2 k}{c^2}t\right) \cos\frac{n\pi x}{c}$$

of the functions (10) and (11) satisfies conditions (1) and (2), provided that any needed convergence, differentiability, and continuity requirements are satisfied. The constants A_n $(n = 0, 1, 2, \ldots)$ in expression (12) are readily obtained from the nonhomogeneous condition (3), namely $u(x, 0) = f(x)$. More precisely, by writing $t = 0$ in expression (12), we have

$$f(x) = \frac{2A_0}{2} + \sum_{n=1}^{\infty} A_n \cos\frac{n\pi x}{c} \qquad (0 < x < c).$$

Since this is a Fourier cosine series on $0 < x < c$ (see Secs. 8 and 15), it follows that

$$(13) \qquad A_0 = \frac{1}{c}\int_0^c f(x)\,dx$$

and

$$(14) \qquad A_n = \frac{2}{c}\int_0^c f(x) \cos\frac{n\pi x}{c}\,dx \qquad (n = 1, 2, \ldots).$$

The formal solution of our temperature problem is now complete. It consists of expression (12) together with coefficients (13) and (14). Note that the steady-state temperatures, occurring when t tends to infinity, are A_0. That constant temperature is evidently the mean, or average, value of the initial temperatures $f(x)$ over the interval $0 < x < c$.

EXAMPLE. Suppose that the thickness c of the slab is unity and that the initial temperatures are $f(x) = x$ $(0 \leq x \leq 1)$. Here

$$A_0 = \int_0^1 x\,dx = \frac{1}{2}.$$

Using integration by parts, or Kronecker's method (Sec. 5), and observing that

$$\sin n\pi = 0 \qquad \text{and} \qquad \cos n\pi = (-1)^n$$

when n is an integer, we find that

$$A_n = 2 \int_0^1 x \cos n\pi x \, dx = 2 \left[\frac{x \sin n\pi x}{n\pi} + \frac{\cos n\pi x}{n^2\pi^2} \right]_0^1 = \frac{2}{\pi^2} \cdot \frac{(-1)^n - 1}{n^2}$$

$$(n = 1, 2, \ldots).$$

When $c = 1$ and these values for A_n ($n = 0, 1, 2, \ldots$) are used, expression (12) becomes

$$u(x, t) = \frac{1}{2} + \frac{2}{\pi^2} \sum_{n=1}^{\infty} \frac{(-1)^n - 1}{n^2} \exp(-n^2\pi^2 kt) \cos n\pi x,$$

or[†]

$$(15) \qquad u(x, t) = \frac{1}{2} - \frac{4}{\pi^2} \sum_{n=1}^{\infty} \frac{\exp[-(2n-1)^2\pi^2 kt]}{(2n-1)^2} \cos(2n-1)\pi x.$$

37. A VIBRATING STRING PROBLEM

To illustrate further the Fourier method, we now consider a boundary value problem for displacements in a vibrating string. This time, the nonhomogeneous condition will require us to expand a function $f(x)$ into a sine series, rather than a cosine series.

Let us find an expression for the transverse displacements $y(x, t)$ in a string, stretched between the points $x = 0$ and $x = c$ on the x axis and with no external forces acting along it, if the string is initially displaced into a position $y = f(x)$ and released at rest from that position. The function $y(x, t)$ must satisfy the wave equation (Sec. 28)

$$(1) \qquad\qquad y_{tt}(x, t) = a^2 y_{xx}(x, t) \qquad\qquad (0 < x < c, t > 0).$$

It must also satisfy the boundary conditions

$$(2) \qquad\qquad y(0, t) = 0, \qquad y(c, t) = 0, \qquad y_t(x, 0) = 0,$$

$$(3) \qquad\qquad\qquad y(x, 0) = f(x) \qquad\qquad\qquad (0 \le x \le c),$$

where the prescribed displacement function f is continuous on the interval $0 \le x \le c$ and where $f(0) = f(c) = 0$.

We assume a product solution

$$(4) \qquad\qquad\qquad y = X(x)T(t)$$

[†]Since the coefficients in this series are zero when n is even, the index n can be replaced by $2n - 1$ wherever it appears after the summation symbol. Compare with Example 1, Sec. 3.

of the homogeneous conditions (1) and (2) and substitute it into those conditions. This leads to the two homogeneous problems

$$(5) \qquad\qquad X''(x) + \lambda X(x) = 0, \qquad X(0) = 0, \qquad X(c) = 0,$$

$$(6) \qquad\qquad T''(t) + \lambda a^2 T(t) = 0, \qquad T'(0) = 0.$$

Problem (5) is the second Sturm-Liouville problem mentioned in Sec. 35, where it was left to the reader to show that its eigenvalues are

$$(7) \qquad\qquad \lambda_n = \left(\frac{n\pi}{c}\right)^2 \qquad\qquad (n = 1, 2, \ldots)$$

and that the corresponding eigenfunctions are

$$(8) \qquad\qquad X_n(x) = \sin\frac{n\pi x}{c} \qquad\qquad (n = 1, 2, \ldots).$$

When $\lambda = \lambda_n$, problem (6) becomes

$$T''(t) + \left(\frac{n\pi a}{c}\right)^2 T(t) = 0, \qquad T'(0) = 0;$$

and it follows that except for a constant factor, the solution is

$$(9) \qquad\qquad T_n(t) = \cos\frac{n\pi a t}{c} \qquad\qquad (n = 1, 2, \ldots).$$

Consequently, each of the products

$$(10) \qquad\qquad y_n = X_n(x)\,T_n(t) = \sin\frac{n\pi x}{c}\cos\frac{n\pi a t}{c} \qquad (n = 1, 2, \ldots)$$

satisfies the homogeneous conditions (1) and (2).

According to Example 2 in Sec. 34, the generalized linear combination

$$(11) \qquad\qquad y(x, t) = \sum_{n=1}^{\infty} B_n \sin\frac{n\pi x}{c}\cos\frac{n\pi a t}{c}$$

also satisfies the homogeneous conditions (1) and (2), provided that the constants B_n can be restricted so that the infinite series is suitably convergent and differentiable. That series will satisfy the nonhomogeneous condition (3) if the B_n are such that

$$(12) \qquad\qquad f(x) = \sum_{n=1}^{\infty} B_n \sin\frac{n\pi x}{c} \qquad\qquad (0 < x < c).$$

Because representation (12) is a Fourier sine series representation on the interval $0 < x < c$, we know from Sec. 15 that

$$(13) \qquad B_n = \frac{2}{c} \int_0^c f(x) \sin \frac{n\pi x}{c} \, dx \qquad (n = 1, 2, \dots).$$

The formal solution of our boundary value problem is, therefore, series (11) with coefficients (13). Note that series (11) converges to zero at the endpoints $x = 0$ and $x = c$ of the interval $0 < x < c$.

EXAMPLE. Consider a harp string of length $c = 2$ whose midpoint is initially raised to a height h above the horizontal axis. The rest position from which the string is released thus consists of two line segments (Fig. 30).

FIGURE 30

The function f, which describes the initial position of this plucked string, is given by the equations

$$(14) \qquad f(x) = \begin{cases} hx & \text{when } 0 \le x \le 1, \\ -h(x - 2) & \text{when } 1 < x \le 2; \end{cases}$$

and the coefficients B_n in the Fourier sine series for that function on the interval $0 < x < 2$ can be written

$$B_n = \int_0^2 f(x) \sin \frac{n\pi x}{2} \, dx = h \int_0^1 x \sin \frac{n\pi x}{2} \, dx - h \int_1^2 (x - 2) \sin \frac{n\pi x}{2} \, dx.$$

After integrating by parts, or using Kronecker's method (Sec. 5), and simplifying, we find that

$$B_n = \frac{8h}{\pi^2} \cdot \frac{1}{n^2} \sin \frac{n\pi}{2} \qquad (n = 1, 2, \dots).$$

Series (11) then becomes

$$(15) \qquad y(x, t) = \frac{8h}{\pi^2} \sum_{n=1}^{\infty} \frac{1}{n^2} \sin \frac{n\pi}{2} \sin \frac{n\pi x}{2} \cos \frac{n\pi at}{2}.$$

Since

$$\sin \frac{n\pi}{2} = 0$$

when n is even and since

$$\sin \frac{(2n - 1)\pi}{2} = \sin \left(n\pi - \frac{\pi}{2} \right) = -\cos n\pi = (-1)^{n+1} \qquad (n = 1, 2, \dots),$$

expression (15) for the displacements of points on the string in question can also be written[†]

$$(16) \qquad y(x, t) = \frac{8h}{\pi^2} \sum_{n=1}^{\infty} \frac{(-1)^{n+1}}{(2n-1)^2} \sin \frac{(2n-1)\pi x}{2} \cos \frac{(2n-1)\pi a t}{2}.$$

PROBLEMS

1. In Problem 3, Sec. 34, the functions

$$u_0 = y, \qquad u_n = \sinh ny \cos nx \qquad (n = 1, 2, \ldots)$$

were shown to satisfy Laplace's equation

$$u_{xx}(x, y) + u_{yy}(x, y) = 0 \qquad (0 < x < \pi,\ 0 < y < 2)$$

and the homogeneous boundary conditions

$$u_x(0, y) = u_x(\pi, y) = 0, \qquad u(x, 0) = 0.$$

After writing $u = X(x)Y(y)$ and separating variables, use the solutions of the Sturm-Liouville problem (1) in Sec. 35 to show how the functions u_0 and u_n $(n = 1, 2, \ldots)$ can be discovered. Then, by proceeding formally, derive the following solution of the boundary value problem that results when the nonhomogeneous condition $u(x, 2) = f(x)$ is included:

$$u(x, y) = A_0 y + \sum_{n=1}^{\infty} A_n \sinh ny \cos nx,$$

where

$$A_0 = \frac{1}{2\pi} \int_0^{\pi} f(x)\, dx, \qquad A_n = \frac{2}{\pi \sinh 2n} \int_0^{\pi} f(x) \cos nx\, dx \quad (n = 1, 2, \ldots).$$

2. Suppose that in Sec. 36 we had written

$$\frac{T'(t)}{T(t)} = k \frac{X''(x)}{X(x)} \qquad \text{instead of} \qquad \frac{T'(t)}{kT(t)} = \frac{X''(x)}{X(x)}.$$

Continuing with

$$\frac{T'(t)}{T(t)} = k \frac{X''(x)}{X(x)} = -\lambda,$$

where λ is a separation constant, show how the products (10) and (11) in Sec. 36 still follow. (This illustrates how it is generally simpler to keep the physical constants out of the Sturm-Liouville problem, as we did in Sec. 36.)

3. For each of the following partial differential equations in $u = u(x, t)$, determine if it is possible to write $u = X(x)T(t)$ and separate variables to obtain ordinary differential equations in X and T. If it can be done, find those ordinary differential equations.

(a) $u_{xx} - xt u_{tt} = 0$;   (b) $(x + t)u_{xx} - u_t = 0$;

(c) $xu_{xx} + u_{xt} + tu_{tt} = 0$;   (d) $u_{xx} - u_{tt} - u_t = 0$.

[†]See the footnote with the example in Sec. 36.

4. By assuming a product solution $y = X(x)T(t)$, obtain conditions (5) and (6) on X and T in Sec. 37 from the homogeneous conditions (1) and (2) of the string problem there.

5. Derive the eigenvalues and eigenfunctions, stated in Sec. 35, of the Sturm-Liouville problem

$$X''(x) + \lambda X(x) = 0, \qquad X(0) = 0, \qquad X(c) = 0.$$

6. Point out how it follows from expression (11), Sec. 37, that, for each fixed x, the displacement function $y(x, t)$ is periodic in t with period

$$T_0 = \frac{2c}{a}.$$

38. HISTORICAL DEVELOPMENT

Mathematical sciences experienced a burst of activity following the invention of calculus by Newton (1642–1727) and Leibnitz (1646–1716). Among topics in mathematical physics that attracted the attention of great scientists during that period were boundary value problems in vibrations of strings, elastic bars, and columns of air, all associated with mathematical theories of musical vibrations. Early contributors to the theory of vibrating strings included the English mathematician Brook Taylor (1685–1731), the Swiss mathematicians Daniel Bernoulli (1700–1782) and Leonhard Euler (1707–1783), and Jean d'Alembert (1717–1783) in France.

By the 1750s d'Alembert, Bernoulli, and Euler had advanced the theory of vibrating strings to the stage where the wave equation $y_{tt} = a^2 y_{xx}$ was known and a solution of a boundary value problem for strings had been found from the general solution of that equation. Further studies, moreover, led them to the notion of superposition of solutions, to a solution of the form (11), Sec. 37, where a series of trigonometric functions appears, and thus to the matter of representing arbitrary functions by trigonometric series. Euler later found expressions for the coefficients in those series. But the concept of a function had not been clarified, and a lengthy controversy took place over the question of representing arbitrary functions on a bounded interval by such series. The question of representation was finally settled by the German mathematician Peter Gustav Lejeune Dirichlet (1805–1859) about 70 years later.

The French mathematical physicist Jean Baptiste Joseph Fourier (1768–1830) presented many instructive examples of expansions in trigonometric series in connection with boundary value problems in the conduction of heat. His book *Théorie analytique de la chaleur,* published in 1822, is a classic in the theory of heat conduction. It was actually the third version of a monograph that he originally submitted to the Institut de France on December 21, 1807.[†] He effectively illustrated the basic procedures of separation of variables and superposition, and his work did much toward arousing interest in trigonometric series representations.

[†] A. Freeman's early translation of Fourier's book into English was first reprinted by Dover, New York, in 1955. The original 1807 monograph itself remained unpublished until 1972, when the critical edition by Grattan-Guinness that is listed in the Bibliography appeared.

But Fourier's contributions to the representation problem did not include conditions of validity; he was interested in applications and methods. As noted above, Dirichlet was the first to give such conditions. In 1829 he firmly established general conditions on a function sufficient to ensure that it can be represented by a series of sine and cosine functions.[‡]

Representation theory has been refined and greatly extended since the time of Dirichlet. It is still growing.

[‡]For supplementary reading on the history of these series, see the articles by Langer (1947) and Van Vleck (1914), listed in the Bibliography.

CHAPTER
5

BOUNDARY VALUE PROBLEMS

This chapter is devoted to the use of Fourier series in solving various boundary value problems that are mathematical formulations of problems in physics. The basic method has already been described in Chap. 4.

Except for the final section of this chapter (Sec. 49), we shall limit our attention to problems whose solutions follow from the solutions of the two Sturm-Liouville problems needed in Secs. 36 and 37 of Chap. 4. To be specific, we saw in Sec. 35 that the Sturm-Liouville problem

$$(1) \qquad X''(x) + \lambda X(x) = 0, \qquad X'(0) = 0, \qquad X'(c) = 0$$

on the interval $0 \le x \le c$ has nontrivial solutions when λ is one of the eigenvalues

$$\lambda_0 = 0, \qquad \lambda_n = \left(\frac{n\pi}{c}\right)^2 \qquad\qquad (n = 1, 2, \ldots)$$

and that the corresponding solutions, or eigenfunctions, are

$$X_0(x) = 1, \qquad X_n(x) = \cos\frac{n\pi x}{c} \qquad\qquad (n = 1, 2, \ldots).$$

Moreover, for the Sturm-Liouville problem

$$(2) \qquad X''(x) + \lambda X(x) = 0, \qquad X(0) = 0, \qquad X(c) = 0,$$

on the same interval $0 \le x \le c$,

$$\lambda_n = \left(\frac{n\pi}{c}\right)^2 \qquad\qquad (n = 1, 2, \ldots)$$

113

and

$$X_n(x) = \sin \frac{n\pi x}{c} \qquad\qquad (n = 1, 2, \ldots).$$

As illustrated in Chap. 4, the solutions of problems (1) and (2) lead to Fourier cosine and sine series representations, respectively. A third Sturm-Liouville problem, to be solved in Sec. 49, leads to Fourier series with *both* cosines and sines. Boundary value problems whose solutions involve terms other than

$$\cos \frac{n\pi x}{c} \quad \text{and} \quad \sin \frac{n\pi x}{c}$$

are taken up in Chap. 8, where the general theory of Sturm-Liouville problems is developed, and in subsequent chapters.

Once it is shown that a solution found for a given boundary value problem truly satisfies the partial differential equation and all of the boundary conditions and continuity requirements, the solution is rigorously established. But, even for many of the simpler problems, the verification of solutions may be lengthy or difficult. The boundary value problems in this chapter will be solved only *formally* in the sense that we shall not always explicitly mention needed conditions on functions whose Fourier series are used, and in most cases we shall not verify the solutions.

We shall also ignore questions of uniqueness, but the physical requirements of a given boundary value problem that is well posed generally suggest that there should be only one solution of that problem. In Chap. 11 we shall give some attention to uniqueness of solutions, in addition to their verification.

39. A SLAB WITH FACES AT PRESCRIBED TEMPERATURES

We consider here the problem of finding temperatures in the same slab as in Sec. 36 when its faces, or boundary surfaces, are kept at certain specified temperatures. For convenience, however, we take the thickness of the slab to be π units, keeping in mind that we shall illustrate in Example 1, Sec. 40, how temperature formulas for a slab of arbitrary thickness c follow readily once they are found when $c = \pi$. In each of the examples below, the temperature function $u = u(x, t)$ is to satisfy the one-dimensional heat equation

$$(1) \qquad\qquad u_t(x, t) = k u_{xx}(x, t) \qquad\qquad (0 < x < \pi, t > 0).$$

EXAMPLE 1. If both faces of the slab are kept at temperature zero and the initial temperatures are $f(x)$ (Fig. 31), then

$$(2) \qquad u(0, t) = 0, \qquad u(\pi, t) = 0, \qquad \text{and} \qquad u(x, 0) = f(x).$$

Conditions (1) and (2) make up the boundary value problem; and, by separation of variables, we find that a function $u = X(x)T(t)$ satisfies the homogeneous conditions if

$$(3) \qquad\qquad X''(x) + \lambda X(x) = 0, \qquad X(0) = 0, \qquad X(\pi) = 0$$

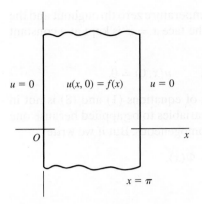

$u = 0$ $u(x, 0) = f(x)$ $u = 0$

O x

$x = \pi$

FIGURE 31

and

(4) $$T'(t) + \lambda k T(t) = 0.$$

According to Sec. 35, the Sturm-Liouville problem (3) has eigenvalues and eigenfunctions

$$\lambda = n^2, \qquad X_n(x) = \sin nx \qquad\qquad (n = 1, 2, \ldots).$$

The corresponding functions of t arising from equation (4) are, except for constant factors,

$$T_n(t) = e^{-n^2 kt} \qquad\qquad (n = 1, 2, \ldots).$$

Formally, then, the function

(5) $$u(x, t) = \sum_{n=1}^{\infty} B_n e^{-n^2 kt} \sin nx$$

satisfies all of the conditions in the boundary value problem, including the non-homogeneous condition $u(x, 0) = f(x)$, if

(6) $$f(x) = \sum_{n=1}^{\infty} B_n \sin nx \qquad\qquad (0 < x < \pi).$$

Let us assume that f is piecewise smooth on the interval $0 < x < \pi$. Then $f(x)$ is represented by its Fourier sine series (6), where

(7) $$B_n = \frac{2}{\pi} \int_0^{\pi} f(x) \sin nx \, dx \qquad\qquad (n = 1, 2, \ldots).$$

The function (5), with coefficients (7), is our formal solution of the boundary value problem (1)–(2). It can be expressed more compactly in the form

$$u(x, t) = \frac{2}{\pi} \sum_{n=1}^{\infty} e^{-n^2 kt} \sin nx \int_0^{\pi} f(s) \sin ns \, ds,$$

where the variable of integration s is used in order to avoid confusion with the free variable x.

EXAMPLE 2. If the slab is initially at temperature zero throughout and the face $x = 0$ is kept at that temperature, while the face $x = \pi$ is kept at a constant temperature u_0 when $t > 0$, then

$$(8) \qquad u(0, t) = 0, \qquad u(\pi, t) = u_0, \qquad u(x, 0) = 0.$$

The boundary value problem consisting of equations (1) and (8) is not in proper form for the method of separation of variables to be applied because one of the two-point boundary conditions is nonhomogeneous. But if we write

$$(9) \qquad u(x, t) = U(x, t) + \Phi(x),$$

equations (1) and (8) become

$$U_t(x, t) = k[U_{xx}(x, t) + \Phi''(x)]$$

and

$$U(0, t) + \Phi(0) = 0, \qquad U(\pi, t) + \Phi(\pi) = u_0, \qquad U(x, 0) + \Phi(x) = 0.$$

Suppose now that

$$(10) \qquad \Phi''(x) = 0 \quad \text{and} \quad \Phi(0) = 0, \qquad \Phi(\pi) = u_0.$$

Then $U(x, t)$ satisfies the boundary value problem

$$(11) \quad U_t(x, t) = kU_{xx}(x, t), \quad U(0, t) = 0, \quad U(\pi, t) = 0, \quad U(x, 0) = -\Phi(x).$$

Conditions (10) tell us that

$$(12) \qquad \Phi(x) = \frac{u_0}{\pi} x.$$

Hence problem (11) is a special case of the one in Example 1, where

$$(13) \qquad f(x) = -\frac{u_0}{\pi} x.$$

When $f(x)$ is this particular function, the coefficients B_n in solution (5) can be found by evaluating the integrals in expression (7). But since we already know from Example 1, Sec. 5, that

$$(14) \qquad x = \sum_{n=1}^{\infty} 2 \frac{(-1)^{n+1}}{n} \sin nx \qquad (0 < x < \pi)$$

and since the numbers B_n are the coefficients in the Fourier sine series for the function (13) on the interval $0 < x < \pi$, we can see at once that

$$B_n = -\frac{u_0}{\pi} 2 \frac{(-1)^{n+1}}{n} = \frac{u_0}{\pi} 2 \cdot \frac{(-1)^n}{n} \qquad (n = 1, 2, \ldots).$$

Consequently,

$$U(x, t) = \frac{u_0}{\pi} 2 \sum_{n=1}^{\infty} \frac{(-1)^n}{n} e^{-n^2 kt} \sin nx;$$

and so, in view of expressions (9) and (12),

$$(15) \qquad u(x, t) = \frac{u_0}{\pi} \left[x + 2 \sum_{n=1}^{\infty} \frac{(-1)^n}{n} e^{-n^2 kt} \sin nx \right].$$

By letting t tend to infinity in solution (15), we find that the function (12) represents *steady-state* temperatures in the slab. In fact, conditions (10) consist of Laplace's equation in one dimension together with the conditions that the temperature be 0 and u_0 at $x = 0$ and $x = \pi$, respectively. Expression (9), in the form

$$U(x, t) = u(x, t) - \Phi(x),$$

reveals that $U(x, t)$ is merely the desired solution minus the steady-state temperatures.

Finally, note that one can replace the term x in solution (15) by its representation (14) and write that solution as

$$(16) \qquad u(x, t) = \frac{2u_0}{\pi} \sum_{n=1}^{\infty} \frac{(-1)^{n+1}}{n} (1 - e^{-n^2 kt}) \sin nx.$$

This alternative form can be more useful in approximating $u(x, t)$ by a few terms of the series when t is small, since the factors $1 - \exp(-n^2 kt)$ are then small compared to the factors $\exp(-n^2 kt)$ in expression (15). Hence the terms that are discarded are smaller. The terms in series (15) are, of course, smaller when t is large.

PROBLEMS[†]

1. Let the initial temperature distribution be uniform over the slab in Example 1, Sec. 39, so that $f(x) = u_0$. Find $u(x, t)$ and the flux $\Phi(x_0, t) = -Ku_x(x_0, t)$ (see Sec. 22) across a plane $x = x_0$ $(0 \le x_0 \le \pi)$ when $t > 0$. Show that no heat flows across the center plane $x = \pi/2$.

2. Suppose that $f(x) = \sin x$ in Example 1, Sec. 39. Find $u(x, t)$ and verify the result fully.
   Suggestion: Use the integration formula obtained in Problem 9, Sec. 5.
   Answer: $u(x, t) = e^{-kt} \sin x$.

3. Let $v(x, t)$ and $w(x, t)$ denote the solutions found in Examples 1 and 2 in Sec. 39. Assuming that those solutions are valid, show that the sum $u = v + w$ gives a temperature formula for a slab $0 \le x \le \pi$ whose faces $x = 0$ and $x = \pi$ are kept at temperatures 0 and u_0, respectively, and whose initial temperature distribution is $f(x)$.

4. Suppose that the conditions on the faces of the slab in Example 2, Sec. 39, are reversed, so that

$$u(0, t) = u_0 \quad \text{and} \quad u(\pi, t) = 0.$$

By replacing x with $\pi - x$ in solution (15) in that example, show that the solution of this new boundary value problem is

$$u(x, t) = u_0 \left[1 - \frac{x}{\pi} - \frac{2}{\pi} \sum_{n=1}^{\infty} \frac{1}{n} e^{-n^2 kt} \sin nx \right].$$

[†]Only formal solutions of the boundary value problems here and in the sets of problems to follow are expected, unless the problem specifically states that the solution is to be fully verified. Partial verification is often easy and helpful.

5. Let the face $x = 0$ of the slab in Problem 4 be maintained at temperatures $u(0, t) = F(t)$, instead of $u(0, t) = u_0$, where $F(t)$ is continuous and differentiable when $t \geq 0$ and where $F(0) = 0$. Use the solution in Problem 4 together with Duhamel's principle in Sec. 27 to show that

$$u(x, t) = \frac{2k}{\pi} \sum_{n=1}^{\infty} n \sin nx \int_0^t F(\tau) e^{-n^2 k(t-\tau)} d\tau.$$

(Compare with the example in Sec. 27.)

40. RELATED TEMPERATURE PROBLEMS

As indicated in Example 2, Sec. 39, a given boundary value problem can sometimes be reduced to one already solved. The examples in this and the following section illustrate this further.

EXAMPLE 1. Consider the boundary value problem consisting of the conditions

(1) $$u_t(x, t) = k u_{xx}(x, t) \qquad (0 < x < c, t > 0),$$

(2) $$u(0, t) = 0, \qquad u(c, t) = 0, \qquad u(x, 0) = f(x).$$

This is the problem for the temperatures in an infinite slab that was solved in Example 1, Sec. 39, when $c = \pi$. It is also the problem of determining temperatures in a bar of uniform cross section, such as one in the shape of a right circular cylinder (Fig. 32), when its bases in the planes $x = 0$ and $x = c$ are kept at temperature zero, its lateral surface is insulated and parallel to the x axis, and its initial temperatures are $f(x)$ $(0 < x < c)$.

$u = 0$ $u(x, 0) = f(x)$ $u = 0$

$x = 0$ $x = c$

FIGURE 32

The problem in Example 1, Sec. 39, where $c = \pi$, suggests that we make the substitution

(3) $$s = \frac{\pi x}{c}$$

in the problem here and then refer to the solution in that earlier example. Since

$$\frac{\partial u}{\partial x} = \frac{\partial u}{\partial s} \frac{ds}{dx} = \frac{\pi}{c} \frac{\partial u}{\partial s}$$

and

$$\frac{\partial^2 u}{\partial x^2} = \frac{\partial}{\partial x}\left(\frac{\partial u}{\partial x}\right) = \frac{\partial}{\partial s}\left(\frac{\pi}{c} \frac{\partial u}{\partial s}\right)\frac{ds}{dx} = \frac{\pi^2}{c^2} \frac{\partial^2 u}{\partial s^2},$$

equation (1) becomes

(4) $$\frac{\partial u}{\partial t} = \left(\frac{\pi^2 k}{c^2}\right)\frac{\partial^2 u}{\partial s^2} \qquad (0 < s < \pi, t > 0).$$

Conditions (2) tell us that

(5) $u = 0$ when $s = 0$ and $u = 0$ when $s = \pi$

and that

(6) $$u = f\left(\frac{cs}{\pi}\right) \qquad \text{when} \quad t = 0.$$

Except for notation, conditions (4), (5), and (6) make up the earlier boundary value problem in Example 1, Sec. 39. From that example, we know that

$$u = \sum_{n=1}^{\infty} B_n \exp\left(-\frac{n^2\pi^2 k}{c^2}t\right)\sin ns,$$

where

$$B_n = \frac{2}{\pi}\int_0^\pi f\left(\frac{cs}{\pi}\right)\sin ns \, ds \qquad (n = 1, 2, \ldots).$$

Finally, then, substitution (3) gives us the solution of the boundary value problem (1)–(2):

(7) $$u(x, t) = \sum_{n=1}^{\infty} B_n \exp\left(-\frac{n^2\pi^2 k}{c^2}t\right)\sin\frac{n\pi x}{c},$$

where

(8) $$B_n = \frac{2}{c}\int_0^c f(x)\sin\frac{n\pi x}{c}\, dx \qquad (n = 1, 2, \ldots).$$

EXAMPLE 2. Suppose that the face $x = 0$ of a slab of thickness π is kept at temperature zero and that the face $x = \pi$ is insulated. Then, in addition to satisfying the heat equation

(9) $$u_t(x, t) = ku_{xx}(x, t) \qquad (0 < x < \pi, t > 0),$$

u satisfies the homogeneous conditions

(10) $u(0, t) = 0$ and $u_x(\pi, t) = 0$ $(t > 0)$.

Also, let the initial temperatures be

(11) $$u(x, 0) = f(x) \qquad (0 < x < \pi),$$

where f is piecewise smooth. By writing $u = X(x)T(t)$ and separating variables in conditions (9) and (10), we find that

$$X''(x) + \lambda X(x) = 0, \qquad X(0) = 0, \qquad X'(\pi) = 0.$$

Although this problem in X can be treated by methods to be developed in Chap. 8, we are not fully prepared to handle it at this time. The stated temperature problem can, however, be solved here by considering a related problem in a larger slab $0 \le x \le 2\pi$ (Fig. 33).

FIGURE 33

Let the two faces $x = 0$ and $x = 2\pi$ of that larger slab be kept at temperature zero, and let the initial temperatures be

$$(12) \qquad\qquad\qquad u(x, 0) = F(x) \qquad\qquad\qquad (0 < x < 2\pi)$$

where

$$(13) \qquad\qquad F(x) = \begin{cases} f(x) & \text{when} \quad 0 < x < \pi, \\ f(2\pi - x) & \text{when} \quad \pi < x < 2\pi. \end{cases}$$

The function F is a piecewise smooth extension of the function f on the interval $0 < x < 2\pi$, and the graph of $y = F(x)$ is symmetric with respect to the line $x = \pi$. This procedure is suggested by the fact that with the initial condition (12) no heat will flow across the midsection $x = \pi$ of the larger slab. So, when the variable x is restricted to the interval $0 < x < \pi$, the temperature function for the larger slab will be the desired one for the original slab.

According to Example 1, the temperature function for the larger slab is

$$(14) \qquad\qquad u(x, t) = \sum_{n=1}^{\infty} B_n \exp\left(-\frac{n^2 k}{4} t\right) \sin \frac{nx}{2},$$

where B_n are the coefficients in the Fourier sine series for the function F on the interval $0 < x < 2\pi$:

$$B_n = \frac{1}{\pi} \int_0^{2\pi} F(x) \sin \frac{nx}{2}\, dx \qquad\qquad (n = 1, 2, \ldots).$$

This integral can be written in terms of the original function $f(x)$ by simply referring to Problem 6, Sec. 15, which tells us that

$$B_n = \frac{1 - (-1)^n}{\pi} \int_0^{\pi} f(x) \sin \frac{nx}{2}\, dx \qquad\qquad (n = 1, 2, \ldots);$$

that is, $B_{2n} = 0$ and

$$(15) \qquad\qquad B_{2n-1} = \frac{2}{\pi} \int_0^{\pi} f(x) \sin \frac{(2n-1)x}{2}\, dx \qquad\qquad (n = 1, 2, \ldots).$$

Solution (14) then becomes

(16) $$u(x, t) = \sum_{n=1}^{\infty} B_{2n-1} \exp\left[-\frac{(2n-1)^2 k}{4} t\right] \sin \frac{(2n-1)x}{2},$$

with coefficients (15).

PROBLEMS

1. The initial temperature of a slab $0 \leq x \leq \pi$ is zero throughout, and the face $x = 0$ is kept at that temperature. Heat is supplied through the face $x = \pi$ at a constant rate $A\,(A > 0)$ per unit area, so that $Ku_x(\pi, t) = A$ (see Sec. 26). Write

$$u(x, t) = U(x, t) + \Phi(x)$$

and use the solution of the problem in Example 2, Sec. 40, to derive the expression

$$u(x, t) = \frac{A}{K}\left\{x + \frac{8}{\pi} \sum_{n=1}^{\infty} \frac{(-1)^n}{(2n-1)^2} \exp\left[-\frac{(2n-1)^2 k}{4} t\right] \sin \frac{(2n-1)x}{2}\right\}$$

   for the temperatures in this slab.

2. Solve this temperature problem by making the substitution $s = \pi x$, proceeding as in Example 1, Sec. 40, and then referring to solution (15) that was obtained in Example 2, Sec. 39:

$$u_t(x, t) = k u_{xx}(x, t) \qquad (0 < x < 1, t > 0),$$

$$u(0, t) = 0, \quad u(1, t) = u_0, \quad u(x, 0) = 0.$$

   Answer: $u(x, t) = u_0\left[x + \dfrac{2}{\pi} \sum_{n=1}^{\infty} \dfrac{(-1)^n}{n} e^{-n^2\pi^2 kt} \sin n\pi x\right].$

3. Let $v(x, t)$ denote temperatures in a slender wire lying along the x axis. Variations of the temperature over each cross section are to be neglected. At the lateral surface, the linear law of surface heat transfer between the wire and its surroundings is assumed to apply (see Problem 6, Sec. 27). Let the surroundings be at temperature zero; then

$$v_t(x, t) = k v_{xx}(x, t) - bv(x, t),$$

   where b is a positive constant. The ends $x = 0$ and $x = c$ of the wire are insulated (Fig. 34), and the initial temperature distribution is $f(x)$. Solve the boundary value problem for v by separation of variables. Then show that

$$v(x, t) = u(x, t) e^{-bt}$$

   where u is the temperature function found in Sec. 36.

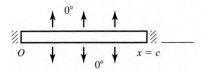

FIGURE 34

4. Solve the boundary value problem consisting of the differential equation

$$u_t(x, t) = u_{xx}(x, t) - bu(x, t) \qquad (0 < x < \pi, t > 0),$$

where b is a positive constant, and the boundary conditions

$$u(0, t) = 0, \qquad u(\pi, t) = 1, \qquad u(x, 0) = 0.$$

Also, give a physical interpretation of this problem (see Problem 3).
Suggestion: The Fourier series for $\sinh ax$ in Example 2, Sec. 19, is useful here.

$$\textit{Answer:}\ \ u(x, t) = \frac{\sinh x\sqrt{b}}{\sinh \pi \sqrt{b}} + \frac{2}{\pi} e^{-bt} \sum_{n=1}^{\infty} (-1)^n \frac{n}{n^2 + b} e^{-n^2 t} \sin nx.$$

41. TEMPERATURES IN A SPHERE

In this section we consider temperatures $u(r, t)$ in a solid sphere $r \leq 1$ with certain boundary and initial conditions. The variable r is, of course, the spherical coordinate in Sec. 24, and u is independent of the other coordinates ϕ and θ. It follows from expression (8), Sec. 24, for the laplacian that

$$\nabla^2 u = \frac{1}{r}(ru)_{rr}$$

and hence that the heat equation $u_t = k\nabla^2 u$ to be used here takes the form

$$(1) \qquad\qquad u_t = \frac{k}{r}(ru)_{rr} \qquad\qquad (0 < r < 1, t > 0).$$

EXAMPLE 1. In this example, the solid sphere is initially at temperatures $f(r)$ and its surface $r = 1$ is kept at temperature zero (Fig. 35). The differential equation (1) and the boundary conditions

$$(2) \qquad\qquad u(1, t) = 0, \qquad u(r, 0) = f(r)$$

evidently make up the boundary value problem for the temperatures $u(r, t)$ in the sphere.

To solve this problem, we introduce the function

$$(3) \qquad\qquad U(r, t) = ru(r, t).$$

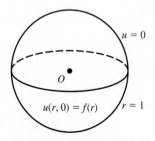

FIGURE 35

to obtain the new boundary value problem

(4) $U_t(r, t) = kU_{rr}(r, t)$ $(0 < r < 1, t > 0)$,

(5) $U(0, t) = 0$, $U(1, t) = 0$, $U(r, 0) = rf(r)$

in $U(r, t)$. The first of conditions (5) follows from relation (3) and the fact that
$u(r, t)$ is expected to be continuous at the center $r = 0$ of the sphere. The solution
of the problem consisting of conditions (4) and (5) follows immediately from the
final result in Example 1, Sec. 40, when $c = 1$ there. In view of relation (3), then,
we arrive at the temperatures in our sphere:

(6) $$u(r, t) = \frac{1}{r} \sum_{n=1}^{\infty} B_n \exp(-n^2\pi^2 kt) \sin n\pi r$$

where

(7) $$B_n = 2 \int_0^1 rf(r) \sin n\pi r\, dr$$ $(n = 1, 2, \ldots)$.

EXAMPLE 2. Consider now the same sphere as in Example 1, but let the
surface $r = 1$ be at temperature $F(t)$, where $F(t)$ is continuous and differentiable
when $t \geq 0$ and where $F(0) = 0$. Also, suppose that the initial temperature of the
sphere is zero. The boundary value problem is, then, equation (1) together with
the conditions

(8) $u(1, t) = F(t)$, $u(r, 0) = 0$.

By writing $U(r, t) = ru(r, t)$, as we did in Example 1, we have the boundary
value problem

(9) $U_t(r, t) = kU_{rr}(r, t)$ $(0 < r < 1, t > 0)$,

(10) $U(0, t) = 0$, $U(1, t) = F(t)$, $U(r, 0) = 0$.

Now, according to Problem 2, Sec. 40, the problem

$$v_t(r, t) = kv_{rr}(r, t) \qquad (0 < r < 1, t > 0),$$

$$v(0, t) = 0, \quad v(1, t) = 1, \quad v(r, 0) = 0$$

has solution

$$v(r, t) = r + \frac{2}{\pi} \sum_{n=1}^{\infty} \frac{(-1)^n}{n} e^{-n^2\pi^2 kt} \sin n\pi r;$$

and Duhamel's principle in Sec. 27 tells us that

(11) $$U(r, t) = \int_0^t F(\tau)v_t(r, t - \tau)d\tau.$$

Inasmuch as

$$v_t(r, t) = 2\pi k \sum_{n=1}^{\infty} (-1)^{n+1} n e^{-n^2\pi^2 kt} \sin n\pi r,$$

it now follows from the relation $u(r, t) = U(r, t)/r$ and expression (11) that

$$(12) \qquad u(t, t) = \frac{2\pi k}{r} \sum_{n=1}^{\infty} (-1)^{n+1} n \sin n\pi r \int_0^t e^{-n^2\pi^2 k(t-\tau)} F(\tau) d\tau.$$

The special case in which $F(t) = t$ is treated in Problem 1 below.

PROBLEMS

1. Derive this special case of the temperature function (12) in Example 2, Sec. 41, when $F(t) = t$:

$$u(r, t) = t - \frac{2}{\pi^3 kr} \sum_{n=1}^{\infty} \frac{(-1)^{n+1}}{n^3} \left(1 - e^{-n^2\pi^2 kt} \right) \sin n\pi r.$$

Suggestion: The summation formula (see Problem 1, Sec. 8)

$$\frac{2}{\pi} \sum_{n=1}^{\infty} \frac{(-1)^{n+1}}{n} \sin n\pi r = r \qquad (0 < r < 1)$$

will be useful here.

2. A solid sphere $r \leq 1$ is initially at temperature zero, and its surface is kept at that temperature. Heat is generated at a constant uniform rate per unit volume throughout the interior of the sphere, so that the temperature function $u = u(r, t)$ satisfies the nonhomogeneous heat equation (see Sec. 23)

$$\frac{\partial u}{\partial t} = \frac{k}{r} \frac{\partial^2}{\partial r^2} (ru) + q_0 \qquad (0 < r < 1, t > 0),$$

where q_0 is a positive constant. Make the substitution

$$u(r, t) = U(r, t) + \Phi(r)$$

in the temperature problem for this sphere, where U and Φ are to be continuous when $r = 0$. [Note that this continuity condition implies that $r\Phi(r)$ tends to zero as r tends to zero.] Then refer to the solution derived in Example 1, Sec. 41, to write the solution of a new boundary value problem for $U(r, t)$ and thus show that

$$u(r, t) = \frac{q_0}{kr} \left[\frac{1}{6} r(1 - r^2) + \frac{2}{\pi^3} \sum_{n=1}^{\infty} \frac{(-1)^n}{n^3} e^{-n^2\pi^2 kt} \sin n\pi r \right].$$

Suggestion: It is useful to note that in view of the formula for the coefficients in a Fourier sine series, the values of certain integrals that arise are, except for a constant factor, the coefficients in the following series [see Problem 4(a), Sec. 8]:

$$r(1 - r^2) = \frac{12}{\pi^3} \sum_{n=11}^{\infty} \frac{(-1)^{n+1}}{n^3} \sin n\pi r \qquad (0 < r < 1).$$

3. A *hollow* sphere $1 \leq r \leq 2$ is initially at temperature zero. The interior surface is kept at that temperature, and the outer one is maintained at a constant temperature u_0. Set up the boundary value problem for the temperatures

$$u = u(r, t) \qquad (1 < r < 2, t > 0)$$

and follow these steps to solve it:

(a) Write $v(r, t) = ru(r, t)$ to obtain a new boundary value problem for $v(r, t)$. Then put $s = r - 1$ to obtain the problem

$$v_t = kv_{ss} \qquad\qquad (0 < s < 1, t > 0),$$

$$v = 0 \text{ when } s = 0, \qquad v = 2u_0 \text{ when } s = 1,$$

$$v = 0 \text{ when } t = 0.$$

(b) Use the result in Problem 2, Sec. 40, to write a solution of the boundary value problem reached in part (a). Then show how it follows from the substitutions made in part (a) that

$$u(r, t) = 2u_0 \left[1 - \frac{1}{r} + \frac{2}{\pi r} \sum_{n=1}^{\infty} \frac{(-1)^n}{n} e^{-n^2\pi^2 kt} \sin n\pi (r-1) \right].$$

42. A SLAB WITH INTERNALLY GENERATED HEAT

We consider here the same infinite slab $0 \le x \le \pi$ as in Sec. 39, but we assume that there is a source that generates heat at a rate per unit volume which depends on time. The slab is initially at temperatures $f(x)$, and both faces are maintained at temperature zero. According to Sec. 22, the temperatures $u(x, t)$ in the slab must satisfy the modified form

(1) $$u_t(x, t) = ku_{xx}(x, t) + q(t) \qquad\qquad (0 < x < \pi, t > 0)$$

of the one-dimensional heat equation, where $q(t)$ is assumed to be a continuous function of t. The conditions

(2) $$u(0, t) = 0, \qquad u(\pi, t) = 0, \qquad \text{and} \qquad u(x, 0) = f(x)$$

complete the statement of this boundary value problem.

Since the differential equation (1) is nonhomogeneous, the method of separation of variables cannot be applied directly. We shall use here, instead, the *method of variation of parameters*. Also called the method of eigenfunction expansions, it is often useful when the differential equation is nonhomogeneous, especially when the term making it so is time-dependent. To be specific, we seek a solution of the boundary value problem in the form

(3) $$u(x, t) = \sum_{n=1}^{\infty} B_n(t) \sin nx$$

of a Fourier sine series whose coefficients $B_n(t)$ are differentiable functions of t. The form (3) is suggested by Example 1, Sec. 39, where the problem is the same as this one when $q(t) \equiv 0$ in equation (1). We anticipate that the function $q(t)$ in equation (1) will cause the coefficients B_n in the solution

$$u(x, t) = \sum_{n=1}^{\infty} B_n e^{-n^2 kt} \sin nx$$

that we obtained for the homogeneous part of that earlier problem to depend on t. Instead of writing the coefficients of $\sin nx$ as

$$B_n(t) e^{-n^2 kt},$$

we simply write $B_n(t)$ since it is only important that these coefficients depend on t and that they do not depend on x. So our approach here is to start with a generalized linear combination, with coefficients depending on t, of the eigenfunctions

$$X_n(x) = \sin nx \qquad (n = 1, 2, \ldots)$$

of the Sturm-Liouville problem arising in Example 1, Sec. 39. The reader will note that the method of finding a solution of the form (3) is similar in spirit to the method of variation of parameters used in solving linear *ordinary* differential equations that are nonhomogeneous.

We assume that series (3) can be differentiated term by term. Then, by substituting it into equation (1) and recalling [Problem 1(*b*), Sec. 5] that

$$1 = \sum_{n=1}^{\infty} \frac{2\left[1 - (-1)^n\right]}{n\pi} \sin nx \qquad (0 < x < \pi),$$

we may write

$$\sum_{n=1}^{\infty} B_n'(t) \sin nx = k \sum_{n=1}^{\infty} \left[-n^2 B_n(t)\right] \sin nx + q(t) \sum_{n=1}^{\infty} \frac{2\left[1 - (-1)^n\right]}{n\pi} \sin nx,$$

or

$$\sum_{n=1}^{\infty} \left[B_n'(t) + n^2 k B_n(t)\right] \sin nx = \sum_{n=1}^{\infty} \frac{2\left[1 - (-1)^n\right]}{n\pi} q(t) \sin nx.$$

By identifying the coefficients in the sine series on each side of this last equation, we now see that

(4) $$B_n'(t) + n^2 k B_n(t) = \frac{2\left[1 - (-1)^n\right]}{n\pi} q(t) \qquad (n = 1, 2, \ldots).$$

Moreover, according to the third of conditions (2),

$$\sum_{n=1}^{\infty} B_n(0) \sin nx = f(x) \qquad (0 < x < \pi);$$

and this means that

(5) $$B_n(0) = b_n \qquad (n = 1, 2, \ldots),$$

where b_n are the coefficients

(6) $$b_n = \frac{2}{\pi} \int_0^{\pi} f(x) \sin nx \, dx \qquad (n = 1, 2, \ldots)$$

in the Fourier sine series for $f(x)$ on the interval $0 < x < \pi$.

For each value of n, equations (4) and (5) make up an initial value problem in ordinary differential equations. To solve the linear differential equation (4), we observe that an integrating factor is[†]

$$\exp\left(\int n^2 k\,dt\right) = \exp n^2 kt.$$

Multiplication through equation (4) by this integrating factor puts it in the form

$$\frac{d}{dt}[e^{n^2 kt}\,B_n(t)] = \frac{2\,[1-(-1)^n]}{n\pi}\,e^{n^2 kt}q(t),$$

where the left-hand side is an exact derivative. If we replace the variable t here by τ and integrate each side from $\tau = 0$ to $\tau = t$, we find that

$$[e^{n^2 k\tau}\,B_n(\tau)]_0^t = \frac{2\,[1-(-1)^n]}{n\pi}\int_0^t e^{n^2 k\tau}q(\tau)\,d\tau.$$

In view of condition (5), then,

(7) $$B_n(t) = b_n\,e^{-n^2 kt} + \frac{2\,[1-(-1)^n]}{n\pi}\int_0^t e^{-n^2 k(t-\tau)}q(\tau)\,d\tau.$$

Finally, by substituting this expression for $B_n(t)$ into series (3), we arrive at the formal solution of our boundary value problem:

(8) $$u(x,t) = \sum_{n=1}^{\infty} b_n\,e^{-n^2 kt}\,\sin nx$$

$$+\frac{4}{\pi}\sum_{n=1}^{\infty}\frac{\sin(2n-1)x}{2n-1}\int_0^t e^{-(2n-1)^2 k(t-\tau)}q(\tau)\,d\tau.$$

Observe that the first of these series represents the solution of the boundary value problem in Example 1, Sec. 39, where $q(t) \equiv 0$.

To illustrate how interesting special cases of solution (8) are readily obtained, suppose now that $f(x) \equiv 0$ in the third of conditions (2) and that $q(t)$ is the constant function $q(t) = q_0$. Since $b_n = 0$ $(n = 1, 2, \ldots)$ and

$$\int_0^t e^{-(2n-1)^2 k(t-\tau)}q_0\,d\tau = \frac{q_0}{k}\cdot\frac{1-\exp[-(2n-1)^2 kt]}{(2n-1)^2},$$

solution (8) reduces to[‡]

(9) $$u(x,t) = \frac{4q_0}{\pi k}\sum_{n=1}^{\infty}\frac{1-\exp[-(2n-1)^2 kt]}{(2n-1)^3}\sin(2n-1)x.$$

[†]The reader will recall that any linear first-order equation $y' + p(t)y = g(t)$ has an integrating factor of the form $\exp[\int p(t)\,dt]$. See, for instance, the book by Boyce and DiPrima (2009, Sec. 2.1), listed in the Bibliography.

[‡]This result occurs, for example, in the theory of gluing of wood with the aid of radio-frequency heating. See G. H. Brown, *Proc. Inst. Radio Engrs.*, vol. 31, no. 10, pp. 537–548, 1943, where operational methods are used.

In view of the Fourier sine series representation (Problem 5, Sec. 5)

$$x(\pi - x) = \frac{8}{\pi} \sum_{n=1}^{\infty} \frac{\sin(2n-1)x}{(2n-1)^3} \qquad (0 < x < \pi),$$

solution (9) can also be written

$$(10) \qquad u(x,t) = \frac{q_0}{2k} x(\pi - x) - \frac{4q_0}{\pi k} \sum_{n=1}^{\infty} \frac{\exp[-(2n-1)^2 kt]}{(2n-1)^3} \sin(2n-1)x.$$

(See remarks at the end of Example 2, Sec. 39.)

PROBLEMS

1. The boundary value problem

$$u_t(x,t) = u_{xx}(x,t) + x p(t) \qquad (0 < x < 1, t > 0),$$

$$u(0,t) = 0, \qquad u(1,t) = 0, \qquad u(x,0) = 0$$

describes temperatures in an internally heated slab, where the units for t are chosen so that the thermal conductivity k of the material can be taken as unity (compare with Problem 3, Sec. 23). Solve this problem with the aid of the expansion (see Problem 1, Sec. 8)

$$x = \frac{2}{\pi} \sum_{n=1}^{\infty} \frac{(-1)^{n+1}}{n} \sin n\pi x \qquad (0 < x < 1)$$

and using the method of variation of parameters.

Answer: $u(x,t) = \dfrac{2}{\pi} \displaystyle\sum_{n=1}^{\infty} \dfrac{(-1)^{n+1}}{n} \sin n\pi x \displaystyle\int_0^t e^{-n^2\pi^2(t-\tau)} p(\tau)\, d\tau.$

2. Let $u(x,t)$ denote temperatures in a slab $0 \le x \le 1$ that is initially at temperature zero throughout and whose faces are at temperatures

$$u(0,t) = 0 \qquad \text{and} \qquad u(1,t) = F(t),$$

where $F(t)$ and $F'(t)$ are continuous when $t \ge 0$ and where $F(0) = 0$. The unit of time is chosen so that the one-dimensional heat equation has the form $u_t(x,t) = u_{xx}(x,t)$. Write

$$u(x,t) = U(x,t) + x F(t),$$

and observe how it follows from the stated conditions on the faces of the slab that

$$U(0,t) = 0 \qquad \text{and} \qquad U(1,t) = 0.$$

Transform the remaining conditions on $u(x,t)$ into conditions on $U(x,t)$, and then refer to the solution found in Problem 1 to show that

$$u(x,t) = x F(t) + \frac{2}{\pi} \sum_{n=1}^{\infty} \frac{(-1)^n}{n} \sin n\pi x \int_0^t e^{-n^2\pi^2(t-\tau)} F'(\tau)\, d\tau.$$

(Compare with Example 3, Sec. 39.)

3. Show that when $F(t) = At$, where A is a constant, the expression for $u(x, t)$ obtained in Problem 2 becomes

$$u(x, t) = A\left[xt + \frac{2}{\pi^3}\sum_{n=1}^{\infty}(-1)^n\frac{1 - \exp(-n^2\pi^2 t)}{n^3}\sin n\pi x\right].$$

4. A bar, with its lateral surface insulated, is initially at temperature zero, and its ends $x = 0$ and $x = c$ are kept at that temperature. Because of internally generated heat, the temperatures in the bar satisfy the differential equation

$$u_t(x, t) = ku_{xx}(x, t) + q(x, t) \qquad\qquad (0 < x < c, t > 0).$$

Use the method of variation of parameters to derive the temperature formula

$$u(x, t) = \frac{2}{c}\sum_{n=1}^{\infty}I_n(t)\sin\frac{n\pi x}{c},$$

where $I_n(t)$ denotes the iterated integrals

$$I_n(t) = \int_0^t\exp\left[-\frac{n^2\pi^2 k}{c^2}(t - \tau)\right]\int_0^c q(x, \tau)\sin\frac{n\pi x}{c}\,dx\,d\tau \qquad (n = 1, 2, \ldots).$$

Suggestion: Write

$$q(x, t) = \sum_{n=1}^{\infty}b_n(t)\sin\frac{n\pi x}{c} \qquad\text{where}\qquad b_n(t) = \frac{2}{c}\int_0^c q(x, t)\sin\frac{n\pi x}{c}\,dx.$$

5. By writing $c = 1$, $k = 1$, and $q(x, t) = xp(t)$ in the solution found in Problem 4, obtain the solution already found in Problem 1.

6. Solve the boundary value problem (1)–(2) in Sec. 42 when $q(t) = q_0$ by writing

$$u(x, t) = U(x, t) + \Phi(x)$$

and referring to the solution of the problem treated in Example 1, Sec. 39.

Answer: $u(x, t) = \dfrac{q_0}{2k}x(\pi - x) + \displaystyle\sum_{n=1}^{\infty}b_n\,e^{-n^2kt}\sin nx,$

where

$$b_n = \frac{2}{\pi}\int_0^\pi\left[f(x) - \frac{q_0}{2k}x(\pi - x)\right]\sin nx\,dx \qquad (n = 1, 2, \ldots).$$

7. Show that when $f(x) \equiv 0$, the solution obtained in Problem 6 can be put in the form (9), Sec. 42.

8. Using a series of the form

$$u(x, t) = A_0(t) + \sum_{n=1}^{\infty}A_n(t)\cos\frac{n\pi x}{c}$$

and the expansion (see Example 1 in Sec. 8)

$$x^2 = \frac{c^2}{3} + \frac{4c^2}{\pi^2}\sum_{n=1}^{\infty}\frac{(-1)^n}{n^2}\cos\frac{n\pi x}{c} \qquad\qquad (0 < x < c),$$

solve the following temperature problem for a slab $0 \le x \le c$ with insulated faces:

$$u_t(x, t) = ku_{xx}(x, t) + ax^2 \qquad\qquad (0 < x < c, t > 0),$$
$$u_x(0, t) = 0, \qquad u_x(c, t) = 0, \qquad u(x, 0) = 0,$$

where a is a constant. Thus, show that

$$u(x, t) = ac^2 \left\{ \frac{t}{3} + \frac{4c^2}{\pi^4 k} \sum_{n=1}^{\infty} \frac{(-1)^n}{n^4} \left[1 - \exp\left(-\frac{n^2 \pi^2 k}{c^2} t \right) \right] \cos \frac{n\pi x}{c} \right\}.$$

9. The boundary value problem

$$\frac{\partial u}{\partial t} = \frac{1}{r} \frac{\partial^2}{\partial r^2}(ru) + q(t) \qquad (0 < r < 1, t > 0),$$

$$u(1, t) = 0, \qquad u(r, 0) = 0$$

for temperatures $u = u(r, t)$ in a solid sphere with heat generated internally reduces to Problem 2, Sec. 41, with $k = 1$, when $q(t) = q_0$.

(a) By writing $v(r, t) = ru(r, t)$ and transforming the problem here into a new one for $v(r, t)$ and then using the solution of Problem 1 above, show that

$$u(r, t) = \frac{2}{\pi r} \sum_{n=1}^{\infty} \frac{(-1)^{n+1}}{n} \sin n\pi r \int_0^t e^{-n^2 \pi^2 (t-\tau)} q(\tau) \, d\tau.$$

(b) Show that when $q(t) = q_0$, the solution obtained in part (a) becomes

$$u(r, t) = \frac{2q_0}{\pi^3 r} \sum_{n=1}^{\infty} \frac{(-1)^{n+1}}{n^3} \left(1 - e^{-n^2 \pi^2 t} \right) \sin n\pi r.$$

(c) Use the Fourier sine series in the suggestion with Problem 2, Sec. 41, to put the solution in part (b) in the form

$$u(r, t) = \frac{q_0}{r} \left[\frac{1}{6} r(1 - r^2) + \frac{2}{\pi^3} \sum_{n=1}^{\infty} \frac{(-1)^n}{n^3} e^{-n^2 \pi^2 t} \sin n\pi r \right].$$

(This is the solution found in Problem 2, Sec. 41, when $k = 1$ there.)

10. Use the method of variation of parameters to solve the temperature problem

$$u_t(x, t) = u_{xx}(x, t) - b(t) u(x, t) + q_0 \qquad (0 < x < \pi, t > 0),$$

$$u(0, t) = 0, \qquad u(\pi, t) = 0, \qquad u(x, 0) = 0,$$

where q_0 is a constant.[†] (See Problem 6, Sec. 27.)

$$\textit{Answer: } u(x, t) = \frac{4q_0}{\pi a(t)} \sum_{n=1}^{\infty} \frac{\sin(2n - 1)x}{2n - 1} \int_0^t e^{-(2n-1)^2(t-\tau)} a(\tau) \, d\tau,$$

where

$$a(t) = \exp\left[\int_0^t b(\sigma) \, d\sigma \right].$$

[†] In finding an integrating factor for the ordinary differential equation that arises, it is useful to note that $\int_0^t b(\sigma) \, d\sigma$ is an antiderivative of $b(t)$.

43. STEADY TEMPERATURES IN RECTANGULAR COORDINATES

We now illustrate the use of the Fourier method in finding *steady temperatures* $u(x, y)$ in plates whose faces are insulated. According to Sec. 23, these temperatures must satisfy Laplace's equation $\nabla^2 u = 0$ in the interiors of the regions occupied by the plates and are said to be harmonic there. The boundary value problems in the following two examples are, in fact, Dirichlet problems (Sec. 31) since each has prescribed values of $u(x, y)$ along the entire boundary of the region involved.

EXAMPLE 1. Let $u(x, y)$ be harmonic in the interior of a rectangular region $0 \leq x \leq a, 0 \leq y \leq b$, so that

(1) $$u_{xx}(x, y) + u_{yy}(x, y) = 0 \qquad (0 < x < a, 0 < y < b).$$

The boundary values are (Fig. 36)

(2) $$u(0, y) = 0, \qquad u(a, y) = 0 \qquad\qquad (0 < y < b),$$

(3) $$u(x, 0) = 0, \qquad u(x, b) = f(x) \qquad\qquad (0 < x < a).$$

FIGURE 36

With these boundary conditions, the function $u(x, y)$ represents steady temperatures in a plate $0 < x < a, 0 < y < b$ when $u = f(x)$ on the edge $y = b$ and $u = 0$ on the other three edges. The function $u(x, y)$ also represents the electrostatic potential in a space formed by the planes $x = 0, x = a, y = 0$, and $y = b$ when the space is free of charges and the planar surfaces are kept at potentials given by conditions (2) and (3).

Separation of variables, with $u = X(x)Y(y)$, transforms the homogeneous conditions into the Sturm-Liouville problem

(4) $$X''(x) + \lambda X(x) = 0, \qquad X(0) = 0, \qquad X(a) = 0,$$

whose eigenvalues and eigenfunctions are (Sec. 35)

$$\lambda_n = \left(\frac{n\pi}{a}\right)^2, \qquad X_n(x) = \sin\frac{n\pi x}{a} \qquad (n = 1, 2, \ldots),$$

as well as the equations

(5) $$Y''(y) - \lambda Y(y) = 0, \qquad Y(0) = 0.$$

When λ is a particular eigenvalue λ_n of the Sturm-Liouville problem (4), the function $Y(y)$ satisfying conditions (5) is found to be

$$Y(y) = C_1 \left[\exp\left(\frac{n\pi y}{a}\right) - \exp\left(-\frac{n\pi y}{a}\right) \right],$$

where C_1 denotes an arbitrary nonzero constant. Instead of writing $C_1 = 1$, as we have always done in such cases, let us write $C_1 = 1/2$. Then

$$Y_n(y) = \sinh\frac{n\pi y}{a} \qquad (n = 1, 2, \ldots).$$

Thus the function

(6) $$u(x, y) = \sum_{n=1}^{\infty} B_n \sinh\frac{n\pi y}{a} \sin\frac{n\pi x}{a}$$

formally satisfies all of the conditions (1) through (3), provided that

(7) $$f(x) = \sum_{n=1}^{\infty} B_n \sinh\frac{n\pi b}{a} \sin\frac{n\pi x}{a} \qquad (0 < x < a).$$

We assume that f is piecewise smooth. Then series (7) is the Fourier sine series representation of $f(x)$ on the interval $0 < x < a$ if

$$B_n \sinh\frac{n\pi b}{a} = \frac{2}{a} \int_0^a f(x) \sin\frac{n\pi x}{a}\, dx \qquad (n = 1, 2, \ldots).$$

The function defined by means of equation (6), with coefficients

(8) $$B_n = \frac{2}{a \sinh(n\pi b/a)} \int_0^a f(x) \sin\frac{n\pi x}{a}\, dx \qquad (n = 1, 2, \ldots),$$

is, therefore, our formal solution.

If the boundary conditions (3) are changed to

(9) $$u(x, 0) = g(x), \quad u(x, b) = 0 \qquad (0 < x < a),$$

conditions (5) become

$$Y''(y) - \lambda Y(y) = 0, \quad Y(b) = 0,$$

and so

$$Y(y) = C_1 \left[\exp\frac{n\pi y}{a} - \exp\frac{n\pi (2b - y)}{a} \right],$$

where C_1 is an arbitrary nonzero constant. Then, by writing

$$C_1 = -\frac{1}{2}\exp\left(-\frac{n\pi b}{a}\right),$$

we have

$$Y_n(y) = \sinh\frac{n\pi (b - y)}{a}.$$

Hence the solution of our modified boundary value problem involving conditions (9) instead of conditions (3) is

$$(10) \qquad u(x, y) = \sum_{n=1}^{\infty} B_n \sinh \frac{n\pi (b - y)}{a} \sin \frac{n\pi x}{a},$$

where

$$(11) \qquad B_n = \frac{2}{a \sinh(n\pi b/a)} \int_0^a g(x) \sin \frac{n\pi x}{a} dx \qquad (n = 1, 2, \ldots).$$

This solution is, of course, expected since it can also be obtained by replacing y by $b - y$ in series (6) and $f(x)$ by $g(x)$ in expression (8).

EXAMPLE 2. We consider here steady temperatures $u(x, y)$ in a semi-infinite plate $x \geq 0, 0 \leq y \leq \pi$, whose faces are insulated, when the edges are kept at the temperatures shown in Fig. 37. The boundary value problem is, then,

$$(12) \qquad u_{xx}(x, y) + u_{yy}(x, y) = 0, \qquad (x > 0, 0 < y < \pi),$$

$$(13) \qquad u(x, 0) = 0, \quad u(x, \pi) = 0 \qquad (x \geq 0),$$

$$(14) \qquad u(0, y) = f(y) \qquad (0 < y < \pi).$$

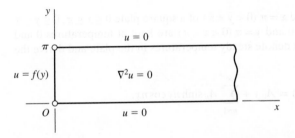

FIGURE 37

We agree that f is piecewise smooth and that $u(x, y)$ is to be bounded. So there is a positive constant M such that $|u(x, y)| \leq M$ at all points in the plate. This boundedness condition serves as a condition at the missing right-hand end of the plate.

By substituting $u = X(x)Y(y)$ into the homogeneous conditions (12) and (13), we have the ordinary differential equation

$$(15) \qquad X''(x) - \lambda X(x) = 0$$

and the Sturm-Liouville problem

$$(16) \qquad Y''(y) + \lambda Y(y) = 0, \quad Y(0) = 0, \quad Y(\pi) = 0.$$

The eigenvalues and eigenfunctions of problem (16) are (Sec. 35)

$$\lambda_n = n^2, \quad Y_n(y) = \sin ny \qquad (n = 1, 2, \ldots);$$

and, when λ is any one of the eigenvalues λ_n,

$$X(x) = C_1 e^{nx} + C_2 e^{-nx} \qquad (x > 0).$$

Now $e^{nx} \to \infty$ as $x \to \infty$. So $C_1 = 0$; and, except for constant factors,

$$X_n(x) = e^{-nx} \qquad\qquad (n = 1, 2, \ldots).$$

Consequently, the function

(17)
$$u(x, y) = \sum_{n=1}^{\infty} B_n e^{-nx} \sin ny$$

satisfies conditions (12) and (13)

Finally, since the nonhomogeneous condition (14) requires that

$$f(y) = \sum_{n=1}^{\infty} B_n \sin ny \qquad\qquad (0 < y < \pi),$$

we know that

(18)
$$B_n = \frac{2}{\pi} \int_0^{\pi} f(y) \sin ny \, dy \qquad\qquad (n = 1, 2, \ldots).$$

Expressions (17) and (18) thus make up the solutions of our boundary value problem.

PROBLEMS

1. The faces and edges $x = 0$ and $x = \pi$ $(0 < y < \pi)$ of a square plate $0 \le x \le \pi, 0 \le y \le \pi$ are insulated. The edges $y = 0$ and $y = \pi$ $(0 < x < \pi)$ are kept at temperatures 0 and $f(x)$, respectively. Let $u(x, y)$ denote steady temperatures in the plate and derive the expression

$$u(x, y) = A_0 \, y + \sum_{n=1}^{\infty} A_n \sinh ny \cos nx,$$

where

$$A_0 = \frac{1}{\pi^2} \int_0^{\pi} f(x) \, dx \qquad \text{and} \qquad A_n = \frac{2}{\pi \sinh n\pi} \int_0^{\pi} f(x) \cos nx \, dx$$

$$(n = 1, 2, \ldots).$$

Find $u(x, y)$ when $f(x) = u_0$, where u_0 is a constant.

2. The faces and edge $y = 0$ $(0 < x < \pi)$ of a rectangular plate $0 \le x \le \pi, 0 \le y \le y_0$ are insulated. The other three edges are maintained at the temperatures indicated in Fig. 38.

FIGURE 38

By making the substitution $u(x, y) = U(x, y) + \Phi(x)$ in the boundary value problem for the steady temperatures $u(x, y)$ in the plate and using the method described in Example 2, Sec. 39, derive the temperature formula

$$u(x, y) = \frac{1}{\pi} \left[x + 2 \sum_{n=1}^{\infty} \frac{(-1)^n}{n} \cdot \frac{\cosh ny}{\cosh ny_0} \sin nx \right].$$

Suggestion: The series representation (Example 1, Sec. 5)

$$x = 2 \sum_{n=1}^{\infty} \frac{(-1)^{n+1}}{n} \sin nx \qquad (0 < x < \pi)$$

is useful in finding $U(x, y)$.

3. One edge of a square plate with insulated faces is kept at a uniform temperature u_0, and the other three edges are kept at temperature zero. Without solving a boundary value problem, but by superposition of solutions of like problems to obtain the trivial case in which all four edges are at temperature u_0, show why the steady temperature at the center of the given plate must be $u_0/4$.

4. Suppose that in the plate described in Example 2, Sec. 43, there is a heat source depending on the variable y and that the entire boundary is kept at temperature zero. According to Sec. 23, the steady temperatures $u(x, y)$ in the plate must now satisfy *Poisson's equation*

$$u_{xx}(x, y) + u_{yy}(x, y) + q(y) = 0 \qquad (x > 0, 0 < y < \pi).$$

(a) By assuming a (bounded) solution of the form

$$u(x, y) = \sum_{n=1}^{\infty} B_n(x) \sin ny$$

of this temperature problem and using the method of variation of parameters (Sec. 42), show formally that

$$B_n(x) = \frac{q_n}{n^2} (1 - e^{-nx}) \qquad (n = 1, 2, \ldots),$$

where q_n are the coefficients in the Fourier sine series for $q(y)$ on the interval $0 < y < \pi$.

(b) Show that when $q(y)$ is the constant function $q(y) = Q$, the solution in part (a) becomes

$$u(x, y) = \frac{4Q}{\pi} \sum_{n=1}^{\infty} \frac{1 - \exp[-(2n-1)x]}{(2n-1)^3} \sin(2n-1)y.$$

Suggestion: In part (a), recall that the general solution of a linear second-order equation $y'' + p(x)y = g(x)$ is of the form $y = y_c + y_p$, where y_p is any particular solution and y_c is the general solution of the complementary equation

$$y'' + p(x)y = 0.^\dagger$$

5. Derive an expression for the bounded steady temperatures $u(x, y)$ in a semi-infinite slab $0 \le x \le c$, $y \ge 0$ whose faces in the planes $x = 0$ and $x = c$ are insulated and where $u(x, 0) = f(x)$. Assume that f is piecewise smooth on the interval $0 < x < c$.

---

†See, for instance, the book by Boyce and DiPrima (2009, Sec. 3.5), listed in the Bibliography.

44. STEADY TEMPERATURES IN CYLINDRICAL COORDINATES

In this section, we solve two boundary value problems involving cylindrical coordinates. The first is a Dirichlet problem, and the second involves steady temperatures in a long rod part of whose surface is insulated.

EXAMPLE 1. Let $u(\rho, \phi)$ denote a function of the cylindrical, or polar, coordinates ρ and ϕ that is harmonic in the domain $1 < \rho < b, 0 < \phi < \pi$ of the plane $z = 0$ (Fig. 39). Thus, (Sec. 24)

$$(1) \qquad \rho^2 u_{\rho\rho}(\rho, \phi) + \rho u_\rho(\rho, \phi) + u_{\phi\phi}(\rho, \phi) = 0 \qquad (1 < \rho < b, 0 < \phi < \pi).$$

Suppose further that

$$(2) \qquad u(\rho, 0) = 0, \qquad u(\rho, \pi) = 0 \qquad (1 < \rho < b),$$

$$(3) \qquad u(1, \phi) = 0, \qquad u(b, \phi) = u_0 \qquad (0 < \phi < \pi),$$

where u_0 is a constant.

FIGURE 39

Substituting $u = R(\rho)\Phi(\phi)$ into the homogeneous conditions and separating variables, we find that

$$(4) \qquad \rho^2 R''(\rho) + \rho R'(\rho) - \lambda R(\rho) = 0, \qquad R(1) = 0$$

and

$$(5) \qquad \Phi''(\phi) + \lambda \Phi(\phi) = 0, \qquad \Phi(0) = 0, \qquad \Phi(\pi) = 0.$$

Except for notation, the problem in Φ is the Sturm-Liouville problem (4) in Sec. 35 with $c = \pi$. The eigenvalues and eigenfunctions are

$$\lambda_n = n^2, \qquad \Phi_n(\phi) = \sin n\phi \qquad (n = 1, 2, \ldots).$$

The corresponding functions $R_n(\rho)$ are determined by solving the differential equation

$$\rho^2 R''(\rho) + \rho R'(\rho) - n^2 R(\rho) = 0 \qquad (1 < \rho < b),$$

where $R(1) = 0$. This is a Cauchy-Euler equation (see Problem 1), and the substitution $\rho = \exp s$ transforms it into the differential equation

$$\frac{d^2 R}{ds^2} - n^2 R = 0.$$

Hence

$$R = C_1 e^{ns} + C_2 e^{-ns};$$

and because $s = \ln \rho$,

$$R(\rho) = C_1 e^{n \ln \rho} + C_2 e^{-n \ln \rho} = C_1 \rho^n + C_2 \rho^{-n}.$$

In view of the condition $R(1) = 0$, it follows that $C_2 = -C_1$. So, except for constant factors, the desired functions of ρ are

$$R_n(\rho) = \rho^n - \rho^{-n} \qquad\qquad (n = 1, 2, \ldots).$$

Formally, then,

$$u(\rho, \phi) = \sum_{n=1}^{\infty} B_n \left(\rho^n - \rho^{-n} \right) \sin n\phi$$

where, according to the second of conditions (3), the constants B_n are such that

$$u_0 = \sum_{n=1}^{\infty} B_n \left(b^n - b^{-n} \right) \sin n\phi \qquad\qquad (0 < \phi < \pi).$$

Since this is in the form of a Fourier sine series representation for the constant function u_0 on the interval $0 < \phi < \pi$,

$$B_n \left(b^n - b^{-n} \right) = \frac{2}{\pi} \int_0^\pi u_0 \sin n\phi \, d\phi = \frac{2u_0}{\pi} \cdot \frac{1 - (-1)^n}{n} \qquad (n = 1, 2, \ldots).$$

The complete solution of our Dirichlet problem is, therefore,

$$u(\rho, \phi) = \frac{2u_0}{\pi} \sum_{n=1}^{\infty} \frac{\rho^n - \rho^{-n}}{b^n - b^{-n}} \cdot \frac{1 - (-1)^n}{n} \sin n\phi,$$

or

(6) $$u(\rho, \phi) = \frac{4u_0}{\pi} \sum_{n=1}^{\infty} \frac{\rho^{2n-1} - \rho^{-(2n-1)}}{b^{2n-1} - b^{-(2n-1)}} \cdot \frac{\sin (2n-1)\phi}{2n-1}.$$

EXAMPLE 2. Using cylindrical coordinates, let us derive an expression for the steady temperatures $u = u(\rho, \phi)$ in a long rod, with a uniform semicircular cross section and occupying the region $0 \leq \rho \leq a, 0 \leq \phi \leq \pi$, when it is insulated on its planar surface and maintained at temperatures $f(\phi)$ on the semicircular part (Fig. 40). The reader will find that the fundamental difference between this

FIGURE 40

example and Example 1 is that the origin was not on the boundary in the first example but it is in this one.

As in Example 1, $u(\rho, \phi)$ satisfies Laplace's equation

$$(7) \qquad \rho^2 u_{\rho\rho}(\rho, \phi) + \rho u_\rho(\rho, \phi) + u_{\phi\phi}(\rho, \phi) = 0,$$

but now in the domain $0 < \rho < a, 0 < \phi < \pi$. It also satisfies the homogeneous conditions (see Example 2, Sec. 26)

$$(8) \qquad u_\phi(\rho, 0) = 0, \qquad u_\phi(\rho, \pi) = 0 \qquad\qquad (0 < \rho < a),$$

as well as the nonhomogeneous one

$$(9) \qquad u(a, \phi) = f(\phi) \qquad\qquad (0 < \phi < \pi).$$

The function f is understood to be piecewise smooth and therefore bounded. We assume further that $|u(\rho, \phi)| \leq M$, where M denotes some positive constant. The need for such a boundedness condition is physically evident and has been only tacitly assumed in most earlier problems. Here it serves as a condition at the origin, which may be thought of as the limiting case of a smaller semicircle (compare with Fig. 39 in Example 1) as its radius tends to zero.

Substituting $u = R(\rho)\Phi(\phi)$ into the homogeneous conditions (7) and (8) leads to the condition

$$(10) \qquad \rho^2 R''(\rho) + \rho R'(\rho) - \lambda R(\rho) = 0 \qquad\qquad (0 < \rho < a)$$

on $R(\rho)$ and to the Sturm-Liouville problem

$$(11) \qquad \Phi''(\phi) + \lambda\Phi(\phi) = 0, \qquad \Phi'(0) = 0, \qquad \Phi'(\pi) = 0,$$

whose eigenvalues and eigenfunctions are

$$\lambda_0 = 0, \qquad \lambda_n = n^2 \qquad\qquad (n = 1, 2, \ldots)$$

and

$$\Phi_0(\phi) = 1, \qquad \Phi_n(\phi) = \cos n\phi \qquad\qquad (n = 1, 2, \ldots),$$

according to Sec. 35.

Equation (10) is a Cauchy-Euler equation, similar to the one in Example 1; and with the substitution $\rho = \exp s$, Problem 1 tells us that it becomes

$$\frac{d^2 R}{ds^2} = 0$$

when $\lambda = \lambda_0$. So, for the eigenvalue λ_0,

$$R = As + B = A \ln\rho + B \qquad\qquad (0 < \rho < a),$$

where A and B are constants. But since the product $R(\rho)\Phi(\phi)$ is expected to be bounded in the domain $0 < \rho < a$, $0 < \phi < \pi$ and since $\ln \rho$ tends to $-\infty$ as ρ tends to 0 through positive values, the constant A must be zero. Hence, except for a constant factor,

$$R_0(\rho) = 1.$$

When $\lambda = \lambda_n = n^2$ $(n = 1, 2, \ldots)$, our boundedness condition requires that the constant C_2 in the general solution

$$R(\rho) = C_1 \rho^n + C_2 \rho^{-n} = C_1 \rho^n + \frac{C_2}{\rho^n} \qquad (0 < \rho < a)$$

of equation (10) be zero. Hence we may write

$$R_n(\rho) = \rho^n \qquad (n = 1, 2, \ldots),$$

and the homogeneous conditions (7) and (8) are formally satisfied by the function

$$(12) \qquad u(\rho, \phi) = A_0 + \sum_{n=1}^{\infty} A_n \rho^n \cos n\phi,$$

where the constants A_n $(n = 0, 1, 2, \ldots)$ are yet to be determined.

In view of the nonhomogeneous condition (9),

$$f(\phi) = \frac{2A_0}{2} + \sum_{n=1}^{\infty} \left(A_n a^n \right) \cos n\phi \qquad (0 < \phi < \pi).$$

Consequently,

$$(13) \qquad A_0 = \frac{1}{\pi} \int_0^{\pi} f(\phi)\, d\phi \qquad \text{and} \qquad A_n = \frac{2}{\pi a^n} \int_0^{\pi} f(\phi) \cos n\phi\, d\phi$$

$$(n = 1, 2, \ldots).$$

The complete solution of our boundary value problem is, then, given by series (12) with coefficients (13). This solution can, of course, be alternatively written as

$$(14) \quad u(\rho, \phi) = \frac{1}{\pi} \int_0^{\pi} f(\psi)\, d\psi + \frac{2}{\pi} \sum_{n=1}^{\infty} \left(\frac{\rho}{a} \right)^n \cos n\phi \int_0^{\pi} f(\psi) \cos n\psi\, d\psi,$$

where the variable of integration ψ is to be distinguished from the free variable ϕ.

PROBLEMS

1. If A, B, and C, are constants, the differential equation

$$Ax^2 y'' + Bxy' + Cy = 0$$

is called a *Cauchy-Euler equation*. Show that with the substitution $x = \exp s$ $(s = \ln x)$, it can be transformed into the constant-coefficient differential equation

$$A\frac{d^2 y}{ds^2} + (B - A)\frac{dy}{ds} + Cy = 0.$$

Suggestion: Use the chain rule to show that

$$y' = \frac{dy}{dx} = \frac{dy}{ds}\frac{ds}{dx} = e^{-s}\frac{dy}{ds}$$

and then

$$y'' = (y')' = e^{-s}\frac{dy'}{ds} = e^{-s}\frac{d}{ds}\left(e^{-s}\frac{dy}{ds} \right) = e^{-2s}\left(\frac{d^2 y}{ds^2} - \frac{dy}{ds} \right).$$

2. Let the faces of a plate in the shape of a wedge $0 \le \rho \le a, 0 \le \phi \le \alpha$ in the first quadrant (Fig. 41) be insulated. Find the steady temperatures $u(\rho, \phi)$ in the plate when $u = 0$ on the two rays $\phi = 0, \phi = \alpha \; (0 < \rho < a)$ and $u = f(\phi)$ on the arc $\rho = a \; (0 < \phi < \alpha)$. Assume that f is piecewise smooth and that u is bounded.

$$\text{Answer: } u(\rho, \phi) = \frac{2}{\alpha} \sum_{n=1}^{\infty} \left(\frac{\rho}{a}\right)^{n\pi/\alpha} \sin \frac{n\pi\phi}{\alpha} \int_0^{\alpha} f(\psi) \sin \frac{n\pi\psi}{\alpha} \, d\psi.$$

FIGURE 41

3. Let $\rho, \phi,$ and z be cylindrical coordinates. Find the harmonic function $u(\rho, \phi)$ in the domain $1 < \rho < b, 0 < \phi < \pi/2$ of the plane $z = 0$ when

$$u(1, \phi) = 0, \qquad u(b, \phi) = f(\phi) \qquad\qquad (0 < \phi < \pi/2)$$

and

$$u_\phi(\rho, 0) = 0, \qquad u_\phi(\rho, \pi/2) = 0 \qquad\qquad (1 < \rho < b).$$

Give a physical interpretation of this problem.

$$\text{Answer: } u(\rho, \phi) = A_0 \ln \rho + \sum_{n=1}^{\infty} A_n (\rho^{2n} - \rho^{-2n}) \cos 2n\phi,$$

where

$$A_0 = \frac{2}{\pi \ln b} \int_0^{\pi/2} f(\phi) \, d\phi$$

and

$$A_n = \frac{4}{\pi (b^{2n} - b^{-2n})} \int_0^{\pi/2} f(\phi) \cos 2n\phi \, d\phi \qquad\qquad (n = 1, 2, \ldots).$$

45. A STRING WITH PRESCRIBED INITIAL CONDITIONS

In this section we examine the displacements in a string of finite length when three different types of initial conditions are used.

(i) Prescribed Initial Displacements

Section 37 was devoted to solving the boundary value problem

$$(1) \qquad\qquad y_{tt}(x, t) = a^2 y_{xx}(x, t) \qquad\qquad (0 < x < c, t > 0),$$

$$(2) \qquad\qquad y(0, t) = 0, \qquad y(c, t) = 0,$$

$$(3) \qquad\qquad y(x, 0) = f(x), \qquad y_t(x, 0) = 0$$

for the transverse displacements $y(x, t)$ in a finite string that starts with displacements $y = f(x)$ and is initially at rest. We recall that f was continuous on $0 \le x \le c$ and that

$$f(0) = f(c) = 0.$$

We obtained the solution

(4) $$y(x, t) = \sum_{n=1}^{\infty} B_n \sin \frac{n\pi x}{c} \cos \frac{n\pi at}{c},$$

where

(5) $$B_n = \frac{2}{c} \int_0^c f(x) \sin \frac{n\pi x}{c}\, dx \qquad (n = 1, 2, \ldots).$$

Solution (4) is easily written in a closed form that does not involve infinite series. We can do this with the aid of the trigonometric identity

$$2 \sin A \cos B = \sin(A + B) + \sin(A - B)$$

by first noting that

(6) $$\sin \frac{n\pi x}{c} \cos \frac{n\pi at}{c} = \frac{1}{2}\left[\sin \frac{n\pi(x + at)}{c} + \sin \frac{n\pi(x - at)}{c} \right].$$

Series (4) then becomes

(7) $$y(x, t) = \frac{1}{2}\left[\sum_{n=1}^{\infty} B_n \sin \frac{n\pi(x + at)}{c} + \sum_{n=1}^{\infty} B_n \sin \frac{n\pi(x - at)}{c} \right].$$

Next, we let F denote the odd periodic extension, with period $2c$, of the function f. That is (see Fig. 42),

$$F(x) = f(x) \qquad\qquad\qquad \text{when } 0 \le x \le c$$

and

$$F(-x) = -F(x), \qquad F(x + 2c) = F(x) \qquad\qquad \text{for all } x.$$

FIGURE 42

Under the assumption that the Fourier sine series representation

$$f(x) = \sum_{n=1}^{\infty} B_n \sin \frac{n\pi x}{c} \qquad\qquad (0 < x < c)$$

is valid when coefficients (5) are used, it follows from the fact that each of the functions $\sin(n\pi x/c)$ is odd and periodic with period $2c$ that $F(x)$ is represented for all x by the same series:

$$(8) \qquad F(x) = \sum_{n=1}^{\infty} B_n \sin \frac{n\pi x}{c} \qquad (-\infty < x < \infty).$$

Consequently, expression (7) can be written

$$(9) \qquad y(x,\, t) = \frac{1}{2}\,[F(x + at) + F(x - at)].$$

(Compare with d'Alembert's solution in Example 1, Sec. 30.) The form (9) of our solution will be verified in Chap. 11 (Sec. 112).

(ii) Prescribed Initial Velocities

When, initially, the string is in its position of equilibrium $y = 0$ and has a prescribed distribution of velocities $g(x)$ parallel to the y axis, the boundary value problem for the displacements $y(x, t)$ becomes

$$(10) \qquad y_{tt}(x,\, t) = a^2 y_{xx}(x,\, t) \qquad (0 < x < c,\ t > 0),$$

$$(11) \qquad y(0,\, t) = 0, \qquad y(c,\, t) = 0,$$

$$(12) \qquad y(x,\, 0) = 0, \qquad y_t(x,\, 0) = g(x).$$

If the xy plane, with the string lying on the x axis, is moving parallel to the y axis and is brought to rest at the instant $t = 0$, the function $g(x)$ is a constant. The hammer action in a piano may produce approximately a uniform initial velocity over a short span of a piano wire, in which case $g(x)$ may be considered to be a step function.

As in Sec. 37, we seek functions of the type $y = X(x)T(t)$ that satisfy all of the homogeneous conditions in the boundary value problem. The Sturm-Liouville problem that arises is the same as the one in Sec. 37:

$$X''(x) + \lambda X(x) = 0, \qquad X(0) = 0, \qquad X(c) = 0.$$

We recall that the eigenvalues and corresponding eigenfunctions are

$$\lambda_n = \left(\frac{n\pi}{c}\right)^2, \qquad X_n(x) = \sin \frac{n\pi x}{c} \qquad (n = 1, 2, \ldots).$$

Since the conditions on $T(t)$ are

$$T''(t) + \lambda a^2 T(t) = 0, \qquad T(0) = 0,$$

the corresponding functions of t are, except for constant factors,

$$T_n(t) = \sin \frac{n\pi a t}{c} \qquad (n = 1, 2, \ldots).$$

Thus the homogeneous conditions in the boundary value problem are formally satisfied by the function

$$(13) \qquad y(x,\, t) = \sum_{n=1}^{\infty} C_n \sin \frac{n\pi x}{c} \sin \frac{n\pi a t}{c},$$

where the constants C_n must be determined. To find those constants, we use expression (13) to write

$$(14) \qquad y_t(x, t) = \sum_{n=1}^{\infty} \frac{n\pi a}{c} C_n \sin \frac{n\pi x}{c} \cos \frac{n\pi a t}{c};$$

and, from this and the second of conditions (12), we see that

$$(15) \qquad g(x) = \sum_{n=1}^{\infty} \frac{n\pi a}{c} C_n \sin \frac{n\pi x}{c} \qquad\qquad (0 < x < c).$$

Because this is a Fourier sine series for $g(x)$ on $0 < x < c$, then,

$$\frac{n\pi a}{c} C_n = \frac{2}{c} \int_0^c g(x) \sin \frac{n\pi x}{c} \, dx \qquad\qquad (n = 1, 2, \ldots).$$

That is,

$$(16) \qquad C_n = \frac{2}{n\pi a} \int_0^c g(x) \sin \frac{n\pi x}{c} \, dx \qquad\qquad (n = 1, 2, \ldots).$$

We can sum the series (13), with the aid of expressions (14) and (6), by writing

$$y_t(x, t) = \frac{1}{2} \left[\sum_{n=1}^{\infty} \frac{n\pi a}{c} C_n \sin \frac{n\pi(x + at)}{c} + \sum_{n=1}^{\infty} \frac{n\pi a}{c} C_n \sin \frac{n\pi(x - at)}{c} \right]$$

and noting how it follows from representation (15) that

$$y_t(x, t) = \frac{1}{2} [G(x + at) + G(x - at)]$$

where G is the odd periodic extension, with period $2c$, of the function g. Then, since $y(x, 0) = 0$, we have[†]

$$y(x, t) = \frac{1}{2} \left[\int_0^t G(x + a\tau) \, d\tau + \int_0^t G(x - a\tau) \, d\tau \right].$$

After substituting $s = x + a\tau$ in the first of these integrals and $s = x - a\tau$ in the second, we arrive at the expression

$$y(x, t) = \frac{1}{2a} \left[\int_x^{x+at} G(s) \, ds - \int_x^{x-at} G(s) \, ds \right],$$

or

$$(17) \qquad y(x, t) = \frac{1}{2a} \int_{x-at}^{x+at} G(s) \, ds.$$

(iii) Initial Displacements and Velocities both Specified

If points on the string are given both nonzero initial displacements and nonzero initial velocities, so that

$$(18) \qquad y(x, 0) = f(x) \qquad \text{and} \qquad y_t(x, 0) = g(x),$$

[†]See also the footnote with Problem 10, Sec. 42, regarding antiderivatives.

the displacements $y(x, t)$ can be written as the sum

(19) $$y(x, t) = \frac{1}{2}[F(x + at) + F(x - at)] + \frac{1}{2a}\int_{x-at}^{x+at} G(s)\,ds$$

of the solutions (9) and (17) above. (Compare with Problem 2, Sec. 30.) To see that this is so, let $Y(x, t)$ and $Z(x, t)$ denote those two solutions, respectively. The principle of superposition in Sec. 33, applied to just two functions, ensures that the sum

$$y(x, t) = Y(x, t) + Z(x, t)$$

satisfies the linear homogeneous conditions (1) and (2), which are the same as conditions (10) and (11). Furthermore, in view of conditions (3) and (12),

$$y(x, 0) = Y(x, 0) + Z(x, 0) = f(x) + 0 = f(x)$$

and

$$y_t(x, 0) = Y_t(x, 0) + Z_t(x, 0) = 0 + g(x) = g(x).$$

In general, the solution of a linear problem containing more than one non-homogeneous condition can be written as a sum of solutions of problems each of which contains only one nonhomogeneous condition. The resolution of the original problem in this way, although not an essential step, often simplifies the process of solving it.

PROBLEMS

1. A string is stretched between the fixed points 0 and 1 on the x axis and released at rest from the position $y = A\sin \pi x$, where A is a constant. Obtain from expression (9), Sec. 45, the subsequent displacements $y(x, t)$, and verify the result fully. Sketch the position of the string at several instants of time.

    Answer: $y(x, t) = A\sin \pi x \cos \pi a t$.

2. Solve Problem 1 when the initial displacement there is changed to $y = B\sin 2\pi x$, where B is a constant.

    Answer: $y(x, t) = B\sin 2\pi x \cos 2\pi a t$.

3. Show why the sum of the two functions $y(x, t)$ found in Problems 1 and 2 represents the displacements after the string is released at rest from the position

$$y = A\sin \pi x + B\sin 2\pi x.$$

4. A string, stretched between the points 0 and π on the x axis and initially at rest, is released from the position $y = f(x)$. Its motion is opposed by air resistance, which is proportional to the velocity at each point (Sec. 28). Let the unit of time be chosen so that the equation of motion becomes

$$y_{tt}(x, t) = y_{xx}(x, t) - 2\beta y_t(x, t) \qquad (0 < x < \pi, t > 0),$$

where β is a positive constant. Assuming that $0 < \beta < 1$, derive the expression

$$y(x, t) = e^{-\beta t}\sum_{n=1}^{\infty} B_n\left(\cos \alpha_n t + \frac{\beta}{\alpha_n}\sin \alpha_n t\right)\sin nx,$$

where

$$\alpha_n = \sqrt{n^2 - \beta^2}, \qquad B_n = \frac{2}{\pi} \int_0^\pi f(x) \sin nx \, dx \qquad (n = 1, 2, \ldots),$$

for the transverse displacements.

5. Suppose that the string in Problem 4 is initially straight with a uniform velocity in the direction of the y axis, as if a moving frame supporting the endpoints is brought to rest at the instant $t = 0$. The transverse displacements $y(x, t)$ thus satisfy the same differential equation, where $0 < \beta < 1$, and the boundary conditions

$$y(0, t) = y(\pi, t) = 0, \qquad y(x, 0) = 0, \qquad y_t(x, 0) = v_0.$$

Derive this expression for those displacements:

$$y(x, t) = \frac{4v_0}{\pi} e^{-\beta t} \sum_{n=1}^{\infty} \frac{\sin(2n - 1)x}{(2n - 1)\alpha_n} \sin \alpha_n t,$$

where $\alpha_n = \sqrt{(2n - 1)^2 - \beta^2}$.

6. The ends of a stretched string are fixed at the origin and at the point $x = \pi$ on the horizontal x axis. The string is initially at rest along the x axis and then drops under its own weight. The vertical displacements $y(x, t)$ thus satisfy the differential equation (Sec. 28)

$$y_{tt}(x, t) = a^2 y_{xx}(x, t) - g \qquad (0 < x < \pi, t > 0),$$

where g is acceleration due to gravity.

(a) Use the method of variation of parameters (Sec. 42) to derive the expression

$$y(x, t) = \frac{4g}{\pi a^2} \left[\sum_{n=1}^{\infty} \frac{\sin(2n - 1)x}{(2n - 1)^3} \cos(2n - 1)at - \frac{\pi}{8} x(\pi - x) \right]$$

for those displacements.

(b) With the aid of the trigonometric identity

$$2 \sin A \cos B = \sin(A + B) + \sin(A - B),$$

show that the expression found in part (a) can be put in the closed form

$$y(x, t) = \frac{g}{2a^2} \left[\frac{P(x + at) + P(x - at)}{2} - x(\pi - x) \right]$$

where the function $P(x)$ is the odd periodic extension, with period 2π, of the function $x(\pi - x)$ $(0 \le x \le \pi)$.

Suggestion: In both parts (a) and (b), the Fourier sine series representation (Problem 5, Sec. 5)

$$x(\pi - x) = \frac{8}{\pi} \sum_{n=1}^{\infty} \frac{\sin(2n - 1)x}{(2n - 1)^3} \qquad (0 \le x \le \pi)$$

is needed. Also, for part (a), see the suggestion with Problem 4, Sec. 43.

46.   RESONANCE

A stretched string, of length unity and with fixed ends, is initially at rest in its position of equilibrium. A simple periodic transverse force acts uniformly on all elements of the string, so that the transverse displacements $y(x, t)$ satisfy this modified form (see Sec. 28) of the wave equation:

$$(1) \qquad y_{tt}(x, t) = y_{xx}(x, t) + A \sin \omega t \qquad\qquad (0 < x < 1, t > 0),$$

where A is a constant. Equation (1) and the boundary conditions

$$(2) \qquad\qquad y(0, t) = 0, \qquad y(1, t) = 0,$$

$$(3) \qquad\qquad y(x, 0) = 0, \qquad y_t(x, 0) = 0,$$

just described, make up a boundary value problem to which the method of variation of parameters (Sec. 42) can be applied.

We note from Sec. 37 that if the constant A were actually zero, the Sturm-Liouville problem arising would have eigenfunctions $\sin n\pi x$ $(n = 1, 2, \ldots)$. Hence we seek a solution of our boundary value problem having the form

$$(4) \qquad\qquad y(x, t) = \sum_{n=1}^{\infty} B_n(t) \sin n\pi x,$$

where the coefficients $B_n(t)$ are to be determined. To do this, we need the Fourier sine series representation

$$(5) \qquad 1 = \sum_{n=1}^{\infty} \frac{2[1 - (-1)^n]}{n\pi} \sin n\pi x \qquad\qquad (0 < x < 1),$$

which is easily obtained by replacing x by πx in the known [Problem 1(b), Sec. 5] representation

$$1 = \sum_{n=1}^{\infty} \frac{2[1 - (-1)^n]}{n\pi} \sin nx \qquad\qquad (0 < x < \pi).$$

Substitution of series (4) and (5) into the differential equation (1) enables us to write

$$\sum_{n=1}^{\infty} B_n''(t) \sin n\pi x = \sum_{n=1}^{\infty} [-(n\pi)^2 B_n(t)] \sin n\pi x$$

$$+ A \sin \omega t \sum_{n=1}^{\infty} \frac{2[1 - (-1)^n]}{n\pi} \sin n\pi x,$$

or

$$\sum_{n=1}^{\infty} [B_n''(t) + (n\pi)^2 B_n(t)] \sin n\pi x = \sum_{n=1}^{\infty} \frac{2A[1 - (-1)^n]}{n\pi} \sin \omega t \sin n\pi x.$$

Thus,

$$(6) \qquad B_n''(t) + (n\pi)^2 B_n(t) = \frac{2A[1 - (-1)^n]}{n\pi} \sin \omega t \qquad\qquad (n = 1, 2, \ldots),$$

and conditions (3) yield the initial conditions

(7) $$B_n(0) = 0 \quad \text{and} \quad B_n'(0) = 0 \qquad (n = 1, 2, \ldots)$$

on $B_n(t)$.

When n is replaced by $2n$ in equations (6) and (7), we have

(8) $$B_{2n}''(t) + (2n\pi)^2 B_{2n}(t) = 0,$$

(9) $$B_{2n}(0) = 0, \qquad B_{2n}'(0) = 0.$$

Solving this initial value problem, we find that $B_{2n}(t) \equiv 0$ $(n = 1, 2, \ldots)$. That is, $B_n(t)$ is identically equal to zero when n is even.

To find $B_n(t)$ when n is odd, we replace n by $2n - 1$ in equations (6) and (7) and write

(10) $$\omega_n = (2n - 1)\pi \qquad (n = 1, 2, \ldots).$$

The initial value problem for $B_{2n-1}(t)$ is then

(11) $$B_{2n-1}''(t) + \omega_n^2 B_{2n-1}(t) = \frac{4A}{\omega_n} \sin \omega t,$$

(12) $$B_{2n-1}(0) = 0, \qquad B_{2n-1}'(0) = 0.$$

We may now refer to Problem 3 below. In that problem, methods learned in an introductory course in ordinary differential equations are used to solve the initial value problem

(13) $$y''(t) + a^2 y(t) = b \sin \omega t,$$

(14) $$y(0) = 0, \qquad y'(0) = 0,$$

where a and b are constants.

To be specific, if $\omega \neq a$,

(15) $$y(t) = \frac{b}{\omega^2 - a^2} \left(\frac{\omega}{a} \sin at - \sin \omega t \right).$$

Thus, we see that if $\omega \neq \omega_n$ for any value of n $(n = 1, 2, \ldots)$, the solution of problem (11)–(12) is

$$B_{2n-1}(t) = \frac{4A}{\omega_n (\omega^2 - \omega_n^2)} \left(\frac{\omega}{\omega_n} \sin \omega_n t - \sin \omega t \right) \qquad (n = 1, 2, \ldots);$$

and it follows from equation (4) that

(16) $$y(x, t) = 4A \sum_{n=1}^{\infty} \frac{\sin \omega_n x}{\omega_n (\omega^2 - \omega_n^2)} \left(\frac{\omega}{\omega_n} \sin \omega_n t - \sin \omega t \right).$$

It is also shown in Problem 3 that if $\omega = a$, the solution of differential equation (13), with conditions (14), is

(17) $$y(t) = \frac{b}{2a} \left(\frac{1}{a} \sin at - t \cos at \right).$$

Hence, when there is a value N of n $(n = 1, 2, \ldots)$ such that $\omega = \omega_N$,

$$(18) \qquad B_{2N-1}(t) = \frac{2A}{\omega_N^2}\left(\frac{1}{\omega_N}\sin\omega_N t - t\cos\omega_N t\right).$$

Because of the factor t with the cosine function here, this means that series (4) contains an *unstable* component. Such a phenomenon is called *resonance*. The periodic external force is evidently in resonance with the string when the frequency ω of that force coincides with any one of the resonant frequencies (10). Those frequencies depend, in general, on the physical properties of the string and the manner in which it is supported.

PROBLEMS

1. The boundary value problem

$$y_{tt}(x, t) = a^2 y_{xx}(x, t) + Ax\sin\omega t \qquad (0 < x < c, t > 0),$$
$$y(0, t) = y(c, t) = 0, \qquad y(x, 0) = y_t(x, 0) = 0$$

describes transverse displacements in a vibrating string. [Compare with equation (1), Sec. 46, where the term that was $A\sin\omega t$ is now $Ax\sin\omega t$.] Show that resonance occurs when ω has one of the values

$$\omega_n = \frac{n\pi a}{c} \qquad\qquad (n = 1, 2, \ldots).$$

2. Let a, b, and ω denote nonzero constants. The general solution of the ordinary differential equation

$$y''(t) + a^2 y(t) = b\sin\omega t$$

is of the form $y = y_c + y_p$, where y_c is the general solution of the complementary equation $y''(t) + a^2 y(t) = 0$ and y_p is any particular solution of the original nonhomogeneous equation.[†]

(*a*) Suppose that $\omega \neq a$. After substituting

$$y_p = A\cos\omega t + B\sin\omega t,$$

where A and B are constants, into the given differential equation, determine values of A and B such that y_p is a solution. Thus, derive the general solution

$$y(t) = C_1\cos at + C_2\sin at + \frac{b}{a^2 - \omega^2}\sin\omega t$$

of that equation.

(*b*) Suppose that $\omega = a$ and find constants A and B such that

$$y_p = At\cos\omega t + Bt\sin\omega t$$

is a particular solution of the given differential equation. Thus obtain the general solution

$$y(t) = C_1\cos at + C_2\sin at - \frac{b}{2a}t\cos at.$$

[†]For the method of solution to be used here, which is known as the *method of undetermined coefficients*, see, for instance, the book by Boyce and DiPrima (2009) or the one by Rainville, Bedient, and Bedient (1997). Both books are listed in the Bibliography.

3. Use the general solutions derived in Problem 2 to obtain the following solutions of the initial value problem

$$y''(t) + a^2 y(t) = b \sin \omega t, \qquad y(0) = 0, \qquad y'(0) = 0:$$

$$y(t) = \begin{cases} \dfrac{b}{\omega^2 - a^2}\left(\dfrac{\omega}{a}\sin at - \sin \omega t\right) & \text{when } \omega \neq a, \\[4mm] \dfrac{b}{2a}\left(\dfrac{1}{a}\sin at - t \cos at\right) & \text{when } \omega = a. \end{cases}$$

47. AN ELASTIC BAR

Boundary value problems for longitudinal displacements in elastic bars are similar to problems for transverse displacements in a stretched string.

     EXAMPLE. A cylindrical bar of natural length c is initially stretched by an amount bc (Fig. 43) and starts its motion from rest. The initial longitudinal displacements of its sections are then proportional to the distance from the fixed end $x = 0$. At the instant $t = 0$, both ends are released and left free. The longitudinal displacements $y(x, t)$ satisfy the following boundary value problem, where $a^2 = E/\delta$ (Sec. 29):

(1)	$y_{tt}(x, t) = a^2 y_{xx}(x, t)$	$(0 < x < c, t > 0),$
(2)	$y_x(0, t) = 0, \qquad y_x(c, t) = 0,$	
(3)	$y(x, 0) = bx, \qquad y_t(x, 0) = 0.$	

The homogeneous two-point boundary conditions (2) state that the force per unit area on the end sections is zero.

FIGURE 43

     The function $y(x, t)$ can also be interpreted as representing transverse displacements in a stretched string, released at rest from the position $y(x, 0) = bx$, when the ends are looped around perfectly smooth rods lying along the lines $x = 0$ and $x = c$. In that case, $a^2 = H/\delta$; and the boundary conditions (2) state that no forces act in the y direction at the ends of the string (see Sec. 28).

     The products $y = X(x)T(t)$ satisfy all of the homogeneous conditions above when $X(x)$ is an eigenfunction of the problem

(4)	$X''(x) + \lambda X(x) = 0, \qquad X'(0) = 0, \qquad X'(c) = 0$

and when, for the same eigenvalue λ,

(5)	$T''(t) + \lambda a^2 T(t) = 0, \qquad T'(0) = 0.$

Those eigenvalues are (Sec. 35)

$$\lambda_0 = 0 \quad \text{and} \quad \lambda_n = \left(\frac{n\pi}{c}\right)^2 \qquad (n = 1, 2, \ldots),$$

with eigenfunctions

$$X_0(x) = 1 \quad \text{and} \quad X_n(x) = \cos\frac{n\pi x}{c} \qquad (n = 1, 2, \ldots).$$

The corresponding functions of t are

$$T_0(t) = 1 \quad \text{and} \quad T_n(t) = \cos\frac{n\pi a t}{c} \qquad (n = 1, 2, \ldots).$$

Formally, then, the generalized linear combination

$$(6) \qquad y(x, t) = A_0 + \sum_{n=1}^{\infty} A_n \cos\frac{n\pi x}{c} \cos\frac{n\pi a t}{c}$$

satisfies conditions (1) through (3), provided that

$$(7) \qquad bx = A_0 + \sum_{n=1}^{\infty} A_n \cos\frac{n\pi x}{c} \qquad (0 < x < c).$$

The coefficients in this Fourier cosine series, which is actually valid on the closed interval $0 \le x \le c$, are

$$A_0 = \frac{b}{c}\int_0^c x\,dx, \qquad A_n = \frac{2b}{c}\int_0^c x\cos\frac{n\pi x}{c}\,dx \qquad (n = 1, 2, \ldots).$$

Consequently,

$$(8) \qquad A_0 = \frac{bc}{2}, \qquad A_n = -\frac{2bc}{\pi^2}\cdot\frac{1-(-1)^n}{n^2} \qquad (n = 1, 2, \ldots);$$

and we arrive at the solution

$$(9) \qquad y(x, t) = \frac{bc}{2} - \frac{4bc}{\pi^2}\sum_{n=1}^{\infty}\frac{1}{(2n-1)^2}\cos\frac{(2n-1)\pi x}{c}\cos\frac{(2n-1)\pi a t}{c}.$$

By a method already used in Sec. 45, we can put this series solution in closed form, involving the *even* periodic extension $P(x)$, with period $2c$, of the function bx $(0 \le x \le c)$. To be specific, we know from the trigonometric identity

$$2\cos A\cos B = \cos(A+B) + \cos(A-B)$$

that

$$2\cos\frac{n\pi x}{c}\cos\frac{n\pi a t}{c} = \cos\frac{n\pi(x+at)}{c} + \cos\frac{n\pi(x-at)}{c}.$$

Hence expression (6) can be written

$$(10) \quad y(x, t) = \frac{1}{2}\left[A_0 + \sum_{n=1}^{\infty}A_n\cos\frac{n\pi(x+at)}{c} + A_0 + \sum_{n=1}^{\infty}A_n\cos\frac{n\pi(x-at)}{c}\right].$$

But series (7) represents $P(x)$ for all values of x when the values (8) of the coefficients A_n $(n = 0, 1, 2, \ldots)$ are used. Hence expression (10), with those values of

A_n, reduces to

(11) $$y(x, t) = \frac{1}{2}[P(x + at) + P(x - at)].$$

This is the desired closed form of solution (9).

PROBLEMS

1. Show that the motion of each cross section of the elastic bar treated in Sec. 47 is periodic in t, with period $2c/a$.

2. From expression (11), Sec. 47, shows that $y(0, t) = P(at)$ and hence that the end $x = 0$ of the bar moves with the constant velocity ab during the half period $0 < t < c/a$ (see Problem 1) and with velocity $-ab$ during the next half-period.

3. The end $x = 0$ of an elastic bar is free, and a constant longitudinal force F_0 per unit area is applied at the end $x = c$ (Fig. 44). The bar is initially unstrained and at rest. Set up the boundary value problem for the longitudinal displacements $y(x, t)$, the conditions at the ends of the bar being $y_x(0, t) = 0$ and $y_x(c, t) = F_0/E$ (Sec. 29). After noting that the method of separation of variables cannot be applied directly, follow the steps below to find $y(x, t)$.

FIGURE 44

(a) By writing $y(x, t) = Y(x, t) + Ax^2$, determine a value of A that leads to the new boundary value problem

$$Y_{tt}(x, t) = a^2 Y_{xx}(x, t) + \frac{F_0 a^2}{cE} \qquad (0 < x < c, t > 0),$$

$$Y_x(0, t) = 0, \qquad Y_x(c, t) = 0,$$

$$Y(x, 0) = -\frac{F_0}{2cE}x^2, \qquad Y_t(x, 0) = 0.$$

(b) Point out why it is reasonable to expect that the new boundary value problem in part (a) has a solution of the form

$$Y(x, t) = A_0(t) + \sum_{n=1}^{\infty} A_n(t) \cos \frac{n\pi x}{c}.$$

Then use the method of variation of parameters (Sec. 42) to find $Y(x, t)$ and thereby derive the solution

$$y(x, t) = \frac{F_0}{6cE}\left[3(x^2 + a^2 t^2) - c^2 + \frac{12c^2}{\pi^2}\sum_{n=1}^{\infty}\frac{(-1)^{n+1}}{n^2}\cos\frac{n\pi at}{c}\cos\frac{n\pi x}{c}\right]$$

of the original problem.

(c) Use the trigonometric identity

$$2\cos A \cos B = \cos(A + B) + \cos(A - B)$$

and the series representation

$$x^2 = \frac{c^2}{3} + \frac{4c^2}{\pi^2} \sum_{n=1}^{\infty} \frac{(-1)^n}{n^2} \cos \frac{n\pi x}{c} \qquad (-c \leq x \leq c),$$

which follows from Example 1 in Sec. 8, to write the expression for $y(x, t)$ in part (b) as

$$y(x, t) = \frac{F_0}{2cE} \left[x^2 + a^2 t^2 - \frac{P(x+at) + P(x-at)}{2} \right]$$

where $P(x)$ is the periodic extension, with period $2c$, of the function x^2 defined on the interval $-c \leq x \leq c$.

4. Show how it follows from the expression for $y(x, t)$ in Problem 3(c) that the end $x = 0$ of the bar moves with the following velocities:

$$y_t(0, t) = 0 \qquad \text{when} \quad 0 < t < \frac{c}{a},$$

$$y_t(0, t) = v_0 = \frac{2a F_0}{E} \qquad \text{when} \quad \frac{c}{a} < t < \frac{3c}{a},$$

$$y_t(0, t) = 2v_0 \qquad \text{when} \quad \frac{3c}{a} < t < \frac{5c}{a},$$

etc.

48. DOUBLE FOURIER SERIES

The Fourier method is readily adapted to boundary value problems that give rise to so-called double Fourier series. This is illustrated below.

EXAMPLE. Let $z(x, y, t)$ denote the transverse displacement at each point (x, y) at time t in a membrane that is stretched across a rigid square frame in the xy plane. To simplify the notation, we select the origin and the point (π, π) as ends of a diagonal of the frame. If the membrane is released at rest with a given initial displacement $f(x, y)$ that is continuous and vanishes on the boundary of the square, then (Sec. 29)

$$(1) \qquad z_{tt} = a^2(z_{xx} + z_{yy})$$

in the three-dimensional domain $0 < x < \pi, 0 < y < \pi, t > 0$ and

$$(2) \qquad z(0, y, t) = z(\pi, y, t) = z(x, 0, t) = z(x, \pi, t) = 0,$$
$$(3) \qquad z(x, y, 0) = f(x, y), \qquad z_t(x, y, 0) = 0,$$

where $0 \leq x \leq \pi, 0 \leq y \leq \pi$. We assume that the partial derivatives $f_x(x, y)$ and $f_y(x, y)$ are also continuous.

Functions of the type $z = X(x)Y(y)T(t)$ satisfy equation (1) if

$$(4) \qquad \frac{T''(t)}{a^2 T(t)} = \frac{X''(x)}{X(x)} + \frac{Y''(y)}{Y(y)} = -\lambda.$$

Separating variables again, this time in the second of equations (4), we have

$$\frac{Y''(y)}{Y(y)} = -\lambda - \frac{X''(x)}{X(x)} = -\mu,$$

where μ is another separation constant. So we are led to two Sturm-Liouville problems,

$$X''(x) + (\lambda - \mu)X(x) = 0, \qquad X(0) = 0, \qquad X(\pi) = 0$$

and

$$Y''(y) + \mu Y(y) = 0, \qquad Y(0) = 0, \qquad Y(\pi) = 0,$$

and to the conditions

$$T''(t) + \lambda a^2 T(t) = 0, \qquad T'(0) = 0$$

on T.

We turn to the Sturm-Liouville problem in Y first since it involves only one of the separation constants. According to Sec. 35, that problem has eigenvalues $\mu = m^2$ ($m = 1, 2, \ldots$) and corresponding eigenfunctions

$$Y_m(y) = \sin my \qquad\qquad (m = 1, 2, \ldots).$$

When $\lambda - \mu = n^2$ ($n = 1, 2, \ldots$), the eigenfunctions

$$X_n(x) = \sin nx \qquad\qquad (n = 1, 2, \ldots)$$

of the problem in X are also obtained. The conditions on T thus become

$$T''(t) + a^2(m^2 + n^2)T(t) = 0, \qquad T'(0) = 0,$$

where $m = 1, 2, \ldots$ and $n = 1, 2, \ldots$. For any fixed positive integers m and n, the solution of this problem in T is, except for a constant factor,

$$T_{mn}(t) = \cos\left(at\sqrt{m^2 + n^2}\right).$$

The formal solution of our boundary value problem is, therefore,

$$(5) \qquad z(x, y, t) = \sum_{n=1}^{\infty}\sum_{m=1}^{\infty} B_{mn} \sin nx \, \sin my \, \cos\left(at\sqrt{m^2 + n^2}\right),$$

where the coefficients B_{mn} need to be determined so that

$$(6) \qquad f(x, y) = \sum_{n=1}^{\infty}\sum_{m=1}^{\infty} B_{mn} \sin nx \, \sin my$$

when $0 \le x \le \pi$ and $0 \le y \le \pi$. By grouping terms in this double sine series so as to display the total coefficient of $\sin nx$ for each n, one can write, formally,

$$(7) \qquad f(x, y) = \sum_{n=1}^{\infty}\left(\sum_{m=1}^{\infty} B_{mn} \sin my\right)\sin nx.$$

For each fixed y ($0 \le y \le \pi$), equation (7) is a Fourier sine series representation of the function $f(x, y)$, with variable x ($0 \le x \le \pi$), provided that

$$(8) \qquad \sum_{m=1}^{\infty} B_{mn} \sin my = \frac{2}{\pi}\int_0^{\pi} f(x, y)\sin nx \, dx \qquad\qquad (n = 1, 2, \ldots).$$

The right-hand side here is a sequence of functions

$$(9) \qquad F_n(y) = \frac{2}{\pi} \int_0^\pi f(x, y) \sin nx \, dx \qquad\qquad (n = 1, 2, \ldots)$$

of y, each represented by its Fourier sine series

$$F_n(y) = \sum_{m=1}^\infty B_{mn} \sin my$$

on the interval $0 \le y \le \pi$ when

$$(10) \qquad B_{mn} = \frac{2}{\pi} \int_0^\pi F_n(y) \sin my \, dy \qquad\qquad (m = 1, 2, \ldots).$$

Combining expressions (9) and (10), we find that

$$(11) \qquad B_{mn} = \frac{4}{\pi^2} \int_0^\pi \sin my \int_0^\pi f(x, y) \sin nx \, dx \, dy.$$

The solution of our membrane problem is now given by equation (5) with coefficients (11).

Since the numbers $\sqrt{m^2 + n^2}$ do not change by integral multiples of some fixed number as m and n vary through integral values, the cosine functions in equation (5) have no common period in the variable t; so the displacement z is not generally a periodic function of t. Consequently, the vibrating membrane, in contrast to the vibrating string, does not usually produce a musical note. It can be made to do so, however, by giving it the proper initial displacement. If, for example,

$$z(x, y, 0) = A \sin x \sin y$$

where A is a constant, the displacements (5) are given by a single term:

$$z(x, y, t) = A \sin x \sin y \cos(a\sqrt{2}t).$$

Then z is periodic in t, with period $\pi\sqrt{2}/a$.

PROBLEMS

1. All four faces of an infinitely long rectangular prism, formed by the planes $x = 0$, $x = a$, $y = 0$, and $y = b$, are kept at temperature zero. Let the initial temperature distribution be $f(x, y)$, and derive this expression for the temperatures $u(x, y, t)$ in the prism:

$$u(x, y, t) = \sum_{n=1}^\infty \sum_{m=1}^\infty B_{mn} \exp\left[-\pi^2 kt \left(\frac{m^2}{a^2} + \frac{n^2}{b^2}\right)\right] \sin \frac{n\pi x}{a} \sin \frac{m\pi y}{b},$$

where

$$B_{mn} = \frac{4}{ab} \int_0^b \sin \frac{m\pi y}{b} \int_0^a f(x, y) \sin \frac{n\pi x}{a} \, dx \, dy.$$

2. Write $f(x, y) = g(x)h(y)$ in Problem 1 and show that the double series obtained there for u reduces to the product

$$u(x, y, t) = v(x, t)\, w(y, t)$$

of two single series, where v and w represent temperatures in the slabs $0 \le x \le a$ and $0 \le y \le b$ with faces at temperature zero and with initial temperatures $g(x)$ and $h(y)$, respectively.

3. Let the functions $v(x, t)$ and $w(y, t)$ satisfy the heat equation for one-dimensional flow:

$$v_t = k v_{xx}, \qquad w_t = k w_{yy}.$$

Show by differentiation that their product $u = vw$ satisfies the two-dimensional heat equation

$$u_t = k(u_{xx} + u_{yy}).$$

Use this result to arrive at the expression for $u(x, y, t)$ in Problem 2.

49. PERIODIC BOUNDARY CONDITIONS

The solutions of the boundary value problems in this chapter have been based on the solutions of just two Sturm-Liouville problems, which lead to Fourier cosine and sine series representations of prescribed functions. Although Chap. 8 is devoted to the theory and application of many other Sturm-Liouville problems, as well as to the precise definition of such a problem, we conclude this chapter by considering a third problem that arises in certain boundary value problems for regions with circular boundaries:

$$(1) \qquad X''(x) + \lambda X(x) = 0, \qquad X(-\pi) = X(\pi), \qquad X'(-\pi) = X'(\pi).$$

We include it here since its solutions also lead to Fourier series representations, but now involving *both* cosines and sines on the interval $-\pi < x < \pi$, and since most of the general theory of Sturm-Liouville problems is not actually required. We need accept only the fact, to be verified in Chap. 8 (Sec. 69), that each eigenvalue, or value of λ for which problem (1) has a nontrivial solution, is a real number. In anticipation of Chap. 8, we continue to refer to such values of λ as eigenvalues and to the nontrivial solutions as eigenfunctions.

(i) The case $\lambda = 0$
When $\lambda = 0$, problem (1) becomes

$$(2) \qquad X''(x) = 0, \qquad X(-\pi) = X(\pi), \qquad X'(-\pi) = X'(\pi).$$

It is easy to see that $X(x) = Ax + B$, where A and B are constants; and the two boundary conditions require that $A = 0$. Since all of the conditions in problem (2) are linear and homogeneous, we thus find that except for a constant factor, $X(x) = 1$.

(ii) The case $\lambda > 0$
When $\lambda > 0$, we write $\lambda = \alpha^2 (\alpha > 0)$, so that problem (1) is

$$(3) \qquad X''(x) + \alpha^2 X(x) = 0, \qquad X(-\pi) = X(\pi), \qquad X'(-\pi) = X'(\pi).$$

The general solution of this differential equation is, of course,

$$X(x) = C_1 \cos \alpha x + C_2 \sin \alpha x.$$

Now it is straightforward to show that in order for the boundary conditions to be satisfied,

$$C_2 \sin \alpha \pi = 0 \quad \text{and} \quad C_1 \sin \alpha \pi = 0.$$

Since the constants C_1 and C_2 cannot both vanish if $X(x)$ is to be nontrivial, it follows that $X(x)$ is nontrivial only when the positive number α is a positive integer n. That is, $\lambda = n^2$ $(n = 1, 2, \ldots)$; and the corresponding general solution of problem (1) is an arbitrary linear combination of the two linearly independent eigenfunctions $\cos nx$ and $\sin nx$.

(iii) The case $\lambda < 0$

When $\lambda < 0$, one can write problem (1) as

(4) $$X''(x) - \alpha^2 X(x) = 0, \quad X(-\pi) = X(\pi), \quad X'(-\pi) = X'(\pi),$$

where $\lambda = \alpha^2 (\alpha > 0)$. The general solution of this differential equation is

$$X(x) = C_1 e^{\alpha x} + C_2 e^{-\alpha x};$$

and the first boundary condition reveals that

$$C_1 (e^{\alpha \pi} - e^{-\alpha \pi}) = C_2 (e^{\alpha \pi} - e^{-\alpha \pi}),$$

or

(5) $$(C_1 - C_2) \sinh \alpha \pi = 0.$$

Likewise, it follows from the second boundary condition that

(6) $$(C_1 + C_2) \sinh \alpha \pi = 0.$$

Since $\sinh \alpha \pi \neq 0$, equations (5) and (6) tell us that

$$C_1 - C_2 = 0 \quad \text{and} \quad C_1 + C_2 = 0.$$

Solving for C_1 and C_2 here, we have $C_1 = 0$ and $C_2 = 0$. So $X(x) \equiv 0$, and this solution is a trivial one.

So we may conclude from cases (i) and (ii) above that the eigenvalues and corresponding eigenfunctions of problem (1) are

$$\lambda_0 = 0, \qquad \lambda_n = n^2 \qquad\qquad (n = 1, 2, \ldots)$$

and

$$X_0(x) = 1, \qquad X_n(x) = A_n \cos nx + B_n \sin nx \qquad (n = 1, 2, \ldots),$$

where A_n and B_n are arbitrary constants.

We now illustrate the use of this Sturm-Liouville problem, involving *periodic boundary conditions.*

EXAMPLE. Let $u(\rho, \phi)$ denote the steady temperatures in a thin disk $\rho \leq 1$, with insulated surfaces, when its edge $\rho = 1$ is kept at temperatures $f(\phi)$.

The variables ρ and ϕ are, of course, polar coordinates, and u satisfies Laplace's equation $\nabla^2 u = 0$. That is,

$$(7) \qquad \rho^2 u_{\rho\rho}(\rho, \phi) + \rho u_\rho(\rho, \phi) + u_{\phi\phi}(\rho, \phi) = 0 \qquad (0 < \rho < 1, -\pi < \phi < \pi),$$

where

$$(8) \qquad\qquad\qquad u(1, \phi) = f(\phi) \qquad\qquad\qquad (-\pi < \phi < \pi).$$

Also, u and its partial derivatives of the first and second order are continuous and bounded in the interior of the disk. In particular, u and its first-order partial derivatives are continuous on the ray $\phi = \pi$ (Fig. 45).

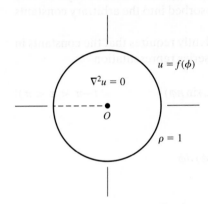

FIGURE 45

If functions of the type $u = R(\rho)\Phi(\phi)$ are to satisfy equation (7) and the continuity requirements, then

$$(9) \qquad\qquad \rho^2 R''(\rho) + \rho R'(\rho) - \lambda R(\rho) = 0 \qquad\qquad (0 < \rho < 1)$$

and

$$(10) \qquad \Phi''(\phi) + \lambda\Phi(\phi) = 0, \qquad \Phi(-\pi) = \Phi(\pi), \qquad \Phi'(-\pi) = \Phi'(\pi),$$

where λ is a separation constant. We now recognize that equations (10) constitute a Sturm-Liouville problem in Φ, with eigenvalues $\lambda_0 = 0$ and $\lambda_n = n^2$ $(n = 1, 2, \ldots)$. The corresponding eigenfunctions are

$$\Phi_0(\phi) = 1 \qquad \text{and} \qquad \Phi_n(\phi) = A_n \cos n\phi + B_n \sin n\phi \qquad (n = 1, 2, \ldots).$$

Equation (9) is a Cauchy-Euler equation (see Problem 1, Sec. 44), and we know from Example 2, Sec. 44, that its bounded solutions are

$$R_0(\rho) = 1 \qquad \text{when } \lambda = 0$$

and

$$R_n(\rho) = \rho^n \qquad \text{when } \lambda = n^2 \qquad\qquad (n = 1, 2, \ldots).$$

By superposition, the generalized linear combination of the products

$$R_0(\rho)\Phi_0(\phi) = 1$$

and

$$R_n(\rho)\Phi_n(\phi) = \rho^n(A_n \cos n\phi + B_n \sin n\phi) \qquad (n = 1, 2, \ldots)$$

is

(11) $$u(\rho, \phi) = A_0 + \sum_{n=1}^{\infty} \rho^n(A_n \cos n\phi + B_n \sin n\phi).$$

Note that if we had multiplied the products $R_n(\rho)\Phi_n(\phi)$ $(n = 1, 2, \ldots)$ by arbitrary constants, those constants would have been absorbed into the arbitrary constants A_n and B_n.

The nonhomogeneous condition (8) evidently requires that the constants in expression (11) be the same as in the Fourier series representation

$$f(\phi) = \frac{2A_0}{2} + \sum_{n=1}^{\infty}(A_n \cos n\phi + B_n \sin n\phi) \qquad (-\pi < x < \pi).$$

Thus,

(12) $$A_0 = \frac{1}{2\pi} \int_{-\pi}^{\pi} f(\phi) \, d\phi$$

and

(13) $$A_n = \frac{1}{\pi} \int_{-\pi}^{\pi} f(\phi) \cos n\phi \, d\phi, \qquad B_n = \frac{1}{\pi} \int_{-\pi}^{\pi} f(\phi) \sin n\phi \, d\phi$$

$$(n = 1, 2, \ldots).$$

We assume that f is piecewise smooth.

The solution obtained in this example can be put in closed form with the aid of the summation formula (Problem 3)

(14) $$\sum_{n=1}^{\infty} a^n \cos n\theta = \frac{a \cos\theta - a^2}{1 - 2a \cos\theta + a^2} \qquad (-1 < a < 1).$$

To do this, we use the variable of integration ψ in expressions (12) and (13):

$$A_0 = \frac{1}{2\pi} \int_{-\pi}^{\pi} f(\psi) \, d\psi,$$

$$A_n = \frac{1}{\pi} \int_{-\pi}^{\pi} f(\psi) \cos n\psi \, d\psi, \qquad B_n = \frac{1}{\pi} \int_{-\pi}^{\pi} f(\psi) \sin n\psi \, d\psi \qquad (n = 1, 2, \ldots).$$

Since

$$A_n \cos n\phi + B_n \sin n\phi = \frac{1}{\pi} \int_{-\pi}^{\pi} f(\psi)(\cos n\phi \cos n\psi + \sin n\phi \sin n\psi) \, d\psi$$

$$= \frac{1}{\pi} \int_{-\pi}^{\pi} f(\psi) \cos n(\phi - \psi) \, d\psi,$$

expression (11) tells us that

$$u(\rho, \phi) = \frac{1}{2\pi} \int_{-\pi}^{\pi} f(\psi) \, d\psi + \sum_{n=1}^{\infty} \rho^n \frac{1}{\pi} \int_{-\pi}^{\pi} f(\psi) \cos n(\phi - \psi) \, d\psi$$

$$= \frac{1}{2\pi} \int_{-\pi}^{\pi} f(\psi) \left[1 + 2 \sum_{n=1}^{\infty} \rho^n \cos n(\phi - \psi) \right] d\psi.$$

Finally, in view of the summation formula (14),

$$1 + 2 \sum_{n=1}^{\infty} \rho^n \cos n(\phi - \psi) = 1 + \frac{2\rho \cos(\phi - \psi) - 2\rho^2}{1 - 2\rho \cos(\phi - \psi) + \rho^2}$$

$$= \frac{1 - \rho^2}{1 - 2\rho \cos(\phi - \psi) + \rho^2};$$

and we arrive at *Poisson's integral formula*[†]

$$(15) \qquad u(\rho, \phi) = \frac{1}{2\pi} \int_{-\pi}^{\pi} f(\psi) \frac{1 - \rho^2}{1 - 2\rho \cos(\phi - \psi) + \rho^2} d\psi$$

for temperatures in the disk $\rho < 1$.

PROBLEMS

1. Using the cylindrical coordinates ρ, ϕ, and z, let $u(\rho, \phi)$ denote steady temperatures in a long hollow cylinder $a \le \rho \le b, -\infty < z < \infty$ when the temperatures on the inner surface $\rho = a$ are $f(\phi)$ and the temperature of the outer surface $\rho = b$ is zero.

   (*a*) Derive the temperature formula

$$u(\rho, \phi) = A_0 \frac{\ln b - \ln \rho}{\ln b - \ln a} + \sum_{n=1}^{\infty} \left(\frac{a}{\rho} \right)^n \frac{b^{2n} - \rho^{2n}}{b^{2n} - a^{2n}} (A_n \cos n\phi + B_n \sin n\phi),$$

   where the coefficients A_n and B_n, including A_0, are given by equations (12) and (13) in Sec. 49.

   (*b*) Use the result in part (*a*) to show that if $f(\phi) = \alpha + \beta \sin \phi$, where α and β are constants, then

$$u(\rho, \phi) = \alpha \frac{\ln b - \ln \rho}{\ln b - \ln a} + \beta \frac{a}{\rho} \cdot \frac{b^2 - \rho^2}{b^2 - a^2} \sin \phi.$$

2. Solve the boundary value problem

$$u_t(x, t) = k u_{xx}(x, t) \qquad\qquad (-\pi < x < \pi, t > 0),$$

$$u(-\pi, t) = u(\pi, t), \qquad u_x(-\pi, t) = u_x(\pi, t), \qquad u(x, 0) = f(x).$$

The solution $u(x, t)$ represents, for example, temperatures in an insulated wire of length 2π that is bent into a unit circle and has a given temperature distribution along it. For

---

[†]This and related formulas are obtained by complex-variable methods in the authors' book (2009, Chap. 12) that is listed in the Bibliography.

convenience, the wire is thought of as being cut at one point and laid on the x axis between $x = -\pi$ and $x = \pi$. The variable x then measures the distance along the wire, starting at the point $x = -\pi$; and the points $x = -\pi$ and $x = \pi$ denote the same point on the circle. The first two boundary conditions in the problem state that the temperatures and the flux must be the same for each of those values of x. This problem was of considerable interest to Fourier himself, and the wire has come to be known as *Fourier's ring.*

$$Answer:\ u(x,\ t) = A_0 + \sum_{n=1}^{\infty} e^{-n^2 kt}(A_n \cos nx + B_n \sin nx),$$

where

$$A_0 = \frac{1}{2\pi}\int_{-\pi}^{\pi} f(x)\,dx$$

and

$$A_n = \frac{1}{\pi}\int_{-\pi}^{\pi} f(x)\cos nx\,dx, \qquad B_n = \frac{1}{\pi}\int_{-\pi}^{\pi} f(x)\sin nx\,dx \qquad (n = 1, 2, \ldots).$$

3. By writing $A = n\theta$ and $B = \theta$ in the trigonometric identity

$$2\cos A \cos B = \cos(A+B) + \cos(A-B),$$

multiplying through the resulting equation by a^n $(-1 < a < 1)$, and then summing each side from $n = 1$ to $n = \infty$, derive the summation formula

$$\sum_{n=1}^{\infty} a^n \cos n\theta = \frac{a\cos\theta - a^2}{1 - 2a\cos\theta + a^2} \qquad (-1 < a < 1),$$

used in Sec. 49. [One can readily see that this series is absolutely convergent by comparing it with the geometric series whose terms are a^n $(n = 1, 2, \ldots)$.]

FOURIER INTEGRALS AND APPLICATIONS

In Chap. 2 (Sec. 15) we saw that a periodic function, with period $2c$, has a Fourier series representation which is valid for all x when it satisfies certain conditions on the fundamental interval $-c < x < c$. In this chapter, we develop the theory of trigonometric representations of functions, defined for all x, that are *not* periodic. Such representations, which are analogous to Fourier series representations, involve improper integrals instead of infinite series.

50. THE FOURIER INTEGRAL FORMULA

From Problem 9, Sec. 8, we know that the Fourier series corresponding to a function $f(x)$ on an interval $-c < x < c$ can be written

$$(1) \qquad \frac{1}{2c} \int_{-c}^{c} f(s)ds + \frac{1}{c} \sum_{n=1}^{\infty} \int_{-c}^{c} f(s) \cos\left[\frac{n\pi}{c}(s-x)\right]ds;$$

and, from Theorem 1 in Sec. 15, we know conditions under which this series converges to $f(x)$ everywhere in the interval $-c < x < c$. Namely, it is sufficient that f be piecewise smooth on the interval and that the value of f at each of its points of discontinuity x be the mean value of the one-sided limits $f(x+)$ and $f(x-)$.

Suppose now that f satisfies such conditions on *every* bounded interval $-c < x < c$. Here c may be given any fixed positive value, arbitrarily large but finite, and series (1) will represent $f(x)$ over the large segment $-c < x < c$ of the x axis. But that series representation cannot apply over the rest of the x axis unless f is periodic, with period $2c$, because the sum of the series has that periodicity.

161

In seeking a representation that is valid for all real x when f is not periodic, it is natural to try to modify series (1) by letting c tend to infinity. The first term in the series will then vanish, provided that the improper integral

$$\int_{-\infty}^{\infty} f(s)\, ds$$

exists. If we write $\Delta \alpha = \pi / c$, the remaining terms take the form

$$(2) \qquad \frac{1}{\pi} \sum_{n=1}^{\infty} \Delta \alpha \int_{-c}^{c} f(s) \cos\left[n\Delta\alpha\,(s - x)\right] ds,$$

which is the same as

$$(3) \qquad \frac{1}{\pi} \sum_{n=1}^{\infty} F_c(n\Delta\alpha, x)\, \Delta\alpha \qquad\qquad \left(\Delta\alpha = \frac{\pi}{c} \right),$$

where

$$(4) \qquad\qquad F_c(\alpha, x) = \int_{-c}^{c} f(s) \cos\alpha(s - x)\, ds.$$

Let the value of x be fixed and c be large, so that $\Delta\alpha$ is a small positive number. The points $n\Delta\alpha$ $(n = 1, 2, \ldots)$ are equally spaced along the entire positive α axis; and, because of the resemblance of the series in expression (3) to a sum of areas of rectangles used in defining definite integrals (see Fig. 46), one might expect the partial sums of that series to approach

$$(5) \qquad\qquad \int_{0}^{\infty} F_c(\alpha, x)\, d\alpha,$$

or possibly

$$(6) \qquad\qquad \int_{0}^{\infty} F_\infty(\alpha, x)\, d\alpha,$$

as $\Delta\alpha$ tends to zero. As the subscript ∞ in integral (6) indicates, however, the function $F_c(\alpha, x)$ changes with $\Delta\alpha$ because $c = \pi / \Delta\alpha$. Also, the limit of the series in expression (3) as $\Delta\alpha$ tends to zero is not, in fact, the definition of the improper integral (5) even if c could be kept fixed.

FIGURE 46

The above manipulations merely *suggest* that under appropriate conditions on f, the function may have the representation

$$(7) \qquad f(x) = \frac{1}{\pi} \int_0^\infty \int_{-\infty}^\infty f(s) \cos \alpha (s - x) \, ds \, d\alpha \qquad (-\infty < x < \infty).$$

This is the *Fourier integral formula* for the function f, to be established rigorously in Sec. 53.

Observe how it follows from the trigonometric identity

$$\cos \alpha (s - x) = \cos \alpha s \cos \alpha x + \sin \alpha s \sin \alpha x$$

that

$$\int_{-\infty}^\infty f(s) \cos \alpha (s - x) \, ds = \int_{-\infty}^\infty f(s) \cos \alpha s \, ds \cos \alpha x + \int_{-\infty}^\infty f(s) \sin \alpha s \, ds \sin \alpha x.$$

Hence formula (7) can be written in terms of separate cosine and sine functions as follows:

$$(8) \qquad f(x) = \int_0^\infty [A(\alpha) \cos \alpha x + B(\alpha) \sin \alpha x] \, d\alpha \qquad (-\infty < x < \infty),$$

where

$$(9) \qquad A(\alpha) = \frac{1}{\pi} \int_{-\infty}^\infty f(x) \cos \alpha x \, dx, \qquad B(\alpha) = \frac{1}{\pi} \int_{-\infty}^\infty f(x) \sin \alpha x \, dx.$$

Expression (8), with coefficients (9), bears a resemblance to a Fourier series representation on $-\pi < x < \pi$.

A reader who wishes to accept the validity of Fourier integral representations in order to proceed more quickly to physical applications can at this time skip to Sec. 54 without serious disruption.

51. DIRICHLET'S INTEGRAL

Just as we prefaced the Fourier theorem in Sec. 12 with some preliminary theory, we include here and in Sec. 52 background that is essential to our proof of a theorem that gives conditions under which representation (7) in Sec. 50 is valid.

This section is devoted to the evaluation of an improper integral, known as *Dirichlet's integral,* that is prominent in applied mathematics. We show here that[†]

$$(1) \qquad \int_0^\infty \frac{\sin x}{x} \, dx = \frac{\pi}{2}.$$

Our method of evaluation requires us to first show that the integral actually converges. We note that the integrand is piecewise continuous on every bounded interval $0 \le x \le c$. This is because that quotient is continuous everywhere except

---

[†]For another approach, see, for instance, the book by Buck (2004). A method of evaluation involving complex variables is given in the authors' book (2009, pp. 279–280). Both books are listed in the Bibliography.

at $x = 0$, where l'Hôpital's rule shows that its right-hand limit exists. Since

$$\int_0^\infty \frac{\sin x}{x}\, dx = \lim_{c\to\infty} \int_0^c \frac{\sin x}{x}\, dx$$

$$= \lim_{c\to\infty} \left(\int_0^1 \frac{\sin x}{x}\, dx + \int_1^c \frac{\sin x}{x}\, dx \right)$$

$$= \int_0^1 \frac{\sin x}{x}\, dx + \lim_{c\to\infty} \int_1^c \frac{\sin x}{x}\, dx,$$

where c is any positive number, it suffices to show that the last limit here exists.

To accomplish this, we note that if

$$u = \frac{1}{x} \quad \text{and} \quad dv = \sin x\, dx,$$

then

$$du = -\frac{1}{x^2}dx \quad \text{and} \quad v = -\cos x.$$

Hence integration by parts yields

$$\int_1^c \frac{\sin x}{x}dx = \int_1^c \frac{1}{x} \sin x\, dx = \left[\frac{-\cos x}{x} \right]_1^c - \int_1^c \frac{\cos x}{x^2}dx,$$

or

(2)
$$\int_1^c \frac{\sin x}{x}dx = -\frac{\cos c}{c} + \cos 1 - \int_1^c \frac{\cos x}{x^2}dx.$$

Because

$$\left| \frac{\cos c}{c} \right| \le \frac{1}{c} \quad \text{and} \quad \left| \frac{\cos x}{x^2} \right| \le \frac{1}{x^2},$$

the first term on the right in equation (2) tends to zero as c tends to infinity; and the improper integral

$$\int_1^\infty \frac{\cos x}{x^2}\, dx = \lim_{c\to\infty} \int_1^c \frac{\cos x}{x^2}\, dx$$

is (absolutely) convergent. The limit of the left-hand side of equation (2) as c tends to infinity therefore exists; that is, integral (1) converges.

Now that we have established that integral (1) converges to some number L, or that

$$\lim_{c\to\infty} \int_0^c \frac{\sin x}{x}\, dx = L,$$

we note that, in particular,

(3)
$$\lim_{N\to\infty} \int_0^{(\frac{1}{2}+N)\pi} \frac{\sin x}{x}\, dx = L$$

as N passes through positive integers. That is,

(4)
$$\lim_{N\to\infty} \int_0^\pi \frac{\sin\left(\frac{1}{2} + N\right) u}{u}\, du = L,$$

where the substitution

$$x = \left(\frac{1}{2} + N\right) u$$

has been made for the variable of integration. Observe that equation (4) can be written

(5) $$\lim_{N \to \infty} \int_0^\pi g(u) D_N(u)\, du = L,$$

where

(6) $$g(u) = \frac{2 \sin \dfrac{u}{2}}{u}$$

and where $D_N(u)$ is the Dirichlet kernel (Sec. 11)

(7) $$D_N(u) = \frac{\sin\left(\dfrac{u}{2} + Nu\right)}{2 \sin \dfrac{u}{2}}.$$

The function $g(u)$, moreover, satisfies the conditions in Lemma 2, Sec. 11 (see Problem 1, Sec. 52); and $g(0 +) = 1$. So, by that lemma, limit (5) has the value $\pi/2$; and, by uniqueness of limits, $L = \pi/2$. Integration formula (1) is now established.

52. TWO LEMMAS

The two lemmas in this section are analogues of the ones in Sec. 11, leading up to a convergence theorem for Fourier series. The statement and proof of the corresponding theorem for Fourier integrals appear in Sec. 53, where these lemmas are needed.

Lemma 1. *If a function $G(u)$ is piecewise continuous on an interval $0 < x < c$, then*

(1) $$\lim_{r \to \infty} \int_0^c G(u) \sin ru\, du = 0. \qquad\qquad (r > 0)$$

This is the general statement of the *Riemann-Lebesgue lemma* involving a sine function. Lemma 1 in Sec. 11 is a special case of it, where $c = \pi$ and r tends to infinity through the half-integers

$$r = \frac{1}{2} + N \qquad\qquad (N = 1, 2, \ldots),$$

rather than continuously as it does here. This lemma also holds when $\sin ru$ is replaced by $\cos ru$; and the proof is similar to the one below involving $\sin ru$.

To verify limit (1), it is sufficient to show that if $G(u)$ is *continuous* at each point in an interval $a \le u \le b$, then

(2) $$\lim_{r \to \infty} \int_a^b G(u) \sin ru\, du = 0.$$

For, in view of the discussion of integrals of piecewise continuous functions in Sec. 1, the integral in limit (1) can be expressed as the sum of a finite number of integrals of the type appearing in limit (2).

Assuming, then, that $G(u)$ is continuous on the closed bounded interval $a \leq u \leq b$, we note that it must also be *uniformly* continuous there. That is, for each positive number ε, there exists a positive number δ such that

$$|G(u) - G(v)| < \varepsilon$$

whenever u and v lie in the interval and satisfy the inequality $|u - v| < \delta$.[†] Writing

$$\varepsilon = \frac{\varepsilon_0}{2(b - a)},$$

where ε_0 is an arbitrary positive number, we are thus assured that there is a positive number δ such that

(3) $$|G(u) - G(v)| < \frac{\varepsilon_0}{2(b - a)} \qquad \text{whenever } |u - v| < \delta.$$

To obtain the limit (2), divide the interval $a \leq u \leq b$ into N subintervals of equal length $(b - a)/N$ by means of the points $a = u_0, u_1, u_2, \ldots, u_N = b$, where $u_0 < u_1 < u_2 < \cdots < u_N$, and let N be so large that the length of each subinterval is less than the number δ in condition (3). Then write

$$\int_a^b G(u) \sin ru \, du = \sum_{n=1}^{N} \int_{u_{n-1}}^{u_n} G(u) \sin ru \, du,$$

or

$$\int_a^b G(u) \sin ru \, du$$

$$= \sum_{n=1}^{N} \int_{u_{n-1}}^{u_n} [G(u) - G(u_n)] \sin ru \, du + \sum_{n=1}^{N} G(u_n) \int_{u_{n-1}}^{u_n} \sin ru \, du,$$

from which it follows that

(4) $$\left| \int_a^b G(u) \sin ru \, du \right|$$

$$\leq \sum_{n=1}^{N} \int_{u_{n-1}}^{u_n} |G(u) - G(u_n)| \, |\sin ru| \, du + \sum_{n=1}^{N} |G(u_n)| \left| \int_{u_{n-1}}^{u_n} \sin ru \, du \right|.$$

In view of condition (3) and the fact that $|\sin ru| \leq 1$, it is easy to see that

$$\int_{u_{n-1}}^{u_n} |G(u) - G(u_n)| \, |\sin ru| \, du < \frac{\varepsilon_0}{2(b - a)} \cdot \frac{b - a}{N} = \frac{\varepsilon_0}{2N} \qquad (n = 1, 2, \ldots, N).$$

Also, since $G(u)$ is continuous on the closed interval $a \leq u \leq b$, it is bounded there; that is, there is a positive number M such that $|G(u)| \leq M$ for all u in that interval.

[†] See, for instance, the book by Taylor and Mann (1983, pp. 529–531), listed in the Bibliography.

Furthermore,

$$\left| \int_{u_{n-1}}^{u_n} \sin ru \, du \right| \leq \frac{|\cos ru_n| + |\cos ru_{n-1}|}{r} \leq \frac{2}{r} \qquad (n = 1, 2, \ldots, N).$$

With these observations, we find that inequality (4) yields the statement

$$\left| \int_a^b G(u) \sin ru \, du \right| < \frac{\varepsilon_0}{2} + \frac{2MN}{r}.$$

Now write

$$R = \frac{4MN}{\varepsilon_0}$$

and observe that

$$\frac{2MN}{r} < \frac{\varepsilon_0}{2} \qquad \text{whenever } r > R.$$

Consequently,

$$\left| \int_a^b G(u) \sin ru \, du \right| < \frac{\varepsilon_0}{2} + \frac{\varepsilon_0}{2} = \varepsilon_0 \qquad \text{whenever } r > R;$$

and limit (2) is established.

Our second lemma makes direct use of the first one.

Lemma 2. *Suppose that a function $g(u)$ is piecewise continuous on every bounded interval of the positive u axis and that the right-hand derivative $g'_+(0)$ exists. If the improper integral*

$$(5) \qquad \qquad \int_0^\infty |g(u)| \, du$$

converges, then

$$(6) \qquad \qquad \lim_{r \to \infty} \int_0^\infty g(u) \frac{\sin ru}{u} \, du = \frac{\pi}{2} g(0+).$$

Observe that the integrand appearing in equation (6) is piecewise continuous on the same intervals as $g(u)$ and that when $u \geq 1$,

$$\left| g(u) \frac{\sin ru}{u} \right| \leq |g(u)|.$$

Hence the convergence of integral (5) ensures the existence of the integral in equation (6).

We begin the proof of the lemma by demonstrating its validity when the interval of integration is replaced by any *bounded* interval $0 < x < c$. That is, we first show that if a function $g(u)$ is piecewise continuous on a bounded interval $0 < x < c$ and $g'_+(0)$ exists, then

$$(7) \qquad \qquad \lim_{r \to \infty} \int_0^c g(u) \frac{\sin ru}{u} \, du = \frac{\pi}{2} g(0+).$$

To prove this, we write

$$\int_0^c g(u) \frac{\sin ru}{u} \, du = I(r) + J(r),$$

where

$$I(r) = \int_0^c \frac{g(u) - g(0+)}{u} \sin ru \, du \qquad \text{and} \qquad J(r) = \int_0^c g(0+) \frac{\sin ru}{u} \, du.$$

Since the function

$$G(u) = \frac{g(u) - g(0+)}{u}$$

is piecewise continuous on the interval $0 < x < c$, where $G(0+) = g'_+(0)$, we need only refer to Lemma 1 to see that

(8)
$$\lim_{r \to \infty} I(r) = 0.$$

On the other hand, if we substitute $x = ru$ in the integral representing $J(r)$, the integration formula in Sec. 51 tells us that

(9)
$$\lim_{r \to \infty} J(r) = g(0+) \lim_{r \to \infty} \int_0^{cr} \frac{\sin x}{x} \, dx = \frac{\pi}{2} g(0+).$$

Limit (7) is evidently now a consequence of limits (8) and (9).

To actually obtain limit (6), we note that

$$\left| \int_c^\infty g(u) \frac{\sin ru}{u} \, du \right| \leq \int_0^\infty |g(u)| \, du,$$

where we assume that $c \geq 1$. We then write

(10)
$$\left| \int_0^\infty g(u) \frac{\sin ru}{u} \, du - \frac{\pi}{2} g(0+) \right|$$

$$\leq \left| \int_0^c g(u) \frac{\sin ru}{u} \, du - \frac{\pi}{2} g(0+) \right| + \int_c^\infty |g(u)| \, du,$$

choosing c to be so large that the value of the last integral on the right, which is the remainder of integral (5), is less than $\varepsilon/2$, where ε is an arbitrary positive number independent of the value of r. In view of limit (7), there exists a positive number R such that whenever $r > R$, the first absolute value on the right-hand side of inequality (10) is also less than $\varepsilon/2$. It then follows that

$$\left| \int_0^\infty g(u) \frac{\sin ru}{u} \, du - \frac{\pi}{2} g(0+) \right| < \frac{\varepsilon}{2} + \frac{\varepsilon}{2} = \varepsilon$$

whenever $r > R$, and this is the same as statement (6).

PROBLEMS

1. Show that the function

$$g(u) = \frac{2 \sin \frac{u}{2}}{u},$$

used in equation (5), Sec. 51, satisfies the conditions in Lemma 2, Sec. 11. To be precise, show that g is piecewise continuous on the interval $0 < x < \pi$ and that $g'_+(0)$ exists.
   Suggestion: To obtain $g'_+(0)$, show that

$$g'_+(0) = \lim_{\substack{u \to 0 \\ u > 0}} \frac{2 \sin \frac{u}{2} - u}{u^2}.$$

Then apply l'Hôpital's rule twice.

2. Prove Lemma 1 in Sec. 52, when $\sin ru$ is replaced by $\cos ru$ in integral (1) there.

3. Assume that a function $f(x)$ has the Fourier integral representation (8), Sec. 50, which can be written

$$f(x) = \lim_{c \to \infty} \int_0^c [A(\alpha) \cos \alpha x + B(\alpha) \sin \alpha x] \, d\alpha.$$

Use the exponential forms (compare with Problem 8, Sec. 15)

$$\cos \theta = \frac{e^{i\theta} + e^{-i\theta}}{2}, \qquad \sin \theta = \frac{e^{i\theta} - e^{-i\theta}}{2i}$$

of the cosine and sine functions to show formally that

$$f(x) = \lim_{c \to \infty} \int_{-c}^c C(\alpha) e^{i\alpha x} \, d\alpha,$$

where

$$C(\alpha) = \frac{A(\alpha) - i B(\alpha)}{2}, \qquad C(-\alpha) = \frac{A(\alpha) + i B(\alpha)}{2} \qquad (\alpha > 0).$$

Then use expressions (9), Sec. 50, for $A(\alpha)$ and $B(\alpha)$ to obtain the single formula[†]

$$C(\alpha) = \frac{1}{2\pi} \int_{-\infty}^{\infty} f(x) e^{-i\alpha x} \, dx \qquad (-\infty < \alpha < \infty).$$

53. A FOURIER INTEGRAL THEOREM

The following theorem gives conditions under which the Fourier integral representation (7), Sec. 50, is valid.[‡]

   Theorem. *Let f denote a function that is piecewise continuous on every bounded interval of the x axis, and suppose that it is absolutely integrable over*

[†]The function $C(\alpha)$ is known as the *exponential Fourier transform* of $f(x)$ and is of particular importance in electrical engineering. For a development of this and other types of Fourier transforms, see, for example, the book by Churchill (1972) that is listed in the Bibliography.

[‡]For other conditions, see the books by Carslaw (1952, pp. 315ff) and Titchmarsh (1986, pp. 13ff), both listed in the Bibliography.

the entire x axis; that is, the improper integral

$$\int_{-\infty}^{\infty} |f(x)| \, dx$$

converges. Then the Fourier integral

(1) $$\frac{1}{\pi} \int_0^{\infty} \int_{-\infty}^{\infty} f(s) \cos \alpha(s - x) \, ds \, d\alpha$$

converges to the mean value

(2) $$\frac{f(x+) + f(x-)}{2}$$

of the one-sided limits of f at each point x $(-\infty < x < \infty)$ where both of the one-sided derivatives $f'_+(x)$ and $f'_-(x)$ exist.

We begin our proof with the observation that integral (1) represents the limit as r tends to infinity of the integral

(3) $$\frac{1}{\pi} \int_0^r \int_{-\infty}^{\infty} f(s) \cos \alpha(s - x) \, ds \, d\alpha = \frac{1}{\pi} [I(r, x) + J(r, x)],$$

where

$$I(r, x) = \int_0^r \int_x^{\infty} f(s) \cos \alpha(s - x) \, ds \, d\alpha,$$

$$J(r, x) = \int_0^r \int_{-\infty}^x f(s) \cos \alpha(s - x) \, ds \, d\alpha.$$

We now show that the individual integrals $I(r, x)$ and $J(r, x)$ exist; and, assuming that $f'_+(x)$ and $f'_-(x)$ exist, we examine the behavior of these integrals as r tends to infinity.

Turning to $I(r, x)$ first, we introduce the new variable of integration $u = s - x$ and write that integral in the form

(4) $$I(r, x) = \int_0^r \int_0^{\infty} f(x + u) \cos \alpha u \, du \, d\alpha.$$

Since

$$|f(x + u) \cos \alpha u| \leq |f(x + u)|$$

and because

$$\int_0^{\infty} |f(x + u)| \, du = \int_x^{\infty} |f(s)| \, ds \leq \int_{-\infty}^{\infty} |f(s)| \, ds,$$

the Weierstrass M-test for improper integrals applies to show that the integral

$$\int_0^{\infty} f(x + u) \cos \alpha u \, du$$

converges uniformly with respect to the variable α. Consequently, not only does the iterated integral (4) exist, but also the order of integration there can be reversed:[†]

$$I(r, x) = \int_0^\infty \int_0^r f(x + u) \cos \alpha u \, d\alpha \, du = \int_0^\infty f(x + u) \frac{\sin ru}{u} \, du.$$

Now the function $g(u) = f(x + u)$ satisfies the conditions in Lemma 2, Sec. 52 (compare with Sec. 12). So, applying that lemma to this last integral, we find that

(5)
$$\lim_{r \to \infty} I(r, x) = \frac{\pi}{2} f(x +).$$

The limit of $J(r, x)$ as r tends to infinity is treated similarly. Here we make the substitution $u = x - s$ and write

$$J(r, x) = \int_0^r \int_0^\infty f(x - u) \cos \alpha u \, du \, d\alpha = \int_0^\infty f(x - u) \frac{\sin ru}{u} \, du.$$

When $g(u) = f(x - u)$, the limit

(6)
$$\lim_{r \to \infty} J(r, x) = \frac{\pi}{2} f(x -)$$

also follows from Lemma 2 in Sec. 52.

Finally, in view of limits (5) and (6), we see that the limit of the left-hand side of equation (3) as r tends to infinity has the value (2), which is, then, the value of integral (1) at any point where the one-sided derivatives of f exist.

Note that since the integrals in expressions (9), Sec. 50, for the coefficients $A(\alpha)$ and $B(\alpha)$ exist when f satisfies the conditions stated in the theorem, the form (8), Sec. 50, of the Fourier integral formula is also justified.

PROBLEMS

1. Verify that all of the conditions in the theorem in Sec. 53 are satisfied by the function f defined by means of the equations

$$f(x) = \begin{cases} 1 & \text{when } |x| < 1, \\ 0 & \text{when } |x| > 1, \end{cases}$$

and $f(\pm 1) = 1/2$. Thus show that for every x $(-\infty < x < \infty)$,

$$f(x) = \frac{1}{\pi} \int_0^\infty \frac{\sin \alpha (1 + x) + \sin \alpha (1 - x)}{\alpha} \, d\alpha = \frac{2}{\pi} \int_0^\infty \frac{\sin \alpha \cos \alpha x}{\alpha} \, d\alpha.$$

2. Show that the function defined by means of the equations

$$f(x) = \begin{cases} 0 & \text{when } x < 0, \\ \exp(-x) & \text{when } x > 0, \end{cases}$$

[†]Theorems on improper integrals used here are developed in the book by Buck (2004), listed in the Bibliography, as well as in most other texts on advanced calculus. The theorems are usually given for integrals with continuous integrands, but they are also valid when the integrands are piecewise continuous.

and $f(0) = 1/2$ satisfies the conditions in the theorem in Sec. 53 and hence that

$$f(x) = \frac{1}{\pi} \int_0^\infty \frac{\cos \alpha x + \alpha \sin \alpha x}{1 + \alpha^2} \, d\alpha \qquad (-\infty < x < \infty).$$

Verify this representation directly at the point $x = 0$.

3. Show how it follows from the result in Problem 2 that

$$\exp(-|x|) = \frac{2}{\pi} \int_0^\infty \frac{\cos \alpha x}{1 + \alpha^2} \, d\alpha \qquad (-\infty < x < \infty).$$

4. Use the theorem in Sec. 53 to show that if

$$f(x) = \begin{cases} 0 & \text{when } x < 0 \text{ or } x > \pi, \\ \sin x & \text{when } 0 \le x \le \pi, \end{cases}$$

then

$$f(x) = \frac{1}{\pi} \int_0^\infty \frac{\cos \alpha x + \cos \alpha (\pi - x)}{1 - \alpha^2} \, d\alpha \qquad (-\infty < x < \infty).$$

In particular, write $x = \pi/2$ to show that

$$\int_0^\infty \frac{\cos(\alpha \pi/2)}{1 - \alpha^2} \, d\alpha = \frac{\pi}{2}.$$

5. Show why the Fourier integral formula fails to represent the function

$$f(x) = 1 \qquad (-\infty < x < \infty).$$

Also, point out which condition in the theorem in Sec. 53 is not satisfied by that function.

6. Give details showing that the integral $J(r, x)$ in Sec. 53 actually exists and that limit (6) in that section holds.

7. Let f be a nonzero function that is periodic, with period $2c$. Point out why the integrals

$$\int_{-\infty}^\infty f(x) \, dx \qquad \text{and} \qquad \int_{-\infty}^\infty |f(x)| \, dx$$

fail to exist.

8. Let $A(\alpha)$ and $B(\alpha)$ denote the coefficients (9), Sec. 50, in the Fourier integral representation (8) in that section for a function $f(x)$ ($-\infty < x < \infty$) that satisfies the conditions in the theorem in Sec. 53.

(a) By considering even and odd functions of α, point out why

$$\int_{-\infty}^\infty [A(\alpha) \cos \alpha x + B(\alpha) \sin \alpha x] \, d\alpha = 2 f(x)$$

and

$$\int_{-\infty}^\infty [B(\alpha) \cos \alpha x + A(\alpha) \sin \alpha x] \, d\alpha = 0.$$

(b) By adding corresponding sides of the equations in part (a), obtain the following symmetric form of the Fourier integral formula:[†]

$$f(x) = \frac{1}{\sqrt{2\pi}} \int_{-\infty}^\infty g(\alpha)(\cos \alpha x + \sin \alpha x) \, d\alpha \qquad (-\infty < x < \infty),$$

[†]This form is useful in certain types of transmission problems. See R. V. L. Hartley, *Proc. Inst. Radio Engrs.*, vol. 30, no. 3, pp. 144–150, 1942.

where

$$g(\alpha) = \frac{1}{\sqrt{2\pi}} \int_{-\infty}^{\infty} f(x)(\cos \alpha x + \sin \alpha x)\,dx.$$

54. THE COSINE AND SINE INTEGRALS

Let f denote a function satisfying the conditions stated in the theorem in Sec. 53. As pointed out in the final paragraph of that section, the Fourier integral representation of $f(x)$ remains valid when written in the form

(1) $$f(x) = \int_0^{\infty} [A(\alpha) \cos \alpha x + B(\alpha) \sin \alpha x]\,d\alpha,$$

where

(2) $$A(\alpha) = \frac{1}{\pi} \int_{-\infty}^{\infty} f(x) \cos \alpha x\,dx, \qquad B(\alpha) = \frac{1}{\pi} \int_{-\infty}^{\infty} f(x) \sin \alpha x\,dx.$$

Also, in view of the theorem in Sec. 9, representation (1) is valid for any function f that is absolutely integrable over the entire x axis and *piecewise smooth* on every bounded interval of it.

Suppose now that $f(x)$ is defined only when $x > 0$ and that

(*i*) f is absolutely integrable over the positive x axis and piecewise smooth on every bounded interval of it;

(*ii*) $f(x)$ at each point of discontinuity of f is the mean value of the one-sided limits $f(x+)$ and $f(x-)$.

The following theorem regarding *Fourier cosine and sine integral formulas* is analogous to Theorem 2 in Sec. 15, which ensures the convergence to $f(x)$ of Fourier cosine and sine series on an interval $0 < x < c$. It is an immediate consequence of the Fourier integral theorem in Sec. 53 and will be especially useful in our applications.

Theorem. *Let f denote a function that is defined on the positive x axis and satisfies conditions* (*i*) *and* (*ii*). *The Fourier cosine integral representation*

(3) $$f(x) = \int_0^{\infty} A(\alpha) \cos \alpha x\,d\alpha,$$

where

(4) $$A(\alpha) = \frac{2}{\pi} \int_0^{\infty} f(x) \cos \alpha x\,dx,$$

is valid for each x $(x > 0)$; and the same is true of the Fourier sine integral representation

(5) $$f(x) = \int_0^{\infty} B(\alpha) \sin \alpha x\,d\alpha,$$

where

(6)
$$B(\alpha) = \frac{2}{\pi} \int_0^\infty f(x) \sin \alpha x \, dx.$$

Note how representations (3) and (5) can also be written

(7)
$$f(x) = \frac{2}{\pi} \int_0^\infty \cos \alpha x \int_0^\infty f(s) \cos \alpha s \, ds \, d\alpha$$

and

(8)
$$f(x) = \frac{2}{\pi} \int_0^\infty \sin \alpha x \int_0^\infty f(s) \sin \alpha s \, ds \, d\alpha,$$

respectively.

To start the proof of the theorem, observe that if f is *even*, $f(x) \sin \alpha x$ is odd in the variable x. The graph of $y = f(x) \sin \alpha x$ is, therefore, symmetric with respect to the origin. Hence $B(\alpha) = 0$ in representation (1), which reduces to equation (3). The function $f(x) \cos \alpha x$ is, moreover, even in x, and so the graph of $y = f(x) \cos \alpha x$ is symmetric with respect to the y axis. Consequently, the coefficient $A(\alpha)$ in representation (1) takes the form (4). If, on the other hand, f is *odd*, $A(\alpha) = 0$; and similar considerations lead to representation (5).

Suppose now that f is defined only when $x > 0$, as in the statement of the theorem. When the even extension is made, so that f is defined on the entire x axis except at $x = 0$, integral (3) represents that extension for every nonzero x and converges to $f(0 +)$ when $x = 0$. Likewise, integral (5) represents the odd extension of $f(x)$ for every nonzero x and converges to zero when $x = 0$. So the theorem here follows from the Fourier integral theorem in Sec. 53.

55. SOME EIGENVALUE PROBLEMS ON UNBOUNDED INTERVALS

The integral representation (3) in the theorem in Sec. 54 is needed in various applications involving the eigenvalue problem

(1)
$$X''(x) + \lambda X(x) = 0, \quad X'(0) = 0, \quad |X(x)| < M \qquad (x > 0),$$

where M is some positive constant. This is another kind of eigenvalue problem which is basically different from the ones solved in Secs. 35 and 49. The difference, to be described further in Chap. 8 (Sec. 68), is that the fundamental interval $x > 0$ here is unbounded. We accept the fact, which can be verified using complex-variable methods, that the eigenvalues λ in this and the other eigenvalue problems in this chapter must be *real* numbers.

To solve problem (1), we consider the cases in which λ is zero, positive, and negative separately.

(i) The case $\lambda = 0$

When $\lambda = 0$, the differential equation is $X'' = 0$. Its solution is $X(x) = Ax + B$, where A and B are arbitrary constants, and the condition $X'(0) = 0$ requires that $A = 0$. Inasmuch as the function $X(x) = B$ is bounded, we find that except for a constant factor, $X(x) = 1$.

(ii) The case $\lambda > 0$

Here we write $\lambda = \alpha^2 (\alpha > 0)$, so that the general solution of the differential equation is

$$X(x) = C_1 \cos \alpha x + C_2 \sin \alpha x,$$

where the constants C_1 and C_2 are arbitrary. Since $\alpha \neq 0$, the condition $X'(0) = 0$ requires that $C_2 = 0$. So, except for a constant factor, $X(x) = \cos \alpha x$, where α takes on all positive values. Note that the corresponding eigenvalues $\lambda = \alpha^2$ are continuous, rather than discrete.

(iii) The case $\lambda < 0$

In this case, we write $\lambda = -\alpha^2 (\alpha > 0)$ and observe that the general solution of the differential equation is $X(x) = C_1 e^{\alpha x} + C_2 e^{-\alpha x}$. The condition $X'(0) = 0$ requires that

$$\alpha(C_1 - C_2) = 0,$$

or that $C_2 = C_1$. Consequently,

$$X(x) = C_1(e^{\alpha x} + e^{-\alpha x}) = 2C_1 \cosh \alpha x,$$

and since $\cosh \alpha x$ is unbounded on the half line $x > 0$, the constant C_1 must be zero. So $X(x)$ is identically equal to zero, and we find that the case $\lambda < 0$ yields no new eigenfunctions.

The eigenvalues and eigenfunctions of Problem 1 are, therefore,

$$(2) \qquad\qquad \lambda = \alpha^2, \qquad X(x) = \cos \alpha x \qquad\qquad (\alpha \geq 0).$$

Although the eigenfunctions $X(x) = \cos \alpha x$ $(\alpha \geq 0)$ have no orthogonality property, the Fourier cosine integral formula (3) in Sec. 54 gives representations of functions $f(x)$ on the interval $x > 0$ that are generalized linear combinations of those eigenfunctions.

Likewise, it is straightforward to show (Problem 7) that

$$(3) \qquad\qquad \lambda = \alpha^2, \qquad X(x) = \sin \alpha x \qquad\qquad (\alpha > 0)$$

are the eigenvalues and eigenfunctions of the problem

$$(4) \qquad X''(x) + \lambda X(x) = 0, \qquad X(0) = 0, \qquad |X(x)| < M \qquad (x > 0);$$

and formula (5) in Sec. 54 represents functions $f(x)$ in terms of $\sin \alpha x$.

Finally, solutions of the eigenvalue problem

$$(5) \qquad\qquad X''(x) + \lambda X(x) = 0, \qquad |X(x)| < M \qquad\qquad (-\infty < x < \infty)$$

are found in Problem 8 and will be used in Sec. 59.

PROBLEMS

1. By applying the Fourier sine integral formula and the theorem in Sec. 54 to the function defined by means of the equations

$$f(x) = \begin{cases} 1 & \text{when } 0 < x < b, \\ 0 & \text{when } \qquad x > b, \end{cases}$$

and $f(b) = 1/2$, obtain the representation

$$f(x) = \frac{2}{\pi} \int_0^\infty \frac{1 - \cos b\alpha}{\alpha} \sin \alpha x \, d\alpha \qquad (x > 0).$$

2. Verify that the function $\exp(-bx)$, where b is a positive constant, satisfies the conditions in the theorem in Sec. 54, and show that the coefficient $B(\alpha)$ in the Fourier sine integral representation of that function is

$$B(\alpha) = \frac{2}{\pi} \int_0^\infty e^{-bx} \sin \alpha x \, dx = \frac{2}{\pi} \cdot \frac{\alpha}{\alpha^2 + b^2}.$$

Thus, prove that

$$e^{-bx} = \frac{2}{\pi} \int_0^\infty \frac{\alpha \sin \alpha x}{\alpha^2 + b^2} \, d\alpha \qquad (b > 0, x > 0).$$

3. Verify the Fourier sine integral representation

$$\frac{x}{x^2 + b^2} = \frac{2}{\pi} \int_0^\infty \sin \alpha x \int_0^\infty \frac{s \sin \alpha s}{s^2 + b^2} \, ds \, d\alpha \qquad (b > 0, x \geq 0)$$

by first observing that according to the final result in Problem 2,

$$\int_0^\infty \frac{s \sin \alpha s}{s^2 + b^2} \, ds = \frac{\pi}{2} e^{-b\alpha} \qquad (b > 0, \alpha > 0).$$

Then, by referring to the expression for $B(\alpha)$ in Problem 2, complete the verification. Show that the function $x/(x^2 + b^2)$ is *not*, however, absolutely integrable over the positive x axis.

4. As already verified in Problem 2, the function $\exp(-bx)$, where b is a positive constant, satisfies the conditions in the theorem in Sec. 54. Show that the coefficient $A(\alpha)$ in the Fourier cosine integral representation of that function is

$$A(\alpha) = \frac{2}{\pi} \int_0^\infty e^{-bx} \cos \alpha x \, dx = \frac{2}{\pi} \cdot \frac{b}{\alpha^2 + b^2}.$$

Thus prove that

$$e^{-bx} = \frac{2b}{\pi} \int_0^\infty \frac{\cos \alpha x}{\alpha^2 + b^2} \, d\alpha \qquad (b > 0, x \geq 0).$$

5. By regarding the positive constant b in the final equation obtained in Problem 4 as a variable and then differentiating each side of that equation with respect to b, show *formally* that

$$(1 + x) e^{-x} = \frac{4}{\pi} \int_0^\infty \frac{\cos \alpha x}{(\alpha^2 + 1)^2} \, d\alpha \qquad (x \geq 0).$$

6. Verify that the function $e^{-x} \cos x$ satisfies the conditions in the theorem in Sec. 54, and show that the coefficient $A(\alpha)$ in the Fourier cosine integral representation of that function can be written

$$A(\alpha) = \frac{1}{\pi} \int_0^\infty e^{-x} \cos(\alpha + 1)x \, dx + \frac{1}{\pi} \int_0^\infty e^{-x} \cos(\alpha - 1)x \, dx.$$

Then use the expression for the corresponding coefficients in Problem 4 to prove that

$$e^{-x} \cos x = \frac{2}{\pi} \int_0^\infty \frac{\alpha^2 + 2}{\alpha^4 + 4} \cos \alpha x \, d\alpha \qquad (x \geq 0).$$

7. In Sec. 55, show that the solutions of the eigenvalue problem (4) are as stated there.

8. Show that the eigenvalues of the eigenvalue problem

$$X''(x) + \lambda X(x) = 0, \qquad |X(x)| < M \qquad (-\infty < x < \infty),$$

where M is a positive constant, are $\lambda = \alpha^2$ ($\alpha \geq 0$) and that the corresponding eigen-functions are constant multiples of unity when $\alpha = 0$ and arbitrary linear combinations of $\cos \alpha x$ and $\sin \alpha x$ when $\alpha > 0$. (Compare with the solutions of the eigenvalue problem in Sec. 49.)

56. MORE ON SUPERPOSITION OF SOLUTIONS

In Sec. 33 we showed that if $u_1, u_2, \ldots$ are solutions of a given linear homogeneous differential equation or boundary condition, then so is any generalized linear combination

$$u = \sum_{n=1}^{\infty} c_n u_n$$

of those functions, provided that needed differentiability and continuity conditions are satisfied. We thus had the basis of the technique for solving boundary value problems in Chap. 5. Another important version of that principle of superposition is illustrated in the following example, where superposition consists of integration with respect to a parameter α instead of summation with respect to an index n. It will enable us to solve certain boundary value problems in which Fourier integrals, rather than Fourier series, are required.

EXAMPLE. Consider the set of functions $u = e^{-\alpha y} \sin \alpha x$, where each func-tion corresponds to a value of the parameter α ($\alpha > 0$) and where α is independent of x and y. Each function satisfies Laplace's equation

$$(1) \hspace{3cm} u_{xx}(x, y) + u_{yy}(x, y) = 0 \hspace{3cm} (x > 0, y > 0)$$

and the boundary condition

$$(2) \hspace{4cm} u(0, y) = 0 \hspace{4cm} (y > 0).$$

These functions are bounded in the domain $x > 0$, $y > 0$ (Fig. 47) and are obtained from conditions (1) and (2) by the method of separation of variables when that boundedness condition is included (Problem 1, Sec. 57).

We now show that their superposition of the type

$$(3) \hspace{2cm} u(x, y) = \int_0^\infty B(\alpha) \, e^{-\alpha y} \sin \alpha x \, d\alpha \hspace{2cm} (x > 0, y > 0)$$

also represents a solution of the homogeneous conditions (1) and (2) which is bounded in the domain $x > 0$, $y > 0$ for each function $B(\alpha)$ that is bounded and continuous on the half-line $\alpha > 0$ and absolutely integrable over it.

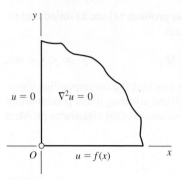

FIGURE 47

To accomplish this, we use tests for improper integrals that are analogous to those for infinite series.[†] The integral in equation (3) converges absolutely and uniformly with respect to x and y because

$$(4) \qquad\qquad |B(\alpha)\, e^{-\alpha y} \sin \alpha x| \leq |B(\alpha)| \qquad\qquad (x \geq 0,\, y \geq 0)$$

and because $B(\alpha)$ is independent of x and y and absolutely integrable from zero to infinity with respect to α. Moreover, since

$$(5) \qquad |u(x, y)| \leq \int_0^\infty |B(\alpha)\, e^{-\alpha y} \sin \alpha x|\, d\alpha \leq \int_0^\infty |B(\alpha)|\, d\alpha,$$

u is bounded. It is also a continuous function of x and y ($x \geq 0,\, y \geq 0$) because of the uniform convergence of the integral in equation (3) and the continuity of the integrand. Clearly, $u = 0$ when $x = 0$.

When $y > 0$,

$$(6) \qquad \frac{\partial u}{\partial x} = \frac{\partial}{\partial x} \int_0^\infty B(\alpha)\, e^{-\alpha y} \sin \alpha x\, d\alpha = \int_0^\infty \frac{\partial}{\partial x} [B(\alpha)\, e^{-\alpha y} \sin \alpha x]\, d\alpha;$$

for if $|B(\alpha)| \leq B_0$ and $y \geq y_0$, where y_0 is some small positive number, then the absolute value of the integrand of the integral on the far right does not exceed $B_0\, \alpha \exp(-\alpha y_0)$, which is independent of x and y and integrable over the semi-infinite interval $0 \leq \alpha < \infty$. Hence that integral is uniformly convergent. Integral (3) is then differentiable with respect to x, and similarly for the other derivatives involved in the laplacian operator $\nabla^2 = \partial^2/\partial x^2 + \partial^2/\partial y^2$. Therefore,

$$(7) \qquad \nabla^2 u = \int_0^\infty B(\alpha) \nabla^2 (e^{-\alpha y} \sin \alpha x)\, d\alpha = 0 \qquad\qquad (x > 0,\, y > 0).$$

Suppose now that the function (3) is also required to satisfy the nonhomogeneous boundary condition

$$(8) \qquad\qquad\qquad u(x, 0) = f(x) \qquad\qquad\qquad (x > 0),$$

[†]See the book by Kaplan (2003, pp. 447ff) or the one by Taylor and Mann (1983, pp. 682ff), both listed in the Bibliography.

where f is a given function satisfying conditions (i) and (ii) in Sec. 54. We need to determine the function $B(\alpha)$ in equation (3) so that

$$(9) \qquad\qquad f(x) = \int_0^\infty B(\alpha) \sin \alpha x \, d\alpha \qquad\qquad (x > 0).$$

This is easily done since representation (9) is the Fourier sine integral formula in the theorem in Sec. 54 when

$$(10) \qquad\qquad B(\alpha) = \frac{2}{\pi} \int_0^\infty f(x) \sin \alpha x \, dx \qquad\qquad (\alpha > 0).$$

We have shown here that the function (3), with $B(\alpha)$ given by equation (10), is a solution of the boundary value problem consisting of equations (1), (2), and (8), together with the requirement that u be bounded.

57. STEADY TEMPERATURES IN A SEMI-INFINITE STRIP

Here we let $u(x, y)$ denote the bounded steady temperatures in a semi-infinite strip $x > 0, 0 < y < 1$ whose left-hand and bottom edges are insulated and whose top edge is kept at the temperatures shown in Fig. 48. The boundary value problem satisfied by the temperature function $u(x, y)$ is evidently

$$(1) \qquad\qquad u_{xx}(x, y) + u_{yy}(x, y) = 0 \qquad\qquad (x > 0, 0 < y < 1),$$

$$(2) \qquad\qquad u_x(0, y) = 0, \quad u_y(x, 0) = 0,$$

$$(3) \qquad\qquad u(x, 1) = e^{-x},$$

along with the boundedness condition $|u(x, y)| < M$, where M is some positive constant.

FIGURE 48

When $u = X(x)Y(y)$ and the method of separation of variables is applied to the homogeneous conditions (1) and (2), we have the eigenvalue problem

$$(4) \qquad X''(x) + \lambda X(x) = 0, \quad X'(0) = 0, \quad |X(x)| < M_1 \qquad (x > 0),$$

where M_1 is some positive constant, as well as the conditions

$$(5) \qquad\qquad Y''(x) - \lambda Y(x) = 0, \quad Y'(0) = 0 \qquad\qquad (0 < y < 1).$$

The eigenvalues and eigenfunctions of problem (4) are (see Sec. 55)

$$\lambda = \alpha^2, \quad X(x) = \cos \alpha x \qquad\qquad (\alpha \geq 0),$$

and the general solution of the corresponding differential equation

$$Y''(y) - \alpha^2 Y(y) = 0 \qquad\qquad (0 < y < 1)$$

is

$$Y(y) = C_1 e^{\alpha y} + C_2 e^{-\alpha y},$$

where the constants C_1 and C_2 are arbitrary. The condition $Y'(0) = 0$ tells us that $\alpha(C_1 - C_2) = 0$; and when $\alpha > 0$, we find that $C_2 = C_1$. Hence

$$Y(y) = C_1(e^{\alpha y} + e^{-\alpha y}) = 2C_1 \cosh \alpha y \qquad\qquad (\alpha > 0),$$

where C_1 is nonzero. By writing $C_1 = 1/2$, one can see that any constant multiple of $Y(y) = \cosh \alpha y$ satisfies the homogeneous conditions (5) and that

$$(6) \qquad\qquad X(x)Y(y) = \cos \alpha x \cosh \alpha y \qquad\qquad (\alpha > 0).$$

So the generalized linear combination (see Sec. 56)

$$(7) \quad u(x, y) = \int_0^\infty A(\alpha) \cos \alpha x \cosh \alpha y \, d\alpha = \int_0^\infty [A(\alpha) \cosh \alpha y] \cos \alpha x \, d\alpha$$

satisfies the homogeneous conditions (1) and (2) in our temperature problem.

The nonhomogeneous condition (3) is satisfied once $A(\alpha)$ is determined. To accomplish this, we note how it follows from the theorem in Sec. 54 that

$$e^{-x} = \int_0^\infty [A(\alpha) \cosh \alpha] \cos \alpha x \, d\alpha$$

if

$$(8) \qquad\qquad A(\alpha) \cosh \alpha = \frac{2}{\pi} \int_0^\infty e^{-x} \cos \alpha x \, dx.$$

The easiest way to evaluate this last integral is to refer to Problem 4, Sec. 55, according to which equation (8) becomes

$$A(\alpha) \cosh \alpha = \frac{2}{\pi} \cdot \frac{1}{(\alpha^2 + 1)}$$

Consequently, the formal solution of our temperature problem is

$$(9) \qquad\qquad u(x, y) = \frac{2}{\pi} \int_0^\infty \frac{\cos \alpha x \cosh \alpha y}{(\alpha^2 + 1) \cosh \alpha} \, d\alpha.$$

PROBLEMS

1. Give details showing how the functions $e^{-\alpha y} \sin \alpha x$ $(\alpha > 0)$ arise by means of separation of variables from conditions (1) and (2), Sec. 56, and the condition that the function $u(x, y)$ there be bounded when $x > 0$, $y > 0$.

2. (*a*) Substitute expression (10), Sec. 56, for the function $B(\alpha)$ into equation (3) of that section. Then, by formally reversing the order of integration, show that the solution of the boundary value problem treated in Sec. 56 can be written

$$u(x, y) = \frac{y}{\pi} \int_0^\infty f(s) \left[\frac{1}{(s - x)^2 + y^2} - \frac{1}{(s + x)^2 + y^2} \right] ds.$$

(b) Show that when $f(x) = 1$, the form of the solution obtained in part (a) can be written in terms of the inverse tangent function as

$$u(x, y) = \frac{2}{\pi} \tan^{-1}\left(\frac{x}{y}\right).$$

3. A semi-infinite string, with one end fixed at the origin, is stretched along the positive half of the x axis and released at rest from a position $y = f(x)$ ($x \geq 0$). Derive the expression

$$y(x, t) = \frac{2}{\pi} \int_0^\infty \cos \alpha at \sin \alpha x \int_0^\infty f(s) \sin \alpha s \, ds \, d\alpha$$

for the transverse displacements. Let $F(x)$ ($-\infty < x < \infty$) denote the odd extension of $f(x)$, and show how this result reduces to the form

$$y(x, t) = \frac{1}{2}[F(x + at) + F(x - at)].$$

[Compare with solution (9), Sec. 45, of a string problem treated in that section.]

4. Find $u(x, y)$ when the boundary conditions in Sec. 57 are replaced by the conditions

$$u_x(0, y) = 0, \qquad u_y(x, 1) = -u(x, 1), \qquad u(x, 0) = f(x),$$

where

$$f(x) = \begin{cases} 1 & \text{when } 0 < x < 1, \\ 0 & \text{when } \quad x > 1. \end{cases}$$

Interpret this problem physically.

Answer: $u(x, y) = \dfrac{2}{\pi} \displaystyle\int_0^\infty \dfrac{\alpha \cosh \alpha (1 - y) + \sinh \alpha (1 - y)}{\alpha^2 \cosh \alpha + \alpha \sinh \alpha} \sin \alpha \cos \alpha x \, d\alpha.$

5. Find the bounded harmonic function $u(x, y)$ in the semi-infinite strip $0 < x < 1, y > 0$ that satisfies the conditions

$$u_y(x, 0) = 0, \qquad u(0, y) = 0, \qquad u_x(1, y) = f(y).$$

Answer: $u(x, y) = \dfrac{2}{\pi} \displaystyle\int_0^\infty \dfrac{\sinh \alpha x \cos \alpha y}{\alpha \cosh \alpha} \int_0^\infty f(s) \cos \alpha s \, ds \, d\alpha.$

6. Solve the following boundary value problem for steady temperatures $u(x, y)$ in a thin plate in the shape of a semi-infinite strip when heat transfer to the surroundings at temperature zero takes place at the faces of the plate:

$$u_{xx}(x, y) + u_{yy}(x, y) - bu(x, y) = 0 \qquad (x > 0, 0 < y < 1),$$

$$u_x(0, y) = 0 \qquad (0 < y < 1),$$

$$u(x, 0) = 0, \qquad u(x, 1) = f(x) \qquad (x > 0),$$

where b is a positive constant and

$$f(x) = \begin{cases} 1 & \text{when } 0 < x < c, \\ 0 & \text{when } \quad x > c. \end{cases}$$

Answer: $u(x, y) = \dfrac{2}{\pi} \displaystyle\int_0^\infty \dfrac{\sin \alpha c \, \cos \alpha x \, \sinh\left(y\sqrt{\alpha^2 + b}\right)}{\alpha \sinh \sqrt{\alpha^2 + b}} \, d\alpha.$

58. TEMPERATURES IN A SEMI-INFINITE SOLID

The face $x = 0$ of a semi-infinite solid $x \geq 0$ is kept at temperature zero (Fig. 49). Let us find the temperatures $u(x, t)$ in the solid when the initial temperature distribution is $f(x)$, assuming for now that f is piecewise smooth on each bounded interval of the positive x axis and that f is bounded and absolutely integrable from $x = 0$ to $x = \infty$.

$u = 0$ $u(x, 0) = f(x)$

O x

FIGURE 49

If the solid is considered as a limiting case of a slab $0 \leq x \leq c$ as c increases, some condition corresponding to a thermal condition on the face $x = c$ seems to be needed. Otherwise, the temperatures on that face may be increased in any manner as c increases. We require that our function u be bounded; that condition also implies that there is no instantaneous source of heat on the face $x = 0$ at the instant $t = 0$. Then

$$(1) \qquad u_t(x, t) = k u_{xx}(x, t) \qquad (x > 0, t > 0),$$

$$(2) \qquad u(0, t) = 0 \qquad (t > 0),$$

$$(3) \qquad u(x, 0) = f(x) \qquad (x > 0),$$

and $|u(x, t)| < M$, where M is some positive constant.

Linear combinations of functions $u = X(x)T(t)$ will not ordinarily be bounded unless X and T are themselves bounded. Upon separating variables, we thus have the conditions

$$(4) \qquad X''(x) + \lambda X(x) = 0, \qquad X(0) = 0, \qquad |X(x)| < M_1 \qquad (x > 0)$$

and

$$(5) \qquad T'(t) + \lambda k T(t) = 0, \qquad |T(t)| < M_2 \qquad (t > 0),$$

where M_1 and M_2 are positive constants. As stated in Sec. 55, the eigenvalue problem (4) has continuous eigenvalues $\lambda = \alpha^2$, where α represents *all positive real numbers*, and $X(x) = \sin \alpha x$ are the eigenfunctions. In this case, the corresponding functions

$$T(t) = e^{-\alpha^2 kt} \qquad (a > 0)$$

are bounded. The generalized linear combination (see Sec. 56)

$$(6) \qquad u(x, t) = \int_0^\infty B(\alpha) e^{-\alpha^2 kt} \sin \alpha x \, d\alpha$$

of the functions $X(x)T(t)$ will formally satisfy all the conditions in the boundary value problem, including condition (3), if $B(\alpha)$ can be determined so that

$$(7) \qquad\qquad f(x) = \int_0^\infty B(\alpha) \sin \alpha x \, d\alpha \qquad\qquad (x > 0).$$

As in Sec. 56, we note that representation (7) is the Fourier sine integral formula (5), Sec. 54, for $f(x)$ if

$$(8) \qquad\qquad B(\alpha) = \frac{2}{\pi} \int_0^\infty f(x) \sin \alpha x \, dx \qquad\qquad (\alpha > 0).$$

Our formal solution (6), with $B(\alpha)$ defined by equation (8), can also be written

$$(9) \qquad\qquad u(x, t) = \frac{2}{\pi} \int_0^\infty e^{-\alpha^2 kt} \sin \alpha x \int_0^\infty f(s) \sin \alpha s \, ds \, d\alpha.$$

One can simplify this result by formally reversing the order of integration, replacing $2 \sin \alpha s \sin \alpha x$ by $\cos \alpha (s - x) - \cos \alpha (s + x)$, and then applying the integration formula (Problem 10)

$$(10) \qquad\qquad \int_0^\infty e^{-\alpha^2 a} \cos \alpha b \, d\alpha = \frac{1}{2} \sqrt{\frac{\pi}{a}} \exp\left(-\frac{b^2}{4a}\right) \qquad\qquad (a > 0).$$

Equation (9) then becomes

$$(11) \quad u(x, t) = \frac{1}{2\sqrt{\pi kt}} \int_0^\infty f(s) \left\{ \exp\left[-\frac{(s - x)^2}{4kt}\right] - \exp\left[-\frac{(s + x)^2}{4kt}\right] \right\} ds,$$

or

$$u(x, t) = \frac{1}{2\sqrt{\pi kt}} \int_0^\infty f(s) \exp\left[-\frac{(s - x)^2}{4kt}\right] ds$$
$$- \frac{1}{2\sqrt{\pi kt}} \int_0^\infty f(s) \exp\left[-\frac{(s + x)^2}{4kt}\right] ds,$$

when $t > 0$. By writing

$$s = x + 2\sigma\sqrt{kt} \qquad \text{and} \qquad s = -x + 2\sigma\sqrt{kt}$$

in these last two integrals, respectively, we have this alternative form of expression (11):

$$(12) \qquad u(x, t) = \frac{1}{\sqrt{\pi}} \int_{-x/(2\sqrt{kt})}^\infty f(x + 2\sigma\sqrt{kt}) e^{-\sigma^2} d\sigma$$
$$- \frac{1}{\sqrt{\pi}} \int_{x/(2\sqrt{kt})}^\infty f(-x + 2\sigma\sqrt{kt}) e^{-\sigma^2} d\sigma.$$

Our use of the Fourier sine integral formula in obtaining solution (9) suggests that we apply the theorem in Sec. 54 in verifying that solution. The forms (11) and (12) suggest, however, that the condition in the theorem that $|f(x)|$ be integrable from zero to infinity can be relaxed in the verification. More precisely, when s is kept fixed and $t > 0$, the functions

$$\frac{1}{\sqrt{t}} \exp\left[-\frac{(s \pm x)^2}{4kt}\right]$$

satisfy the heat equation (1). Then, under the assumption that $f(x)$ is continuous and bounded when $x \geq 0$, it is possible to show that the function (11) is bounded and satisfies the heat equation when $x_0 < x < x_1$ and $t_0 < t < t_1$, where x_0, x_1, t_0, and t_1 are any positive numbers. Conditions (2) and (3) can be verified by using expression (12). By adding step functions to f (see Problem 2), we can allow f to have a finite number of jumps on the half-line $x > 0$. Except for special cases, details in the verification of formal solutions of this problem are, however, tedious.

If $f(x) = u_0$, where u_0 is a constant, it follows from equation (12) that

$$(13) \qquad u(x, t) = \frac{u_0}{\sqrt{\pi}} \left(\int_{-x/(2\sqrt{kt})}^{\infty} e^{-\sigma^2} \, d\sigma - \int_{x/(2\sqrt{kt})}^{\infty} e^{-\sigma^2} \, d\sigma \right).$$

In terms of the *error function*

$$(14) \qquad \operatorname{erf}(x) = \frac{2}{\sqrt{\pi}} \int_0^x e^{-\sigma^2} \, d\sigma,$$

expression (13) can be written

$$(15) \qquad u(x, t) = u_0 \operatorname{erf}\left(\frac{x}{2\sqrt{kt}}\right).$$

The verification of this is not difficult, since $\exp(-\sigma^2)$ is an even function of σ. Note that because (see Problem 9)

$$(16) \qquad \int_0^{\infty} e^{-\sigma^2} \, d\sigma = \frac{\sqrt{\pi}}{2},$$

$\operatorname{erf}(x)$ tends to unity as x tends to infinity. Thus, if $f(x) = u_0$, the temperatures $u(x, t)$ in the solid tend to u_0 when x tends to infinity, as would be expected.

PROBLEMS

1. Verify that when $x > 0$ and $t > 0$, the function [see expression (14) in Sec. 58]

$$u(x, t) = \operatorname{erf}\left(\frac{x}{2\sqrt{kt}}\right)$$

satisfies the heat equation $u_t(x, t) = k u_{xx}(x, t)$ as well as the conditions

$$u(0+, t) = 0, \qquad u(x, 0+) = 1, \qquad \text{and} \qquad |u(x, t)| < 1.$$

2. Show that if

$$f(x) = \begin{cases} 0 & \text{when } 0 < x < c, \\ 1 & \text{when } \quad x > c, \end{cases}$$

expression (12), Sec. 58, reduces to

$$u(x, t) = \frac{1}{2} \operatorname{erf}\left(\frac{c + x}{2\sqrt{kt}}\right) - \frac{1}{2} \operatorname{erf}\left(\frac{c - x}{2\sqrt{kt}}\right).$$

Verify this solution of the boundary value problem in Sec. 58, when f is this function.

3. (a) The face $x = 0$ of a semi-infinite solid $x \geq 0$ is kept at a constant temperature u_0 after the interior $x > 0$ is initially at temperature zero throughout. By writing $u(x, t) = U(x, t) + \Phi(x)$ (compare with Example 2, Sec. 39), where $\Phi(x)$ is to be bounded for $x \geq 0$, and referring to solution (15), Sec. 58, of the special case of the boundary value problem noted there, derive the temperature formula

$$u(x, t) = u_0 \left[1 - \operatorname{erf}\left(\frac{x}{2\sqrt{kt}} \right) \right].$$

(b) Use equations (14) and (16) in Sec. 58 to rewrite the solution in part (a) as

$$u(x, t) = \frac{2u_0}{\sqrt{\pi}} \int_{x/(2\sqrt{kt})}^{\infty} e^{-\sigma^2} d\sigma.$$

4. Replace the constant temperature u_0 in Problem 3 by a time-dependent temperature $F(t)$, where $F(t)$ is continuous and differentiable when $t \geq 0$ and $F(0) = 0$. Then use the solution obtained in part (b) of Problem 3, together with the special case of Duhamel's principle described in Sec. 27, to derive the solution

$$u(x, t) = \frac{x}{2\sqrt{\pi k}} \int_0^t \frac{F(\tau)}{\sqrt{(t - \tau)^3}} \exp\left[-\frac{x^2}{4k(t - \tau)} \right] d\tau$$

of the temperature problem here.

5. (a) The face $x = 0$ of a semi-infinite solid $x \geq 0$ is insulated, and the initial temperature distribution is $f(x)$. Derive the temperature formula

$$u(x, t) = \frac{1}{\sqrt{\pi}} \int_{-x/(2\sqrt{kt})}^{\infty} f(x + 2\sigma\sqrt{kt}) e^{-\sigma^2} d\sigma$$

$$+ \frac{1}{\sqrt{\pi}} \int_{x/(2\sqrt{kt})}^{\infty} f(-x + 2\sigma\sqrt{kt}) e^{-\sigma^2} d\sigma.$$

(b) Show that if the function f in part (a) is defined by means of the equations

$$f(x) = \begin{cases} 1 & \text{when } 0 < x < c, \\ 0 & \text{when } \quad x > c, \end{cases}$$

then

$$u(x, t) = \frac{1}{2} \operatorname{erf}\left(\frac{c + x}{2\sqrt{kt}} \right) + \frac{1}{2} \operatorname{erf}\left(\frac{c - x}{2\sqrt{kt}} \right).$$

6. Let a semi-infinite solid $x \geq 0$, which is initially at a uniform temperature, be cooled or heated by keeping its boundary at a uniform constant temperature (Sec. 58). Show that the times required for two interior points to reach the same temperature are proportional to the squares of the distances of those points from the boundary plane.

7. Verify that for any constant C, the function

$$v(x, t) = C x t^{-3/2} \exp\left(-\frac{x^2}{4kt} \right)$$

satisfies the heat equation $v_t = k v_{xx}$ when $x > 0$ and $t > 0$. Also, verify that for those values of x and t,

$$v(0+, t) = 0 \quad \text{and} \quad v(x, 0+) = 0.$$

Thus show that $v(x, t)$ can be added to the solution (9) found in Sec. 58 to form other solutions of the problem there if the temperature function is not required to be bounded.
Note that v is unbounded as x and t tend to zero (this can be seen by letting x vanish
while $t = x^2$).

8. Let $u = u(x, y, t)$ denote the bounded solution of the two-dimensional temperature
problem indicated in Fig. 50, where

$$u_t = k(u_{xx} + u_{yy}) \qquad (x > 0, 0 < y < 1, t > 0),$$

and let $v = v(x, t)$ and $w = w(y, t)$ denote the bounded solutions of the following
one-dimensional temperature problems:

$$v_t = kv_{xx}, \qquad v(0, t) = 0, \qquad v(x, 0) = 1 \qquad\qquad (x > 0, t > 0),$$

$$w_t = kw_{yy}, \qquad w(0, t) = w(1, t) = 0, \qquad w(y, 0) = 1 \qquad (0 < y < 1, t > 0).$$

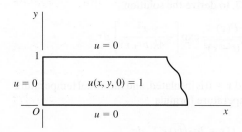

FIGURE 50

(a) With the aid of the result obtained in Problem 3, Sec. 48, show that $u = vw$.

(b) By referring to the solution (15), Sec. 58 of the temperature problem there and to
the temperature function found in Example 1, Sec. 40, write explicit expressions
for v and w. Then use the result in part (a) to show that

$$u(x, y, t) = \frac{4}{\pi} \operatorname{erf}\left(\frac{x}{2\sqrt{kt}}\right) \sum_{n=1}^{\infty} \frac{\sin(2n-1)\pi y}{2n-1} \exp[-(2n-1)^2 \pi^2 kt].$$

9. Use the following method to show that

$$\int_0^{\infty} e^{-\sigma^2}\, d\sigma = \frac{\sqrt{\pi}}{2},$$

as stated in Sec. 58. Do this by denoting the integral by I, writing

$$I^2 = \int_0^{\infty} e^{-x^2}\, dx \int_0^{\infty} e^{-y^2}\, dy = \int_0^{\infty} \int_0^{\infty} e^{-(x^2+y^2)}\, dx\, dy,$$

and then evaluating this iterated integral by switching to polar coordinates.

10. Derive the integration formula (10), Sec. 58, by first writing

$$y(x) = \int_0^{\infty} e^{-\alpha^2 a} \cos \alpha x\, d\alpha \qquad\qquad (a > 0)$$

and differentiating the integral to find $y'(x)$. Then integrate the new integral by parts to show that $2ay'(x) = -xy(x)$, point out why

$$y(0) = \frac{1}{2}\sqrt{\frac{\pi}{a}}$$

(see Problem 9), and solve for $y(x)$. The desired result is the value of y when $x = b.$[†]

59. TEMPERATURES IN AN UNLIMITED MEDIUM

For an application of the general Fourier integral formula in Sec. 50, we now derive expressions for the temperatures $u(x, t)$ in a medium that occupies all space, where the initial temperature distribution is $f(x)$. We assume that $f(x)$ is bounded and, moreover, that it satisfies conditions under which it is represented by its Fourier integral formula. The boundary value problem consists of a boundedness condition $|u(x, t)| < M$ and the conditions

$$(1) \qquad\qquad u_t(x, t) = ku_{xx}(x, t) \qquad\qquad (-\infty < x < \infty, t > 0),$$

$$(2) \qquad\qquad u(x, 0) = f(x) \qquad\qquad (-\infty < x < \infty).$$

Writing $u = X(x)T(t)$ and separating variables, we have the eigenvalue problem

$$X''(x) + \lambda X(x) = 0, \qquad |X(x)| < M_1 \qquad\qquad (-\infty < x < \infty),$$

whose eigenvalues are $\lambda = \alpha^2$ $(\alpha \geq 0)$ and whose eigenfunctions are constant multiples of unity when $\alpha = 0$ and arbitrary linear combinations of $\cos \alpha x$ and $\sin \alpha x$ when $\alpha > 0$ (Problem 8, Sec. 55). The solutions of the differential equation

$$T'(t) + \lambda kT(t) = 0, \qquad |T(t)| < M_2 \qquad\qquad (t > 0)$$

that arise are constant multiples of

$$T(t) = e^{-\alpha^2 kt} \qquad\qquad (\alpha \geq 0).$$

Our generalized linear combination of the products $u = X(x)T(t)$ is then

$$(3) \qquad\qquad u(x, t) = \int_0^\infty e^{-\alpha^2 kt} \left[A(\alpha) \cos \alpha x + B(\alpha) \sin \alpha x\right] d\alpha.$$

The coefficients $A(\alpha)$ and $B(\alpha)$ are to be determined so that the integral here represents $f(x)$ $(-\infty < x < \infty)$ when $t = 0$. According to equations (8) and (9) in Sec. 50 and our Fourier integral theorem (Sec. 53), the representation is valid if

$$A(\alpha) = \frac{1}{\pi} \int_{-\infty}^\infty f(x) \cos \alpha x \, dx, \qquad B(\alpha) = \frac{1}{\pi} \int_{-\infty}^\infty f(x) \sin \alpha x \, dx.$$

[†]Another derivation is indicated in the authors' book (2009, pp. 161–162), listed in the Bibliography.

Thus

(4) $$u(x, t) = \frac{1}{\pi} \int_0^\infty e^{-\alpha^2 kt} \int_{-\infty}^\infty f(s) \cos \alpha (s - x) \, ds \, d\alpha.$$

If we formally reverse the order of integration here, the integration formula (10) in Sec. 58 can be used to write equation (4) as

(5) $$u(x, t) = \frac{1}{2\sqrt{\pi kt}} \int_{-\infty}^\infty f(s) \exp\left[-\frac{(s - x)^2}{4kt}\right] ds \qquad (t > 0).$$

An alternative form of this is

(6) $$u(x, t) = \frac{1}{\sqrt{\pi}} \int_{-\infty}^\infty f(x + 2\sigma \sqrt{kt}) \, e^{-\sigma^2} \, d\sigma.$$

[Compare with expression (12), Sec. 58.]

Forms (5) and (6) can be verified by assuming only that f is piecewise continuous over some bounded interval $|x| < c$ and continuous and bounded over the rest of the x axis, or when $|x| \geq c$. If f is an odd function, $u(x, t)$ becomes the function found in Sec. 58 for positive values of x.

PROBLEMS

1. Let the initial temperature distribution $f(x)$ in the unlimited medium in Sec. 59 be defined by means of the equations

$$f(x) = \begin{cases} 0 & \text{when } x < 0, \\ 1 & \text{when } x > 0. \end{cases}$$

   Show that

$$u(x, t) = \frac{1}{2} + \frac{1}{2} \operatorname{erf}\left(\frac{x}{2\sqrt{kt}}\right).$$

   Verify this solution of the boundary value problem in Sec. 59 when f is this function.

2. Derive this solution of the wave equation $y_{tt} = a^2 y_{xx}$ $(-\infty < x < \infty, t > 0)$, which satisfies the conditions $y(x, 0) = f(x)$ and $y_t(x, 0) = 0$ when $-\infty < x < \infty$:

$$y(x, t) = \frac{1}{\pi} \int_0^\infty \cos \alpha at \int_{-\infty}^\infty f(s) \cos \alpha (s - x) \, ds \, d\alpha.$$

   Also, reduce the solution to the form obtained in Example 1, Sec. 30:

$$y(x, t) = \frac{1}{2} [f(x + at) + f(x - at)].$$

3. Find the bounded harmonic function $u(x, y)$ in the strip $-\infty < x < \infty, 0 < y < b$ such that $u(x, 0) = 0$ and $u(x, b) = f(x)$ $(-\infty < x < \infty)$, where f is bounded and represented by its Fourier integral.

$$\textit{Answer: } u(x, y) = \frac{1}{\pi} \int_0^\infty \frac{\sinh \alpha y}{\sinh \alpha b} \int_{-\infty}^\infty f(s) \cos \alpha (s - x) \, ds \, d\alpha.$$

CHAPTER
7

ORTHONORMAL
SETS

In this chapter, we provide a brief introduction to the theory of so-called orthonormal sets of functions. The chapter will not only clarify underlying concepts behind the several types of Fourier series that we have encountered but will also lay the foundation for finding other series representations that are needed in chapters to follow.

60. INNER PRODUCTS
AND ORTHONORMAL SETS

Let f and g denote any two functions that are continuous on a closed bounded interval $a \leq x \leq b$. Dividing that interval into N closed subintervals of equal length $\Delta x = (b - a)/N$ and letting x_k denote any point in the kth subinterval, we recall from calculus that

$$\int_a^b f(x) g(x) \, dx \doteq \sum_{k=1}^{N} f(x_k) g(x_k) \Delta x$$

when N is large, the symbol $\doteq$ here denoting approximate equality. That is,

$$(1) \qquad \int_a^b f(x) g(x) \, dx \doteq \sum_{k=1}^{N} a_k b_k$$

where

$$a_k = f(x_k) \sqrt{\Delta x} \qquad \text{and} \qquad b_k = g(x_k) \sqrt{\Delta x}.$$

The left-hand side of expression (1) is, then, approximately equal to the inner product of two vectors in N-dimensional space when N is large. The approximation becomes exact in the limit as N tends to infinity.[†] This suggests defining an *inner product* of the functions f and g:

$$(2) \qquad (f, g) = \int_a^b f(x)g(x)\, dx.$$

The integral here is, of course, well defined when f and g are piecewise continuous on the *fundamental interval* $a < x < b$. Equation (2) can, therefore, be used to define an inner product of *any* two functions f and g in the function space $C_p(a, b)$ that was introduced in Sec. 1.

The function space $C_p(a, b)$, with inner product (2), is analogous to ordinary three-dimensional space. Indeed, the following counterparts of familiar properties of vectors in three-dimensional space clearly hold for any functions f, g, and h in $C_p(a, b)$:

$$(3) \qquad (f, g) = (g, f),$$

$$(4) \qquad (f, g + h) = (f, g) + (f, h),$$

$$(5) \qquad (cf, g) = c(f, g),$$

where c is any constant, and

$$(6) \qquad (f, f) \geq 0.$$

The analogy is continued with the introduction of the *norm*

$$(7) \qquad \|f\| = (f, f)^{1/2}$$

of a function f in $C_p(a, b)$. According to equation (2), the norm of f can be written

$$(8) \qquad \|f\| = \left\{ \int_a^b [f(x)]^2\, dx \right\}^{1/2}.$$

The norm of the difference of two functions f and g,

$$(9) \qquad \|f - g\| = \left\{ \int_a^b [f(x) - g(x)]^2\, dx \right\}^{1/2},$$

is a measure of the area of the region between the graphs of $y = f(x)$ and $y = g(x)$ (Fig. 51). To be specific, the quotient

$$\frac{\|f - g\|^2}{b - a} = \frac{1}{b - a} \int_a^b [f(x) - g(x)]^2 dx$$

is the mean, or average, value of the squares of the vertical distances $|f(x) - g(x)|$ between points on those graphs over the interval $a < x < b$. The quantity $\|f - g\|^2$ is called the *mean square deviation* of one of the functions f and g from the other.

Two functions f and g in $C_p(a, b)$ are *orthogonal* if $(f, g) = 0$, or

$$(10) \qquad \int_a^b f(x)g(x)\, dx = 0,$$

[†]See the book by Lanczos (1966, pp. 210ff), listed in the Bibliography, for an elaboration of this idea.

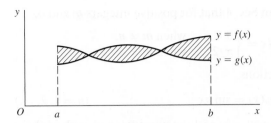

FIGURE 51

where it is understood that neither function is identically equal to zero on the fundamental interval $a < x < b$. We have carried the analogy of $C_p(a, b)$ to three-dimensional space too far to preserve the original meaning of the geometric terminology used here. The orthogonality of two functions f and g signifies nothing about perpendicularity. It says only that the product fg assumes both positive and negative values on the fundamental interval in such a way that equation (10) holds.

Consider now a set of functions

$$\tag{11} \psi_n(x) \qquad\qquad (n = 1, 2, \ldots)$$

in $C_p(a, b)$ that are mutually orthogonal, so that $(\psi_m, \psi_n) = 0$ when $m \neq n$. We say that $\{\psi_n(x)\}$ is an *orthogonal set*; and, assuming that none of the functions $\psi_n(x)$ has zero norm (see Problem 4, Sec. 61), we have the *normalized* functions

$$\tag{12} \phi_n(x) = \frac{\psi_n(x)}{\|\psi_n\|} \qquad\qquad (n = 1, 2, \ldots),$$

whose norms $\|\phi_n\|$ are unity. One can show that $\|\phi_n\| = 1$ for all values of n by writing

$$\tag{13} (\phi_m, \phi_n) = \left(\frac{\psi_m}{\|\psi_m\|}, \frac{\psi_n}{\|\psi_n\|} \right) = \frac{(\psi_m, \psi_n)}{\|\psi_m\|\|\psi_n\|}$$

and nothing from this that

$$\|\phi_n\|^2 = (\phi_n, \phi_n) = \frac{(\psi_n, \psi_n)}{\|\psi_n\|\|\psi_n\|} = \frac{\|\psi_n\|^2}{\|\psi_n\|^2} = 1.$$

Because the set $\{\psi_n(x)\}$ is orthogonal, it follows from equations (13) that $\{\phi_n(x)\}$ is too. The set $\{\phi_n(x)\}$ is, then, *orthonormal* in the sense that it is orthogonal and each function in it has norm unity. Observe that such a set is also characterized by the equations

$$\tag{14} (\phi_m, \phi_n) = \int_a^b \phi_m(x)\phi_n(x)\, dx = \begin{cases} 0 & \text{when } m \neq n, \\ 1 & \text{when } m = n. \end{cases}$$

61. EXAMPLES

We present here three examples of orthonormal sets of functions. These sets are related to the various types of Fourier series introduced in Chap. 1 and will serve to illustrate much of the theory of those series that appears in the present chapter.

EXAMPLE 1. We recall from Sec. 4 that for positive integers m and n,

(1)
$$\int_0^\pi \sin mx \sin nx \, dx = \begin{cases} 0 & \text{when } m \neq n, \\ \pi/2 & \text{when } m = n. \end{cases}$$

Evidently, then, the set of sine functions

$$\psi_n(x) = \sin nx \qquad\qquad (n = 1, 2, \ldots)$$

is orthogonal on the interval of $0 < x < \pi$; and the norm $\|\psi_n\|$ of each of these functions is

$$\|\psi_n\| = \left\{ \int_0^\pi \sin^2 nx \, dx \right\}^{1/2} = \sqrt{\frac{\pi}{2}}.$$

Hence, the corresponding orthonormal set $\{\phi_n(x)\}$ consists of the functions

(2)
$$\phi_n(x) = \sqrt{\frac{2}{\pi}} \sin nx \qquad\qquad (n = 1, 2, \ldots).$$

It is sometimes more convenient to index an infinite orthogonal or orthonormal set by starting with $n = 0$, rather than $n = 1$. This is the case in Examples 2 and 3 below.

EXAMPLE 2. The functions

(3)
$$\phi_0(x) = \frac{1}{\sqrt{\pi}}, \qquad \phi_n(x) = \sqrt{\frac{2}{\pi}} \cos nx \qquad\qquad (n = 1, 2, \ldots)$$

constitute a set $\{\phi_n(x)\}$ $(n = 0, 1, 2, \ldots)$ that is orthonormal on the same interval $0 < x < \pi$ as in Example 1.

To verify this, we start with the observations that

$$(\phi_0, \phi_n) = \frac{\sqrt{2}}{\pi} \int_0^\pi \cos nx \, dx = \frac{\sqrt{2}}{\pi} \left[\frac{\sin nx}{n} \right]_0^\pi = 0 \qquad (n = 1, 2, \ldots)$$

and

$$\|\phi_0\|^2 = (\phi_0, \phi_0) = \frac{1}{\pi} \int_0^\pi dx = 1.$$

Next, we let m and n denote positive integers and recall from Sec. 2 that

(4)
$$\int_0^\pi \cos mx \cos nx \, dx = \begin{cases} 0 & \text{when } m \neq n, \\ \pi/2 & \text{when } m = n. \end{cases}$$

This tells us that for *distinct* positive integers m and n,

$$(\phi_m, \phi_n) = \frac{2}{\pi} \int_0^\pi \cos mx \cos nx \, dx = 0$$

and that

$$\|\phi_n\|^2 = (\phi_n, \phi_n) = \frac{2}{\pi} \int_0^\pi \cos nx \cos nx \, dx = 1 \qquad (n = 1, 2, \ldots).$$

The verification that the set (3) is orthonormal is now complete.

EXAMPLE 3. The set $\{\phi_n(x)\}$ $(n = 0, 1, 2, \ldots)$ consisting of the functions

(5) $\phi_0(x) = \dfrac{1}{\sqrt{2\pi}},$ $\phi_{2n-1}(x) = \dfrac{1}{\sqrt{\pi}} \cos nx,$ $\phi_{2n}(x) = \dfrac{1}{\sqrt{\pi}} \sin nx$

$$(n = 1, 2, \ldots)$$

is orthonormal on the interval $-\pi < x < \pi$.

Steps needed in the verification are as follows. Simple integration reveals that

$$(\phi_0, \phi_{2n-1}) = \frac{1}{\sqrt{2\pi}} \int_{-\pi}^{\pi} \cos nx \, dx = 0 \quad \text{and} \quad (\phi_0, \phi_{2n}) = \frac{1}{\sqrt{2\pi}} \int_{-\pi}^{\pi} \sin nx \, dx = 0$$

$$(n = 1, 2, \ldots)$$

and that

$$\|\phi_0\|^2 = \frac{1}{2\pi} \int_{-\pi}^{\pi} dx = 1.$$

The remaining steps depend on integration formulas (1) and (4), together with the observations that

$$\int_{-\pi}^{\pi} f(x) \, dx = 2 \int_{0}^{\pi} f(x) \, dx$$

when a given continuous function f is even and

$$\int_{-\pi}^{\pi} f(x) \, dx = 0$$

when it is odd.

To be specific, for *distinct* positive integers m and n,

$$(\phi_{2m-1}, \phi_{2n-1}) = \frac{1}{\pi} \int_{-\pi}^{\pi} \cos mx \cos nx \, dx = \frac{2}{\pi} \int_{0}^{\pi} \cos mx \cos nx \, dx = 0$$

and

$$(\phi_{2m}, \phi_{2n}) = \frac{1}{\pi} \int_{-\pi}^{\pi} \sin mx \sin nx \, dx = \frac{2}{\pi} \int_{0}^{\pi} \sin mx \sin nx \, dx = 0.$$

Also, for *any* positive integers m and n,

$$(\phi_{2m-1}, \phi_{2n}) = \frac{1}{\pi} \int_{-\pi}^{\pi} \cos mx \sin nx \, dx = 0.$$

Finally, we know from equations (4) and (1) that when $n = 1, 2, \ldots,$

$$\|\phi_{2n-1}\|^2 = \frac{1}{\pi} \int_{-\pi}^{\pi} \cos^2 nx \, dx = \frac{2}{\pi} \int_{0}^{\pi} \cos^2 nx \, dx = 1$$

and

$$\|\phi_{2n}\|^2 = \frac{1}{\pi} \int_{-\pi}^{\pi} \sin^2 nx \, dx = \frac{2}{\pi} \int_{0}^{\pi} \sin^2 nx \, dx = 1.$$

PROBLEMS

1. Show that the functions $\psi_1(x) = 1$ and $\psi_2(x) = x$ are orthogonal on the interval $-1 < x < 1$, and determine constants A and B such that the function

$$\psi_3(x) = 1 + Ax + Bx^2$$

is orthogonal to both ψ_1 and ψ_2 on that interval.
   Answer: $A = 0$, $B = -3$.

2. Suppose that two continuous functions $f(x)$ and $\psi_1(x)$, with positive norms, are linearly independent on an interval $a \leq x \leq b$; that is, one is not a constant times the other. By determining the linear combination $f + A\psi_1$ of those functions that is orthogonal to ψ_1 on the fundamental interval $a < x < b$, obtain an orthogonal pair ψ_1, ψ_2 where

$$\psi_2(x) = f(x) - \frac{(f, \psi_1)}{\|\psi_1\|^2} \psi_1(x).$$

Interpret this expression geometrically when f, ψ_1, and ψ_2 represent vectors in three-dimensional space.

3. In Problem 2, suppose that the fundamental interval is $-\pi < x < \pi$ and that

$$f(x) = \cos nx + \sin nx \quad \text{and} \quad \psi_1(x) = \cos nx,$$

where n is a fixed positive integer. Show that the function $\psi_2(x)$ there turns out to be

$$\psi_2(x) = \sin nx.$$

   Suggestion: One can avoid evaluating any integrals by using the fact that the set in Example 3, Sec. 61, is orthogonal on the interval $-\pi < x < \pi$.

4. Verify the following two statements, regarding functions f in the space $C_p(a, b)$:
   (a) if $f(x) = 0$, except possibly at a finite number of points, in the interval $a < x < b$, then $\|f\| = 0$;
   (b) conversely, if $\|f\| = 0$, then $f(x) = 0$, except possibly at a finite number of points, in the interval $a < x < b$.

   Suggestion: In part (b), use the fact that a definite integral of a nonnegative continuous function over a bounded interval has positive value if the function has a positive value somewhere in that interval.

5. Verify that for any two functions f and g in the space $C_p(a, b)$,

$$\frac{1}{2} \int_a^b \int_a^b [f(x)g(y) - g(x)f(y)]^2 \, dx \, dy = \|f\|^2 \|g\|^2 - (f, g)^2.$$

Thus, establish the *Schwarz inequality*

$$|(f, g)| \leq \|f\| \|g\|,$$

which is also valid when f and g denote vectors in three-dimensional space. In that case, it is known as Cauchy's inequality.

6. Let f and g denote any two functions in the space $C_p(a, b)$. Use the Schwarz inequality (Problem 5) to show that if either function has zero norm, then $(f, g) = 0$.

7. Prove that if f and g are functions in the space $C_p(a, b)$, then

$$\|f + g\| \leq \|f\| + \|g\|.$$

If f and g denote, instead, vectors in three-dimensional space, this is the familiar triangle inequality, which states that the length of one side of a triangle is less than or equal to the sum of the lengths of the other two sides.

Suggestion: Start the proof by showing that

$$\|f + g\|^2 = \|f\|^2 + 2(f, g) + \|g\|^2,$$

and then use the Schwarz inequality (Problem 5).

62. GENERALIZED FOURIER SERIES

Let f be any given function in $C_p(a, b)$, the space of piecewise continuous functions defined on the interval $a < x < b$. When an orthonormal set of functions $\phi_n(x)$ ($n = 1, 2, \ldots$) in $C_p(a, b)$ is specified, it *may* be possible to represent $f(x)$ by a linear combination of those functions, generalized to an infinite series that converges to $f(x)$ at all but possibly a finite number of points in the interval $a < x < b$:

$$(1) \qquad\qquad f(x) = \sum_{n=1}^{\infty} c_n \phi_n(x) \qquad\qquad (a < x < b).$$

This is analogous to the expression for any vector in three-dimensional space in terms of three mutually orthogonal vectors of unit length, such as $\mathbf{i}, \mathbf{j}$, and $\mathbf{k}$.

In order to discover an expression for the coefficients c_n in representation (1), if such a representation actually exists, we use the index of summation m, rather than n, to write

$$(2) \qquad\qquad f(x) = \sum_{m=1}^{\infty} c_m \phi_m(x) \qquad\qquad (a < x < b).$$

We also assume that after each of the terms here is multiplied by a specific $\phi_n(x)$, the resulting series is integrable term by term over the interval $a < x < b$. This enables us to write

$$\int_a^b f(x) \phi_n(x)\, dx = \sum_{m=1}^{\infty} c_m \int_a^b \phi_m(x) \phi_n(x)\, dx,$$

or

$$(3) \qquad\qquad (f, \phi_n) = \sum_{m=1}^{\infty} c_m (\phi_m, \phi_n).$$

But $(\phi_m, \phi_n) = 0$ for all values of m here except when $m = n$, in which case $(\phi_m, \phi_n) = \|\phi_n\|^2 = 1$. Hence equation (3) becomes $(f, \phi_n) = c_n$, and c_n is evidently the inner product of f and ϕ_n.

As indicated above, one cannot be certain that representation (1), with coefficients $c_n = (f, \phi_n)$, is actually valid for a specific f and a given orthonormal set $\{\phi_n\}$. Hence, we write

$$(4) \qquad\qquad f(x) \sim \sum_{n=1}^{\infty} c_n \phi_n(x) \qquad\qquad (a < x < b),$$

where the tilde symbol $\sim$ merely denotes correspondence when

$$(5) \qquad\qquad c_n = (f, \phi_n) = \int_a^b f(x) \phi_n(x)\, dx \qquad\qquad (n = 1, 2, \ldots).$$

To strengthen the analogy with vectors, we recall that if a vector $\mathbf{A}$ in three-dimensional space is to be written in terms of the orthonormal set $\{\mathbf{i}, \mathbf{j}, \mathbf{k}\}$ as

$$\mathbf{A} = a_1\mathbf{i} + a_2\mathbf{j} + a_3\mathbf{k},$$

the components can be obtained by taking the inner product of $\mathbf{A}$ with each of the vectors of that set. That is, the inner product of $\mathbf{A}$ with $\mathbf{i}$ is a_1, etc.

The series in correspondence (4) is the *generalized Fourier series*, with respect to the orthonormal set $\{\phi_n\}$, for the function f on the interval $a < x < b$. The coefficients c_n are known as *Fourier constants*.

The generalized Fourier series that we shall encounter will always involve orthonormal sets and functions f in a space of the type $C_p(a, b)$, or subspaces of it; and we say that representation (1) is *valid* for functions f in a given space if equality holds everywhere except possibly at a finite number of points in the fundamental interval $a < x < b$.

Representation (1) will not, however, always be valid even in some very restricted function spaces. We may anticipate this limitation in the following way. If just the two vectors $\mathbf{i}$ and $\mathbf{j}$ make up an orthonormal set in three-dimensional space, any vector $\mathbf{A}$ that is not parallel to the xy plane fails to have a representation of the form $\mathbf{A} = a_1\mathbf{i} + a_2\mathbf{j}$. In particular, the nonzero vector $\mathbf{A} = \mathbf{k}$ is orthogonal to both $\mathbf{i}$ and $\mathbf{j}$, in which case the components $a_1 = \mathbf{k} \cdot \mathbf{i}$ and $a_2 = \mathbf{k} \cdot \mathbf{j}$ would both be zero. Similarly, an orthonormal set $\{\phi_n(x)\}$ may not be large enough to write a generalized Fourier series representation. To be specific, if the function $f(x)$ in correspondence (4) is orthogonal to each function in the orthonormal set $\{\phi_n(x)\}$, we find that the Fourier constants $c_n = (f, \phi_n)$ are all zero. This means, of course, that the sum of the series is the zero function, whose norm is zero. Consequently, if f has a positive norm, the series is not a valid representation on the fundamental interval.

An orthonormal set $\{\phi_n(x)\}$ is *closed* in $C_p(a, b)$, or a subspace of it, if there is no function f in the space, with positive norm, that is orthogonal to each of the functions $\phi_n(x)$. Thus, according to the preceding paragraph, the following two statements, which are equivalent, are true:

(*i*) if an orthonormal set $\{\phi_n(x)\}$ is not closed in $C_p(a, b)$, or a subspace of it, then representation (1) cannot be valid for every function f in that space or subspace;

(*ii*) if representation (1), with respect to a given orthonormal set $\{\phi_n(x)\}$, is valid for every function f in $C_p(a, b)$, or a subspace of it, then the set must be closed in that space or subspace.

63.   EXAMPLES

This section is devoted to familiar examples of generalized Fourier series, namely Fourier sine and cosine series on the fundamental interval $0 < x < \pi$ and Fourier series involving both sines and cosines on $-\pi < x < \pi$. These special cases of series (4), Sec. 62, will be based on the examples in Sec. 61.

EXAMPLE 1. We saw in Example 1, Sec. 61, that the sine functions

$$\phi_n(x) = \sqrt{\frac{2}{\pi}} \sin nx \qquad (n = 1, 2, \ldots) \tag{1}$$

constitute an orthonormal set on the interval $0 < x < \pi$. The generalized Fourier series correspondence (4), Sec. 62, for a function $f(x)$ in $C_p(0, \pi)$ is then

$$f(x) \sim \sum_{n=1}^{\infty} c_n \sqrt{\frac{2}{\pi}} \sin nx \qquad (0 < x < \pi),$$

where

$$c_n = (f, \phi_n) = \sqrt{\frac{2}{\pi}} \int_0^\pi f(x) \sin nx \, dx \qquad (n = 1, 2, \ldots).$$

Upon writing

$$b_n = c_n \sqrt{\frac{2}{\pi}} \qquad (n = 1, 2, \ldots),$$

we have the Fourier sine series correspondence (Sec. 4)

$$f(x) \sim \sum_{n=1}^{\infty} b_n \sin nx \qquad (0 < x < \pi), \tag{2}$$

where

$$b_n = \frac{2}{\pi} \int_0^\pi f(x) \sin nx \, dx \qquad (n = 1, 2, \ldots). \tag{3}$$

EXAMPLE 2. Let f be any function in $C_p(0, \pi)$. We know from Example 2 in Sec. 61 that the set $\{\phi_n(x)\}$ $(n = 0, 1, 2, \ldots)$ consisting of the functions

$$\phi_0(x) = \frac{1}{\sqrt{\pi}}, \qquad \phi_n(x) = \sqrt{\frac{2}{\pi}} \cos nx \qquad (n = 1, 2, \ldots) \tag{4}$$

is orthonormal on the interval $0 < x < \pi$. The correspondence

$$f(x) \sim \sum_{n=0}^{\infty} c_n \phi_n(x) \qquad (0 < x < \pi), \tag{5}$$

which is correspondence (4), Sec. 62, with the summation starting from $n = 0$, becomes

$$f(x) \sim \frac{c_0}{\sqrt{\pi}} + \sum_{n=1}^{\infty} c_n \sqrt{\frac{2}{\pi}} \cos nx \qquad (0 < x < \pi).$$

Moreover,

$$c_0 = (f, \phi_0) = \frac{1}{\sqrt{\pi}} \int_0^\pi f(x) \, dx, \qquad c_n = (f, \phi_n) = \sqrt{\frac{2}{\pi}} \int_0^\pi f(x) \cos nx \, dx$$
$$(n = 1, 2, \ldots).$$

By writing

$$a_0 = 2\frac{c_0}{\sqrt{\pi}}, \qquad a_n = c_n \sqrt{\frac{2}{\pi}} \qquad (n = 1, 2, \ldots),$$

we thus arrive at the Fourier cosine series correspondence (Sec. 2)

$$(6) \qquad\qquad f(x) \sim \frac{a_0}{2} + \sum_{n=1}^{\infty} a_n \cos nx \qquad\qquad (0 < x < \pi),$$

where

$$(7) \qquad\qquad a_n = \frac{2}{\pi} \int_0^{\pi} f(x) \cos nx \, dx \qquad\qquad (n = 0, 1, 2, \ldots).$$

We know from the discussion of the convergence of Fourier cosine and sine series just after Example 1 in Sec. 14 and also from Theorem 2 in Sec. 15 that correspondence (6) yields a valid representation for each function f in the subspace $C_p'(0, \pi)$ of $C_p(0, \pi)$ consisting of all piecewise smooth functions defined on $0 < x < \pi$. It follows, then, from statement (*ii*) at the end of Sec. 62 that the set (4) is closed in $C_p'(0, \pi)$.

But if the function $\phi_0(x)$, for instance, is not included with the rest of the functions (4), the resulting set

$$(8) \qquad\qquad \phi_n(x) = \sqrt{\frac{2}{\pi}} \cos nx \qquad\qquad (n = 1, 2, \ldots)$$

is not closed because $\phi_0(x)$ is orthogonal to each of the functions in that smaller set. Statement (*i*) near the end of Sec. 62 thus tells us that the functions $\phi_0(x)$ is needed in series (5) in order to provide valid representations for *all* functions f in $C_p'(0, \pi)$. Hence a_0 must, in general, be included in the Fourier cosine series (6).

EXAMPLE 3. In Example 3, Sec. 61, we saw that the functions

$$(9) \qquad \phi_0(x) = \frac{1}{\sqrt{2\pi}}, \qquad \phi_{2n-1}(x) = \frac{1}{\sqrt{\pi}} \cos nx, \qquad \phi_{2n}(x) = \frac{1}{\sqrt{\pi}} \sin nx$$
$$(n = 1, 2, \ldots)$$

form an orthonormal set on the fundamental interval $-\pi < x < \pi$. The generalized Fourier series corresponding to a function $f(x)$ in $C_p(-\pi, \pi)$ is, therefore,

$$\sum_{n=0}^{\infty} c_n \phi_n(x) = c_0 \phi_0(x) + \sum_{n=1}^{\infty} [c_{2n-1} \phi_{2n-1}(x) + c_{2n} \phi_{2n}(x)].$$

That is,

$$(10) \qquad f(x) \sim \frac{c_0}{\sqrt{2\pi}} + \sum_{n=1}^{\infty} \left(\frac{c_{2n-1}}{\sqrt{\pi}} \cos nx + \frac{c_{2n}}{\sqrt{\pi}} \sin nx \right) \qquad (-\pi < x < \pi)$$

where

$$c_0 = (f, \phi_0) = \frac{1}{\sqrt{2\pi}} \int_{-\pi}^{\pi} f(x) \, dx$$

and

$$c_{2n-1} = (f, \phi_{2n-1}) = \frac{1}{\sqrt{\pi}} \int_{-\pi}^{\pi} f(x) \cos nx \, dx \qquad (n = 1, 2, \ldots),$$

$$c_{2n} = (f, \phi_{2n}) = \frac{1}{\sqrt{\pi}} \int_{-\pi}^{\pi} f(x) \sin nx \, dx \qquad (n = 1, 2, \ldots).$$

So if we write

$$a_0 = 2\frac{c_0}{\sqrt{2\pi}}, \qquad a_n = \frac{c_{2n-1}}{\sqrt{\pi}}, \qquad b_n = \frac{c_{2n}}{\sqrt{\pi}} \qquad (n = 1, 2, \ldots),$$

correspondence (10) becomes (see Sec. 6)

$$(11) \qquad\qquad f(x) \sim \frac{a_0}{2} + \sum_{n=1}^{\infty}(a_n \cos nx + b_n \sin nx) \qquad (-\pi < x < \pi),$$

where

$$(12) \qquad\qquad a_n = \frac{1}{\pi}\int_{-\pi}^{\pi} f(x)\cos nx\, dx \qquad\qquad (n = 0, 1, 2, \ldots)$$

and

$$(13) \qquad\qquad b_n = \frac{1}{\pi}\int_{-\pi}^{\pi} f(x)\sin nx\, dx \qquad\qquad (n = 1, 2, \ldots).$$

PROBLEMS

1. Let $\{\psi_n(x)\}$ $(n = 1, 2, \ldots)$ denote an orthogonal, but not necessarily orthonormal, set on a fundamental interval $a < x < b$. Show that the correspondence between a piecewise continuous function $f(x)$ and its generalized Fourier series with respect to the *orthonormal* set

$$\phi_n(x) = \frac{\psi_n(x)}{\|\psi_n\|} \qquad\qquad (n = 1, 2, \ldots)$$

can be written

$$f(x) \sim \sum_{n=1}^{\infty} \gamma_n \psi_n(x) \qquad \text{where} \qquad \gamma_n = \frac{(f, \psi_n)}{\|\psi_n\|^2}.$$

2. State why the orthonormal set (8) in Example 2, Sec. 63, is closed in the space of all functions f that are piecewise smooth on the interval $0 < x < \pi$ and satisfy the condition

$$\int_0^{\pi} f(x)\, dx = 0.$$

   Suggestion: Refer to statement (*ii*) at the end of Sec. 62.

3. In the space of *continuous* functions on the interval $a \leq x \leq b$, prove that if two functions f and g have the same Fourier constants with respect to a *closed* (Sec. 62) orthonormal set $\{\phi_n(x)\}$, then f and g must be identical. Thus show that f is uniquely determined by its Fourier constants.

   Suggestion: Note that $(f - g, \phi_n) = 0$ for all values of n when

$$(f, \phi_n) = (g, \phi_n)$$

   for all n. Then use the definition of a closed orthonormal set to show that $\|f - g\| = 0$. Finally, refer to the suggestion with Problem 4, Sec. 61.

4. Let $\{\phi_n(x)\}$ be an orthonormal set in the space of *continuous* functions on the interval $a \leq x \leq b$, and suppose that the generalized Fourier series for a function $f(x)$ in that space converges *uniformly* (Sec. 17) to a sum $s(x)$ on that interval.

(a) Show that $s(x)$ and $f(x)$ have the same Fourier constants with respect to $\{\phi_n(x)\}$.

(b) Use results in part (a) and Problem 3 to show that if $\{\phi_n(x)\}$ is *closed* (Sec. 62), then $s(x) = f(x)$ on the interval $a \leq x \leq b$.

Suggestion: Recall from Sec. 17 that the sum of a uniformly convergent series of continuous functions is continuous and that such a series can be integrated term by term.

64.   BEST APPROXIMATION IN THE MEAN

Since the material in this and the next two sections is not essential for subsequent chapters, the reader may at this time pass directly to Chap. 8 without loss of continuity.

Let f be a function in $C_p(a, b)$ and $\{\phi_n(x)\}$ $(n = 1, 2, \ldots)$ an orthonormal set in that space. We consider here the first N functions $\phi_1(x), \phi_2(x), \ldots, \phi_N(x)$ of the orthonormal set and let $\Phi_N(x)$ denote *any* linear combination of them:

$$(1) \qquad \Phi_N(x) = \gamma_1\,\phi_1(x) + \gamma_2\,\phi_2(x) + \cdots + \gamma_N\,\phi_N(x).$$

The norm

$$\| f - \Phi_N \| = \left\{ \int_a^b [f(x) - \Phi_N(x)]^2 \, dx \right\}^{1/2}$$

is a measure of the deviation of the sum Φ_N from a given function f in $C_p(a, b)$ (see Sec. 60). Let us determine values of the constants γ_n $(n = 1, 2, \ldots, N)$ in expression (1) that make $\| f - \Phi_N \|$, or the quantity

$$(2) \qquad E = \| f - \Phi_N \|^2 = \int_a^b [f(x) - \Phi_N(x)]^2 \, dx,$$

as small as possible. The nonnegative number E represents the *mean square error* in the approximation by the function Φ_N to the function f, and we seek the *best approximation in the mean*.[†]

We start with the observation that

$$(f - \Phi_N)^2 = \left(f - \sum_{n=1}^{N} \gamma_n\phi_n \right)^2 = f^2 - 2f\sum_{n=1}^{N} \gamma_n\phi_n + \left(\sum_{n=1}^{N} \gamma_n\phi_n \right)^2.$$

But

$$\left(\sum_{n=1}^{N} \gamma_n\phi_n \right)^2 = \left(\sum_{m=1}^{N} \gamma_m\phi_m \right) \left(\sum_{n=1}^{N} \gamma_n\phi_n \right)$$

$$= \sum_{n=1}^{N} \left(\sum_{m=1}^{N} \gamma_m\phi_m \right) \gamma_n\phi_n$$

$$= \sum_{n=1}^{N} \left(\sum_{m=1}^{N} \gamma_m\gamma_n\phi_m\phi_n \right),$$

[†]The approximation sought here is also called a *least squares approximation*.

and this enables us to write

$$(f - \Phi_N)^2 = f^2 + \sum_{n=1}^{N} \left[\left(\sum_{m=1}^{N} \gamma_m \gamma_n \phi_m \phi_n \right) - 2\gamma_n f \phi_n \right].$$

Integrating each side here over the interval $a < x < b$ and then using the relations

$$\int_a^b \phi_m(x) \, \phi_n(x) \, dx = \begin{cases} 0 & \text{when } m \neq n, \\ 1 & \text{when } m = n \end{cases}$$

and

$$\int_a^b f(x) \, \phi_n(x) \, dx = c_n,$$

where c_n are Fourier constants (Sec. 62), we arrive at the following expression for the error E, defined by equations (2):

$$E = \| f \|^2 + \sum_{n=1}^{N} \left(\gamma_n^2 - 2\gamma_n c_n \right).$$

If we complete the squares in the terms being summed here and write

$$\gamma_n^2 - 2\gamma_n c_n = \left(\gamma_n^2 - 2c_n \gamma_n + c_n^2 \right) - c_n^2 = (\gamma_n - c_n)^2 - c_n^2,$$

this expression for E takes the form

(3) $$E = \| f \|^2 + \sum_{n=1}^{N} (\gamma_n - c_n)^2 - \sum_{n=1}^{N} c_n^2.$$

In view of the squares in the first summation appearing in equation (3), the smallest possible value of E is, then, obtained when $\gamma_n = c_n$ $(n = 1, 2, \ldots, N)$, that value being

(4) $$E = \| f \|^2 - \sum_{n=1}^{N} c_n^2.$$

We state the result as a theorem.

Theorem. *Let c_n $(n = 1, 2, \ldots)$ be the Fourier constants for a function f in $C_p(a, b)$ with respect to an orthonormal set $\{\phi_n(x)\}$ $(n = 1, 2, \ldots)$ in that space. Then, of all possible linear combinations of the functions $\phi_1(x), \phi_2(x), \ldots, \phi_N(x)$, the combination*

$$c_1 \phi_1(x) + c_2 \phi_2(x) + \cdots + c_N \phi_N(x)$$

is the best approximation in the mean to $f(x)$ on the fundamental interval $a < x < b$. In that case, the mean square error E is given by equation (4).

This theorem is analogous to, and even suggested by, a corresponding result in three-dimensional space. Namely, suppose that we wish to approximate a vector $\mathbf{A} = a_1 \mathbf{i} + a_2 \mathbf{j} + a_3 \mathbf{k}$ by a linear combination of just the two basis vectors $\mathbf{i}$ and $\mathbf{j}$. If we interpret $\mathbf{A}$ and any linear combination $\gamma_1 \mathbf{i} + \gamma_2 \mathbf{j}$ as radius vectors, it is geometrically evident that the shortest distance d between their tips occurs when $\gamma_1 \mathbf{i} + \gamma_2 \mathbf{j}$ is the vector projection of $\mathbf{A}$ onto the plane of $\mathbf{i}$ and $\mathbf{j}$. That projection is, of course, the vector $a_1 \mathbf{i} + a_2 \mathbf{j}$ (see Fig. 52), the components a_1 and a_2 being the inner products of $\mathbf{A}$ with $\mathbf{i}$ and $\mathbf{j}$, respectively.

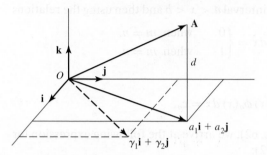

FIGURE 52

EXAMPLE. We recall from Example 3, Sec. 63, that when the orthonormal set of functions

$$\phi_0(x) = \frac{1}{\sqrt{2\pi}}, \qquad \phi_{2n-1}(x) = \frac{1}{\sqrt{\pi}} \cos nx, \qquad \phi_{2n}(x) = \frac{1}{\sqrt{\pi}} \sin nx$$

$$(n = 1, 2, \ldots)$$

in $C_p(-\pi, \pi)$ is used, the generalized Fourier series

$$(5) \quad \sum_{n=0}^{\infty} c_n \phi_n(x) = c_0 \phi_0(x) + \sum_{n=1}^{\infty} [c_{2n-1} \phi_{2n-1}(x) + c_{2n} \phi_{2n}(x)] \quad (-\pi < x < \pi)$$

corresponding to a function f in $C_p(-\pi, \pi)$ is the ordinary Fourier series

$$(6) \qquad \frac{a_0}{2} + \sum_{n=1}^{\infty} (a_n \cos nx + b_n \sin nx) \qquad (-\pi < x < \pi),$$

where

$$a_0 = 2\frac{c_0}{\sqrt{2\pi}}, \qquad a_n = \frac{c_{2n-1}}{\sqrt{\pi}}, \qquad b_n = \frac{c_{2n}}{\sqrt{\pi}} \qquad (n = 1, 2, \ldots).$$

The above theorem now tells us that of all possible linear combinations of the functions $\phi_n(x)$ $(n = 0, 1, 2, \ldots, 2N)$, the partial sum

$$\sum_{n=0}^{2N} c_n \phi_n(x) = c_0 \phi_0(x) + \sum_{n=1}^{N} [c_{2n-1} \phi_{2n-1}(x) + c_{2n} \phi_{2n}(x)]$$

of series (5) is the best approximation in the mean to f on the interval $-\pi < x < \pi$. That is, the partial sum

$$(7) \qquad S_N(x) = \frac{a_0}{2} + \sum_{n=1}^{N} (a_n \cos nx + b_n \sin nx) \qquad (-\pi < x < \pi)$$

of series (6) is the best approximation of all linear combinations of the $2N + 1$ functions 1, and $\cos nx$, $\sin nx$ $(n = 1, 2, \ldots, N)$.

65. BESSEL'S INEQUALITY AND PARSEVAL'S EQUATION

Because the mean square error E, defined by equations (2) in Sec. 64, is non-negative, we know from expression (4) there that

$$\|f\|^2 - \sum_{n=1}^{N} c_n^2 \geq 0 \qquad\qquad (N = 1, 2, \ldots),$$

or

$$(1) \qquad\qquad \sum_{n=1}^{N} c_n^2 \leq \|f\|^2 \qquad\qquad (N = 1, 2, \ldots).$$

This is *Bessel's inequality* for the Fourier constants c_n. The following important theorem is an immediate consequence of it.

    Theorem 1. *If c_n ($n = 1, 2, \ldots$) are the Fourier constants for a function f in $C_p(a, b)$ with respect to an orthonormal set in that space, then*

$$(2) \qquad\qquad \lim_{n\to\infty} c_n = 0.$$

    Our proof of this theorem is similar to an argument in Sec. 10, based on a special case of inequality (1) (see Problem 3, Sec. 66), showing that the coefficients a_n in a Fourier cosine series on $0 < x < \pi$ tend to zero as n tends to infinity. We start here with the fact that since $\|f\|^2$ is independent of N, the sums of the squares c_n^2 on the left-hand side of inequality (1) form a sequence that is bounded and nondecreasing as N increases. Such a sequence must converge; and since it is the sequence of partial sums of the series whose terms are c_n^2 ($n = 1, 2, \ldots$), that series must converge. Finally, because the nth term of a convergent series tends to zero as n tends to infinity, limit (2) is established.

    We turn now to a modification of inequality (1) in which the inequality is actually an equality. A sequence of functions $s_N(x)$ ($N = 1, 2, \ldots$) in $C_p(a, b)$ is said to *converge in the mean* to a function $f(x)$ in $C_p(a, b)$ if the mean square error (Sec. 64)

$$(3) \qquad\qquad E = \|f - s_N\|^2 = \int_a^b [f(x) - s_N(x)]^2 \, dx$$

in the approximation by s_N to f tends to zero as N tends to infinity. That is, convergence in the mean occurs when

$$(4) \qquad\qquad \lim_{N\to\infty} \|f - s_N\| = 0.$$

Sometimes condition (4) is also written

$$(5) \qquad\qquad \underset{N\to\infty}{\text{l.i.m.}}\, s_N(x) = f(x),$$

where the abbreviation "l.i.m." stands for *limit in the mean*.

    It should be emphasized that statement (5) is *not* the same as the statement

$$(6) \qquad\qquad \lim_{N\to\infty} s_N(x) = f(x) \qquad\qquad (a < x < b),$$

even if a finite number of points in the interval are ignored.[†] In fact, neither of the statements (5) and (6) implies the other, as the following example and Problem 5, Sec. 66 will show.

EXAMPLE. Consider the sequence of functions $s_N(x)$ ($N = 1, 2, \ldots$) in $C_p(0, 1)$ that are defined by means of the equations (see Fig. 53)

$$
s_N(x) = \begin{cases} 0 & \text{when } 0 \le x \le \dfrac{1}{N}, \\[2mm] \sqrt{N} & \text{when } \dfrac{1}{N} < x < \dfrac{2}{N}, \\[2mm] 0 & \text{when } \dfrac{2}{N} \le x \le 1. \end{cases}
$$

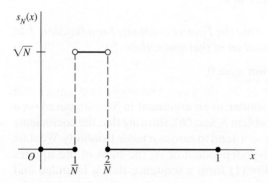

FIGURE 53

It evidently converges to zero at each point x in the interval $0 \le x \le 1$ since $s_N(0) = 0$ for all N and since $s_N(x) = 0$ when $0 < x \le 1$ and N is so large that $2/N < x$. Hence, the sequence $s_N(x)$ ($N = 1, 2, \ldots$) converges pointwise to the function $f(x) = 0$ ($0 \le x \le 1$). It does not, however, converge in the mean to that function. This is seen by writing

$$
\| f - s_N \|^2 = \int_0^1 [s_N(x)]^2 \, dx = \int_{1/N}^{2/N} N \, dx = 1
$$

and referring to definition (4) in Sec. 65 of convergence in the mean.

Let $s_N(x)$ denote the partial sums of a generalized Fourier series (Sec. 62) corresponding to some function f on a fundamental interval $a < x < b$:

$$
(7) \qquad\qquad s_N(x) = \sum_{n=1}^{N} c_n \, \phi_n(x).
$$

[†]An example of a sequence of functions that converges in the mean to zero but *diverges at each point* of the interval is given in the book by Franklin (1964, p. 408), listed in the Bibliography.

This is the linear combination $\Phi_N(x)$ in Sec. 64, when $\gamma_n = c_n$ there. If condition (4) is satisfied by each function f in our function space $C_p(a, b)$, or possibly a subspace containing the orthonormal set $\{\phi_n(x)\}$, we say that $\{\phi_n(x)\}$ is *complete* in that space or subspace.[†] Thus each function $f(x)$ can be approximated arbitrarily closely in the mean by some linear combination of the functions $\phi_n(x)$ of a complete set, namely the linear combination (7) when N is large enough.

According to equation (4), Sec. 64, the mean square error in the approximation by $s_N(x)$ to $f(x)$ is

$$(8) \qquad \| f - s_N \|^2 = \| f \|^2 - \sum_{n=1}^{N} c_n^2.$$

Hence, when $\{\phi_n(x)\}$ is complete, it is always true that

$$(9) \qquad \sum_{n=1}^{\infty} c_n^2 = \| f \|^2.$$

Equation (9) is known as *Parseval's equation*. It identifies the sum of the squares of the Fourier constants for f, with respect to the orthonormal set $\{\phi_n(x)\}$, as the square of the norm of f.

Conversely, if each function f in the space satisfies Parseval's equation, the set $\{\phi_n(x)\}$ is complete in the sense of mean convergence. This is because, in view of equation (8), limit (4) is merely a restatement of equation (9). We now have a theorem that provides an alternative characterization of complete sets.

Theorem 2. *A necessary and sufficient condition for an orthonormal set* $\{\phi_n(x)\}$ $(n = 1, 2, \ldots)$ *to be complete is that for each function f in the space considered, Parseval's equation*

$$(10) \qquad \sum_{n=1}^{\infty} c_n^2 = \| f \|^2,$$

where c_n are the Fourier constants $c_n = (f, \phi_n)$, is satisfied.

Each of the theorems in this section will be illustrated in Sec. 66, with applications to ordinary Fourier series.

66. APPLICATIONS TO FOURIER SERIES

In Example 3, Sec. 61, we saw that the functions

$$(1) \qquad \phi_0(x) = \frac{1}{\sqrt{2\pi}}, \qquad \phi_{2n-1}(x) = \frac{1}{\sqrt{\pi}} \cos nx, \qquad \phi_{2n}(x) = \frac{1}{\sqrt{\pi}} \sin nx$$

$$(n = 1, 2, \ldots)$$

[†]In the mathematical literature, including some earlier editions of this text, the terms *complete* and *closed* are sometimes applied to sets that we have called *closed* (Sec. 62) and *complete,* respectively.

form an orthonormal set on the fundamental interval $-\pi < x < \pi$. The Fourier constants c_n ($n = 0, 1, 2, \ldots$) in the generalized Fourier series for a function f in $C_p(-\pi, \pi)$ with respect to this set were then used in Example 3, Sec. 63, to define the constants

(2) $\qquad a_0 = 2\dfrac{c_0}{\sqrt{2\pi}}, \qquad a_n = \dfrac{c_{2n-1}}{\sqrt{\pi}}, \qquad b_n = \dfrac{c_{2n}}{\sqrt{\pi}} \qquad\qquad (n = 1, 2, \ldots).$

That gave rise to the Fourier series correspondence

(3) $\qquad f(x) \sim \dfrac{a_0}{2} + \displaystyle\sum_{n=1}^{\infty}(a_n \cos nx + b_n \sin nx) \qquad\qquad (-\pi < x < \pi),$

where

(4) $\qquad a_n = \dfrac{1}{\pi}\displaystyle\int_{-\pi}^{\pi} f(x)\cos nx\,dx \qquad\qquad (n = 0, 1, 2, \ldots)$

and

(5) $\qquad b_n = \dfrac{1}{\pi}\displaystyle\int_{-\pi}^{\pi} f(x)\sin nx\,dx \qquad\qquad (n = 1, 2, \ldots).$

Bessel's inequality (1), Sec. 65, involving $2N+1$ terms in the sum there, is

$$c_0^2 + \sum_{n=1}^{N}\left(c_{2n-1}^2 + c_{2n}^2\right) \le \|f\|^2 \qquad\qquad (N = 1, 2, \ldots);$$

and, in view of relations (2), this is the same as (compare with Problem 4, Sec. 11)

(6) $\qquad \dfrac{a_0^2}{2} + \displaystyle\sum_{n=1}^{N}\left(a_n^2 + b_n^2\right) \le \dfrac{1}{\pi}\int_{-\pi}^{\pi}[f(x)]^2\,dx \qquad\qquad (N = 1, 2, \ldots).$

Theorem 1 in Sec. 65 tells us, moreover, that

(7) $\qquad\qquad \displaystyle\lim_{n\to\infty} a_n = 0 \quad \text{and} \quad \lim_{n\to\infty} b_n = 0.$

Limits (7) were obtained directly in Sec. 10, where a_n and b_n were also the coefficients in the Fourier cosine and sine series for certain functions related to f. (See Problems 2 and 3, where the Bessel inequalities appearing in Sec. 10 are derived from orthonormal sets.)

We now prove a theorem that follows from Theorem 2 in Sec. 65 and states that the orthonormal set (1) is complete in the space consisting of functions satisfying the same conditions as in the lemma in Sec. 16, as well as in the theorems in Secs. 17 and 19.

Theorem. *The orthonormal set* (1) *is complete in the space in which each function f has these properties:*

(i) *f is continuous on the interval* $-\pi \le x \le \pi$;

(ii) $f(-\pi) = f(\pi)$;

(iii) *its derivative f' is piecewise continuous on the interval* $-\pi < x < \pi$.

Observe that, just as Bessel's inequality in Sec. 65 becomes inequality (6) when the set (1) is used, Parseval's equation (10) in Sec. 65 becomes

$$(8) \qquad \frac{a_0^2}{2} + \sum_{n=1}^{\infty} (a_n^2 + b_n^2) = \frac{1}{\pi} \int_{-\pi}^{\pi} [f(x)]^2 \, dx.$$

Hence, once we show that the coefficients (4) and (5) actually satisfy equation (8), the theorem here is proved.

The fact that equation (8) is satisfied is an easy consequence of the theorem in Sec. 17, which tells us that for the functions f in the space considered here the series in correspondence (3) converges uniformly to $f(x)$ on the interval $-\pi \le x \le \pi$:

$$(9) \qquad f(x) = \frac{a_0}{2} + \sum_{n=1}^{\infty} (a_n \cos nx + b_n \sin nx) \qquad (-\pi \le x \le \pi).$$

Now a uniformly convergent series of continuous functions can be integrated term by term (Sec. 17). Hence we may multiply each term in equation (9) by $f(x)$ itself, thus leaving the series still uniformly convergent, and then integrate over the fundamental interval:

$$\int_{-\pi}^{\pi} [f(x)]^2 \, dx$$
$$= \frac{a_0}{2} \int_{-\pi}^{\pi} f(x) \, dx + \sum_{n=1}^{\infty} \left[a_n \int_{-\pi}^{\pi} f(x) \cos nx \, dx + b_n \int_{-\pi}^{\pi} f(x) \sin nx \, dx \right].$$

In view of expressions (4) and (5), the integrals on the right here can be written in terms of a_n and b_n; and we find that

$$\int_{-\pi}^{\pi} [f(x)]^2 \, dx = \pi \left[\frac{a_0^2}{2} + \sum_{n=1}^{\infty} (a_n^2 + b_n^2) \right].$$

Since this is the same as Parseval's equation (8), the proof is finished.

The theorem above is readily modified so as to apply to the orthonormal sets leading to Fourier cosine and sine series on the interval $0 < x < \pi$. More specifically, the set of normalized cosine functions in Example 2, Sec. 61, is complete in the space of continuous functions f, on the interval $0 \le x \le \pi$, whose derivatives f' are piecewise continuous. When the normalized sine functions in Example 1, Sec. 61, are used to obtain a sine series, the conditions $f(0) = f(\pi) = 0$ are also needed in order for the set to be complete.

The function space in the theorem is quite restricted. It can be shown that Parseval's equation (8) holds for any function f whose square is integrable over the interval $-\pi < x < \pi$.[†]

[†]See, for instance, the book by Tolstov (1976, pp. 54–57 and 117–120), which is listed in the Bibliography.

PROBLEMS

1. Use Theorem 2 in Sec. 65 to show that *an orthonormal set $\{\phi_n(x)\}$ is closed* (Sec. 62) *in a given function space if it is complete in that space.*

2. Apply Bessel's inequality (1), Sec. 65, to the orthonormal set (Example 1, Sec. 61)

$$\phi_n(x) = \sqrt{\frac{2}{\pi}} \sin nx \qquad (n = 1, 2, \ldots)$$

in $C_p(0, \pi)$ to show that

$$\sum_{n=1}^{N} b_n^2 \le \frac{2}{\pi} \int_0^{\pi} [f(x)]^2 \, dx \qquad (N = 1, 2, \ldots)$$

when f is in $C_p(0, \pi)$ and b_n are the coefficients in its Fourier sine series.

3. Let a_n $(n = 0, 1, 2, \ldots)$ be the usual coefficients in the Fourier cosine series for a function f in $C_p(0, \pi)$. By referring to the orthonormal set (Example 2, Sec. 61)

$$\phi_0(x) = \frac{1}{\sqrt{\pi}}, \qquad \phi_n(x) = \sqrt{\frac{2}{\pi}} \cos nx \qquad (n = 1, 2, \ldots)$$

and using Bessel's inequality (1), Sec. 65, show that

$$\frac{a_0^2}{2} + \sum_{n=1}^{N} a_n^2 \le \frac{2}{\pi} \int_0^{\pi} [f(x)]^2 \, dx \qquad (N = 1, 2, \ldots).$$

4. (a) Use the same steps as in Example 3, Sec. 61, to verify that the set of functions

$$\phi_0(x) = \frac{1}{\sqrt{2c}}, \qquad \phi_{2n-1}(x) = \frac{1}{\sqrt{c}} \cos \frac{n\pi x}{c}, \qquad \phi_{2n}(x) = \frac{1}{\sqrt{c}} \sin \frac{n\pi x}{c}$$

$$(n = 1, 2, \ldots)$$

is orthonormal on the interval $-c < x < c$. (This set becomes the one in that example when $c = \pi$.)

(b) By proceeding as in Example 3, Sec. 63, show that the generalized Fourier series corresponding to a function $f(x)$ in $C_p(-c, c)$ with respect to the orthonormal set in part (a) can be written as an ordinary Fourier series on $-c < x < c$ (Sec. 15), with the usual coefficients a_n and b_n.

(c) Derive Bessel's inequality

$$\frac{a_0^2}{2} + \sum_{n=1}^{N} \left(a_n^2 + b_n^2\right) \le \frac{1}{c} \int_{-c}^{c} [f(x)]^2 \, dx \qquad (N = 1, 2, \ldots)$$

for the coefficients a_n and b_n in part (b) from the general form (1), Sec. 65, of that inequality for Fourier constants. [Compare with inequality (6), Sec. 66.]

Suggestion: In part (a), some integrals to be used can be evaluated by writing

$$x = \frac{\pi}{c} s$$

in integrals (1) and (4), Sec. 61.

5. Let $s_N(x)$ $(N = 1, 2, \ldots)$ be a sequence of functions defined on the interval $0 \le x \le 1$ by means of the equations

$$s_N(x) = \begin{cases} 0 & \text{when } x = 1, \dfrac{1}{2}, \ldots, \dfrac{1}{N}, \\[2ex] 1 & \text{when } x \neq 1, \dfrac{1}{2}, \ldots, \dfrac{1}{N}. \end{cases}$$

Show that this sequence converges in the mean to the function $f(x) = 1$ in $C_p(0, 1)$ but that for each positive integer p,

$$\lim_{N \to \infty} s_N\left(\frac{1}{p}\right) = 0.$$

Suggestion: Observe that

$$s_N\left(\frac{1}{p}\right) = 0 \qquad \text{when} \qquad N \ge p.$$

CHAPTER
8

STURM-LIOUVILLE
PROBLEMS
AND
APPLICATIONS

We turn now to a careful presentation of the basic theory of Sturm-Liouville problems and their solutions. Once that is done, we shall illustrate the Fourier method in solving physical problems that involve eigenfunctions not encountered in earlier chapters.

67. REGULAR STURM-LIOUVILLE PROBLEMS

In Chap. 5, we found solutions of various boundary value problems by the Fourier method. Except in Sec. 49, the method always led to the need for a Fourier cosine or sine series representation of a given function. The cosine and sine functions in the series were the eigenfunctions of one of the following two Sturm-Liouville problems on an interval $0 \leq x \leq c$:

(1) $\qquad X''(x) + \lambda X(x) = 0, \qquad X'(0) = 0, \qquad X'(c) = 0,$

(2) $\qquad X''(x) + \lambda X(x) = 0, \qquad X(0) = 0, \qquad X(c) = 0.$

When applied to many other boundary value problems in partial differential equations, the Fourier method continues to involve a Sturm-Liouville problem consisting of a linear homogeneous ordinary differential equation of the type

(3) $\qquad [r(x)X'(x)]' + [q(x) + \lambda p(x)]X(x) = 0 \qquad (a < x < b),$

together with a pair of *separated* boundary conditions

(4) $\qquad a_1 X(a) + a_2 X'(a) = 0, \qquad b_1 X(b) + b_2 X'(b) = 0.$

210

The interval $a < x < b$ is understood to be bounded. We agree, moreover, that a_1 and a_2 are not both zero and that the same is true of the constants b_1 and b_2. Values of the parameter λ and corresponding nontrivial solutions $X(x)$ are to be determined.

The parameter λ appears in a Sturm-Liouville problem only as indicated above. That is, the real-valued functions p, q, and r in the differential equation (3) are independent of λ, and the real numbers a_1, a_2, b_1, b_2 in boundary conditions (4) are also independent of λ. The Sturm-Liouville problem is said to be *regular* when[†]

(i) p, q, r, and r' are continuous on the closed interval $a \leq x \leq b$;
(ii) $p(x) > 0$ and $r(x) > 0$ when $a \leq x \leq b$.

EXAMPLES. Problems (1) and (2) are regular Sturm-Liouville problems. Other examples, to be solved later in this chapter, are

$$X''(x) + \lambda X(x) = 0 \qquad (0 < x < c),$$

$$X'(0) = 0, \qquad hX(c) + X'(c) = 0,$$

where h denotes a positive constant, and

$$[x^2 X'(x)]' + \lambda X(x) = 0 \qquad (1 < x < b),$$

$$X(1) = 0, \qquad X(b) = 0,$$

as well as

$$[xX'(x)]' + \frac{\lambda}{x} X(x) = 0 \qquad (1 < x < b),$$

$$X'(1) = 0, \qquad X(b) = 0.$$

As was the case with problems (1) and (2), a value of λ for which problem (3)–(4) has a nontrivial solution is called an *eigenvalue*; and the nontrivial solution is called an *eigenfunction*. Note that if $X(x)$ is an eigenfunction, then so is $CX(x)$, where C is any nonzero constant. It is understood that for $X(x)$ to be an eigenfunction, $X(x)$ *and* $X'(x)$ *must be continuous on the closed interval* $a \leq x \leq b$. Such continuity conditions are usually required of solutions of boundary value problems in ordinary differential equations.

The set of eigenvalues of problem (3)–(4) is called the *spectrum* of the problem. The spectrum of a regular Sturm-Liouville problem consists of an infinite number of eigenvalues $\lambda_1, \lambda_2, \ldots$. We state this fact without proof, which is quite involved.[‡] In special cases, the eigenvalues will be found; and so their existence will not be in doubt. When eigenvalues are sought, however, it is useful to know

[†]Papers by J. C. F. Sturm and J. Liouville giving the first extensive development of the theory of this problem appeared in vols. 1–3 of the *Journal de mathématique* (1836–1838).

[‡]For verification of statements in this section that we do not prove, see the book by Churchill (1972, Chap. 9), which contains proofs when $a_2 = b_2 = 0$ in conditions (4), and the one by Birkhoff and Rota (1989). Also, extensive treatments of Sturm-Liouville theory appear in the books by Ince (1956) and Titchmarsh (1962). These references are all listed in the Bibliography.

that they are all real and hence that there is no possibility of discovering others in the complex plane. The proof that the eigenvalues must be real is given in
Sec. 69, and we agree that they are to be arranged in ascending order of magnitude,
so that $\lambda_n < \lambda_{n+1}$ $(n = 1, 2, \ldots)$. It can be shown that $\lambda_n \to \infty$ as $n \to \infty$.

68. MODIFICATIONS

Although we are mainly concerned in this chapter with the theory and application of *regular* Sturm-Liouville problems, described in Sec. 67, certain important
modifications are also of interest in practice. We mention them here since some of
their theory is conveniently included in the discussion of regular Sturm-Liouville
problems in Sec. 69.

A Sturm-Liouville problem

(1) $$[r(x) X'(x)]' + [q(x) + \lambda p(x)] X(x) = 0 \qquad (a < x < b),$$

(2) $$a_1 X(a) + a_2 X'(a) = 0, \qquad b_1 X(b) + b_2 X'(b) = 0$$

is said to be *singular* if

(i) at least one of the regularity conditions stated in Sec. 67 fails to be satisfied;

(ii) or the interval on which the problem is defined is unbounded.

Note that the problem is singular if, for instance, the function q has an infinite
discontinuity at an end point of the interval $a \le x \le b$. Also, it is singular if $p(x)$ or
$r(x)$ vanishes at an endpoint. When $r(x)$ does this, we drop the boundary condition
at the endpoint in question. Note that the dropping of the boundary condition at
$x = a$ is the same as letting both of the coefficients a_1 and a_2 in that condition be
zero; a similar remark can be made when the condition at $x = b$ is to be dropped.
Finally, we recall that eigenvalue problems involving unbounded intervals have
already been encountered in Sec. 55 of Chap. 6.

EXAMPLE 1. One singular Sturm-Liouville problem to be studied in
Chap. 9 consists of the differential equation

$$[x X'(x)]' + \left(-\frac{n^2}{x} + \lambda x\right) X(x) = 0 \qquad (0 < x < c),$$

where $n = 0, 1, 2, \ldots$, and the single boundary condition $X(c) = 0$. Observe that
the functions $p(x) = x$ and $r(x) = x$ both vanish at $x = 0$ and that the function
$q(x) = -n^2/x$ has an infinite discontinuity there when n is positive.

EXAMPLE 2. The differential equation

$$[(1 - x^2) X'(x)]' + \lambda X(x) = 0 \qquad (-1 < x < 1),$$

with no boundary conditions, constitutes a singular Sturm-Liouville problem.
Here the function $r(x) = 1 - x^2$ vanishes at both ends $x = \pm 1$ of the interval
$-1 \le x \le 1$. This problem is the main one that is solved and used in Chap. 10.

The singular problems in Chap. 6 had *continuous* spectra, consisting of either
all nonnegative or all positive values of λ, and it will turn out that the problems in

Examples 1 and 2 just above have the *discrete* spectra of regular Sturm-Liouville problems, where the eigenvalues may be indexed with nonnegative or positive integers. As already indicated in Sec. 67, the nature of the spectrum of any particular problem will be determined by actually finding the eigenvalues.

Finally, in addition to singular problems, another modification of problem (1)–(2) occurs when $r(a) = r(b)$ and conditions (2) are replaced by the *periodic* boundary conditions

$$(3) \qquad\qquad X(a) = X(b), \qquad X'(a) = X'(b).$$

EXAMPLE 3. The problem

$$X''(x) + \lambda X(x) = 0, \qquad X(-\pi) = X(\pi), \qquad X'(-\pi) = X'(\pi),$$

already solved in Sec. 49, has periodic boundary conditions.

69. ORTHOGONAL EIGENFUNCTIONS AND REAL EIGENVALUES

As pointed out in Sec. 67, a regular Sturm-Liouville problem always has an infinite number of eigenvalues $\lambda_1, \lambda_2, \ldots$. In this section, we shall establish the orthogonality of eigenfunctions corresponding to *distinct* eigenvalues. The concept of orthogonality to be used here is, however, a slight generalization of the one originally introduced in Sec. 60. To be specific, a set $\{\psi_n(x)\}$ $(n = 1, 2, \ldots)$ is orthogonal on an interval $a < x < b$ with respect to a *weight function* $p(x)$, which is piecewise continuous and positive on that interval, if

$$\int_a^b p(x)\psi_m(x)\psi_n(x)\, dx = 0 \qquad \text{when } m \neq n.$$

The integral here represents an inner product (ψ_m, ψ_n) with respect to the weight function. The set is normalized by dividing each $\psi_n(x)$ by $\|\psi_n\|$, where

$$\|\psi_n\|^2 = (\psi_n, \psi_n) = \int_a^b p(x)[\psi_n(x)]^2\, dx$$

and where it is assumed that $\|\psi_n\| \neq 0$. This type of orthogonality can, of course, be reduced to that in Sec. 60 by using the products $\sqrt{p(x)}\psi_n(x)$ as functions of the set. In Sec. 73, we shall illustrate how expansions of arbitrary functions in series of such normalized eigenfunctions follow from our earlier discussion of generalized Fourier series (Sec. 62).

The following theorem states that eigenfunctions associated with distinct eigenvalues of a regular Sturm-Liouville problem

$$(1) \qquad\qquad [r(x)X'(x)]' + [q(x) + \lambda p(x)]X(x) = 0 \qquad\qquad (a < x < b),$$

$$(2) \qquad\qquad a_1 X(a) + a_2 X'(a) = 0, \qquad b_1 X(b) + b_2 X'(b) = 0$$

are orthogonal on the interval $a < x < b$ with respect to the weight function $p(x)$, where $p(x)$ is the same function as in equation (1). In presenting the theorem, we relax the conditions of regularity on the coefficients in the differential equation (1) so that the result can also be applied to eigenfunctions that are found for some of the modifications of regular Sturm-Liouville problems mentioned in Sec. 68. We retain all of the conditions for a regular problem, stated in Sec. 67, except that now q may be discontinuous at an endpoint of the interval $a \leq x \leq b$ and $p(x)$ and $r(x)$ may vanish at an endpoint. That is,

(i) p, r, and r' are continuous on the closed interval $a \leq x \leq b$, and q is continuous on the open interval $a < x < b$;

(ii) $p(x) > 0$ and $r(x) > 0$ when $a < x < b$.

   Theorem 1. *If λ_m and λ_n are distinct eigenvalues of the Sturm-Liouville problem (1)–(2), then corresponding eigenfunctions $X_m(x)$ and $X_n(x)$ are orthogonal with respect to the weight function $p(x)$ on the interval $a < x < b$. The orthogonality also holds in each of the following cases:*

(a) *when $r(a) = 0$ and the first of boundary conditions (2) is dropped from the problem;*

(b) *when $r(b) = 0$ and the second of conditions (2) is dropped;*

(c) *when $r(a) = r(b)$ and conditions (2) are replaced by the conditions*

$$X(a) = X(b), \qquad X'(a) = X'(b).$$

   Note that *both* cases (a) and (b) here may apply to a single Sturm-Liouville problem (see Example 2, Sec. 68).

   To prove the theorem, we first observe that

$$(rX'_m)' + qX_m = -\lambda_m pX_m, \qquad (rX'_n)' + qX_n = -\lambda_n pX_n$$

since each eigenfunction satisfies equation (1) when λ is the eigenvalue to which it corresponds. We then multiply each side of these two equations by X_n and X_m, respectively, and subtract:

$$(\lambda_m - \lambda_n)pX_mX_n = X_m(rX'_n)' - X_n(rX'_m)'.$$

Since the right-hand side of this last equation can be written

$$[X_m(rX'_n)' + X'_m(rX'_n)] - [X_n(rX'_m)' + X'_n(rX'_m)],$$

or

$$\frac{d}{dx}[X_m(rX'_n) - X_n(rX'_m)],$$

it follows that

(3) $$\qquad (\lambda_m - \lambda_n)pX_mX_n = \frac{d}{dx}[r(X_mX'_n - X_nX'_m)].$$

   The function q has now been eliminated, and the continuity conditions on the remaining functions allow us to write

(4) $$\qquad (\lambda_m - \lambda_n)\int_a^b pX_mX_n\, dx = [r(x)\, \Delta(x)]_a^b,$$

where $\Delta(x)$ is the determinant

$$(5) \qquad \Delta(x) = \begin{vmatrix} X_m(x) & X'_m(x) \\ X_n(x) & X'_n(x) \end{vmatrix} = X_m(x)\,X'_n(x) - X_n(x)\,X'_m(x).$$

That is,

$$(6) \qquad (\lambda_m - \lambda_n) \int_a^b pX_mX_n\,dx = r(b)\Delta(b) - r(a)\Delta(a).$$

The first of boundary conditions (2) requires that

$$a_1 X_m(a) + a_2 X'_m(a) = 0,$$
$$a_1 X_n(a) + a_2 X'_n(a) = 0;$$

and for this pair of linear homogeneous equations in a_1 and a_2 to be satisfied by numbers a_1 and a_2, not both zero, it is necessary that the determinant $\Delta(a)$ be zero. Similarly, from the second boundary condition, where b_1 and b_2 are not both zero, we see that $\Delta(b) = 0$. Thus, according to equation (6),

$$(7) \qquad (\lambda_m - \lambda_n) \int_a^b pX_mX_n\,dx = 0;$$

and since $\lambda_m \neq \lambda_n$, the desired orthogonality property follows:

$$(8) \qquad \int_a^b p(x)X_m(x)X_n(x)\,dx = 0.$$

If $r(a) = 0$, property (8) follows from equation (6) even when $\Delta(a) \neq 0$ or when $a_1 = a_2 = 0$, in which case the first of boundary conditions (2) disappears. Similarly, if $r(b) = 0$, the second of those conditions is not used.

If $r(a) = r(b)$ and the periodic boundary conditions (Sec. 49)

$$X(a) = X(b), \qquad X'(a) = X'(b)$$

are used in place of conditions (2), then $\Delta(a) = \Delta(b)$. Hence,

$$r(b)\Delta(b) = r(a)\Delta(a);$$

and, again, property (8) follows. This completes the proof of Theorem 1.

EXAMPLE 1. The eigenfunctions of the regular Sturm-Liouville problem

$$X''(x) + \lambda X(x) = 0 \qquad\qquad (0 < x < c),$$

$$X(0) = 0, \qquad X(c) = 0$$

are (Sec. 35)

$$X_n(x) = \sin\frac{n\pi x}{c} \qquad\qquad (n = 1, 2, \ldots).$$

The theorem tells us that any two distinct eigenfunctions $X_m(x)$ and $X_n(x)$ are orthogonal on the interval $0 < x < c$ with weight function $p(x) = 1$:

$$(9) \qquad \int_0^c \sin\frac{m\pi x}{c} \sin\frac{n\pi x}{c}\,dx = 0 \qquad\qquad (m \neq n).$$

We recall that the value of this integral was established directly when $c = \pi$ in Problem 9, Sec. 5.

EXAMPLE 2. Eigenfunctions corresponding to distinct eigenvalues of the regular Sturm-Liouville problem

$$[xX'(x)]' + \frac{\lambda}{x} X(x) = 0 \qquad (1 < x < b),$$

$$X(1) = 0, \qquad X(b) = 0$$

are, according to the theorem, orthogonal on the interval $1 < x < b$ with weight function $p(x) = 1/x$. In Problem 1 the eigenfunctions are actually found, and the orthogonality is verified.

The following theorem is an immediate consequence of Theorem 1.

Theorem 2. *If λ is an eigenvalue of the Sturm-Liouville problem (1)–(2), then it must be a real number. The same is true in cases (a), (b), and (c), that were treated in Theorem 1.*

We begin the proof by writing the eigenvalue as $\lambda = \alpha + i\beta$, where α and β are real numbers. If X denotes a corresponding eigenfunction, which is nontrivial and may be complex-valued, conditions (1) and (2) are satisfied. Now the complex conjugate of λ is the number $\bar{\lambda} = \alpha - i\beta$; and if

$$X(x) = u(x) + iv(x),$$

then

$$\bar{X} = u - iv \qquad \text{and} \qquad X' = u' + iv'.$$

Also, the conjugate of a sum or product of two complex numbers is the sum or product, respectively, of the conjugates of those numbers. Hence, by taking the conjugates of both sides of the equations in conditions (1) and (2) and keeping in mind that the functions p, q, and r are real-valued and that the coefficients in conditions (2) are real numbers, we see that

$$(r\bar{X}')' + (q + \bar{\lambda}p)\bar{X} = 0,$$

$$a_1\bar{X}(a) + a_2\bar{X}'(a) = 0, \qquad b_1\bar{X}(b) + b_2\bar{X}'(b) = 0.$$

Thus, the nontrivial function $\bar{X}$ is an eigenfunction corresponding to $\bar{\lambda}$.

If we assume that $\beta \neq 0$, then $\bar{\lambda} \neq \lambda$; and Theorem 1 tells us that X and $\bar{X}$ are orthogonal on the interval $a < x < b$ with respect to the weight function $p(x)$, even in cases (a), (b), and (c):

$$(10) \qquad \int_a^b p(x)X(x)\bar{X}(x)\,dx = 0.$$

But $p(x) > 0$ when $a < x < b$. Moreover,

$$X\bar{X} = u^2 + v^2 = |X|^2 \geq 0$$

when $a \leq x \leq b$; and $|X|^2$ is not identically equal to zero since X is an eigen-function. So integral (10) has positive value, and our assumption that $\beta \neq 0$ has led us to a contradiction. Hence, we must conclude that $\beta = 0$, or that λ is real.

PROBLEMS

1. (a) After writing the differential equation in the regular Sturm-Liouville problem

$$[xX'(x)]' + \frac{\lambda}{x} X(x) = 0 \qquad\qquad (1 < x < b),$$

$$X(1) = 0, \qquad X(b) = 0$$

in Cauchy-Euler form (see Problem 1, Sec. 44), use the substitution $x = \exp s$ to transform the problem into one consisting of the differential equation

$$\frac{d^2 X}{ds^2} + \lambda X = 0 \qquad\qquad (0 < s < \ln b)$$

and the boundary conditions

$$X = 0 \quad \text{when} \quad s = 0 \quad \text{and} \quad X = 0 \quad \text{when} \quad s = \ln b.$$

Then, by simply referring to the solutions of the Sturm-Liouville problem (4) in Sec. 35, show that the eigenvalues and eigenfunctions of the original problem here are

$$\lambda_n = \alpha_n^2, \qquad X_n(x) = \sin(\alpha_n \ln x) \qquad\qquad (n = 1, 2, \ldots),$$

where $\alpha_n = n\pi / \ln b$.
   (b) By making the substitution

$$s = \pi \frac{\ln x}{\ln b}$$

in the integral involved and then referring to Problem 9, Sec. 5, give a direct verification that the set of eigenfunctions $X_n(x)$ obtained in part (a) is orthogonal on the interval $1 < x < b$ with weight function $p(x) = 1/x$, as ensured by Theorem 1 in Sec. 69.

2. Note that the differential equation

$$(rX')' + (q + \lambda p) X = 0$$

in a Sturm-Liouville problem can be put in the form

$$\mathcal{L}[X] + \lambda p X = 0,$$

where $\mathcal{L}$ is the differential operator defined by means of the equation

$$\mathcal{L}[X] = (rX')' + qX.$$

Show that the identity

$$X(rY')' - Y(rX')' = \frac{d}{dx}[r(XY' - YX')],$$

which is obtained by the steps leading up to equation (3) in Sec. 69, can be written

$$X\mathcal{L}[Y] - Y\mathcal{L}[X] = \frac{d}{dx}[r(XY' - YX')].$$

This is called *Lagrange's identity* for the operator $\mathcal{L}$.

3. (a) Suppose that the operator $\mathcal{L}$ in Problem 2 is defined on a space of functions satisfying the conditions

$$a_1 X(a) + a_2 X'(a) = 0, \qquad b_1 X(b) + b_2 X'(b) = 0,$$

where a_1 and a_2 are not both zero and where the same is true of b_1 and b_2. Use Lagrange's identity, obtained in Problem 2, to show that

$$(X, \mathcal{L}[Y]) = (\mathcal{L}[X], Y),$$

where these inner products are on the interval $a < x < b$ with weight function unity.

(b) Let λ_m and λ_n denote distinct eigenvalues of a regular Sturm-Liouville problem whose differential equation is (see Problem 2)

$$\mathcal{L}[X] + \lambda p X = 0.$$

Use the result in part (a) to prove that if X_m and X_n are eigenfunctions corresponding to λ_m and λ_n, then

$$(p X_m, X_n) = 0.$$

Thus show that X_m and X_n are orthogonal on the interval $a < x < b$ with weight function p, as already demonstrated in Sec. 69.

70. REAL-VALUED EIGENFUNCTIONS

In the study of ordinary differential equations, problems in which all boundary data are given at one point are called *initial value problems*. We begin here by stating without proof a fundamental result from the theory of such problems.[†]

Lemma 1. Let P and Q denote functions of x that are continuous on an interval $a \le x \le b$. If x_0 is a point in that interval and A and B are prescribed constants, then there is one and only one function y, which is continuous together with its derivative y' when $a \le x \le b$, that satisfies the differential equation

$$y''(x) + P(x)y'(x) + Q(x)y(x) = 0 \qquad (a < x < b)$$

and the two initial conditions

$$y(x_0) = A, \qquad y'(x_0) = B.$$

Note that $y'' = -Py' - Qy$, and so y'' is continuous when $a \le x \le b$. Also, since any values can be assigned to the constants A and B, the general solution of the differential equation has two arbitrary constants.

Suppose now that X and Y are two eigenfunctions corresponding to the same eigenvalue λ of the regular Sturm-Liouville problem

(1) $$(rX')' + (q + \lambda p)X = 0 \qquad (a < x < b),$$

(2) $$a_1 X(a) + a_2 X'(a) = 0, \qquad b_1 X(b) + b_2 X'(b) = 0.$$

[†]A proof can be found in, for instance, the book by Coddington (1989, Chap. 6), which is listed in the Bibliography.

As stated in Sec. 67, *the functions p, q, r, and r' must be continuous on the interval $a \leq x \leq b$; also, $p(x) > 0$ and $r(x) > 0$ when $a \leq x \leq b$.* The above lemma enables us to prove the following one, which shows that X and Y can differ by, at most, a constant factor.

Lemma 2. *If X and Y are eigenfunctions corresponding to the same eigenvalue of a regular Sturm-Liouville problem, then*

$$(3) \qquad\qquad Y(x) = CX(x) \qquad\qquad (a \leq x \leq b),$$

where C is a nonzero constant.

According to this lemma, a regular Sturm-Liouville problem cannot have two linearly independent eigenfunctions corresponding to the same eigenvalue. For certain modifications of regular Sturm-Liouville problems, however, it is possible to have an eigenvalue with linearly independent eigenfunctions (see Sec. 49).

We let $X(x)$ and $Y(x)$ be as stated in the hypothesis of Lemma 2 and start the proof by observing that in view of the principle of superposition of solutions for linear homogeneous ordinary differential equations, the linear combination

$$(4) \qquad\qquad Z(x) = Y'(a)X(x) - X'(a)Y(x)$$

satisfies the differential equation

$$(5) \qquad\qquad (rZ')' + (q + \lambda p)Z = 0 \qquad\qquad (a < x < b);$$

in addition, $Z'(a) = 0$. Since X and Y satisfy the conditions

$$a_1 X(a) + a_2 X'(a) = 0,$$
$$a_1 Y(a) + a_2 Y'(a) = 0,$$

where a_1 and a_2 are not both zero, and since $Z(a)$ is the determinant of this pair of linear homogeneous equations in a_1 and a_2, we also know that $Z(a) = 0$. According to Lemma 1, then, $Z(x) = 0$ when $a \leq x \leq b$. That is,

$$(6) \qquad\qquad Y'(a)X(x) - X'(a)Y(x) = 0 \qquad\qquad (a \leq x \leq b).$$

Since eigenfunctions cannot be identically equal to zero, it is clear from relation (6) that if either of the values $X'(a)$ or $Y'(a)$ is zero, then so is the other.

Relation (3) now follows from equation (6), provided that $X'(a)$ and $Y'(a)$ are nonzero. That is,

$$Y(x) = \frac{Y'(a)}{X'(a)} X(x) \qquad\qquad (a \leq x \leq b).$$

Suppose, on the other hand, that $X'(a)$ and $Y'(a)$ are zero. Then $X(a)$ and $Y(a)$ are nonzero since, otherwise, $X(x)$ and $Y(x)$ would be identically equal to zero, according to Lemma 1; and zero is not an eigenfunction. So, although equation (6) cannot be used, the procedure that we have applied to $Z(x)$ may now be used to show (Problem 13, Sec. 72) that the linear combination

$$(7) \qquad\qquad W(x) = Y(a)X(x) - X(a)Y(x)$$

is zero when $a \leq x \leq b$ and hence that relation (3) still holds.

It follows from Lemma 2 that each eigenfunction of a regular Sturm-Liouville problem can be made real-valued by multiplying it by some nonzero constant. We state this important result as a theorem.

Theorem. *Each eigenfunction of a regular Sturm-Liouville problem can be made real-valued by multiplying it by an appropriate nonzero constant.*

To show this, we first recall from Theorem 2 in Sec. 69 that the eigenvalue λ to which X corresponds must be real. So if we make the substitution $X = U + iV$, where U and V are real-valued functions, in problem (1)–(2) and separate real and imaginary parts, we find that U and V are themselves eigenfunctions corresponding to λ. Hence, by Lemma 2, there is a nonzero constant β such that $V = \beta U$. Here β is real since U and V are real-valued, and we may conclude that

$$X = U + i\beta U = (1 + i\beta)U.$$

That is, X can be expressed as a nonzero constant times a real-valued function. Since

$$U = \left(\frac{1}{1 + i\beta}\right)X,$$

the theorem is now proved.

71. NONNEGATIVE EIGENVALUES

We know from Theorem 2 in Sec. 69 that each eigenvalue of a regular Sturm-Liouville problem

$$(1) \qquad\qquad (rX')' + (q + \lambda p)X = 0 \qquad\qquad (a < x < b),$$

$$(2) \qquad a_1 X(a) + a_2 X'(a) = 0, \qquad b_1 X(b) + b_2 X'(b) = 0$$

must be real. The theorem in this section is an additional aid in determining eigenvalues since it often eliminates the possibility that there are negative ones.

Theorem. *Let λ be an eigenvalue of the regular Sturm-Liouville problem (1)–(2). If the conditions*

$$q(x) \le 0 \, (a \le x \le b) \qquad and \qquad a_1 a_2 \le 0, \; b_1 b_2 \ge 0$$

are satisfied, then $\lambda \ge 0$.

Since we are considering a *regular* Sturm-Liouville problem, we assume that the functions p, q, r, and r' are continuous when $a \le x \le b$ and that $p(x) > 0$ and $r(x) > 0$ on that closed interval. We start our proof by letting X denote a real-valued eigenfunction (see the theorem in Sec. 70) corresponding to the eigenvalue λ in the statement of the theorem here. Equation (1) is thus satisfied, and we multiply each term of that equation by X and integrate each of the resulting terms from $x = a$ to $x = b$:

$$(3) \qquad \int_a^b X(rX')' \, dx + \int_a^b q X^2 \, dx + \lambda \int_a^b p X^2 \, dx = 0.$$

After applying integration by parts to the first of these integrals, one can write equation (3) in the form

$$(4) \qquad \lambda \int_a^b p X^2 \, dx = \int_a^b (-q X^2) \, dx + \int_a^b r (X')^2 \, dx$$
$$+ r(a) X(a) X'(a) - r(b) X(b) X'(b).$$

Let us now assume that the conditions stated in the theorem are satisfied. Since $-q(x) \geq 0$ and $r(x) > 0$ when $a \leq x \leq b$, the values of the two integrals on the right in equation (4) are clearly nonnegative. As for the third term on the right, we note that if $a_1 = 0$ or $a_2 = 0$ in the first of conditions (2), then $X'(a) = 0$ or $X(a) = 0$, respectively. In either case, the third term is zero. If, on the other hand, neither a_1 nor a_2 is zero, then

$$r(a) X(a) X'(a) = \frac{r(a)[a_1 X(a)]^2}{-a_1 a_2} \geq 0.$$

Similarly, $-r(b) X(b) X'(b) \geq 0$; and it follows that all the terms on the right-hand side of equation (4) are nonnegative. Consequently,

$$\lambda \int_a^b p(x)[X(x)]^2 \, dx \geq 0.$$

But this integral has a positive value, and so $\lambda \geq 0$.

EXAMPLE. Example 1 in the next section is concerned with finding the normalized eigenfunctions of this regular Sturm-Liouville problem:

$$X'' + \lambda X = 0, \quad X'(0) = 0, \quad h X(c) + X'(c) = 0,$$

where h is a positive constant. This is, of course, a special case of the Sturm-Liouville problem (1)–(2), where

$$q(x) \equiv 0, \ (0 \leq x \leq c) \qquad \text{and} \qquad a_1 a_2 = 0, \ b_1 b_2 = h > 0.$$

According to the theorem just proved, the eigenvalues of the Sturm-Liouville problem in this example are all nonnegative.

72. METHODS OF SOLUTION

We turn now to two examples that illustrate methods to be used in finding eigenvalues and eigenfunctions. The basic method has already been touched on in Secs. 35 and 49, where simpler Sturm-Liouville problems were solved. That basic method is illustrated further in our first example here. Our second example illustrates how it is sometimes possible to transform a given Sturm-Liouville problem into one whose solutions are already known.

EXAMPLE 1. Let us solve the regular Sturm-Liouville problem

$$(1) \qquad\qquad\qquad X'' + \lambda X = 0 \qquad\qquad\qquad (0 < x < c),$$

$$(2) \qquad\qquad X'(0) = 0, \qquad h X(c) + X'(c) = 0,$$

where h is a positive constant.

We know from Theorem 2 in Sec. 69 that any eigenvalue of this problem is a real number, and we recall from the example at the end of the preceding section that every such eigenvalue must be nonnegative. So we need only treat the cases $\lambda = 0$ and $\lambda > 0$ here.

(i) The case $\lambda = 0$

If $\lambda = 0$, the general solution of equation (1) is $X(x) = Ax + B$ where A and B are constants; and it follows from boundary conditions (2) that $A = 0$ and $B = 0$. But eigenfunctions cannot be identically equal to zero. Consequently, the number $\lambda = 0$ is not an eigenvalue. This leaves only the possibility that $\lambda > 0$.

(ii) The case $\lambda > 0$

If $\lambda > 0$, we write $\lambda = \alpha^2$ ($\alpha > 0$). The general solution of equation (1) this time is

$$X(x) = C_1 \cos \alpha x + C_2 \sin \alpha x.$$

It reduces to

$$(3) \qquad\qquad X(x) = C_1 \cos \alpha x$$

when the first of boundary conditions (2) is applied. The second boundary condition then requires that

$$(4) \qquad\qquad C_1 (h \cos \alpha c - \alpha \sin \alpha c) = 0.$$

If the function (3) is to be nontrivial, the constant C_1 must be nonzero. Hence the factor in parentheses in equation (4) must be equal to zero. That is, if there is an eigenvalue $\lambda = \alpha^2$ ($\alpha > 0$), the number α must be a positive root of the equation

$$(5) \qquad\qquad \tan \alpha c = \frac{h}{\alpha}.$$

Figure 54, where the graphs of

$$y = \tan \alpha c \qquad \text{and} \qquad y = \frac{h}{\alpha}$$

are plotted, shows that equation (5) has an infinite number of positive roots

$$\alpha_1, \alpha_2, \alpha_3, \ldots \qquad \text{where} \qquad \alpha_n < \alpha_{n+1} \qquad\qquad (n = 1, 2, \ldots);$$

they are the positive values of α for which those graphs intersect. The eigenvalues are, then, the numbers $\lambda_n = \alpha_n^2$ ($n = 1, 2, \ldots$). We identify them by simply writing

$$(6) \qquad\qquad \lambda_n = \alpha_n^2 \qquad \text{where} \qquad \tan \alpha_n c = \frac{h}{\alpha_n} \qquad\qquad (\alpha_n > 0).$$

Note that the dashed vertical lines in Fig. 54 are equally spaced π/c units apart. Also, as n tends to infinity, the numbers α_n tend to be the positive roots of the equation $\tan \alpha c = 0$, which are the same as the positive roots of $\sin \alpha c = 0$. In fact, the numbers $\alpha_n c$ are approximately $(n - 1)\pi$ when n is large. The first few

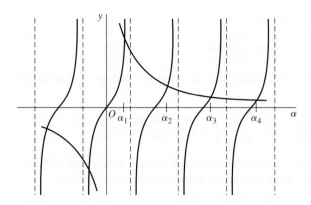

FIGURE 54

positive roots $x_1, x_2, x_3, \ldots$ of the equation[†]

$$\tan x = \frac{a}{x} \qquad\qquad (a = hc)$$

have been tabulated for various values of the constant a, and it follows from equation (5) that

$$\alpha_1 = \frac{x_1}{c}, \qquad \alpha_2 = \frac{x_2}{c}, \qquad \alpha_3 = \frac{x_3}{c}, \qquad \ldots$$

In view of the discussion just above,

$$\lambda_n = \alpha_n^2 \doteq \left[\frac{(n-1)\pi}{c}\right]^2 \qquad \text{when } n \text{ is large,}$$

where the symbol $\doteq$ denotes approximate equality. This is in agreement with the statement made earlier in Sec. 67 that if λ_n are the eigenvalues of a regular Sturm-Liouville problem, arranged in ascending order of magnitude, then it is always true that $\lambda_n \to \infty$ as $n \to \infty$.

Expression (3) now tells us that except for constant factors, the corresponding eigenfunctions are $X_n(x) = \cos\alpha_n x$ $(n = 1, 2, \ldots)$. Let us put these eigenfunctions in *normalized* form (Sec. 60), the form that we shall need in the applications. To accomplish this, we note that since the functions $X_n(x)$ are orthogonal on the interval $0 < x < c$ with weight function unity, according to the theorem in Sec. 69,

$$\|X_n\|^2 = \int_0^c \cos^2\alpha_n x \, dx = \frac{1}{2}\int_0^c (1 + \cos 2\alpha_n x)\, dx = \frac{1}{2}\left(c + \frac{\sin 2\alpha_n c}{2\alpha_n}\right).$$

The trigonometric identity

$$\sin 2\alpha_n c = 2 \sin\alpha_n c \cos\alpha_n c$$

[†]Roots of this and the related equation $\tan x = ax$, arising elsewhere in this chapter, are tabulated in, for example, the handbook edited by Abramowitz and Stegun (1972, pp. 224–225). They can also be found in the book edited by Özişik (2003, pp. 481–482), as well as the one by Carslaw and Jaeger (1986, pp. 491–492). These references are all listed in the Bibliography.

and the expression

$$\frac{1}{\alpha_n} = \frac{\sin \alpha_n c}{h \cos \alpha_n c},$$

which is equivalent to the second equation in statement (6), now enable us to put $\|X_n\|^2$ in the form

(7) $$\|X_n\|^2 = \frac{1}{2}\left(c + \frac{\sin^2 \alpha_n c}{h}\right) = \frac{hc + \sin^2 \alpha_n c}{2h}.$$

Note that this last expression is obviously positive since h and c are positive. Dividing each $X_n(x)$ by $\|X_n\|$, we arrive at the normalized eigenfunctions

(8) $$\phi_n(x) = \sqrt{\frac{2h}{hc + \sin^2 \alpha_n c}} \cos \alpha_n x \qquad (n = 1, 2, \ldots).$$

The solutions of a given Sturm-Liouville problem sometimes follow from the solutions of a problem related to it. This has already been indicated in Problem 1(a), Sec. 69, and the next example illustrates the method more fully.

EXAMPLE 2. We consider here the problem

(9) $$(xX')' + \frac{\lambda}{x}X = 0 \qquad (1 < x < b),$$

(10) $$X'(1) = 0, \qquad hX(b) + X'(b) = 0,$$

where h is a positive constant.

Since equation (9) can be put in the Cauchy-Euler form (see Problem 1, Sec. 44)

$$x^2 X'' + xX' + \lambda X = 0,$$

the substitution $x = \exp s$ transforms it into the equation

(11) $$\frac{d^2 X}{ds^2} + \lambda X = 0 \qquad (0 < s < \ln b).$$

Also, since

$$\frac{dX}{dx} = \frac{dX}{ds} e^{-s},$$

the boundary conditions (10) become

(12) $$\frac{dX}{ds} = 0 \text{ when } s = 0, \qquad (hb)X + \frac{dX}{ds} = 0 \text{ when } s = \ln b.$$

Hence, by referring to Example 1, we see immediately that the eigenvalues of problem (11)–(12), and therefore of problem (9)–(10), are the numbers

(13) $$\lambda_n = \alpha_n^2, \qquad \text{where} \qquad \tan (\alpha_n \ln b) = \frac{hb}{\alpha_n} \qquad (\alpha_n > 0).$$

The corresponding eigenfunctions are evidently

$$X_n = \cos \alpha_n s = \cos(\alpha_n \ln x) \qquad (n = 1, 2, \ldots).$$

From equations (9) and (11), we know that the weight functions for the eigenfunctions $X_n = \cos(\alpha_n \ln x)$ and $X_n = \cos \alpha_n s$ are $1/x$ and 1, respectively. The value of the norm $\| X_n \|$ is, however, the same regardless of whether we think of X_n as a function of x or s. This is because, with the substitution $x = \exp s$ ($s = \ln x$), the values of the two integrals

$$\int_1^b \frac{1}{x} \cos^2(\alpha_n \ln x)dx, \qquad \int_0^{\ln b} \cos^2 \alpha_n s \; ds$$

are found to be the same. So, if we replace c by $\ln b$ and h by hb in expression (7), we see that for this problem,

$$\| X_n \|^2 = \frac{hb \ln b + \sin^2(\alpha_n \ln b)}{2hb}.$$

The normalized eigenfunctions are, therefore,

$$(14) \qquad \phi_n(x) = \sqrt{\frac{2hb}{hb \ln b + \sin^2(\alpha_n \ln b)}} \cos(\alpha_n \ln x) \qquad (n = 1, 2, \ldots).$$

PROBLEMS

In Problems 1 through 5, solve directly (without referring to any other problems) for the eigenvalues and normalized eigenfunctions.

1. $X'' + \lambda X = 0, \qquad X(0) = 0, \qquad X'(1) = 0.$

Answer: $\lambda_n = \alpha_n^2, \quad \phi_n(x) = \sqrt{2} \sin \alpha_n x \quad (n = 1, 2, \ldots); \quad \alpha_n = \dfrac{(2n - 1)\pi}{2}.$

2. $X'' + \lambda X = 0, \qquad X(0) = 0, \qquad hX(1) + X'(1) = 0 \quad (h > 0).$

Answer: $\lambda_n = \alpha_n^2, \quad \phi_n(x) = \sqrt{\dfrac{2h}{h + \cos^2 \alpha_n}} \sin \alpha_n x \quad (n = 1, 2, \ldots);$

$\tan \alpha_n = -\dfrac{\alpha_n}{h} \quad (\alpha_n > 0).$

3. $X'' + \lambda X = 0, \qquad X'(0) = 0, \qquad X(c) = 0.$

Answer: $\lambda_n = \alpha_n^2, \quad \phi_n(x) = \sqrt{\dfrac{2}{c}} \cos \alpha_n x \quad (n = 1, 2, \ldots); \quad \alpha_n = \dfrac{(2n - 1)\pi}{2c}.$

4. $X'' + \lambda X = 0, \qquad X(0) = 0, \qquad X(1) - X'(1) = 0.$
Suggestion: The trigonometric identity

$$\cos^2 A = \frac{1}{1 + \tan^2 A}$$

is useful in putting $\| X_n \|^2$ in a form that leads to the expression for $\phi_n(x)$ in the answer below.

Answer: $\lambda_0 = 0, \quad \lambda_n = \alpha_n^2, \quad \phi_0(x) = \sqrt{3}x, \quad \phi_n(x) = \dfrac{\sqrt{2(\alpha_n^2 + 1)}}{\alpha_n} \sin \alpha_n x$

$(n = 1, 2, \ldots);$ $\tan \alpha_n = \alpha_n \; (\alpha_n > 0).$

5. $X'' + \lambda X = 0, \qquad hX(0) - X'(0) = 0 \quad (h > 0), \qquad X(1) = 0.$

Answer: $\lambda_n = \alpha_n^2, \quad \phi_n(x) = \sqrt{\dfrac{2h}{h + \cos^2 \alpha_n}} \sin \alpha_n (1 - x) \quad (n = 1, 2, \ldots);$

$\tan \alpha_n = -\dfrac{\alpha_n}{h} \quad (\alpha_n > 0).$

6. In Problem 1(*a*), Sec. 69, the eigenvalues and eigenfunctions of the Sturm-Liouville problem

$$(xX')' + \frac{\lambda}{x}X = 0, \qquad X(1) = 0, \qquad X(b) = 0$$

were found to be

$$\lambda_n = \alpha_n^2, \qquad X_n(x) = \sin(\alpha_n \ln x) \qquad\qquad (n = 1, 2, \ldots),$$

where $\alpha_n = n\pi / \ln b$. Show that the *normalized* eigenfunctions are

$$\phi_n(x) = \sqrt{\frac{2}{\ln b}} \sin(\alpha_n \ln x) \qquad\qquad (n = 1, 2, \ldots).$$

Suggestion: The integral that arises can be evaluated by making the substitution

$$s = \pi \frac{\ln x}{\ln b}$$

and then referring to the integration formula established in Problem 9, Sec. 5.

7. Find the eigenvalues and normalized eigenfunctions of the Sturm-Liouville problem

$$X'' + \lambda X = 0, \qquad X(0) = 0, \qquad X'(c) = 0$$

by making the substitution $s = x/c$ and referring to the solutions of Problem 1.

Answer: $\lambda_n = \alpha_n^2, \quad \phi_n(x) = \sqrt{\dfrac{2}{c}} \sin \alpha_n x \quad (n = 1, 2, \ldots); \quad \alpha_n = \dfrac{(2n-1)\pi}{2c}.$

8. (*a*) Show that the solutions obtained in Problem 2 can be written

$$\lambda_n = \alpha_n^2, \qquad \phi_n(x) = \sqrt{\frac{2(\alpha_n^2 + h^2)}{\alpha_n^2 + h^2 + h}} \sin \alpha_n x \qquad\qquad (n = 1, 2, \ldots),$$

where $\alpha_n \cos \alpha_n = -h \sin \alpha_n \ (\alpha_n > 0)$.

(*b*) By referring to the solutions of Problem 1, point out why the solutions in part (*a*) here are actually valid solutions of Problem 2 when $h \geq 0$, not just when $h > 0$.

Suggestion: The trigonometric identity in the suggestion with Problem 4 is useful in part (*a*) here as well.

9. Use the solutions obtained in Problem 3 to find the eigenvalues and normalized eigenfunctions of the Sturm-Liouville problem

$$(xX')' + \frac{\lambda}{x}X = 0, \qquad X'(1) = 0, \qquad X(b) = 0.$$

Answer:

$$\lambda_n = \alpha_n^2, \qquad \phi_n(x) = \sqrt{\frac{2}{\ln b}} \cos(\alpha_n \ln x) \quad (n = 1, 2, \ldots); \qquad \alpha_n = \frac{(2n-1)\pi}{2 \ln b}.$$

10. By making an appropriate substitution and referring to the known solutions of the same problem on a different interval in the section indicated, find the eigenfunctions of the Sturm-Liouville problem

(*a*) $X'' + \lambda X = 0, \qquad X'(-\pi) = 0, \qquad X'(\pi) = 0 \quad$ (Sec. 35);

(*b*) $X'' + \lambda X = 0, \qquad X(-c) = X(c), \qquad X'(-c) = X'(c) \quad$ (Sec. 49).

Answers: (a) $1, \cos \dfrac{n(x+\pi)}{2} \quad (n = 1, 2, \ldots);$

(b) $1, \cos \dfrac{n\pi x}{c}, \sin \dfrac{n\pi x}{c} \quad (n = 1, 2, \ldots).$

11. (a) By making the substitutions

$$X = \frac{Y}{\sqrt{x}} \qquad \text{and} \qquad \lambda = \frac{1}{4} + \mu,$$

transform the regular Sturm-Liouville problem

$$(x^2 X')' + \lambda X = 0, \qquad X(1) = 0, \qquad X(b) = 0,$$

where $b > 1$, into the problem

$$(x Y')' + \frac{\mu}{x} Y = 0, \qquad Y(1) = 0, \qquad Y(b) = 0.$$

(b) Obtain the eigenvalues and normalized eigenfunctions of the new problem in part (a) by referring to Problem 6. Then substitute back to show that for the original problem in part (a), the eigenvalues and normalized eigenfunctions are

$$\lambda_n = \frac{1}{4} + \alpha_n^2, \qquad \phi_n(x) = \sqrt{\frac{2}{x \ln b}} \sin(\alpha_n \ln x) \qquad (n = 1, 2, \ldots),$$

where $\alpha_n = n\pi / \ln b$.

12. Find the eigenfunctions of each of these Sturm-Liouville problems:

(a) $X'' + \lambda X = 0, \qquad X(0) = 0, \qquad hX(1) + X'(1) = 0 \quad (h < -1);$

(b) $(x^3 X')' + \lambda x X = 0, \qquad X(1) = 0, \qquad X(e) = 0.$

Answers: (a) $X_0(x) = \sinh \alpha_0 x,$ where $\tanh \alpha_0 = -\dfrac{\alpha_0}{h} \quad (\alpha_0 > 0),$

$X_n(x) = \sin \alpha_n x \quad (n = 1, 2, \ldots),$ where $\tan \alpha_n = -\dfrac{\alpha_n}{h} \quad (\alpha_n > 0);$

(b) $X_n(x) = \dfrac{1}{x} \sin(n\pi \ln x) \qquad (n = 1, 2, \ldots).$

13. Give details showing that the function $W(x)$ defined by equation (7), Sec. 70, is identically equal to zero on the interval $a \le x \le b$.

73. EXAMPLES OF EIGENFUNCTION EXPANSIONS

We now illustrate how generalized Fourier series representations (Sec. 62)

$$(1) \qquad\qquad f(x) = \sum_{n=1}^{\infty} c_n \phi_n(x) \qquad\qquad (a < x < b)$$

are obtained when the functions $\phi_n(x)$ $(n = 1, 2, \ldots)$ are the normalized eigenfunctions of specific Sturm-Liouville problems. We have, of course, already illustrated the method when the eigenfunctions are the ones leading to Fourier cosine and sine series on the interval $0 < x < \pi$, as well as Fourier series on $-\pi < x < \pi$ (see Sec. 63). For other sets of normalized eigenfunctions $\phi_n(x)$ $(n = 1, 2, \ldots)$, we shall use the expression

$$(2) \qquad\qquad c_n = (f, \phi_n) = \int_a^b p(x) f(x) \phi_n(x) \, dx \qquad\qquad (n = 1, 2, \ldots)$$

for the coefficients c_n in expansion (1) that was found in Sec. 62 when the weight function $p(x)$ was unity.

Except for a few cases in which it is easy to establish the validity of an expansion by transforming it into a known Fourier series representation, in this book we do not treat the convergence of series (1). We merely accept the fact that results analogous to the Fourier theorems in Secs. 12 and 13 exist when specific eigenfunctions are used. Such results are often obtained with the aid of the theory of functions of a complex variable.[†] Proofs are complicated by the fact that explicit solutions of the Sturm-Liouville differential equation with arbitrary coefficients cannot be written.

EXAMPLE 1. According to Problem 6, Sec. 72, the Sturm-Liouville problem

$$(xX')' + \frac{\lambda}{x} X = 0, \qquad X(1) = 0, \qquad X(b) = 0$$

has eigenvalues and normalized eigenfunctions

$$\lambda_n = \alpha_n^2, \qquad \phi_n(x) = \sqrt{\frac{2}{\ln b}} \sin(\alpha_n \ln x) \qquad (n = 1, 2, \ldots),$$

where $\alpha_n = n\pi / \ln b$. Since the orthogonality of the set $\{\phi_n(x)\}$ $(n = 1, 2, \ldots)$ is with respect to the weight function $p(x) = 1/x$, the coefficients in the expansion

$$(3) \qquad\qquad\qquad 1 = \sum_{n=1}^{\infty} c_n \phi_n(x) \qquad\qquad\qquad (1 < x < b)$$

are

$$c_n = (f, \phi_n) = \sqrt{\frac{2}{\ln b}} \int_1^b \frac{1}{x} \sin(\alpha_n \ln x) \, dx.$$

Making the substitution $s = \ln x$ here and noting that

$$\cos(\alpha_n \ln b) = \cos n\pi = (-1)^n,$$

we readily see that

$$\int_1^b \frac{1}{x} \sin(\alpha_n \ln x) \, dx = \int_0^{\ln b} \sin \alpha_n s \, ds = \frac{1 - (-1)^n}{\alpha_n}.$$

Thus,

$$c_n = \sqrt{\frac{2}{\ln b}} \cdot \frac{1 - (-1)^n}{\alpha_n} \qquad\qquad (n = 1, 2, \ldots),$$

and expansion (3) becomes

$$(4) \qquad\qquad\qquad 1 = \frac{4}{\ln b} \sum_{n=1}^{\infty} \frac{\sin(\alpha_{2n-1} \ln x)}{\alpha_{2n-1}} \qquad\qquad (1 < x < b).$$

[†]The theory of eigenfunction expansions is extensively developed in the volumes by Titchmarsh (1962, 1958) that are listed in the Bibliography.

The validity of this representation is evident if we introduce the variable

(5)
$$s = \frac{\alpha_{2n-1} \ln x}{2n - 1}$$

and note that

(6)
$$\alpha_{2n-1} = \frac{(2n - 1)\pi}{\ln b}.$$

Equation (4) then becomes the known Fourier sine series expansion

(7)
$$1 = \frac{4}{\pi} \sum_{n=1}^{\infty} \frac{\sin(2n - 1)s}{2n - 1} \qquad (0 < s < \pi)$$

that was found in Problem 1(b), Sec. 5, and the validity of representation (4) is established since it is just a different form of expansion (7).

EXAMPLE 2. The eigenvalues and normalized eigenfunctions of the Sturm-Liouville problem

$$X'' + \lambda X = 0, \qquad X(0) = 0, \qquad X'(c) = 0$$

are (Problem 7, Sec. 72)

$$\lambda_n = \alpha_n^2, \qquad \phi_n(x) = \sqrt{\frac{2}{c}} \sin \alpha_n x \qquad (n = 1, 2, \ldots),$$

where

$$\alpha_n = \frac{(2n - 1)\pi}{2c}.$$

The weight function is $p(x) = 1$, and we may find the coefficients in the expansion

$$x = \sum_{n=1}^{\infty} c_n \phi_n(x) \qquad (0 < x < c)$$

by writing

$$c_n = (f, \phi_n) = \sqrt{\frac{2}{c}} \int_0^c x \sin \alpha_n x \, dx = \sqrt{\frac{2}{c}} \left[-\frac{x \cos \alpha_n x}{\alpha_n} + \frac{\sin \alpha_n x}{\alpha_n^2} \right]_0^c.$$

Since

$$\cos \alpha_n c = \cos\left(n\pi - \frac{\pi}{2} \right) = \cos n\pi \cos \frac{\pi}{2} + \sin n\pi \sin \frac{\pi}{2} = 0$$

and

$$\sin \alpha_n c = \sin\left(n\pi - \frac{\pi}{2} \right) = \sin n\pi \cos \frac{\pi}{2} - \cos n\pi \sin \frac{\pi}{2} = (-1)^{n+1},$$

we find that

$$c_n = \sqrt{\frac{2}{c}} \cdot \frac{(-1)^{n+1}}{\alpha_n^2} \qquad (n = 1, 2, \ldots).$$

Hence,

(8)
$$x = \frac{2}{c} \sum_{n=1}^{\infty} \frac{(-1)^{n+1}}{\alpha_n^2} \sin \alpha_n x \qquad (0 < x < c).$$

After putting expansion (8) in the form

$$x = \frac{8c}{\pi^2} \sum_{n=1}^{\infty} \frac{(-1)^{n+1}}{(2n-1)^2} \sin \frac{(2n-1)\pi x}{2c} \qquad (0 < x < c),$$

we see from Problem 7, Sec. 15, that it is actually valid on the closed interval $-c \le x \le c$. Furthermore,

(9)
$$\sin \alpha_n (x + 2c) = -\sin \alpha_n x \qquad (n = 1, 2, \ldots)$$

since

$$\sin \alpha_n (x + 2c) = \sin(\alpha_n x + 2c\alpha_n) = \sin \alpha_n x \cos 2c\alpha_n + \cos \alpha_n x \sin 2c\alpha_n$$

and

$$\cos 2c\alpha_n = \cos(2n-1)\pi = (-1)^{2n-1} = -1, \qquad \sin 2c\alpha_n = \sin(2n-1)\pi = 0.$$

In view of equation (9), then, series (8) converges for all x; and if $H(x)$ denotes the sum of that series for each value of x, it is clear that $H(x)$ represents the triangular wave function defined by means of the equations (see Fig. 55)

(10)
$$H(x) = x \qquad (-c \le x \le c),$$

(11)
$$H(x + 2c) = -H(x) \qquad (-\infty < x < \infty).$$

Thus $H(x)$ is an *antiperiodic* function. It is also periodic, with period $4c$, as is seen by writing

$$H(x + 4c) = H(x + 2c + 2c) = -H(x + 2c) = H(x).$$

Note, too, that

$$H(2c - x) = -H(x - 2c) = -H(x + 2c) = H(x).$$

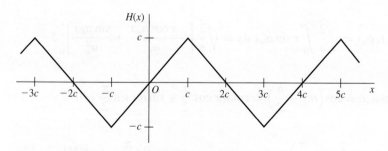

FIGURE 55

We conclude with an example in which the series obtained is a sine series that cannot be transformed into an ordinary Fourier sine series. We must, therefore, accept the representation without verification.

EXAMPLE 3. We consider here the eigenvalues and normalized eigenfunctions of the Sturm-Liouville problem

$$X'' + \lambda X = 0, \qquad X(0) = 0, \qquad X(1) - X'(1) = 0.$$

According to Problem 4, Sec. 72, they are

$$\lambda_0 = 0, \qquad \lambda_n = \alpha_n^2 \qquad\qquad (n = 1, 2, \ldots)$$

and

$$\phi_0(x) = \sqrt{3}\,x, \qquad \phi_n(x) = \frac{\sqrt{2(\alpha_n^2 + 1)}}{\alpha_n}\sin \alpha_n x \qquad (n = 1, 2, \ldots),$$

where $\tan \alpha_n = \alpha_n$ ($\alpha_n > 0$), the weight function being unity. The coefficients in the representation

$$f(x) = c_0\,\phi_0(x) + \sum_{n=1}^{\infty} c_n\,\phi_n(x) \qquad\qquad (0 < x < 1)$$

of a piecewise smooth function $f(x)$ are

$$c_0 = (f, \phi_0) = \sqrt{3}\int_0^1 x f(x)\, dx$$

and

$$c_n = (f, \phi_n) = \frac{\sqrt{2(\alpha_n^2 + 1)}}{\alpha_n}\int_0^1 f(x)\sin \alpha_n x\, dx \qquad (n = 1, 2, \ldots).$$

Consequently,

(12) $$f(x) = B_0\, x + \sum_{n=1}^{\infty} B_n \sin \alpha_n x,$$

where

(13) $$B_0 = 3\int_0^1 x f(x)\, dx \qquad \text{and} \qquad B_n = \frac{2(\alpha_n^2 + 1)}{\alpha_n^2}\int_0^1 f(x)\sin \alpha_n x\, dx$$

$$(n = 1, 2, \ldots).$$

PROBLEMS

1. Use the normalized eigenfunctions in Problem 3, Sec. 72, to derive the representation

$$1 = \frac{2}{c}\sum_{n=1}^{\infty} \frac{(-1)^{n+1}}{\alpha_n}\cos \alpha_n x \qquad\qquad (0 < x < c),$$

where

$$\alpha_n = \frac{(2n - 1)\pi}{2c}.$$

2. Derive the expansion

$$1 = \frac{2}{c}\sum_{n=1}^{\infty} \frac{\sin \alpha_n x}{\alpha_n} \qquad\qquad (0 < x < c),$$

where

$$\alpha_n = \frac{(2n-1)\pi}{2c},$$

using the normalized eigenfunctions in Problem 7, Sec. 72.

3. Use the normalized eigenfunctions in Problem 2, Sec. 72, to derive the expansion

$$1 = 2h \sum_{n=1}^{\infty} \frac{1 - \cos \alpha_n}{\alpha_n(h + \cos^2 \alpha_n)} \sin \alpha_n x \qquad (0 < x < 1),$$

where $\tan \alpha_n = -\alpha_n/h \ (\alpha_n > 0)$.

4. Using the normalized eigenfunctions in Problem 3, Sec. 72, when $c = \pi$, show that

$$\pi^2 - x^2 = \frac{4}{\pi} \sum_{n=1}^{\infty} \frac{(-1)^{n+1}}{\alpha_n^3} \cos \alpha_n x \qquad (0 < x < \pi),$$

where $\alpha_n = (2n-1)/2$.

5. (a) Use the normalized eigenfunctions in Problem 7, Sec. 72, to obtain the expansion

$$x(2c - x) = \frac{4}{c} \sum_{n=1}^{\infty} \frac{\sin \alpha_n x}{\alpha_n^3} \qquad (0 < x < c),$$

where

$$\alpha_n = \frac{(2n-1)\pi}{2c}.$$

(b) Show how it follows from the result in Problem 5, Sec. 8, that the series found in part (a) converges for all x and that its sum is the antiperiodic function (see Example 2, Sec. 73) $Q(x)$ that can be described by means of the equations

$$Q(x) = x(2c - x) \quad (0 \le x \le 2c), \qquad Q(x + 2c) = -Q(x) \quad (-\infty < x < \infty).$$

6. Using the normalized eigenfunctions in Problem 2, Sec. 72, derive the representation

$$x\left(\frac{2+h}{1+h} - x\right) = 4h \sum_{n=1}^{\infty} \frac{1 - \cos \alpha_n}{\alpha_n^3(h + \cos^2 \alpha_n)} \sin \alpha_n x \qquad (0 < x < 1),$$

where $\tan \alpha_n = -\alpha_n/h \ (\alpha_n > 0)$.

Suggestion: In the simplifications, it is useful to note that

$$-h \sin \alpha_n = \alpha_n \cos \alpha_n.$$

7. Use the normalized eigenfunctions in Problem 1, Sec. 72, to show that

$$\sin \omega x = 2\omega \cos \omega \sum_{n=1}^{\infty} \frac{(-1)^n}{\omega^2 - \omega_n^2} \sin \omega_n x \qquad (0 < x < 1),$$

where

$$\omega_n = \frac{(2n-1)\pi}{2} \qquad \text{and} \qquad \omega \ne \omega_n \text{ for any value of } n.$$

Suggestion: The trigonometric identity

$$2 \sin A \sin B = \cos(A - B) - \cos(A + B)$$

is useful in evaluating the integrals that arise.

8. Find the Fourier constants c_n for the function $f(x) = x$ $(1 < x < b)$ with respect to the normalized eigenfunctions in Problem 6, Sec. 72, and reduce those constants to the form

$$c_n = \sqrt{2 \ln b} \; \frac{n\pi[1 + (-1)^{n+1}b]}{(\ln b)^2 + (n\pi)^2} \qquad (n = 1, 2, \ldots).$$

Suggestion: The integration formula

$$\int e^x \sin ax \, dx = \frac{e^x(\sin ax - a \cos ax)}{1 + a^2},$$

derived in calculus, is useful here.

9. Let f be a piecewise smooth function defined on the interval $1 < x < b$.

(a) Use the normalized eigenfunctions in Problem 6, Sec. 72, to show formally that if $\alpha_n = n\pi / \ln b$, then

$$f(x) = \sum_{n=1}^{\infty} B_n \sin(\alpha_n \ln x) \qquad (1 < x < b),$$

where

$$B_n = \frac{2}{\ln b} \int_1^b \frac{1}{x} f(x) \sin(\alpha_n \ln x) \, dx \qquad (n = 1, 2, \ldots).$$

(b) By making the substitution $x = \exp s$ in the series and integral in part (a) and then referring to Theorem 2 in Sec. 15, verify that the series representation in part (a) is valid for all points in the interval $1 < x < b$ at which f is continuous. (Compare with Example 1, Sec. 73.)

10. Suppose that a function f, defined on the interval $0 < x < c$, is piecewise smooth there.

(a) Use the normalized eigenfunctions (Problem 7, Sec. 72)

$$\phi_n(x) = \sqrt{\frac{2}{c}} \sin \alpha_n x \qquad (n = 1, 2, \ldots),$$

where

$$\alpha_n = \frac{(2n-1)\pi}{2c},$$

to show formally that

$$f(x) = \sum_{n=1}^{\infty} B_n \sin \alpha_n x \qquad (0 < x < c),$$

where

$$B_n = \frac{2}{c} \int_0^c f(x) \sin \alpha_n x \, dx \qquad (n = 1, 2, \ldots).$$

(b) Note that according to Problem 6, Sec. 15, the series in part (a) is actually a Fourier sine series for an extension of f on the interval $0 < x < 2c$. Then, with the aid of Theorem 2 in Sec. 15, state why the representation in part (a) is valid for each point x $(0 < x < c)$ at which f is continuous.

11. (a) Use the normalized eigenfunctions

$$\phi_n(x) = \sqrt{2} \sin \alpha_n x \qquad (n = 1, 2, \ldots),$$

where

$$\alpha_n = \frac{(2n-1)\pi}{2},$$

in Problem 1, Sec. 72, to show formally that

$$x\left(1 - \frac{1}{3}x^2\right) = 4\sum_{n=1}^{\infty} \frac{(-1)^{n+1}}{\alpha_n^4} \sin \alpha_n x \qquad (0 < x < 1).$$

(b) According to Problem 10, the series in part (a) here is a Fourier sine series on the interval $0 < x < 2$. With the aid of Theorem 2 in Sec. 15, show that the series just obtained in part (a) converges for all x and that its sum is the antiperiodic function (see Example 2, Sec. 73) $Q(x)$ that is described by means of the equations

$$Q(x) = x\left(1 - \frac{1}{3}x^2\right) \quad (-1 \le x \le 1), \qquad Q(x+2) = -Q(x) \quad (-\infty < x < \infty).$$

74. A TEMPERATURE PROBLEM IN RECTANGULAR COORDINATES

In this and the remaining sections of the chapter, we shall illustrate how the Fourier method can be applied to boundary value problems that lead to Sturm-Liouville problems other than the ones arising in Chap. 5. As was the case in Chap. 5, we seek only *formal* solutions of our boundary value problems.

Let $u(x, t)$ denote temperatures in a slab $0 \le x \le 1$ (Fig. 56), initially at temperatures $f(x)$, when the face $x = 0$ is insulated and surface heat transfer takes place at the face $x = 1$ into a medium at temperature zero (see Sec. 26). The boundary value problem to be solved is evidently

$$(1) \qquad\qquad u_t(x, t) = k u_{xx}(x, t) \qquad\qquad (0 < x < 1, t > 0),$$

$$(2) \qquad u_x(0, t) = 0, \qquad u_x(1, t) = -hu(1, t), \qquad u(x, 0) = f(x),$$

where h is a positive constant.

$u(x, 0) = f(x)$ $0°$

x

$x = 0$ $x = 1$

FIGURE 56

Writing $u = X(x)T(t)$ and separating variables, we arrive at the Sturm-Liouville problem

$$(3) \qquad X''(x) + \lambda X(x) = 0, \qquad X'(0) = 0, \qquad hX(1) + X'(1) = 0,$$

along with the condition $T'(t) + \lambda k T(t) = 0$. The eigenvalues and normalized eigenfunctions of problem (3) are, according to Example 1, Sec. 72,

$$\lambda_n = \alpha_n^2, \qquad X_n = \phi_n(x) = \sqrt{\frac{2h}{h + \sin^2 \alpha_n}} \cos \alpha_n x \qquad (n = 1, 2, \ldots),$$

where $\tan \alpha_n = h / \alpha_n$ ($\alpha_n > 0$). The corresponding functions of t are, moreover, constant multiples of

$$T_n(t) = \exp\left(-\alpha_n^2 k t\right) \qquad (n = 1, 2, \ldots).$$

Hence, the formal solution of our temperature problem is

$$(4) \qquad u(x, t) = \sum_{n=1}^{\infty} \gamma_n \exp\left(-\alpha_n^2 k t\right) \phi_n(x),$$

where, in order that $u(x, 0) = f(x)$ ($0 < x < 1$),

$$(5) \qquad \gamma_n = (f, \phi_n) = \int_0^1 f(x) \phi_n(x)\, dx = \sqrt{\frac{2h}{h + \sin^2 \alpha_n}} \int_0^1 f(x) \cos \alpha_n x\, dx$$
$$(n = 1, 2, \ldots).$$

Observe that series (4), when the expression for the normalized eigenfunctions $\phi_n(x)$ of problem (3) is used, is

$$u(x, t) = \sum_{n=1}^{\infty} \left(\sqrt{\frac{2h}{h + \sin^2 \alpha_n}}\, \gamma_n \right) \exp\left(-\alpha_n^2 k t\right) \cos \alpha_n x.$$

Hence the solution just obtained can be written

$$(6) \qquad u(x, t) = \sum_{n=1}^{\infty} A_n \exp\left(-\alpha_n^2 k t\right) \cos \alpha_n x,$$

where

$$(7) \qquad A_n = \frac{2h}{h + \sin^2 \alpha_n} \int_0^1 f(x) \cos \alpha_n x\, dx \qquad (n = 1, 2, \ldots).$$

It is easy to show that solution (6), with coefficients (7), also satisfies the boundary value problem

$$(8) \qquad u_t(x, t) = k u_{xx}(x, t) \qquad\qquad (-1 < x < 1, t > 0),$$

$$(9) \qquad u_x(-1, t) = h u(-1, t), \qquad u_x(1, t) = -h u(1, t) \qquad (t > 0),$$

$$(10) \qquad u(x, 0) = f(x) \qquad\qquad (-1 < x < 1),$$

when f is an *even* function, or when $f(-x) = f(x)$ ($-1 < x < 1$). For we already know that u satisfies the heat equation and the second of boundary conditions (9). Since the cosine function is even, it is clear from expression (6) that u is even in x; and its partial derivative u_x is odd in x. Hence the first of boundary conditions (9) is also satisfied:

$$u_x(-1, t) = -u_x(1, t) = h u(1, t) = h u(-1, t).$$

Finally, we already know that $u(x, 0) = f(x)$ when $0 < x < 1$; furthermore, when $-1 < x < 0$, the fact that u and f are even in x enables us to write

$$u(x, 0) = u(-x, 0) = f(-x) = f(x).$$

The boundary value problem (8)–(10) is, of course, a temperature problem for a slab $-1 \le x \le 1$ with initial temperatures (10) and with surface heat transfer at both faces into a medium at temperature zero (Fig. 57). The solution of problem (8)–(10) when f is not necessarily even is obtained in the problems.

FIGURE 57

PROBLEMS[†]

1. Show that when $f(x) = 1$ $(0 < x < 1)$ in the boundary value problem (1)–(2) in Sec. 74, the solution (6)–(7) there reduces to

$$u(x, t) = 2h \sum_{n=1}^{\infty} \frac{\sin \alpha_n}{\alpha_n(h + \sin^2 \alpha_n)} \exp\left(-\alpha_n^2 kt\right) \cos \alpha_n x,$$

where $\tan \alpha_n = h/\alpha_n$ $(\alpha_n > 0)$.

2. Use the normalized eigenfunctions of the Sturm-Liouville problem

$$X'' + \lambda X = 0, \qquad X(0) = 0, \qquad X'(\pi) = 0$$

to solve the boundary value problem

$$u_t(x, t) = k u_{xx}(x, t) \qquad\qquad (0 < x < \pi, t > 0),$$

$$u(0, t) = 0, \qquad u_x(\pi, t) = 0, \qquad u(x, 0) = f(x).$$

Show that the solution can be written

$$u(x, t) = \sum_{n=1}^{\infty} B_{2n-1} \exp\left[-\frac{(2n-1)^2 k}{4} t\right] \sin \frac{(2n-1)x}{2},$$

[†]The eigenvalues and (normalized) eigenfunctions of any Sturm-Liouville problem that arises have already been found in Sec. 72 or in the problem set with that section.

where

$$B_{2n-1} = \frac{2}{\pi} \int_0^\pi f(x) \sin \frac{(2n-1)x}{2} \, dx \qquad (n = 1, 2, \ldots).$$

(The solution in this form was obtained in another way in Example 2, Sec. 40.)

3. Give a full physical interpretation of the following temperature problem, involving a time-dependent diffusivity, and derive its solution:

$$(1+t)u_t(x, t) = u_{xx}(x, t) \qquad (0 < x < 1, t > 0),$$

$$u(0, t) = 0, \qquad u_x(1, t) = 0, \qquad u(x, 0) = 1.$$

Answer: $u(x, t) = 2 \sum_{n=1}^\infty \frac{\sin \alpha_n x}{\alpha_n} (1+t)^{-\alpha_n^2}$, where $\alpha_n = \dfrac{(2n-1)\pi}{2}$.

4. (*a*) Give a physical interpretation of the boundary value problem

$$u_t(x, t) = k u_{xx}(x, t) \qquad (0 < x < 1, t > 0),$$

$$u(0, t) = 0, \qquad u_x(1, t) = -h u(1, t), \qquad u(x, 0) = f(x),$$

where h is a positive constant. Then derive the solution

$$u(x, t) = \sum_{n=1}^\infty B_n \exp\left(-\alpha_n^2 k t\right) \sin \alpha_n x,$$

where $\tan \alpha_n = -\alpha_n/h \ (\alpha_n > 0)$ and

$$B_n = \frac{2h}{h + \cos^2 \alpha_n} \int_0^1 f(x) \sin \alpha_n x \, dx \qquad (n = 1, 2, \ldots).$$

(*b*) Use an argument similar to the one at the end of Sec. 74 to show that the solution found in part (*a*) formally satisfies the boundary value problem (8)–(10) in that section when the function f there is *odd*, or when

$$f(-x) = -f(x) \qquad (-1 < x < 1).$$

5. Use the following method to solve the temperature problem (see Fig. 57 in Sec. 74)

$$u_t(x, t) = k u_{xx}(x, t) \qquad (-1 < x < 1, t > 0),$$

$$u_x(-1, t) = h u(-1, t), \qquad u_x(1, t) = -h u(1, t) \qquad (t > 0),$$

$$u(x, 0) = f(x) \qquad (-1 < x < 1)$$

when the function f is not necessarily even or odd, as it was in condition (10), Sec. 74, and Problem 4(*b*), respectively.

(*a*) Show that if $v(x, t)$ is the solution of the problem when $f(x)$ is replaced by the function

$$G(x) = \frac{f(x) + f(-x)}{2}$$

and if $w(x, t)$ is the solution when $f(x)$ is replaced by

$$H(x) = \frac{f(x) - f(-x)}{2},$$

then the sum $u(x, t) = v(x, t) + w(x, t)$ satisfies the above boundary value problem.

(b) After noting that the functions G and H in part (a) are even and odd, respectively, apply the result there, together with results in Sec. 74 and Problem 4, to show that

$$u(x, t) = \sum_{n=1}^{\infty} A_n \exp\left(-\alpha_n^2 kt\right) \cos \alpha_n x + \sum_{n=1}^{\infty} B_n \exp\left(-\beta_n^2 kt\right) \sin \beta_n x,$$

where

$$\tan \alpha_n = \frac{h}{\alpha_n} \quad (\alpha_n > 0), \qquad \tan \beta_n = -\frac{\beta_n}{h} \quad (\beta_n > 0)$$

and

$$A_n = \frac{h}{h + \sin^2 \alpha_n} \int_{-1}^{1} f(x) \cos \alpha_n x \, dx, \qquad B_n = \frac{h}{h + \cos^2 \beta_n} \int_{-1}^{1} f(x) \sin \beta_n x \, dx.$$

Suggestion: In part (b), write

$$\int_0^1 G(x) \cos \alpha_n x \, dx = \frac{1}{2} \left[\int_0^1 f(x) \cos \alpha_n x \, dx + \int_0^1 f(-s) \cos \alpha_n s \, ds \right]$$

and

$$\int_0^1 H(x) \sin \beta_n x \, dx = \frac{1}{2} \left[\int_0^1 f(x) \sin \beta_n x \, dx - \int_0^1 f(-s) \sin \beta_n s \, ds \right],$$

where $G(x)$ and $H(x)$ are the functions appearing in part (a). Then make the substitution $x = -s$ in the second integrals on the right-hand sides of these equations.

75. STEADY TEMPERATURES

In this section, we treat two steady temperature problems.

EXAMPLE 1. Let $u(x, y)$ represent a function that is harmonic inside a square whose edges are of unit length:

$$(1) \qquad u_{xx}(x, y) + u_{yy}(x, y) = 0 \qquad (0 < x < 1, 0 < y < 1).$$

The function is to satisfy the boundary conditions

$$(2) \qquad u(x, 0) = 0, \qquad u_y(x, 1) = -hu(x, 1) \qquad (0 < x < 1),$$

where h is a positive constant, and

$$(3) \qquad u(0, y) = 0, \qquad u(1, y) = f(y) \qquad (0 < y < 1).$$

This can be thought of as a problem in steady temperatures in a long rod with a square cross section. The temperatures on three of its surfaces are as shown in Fig. 58, and there is surface heat transfer into a medium at temperature zero through the fourth surface.

We start the solution of this boundary value problem by substituting the product $u = X(x)Y(y)$ into conditions (1) and (2) and writing

$$(4) \qquad Y''(y) + \lambda Y(y) = 0, \qquad Y(0) = 0, \qquad hY(1) + Y'(1) = 0,$$
$$(5) \qquad X''(x) - \lambda X(x) = 0, \qquad X(0) = 0.$$

FIGURE 58

Problem 2, Sec. 72, tells us that the eigenvalues and normalized eigenfunctions of the Sturm-Liouville problem (4) are

$$\lambda_n = \alpha_n^2, \qquad Y_n = \phi_n(y) = \sqrt{\frac{2h}{h + \cos^2 \alpha_n}} = \sin \alpha_n y \qquad (n = 1, 2, \ldots)$$

where $\tan \alpha_n = -\alpha_n / h \ (\alpha_n > 0)$. When $\lambda = \alpha_n^2$, it follows from conditions (5) that the corresponding functions of x are constant multiples of

$$X_n(x) = \sinh \alpha_n x \qquad (n = 1, 2, \ldots).$$

Thus,

$$(6) \qquad\qquad u(x, y) = \sum_{n=1}^{\infty} \gamma_n \sinh \alpha_n x \, \phi_n(y),$$

where the γ_n are constants whose values are to be found.

Now the second of conditions (3) is satisfied when

$$f(y) = \sum_{n=1}^{\infty} \gamma_n \sinh \alpha_n \, \phi_n(y) \qquad\qquad (0 < y < 1),$$

and so

$$\gamma_n \sinh \alpha_n = (f, \phi_n) = \int_0^1 f(y) \phi_n(y) \, dy = \sqrt{\frac{2h}{h + \cos^2 \alpha_n}} \int_0^1 f(y) \sin \alpha_n y \, dy$$

$$(n = 1, 2, \ldots).$$

That is,

$$(7) \qquad \sqrt{\frac{2h}{h + \cos^2 \alpha_n}} \gamma_n = \frac{1}{\sinh \alpha_n} \cdot \frac{2h}{h + \cos^2 \alpha_n} \int_0^1 f(y) \sin \alpha_n y \, dy \qquad (n = 1, 2, \ldots).$$

Finally, if we rewrite series (6) as

$$u(x, y) = \sum_{n=1}^{\infty} \left(\sqrt{\frac{2h}{h + \cos^2 \alpha_n}} \gamma_n \right) \sinh \alpha_n x \sin \alpha_n y,$$

equation (7) enables us to express our solution in the form

$$(8) \qquad\qquad u(x, y) = \sum_{n=1}^{\infty} B_n \frac{\sinh \alpha_n x}{\sinh \alpha_n} \sin \alpha_n y$$

where

$$(9) \qquad B_n = \frac{2h}{h + \cos^2 \alpha_n} \int_0^1 f(y) \sin \alpha_n y \, dy \qquad\qquad (n = 1, 2, \ldots).$$

EXAMPLE 2. Here $u(x, y)$ denotes the bounded steady temperatures in a semi-infinite slab, bounded by the planes $x = 0$, $x = \pi$, and $y = 0$ (Fig. 59), whose faces are subject to the following conditions. The face in the plane $x = 0$ is insulated, the face in the plane $x = \pi$ is kept at temperature zero, and the flux inward through the face in the plane $y = 0$ (see Sec. 26) is a prescribed function $f(x)$. The boundary value problem for this slab is

$$(10) \qquad u_{xx}(x, y) + u_{yy}(x, y) = 0 \qquad\qquad (0 < x < \pi, y > 0),$$

$$(11) \qquad u_x(0, y) = 0, \qquad u(\pi, y) = 0 \qquad\qquad (y > 0),$$

$$(12) \qquad -K u_y(x, 0) = f(x) \qquad\qquad (0 < x < \pi),$$

where K is a positive constant.

FIGURE 59

By assuming a product solution $u = X(x)Y(y)$ of conditions (10) and (11) and separating variables, we find that

$$(13) \qquad X''(x) + \lambda X(x) = 0, \qquad X'(0) = 0, \qquad X(\pi) = 0$$

and that $Y(y)$ is to be a *bounded* solution of the differential equation

$$(14) \qquad Y''(y) - \lambda Y(y) = 0.$$

According to Problem 3, Sec. 72, the eigenvalues and normalized eigenfunctions of the Sturm-Liouville problem (13) are

$$\lambda_n = \alpha_n^2, \qquad X_n = \phi_n(x) = \sqrt{\frac{2}{\pi}} \cos \alpha_n x \qquad (n = 1, 2, \ldots),$$

where $\alpha_n = (2n - 1)/2$. Also, when $\lambda = \alpha_n^2$, the general solution of equation (14) is

$$Y(y) = C_1 e^{\alpha_n y} + C_2 e^{-\alpha_n y}.$$

In order that this solution be bounded, we need $C_1 = 0$; and the needed bounded solutions of equation (14) are constant multiples of the functions

$$Y_n(y) = \exp(-\alpha_n y) \qquad\qquad (n = 1, 2, \ldots).$$

Consequently,

$$(15) \qquad\qquad u(x, y) = \sum_{n=1}^{\infty} \gamma_n \exp(-\alpha_n y)\, \phi_n(x),$$

where the coefficients γ_n here are to be determined.

Applying the nonhomogeneous condition (12) to expression (15), one can see that the constants γ_n must be such that

$$f(x) = \sum_{n=1}^{\infty} (K\gamma_n \alpha_n)\, \phi_n(x) \qquad\qquad (0 < x < \pi).$$

That is,

$$(16) \qquad K\gamma_n \alpha_n = (f, \phi_n) = \sqrt{\frac{2}{\pi}} \int_0^{\pi} f(x) \cos \alpha_n x\, dx \qquad (n = 1, 2, \ldots).$$

Finally, it follows from expressions (15) and (16) that

$$(17) \qquad\qquad u(x, y) = \frac{1}{K} \sum_{n=1}^{\infty} A_n \frac{\exp(-\alpha_n y)}{\alpha_n} \cos \alpha_n x,$$

where

$$(18) \qquad\qquad A_n = \frac{2}{\pi} \int_0^{\pi} f(x) \cos \alpha_n x\, dx \qquad\qquad (n = 1, 2, \ldots).$$

Since $\alpha_n = (2n - 1)/2$, equations (17) and (18) can, of course, be written in the form

$$(19) \qquad u(x, y) = \frac{2}{K} \sum_{n=1}^{\infty} \frac{A_n}{2n - 1} \exp\left[-\frac{(2n - 1)y}{2}\right] \cos \frac{(2n - 1)x}{2},$$

where

$$(20) \qquad\qquad A_n = \frac{2}{\pi} \int_0^{\pi} f(x) \cos \frac{(2n - 1)x}{2}\, dx \qquad (n = 1, 2, \ldots).$$

PROBLEMS†

1. Solve the boundary value problem

$$u_{xx}(x, y) + u_{yy}(x, y) = 0 \qquad\qquad (0 < x < a, 0 < y < b),$$
$$u_x(0, y) = 0, \qquad u_x(a, y) = -hu(a, y) \qquad\qquad (0 < y < b),$$
$$u(x, 0) = 0, \qquad u(x, b) = f(x) \qquad\qquad (0 < x < a),$$

---

†The footnote with the problem set for Sec. 74 applies here too.

where h is a positive constant, and interpret $u(x, y)$ physically.

$$\textit{Answer: } u(x, y) = 2h \sum_{n=1}^{\infty} \frac{\cos \alpha_n x}{ha + \sin^2 \alpha_n a} \cdot \frac{\sinh \alpha_n y}{\sinh \alpha_n b} \int_0^a f(s) \cos \alpha_n s \, ds,$$

where $\tan \alpha_n a = h/\alpha_n \ (\alpha_n > 0)$.

2. A bounded harmonic function $u(x, y)$ in the semi-infinite strip $x > 0, 0 < y < 1$ is to satisfy the boundary conditions

$$u(x, 0) = 0, \qquad u_y(x, 1) = -hu(x, 1), \qquad u(0, y) = u_0,$$

where $h \ (h > 0)$ and u_0 are constants. Derive the expression

$$u(x, y) = 2hu_0 \sum_{n=1}^{\infty} \frac{1 - \cos \alpha_n}{\alpha_n (h + \cos^2 \alpha_n)} \exp(-\alpha_n x) \sin \alpha_n y,$$

where $\tan \alpha_n = -\alpha_n/h \ (\alpha_n > 0)$. Interpret $u(x, y)$ physically.

3. Find the bounded harmonic function $u(x, y)$ in the semi-infinite strip $0 < x < 1, y > 0$ that satisfies the boundary conditions

$$u_x(0, y) = 0, \qquad u_x(1, y) = -hu(1, y), \qquad u(x, 0) = f(x),$$

where h is a positive constant, and interpret $u(x, y)$ physically.

$$\textit{Answer: } u(x, y) = \sum_{n=1}^{\infty} A_n \exp(-\alpha_n y) \cos \alpha_n x,$$

where $\tan \alpha_n = h/\alpha_n \ (\alpha_n > 0)$ and

$$A_n = \frac{2h}{h + \sin^2 \alpha_n} \int_0^1 f(x) \cos \alpha_n x \, dx \qquad (n = 1, 2, \ldots).$$

4. Find the bounded solution of this boundary value problem, where b and h are positive constants:

$$u_{xx}(x, y) + u_{yy}(x, y) - bu(x, y) = 0 \qquad (0 < x < 1, y > 0),$$

$$u(0, y) = 0, \qquad u_x(1, y) = -hu(1, y), \qquad u(x, 0) = f(x).$$

$$\textit{Answer: } u(x, y) = \sum_{n=1}^{\infty} B_n \frac{\sin \alpha_n x}{\exp\left(y\sqrt{b + \alpha_n^2}\right)},$$

where $\tan \alpha_n = -\alpha_n/h \ (\alpha_n > 0)$ and

$$B_n = \frac{2h}{h + \cos^2 \alpha_n} \int_0^1 f(x) \sin \alpha_n x \, dx \qquad (n = 1, 2, \ldots).$$

76. OTHER COORDINATES

To illustrate the methods of this chapter in other than rectangular coordinates, we next consider a problem involving polar coordinates. In addition, two of the problems immediately following this section involve spherical coordinates.

    We seek here a function $u(\rho, \phi)$ that satisfies a Dirichlet problem (Sec. 31) consisting of Laplace's equation

(1) $$\rho^2 u_{\rho\rho}(\rho, \phi) + \rho u_\rho(\rho, \phi) + u_{\phi\phi}(\rho, \phi) = 0 \qquad (1 < \rho < b, 0 < \phi < \pi)$$

and the boundary conditions (Fig. 60)

(2) $\qquad\qquad\qquad u(\rho, 0) = 0, \qquad u(\rho, \pi) = u_0 \qquad\qquad (1 < \rho < b),$

(3) $\qquad\qquad\qquad u(1, \phi) = 0, \qquad u(b, \phi) = 0 \qquad\qquad (0 < \phi < \pi),$

where u_0 is a constant.

FIGURE 60

Substitution of the product $u = R(\rho)\Phi(\varphi)$ into the differential equation (1), followed by separation of variables, yields

$$\frac{\rho^2 R''}{R} + \frac{\rho R'}{R} = -\frac{\Phi''}{\Phi} = -\lambda,$$

where $-\lambda$, rather than λ, is chosen as the separation constant in order to obtain a Sturm-Liouville problem in standard form. More precisely, we have the conditions

(4) $\qquad\qquad (\rho R')' + \dfrac{\lambda}{\rho} R = 0, \qquad R(1) = 0, \qquad R(b) = 0,$

(5) $\qquad\qquad\qquad \Phi'' - \lambda\Phi = 0, \qquad \Phi(0) = 0.$

and need only refer to Problem 6, Sec. 72, to see that the eigenvalues of problem (4) are $\lambda_n = \alpha_n^2$ $(n = 1, 2, \ldots)$, where $\alpha_n = n\pi / \ln b$, and that the normalized eigenfunctions are

$$R_n = \phi_n(\rho) = \sqrt{\frac{2}{\ln b}} \sin(\alpha_n \ln \rho) \qquad\qquad (n = 1, 2, \ldots).$$

The weight function for these eigenfunctions is, moreover, $1/\rho$. Except for constant factors, the corresponding functions of ϕ, arising from conditions (5) when $\lambda = \alpha_n^2$, are

$$\Phi_n = \sinh \alpha_n \phi \qquad\qquad (n = 1, 2, \ldots).$$

Hence,

(6) $\qquad\qquad\qquad u(\rho, \phi) = \sum_{n=1}^{\infty} (\gamma_n \sinh \alpha_n \phi)\, \phi_n(\rho).$

Turning to the nonhomogeneous condition $u(\rho, \pi) = u_0$, we set $\phi = \pi$ in expression (6) and write

$$u_0 = \sum_{n=1}^{\infty} (\gamma_n \sinh \alpha_n \pi)\, \phi_n(\rho) \qquad\qquad (1 < \rho < b).$$

Evidently, then, the products $\gamma_n \sinh \alpha_n \pi$ are the Fourier constants in this expansion, and so

$$\gamma_n \sinh \alpha_n \pi = (u_0, \phi_n) = u_0 \sqrt{\frac{2}{\ln b}} \int_1^b \frac{1}{\rho} \sin(\alpha_n \ln \rho) \, d\rho.$$

This integral is readily evaluated by making the substitution $\rho = \exp s$; and by recalling that $\alpha_n = n\pi / \ln b$, one can simplify the result to show that

$$\tag{7} \gamma_n \sinh \alpha_n \pi = \frac{u_0 \sqrt{2 \ln b}}{\pi} \cdot \frac{1 - (-1)^n}{n}.$$

So, in view of expressions (6) and (7),

$$u(\rho, \phi) = \frac{2u_0}{\pi} \sum_{n=1}^{\infty} \frac{1 - (-1)^n}{n} \cdot \frac{\sinh \alpha_n \phi}{\sinh \alpha_n \pi} \sin(\alpha_n \ln \rho).$$

That is,

$$\tag{8} u(\rho, \phi) = \frac{4u_0}{\pi} \sum_{n=1}^{\infty} \frac{\sinh \alpha_{2n-1}\phi}{\sinh \alpha_{2n-1}\pi} \cdot \frac{\sin(\alpha_{2n-1} \ln \rho)}{2n - 1}.$$

It is interesting to contrast this solution with the one obtained in Example 1, Sec. 44, for a Dirichlet problem involving the same region but with the nonhomogeneous condition $u = u_0$ occurring when $\rho = b$ instead of when $\phi = \pi$.

PROBLEMS[†]

1. Show that if the condition $u(\rho, \pi) = u_0$ $(1 < \rho < b)$ in Sec. 76 is replaced by the condition $u(\rho, \pi) = \rho$ $(1 < \rho < b)$, then

$$u(\rho, \phi) = 2\pi \sum_{n=1}^{\infty} \frac{n[1 + (-1)^{n+1}b]}{(\ln b)^2 + (n\pi)^2} \cdot \frac{\sinh \alpha_n \phi}{\sinh \alpha_n \pi} \sin(\alpha_n \ln \rho),$$

where $\alpha_n = n\pi / \ln b$.

Suggestion: The Fourier constants found in Problem 8, Sec. 73, can be used here.

2. Let ρ, ϕ, z denote cylindrical coordinates, and solve the following boundary value problem in the region $1 \le \rho \le b, 0 \le \phi \le \pi$ of the plane $z = 0$:

$$\rho^2 u_{\rho\rho}(\rho, \phi) + \rho u_\rho(\rho, \phi) + u_{\phi\phi}(\rho, \phi) = 0 \qquad (1 < \rho < b, 0 < \phi < \pi),$$

$$u_\rho(1, \phi) = 0, \qquad u_\rho(b, \phi) = -hu(b, \phi) \qquad (0 < \phi < \pi),$$

$$u_\phi(\rho, 0) = 0, \qquad u(\rho, \pi) = u_0 \qquad (1 < \rho < b),$$

where h $(h > 0)$ and u_0 are constants. Interpret the function $u(\rho, \phi)$ physically.

Answer: $u(\rho, \phi) = 2hbu_0 \sum_{n=1}^{\infty} \frac{\cosh \alpha_n \phi}{\cosh \alpha_n \pi} \cdot \frac{\sin(\alpha_n \ln b) \cos(\alpha_n \ln \rho)}{\alpha_n [hb \ln b + \sin^2(\alpha_n \ln b)]},$

where $\tan(\alpha_n \ln b) = hb/\alpha_n$ $(\alpha_n > 0)$.

[†]See the footnote with the problem set for Sec. 74.

3. The boundary $r = 1$ of a *solid sphere* is kept insulated and that solid is initially at temperatures $f(r)$, where r is the spherical coordinate described in Sec. 24. If $u(r, t)$ denotes subsequent temperatures, then

$$\frac{\partial u}{\partial t} = \frac{k}{r} \frac{\partial^2}{\partial r^2} (ru), \qquad u_r(1, t) = 0, \qquad u(r, 0) = f(r).$$

By writing $v(r, t) = ru(r, t)$ and requiring that u be continuous when $r = 0$ (compare with Example 1, Sec. 41), set up a boundary value problem in v, involving the boundary conditions

$$v(0, t) = 0, \qquad v(1, t) = v_r(1, t), \qquad v(r, 0) = rf(r).$$

Then derive the temperature formula

$$u(r, t) = B_0 + \sum_{n=1}^{\infty} B_n \frac{\sin \alpha_n r}{\alpha_n r} \exp(-\alpha_n^2 kt),$$

where $\tan \alpha_n = \alpha_n$ ($\alpha_n > 0$) and

$$B_0 = 3 \int_0^1 r^2 f(r) \, dr, \qquad B_n = 2 \left(\alpha_n + \frac{1}{\alpha_n} \right) \int_0^1 rf(r) \sin \alpha_n r \, dr \qquad (n = 1, 2, \ldots).$$

(An eigenfunction expansion similar to the one required here was found in Example 3, Sec. 73.)

4. By writing $v(r, t) = ru(r, t)$, find the temperatures $u = u(r, t)$ in the solid sphere of Problem 3 when the conditions there are replaced by

$$\frac{\partial u}{\partial t} = \frac{k}{r} \frac{\partial^2}{\partial r^2} (ru), \qquad u_r(1, t) = -hu(1, t), \qquad u(r, 0) = f(r),$$

where the constant h is larger than 1. Interpret this problem physically and derive the temperature formula

$$u(r, t) = \sum_{n=1}^{\infty} B_n \frac{\sin \alpha_n r}{r} \exp(-\alpha_n^2 kt),$$

where

$$\tan \alpha_n = -\frac{\alpha_n}{h-1} \qquad (\alpha_n > 0)$$

and

$$B_n = \frac{2(h-1)}{h - 1 + \cos^2 \alpha_n} \int_0^1 rf(r) \sin \alpha_n r \, dr \qquad (n = 1, 2, \ldots).$$

Suggestion: The Solution of the problem

$$\frac{\partial v}{\partial t} = k \frac{\partial^2 v}{\partial x^2}, \qquad v(0, t) = 0, \qquad v_r(1, t) = -(h - 1)v(1, t), \qquad v(r, 0) = rf(r)$$

in $v(r, t)$ is readily found by referring to Problem 4(a), Sec 74.

77. A MODIFICATION OF THE METHOD

We now illustrate a certain modification of the Fourier method that can often be used when generalized Fourier series arise. Another such modification is illustrated in Sec. 78. Both types of modifications were used in Chap. 5 when ordinary Fourier cosine and sine series were involved.

Assume that heat is introduced through the face $x = 1$ of a slab $0 \le x \le 1$ at a uniform rate $A \, (A > 0)$ per unit area (Sec. 26), while the face $x = 0$ is kept at the initial temperature zero of the slab. The temperature function $u(x, t)$ must satisfy the conditions

$$(1) \qquad\qquad u_t(x, t) = k u_{xx}(x, t) \qquad\qquad (0 < x < 1, t > 0),$$

$$(2) \qquad\qquad u(0, t) = 0, \qquad K u_x(1, t) = A \qquad\qquad (t > 0),$$

$$(3) \qquad\qquad u(x, 0) = 0 \qquad\qquad (0 < x < 1).$$

Because the second of conditions (2) is nonhomogeneous, we do not have two-point boundary conditions leading to a Sturm-Liouville problem. But, by writing

$$(4) \qquad\qquad u(x, t) = U(x, t) + \Phi(x)$$

(compare with Example 2, Sec. 39), we find that conditions (1)–(3) become

$$U_t(x, t) = k[U_{xx}(x, t) + \Phi''(x)],$$

$$U(0, t) + \Phi(0) = 0, \qquad K[U_x(1, t) + \Phi'(1)] = A,$$

and

$$U(x, 0) + \Phi(x) = 0.$$

Hence, if we require that

$$(5) \qquad \Phi''(x) = 0 \quad \text{and} \quad \Phi(0) = 0, \qquad K\Phi'(1) = A,$$

we have the boundary value problem

$$(6) \quad U_t(x, t) = k U_{xx}(x, t), \quad U(0, t) = 0, \quad U_x(1, t) = 0, \quad U(x, 0) = -\Phi(x)$$

for $U(x, t)$ that does have two-point boundary conditions leading to a Sturm-Liouville problem.

It follows readily from conditions (5) that

$$(7) \qquad\qquad \Phi(x) = \frac{A}{K} x.$$

Also, by assuming a product solution $U = X(x)T(t)$ of the homogeneous conditions in problem (6), we see that

$$(8) \qquad X''(x) + \lambda X(x) = 0, \qquad X(0) = 0, \qquad X'(1) = 0$$

and $T'(t) + \lambda k T(t) = 0$. According to Problem 1, Sec. 72, the Sturm-Liouville problem (8) has the eigenvalues and normalized eigenfunctions

$$\lambda_n = \alpha_n^2, \qquad X_n = \phi_n(x) = \sqrt{2} \sin \alpha_n x \qquad (n = 1, 2, \ldots),$$

where $\alpha_n = (2n - 1)\pi/2$; and the corresponding functions of t are

$$T_n(t) = \exp(-\alpha_n^2 k t) \qquad (n = 1, 2, \ldots).$$

Hence,

$$(9) \qquad\qquad U(x, t) = \sum_{n=1}^{\infty} \gamma_n \exp(-\alpha_n^2 kt)\, \phi_n(x)$$

where, in view of the last of conditions (6),

$$-\frac{A}{K} x = \sum_{n=1}^{\infty} \gamma_n \phi_n(x) \qquad\qquad (0 < x < 1).$$

Now the Fourier constants for x $(0 < x < 1)$ with respect to the normalized eigenfunctions here are already known to us (see Example 2, Sec. 73, when $c = 1$), and that earlier result tells us that

$$\gamma_n = \sqrt{2}\, \frac{A}{K} \cdot \frac{(-1)^n}{\alpha_n^2}.$$

After substituting these values of γ_n into expression (9) and then simplifying and combining the result with expression (7), as indicated in equation (4), we arrive at the desired temperature function:

$$(10) \qquad u(x, t) = \frac{A}{K} \left[x + 2 \sum_{n=1}^{\infty} \frac{(-1)^n}{\alpha_n^2} \exp(-\alpha_n^2 kt) \sin \alpha_n x \right],$$

where $\alpha_n = (2n - 1)\pi/2$.

PROBLEMS†

1. With the aid of representation (8) in Example 2, Sec. 73, show that the temperature function (10) in Sec. 77 can be written in the form

$$u(x, t) = \frac{2A}{K} \sum_{n=1}^{\infty} \frac{(-1)^{n+1}}{\alpha_n^2} [1 - \exp(-\alpha_n^2 kt)] \sin \alpha_n x,$$

where $\alpha_n = (2n - 1)\pi/2$.

2. Heat transfer takes place at the surface $x = 0$ of a slab $0 \le x \le 1$ into a medium at temperature zero, according to the linear law of surface heat transfer, so that (Sec. 26)

$$u_x(0, t) = hu(0, t) \qquad\qquad (h > 0).$$

The other boundary conditions are as indicated in Fig. 61, and the unit of time is chosen so that $k = 1$ in the heat equation. By proceeding as in Sec. 77, derive the temperature formula

$$u(x, t) = \frac{hx + 1}{h + 1} - 2h \sum_{n=1}^{\infty} \frac{\sin \alpha_n (1 - x)}{\alpha_n (h + \cos^2 \alpha_n)} \exp(-\alpha_n^2 t),$$

where $\tan \alpha_n = -\alpha_n / h$ $(\alpha_n > 0)$.

---

†The footnote with the problem set for Sec. 74 also applies here.

$0°$ $u(x, 0) = 0$ $u = 1$

x

$x = 0$ $x = 1$

FIGURE 61

Suggestion: In simplifying the expression for the Fourier constants that arise, it is useful to note that

$$-\frac{h \sin \alpha_n}{\alpha_n^2} = \frac{\cos \alpha_n}{\alpha_n}.$$

3. Give a physical interpretation of the boundary value problem

$$u_t(x, t) = k u_{xx}(x, t) \qquad (0 < x < 1, t > 0),$$
$$u_x(0, t) = 0, \qquad u_x(1, t) = h[T - u(1, t)] \qquad (h > 0),$$
$$u(x, 0) = 0,$$

where T is a constant (see Sec. 26). By making the substitution

$$u(x, t) = U(x, t) + \Phi(x)$$

and referring to the solution (6)–(7) in Sec. 74 that was found for another boundary value problem, derive the solution

$$u(x, t) = T\left[1 - 2h\sum_{n=1}^{\infty} \frac{\sin \alpha_n \cos \alpha_n x}{\alpha_n(h + \sin^2 \alpha_n)} \exp\left(-\alpha_n^2 kt\right)\right],$$

where $\tan \alpha_n = h/\alpha_n$ $(\alpha_n > 0)$, of the boundary value problem here.

4. Use the same substitution as in Problem 3 and the same solution of an earlier boundary value problem to solve the temperature problem

$$u_t(x, t) = k u_{xx}(x, t) + q_0 \qquad (0 < x < 1, t > 0),$$
$$u_x(0, t) = 0, \qquad u_x(1, t) = -hu(1, t) \qquad (h > 0),$$
$$u(x, 0) = 0,$$

where q_0 is a constant.

Answer: $u(x, t) = \dfrac{q_0}{2k}\left[\dfrac{2}{h} + 1 - x^2 - 4h\displaystyle\sum_{n=1}^{\infty} \dfrac{\sin \alpha_n \cos \alpha_n x}{\alpha_n^3(h + \sin^2 \alpha_n)} \exp\left(-\alpha_n^2 kt\right)\right],$

where $\tan \alpha_n = h/\alpha_n$ $(\alpha_n > 0)$.

5. Use the method in Sec. 77 to solve the boundary value problem

$$(1 + t)u_t(x, t) = u_{xx}(x, t) \qquad (0 < x < 1, t > 0),$$
$$u_x(0, t) = -1, \qquad u(1, t) = 0, \qquad u(x, 0) = 0.$$

Interpret this problem physically (compare with Problem 3, Sec. 74).

Answer: $u(x, t) = 1 - x - 2\displaystyle\sum_{n=1}^{\infty} \dfrac{\cos \alpha_n x}{\alpha_n^2}(1 + t)^{-\alpha_n^2}$, where $\alpha_n = \dfrac{(2n - 1)\pi}{2}.$

78. ANOTHER MODIFICATION

Let $u(x, t)$ denote temperatures in a slab $0 \leq x \leq \pi$ (Fig. 62) that is initially at temperature zero and whose face $x = 0$ is insulated, while the face $x = \pi$ has temperatures $u(\pi, t) = t$ $(t \geq 0)$. If the unit of time is chosen so that the thermal diffusivity k in the heat equation is unity, the boundary value problem for $u(x, t)$ is

$$
\text{(1)} \qquad\qquad\qquad u_t(x, t) = u_{xx}(x, t) \qquad\qquad (0 < x < \pi, t > 0),
$$

$$
\text{(2)} \qquad\qquad u_x(0, t) = 0, \qquad u(\pi, t) = t, \qquad u(x, 0) = 0.
$$

$u(x, 0) = 0$ $u = t$

x

$x = 0$ $x = \pi$

FIGURE 62

Observe that if $u(x, t)$ satisfies the first two of conditions (2), then the related function $U(x, t) = u(x, t) - t$ satisfies the conditions

$$
\text{(3)} \qquad\qquad U_x(0, t) = 0 \qquad \text{and} \qquad U(\pi, t) = 0,
$$

both of which are homogeneous. In fact, by writing

$$
u(x, t) = U(x, t) + t,
$$

we have the related boundary value problem consisting of the differential equation

$$
\text{(4)} \qquad\qquad\qquad U_t(x, t) = U_{xx}(x, t) - 1
$$

and conditions (3), along with the condition

$$
\text{(5)} \qquad\qquad\qquad U(x, 0) = 0.
$$

The nonhomogeneity in the second of conditions (2) is now transferred to the differential equation in the new boundary value problem, and this suggests applying the method of variation of parameters, first used in Sec. 42.

We begin by noting that when the method of separation of variables is applied to the homogeneous differential equation $U_t(x, t) = U_{xx}(x, t)$, which is equation (4) with the term -1 deleted, and to conditions (3), the Sturm-Liouville problem

$$
X''(x) + \lambda X(x) = 0, \qquad X'(0) = 0, \qquad X(\pi) = 0
$$

arises. Furthermore, from Problem 3, Sec. 72, we know that the eigenfunctions of this problem are the cosine functions

$$
X_n(x) = \cos \alpha_n x \qquad \text{where} \qquad \alpha_n = \frac{2n - 1}{2} \qquad (n = 1, 2, \ldots).
$$

We thus seek a solution of the boundary value problem (3)–(5) having the form

$$(6) \qquad U(x,t) = \sum_{n=1}^{\infty} A_n(t) \cos \alpha_n x.$$

By substituting series (6) into equation (4) and referring to Problem 1, Sec. 73, for the expansion

$$1 = \frac{2}{\pi} \sum_{n=1}^{\infty} \frac{(-1)^{n+1}}{\alpha_n} \cos \alpha_n x \qquad (0 < x < \pi),$$

we find that

$$\sum_{n=1}^{\infty} \left[A'_n(t) + \alpha_n^2 A_n(t) \right] \cos \alpha_n x = \sum_{n=1}^{\infty} \frac{2(-1)^n}{\pi \alpha_n} \cos \alpha_n x.$$

Then, by identifying the coefficients in the series on each side here, we have the differential equation

$$(7) \qquad A'_n(t) + \alpha_n^2 A_n(t) = \frac{2(-1)^n}{\pi \alpha_n} \qquad (n = 1, 2, \ldots).$$

Also, condition (5) tells us that

$$\sum_{n=1}^{\infty} A_n(0) \cos \alpha_n x = 0,$$

or $A_n(0) = 0$ $(n = 1, 2, \ldots)$.

Now an integrating factor for the linear first-order differential equation (7) is

$$\exp \left(\int \alpha_n^2 \, dt \right) = \exp \alpha_n^2 t.$$

Hence, if we multiply through the differential equation by this integrating factor, we have

$$\frac{d}{dt} \left[(\exp \alpha_n^2 t) A_n(t) \right] = \frac{2(-1)^n}{\pi \alpha_n} \exp \alpha_n^2 t.$$

By replacing the variable t here by τ, integrating the result from $\tau = 0$ to $\tau = t$, and keeping in mind the requirement that $A_n(0) = 0$, we see that

$$(\exp \alpha_n^2 t) A_n(t) = \frac{2(-1)^n}{\pi \alpha_n^3} (\exp \alpha_n^2 t - 1),$$

or

$$A_n(t) = \frac{2}{\pi} \cdot \frac{(-1)^n}{\alpha_n^3} \left[1 - \exp(-\alpha_n^2 t) \right] \qquad (n = 1, 2, \ldots).$$

Finally, by substituting this expression for $A_n(t)$ into equation (6) and then recalling that $u(x,t) = U(x,t) + t$, we obtain the solution of the original boundary value problem:

$$(8) \qquad u(x,t) = t + \frac{2}{\pi} \sum_{n=1}^{\infty} \frac{(-1)^n}{\alpha_n^3} \left[1 - \exp(-\alpha_n^2 t) \right] \cos \alpha_n x,$$

where

(9)
$$\alpha_n = \frac{2n-1}{2} \qquad (n = 1, 2, \ldots).$$

Note that in view of the representation

$$\pi^2 - x^2 = \frac{4}{\pi} \sum_{n=1}^{\infty} \frac{(-1)^{n+1}}{\alpha_n^3} \cos \alpha_n x \qquad (0 < x < \pi),$$

found in Problem 4, Sec. 73, this solution can be written

(10)
$$u(x, t) = t - \frac{\pi^2 - x^2}{2} - \frac{2}{\pi} \sum_{n=1}^{\infty} \frac{(-1)^n}{\alpha_n^3} \exp\left(-\alpha_n^2 t\right) \cos \alpha_n x.$$

PROBLEMS†

1. Use the method of variation of parameters to solve the boundary value problem

$$u_t(x, t) = k u_{xx}(x, t) + q(t) \qquad (0 < x < 1, t > 0),$$

$$u_x(0, t) = 0, \qquad u(1, t) = 0, \qquad u(x, 0) = 0$$

for temperatures in an internally heated slab.

   Suggestion: The representation, with $c = 1$, that was found in Problem 1, Sec. 73, is needed here.

   Answer: $u(x, t) = 2 \sum_{n=1}^{\infty} \frac{(-1)^{n+1}}{\alpha_n} \cos \alpha_n x \int_0^t \exp\left[-\alpha_n^2 k(t - \tau)\right] q(\tau)\, d\tau,$

   where $\alpha_n = (2n - 1)\pi/2$.

2. Solve the temperature problem

$$u_t(x, t) = u_{xx}(x, t) \qquad (0 < x < 1, t > 0),$$

$$u_x(0, t) = 0, \qquad u(1, t) = F(t), \qquad u(x, 0) = 0,$$

   where F is continuous and $F(0) = 0$. [Compare this problem with the boundary value problem (1)–(2) in Sec. 78.] Express the answer in the form

$$u(x, t) = F(t) + 2 \sum_{n=1}^{\infty} \frac{(-1)^n}{\alpha_n} \cos \alpha_n x \int_0^t \exp\left[-\alpha_n^2(t - \tau)\right] F'(\tau)\, d\tau,$$

   where $\alpha_n = (2n - 1)\pi/2$.

3. By using the method of variation of parameters, derive the bounded solution of this problem:

$$u_{xx}(x, y) + u_{yy}(x, y) + q_0 = 0 \qquad (0 < x < 1, y > 0),$$

$$u(0, y) = 0, \qquad u_x(1, y) = -hu(1, y) \quad (h > 0), \qquad u(x, 0) = 0,$$

   where q_0 and h are constants. Interpret the problem physically.

---

† See the footnote with the problem set for Sec. 74.

Suggestion: The representation found in Problem 3, Sec. 73, is needed here. Also, for general comments on solving the nonhomogeneous linear second-order differential equation that arises, see the suggestion with Problem 4, Sec. 43.

Answer: $u(x, y) = 2q_0 h \sum\limits_{n=1}^{\infty} \dfrac{1 - \cos \alpha_n}{\alpha_n^3(h + \cos^2 \alpha_n)} [1 - \exp(-\alpha_n y)] \sin \alpha_n x,$

where $\tan \alpha_n = -\alpha_n/h \ (\alpha_n > 0).$

4. With the aid of the representation found in Problem 6, Sec. 73, write the solution in Problem 3 just above as

$$u(x, t) = \frac{q_0}{2} \left[x \left(\frac{2+h}{1+h} - x \right) - 4h \sum_{n=1}^{\infty} \frac{1 - \cos \alpha_n}{\alpha_n^3(h + \cos^2 \alpha_n)} \exp(-\alpha_n y) \sin \alpha_n x \right],$$

where $\tan \alpha_n = -\alpha_n/h \ (\alpha_n > 0)$. Then observe how it follows that

$$\lim_{y \to \infty} u(x, y) = \frac{q_0}{2} x \left(\frac{2+h}{1+h} - x \right).$$

79. A VERTICALLY HUNG ELASTIC BAR

An unstrained elastic bar, or heavy coiled spring, is clamped along its length c in order to prevent longitudinal displacements and then hung from its end $x = 0$ (Fig. 63). At the instant $t = 0$, the clamp is released and the bar vibrates longitudinally because of its own weight. If $y(x, t)$ denotes longitudinal displacements in the bar once it is released, then $y(x, t)$ satisfies the modified form (Problem 3, Sec. 29)

(1) $\qquad\qquad y_{tt}(x, t) = a^2 y_{xx}(x, t) + g \qquad\qquad (0 < x < c, t > 0)$

of the wave equation, where g is acceleration due to gravity. The stated conditions at the ends of the bar tell us that (see Sec. 29)

(2) $\qquad\qquad y(0, t) = 0, \qquad y_x(c, t) = 0,$

the initial conditions being

(3) $\qquad\qquad y(x, 0) = 0, \qquad y_t(x, 0) = 0.$

FIGURE 63

The fact that equation (1) is nonhomogeneous suggests that we use the method of variation of parameters, first used in Sec. 42. We begin with the observation that the sine functions

$$X_n(x) = \sin \alpha_n x \qquad \text{where} \qquad \alpha_n = \frac{(2n-1)\pi}{2c} \qquad (n = 1, 2, \ldots)$$

are the eigenfunctions (Problem 7, Sec. 72) of the Sturm-Liouville problem

$$X''(x) + \lambda X(x) = 0, \qquad X(0) = 0, \qquad X'(c) = 0,$$

which arises when the method of separation of variables is applied to the homogeneous wave equation $y_{xx}(x, t) = a^2 y_{tt}(x, t)$ and conditions (2). To be specific, we seek a solution of the boundary value problem (1)–(3) having the form

$$(4) \qquad\qquad y(x, t) = \sum_{n=1}^{\infty} B_n(t) \sin \alpha_n x,$$

where

$$(5) \qquad\qquad \alpha_n = \frac{(2n-1)\pi}{2c}.$$

Substituting series (4) into equation (1) and recalling the representation (Problem 2, Sec. 73)

$$1 = \frac{2}{c} \sum_{n=1}^{\infty} \frac{\sin \alpha_n x}{\alpha_n} \qquad\qquad (0 < x < c),$$

we find that

$$\sum_{n=1}^{\infty} B_n''(t) \sin \alpha_n x = a^2 \sum_{n=1}^{\infty} [-\alpha_n^2 B_n(t) \sin \alpha_n x] + \frac{2g}{c} \sum_{n=1}^{\infty} \frac{\sin \alpha_n x}{\alpha_n},$$

or

$$\sum_{n=1}^{\infty} [B_n''(t) + (\alpha_n a)^2 B_n(t)] \sin \alpha_n x = \sum_{n=1}^{\infty} \frac{2g}{c\alpha_n} \sin \alpha_n x.$$

That is,

$$(6) \qquad\qquad B_n''(t) + (\alpha_n a)^2 B_n(t) = \frac{2g}{c\alpha_n} \qquad (n = 1, 2, \ldots).$$

It follows, moreover, from conditions (3) that

$$(7) \qquad\qquad B_n(0) = 0, \qquad B_n'(0) = 0 \qquad (n = 1, 2, \ldots).$$

Now the general solution of the complementary equation

$$B_n''(t) + (\alpha_n a)^2 B_n(t) = 0$$

is

$$B_n(t) = C_1 \cos \alpha_n a t + C_2 \sin \alpha_n a t,$$

where C_1 and C_2 are arbitrary constants, and it is easy to see that a particular solution of equation (6) is

$$B_n(t) = \frac{2g}{a^2 c \alpha_n^3}.$$

Hence, the general solution of equation (6) is

(8) $$B_n(t) = C_1 \cos \alpha_n at + C_2 \sin \alpha_n at + \frac{2g}{a^2 c \alpha_n^3}.$$

The constants C_1 and C_2 are readily determined by imposing conditions (7) on expression (8). The result is

$$B_n(t) = \frac{2g}{a^2 c \alpha_n^3} (1 - \cos \alpha_n at);$$

and in view of equation (4), it follows that

(9) $$y(x, t) = \frac{2g}{a^2 c} \sum_{n=1}^{\infty} \frac{\sin \alpha_n x}{\alpha_n^3} (1 - \cos \alpha_n at).$$

This solution can actually be written in closed form in the following way, which is based on the fact (Problem 5, Sec. 73) that

(10) $$\frac{4}{c} \sum_{n=1}^{\infty} \frac{\sin \alpha_n x}{\alpha_n^3} = Q(x) \qquad (-\infty < x < \infty),$$

where $Q(x)$ is the antiperiodic function described by means of the equations

(11) $$Q(x) = x(2c - x) \qquad (0 \le x \le 2c),$$

(12) $$Q(x + 2c) = -Q(x) \qquad (-\infty < x < \infty).$$

First, we put expression (9) in the form

(13) $$y(x, t) = \frac{g}{2a^2} \left[x(2c - x) - \frac{4}{c} \sum_{n=1}^{\infty} \frac{\sin \alpha_n x \cos \alpha_n at}{\alpha_n^3} \right].$$

As for the remaining series here, the trigonometric identity

$$2 \sin A \cos B = \sin(A + B) + \sin(A - B)$$

enables us to write

$$2 \sum_{n=1}^{\infty} \frac{\sin \alpha_n x \cos \alpha_n at}{\alpha_n^3} = \sum_{n=1}^{\infty} \frac{\sin \alpha_n (x + at)}{\alpha_n^3} + \sum_{n=1}^{\infty} \frac{\sin \alpha_n (x - at)}{\alpha_n^3},$$

or

$$\frac{4}{c} \sum_{n=1}^{\infty} \frac{\sin \alpha_n x \cos \alpha_n at}{\alpha_n^3} = \frac{Q(x + at) + Q(x - at)}{2}.$$

Finally, then,

(14) $$y(x, t) = \frac{g}{2a^2} \left[x(2c - x) - \frac{Q(x + at) + Q(x - at)}{2} \right].$$

PROBLEMS†

1. A horizontal elastic bar, with its end $x = 0$ kept fixed, is initially stretched so that its longitudinal displacements are $y(x, 0) = bx$ $(0 \le x \le c)$. It is released from rest in that position at the instant $t = 0$; and its end $x = c$ is kept free, so that $y_x(c, t) = 0$. Derive this expression for the displacements:

$$y(x, t) = b \left[\frac{H(x + at) + H(x - at)}{2} \right],$$

   where $H(x)$ is the triangular wave function (6) in Example 2, Sec. 73. (Except for the condition at $x = 0$, the boundary value problem here is the same as the one solved in Sec. 47.)

2. Suppose that the end $x = 0$ of a horizontal elastic bar of length c is kept fixed and that a constant force F_0 per unit area acts parallel to the bar at the end $x = c$. Let all parts of the bar be initially unstrained and at rest. The displacements $y(x, t)$ then satisfy the boundary value problem

   $$y_{tt}(x, t) = a^2 y_{xx}(x, t) \qquad\qquad (0 < x < c, t > 0),$$

   $$y(0, t) = 0, \qquad\quad Ey_x(c, t) = F_0,$$

   $$y(x, 0) = 0, \qquad\quad y_t(x, 0) = 0,$$

   where $a^2 = E/\delta$, the constant E is Young's modulus of elasticity, and δ is the mass per unit volume of the material (see Sec. 29).
   (a) Write $y(x, t) = Y(x, t) + \Phi(x)$ (compare with Sec. 77) and determine $\Phi(x)$ such that $Y(x, t)$ satisfies a boundary value problem whose solution is obtained by simply referring to the solution in Problem 1. Thus show that

   $$y(x, t) = \frac{F_0}{E} \left[x - \frac{H(x + at) + H(x - at)}{2} \right],$$

   where $H(x)$ is the same triangular wave function as in Problem 1.
   (b) Use the expression for $y(x, t)$ in part (a) to show that those displacements are periodic in t, with period

   $$T_0 = \frac{4c}{a} = 4c \sqrt{\frac{\delta}{E}}.$$

   That is, show that $y(x, t + T_0) = y(x, t)$.

3. Show that the displacements at the end $x = c$ of the bar in Problem 2 are

   $$y(c, t) = \frac{F_0}{E} [c + H(at - c)]$$

   and that the graph of this function is as shown in Fig. 64.

---

†The footnote with the problem set for Sec. 74 applies here as well.

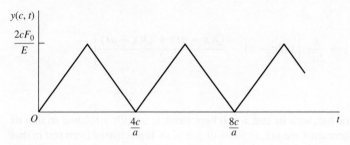

FIGURE 64

4. Show that the force per unit area exerted by the bar in Problem 2 on the support at the end $x = 0$ is the function (see Sec. 29)

$$Ey_x(0, t) = F_0 [1 - H'(at)]$$

and that the graph of this function is as shown in Fig. 65. (Note that this force becomes twice the applied force during regularly spaced intervals of time.)

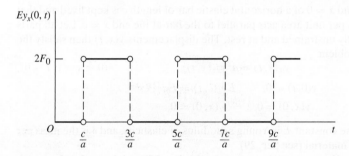

FIGURE 65

5. Let the constant F_0 in Problem 2 be replaced by a finite impulse of duration $4c/a$:

$$F(t) = \begin{cases} F_0 & \text{when } 0 < t < \dfrac{4c}{a}, \\ 0 & \text{when } \quad t > \dfrac{4c}{a}. \end{cases}$$

(a) State why the displacements $y(x, t)$ between the times $t = 0$ and $t = 4c/a$ are the same as in Problem 2. Then, after showing that

$$y\left(x, \frac{4c}{a}\right) = 0 \quad \text{and} \quad y_t\left(x, \frac{4c}{a}\right) = 0$$

when $y(x, t)$ is the solution in Problem 2, state why there is no motion in the bar here after time $t = 4c/a$.

(b) Use results in part (a) and Problem 3 to show that if

$$t_0 = \frac{2c}{a} \quad \text{and} \quad v_0 = \frac{aF_0}{E},$$

the end $x = c$ of the bar moves with velocity

$$y_t(c, t) = \begin{cases} v_0 & \text{when } 0 < t < t_0, \\ -v_0 & \text{when } t_0 < t < 2t_0, \end{cases}$$

and that it remains stationary after time $t = 2t_0$.

6. The end $x = 1$ of a stretched string is elastically supported (Fig. 66), so that the transverse displacements $y(x, t)$ satisfy the condition $y_x(1, t) = -hy(1, t)$, where h is a positive constant. Also,

$$y(0, t) = 0, \qquad y(x, 0) = bx, \qquad y_t(x, 0) = 0,$$

where b is a positive constant; and the wave equation $y_{tt} = y_{xx}$ is satisfied. Derive the following expression for the displacements:

$$y(x, t) = 2bh(h + 1) \sum_{n=1}^{\infty} \frac{\sin \alpha_n \sin \alpha_n x}{\alpha_n^2(h + \cos^2 \alpha_n)} \cos \alpha_n t,$$

where $\tan \alpha_n = -\alpha_n/h \ (\alpha_n > 0)$.

Suggestion: In simplifying the solution to the form given here, note that

$$-\frac{\cos \alpha_n}{\alpha_n} = \frac{h \sin \alpha_n}{\alpha_n^2}.$$

FIGURE 66

7. An unstrained elastic bar of length c, whose cross sections have area A and whose modulus of elasticity (Sec. 29) is E, is moving lengthwise with velocity v_0 when at the instant $t = 0$ its right-hand end $x = c$ meets and adheres to a rigid support (Fig. 67). The displacements $y(x, t)$ thus satisfy the wave equation $y_{tt} = a^2 y_{xx}$ and the end conditions $y_x(0, t) = y(c, t) = 0$, as well as the initial conditions

$$y(x, 0) = 0, \qquad y_t(x, 0) = v_0.$$

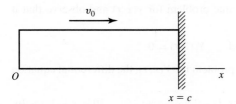

FIGURE 67

(a) Derive this expression for the displacements:

$$y(x, t) = \frac{2v_0}{ac} \sum_{n=1}^{\infty} \frac{(-1)^{n+1}}{\alpha_n^2} \cos \alpha_n x \sin \alpha_n at,$$

where

$$\alpha_n = \frac{(2n - 1)\pi}{2c} \qquad\qquad (n = 1, 2, \ldots).$$

(b) Use the expression for $y(x, t)$ in part (a) to show that

$$y\left(x, \frac{2c}{a}\right) = 0 \quad \text{and} \quad y_t\left(x, \frac{2c}{a}\right) = -v_0 \qquad (0 < x < c).$$

According to these two equations, if the end $x = c$ of the bar is suddenly freed from the support at time $t = 2c/a$, the bar will move after that time as a rigid unstrained body with velocity $-v_0$.

(c) Show how it follows from the expression in part (a) that as long as the end of the bar continues to adhere to the support, the force on the support can be written

$$- AEy_x(c, t) = \frac{AEv_0}{a} M\left(\frac{2c}{a}, t\right),$$

where $M(c, t)$ $(t > 0)$ is the square wave represented by the series (see Problem 3, Sec. 15)

$$M(c, t) = \frac{4}{\pi} \sum_{n=1}^{\infty} \frac{1}{2n - 1} \sin \frac{(2n - 1)\pi t}{c} \qquad (t \neq c, 2c, 3c, \ldots).$$

8. Let $y(x, t)$ denote longitudinal displacements in an elastic bar of length unity whose end $x = 0$ is fixed and at whose end $x = 1$ a force proportional to t^2 acts longitudinally (Fig. 68), so that

$$y(0, t) = 0 \quad \text{and} \quad y_x(1, t) = At^2 \qquad (A \neq 0).$$

The bar is initially unstrained and at rest, and the unit of time is such that $a = 1$ in the wave equation.

FIGURE 68

(a) Write out the complete boundary value problem for $y(x, t)$ and observe that if $Y(x, t) = y(x, t) - At^2 x$, then

$$Y(0, t) = 0 \quad \text{and} \quad Y_x(1, t) = 0.$$

Set up the complete boundary value problem for $Y(x, t)$, the differential equation being

$$Y_{tt}(x, t) = Y_{xx}(x, t) - 2Ax \qquad (0 < x < 1, t > 0).$$

Then, with the aid of representation (8) in Example 2, Sec. 73, apply the method of variation of parameters to solve the boundary value problem for $Y(x, t)$ and thus derive this solution of the original problem:

$$y(x, t) = A\left[xt^2 - 4\sum_{n=1}^{\infty} \frac{(-1)^{n+1}}{\alpha_n^4}(1 - \cos \alpha_n t) \sin \alpha_n x\right],$$

where

$$\alpha_n = \frac{(2n - 1)\pi}{2} \qquad (n = 1, 2, \ldots).$$

(b) Use the result in Problem 11(b), Sec. 73, to write the solution in part (a) here in the form

$$y(x, t) = A\left[x(t^2 - 1) + \frac{1}{3}x^3 + \frac{Q(x + t) + Q(x - t)}{2}\right],$$

where $Q(x)$ is the antiperiodic function described by means of the equations

$$Q(x) = x\left(1 - \frac{1}{3}x^2\right) \qquad (-1 \le x \le 1),$$

$$Q(x + 2) = -Q(x) \qquad (-\infty < x < \infty).$$

9. Consider the same boundary value problem as in Problem 8 except that the condition at the end $x = 1$ of the bar is now replaced by the condition

$$y_x(1, t) = \sin \omega t.$$

(a) By proceeding in the same manner as in Problem 8, show that if

$$\omega_n = \frac{(2n - 1)\pi}{2} \qquad (n = 1, 2, \ldots)$$

and $\omega \ne \omega_n$ for any value of n, then

$$y(x, t) = x \sin \omega t + 2\omega \sum_{n=1}^{\infty} \frac{(-1)^n}{\omega_n(\omega^2 - \omega_n^2)} \left(\frac{\omega}{\omega_n} \sin \omega t - \sin \omega_n t\right) \sin \omega_n x.$$

(b) Modify part (a) to show that resonance (Sec. 46) occurs when $\omega = \omega_N$ for any value of N.

Suggestion: In each part of this problem, it is helpful to refer to the general solution of a certain ordinary differential equation in Problem 2, Sec. 46.

10. By referring to expansion (8) in Example 2, Sec. 73, and the expansion found in Problem 7, Sec. 73, write the solution in Problem 9(a) just above in the form

$$y(x, t) = \frac{\sin \omega x \sin \omega t}{\omega \cos \omega} + 2\omega \sum_{n=1}^{\infty} \frac{(-1)^{n+1}}{\omega_n(\omega^2 - \omega_n^2)} \sin \omega_n x \sin \omega_n t,$$

where

$$\omega_n = \frac{(2n - 1)\pi}{2} \qquad (n = 1, 2, \ldots).$$

CHAPTER
9

BESSEL FUNCTIONS AND APPLICATIONS

In boundary value problems that involve the laplacian $\nabla^2 u$ expressed in cylindrical or polar coordinates, the method of separation of variables often produces a differential equation of the form

(1)
$$\rho^2 \frac{d^2 y}{d\rho^2} + \rho \frac{dy}{d\rho} + (\lambda\rho^2 - \nu^2)y = 0,$$

where y is a function of the coordinate ρ. In such a problem, $-\lambda$ is a separation constant and the values of λ are the eigenvalues of a singular Sturm-Liouville problem involving equation (1). The parameter ν is a nonnegative number determined by other aspects of the boundary value problem. Usually, ν is either zero or a positive integer.

In our applications, it turns out that $\lambda \geq 0$; and when $\lambda > 0$, the substitution $x = \sqrt{\lambda}\, \rho$ can be used to transform equation (1) into a form that is free of λ:

(2)
$$x^2 y''(x) + xy'(x) + (x^2 - \nu^2)y(x) = 0.$$

This differential equation is known as *Bessel's equation* of order ν. Its solutions are called *Bessel functions,* or sometimes cylindrical functions.

Before turning to the problem of finding solutions of equation (2), we begin with a brief discussion of the so-called gamma function, which plays a central role in studies of those solutions.

260

80.   THE GAMMA FUNCTION

As indicated just above, this section is devoted to some basic properties of the *gamma function*, which can be defined in terms of the independent variable v by means of an improper integral:[†]

$$(1) \qquad\qquad \Gamma(v) = \int_0^\infty e^{-t} t^{v-1} dt \qquad\qquad (v > 0).$$

It is easy to see that

$$\Gamma(1) = \int_0^\infty e^{-t} dt = \left[-e^{-t} \right]_0^\infty = 1.$$

In order to find values of this function for the other positive integers, we write

$$\Gamma(v+1) = \int_0^\infty e^{-t} t^v dt$$

and integrate by parts, using

$$U = t^v \quad \text{and} \quad dV = e^{-t} dt.$$

Then

$$dU = v t^{v-1} dt \quad \text{and} \quad V = -e^{-t},$$

so that

$$\Gamma(v+1) = \left[-\frac{t^v}{e^t} \right]_{t=0}^{t=\infty} + v \int_0^\infty e^{-t} t^{v-1} dt.$$

Since e^t grows faster than t^v as t tends to ∞, we find that

$$(2) \qquad\qquad \Gamma(v+1) = v \, \Gamma(v) \qquad\qquad (v > 0).$$

This *recurrence relation*, together with mathematical induction, reveals that

$$(3) \qquad\qquad \Gamma(n+1) = n! \qquad\qquad (n = 0, 1, 2, \ldots).$$

As for the details, we recall from the beginning of this section that $\Gamma(1) = 0!$ when the convention that $0! = 1$ is used; thus equation (3) is valid when $n = 0$. Given that equation (3) is valid when $n = m$ where m is any nonnegative integer ($m = 0, 1, 2, \ldots$), one can apply recurrence relation (2) to see that

$$\Gamma((m+1)+1) = (m+1) \, \Gamma(m+1) = (m+1) \, (m!) = (m+1)! \, .$$

The validity of equation (3) is now established.
  Recurrence relation (2), in the form

$$(4) \qquad\qquad \Gamma(v) = \frac{\Gamma(v+1)}{v} \qquad\qquad (v > 0),$$

[†]Thorough developments of the gamma function appear in the books by Lebedev (1972, Chap. 1) and Rainville (1972, Chap. 2), which are listed in the Bibliography.

can be used to define $\Gamma(\nu)$ when ν is negative but not an integer. To be specific, if $-1 < \nu < 0$, the inequalities $0 < \nu + 1 < 1$ enable us to use equation (4) to define $\Gamma(\nu)$ when $-1 < \nu < 0$. If $-2 < \nu < -1$, so that $-1 < \nu + 1 < 0$, the fact that $\Gamma(\nu)$ is now defined for $-1 < \nu < 0$ allows us to use equation (4) once again, this time to define $\Gamma(\nu)$ when $-2 < \nu < -1$. Continuing in this way, we now have $\Gamma(\nu)$ defined for every negative value of ν that is not an integer (Fig. 69).

FIGURE 69

It can be shown that $\Gamma(\nu)$ is continuous and positive when $\nu > 0$. So it follows from relation (4) that $\Gamma(0+) = \infty$ and, furthermore, that $|\Gamma(\nu)|$ becomes infinite as $\nu \to -n$ $(n = 0, 1, 2, \ldots)$. This means that $1/\Gamma(\nu)$ tends to zero as ν tends to $-n$ $(n = 0, 1, 2, \ldots)$; and, for brevity, we write

(5) $$\frac{1}{\Gamma(-n)} = 0 \quad \text{when } n = 0, 1, 2, \ldots.$$

Note that the reciprocal $1/\Gamma(\nu)$ is then continuous for all ν.

We conclude this discussion of the gamma function by stating two further consequences of relation (2) that will be useful in this chapter and whose verifications are left to the problems. The first is

(6) $$\Gamma(\nu + 1)(\nu + 1)(\nu + 2) \cdots (\nu + k) = \Gamma(\nu + k + 1) \qquad (k = 1, 2, \ldots)$$

when $\nu > 0$, and the second is the expression

(7) $$\Gamma\left(k + \frac{1}{2}\right) = \frac{(2k)!}{k! 2^{2k}} \sqrt{\pi} \qquad (k = 0, 1, 2, \ldots)$$

for the values of the gamma function at the positive half-integers. With the usual convention that $0! = 1$, expression (7) tells us that

(8) $$\Gamma\left(\frac{1}{2}\right) = \sqrt{\pi}.$$

81. BESSEL FUNCTIONS $J_\nu(x)$

Bessel's equation

$$(1) \qquad\qquad x^2 y''(x) + xy'(x) + (x^2 - \nu^2)y(x) = 0 \qquad\qquad (\nu \geq 0)$$

is an ordinary differential equation of the second order that is linear and homogeneous; and, upon comparing it with the standard form

$$(2) \qquad\qquad y''(x) + P(x)y'(x) + Q(x)y(x) = 0$$

of such equations, we see that

$$P(x) = \frac{1}{x} \qquad \text{and} \qquad Q(x) = \frac{x^2 - \nu^2}{x^2}.$$

Since these quotients do not have Maclaurin series representations that are valid in some open interval containing the origin and since the products

$$x P(x) \qquad \text{and} \qquad x^2 Q(x)$$

do, the origin $x = 0$ is a *regular singular point* of Bessel's equation (1). From the theory of ordinary differential equations, it is known that when $x = 0$ is such a point, equation (2) always has a solution of the form [†]

$$y = x^c \sum_{j=0}^{\infty} a_j x^j \qquad\qquad (a_0 \neq 0),$$

which is the same as

$$(3) \qquad\qquad y = \sum_{j=0}^{\infty} a_j x^{c+j} \qquad\qquad (a_0 \neq 0).$$

In order to determine a solution of equation (1) that is of the form (3), we assume that series (3) is differentiable and note that

$$y' = \sum_{j=0}^{\infty} (c + j) a_j x^{c+j-1}$$

and

$$y'' = \sum_{j=0}^{\infty} (c + j)(c + j - 1) a_j x^{c+j-2}.$$

Substituting series (3) and these derivatives into equation (1), we have

$$\sum_{j=0}^{\infty} (c + j)(c + j - 1) a_j x^{c+j} + \sum_{j=0}^{\infty} (c + j) a_j x^{c+j}$$

$$+ \sum_{j=0}^{\infty} a_j x^{c+j+2} - \sum_{j=0}^{\infty} \nu^2 a_j x^{c+j} = 0,$$

[†] The series method used here to solve equation (1) is often referred to as the *method of Frobenius* and is treated in introductory texts on ordinary differential equations, such as the one by Boyce and DiPrima (2009) and the one by Rainville, Bedient, and Bedient (1997). Both are listed in the Bibliography.

or

$$\sum_{j=0}^{\infty} [(c+j)(c+j-1) + (c+j) - v^2]a_j x^{c+j} + \sum_{j=0}^{\infty} a_j x^{c+j+2} = 0.$$

But

$$(c+j)(c+j-1) + (c+j) = (c+j)[(c+j-1)+1] = (c+j)^2$$

in the first series here, and the second series can be written

$$\sum_{j=2}^{\infty} a_{j-2} x^{c+j}.$$

Hence,

$$\sum_{j=0}^{\infty} [(c+j)^2 - v^2]a_j x^{c+j} + \sum_{j=2}^{\infty} a_{j-2} x^{c+j} = 0.$$

Multiplying through this equation by x^{-c} and then writing out the $j=0$ and $j=1$ terms of the first series separately, we have

(4) $\quad (c^2 - v^2)a_0 + [(c+1)^2 - v^2]a_1 x + \sum_{j=2}^{\infty} \{[(c+j)^2 - v^2]a_j + a_{j-2}\}x^j = 0.$

Equation (4) is an identity in x if the coefficient of each power of x vanishes. In particular, the condition $a_0 \neq 0$ with series (3) tells us that $c = v$ or $c = -v$ if the constant term is to vanish, and we make the choice $c = v$. Then $a_1 = 0$, since

$$(v+1)^2 - v^2 = 2v + 1 \neq 0.$$

Furthermore,

$$[(v+j)^2 - v^2]a_j + a_{j-2} = 0 \qquad\qquad (j = 2, 3, \ldots);$$

and since $(v+j)^2 - v^2 = j(2v+j)$, the *recurrence relation*

(5) $$a_j = \frac{-1}{j(2v+j)} a_{j-2} \qquad\qquad (j = 2, 3, \ldots)$$

is obtained. It gives each coefficient $a_j (j = 2, 3, \ldots)$ in terms of the second coefficient preceding it in the series.

Note that if the value $c = -v$, rather than $c = v$, had been chosen, the first factor in the coefficient of x in series (4) would have been

$$(-v+1)^2 - v^2 = -2v + 1,$$

which is zero when $v = 1/2$. Hence a_1 would not need to be zero when $v = 1/2$. Moreover, if $c = -v$, the denominator on the right-hand side of relation (5) would be $j(-2v+j)$; and this means that the relation would not be well defined when v is a positive integer and $j = 2v$.

Since $a_1 = 0$, relation (5) requires that $a_3 = 0$; then $a_5 = 0$, etc. That is,

(6) $$a_{2k+1} = 0 \qquad\qquad (k = 0, 1, 2, \ldots).$$

To obtain the remaining coefficients, we let k denote any positive integer and use relation (5) to write the following k equations:

$$a_2 = \frac{-1}{1(\nu + 1)2^2} a_0,$$

$$a_4 = \frac{-1}{2(\nu + 2)2^2} a_2,$$

$$\vdots$$

$$a_{2k} = \frac{-1}{k(\nu + k)2^2} a_{2k-2}.$$

Upon equating the product of the left-hand sides of these equations to the product of their right-hand sides, and then canceling the common factors $a_2, a_4, \ldots, a_{2k-2}$ on each side of the resulting equation, we arrive at the expression

$$(7) \qquad a_{2k} = \frac{(-1)^k}{k!(\nu + 1)(\nu + 2) \cdots (\nu + k)2^{2k}} a_0 \qquad (k = 1, 2, \ldots).$$

In view of identity (6) and the fact that $c = \nu$, series (3) now takes the form

$$(8) \qquad y = a_0 x^\nu + \sum_{k=1}^{\infty} a_{2k} x^{\nu+2k} \qquad (a_0 \neq 0),$$

where the coefficients a_{2k} $(k = 1, 2, \ldots)$ are those in expression (7). This series is absolutely convergent for all x, according to the ratio test:

$$\lim_{k\to\infty} \left| \frac{a_{2(k+1)} x^{\nu+2(k+1)}}{a_{2k} x^{\nu+2k}} \right| = \lim_{k\to\infty} \frac{1}{(k+1)(\nu + k + 1)} \left(\frac{|x|}{2} \right)^2 = 0.$$

Hence, it represents a continuous function and is differentiable with respect to x any number of times. Since it is differentiable and its coefficients satisfy the recurrence relation needed to make its sum satisfy Bessel's equation (1), series (8) is, indeed, a solution of that equation.

The coefficient a_0 in series (8) may have any nonzero value. If we substitute expression (7) into that series and write

$$y = a_0 x^\nu \left[1 + \sum_{k=1}^{\infty} \frac{(-1)^k}{k!(\nu + 1)(\nu + 2) \cdots (\nu + k)} \left(\frac{x}{2} \right)^{2k} \right],$$

we see that the choice

$$a_0 = \frac{1}{\Gamma(\nu + 1) 2^\nu}$$

enables us to write a solution of Bessel's equation (1) as $y = J_\nu(x)$ where

$$(9) \quad J_\nu(x) = \frac{1}{\Gamma(\nu + 1)} \left(\frac{x}{2} \right)^\nu + \sum_{k=1}^{\infty} \frac{(-1)^k}{k! \Gamma(\nu + 1)(\nu + 1)(\nu + 2) \cdots (\nu + k)} \left(\frac{x}{2} \right)^{\nu+2k}.$$

Finally, the relation (Sec. 80)

$$\Gamma(\nu + 1)(\nu + 1)(\nu + 2) \cdots (\nu + k) = \Gamma(\nu + k + 1) \qquad (k = 1, 2, \ldots)$$

and the convention that $0! = 1$ enable us to write solution (9) more compactly as

$$(10) \qquad\qquad J_\nu(x) = \sum_{k=0}^{\infty} \frac{(-1)^k}{k!\Gamma(\nu+k+1)} \left(\frac{x}{2}\right)^{\nu+2k}.$$

The function $J_\nu(x)$ is known as the *Bessel function of the first kind of order* $\nu(\nu \geq 0)$.

It follows that the related function

$$(11) \qquad\qquad J_{-\nu}(x) = \sum_{k=0}^{\infty} \frac{(-1)^k}{k!\Gamma(-\nu+k+1)} \left(\frac{x}{2}\right)^{-\nu+2k}$$

is also a solution of Bessel's equation (1) when the nonnegative parameter ν is not an integer. One can see this by redoing the derivation of $J_\nu(x)$ using $c = -\nu$ and also referring to Problem 7, Sec. 82. The Bessel function $J_{-\nu}(x)$ is clearly linearly independent of $J_\nu(x)$ since it is not a constant times $J_\nu(x)$. In fact, since $J_{-\nu}(x)$ is the product of $1/x^\nu$ and a power series in x whose initial term $(k = 0)$ is nonzero, it is discontinuous at $x = 0$. But $J_\nu(x)$ tends to zero as $x \to 0$. Thus *the general solution of Bessel's equation* (1) *when* ν *is positive but not an integer is*

$$(12) \qquad\qquad y = C_1 J_\nu(x) + C_2 J_{-\nu}(x), \qquad\qquad (\nu > 0;\ \nu \neq 1, 2, \ldots),$$

where C_1 and C_2 are arbitrary constants.

A solution of Bessel's equation that is linearly independent of $J_\nu(x)$ is more difficult to find when ν is a nonnegative integer $(\nu = 0, 1, 2, \ldots)$. We recall from the paragraph immediately following equation (4) that we chose $c = \nu$ and not $c = -\nu$. If $\nu = 0$, we do not, of course, obtain a new value of c when $c = -\nu$. If ν has one of the values $\nu = 1, 2, \ldots$,we saw that the recurrence relation (5) is not well defined for all values of j. The second (linearly independent) solutions when $\nu = n = 0, 1, 2, \ldots$ are discussed in Sec. 82.

82.   SOLUTIONS WHEN $\nu = 0, 1, 2, \ldots$

This chapter is mainly concerned with solutions of Bessel's equation when the parameter ν is a nonnegative integer n:

$$(1) \qquad\qquad x^2 y''(x) + xy'(x) + (x^2 - n^2)\, y(x) = 0 \qquad\qquad (n = 0, 1, 2, \ldots).$$

From Sec. 80 we know that

$$\Gamma(n+k+1) = (n+k)! \qquad\qquad (k = 0, 1, 2, \ldots),$$

and so the Bessel function of order $\nu(\nu \geq 0)$ that was obtained in Sec. 81 becomes

$$(2) \qquad\qquad J_n(x) = \sum_{k=0}^{\infty} \frac{(-1)^k}{k!(n+k)!} \left(\frac{x}{2}\right)^{n+2k} \qquad\qquad (n = 0, 1, 2, \ldots).$$

The case $n = 0$ will be of special interest to us in the applications. Bessel's equation (1) then becomes

$$(3) \qquad\qquad xy''(x) + y'(x) + xy(x) = 0,$$

and expression (2) reduces to

(4)
$$J_0(x) = \sum_{k=0}^{\infty} \frac{(-1)^k}{(k!)^2} \left(\frac{x}{2}\right)^{2k}.$$

Since

$$(k!)^2 2^{2k} = [(1)(2)(3) \cdots (k)2^k]^2 = [(2)(4)(6) \cdots (2k)]^2 = 2^2 4^2 6^2 \cdots (2k)^2$$

when $k \geq 1$, another form is

(5)
$$J_0(x) = 1 + \sum_{k=1}^{\infty} (-1)^k \frac{x^{2k}}{2^2 4^2 6^2 \cdots (2k)^2} = 1 - \frac{x^2}{2^2} + \frac{x^4}{2^2 4^2} - \frac{x^6}{2^2 4^2 6^2} + \cdots.$$

From expression (2) one can readily see that

(6)
$$J_n(-x) = (-1)^n J_n(x) \qquad\qquad (n = 0, 1, 2, \ldots).$$

Thus J_n is an even function if $n = 0, 2, 4, \ldots$ and odd if $n = 1, 3, 5, \ldots$. Also, it follows immediately from expressions (5) and (2) that $J_0(0) = 1$ and $J_n(0) = 0$ when $n = 1, 2, \ldots$.

Series (5) bears some resemblance to the Maclaurin series for $\cos x$. The differentiation formula $J_0'(x) = -J_1(x)$, to be obtained in Sec. 83, also suggests that $J_1(x)$ might be analogous to $\sin x$. Graphs of $y = J_0(x)$ and $y = J_1(x)$ are shown in Fig. 70. More details regarding these graphs, especially the nature of the zeros of $J_0(x)$ and $J_1(x)$, will be developed later in the chapter.

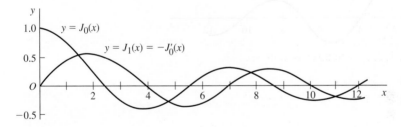

FIGURE 70

A function linearly independent of $J_0(x)$ that satisfies Bessel's equation (3) can be obtained by various methods of a fairly elementary nature. We do not give further details here but only state the results.

A general solution of equation (3) is (see Problems 4 and 10)

(7) $y = A J_0(x)$
$$+ B \left[J_0(x) \ln x + \frac{x^2}{2^2} - \frac{x^4}{2^2 4^2} \left(1 + \frac{1}{2}\right) + \frac{x^6}{2^2 4^2 6^2} \left(1 + \frac{1}{2} + \frac{1}{3}\right) - \cdots \right],$$

where A and B are arbitrary constants and $x > 0$. Evidently, as long as $B \neq 0$, any choice of A and B yields a solution that is unbounded as x tends to zero through positive values. Such a solution cannot, therefore, be expressed as a constant times $J_0(x)$, which tends to unity as x tends to zero. So $J_0(x)$ and the solution (7) are linearly independent when $B \neq 0$. It is most common to use *Euler's constant*

$\gamma = 0.5772 \cdots$, which is defined as the limit of the sequence (see Problem 5)

$$(8) \qquad s_n = 1 + \frac{1}{2} + \frac{1}{3} + \cdots + \frac{1}{n} - \ln n \qquad (n = 1, 2, \ldots),$$

and to write

$$A = \frac{2}{\pi} (\gamma - \ln 2) \quad \text{and} \quad B = \frac{2}{\pi}.$$

When A and B are assigned those values, the second solution that arises is *Weber's Bessel function of the second kind of order zero.* (Fig. 71): [†]

$$(9) \qquad Y_0(x) = \frac{2}{\pi} \left[\left(\ln \frac{x}{2} + \gamma \right) J_0(x) \right.$$

$$\left. + \frac{x^2}{2^2} - \frac{x^4}{2^2 4^2} \left(1 + \frac{1}{2} \right) + \frac{x^6}{2^2 4^2 6^2} \left(1 + \frac{1}{2} + \frac{1}{3} \right) - \cdots \right].$$

Thus a general solution of equation (3) that is valid when $x > 0$ is

$$(10) \qquad y = C_1 J_0(x) + C_2 Y_0(x),$$

where C_1 and C_2 are arbitrary constants.

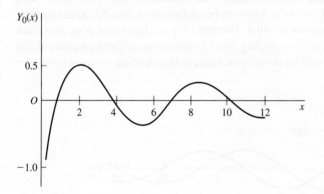

FIGURE 71

We turn now to the case in which ν is a *positive* integer n ($n = 1, 2, \ldots$). Although $J_n(x)$ is a solution of equation (1), $J_{-n}(x)$ is not a linearly independent one. In fact

$$(11) \qquad J_{-n}(x) = (-1)^n J_n(x) \qquad (n = 1, 2, \ldots).$$

To establish this relation, we need only write $\nu = -n(n = 1, 2, \ldots)$ in expression (10), Sec. 81 to see that

$$(12) \qquad J_{-n}(x) = \sum_{k=0}^{\infty} \frac{(-1)^k}{k! \Gamma(-n + k + 1)} \left(\frac{x}{2} \right)^{-n+2k}.$$

[†] There are other Bessel functions, and the notation varies widely throughout the literature. The treatise by Watson (1995) that is listed in the Bibliography is, however, usually regarded as the standard reference.

Because (Sec. 80)

$$\frac{1}{\Gamma(-n)} = 0 \qquad \text{when} \qquad n = 0, 1, 2, \ldots,$$

we know that

$$\frac{1}{\Gamma(-n + k + 1)} = 0 \qquad \text{when} \qquad 0 \le k \le n - 1;$$

and expression (12) becomes

$$J_{-n}(x) = \sum_{k=n}^{\infty} \frac{(-1)^k}{k! \Gamma(-n + k + 1)} \left(\frac{x}{2}\right)^{-n+2k}.$$

Replacing k by $k + n$ in this last series, so that k runs from zero to infinity again, we have

$$J_{-n}(x) = \sum_{k=0}^{\infty} \frac{(-1)^{k+n}}{(k+n)! \Gamma(k+1)} \left(\frac{x}{2}\right)^{n+2k} = (-1)^n \sum_{k=0}^{\infty} \frac{(-1)^k}{k!(n+k)!} \left(\frac{x}{2}\right)^{n+2k}.$$

In view of expression (2), relation (11) now follows.

It is possible to obtain a second solution $Y_n(x)$ of equation (1) that is linearly independent of $J_n(x)$ when $n = 1, 2, \ldots$. As was the case when $n = 0$, the theory of $Y_n(x)$ is considerably more involved than that of $J_n(x)$; and in this chapter, it will be necessary to know only that $Y_n(x)$ is discontinuous at $x = 0$. In view of our discussion of the second (linearly independent) solution of Bessel's equation (1) when $n = 0$, we now know that the general solution of that equation is

(13) $$y = C_1 J_n(x) + C_2 Y_n(x)$$ $(n = 0, 1, 2, \ldots)$

when $x > 0$.

PROBLEMS

1. Use mathematical induction to show that

$$\Gamma(v+1)(v+1)(v+2) \cdots (v+k) = \Gamma(v+k+1) \qquad (k = 1, 2, \ldots)$$

when $v > 0$.

2. Use mathematical induction, together with the definition (Sec. 80)

$$\Gamma(v) = \int_0^\infty e^{-t} t^{v-1} \, dt \qquad (v > 0)$$

of the gamma function and the fact (Sec. 58) that

$$\int_0^\infty e^{-\sigma^2} \, d\sigma = \frac{\sqrt{\pi}}{2},$$

to show that

$$\Gamma\left(k + \frac{1}{2}\right) = \frac{(2k)!}{k! 2^{2k}} \sqrt{\pi} \qquad (k = 0, 1, 2, \ldots).$$

3. Let y be any solution of Bessel's equation $(xy')' + xy = 0$ of order zero, and let $\mathcal{L}$ denote the differential operator defined by means of the equation

$$\mathcal{L}[X] = (xX')' + xX.$$

(a) By writing $X = J_0$ and $Y = y$ in Lagrange's identity (Problem 2, Sec. 69)

$$X\mathcal{L}[Y] - Y\mathcal{L}[X] = \frac{d}{dx}[x(XY' - YX')]$$

for that operator and observing that $\mathcal{L}[X] = 0$ and $\mathcal{L}[Y] = 0$, show that there is a constant B such that

$$\frac{d}{dx}\left[\frac{y(x)}{J_0(x)}\right] = \frac{B}{x[J_0(x)]^2}.$$

(b) Assuming that the function $1/[J_0(x)]^2$ has a Maclaurin series expansion of the form[†]

$$\frac{1}{[J_0(x)]^2} = 1 + \sum_{k=1}^{\infty} c_k x^{2k}$$

and that the expansion obtained by multiplying each side of this by $1/x$ can be integrated term by term, use the result in part (a) to show that y can be put in the form

$$y = AJ_0(x) + B\left[J_0(x)\ln x + \sum_{k=1}^{\infty} d_k x^{2k}\right],$$

where A, B, and d_k $(k = 1, 2, \ldots)$ are constants. [See equation (7), Sec. 82.]

4. According to Problem 3, Bessel's equation $xy'' + y' + xy = 0$ has, in addition to the solution $y_1 = J_0(x)$, a linearly independent solution of the form

$$y_2 = y_1 \ln x + \sum_{k=1}^{\infty} d_k x^{2k}.$$

(a) By substituting this expression for y_2 into Bessel's equation, noting that

$$xy_1'' + y_1' + xy_1 = 0 \quad \text{and} \quad y_1' = -J_1(x) = \sum_{k=0}^{\infty} \frac{(-1)^{k+1}}{k!(k+1)!}\left(\frac{x}{2}\right)^{2k+1},$$

and identifying the coefficients of x^{2k+1} $(k = 0, 1, 2, \ldots)$ in the result, show that

$$d_1 = \frac{1}{2^2}$$

and

$$d_{k+1} = \frac{(-1)^k}{2^{2(k+1)}[(k+1)!]^2}\left[(-1)^{k+1}2^{2k}(k!)^2 d_k + \frac{1}{k+1}\right] \quad (k = 1, 2, \ldots).$$

(b) Use the final result in part (a) and the value of d_1 found there to write expressions for d_2, d_3, and d_4, which suggest that

$$d_k = \frac{(-1)^{k+1}}{2^{2k}(k!)^2}\left(1 + \frac{1}{2} + \frac{1}{3} + \cdots + \frac{1}{k}\right) \quad (k = 1, 2, \ldots).$$

[†]This valid assumption is easily justified by methods from the theory of functions of a complex variable. See the authors' book (2009, Chap. 5), listed in the Bibliography.

Then use mathematical induction to show that this expression for the coefficients d_k is indeed correct. Note that it can also be written [compare with equation (7), Sec. 82]

$$d_k = \frac{(-1)^{k+1}}{2^2 4^2 6^2 \cdots (2k)^2} \left(1 + \frac{1}{2} + \frac{1}{3} + \cdots + \frac{1}{k} \right) \qquad (k = 1, 2, \ldots).$$

5. Let s_n $(n = 1, 2, \ldots)$ be the sequence defined in equation (8), Sec. 82. Show that $s_n > 0$ and $s_n - s_{n+1} > 0$ for each n. Thus show that the sequence is bounded and decreasing and hence that it converges to some number γ. Also, point out why $0 \le \gamma < 1$.

   Suggestion: Observe from the graph of the function $y = 1/x$ that

$$\sum_{k=1}^{n-1} \frac{1}{k} > \int_1^n \frac{dx}{x} = \ln n \qquad (n \ge 2)$$

and

$$\frac{1}{n+1} < \int_n^{n+1} \frac{dx}{x} = \ln (n + 1) - \ln n \qquad (n \ge 1).$$

6. Use the series representations (10) and (11) in Sec. 81, and the identity obtained in Problem 2 to show that

   (a) $J_{1/2}(x) = \sqrt{\dfrac{2}{\pi x}} \sin x;$ (b) $J_{-1/2}(x) = \sqrt{\dfrac{2}{\pi x}} \cos x.$

7. Use the expression for $J_{1/2}(x)$ that was found in Problem 6(a) to verify that $y = J_{1/2}(x)$ is a solution of Bessel's equation

$$x^2 y''(x) + x y'(x) + (x^2 - v^2) y(x) = 0$$

   when $v = 1/2$.

   Suggestion: Since Bessel's equation is linear and homogeneous, it is sufficient to make the substitution $y = x^{-1/2} \sin x$.

8. Show that if y is a differentiable function of x and if $s = \alpha x$, where α is a nonzero constant, then

$$\frac{dy}{dx} = \alpha \frac{dy}{ds} \quad \text{and} \quad \frac{d^2 y}{dx^2} = \alpha^2 \frac{d^2 y}{ds^2}.$$

   Thus, show that the substitution $s = \alpha x$ transforms the *parametric form*

$$x^2 \frac{d^2 y}{dx^2} + x \frac{dy}{dx} + (\alpha^2 x^2 - n^2) y = 0 \qquad (n = 0, 1, 2, \ldots)$$

   of Bessel's equation into

$$s^2 \frac{d^2 y}{ds^2} + s \frac{dy}{ds} + (s^2 - n^2) y = 0 \qquad (n = 0, 1, 2, \ldots),$$

   which is free of α. Conclude that the general solution of the first differential equation here is

$$y = C_1 J_n(\alpha x) + C_2 Y_n(\alpha x).$$

9. The function $I_n(x) = i^{-n} J_n(ix)$, where $i = \sqrt{-1}$, is called the *modified Bessel function of the first kind of order n*.

   (a) Use the series representation (Sec. 82)

$$J_n(x) = \sum_{k=0}^{\infty} \frac{(-1)^k}{k!(n+k)!} \left(\frac{x}{2} \right)^{n+2k} \qquad (n = 0, 1, 2, \ldots)$$

to show that

$$I_n(x) = \sum_{k=0}^{\infty} \frac{1}{k!(n+k)!} \left(\frac{x}{2}\right)^{n+2k} \qquad (n = 0, 1, 2, \ldots).$$

Then, after establishing its convergence for all x, use this last series to show that $I_n(x) > 0$ when $x > 0$ and that

$$I_n(-x) = (-1)^n I_n(x) \qquad (n = 0, 1, 2, \ldots).$$

(b) By referring to the final result in Problem 8, point out why $y = I_n(x)$ is a solution of the *modified Bessel equation*

$$x^2 y''(x) + xy'(x) - (x^2 + n^2) y(x) = 0.$$

10. Follow the steps below to obtain a second solution of Bessel's equation of order zero that is not a constant times $J_0(x)$.[†]

(a) Substitute the series

$$y = x^c \sum_{j=0}^{\infty} a_j x^j \qquad (a_0 \neq 0)$$

into the left-hand side of Bessel's equation

$$xy''(x) + y'(x) + xy(x) = 0$$

of order $n = 0$ to obtain

$$xy''(x) + y'(x) + xy(x) = a_0 c^2 x^{c-1} + a_1 (1+c)^2 x^c$$
$$+ \sum_{j=2}^{\infty} [a_j(j+c)^2 + a_{j-2}] x^{c+j-1},$$

where it is assumed that the parameter c is not a negative integer but is otherwise unrestricted. Write $a_0 = 1$, $a_1 = 0$, and

$$a_j = \frac{-1}{(j+c)^2} a_{j-2} \qquad (j \geq 2).$$

Then show that the function

$$y(x, c) = x^c + \sum_{k=1}^{\infty} a_{2k}(c) x^{2k+c},$$

where

$$a_{2k}(c) = \frac{(-1)^k}{(2+c)^2(4+c)^2(6+c)^2 \cdots (2k+c)^2} \qquad (k \geq 1),$$

satisfies the differential equation

$$x \frac{d^2}{dx^2} y(x, c) + \frac{d}{dx} y(x, c) + xy(x, c) = c^2 x^{c-1}.$$

[†]The method here is a standard one that is used in, for example, the books by Bowman (1958, pp. 6–8) and MacRobert (1967, pp. 224–227), both of which are listed in the Bibliography. The book by MacRobert also uses the method to find a second solution of Bessel's equation of order n when n is any positive integer.

Note that when $c = 0$, one solution of this equation is

$$y_1 = y(x, 0) = J_0(x).$$

(b) Differentiate with respect to c each side of the differential equation at the end of part (a) that is satisfied by $y(x, c)$. Then, by formally reversing the order of differentiation with respect to x and c, show that

$$x \frac{d^2}{dx^2} y_c(x, c) + \frac{d}{dx} y_c(x, c) + x y_c(x, c) = 2c x^{c-1} + c^2 x^{c-1} \ln x$$

and hence, that $y_2 = y_c(x, 0)$ is a second solution of Bessel's equation of order $n = 0$. Also, by differentiating the expression for $y(x, c)$ in part (a) with respect to c, show that

$$y_c(x, c) = y(x, c) \ln x + \sum_{k=1}^{\infty} a'_{2k}(c) x^{2k+c}.$$

(c) Rewrite the expression for $a_{2k}(c)$ in part (a) as

$$\ln[(-1)^k a_{2k}(c)] = -2[\ln(2 + c) + \ln(4 + c) + \ln(6 + c) + \cdots + \ln(2k + c)],$$

differentiate each side here with respect to c, and then set $c = 0$ to obtain

$$a'_{2k}(0) = \frac{(-1)^{k+1}}{2^2 4^2 6^2 \cdots (2k)^2} \left(1 + \frac{1}{2} + \frac{1}{3} + \cdots + \frac{1}{k} \right).$$

Finally, use this expression and the one for $y_c(x, c)$ at the end of part (b) to arrive at the function appearing in brackets in equation (7), Sec. 82. Namely,

$$y_2 = y_c(x, 0) = J_0(x) \ln x + \sum_{k=1}^{\infty} (-1)^{k+1} \frac{x^{2k}}{2^2 4^2 6^2 \cdots (2k)^2} \left(1 + \frac{1}{2} + \frac{1}{3} + \cdots + \frac{1}{k} \right).$$

(Compare with Problem 4.)

83. RECURRENCE RELATIONS

Starting with the expression (Sec. 82)

$$J_n(x) = \sum_{k=0}^{\infty} \frac{(-1)^k}{k!(n+k)!} \left(\frac{x}{2} \right)^{n+2k} \qquad (n = 0, 1, 2, \ldots),$$

write

$$\frac{d}{dx} \left[x^{-n} J_n(x) \right] = \frac{d}{dx} \left[\sum_{k=0}^{\infty} \frac{(-1)^k}{k!(n+k)!} \cdot \frac{x^{2k}}{2^{n+2k}} \right]$$

$$= \sum_{k=0}^{\infty} \frac{(-1)^k}{k!(n+k)!} \cdot \frac{1}{2^{n+2k}} \cdot \frac{d}{dx} x^{2k}$$

$$= \sum_{k=1}^{\infty} \frac{(-1)^k}{(k-1)!(n+k)!} \cdot \frac{x^{2k-1}}{2^{n+2k-1}}.$$

If we replace k by $k+1$ in this last series, so that k runs from zero to infinity again, it follows that

$$\frac{d}{dx}\left[x^{-n}J_n(x)\right] = \sum_{k=0}^{\infty} \frac{(-1)^{k+1}}{k!(n+k+1)!} \cdot \frac{x^{2k+1}}{2^{n+2k+1}}$$

$$= -x^{-n} \sum_{k=0}^{\infty} \frac{(-1)^k}{k!(n+1+k)!} \left(\frac{x}{2}\right)^{n+1+2k},$$

or

(1) $$\frac{d}{dx}\left[x^{-n}J_n(x)\right] = -x^{-n}J_{n+1}(x) \qquad (n=0,1,2,\ldots).$$

The special case

(2) $$J_0'(x) = -J_1(x)$$

was mentioned in Sec. 82.

On the other hand, when $n = 1, 2, \ldots,$

$$\frac{d}{dx}[x^n J_n(x)] = \frac{d}{dx}\left[\sum_{k=0}^{\infty} \frac{(-1)^k}{k!(n+k)!} \cdot \frac{x^{2n+2k}}{2^{n+2k}}\right]$$

$$= \sum_{k=0}^{\infty} \frac{(-1)^k}{k!(n+k)!} \cdot \frac{1}{2^{n+2k}} \cdot \frac{d}{dx} x^{2n+2k}$$

$$= \sum_{k=0}^{\infty} \frac{(-1)^k}{k!(n+k-1)!} \cdot \frac{x^{2n+2k-1}}{2^{n+2k-1}};$$

and we find that

$$\frac{d}{dx}[x^n J_n(x)] = x^n \sum_{k=0}^{\infty} \frac{(-1)^k}{k!(n-1+k)!} \left(\frac{x}{2}\right)^{n-1+2k},$$

or

(3) $$\frac{d}{dx}[x^n J_n(x)] = x^n J_{n-1}(x) \qquad (n=1,2,\ldots).$$

Relations (1) and (3) are called *recurrence relations*. Observe how they can also be written

(4) $$xJ_n'(x) = nJ_n(x) - xJ_{n+1}(x) \qquad (n=0,1,2,\ldots)$$

and

(5) $$xJ_n'(x) = -nJ_n(x) + xJ_{n-1}(x) \qquad (n=1,2,\ldots),$$

respectively; and by eliminating $J_n'(x)$ from these two equations, we find that

(6) $$xJ_{n+1}(x) = 2nJ_n(x) - xJ_{n-1}(x) \qquad (n=1,2,\ldots).$$

This relation, which expresses J_{n+1} in terms of the functions J_n and J_{n-1} of lower orders, is sometimes called a *pure recurrence relation* since it does not involve derivatives.

Integrals involving Bessel functions can sometimes be evaluated with the aid of formulas that follow from relations (1) and (3). Relation (3) tells us, for instance, that when $n = 1, 2, \ldots,$

$$\int_0^x s^n J_{n-1}(s) \, ds = [s^n J_n(s)]_0^x.$$

That is,

$$(7) \qquad \int_0^x s^n J_{n-1}(s) \, ds = x^n J_n(x) \qquad\qquad (n = 1, 2, \ldots).$$

An important special case of this is

$$(8) \qquad \int_0^x s J_0(s) \, ds = x J_1(x).$$

Results in this section will now be used to derive the following *reduction formula*, which is often needed in evaluating certain integrals involving $J_0(x)$:

$$(9) \quad \int_0^x s^n J_0(s) \, ds = x^n J_1(x) + (n-1) x^{n-1} J_0(x) - (n-1)^2 \int_0^x s^{n-2} J_0(s) \, ds$$

$$(n = 2, 3, \ldots).$$

Note that in view of equation (8), formula (9) can be applied successively to completely evaluate the integral on the left-hand side when the integer n is *odd*.[†]

Our derivation of formula (9) uses integration by parts twice. We start by writing

$$\int_0^x s^n J_0(s) \, ds = \int_0^x s^{n-1} s J_0(s) \, ds.$$

If we put

$$U = s^{n-1} \quad \text{and} \quad dV = s J_0(s) \, ds,$$

we see that in view of relation (3),

$$dU = (n-1) s^{n-2} \, ds \quad \text{and} \quad V = s J_1(s).$$

Hence,

$$\int_0^x s^n J_0(s) \, ds = [s^n J_1(s)]_0^x - (n-1) \int_0^x s^{n-1} J_1(s) \, ds,$$

or

$$(10) \qquad \int_0^x s^n J_0(s) \, ds = x^n J_1(x) - (n-1) \int_0^x s^{n-1} J_1(s) \, ds.$$

As for the integral on the right here, we put

$$U = s^{n-1} \quad \text{and} \quad dV = J_1(s) \, ds;$$

[†]Note, too, that when n is *even*, the reduction formula can be used to transform the problem of evaluating $\int_0^x s^n J_0(s) \, ds$ into that of evaluating $\int_0^x J_0(s) \, ds$, which is tabulated for various values of x in, for example, the book edited by Abramowitz and Stegun (1972, pp. 492–493), listed in the Bibliography. Further references are given on pp. 490–491 of that book.

and with the aid of relation (2), we have

$$dU = (n-1)s^{n-2} \quad \text{and} \quad V = -J_0(s).$$

Then,

$$\int_0^x s^{n-1} J_1(s)\, ds = \left[-s^{n-1} J_0(s)\right]_0^x + (n-1)\int_0^x s^{n-2} J_0(s)\, ds,$$

and we arrive at

(11) $$\int_0^x s^{n-1} J_1(s)\, ds = -x^{n-1} J_0(x) + (n-1)\int_0^x s^{n-2} J_0(s)\, ds.$$

Formula (9) is now a combination of equations (10) and (11).

EXAMPLE. Formula (9) can be used to show that

(12) $$\int_0^x s^5 J_0(s)\, ds = x\,(x^2-8)^2 J_1(x) + 4x^2(x^2-8)J_0(x).$$

To be specific, one application of formula (9) yields

$$\int_0^x s^5 J_0(s)\, ds = x^5 J_1(x) + 4x^4 J_0(x) - 16\int_0^x s^3 J_0(s)\, ds,$$

and another gives us

$$\int_0^x s^3 J_0(s)\, ds = x^3 J_1(x) + 2x^2 J_0(x) - 4\int_0^x s J_0(s)\, ds.$$

Thus,

$$\int_0^x s^5 J_0(s)\, ds = (x^5 - 16x^3)J_1(x) + (4x^4 - 32x^2)J_0(x) + 64\int_0^x s J_0(s)\, ds.$$

Referring to the integration formula (8), we now arrive at

$$\int_0^x s^5 J_0(s)\, ds = (x^5 - 16x^3 + 64x)\,J_1(s) + (4x^4 - 32x^2)\,J_0(x),$$

which is the same as equation (12).

Finally, we note that relations (1), (3), and (6) remain valid when n is replaced by the unrestricted parameter ν. Modifications in the derivations simply consist of writing

$$\Gamma(\nu + k + 1) \quad \text{or} \quad (\nu + k)\Gamma(\nu + k)$$

in place of $(n+k)!$.

PROBLEMS

1. By differentiating each side of the recurrence relation (4) in Sec. 83 and then referring to both of the relations (4) and (5) there, show that

$$x^2 J_n''(x) = (n^2 - n - x^2)J_n(x) + x J_{n+1}(x) \qquad (n = 0, 1, 2, \ldots).$$

2. Derive the differentiation formula

$$\frac{d}{dx}[x^{-\nu}J_\nu(x)] = -x^{-\nu}J_{\nu+1}(x),$$

where $\nu > 0$, and point out why it is also valid when ν is replaced by $-\nu$ ($\nu > 0$). [Compare with relation (1), Sec. 83.]

3. Use results in Problems 2 above and 6(a), Sec. 83, to show that

$$J_{3/2}(x) = \sqrt{\frac{2}{\pi x}}\left(\frac{\sin x}{x} - \cos x\right).$$

84. BESSEL'S INTEGRAL FORM

We now derive a useful integral representation for $J_n(x)$. To do this, we first note that the series in the expansions

(1) $$\exp\left(\frac{xt}{2}\right) = \sum_{j=0}^{\infty}\frac{x^j}{j!2^j}t^j, \qquad \exp\left(-\frac{x}{2t}\right) = \sum_{k=0}^{\infty}\frac{(-1)^k x^k}{k!2^k}t^{-k}$$

are absolutely convergent when x is any number and $t \neq 0$. Hence, the product of these exponential functions is itself represented by a series formed by multiplying each term in one series by every term in the other and then summing the resulting terms *in any order.*[†] Clearly, the variable t occurs in each of those resulting terms as a factor t^n ($n = 0, 1, 2, \ldots$) or t^{-n} ($n = 1, 2, \ldots$); and the terms involving any particular power of t may be collected as a sum.

In the case of t^n ($n = 0, 1, 2, \ldots$), that sum is obtained by multiplying the kth term in the second series by the term in the first series whose index is $j = n + k$ and then summing from $k = 0$ to $k = \infty$:

$$\sum_{k=0}^{\infty}\left[\frac{(-1)^k x^k}{k!2^k}t^{-k} \cdot \frac{x^{n+k}}{(n+k)!2^{n+k}}t^{n+k}\right]$$

$$= \sum_{k=0}^{\infty}\frac{(-1)^k}{k!(n+k)!}\left(\frac{x}{2}\right)^{n+2k}t^n = J_n(x)t^n.$$

Similarly, the sum of the terms involving t^{-n} ($n = 1, 2, \ldots$) is found by multiplying the jth term in the first series by the term in the second series with index $k = n + j$ and summing from $j = 0$ to $j = \infty$:

$$\sum_{j=0}^{\infty}\left[\frac{x^j}{j!2^j}t^j \cdot \frac{(-1)^{n+j}x^{n+j}}{(n+j)!2^{n+j}}t^{-n-j}\right]$$

$$= (-1)^n\sum_{j=0}^{\infty}\frac{(-1)^j}{j!(n+j)!}\left(\frac{x}{2}\right)^{n+2j}t^{-n} = (-1)^n J_n(x)t^{-n}.$$

[†]For a justification of this procedure, see, for example, the book by Taylor and Mann (1983, pp. 601–602), which is listed in the Bibliography.

A series representation for the product of the exponential functions (1) is, therefore,

$$(2) \qquad \exp\left[\frac{x}{2}\left(t - \frac{1}{t}\right)\right] = J_0(x) + \sum_{n=1}^{\infty}\left[J_n(x)\, t^n + (-1)^n J_n(x)\, t^{-n}\right].$$

Let us write $t = e^{i\phi}$, where $i = \sqrt{-1}$, in equation (2):

$$(3) \qquad \exp\left[\frac{x}{2}\left(e^{i\phi} - e^{-i\phi}\right)\right] = J_0(x) + \sum_{n=1}^{\infty}\left[J_n(x)\, e^{in\phi} + (-1)^n J_n(x)\, e^{-in\phi}\right].$$

In view of Euler's formula $e^{i\phi} = \cos\phi + i\sin\phi,^{\dagger}$ we know that

$$e^{i\phi} - e^{-i\phi} = 2i\sin\phi$$

and

$$e^{in\phi} = \cos n\phi + i\sin n\phi, \qquad e^{-in\phi} = \cos n\phi - i\sin n\phi.$$

It thus follows from equation (3) that

$$(4) \qquad \exp(ix\sin\phi) = J_0(x) + \sum_{n=1}^{\infty}\left[1 + (-1)^n\right] J_n(x) \cos n\phi$$

$$+ i \sum_{n=1}^{\infty}\left[1 - (-1)^n\right] J_n(x) \sin n\phi.$$

Now, again by Euler's formula,

$$\exp(ix\sin\phi) = \cos(x\sin\phi) + i\sin(x\sin\phi);$$

and if we equate the real parts on each side of equation (4), we find that

$$(5) \qquad \cos(x\sin\phi) = J_0(x) + \sum_{n=1}^{\infty}\left[1 + (-1)^n\right] J_n(x) \cos n\phi.$$

Holding x fixed and regarding this equation as a Fourier cosine series representation of the function $\cos(x\sin\phi)$ on the interval $0 < \phi < \pi$, we need only recall (Sec. 2) the formula for the coefficients in such a series to write

$$(6) \qquad \left[1 + (-1)^n\right] J_n(x) = \frac{2}{\pi}\int_0^{\pi} \cos(x\sin\phi) \cos n\phi\, d\phi \qquad (n = 0, 1, 2, \ldots).$$

If, on the other hand, we equate the imaginary parts on each side of equation (4), we obtain the Fourier sine series representation

$$(7) \qquad \sin(x\sin\phi) = \sum_{n=1}^{\infty}\left[1 - (-1)^n\right] J_n(x) \sin n\phi$$

for $\sin(x\sin\phi)$ on the same interval. Consequently (see Sec. 4),

$$(8) \qquad \left[1 - (-1)^n\right] J_n(x) = \frac{2}{\pi}\int_0^{\pi} \sin(x\sin\phi) \sin n\phi\, d\phi \qquad (n = 1, 2, \ldots).$$

---

†See the footnote with Problem 4, Sec. 7.

According to expressions (6) and (8), then,

$$(9) \qquad J_{2n}(x) = \frac{1}{\pi} \int_0^\pi \cos(x \sin \phi) \cos 2n\phi \, d\phi \qquad\qquad (n = 0, 1, 2, \ldots)$$

and

$$(10) \qquad J_{2n-1}(x) = \frac{1}{\pi} \int_0^\pi \sin(x \sin \phi) \sin(2n - 1)\phi \, d\phi \qquad\qquad (n = 1, 2, \ldots).$$

A single expression for $J_n(x)$ can be obtained by adding corresponding sides of equations (6) and (8) and writing

$$2 J_n(x) = \frac{2}{\pi} \int_0^\pi [\cos n\phi \cos(x \sin \phi) + \sin n\phi \sin(x \sin \phi)] \, d\phi.$$

That is,

$$(11) \qquad J_n(x) = \frac{1}{\pi} \int_0^\pi \cos(n\phi - x \sin \phi) \, d\phi \qquad\qquad (n = 0, 1, 2, \ldots).$$

This is known as *Bessel's integral form* of $J_n(x)$.

85. SOME CONSEQUENCES OF THE INTEGRAL FORMS

A number of important properties of Bessel functions follow readily from integral representations in Sec. 84. The *boundedness properties*

$$(1) \qquad |J_n(x)| \leq 1, \qquad \left| \frac{d^k}{dx^k} J_n(x) \right| \leq 1 \qquad\qquad (k = 1, 2, \ldots)$$

are, for example, immediate consequences of Bessel's integral form

$$J_n(x) = \frac{1}{\pi} \int_0^\pi \cos(n\phi - x \sin \phi) \, d\phi \qquad\qquad (n = 0, 1, 2, \ldots).$$

More precisely, since $|\cos(n\phi - x \sin \phi)| \leq 1$, we find that

$$|J_n(x)| \leq \frac{1}{\pi} \int_0^\pi |\cos(n\phi - x \sin \phi)| \, d\phi \leq \frac{1}{\pi} \int_0^\pi d\phi = 1.$$

Furthermore,

$$J_n'(x) = \frac{1}{\pi} \frac{d}{dx} \int_0^\pi \cos(n\phi - x \sin \phi) \, d\phi$$

$$= \frac{1}{\pi} \int_0^\pi \frac{\partial}{\partial x} \cos(n\phi - x \sin \phi) \, d\phi$$

$$= \frac{1}{\pi} \int_0^\pi \sin(n\phi - x \sin \phi) \sin \phi \, d\phi;$$

and continued differentiation yields integral representations for $J_n''(x)$, etc. Since, in each case, the absolute value of the integrand does not exceed unity, the rest of inequalities (1) also hold.

Sometimes it is useful to write the integral representations

$$J_{2n}(x) = \frac{1}{\pi} \int_0^\pi \cos(x \sin \phi) \cos 2n\phi \, d\phi \qquad (n = 0, 1, 2, \ldots),$$

and

$$J_{2n-1}(x) = \frac{1}{\pi} \int_0^\pi \sin(x \sin \phi) \sin(2n - 1)\phi \, d\phi \qquad (n = 1, 2, \ldots)$$

in Sec. 84 as

(2)
$$J_{2n}(x) = \frac{2}{\pi} \int_0^{\pi/2} \cos(x \sin \phi) \cos 2n\phi \, d\phi \qquad (n = 0, 1, 2, \ldots)$$

and

(3)
$$J_{2n-1}(x) = \frac{2}{\pi} \int_0^{\pi/2} \sin(x \sin \phi) \sin(2n - 1)\phi \, d\phi \qquad (n = 1, 2, \ldots).$$

Expressions (2) and (3) follow from the fact that when x is fixed, the graphs of the integrands

$$y = g(\phi) = \cos(x \sin \phi) \cos 2n\phi,$$
$$y = h(\phi) = \sin(x \sin \phi) \sin(2n - 1)\phi$$

are symmetric with respect to the line $\phi = \pi/2$:

$$g(\pi - \phi) = g(\phi), \qquad h(\pi - \phi) = h(\phi) \qquad (0 \le \phi \le \pi/2).$$

We note the special case

(4)
$$J_0(x) = \frac{2}{\pi} \int_0^{\pi/2} \cos(x \sin \phi) \, d\phi$$

of representation (2). It can also be written

(5)
$$J_0(x) = \frac{2}{\pi} \int_0^{\pi/2} \cos(x \cos \theta) \, d\theta$$

by means of the substitution

$$\theta = \frac{\pi}{2} - \phi.$$

Representations (2) and (3) may be used to verify that for each fixed n $(n = 0, 1, 2, \ldots)$,

(6)
$$\lim_{x \to \infty} J_n(x) = 0.$$

To give the details when $n = 0$, we substitute $u = \sin \phi$ into equation (4) and obtain *Hankel's integral representation*

$$J_0(x) = \frac{2}{\pi} \int_0^1 \frac{\cos xu}{\sqrt{1 - u^2}} \, du,$$

which can also be written

$$\frac{\pi}{2} J_0(x) = \int_0^c \frac{\cos xu}{\sqrt{1 - u^2}} \, du + \int_c^1 \frac{\cos xu}{\sqrt{1 - u^2}} \, du \qquad (0 < c < 1).$$

The second integral here is improper but uniformly convergent with respect to x.[†]
Hence, for any given positive number ε, the absolute value of that integral can be
made less than $\varepsilon/2$, uniformly for all x, by selecting c so that the difference $1 - c$
is sufficiently small and positive. The Riemann-Lebesgue lemma (Sec. 52)

$$(7) \qquad\qquad \lim_{r \to \infty} \int_0^c G(u) \cos ru \, du = 0 \qquad\qquad (r > 0),$$

involving a piecewise continuous function $G(u)$ and a cosine function, then applies
to the first integral with that value of c. That is, there is a number x_ε such that the
absolute value of the first integral is less than $\varepsilon/2$ whenever $x > x_\varepsilon$. Therefore,

$$\frac{\pi}{2}|J_0(x)| < \frac{\varepsilon}{2} + \frac{\varepsilon}{2} = \varepsilon \qquad\qquad \text{whenever } x > x_\varepsilon;$$

and this establishes property (6) when $n = 0$. Verification when n is a positive
integer is left to the problems.

It is interesting to contrast limit (6) with the limit

$$(8) \qquad\qquad \lim_{n \to \infty} J_n(x) = 0,$$

which is valid for each $x \, (-\infty < x < \infty)$. This limit follows from the Riemann-
Lebesgue lemma (7) and its version (Sec. 52)

$$(9) \qquad\qquad \lim_{r \to \infty} \int_0^c G(u) \sin ru \, du = 0 \qquad\qquad (r > 0),$$

involving a sine function, when that lemma is applied to the integral representations (2) and (3) for $J_{2n}(x)$ and $J_{2n-1}(x)$, respectively.

PROBLEMS

1. Use integral representations for $J_n(x)$ to verify that

(a) $J_0(0) = 1$;   (b) $J_n(0) = 0 \ (n = 1, 2, \ldots)$;   (c) $J_0'(x) = -J_1(x)$.

2. Derive representation (2), Sec. 85, for $J_{2n}(x)$ by writing the Fourier cosine series (5),
Sec. 84, as

$$\cos(x \sin \phi) = J_0(x) + 2 \sum_{n=1}^{\infty} J_{2n}(x) \cos 2n\phi$$

and then interpreting it as a Fourier cosine series on the interval $0 < \phi < \pi/2$.

3. Deduce from expression (2), Sec. 85, that

$$J_{2n}(x) = (-1)^n \frac{2}{\pi} \int_0^{\pi/2} \cos(x \cos \theta) \cos 2n\theta \, d\theta \qquad\qquad (n = 0, 1, 2, \ldots).$$

4. Deduce from expression (3), Sec. 85, that

$$J_{2n-1}(x) = (-1)^{n+1} \frac{2}{\pi} \int_0^{\pi/2} \sin(x \cos \theta) \cos(2n - 1)\theta \, d\theta \qquad\qquad (n = 1, 2, \ldots).$$

[†]See, for instance, the book by Kaplan (2003, pp. 453–455) that is listed in the Bibliography.

5. Complete the verification of property (6), Sec. 85, namely

$$\lim_{x \to \infty} J_n(x) = 0$$

for each fixed n ($n = 0, 1, 2, \ldots$).

6. Apply integration by parts to representations (2) and (3) in Sec. 85 and then use the Riemann-Lebesgue lemma (Sec. 52) to show that

$$\lim_{n \to \infty} n J_n(x) = 0$$

for each fixed x.

7. Use the representation (Sec. 85)

$$J_0(x) = \frac{2}{\pi} \int_0^{\pi/2} \cos(x \sin \phi) \, d\phi$$

to show that $J_0(x)$ satisfies Bessel's equation

$$xy''(x) + y'(x) + xy(x) = 0.$$

8. According to Sec. 66, if a function $f(\phi)$ and its derivative $f'(\phi)$ are continuous on the interval $-\pi \le \phi \le \pi$ and if $f(-\pi) = f(\pi)$, then Parseval's equation

$$\frac{1}{\pi} \int_{-\pi}^{\pi} [f(\phi)]^2 \, d\phi = \frac{a_0^2}{2} + \sum_{n=1}^{\infty} \left(a_n^2 + b_n^2 \right)$$

holds, where the numbers a_n ($n = 0, 1, 2, \ldots$) and b_n ($n = 1, 2, \ldots$) are the Fourier coefficients

$$a_n = \frac{1}{\pi} \int_{-\pi}^{\pi} f(\phi) \cos n\phi \, d\phi, \qquad b_n = \frac{1}{\pi} \int_{-\pi}^{\pi} f(\phi) \sin n\phi \, d\phi.$$

(a) By applying that result to $f(\phi) = \cos(x \sin \phi)$, which is an even function of ϕ, and referring to the Fourier (cosine) series (5) for $f(\phi)$ in Sec. 84, show that

$$\frac{1}{\pi} \int_0^{\pi} \cos^2(x \sin \phi) \, d\phi = [J_0(x)]^2 + 2 \sum_{n=1}^{\infty} [J_{2n}(x)]^2 \qquad (-\infty < x < \infty).$$

(b) Similarly, by writing $f(\phi) = \sin(x \sin \phi)$ and referring to the Fourier (sine) series (7) for $f(\phi)$ in Sec. 84, show that

$$\frac{1}{\pi} \int_0^{\pi} \sin^2(x \sin \phi) \, d\phi = 2 \sum_{n=1}^{\infty} [J_{2n-1}(x)]^2 \qquad (-\infty < x < \infty).$$

(c) Combine the results in parts (a) and (b) to show that

$$[J_0(x)]^2 + 2 \sum_{n=1}^{\infty} [J_n(x)]^2 = 1 \qquad (-\infty < x < \infty),$$

and point out how it follows from this identity that

$$|J_0(x)| \le 1 \qquad \text{and} \qquad |J_n(x)| \le \frac{1}{\sqrt{2}} \qquad (n = 1, 2, \ldots)$$

for all x.

9. By writing $t = i$ in the series representation (2), Sec. 84, derive the expansions

$$\cos x = J_0(x) + 2 \sum_{n=1}^{\infty} (-1)^n J_{2n}(x)$$

and

$$\sin x = 2 \sum_{n=1}^{\infty} (-1)^{n+1} J_{2n-1}(x),$$

which are valid for all x.

10. Show that series representation (2), Sec. 84, can be written in the form

$$\exp\left[\frac{x}{2}\left(t - \frac{1}{t}\right)\right] = \lim_{N \to \infty} \sum_{n=-N}^{N} J_n(x)\, t^n \qquad (t \neq 0).$$

This exponential function is, then, a *generating function* for the Bessel functions $J_n(x)$ $(n = 0, \pm 1, \pm 2, \ldots)$.

86. THE ZEROS OF $J_n(x)$

Recall from Sec. 82 that Bessel's equation when $\nu = 0$ is

(1) $$xy''(x) + y'(x) + xy(x) = 0.$$

A modified form of this equation in which the term containing the first derivative is absent will be useful to us here. That form is easily found (see Problem 1, Sec. 87) by making the substitution $y(x) = x^c u(x)$, where c is a constant, in equation (1) and observing that the coefficient of $u'(x)$ in the resulting differential equation,

$$x^2 u''(x) + (1 + 2c) x u'(x) + (x^2 + c^2) u(x) = 0,$$

is zero if $c = -1/2$. The desired modified form of equation (1) is then

(2) $$x^2 u''(x) + \left(x^2 + \frac{1}{4}\right) u(x) = 0,$$

and the function $u(x) = \sqrt{x}\, J_0(x)$ is evidently a solution of equation (2).

We shall now use equation (2) to prove the following important lemma regarding the positive zeros of $J_0(x)$.[†]

Lemma. *The positive zeros of the function $J_0(x)$, or positive roots of the equation $J_0(x) = 0$, form an increasing sequence of numbers x_j $(j = 1, 2, \ldots)$ such that $x_j \to \infty$ as $j \to \infty$.*

To prove this, we continue with the function $u(x) = \sqrt{x}\, J_0(x)$. According to equation (2),

$$-u(x) - u''(x) = \frac{u(x)}{4x^2};$$

[†] Our method is a modification of the one used by A. Czarnecki, *Amer. Math. Monthly*, vol. 71, no. 4, pp. 403–404, 1964, who considers Bessel functions $J_\nu(x)$, when $-1/2 \leq \nu \leq 1/2$.

and multiplying each side of this equation by the function $v(x) = \sin x$ yields

(3)
$$u(x)v''(x) - u''(x)v(x) = u(x)\frac{\sin x}{4x^2}.$$

Also, from the identity

$$u(x)v''(x) - u''(x)v(x) = \frac{d}{dx}[u(x)v'(x) - u'(x)v(x)],$$

we know that

(4)
$$u(x)v''(x) - u''(x)v(x) = \frac{d}{dx}[u(x)\cos x - u'(x)\sin x].$$

By equating the right-hand sides of equations (3) and (4), we obtain

(5)
$$u(x)\frac{\sin x}{4x^2} = \frac{d}{dx}[u(x)\cos x - u'(x)\sin x].$$

Next, let k be any positive integer $(k = 1, 2, \ldots)$. Since

$$\cos(2k\pi + \pi) = -1, \qquad \sin(2k\pi + \pi) = 0$$

and

$$\cos(2k\pi) = 1, \qquad \sin(2k\pi) = 0,$$

it follows from equation (5) that

(6)
$$\int_{2k\pi}^{2k\pi+\pi} u(x)\frac{\sin x}{4x^2}\,dx = [u(x)\cos x - u'(x)\sin x]_{2k\pi}^{2k\pi+\pi}$$
$$= -[u(2k\pi + \pi) + u(2k\pi)].$$

It is now easy to show that our function $u(x) = \sqrt{x}J_0(x)$, and hence $J_0(x)$, has at least one zero in the interval

(7)
$$2k\pi \le x \le 2k\pi + \pi.$$

We do this by assuming that $u(x) \ne 0$ anywhere in that closed interval and obtaining a contradiction. According to our assumption, either $u(x) > 0$ for all x in the interval or $u(x) < 0$ for all such x, since $u(x)$ is continuous and thus cannot change sign without having a zero value at some point in the interval.

Suppose that $u(x) > 0$ everywhere in the interval (7). The integrand in integral (6) is positive when $2k\pi < x < 2k\pi + \pi$. Hence the value of the integral must be positive, while the value $-[u(2k\pi + \pi) + u(2k\pi)]$ that we obtained is evidently negative, giving a contradiction. If, on the other hand, $u(x) < 0$ throughout the interval (7), the value of the integral must be negative; but the value obtained is positive. This is again a contradiction. We thus conclude that $J_0(x)$ has at least one zero in the interval (7).

Actually, $J_0(x)$ can have *at most* a finite number of zeros in any closed bounded interval $a \le x \le b$. To see that this is so, we assume that the interval $a \le x \le b$ *does* contain an infinite number of zeros. From advanced calculus, we know that if a given infinite set of points lies in a closed bounded interval, there is always a sequence of distinct points in that set which converges to a point in the interval.[†] In particular, then, our assumption that the interval $a \leq x \leq b$ contains an infinite number of zeros of $J_0(x)$ implies that there exists a sequence x_m ($m = 1, 2, \ldots$) of distinct zeros such that $x_m \to c$ as $m \to \infty$, where c is a point which also lies in the interval. Since the function $J_0(x)$ is continuous, $J_0(c) = 0$; and by the definition of the limit of a sequence, every interval centered at c contains other zeros of $J_0(x)$. But the fact that $J_0(x)$ is not identically equal to zero and has a Maclaurin series representation which is valid for all x means that there exists some interval centered at c which contains no other zeros.[‡] Since this is contrary to what has just been shown, the number of zeros in the interval $a \leq x \leq b$ cannot, then, be infinite.

It is now evident that the positive zeros of $J_0(x)$ can, in fact, be arranged as an increasing sequence of numbers tending to infinity. The table just below gives the values, correct to four significant figures, of the first five zeros of $J_0(x)$ and the corresponding values of $J_1(x)$. (See Fig. 70 in Sec. 82.) Extensive tables of numerical values of Bessel and related functions, together with their zeros, can be found in books listed in the Bibliography.[§]

$$J_0(x_j) = 0$$

j	1	2	3	4	5
x_j	2.405	5.520	8.654	11.79	14.93
$J_1(x_j)$	0.5191	-0.3403	0.2715	-0.2325	0.2065

The lemma just proved can be extended so as to apply to Bessel functions $J_n(x)$ when n is a positive integer.

Theorem. Let n be any fixed nonnegative integer ($n = 0, 1, 2, \ldots$). The positive zeros of the function $J_n(x)$, or positive roots of the equation

$$(8) \qquad\qquad J_n(x) = 0,$$

form an increasing sequence of numbers x_j ($j = 1, 2, \ldots$) such that $x_j \to \infty$ as $j \to \infty$.

Our proof is by mathematical induction. First, we know from the lemma that this theorem is true when $n = 0$. Assume now that it is true when $n = m$, where m is any nonnegative integer, and let a and b be two distinct positive zeros of $J_m(x)$. This means that the function $x^{-m}J_m(x)$ vanishes when $x = a$ and when $x = b$. It thus follows from Rolle's theorem that the derivative of $x^{-m}J_m(x)$ vanishes for at least one value of x between a and b; furthermore, from relation (1) in Sec. 83,

---

[†] See, for example, the book by Taylor and Mann (1983, pp. 515–519), listed in the Bibliography.

[‡] That is, the zeros of such a function are *isolated*. An argument for this is given in the authors' book (2009, p. 251), listed in the Bibliography.

[§] See especially the book edited by Abramowitz and Stegun (1972) and the ones by Jahnke, Emde, and Lösch (1960), Gray and Mathews (1966), and Watson (1995).

we know that

$$J_{m+1}(x) = -x^m \frac{d}{dx}[x^{-m}J_m(x)].$$

Hence, there is at least one zero of $J_{m+1}(x)$ between any two positive zeros of $J_m(x)$. Also, just as in the case of $J_0(x)$, the function $J_{m+1}(x)$ can have at most a finite number of zeros in any bounded interval. Inasmuch as the zeros of $J_m(x)$ form an unbounded increasing sequence of numbers, it now follows that the same is true of the zeros of $J_{m+1}(x)$. This completes the proof of the theorem.

87. ZEROS OF RELATED FUNCTIONS

We preface the theorem in this section with a needed lemma. The theorem, in addition to the one in Sec. 86, will be important to us in solving boundary value problems in which Bessel functions arise.

Lemma. *At each positive zero of $J_n(x)$ $(n = 0, 1, 2, \ldots)$, the derivative $J_n'(x)$ is nonzero. Moreover, the values of $J_n'(x)$ alternate in sign at consecutive positive zeros of $J_n(x)$.*

The proof starts with the fact that the function $y = J_n(x)$ satisfies Bessel's equation (Sec. 82)

(1) $$x^2 y''(x) + xy'(x) + (x^2 - n^2)y(x) = 0.$$

When written in the form

$$y''(x) + \frac{1}{x}y'(x) + \frac{x^2 - n^2}{x^2}y(x) = 0,$$

equation (1) is seen to be of the type treated in Lemma 1, Sec. 70, dealing with the uniqueness of solutions of certain second-order linear differential equations. According to that lemma, there is just one continuously differentiable solution of Bessel's equation satisfying the conditions $y(c) = y'(c) = 0$, where $c > 0$, and the solution is identically equal to zero. Consequently, there is no positive number c such that $J_n(c) = J_n'(c) = 0$. That is, $J_n'(x)$ cannot vanish at a positive zero of $J_n(x)$. This means, of course, that $J_n(x)$ must change sign at such a point.

It remains to show that values of $J_n'(x)$ have different signs at consecutive positive zeros a and b $(0 < a < b)$ of $J_n(x)$. If $J_n'(a) > 0$, then $J_n(x) > 0$ $(a < x < b)$ and $J_n(x)$ is decreasing at b; hence, $J_n'(b) < 0$. Similarly, if $J_n'(a) < 0$, then $J_n'(b) > 0$. [See the graphs of $y = J_0(x)$ and $y = J_1(x)$ in Fig. 70 (Sec. 82), where the slopes of these functions alternate at their zeros.] The lemma is now established.

The theorem to follow is similar to the one in Sec. 86 but involves the function $hJ_n(x) + xJ_n'(x)$, where n is a nonnegative integer and h is a nonnegative constant. Although this theorem need not exclude the possibility that h may be negative, such values will not arise in our applications.

> **Theorem.** *Let n be any fixed nonnegative integer ($n = 0, 1, 2, \ldots$), and suppose that h is a nonnegative constant ($h \geq 0$). The positive zeros of the function $hJ_n(x) + xJ'_n(x)$, or positive roots of the equation*

$$(2) \qquad\qquad hJ_n(x) + xJ'_n(x) = 0,$$

> *form an increasing sequence of numbers x_j ($j = 1, 2, \ldots$) such that $x_j \to \infty$ as $j \to \infty$.*

To prove this, we observe that if a and b are consecutive positive zeros of $J_n(x)$, it follows that $hJ_n(x) + xJ'_n(x)$ must have the values $aJ'_n(a)$ and $bJ'_n(b)$ at the points $x = a$ and $x = b$, respectively. Since one of those values is positive and the other negative, according to the above lemma, the function $hJ_n(x) + xJ'_n(x)$ vanishes at some point, or at some finite number of points, between a and b. Consequently, it has an increasing sequence of positive zeros tending to infinity.[†] So the theorem is true.

In this and the preceding section, we have considered only the *positive* zeros of the functions

$$(3) \qquad\qquad J_n(x) \qquad \text{and} \qquad hJ_n(x) + xJ'_n(x) \qquad\qquad (n = 0, 1, 2, \ldots)$$

since they are the ones that will concern us in the applications. But observe that $x = 0$ is a zero of both of these functions when $n = 1, 2, \ldots$ and that it is a zero of the second one when $n = 0$ if $h = 0$.

Furthermore, if $x = c$ is a zero of the first of the functions (3), then $x = -c$ is also a zero since $J_n(-c) = (-1)^n J_n(c)$. The same is true of the second of the functions (3). For, in view of the recurrence relation (Sec. 83)

$$xJ'_n(x) = nJ_n(x) - xJ_{n+1}(x),$$

that second function can be written

$$(4) \qquad\qquad (h + n)J_n(x) - xJ_{n+1}(x);$$

and it follows that

$$(h + n)J_n(-c) - (-c)J_{n+1}(-c) = (-1)^n \left[(h + n)J_n(c) - cJ_{n+1}(c) \right].$$

PROBLEMS

1. By means of the substitution $y(x) = x^c u(x)$, transform Bessel's equation

$$x^2 y''(x) + xy'(x) + (x^2 - v^2)y(x) = 0$$

into the differential equation

$$x^2 u''(x) + (1 + 2c)xu'(x) + (x^2 - v^2 + c^2)u(x) = 0,$$

which becomes equation (2), Sec. 86, when $v = 0$ and $c = -1/2$.

[†]In the important special case $n = 0$, the first few zeros are tabulated for various positive values of h in, for example, the book on heat conduction by Carslaw and Jaeger (1986, p. 493), which is listed in the Bibliography.

2. Use the result in Problem 1 when $c = -1/2$ to obtain a general solution of Bessel's equation when $\nu = 1/2$. Then, using the expressions (Problem 6, Sec. 82)

$$J_{1/2}(x) = \sqrt{\frac{2}{\pi x}} \sin x \quad \text{and} \quad J_{-1/2}(x) = \sqrt{\frac{2}{\pi x}} \cos x,$$

point out how $J_{1/2}(x)$ and $J_{-1/2}(x)$ are special cases of that solution.

3. Let n have any one of the values $n = 0, 1, 2, \ldots$. By substituting bi, where b is any nonzero real number, for the variable x in the expression (Sec. 82)

$$J_n(x) = \sum_{k=0}^{\infty} \frac{(-1)^k}{k!(n+k)!} \left(\frac{x}{2} \right)^{n+2k} \qquad (n = 0, 1, 2, \ldots),$$

show that the Bessel function $J_n(x)$ has no pure imaginary zeros.

88. ORTHOGONAL SETS OF BESSEL FUNCTIONS

The physical applications in this chapter will involve solutions of *singular* Sturm-Liouville problems, on an interval $0 \le x \le c$, whose differential equations are of the form (see Example 1 in Sec. 68)

$$(1) \qquad \frac{d}{dx}\left(x \frac{dX}{dx} \right) + \left(-\frac{n^2}{x} + \lambda x \right) X = 0 \qquad (n = 0, 1, 2, \ldots),$$

where X and X' are to be continuous when $0 \le x \le c$. Observe how the differential equation (1) can be written

$$x^2 \frac{d^2 X}{dx^2} + x \frac{dX}{dx} + (\lambda x^2 - n^2) X = 0 \qquad (n = 0, 1, 2, \ldots)$$

and that it reduces to

$$x \frac{d^2 X}{dx^2} + \frac{dX}{dx} + \lambda x X = 0$$

when $n = 0$. The single boundary condition to be used [see case (a) of Theorem 1 in Sec. 69] will always be a special case of

$$(2) \qquad\qquad b_1 X(c) + b_2 X'(c) = 0,$$

where the coefficients b_1 and b_2 are real and not both zero.

Theorems 1 and 2 below provide solutions of our Sturm-Liouville problems when the special case of condition (2) is one of three different types. These theorems treat the problems when $n = 0$ and when $n = 1, 2, \ldots$ separately. Although the theorems could be combined, it will be more convenient to have them separate in the applications. Their proofs, appearing in Sec. 89, will, however, be combined.

Theorem 1. *For the singular Sturm-Liouville problem consisting of the differential equation*

$$(3) \qquad\qquad x \frac{d^2 X}{dx^2} + \frac{dX}{dx} + \lambda x X = 0 \qquad\qquad (0 < x < c)$$

and one of the boundary conditions

(4) $X(c) = 0,$

(5) $hX(c) + cX'(c) = 0$ $(h > 0),$

(6) $X'(c) = 0,$

the eigenvalues λ_j and corresponding eigenfunctions X_j are as follows:

(a) *when condition (4) is used,*

$$\lambda_j = \alpha_j^2, \qquad X_j = J_0(\alpha_j x) \qquad\qquad (j = 1, 2, \ldots)$$

where $\alpha_j (j = 1, 2, \ldots)$ are the positive roots of the equation

$$J_0(\alpha c) = 0;$$

(b) *when condition (5) is used,*

$$\lambda_j = \alpha_j^2, \qquad X_j = J_0(\alpha_j x) \qquad\qquad (j = 1, 2, \ldots)$$

where $\alpha_j (j = 1, 2, \ldots)$ are the positive roots of the equation

$$hJ_0(\alpha c) + (\alpha c)J_0'(\alpha c) = 0 \qquad\qquad (h > 0);$$

(c) *when condition (6) is used,*

$$\lambda_1 = 0, \quad X_1 = 1 \quad\text{and}\quad \lambda_j = \alpha_j^2, \quad X_j = J_0(\alpha_j x) \quad (j = 2, 3, \ldots)$$

where $\alpha_j (j = 2, 3, \ldots)$ are the positive roots of the equation

$$J_0'(\alpha c) = 0.$$

Observe that since $J_0'(x) = -J_1(x)$ (see Sec. 83), the equations defining the numbers α_j in cases (b) and (c) can be written

$$hJ_0(\alpha c) - (\alpha c)J_1(\alpha c) = 0 \qquad\text{and}\qquad J_1(\alpha c) = 0,$$

respectively.

Theorem 2. *Let n be a positive integer ($n = 1, 2, \ldots$). For the singular Sturm-Liouville problem consisting of the differential equation*

(7) $$x^2 \frac{d^2 X}{dx^2} + x\frac{dX}{dx} + (\lambda x^2 - n^2) X = 0 \qquad\qquad (0 < x < c)$$

and one of the boundary conditions

(8) $X(c) = 0,$

(9) $hX(c) + cX'(c) = 0$ $(h > 0),$

(10) $X'(c) = 0,$

the eigenvalues λ_j and corresponding eigenfunctions X_j are

$$\lambda_j = \alpha_j^2, \qquad X_j = J_n(\alpha_j x) \qquad\qquad (j = 1, 2, \ldots)$$

where the numbers α_j are defined as follows:

(a) *when condition (8) is used, α_j ($j = 1, 2, \ldots$) are the positive roots of the equation*

$$J_n(\alpha c) = 0;$$

(b) *when condition (9) is used, α_j ($j = 1, 2, \ldots$) are the positive roots of the equation*

$$hJ_n(\alpha c) + (\alpha c)J_n'(\alpha c) = 0 \qquad\qquad (h > 0);$$

(c) *when condition (10) is used, α_j ($j = 1, 2, \ldots$) are the positive roots of the equation*

$$J_n'(\alpha c) = 0.$$

Note that because the functions

$$hJ_n(x) + xJ_n'(x) \qquad \text{and} \qquad (h+n)J_n(x) - xJ_{n+1}(x)$$

are the same, as pointed out at the end of Sec. 87, the equation defining the numbers α_j in case (b) of Theorem 2 can be written

(11) $$(h+n)J_n(\alpha c) - (\alpha c)J_{n+1}(\alpha c) = 0.$$

Also, because $xJ_n'(x) = nJ_n(x) - xJ_{n+1}(x)$ (Sec. 83), the equation

(12) $$nJ_n(\alpha c) - (\alpha c)J_{n+1}(\alpha c) = 0$$

is an alternative form of the equation defining the α_j in case (c) of Theorem 2.

For each of the cases in these two theorems, the orthogonality property

(13) $$\int_0^c xJ_n(\alpha_j x)J_n(\alpha_k x)\,dx = 0 \qquad\qquad (j \neq k)$$

follows from case (a) of Theorem 1 in Sec. 69. Observe that this orthogonality of the eigenfunctions with respect to the weight function x, on the interval $0 < x < c$, is the same as ordinary orthogonality with weight function unity of the functions $\sqrt{x}\, J_n(\alpha_j x)$ on the same interval. Also, many orthogonal sets are represented here, depending on the values of c, n, and h. Once we have proved the two theorems, we shall in Secs. 90 and 91 normalize these eigenfunctions and find formulas for the coefficients in generalized Fourier series expansions involving the eigenfunctions. The reader who wishes to reach such expansions and their applications more quickly may pass directly to Sec. 90 without loss of continuity.

89. PROOF OF THE THEOREMS

We turn now to the proof of the two theorems in Sec. 88. Recall how we wrote the differential equation (1) there as

(1) $$x^2 \frac{d^2X}{dx^2} + x\frac{dX}{dx} + (\lambda x^2 - n^2)X = 0 \qquad\qquad (n = 0, 1, 2, \ldots)$$

and combined it with one of the boundary conditions

(2) $$X(c) = 0,$$

(3) $$hX(c) + cX'(c) = 0 \qquad (h > 0),$$

(4) $$X'(c) = 0.$$

Case (a) of Theorem 2 in Sec. 69, applied to the general form (1)–(2), Sec. 88, of these three Sturm-Liouville problems, ensures that any eigenvalue must be a real number; and, keeping in mind that X and X' must be continuous on the closed interval $0 \le x \le c$, we consider the possibilities that λ may be zero, positive, or negative.

(i) The case $\lambda = 0$

When $\lambda = 0$, equation (1) is a Cauchy-Euler equation (see Problem 1, Sec. 44):

(5) $$x^2 \frac{d^2X}{dx^2} + x \frac{dX}{dx} - n^2 X = 0 \qquad (n = 0, 1, 2, \ldots).$$

To solve it, we write $x = \exp s$ and put it in the form

(6) $$\frac{d^2X}{ds^2} - n^2 X = 0 \qquad (n = 0, 1, 2, \ldots).$$

If $n = 0$, equation (6) has solution $X = As + B$, where A and B are arbitrary constants; and the general solution of equation (5) is, therefore, $X(x) = A \ln x + B$ when $n = 0$. The requirement that X and X' be continuous when $0 \le x \le c$ forces A to be zero, and we have $X(x) = B$. When condition (2) or (3) is imposed, $B = 0$. The constant B can, however, remain arbitrary when condition (4) is used. Assigning the value $B = 1$, we then have the eigenfunction $X(x) = 1$, corresponding to $\lambda = 0$. This appears in case (c) of Theorem 1 in Sec. 88 and is the only case there in which $\lambda = 0$ is an eigenvalue. Any eigenfunction corresponding to that eigenvalue is, of course, a constant multiple of $X(x) = 1$.

If, on the other hand, n is positive, the general solution of equation (6) is $X = Ae^{ns} + Be^{-ns}$. That is,

$$X(x) = Ax^n + Bx^{-n} = Ax^n + B\frac{1}{x^n}.$$

Since our solution must be continuous and therefore bounded on $0 \le x \le c$, we require that $B = 0$. Hence, $X(x) = Ax^n$. It is now easy to see that $A = 0$ if any of the conditions (2), (3), or (4) is to be satisfied, and we arrive at only the trivial solution $X(x) \equiv 0$. Thus, in Theorem 2, Sec. 88, zero is not an eigenvalue.

(ii) The case $\lambda > 0$

We consider next the possibility that $\lambda > 0$ and write $\lambda = \alpha^2$ $(\alpha > 0)$. Equation (1) is then

(7) $$x^2 \frac{d^2X}{dx^2} + x \frac{dX}{dx} + (\alpha^2 x^2 - n^2)X = 0 \qquad (n = 0, 1, 2, \ldots),$$

and we know from Problem 8, Sec. 82, that its general solution is

$$X(x) = C_1 J_n(\alpha x) + C_2 Y_n(\alpha x).$$

Our continuity requirements imply that $C_2 = 0$, since $Y_n(\alpha x)$ is discontinuous at $x = 0$ (see Sec. 82). Hence, any nontrivial solution of equation (7) that meets those requirements must be a constant multiple of the function $X(x) = J_n(\alpha x)$.

In applying one of the boundary conditions at $x = c$, we emphasize that *the symbol $J_n'(\alpha x)$ stands for the derivative of $J_n(s)$ with respect to s, evaluated at $s = \alpha x$.* Then, by the chain rule,

$$\frac{d}{dx} J_n(\alpha x) = \frac{d}{ds} J_n(s) \frac{ds}{dx} = J_n'(s)\,\alpha = \alpha J_n'(\alpha x);$$

and conditions (2), (3), and (4) require that

(8) $$J_n(\alpha c) = 0,$$

(9) $$h J_n(\alpha c) + (\alpha c) J_n'(\alpha c) = 0 \qquad\qquad (h > 0),$$

or

(10) $$J_n'(\alpha c) = 0,$$

respectively.

According to the theorems in Secs. 86 and 87, each of the equations (8), (9), and (10) has an infinite number of positive roots

(11) $$\alpha_j = \frac{x_j}{c} \qquad\qquad (j = 1, 2, \ldots),$$

where x_j ($j = 1, 2, \ldots$) is the unbounded increasing sequence in the statement of the theorem in question. The numbers α_j here depend, of course, on the value of n and also on the value of h in the case of equation (9). Our Sturm-Liouville problem thus has eigenvalues $\lambda_j = \alpha_j^2$ ($j = 1, 2, \ldots$), and the corresponding eigenfunctions are

(12) $$X_j(x) = J_n(\alpha_j x) \qquad\qquad (j = 1, 2, \ldots).$$

(iii) The case $\lambda < 0$

There are no negative eigenvalues. In order to show this, we assume that $\lambda > 0$ and write $\lambda = -\alpha^2$ ($\alpha > 0$). Equation (1) then becomes

(13) $$x^2 \frac{d^2 X}{dx^2} + x \frac{dX}{dx} - (\alpha^2 x^2 + n^2) X = 0 \qquad\qquad (n = 0, 1, 2, \ldots).$$

The substitution $s = \alpha x$ can be used here to put equation (13) in the form (compare with Problem 8, Sec. 82)

(14) $$s^2 \frac{d^2 X}{ds^2} + s \frac{dX}{ds} - (s^2 + n^2) X = 0 \qquad\qquad (n = 0, 1, 2, \ldots).$$

From Problem 9, Sec. 82, we know that the modified Bessel function

$$X = I_n(s) = i^{-n} J_n(is)$$

satisfies equation (14); and since $I(s)$ has a power series representation that converges for all s, the function $X(x) = I_n(\alpha x)$ satisfies the continuity requirements in our problem. As was the case with equation (7), equation (13) has a second solution, analogous to $Y_n(\alpha x)$, that is discontinuous at $x = 0$.[†] Hence we know that except for an arbitrary constant factor, $X(x) = I_n(\alpha x)$ is the desired solution of equation (13).

We now show that for each positive value of α, the function $X(x) = I_n(\alpha x)$ fails to satisfy any of the boundary conditions (2), (3), or (4). In each case, our proof rests on the fact that $I_n(x) > 0$ when $x > 0$, as demonstrated in Problem 9, Sec. 82.

Since $I_n(\alpha c) > 0$ when $\alpha > 0$, it is obvious that condition (2), which requires that $I_n(\alpha c) = 0$, fails to be satisfied for any positive number α.

Condition (3), when applied to the function $X(x) = i^{-n}J_n(i\alpha x)$, becomes

$$(15) \qquad\qquad hi^{-n}J_n(i\alpha c) + ci^{-n}i\alpha J_n'(i\alpha c) = 0 \qquad\qquad (h > 0).$$

But we know from the discussion at the end of Sec. 87 that the equation

$$hJ_n(x) + xJ_n'(x) = 0 \qquad\qquad (h \ge 0)$$

has the alternative form

$$(h + n)J_n(x) - xJ_{n+1}(x) = 0 \qquad\qquad (h \ge 0).$$

Hence, equation (15) can be written

$$(h + n)i^{-n}J_n(i\alpha c) + (\alpha c)i^{-(n+1)}J_{n+1}(i\alpha c) = 0 \qquad\qquad (h \ge 0).$$

Since $I_n(\alpha x) = i^{-n}J_n(i\alpha x)$, then,

$$(16) \qquad\qquad (h + n)I_n(\alpha c) + (\alpha c)I_{n+1}(\alpha c) = 0 \qquad\qquad (h \ge 0);$$

and because $\alpha > 0$, the left-hand side of this last equation is positive. So, once again, no positive values of α can occur as roots.

Finally, since condition (4) is really condition (3) if h is allowed to be zero and since relation (16) is valid when $h = 0$, we may conclude that there are no negative eigenvalues arising in either of the theorems in Sec. 88. Those theorems are now completely proved.

Except for the zero eigenvalue in case (c) of Theorem 1 in Sec. 88, the eigenvalues are all represented by the numbers $\lambda_j = \alpha_j^2$ where the α_j are given by equation (11). Since the numbers x_j used in equation (11) form an unbounded increasing sequence, it is clear that the same is true of the eigenvalues λ_j. That is, $\lambda_j < \lambda_{j+1}$ and $\lambda_j \to \infty$ as $j \to \infty$.

PROBLEMS

1. By referring to Theorem 1 in Sec. 88, show that the eigenvalues of the singular Sturm-Liouville problem

$$xX'' + X' + \lambda xX = 0, \qquad X(2) = 0$$

on the interval $0 \le x \le 2$ are the numbers $\lambda_j = \alpha_j^2$ $(j = 1, 2, \ldots)$ where α_j are the positive roots of the equation $J_0(2\alpha) = 0$ and that the corresponding eigenfunctions are

---

[†]For a detailed discussion of this, see, for example, the book by Tranter (1969, pp. 16ff), which is listed in the Bibliography.

$X_j = J_0(\alpha_j x)$ $(j = 1, 2, \ldots)$. With the aid of the table in Sec. 86, obtain the numerical values $\alpha_1 = 1.2$, $\alpha_2 = 2.8$, $\alpha_3 = 4.3$, valid to one decimal place.

2. Write $U(x) = \sqrt{x} J_n(\alpha x)$, where n has any one of the values $n = 0, 1, 2, \ldots$ and α is a positive constant.

   (a) By recalling from Problem 8, Sec. 82, that $y(x) = J_n(\alpha x)$ satisfies the differential equation

   $$x^2 y''(x) + xy'(x) + (\alpha^2 x^2 - n^2) y(x) = 0$$

   and noting that $y(x) = x^{-1/2} U(x)$, show that $U(x)$ satisfies the differential equation

   $$U''(x) + \left(\alpha^2 + \frac{1 - 4n^2}{4x^2} \right) U(x) = 0.$$

   (b) Let c denote any fixed positive number and write

   $$U_j(x) = \sqrt{x} \, J_n(\alpha_j x) \qquad\qquad (j = 1, 2, \ldots),$$

   where α_j are the positive roots of the equation $J_n(\alpha c) = 0$. Use the result in part (a) to show that

   $$\left(\alpha_j^2 - \alpha_k^2 \right) U_j(x) U_k(x) = U_j(x) U_k''(x) - U_j''(x) U_k(x).$$

   (c) With the aid of the identity

   $$U_j(x) U_k''(x) - U_j''(x) U_k(x) = \frac{d}{dx} \left[U_j(x) U_k'(x) - U_j'(x) U_k(x) \right],$$

   show how it follows from the result in part (b) that the set $\{U_j(x)\}$ there is orthogonal on the interval $0 < x < c$ with weight function unity. Thus, give another proof that the set $\{J_n(\alpha_j x)\}$ in case (a) of Theorems 1 and 2 in Sec. 88 is orthogonal on $0 < x < c$ with weight function x.

3. Since our series representation of $J_n(x)(n = 0, 1, 2, \ldots)$ in Sec. 82 converges when x is replaced by any complex number z and since the coefficients of the powers of z in that representation are all real, it follows that $J_n(\bar{z}) = \overline{J_n(z)}$, where $\bar{z}$ denotes the complex conjugate $x - iy$ of the number $z = x + iy$.[†] Also, the proof of orthogonality in Problem 2 remains valid when α is a nonzero complex number and when the set of roots α_j there is allowed to include any nonzero complex roots that may occur. Use these facts to show that if a complex number

   $$\alpha_j = a + ib \qquad\qquad (a \neq 0, b \neq 0)$$

   is a zero of $J_n(z)$, then so is $\overline{\alpha_j} = a - ib$. Thus,

   $$\int_0^1 x \left| J_n(\alpha_j x) \right|^2 dx = \int_0^1 x J_n(\alpha_j x) J_n(\overline{\alpha_j} x) \, dx = 0.$$

   Point out why the first integral here is actually positive. With this contradiction, conclude that if $z = x_j$ $(j = 1, 2, \ldots)$ are the positive zeros of $J_n(z)$, then the only other zeros, real or complex, are $z = -x_j$ $(j = 1, 2, \ldots)$, and also $z = 0$ when n is positive. (Compare with Problem 3, Sec. 87.)

[†]For a discussion of power series representations in the complex plane, see the authors' book (2009, Chap. 5), listed in the Bibliography.

90.   TWO LEMMAS

The orthogonal sets of Bessel functions in Sec. 88 need to be normalized if we are to use the theory of generalized Fourier series to find expansions in terms of those sets. Lemmas 1 and 2 in this section provide the required norms. As we did with the theorems in Sec. 88, we state these lemmas separately when $n = 0$ and when $n = 1, 2, \ldots$. Regardless of the value of n, however, the eigenfunctions of the Sturm-Liouville problem can be written in normalized form as

$$(1) \qquad\qquad \phi_j(x) = \frac{J_n(\alpha_j x)}{\| J_n(\alpha_j x) \|} \qquad\qquad (j = 1, 2, \ldots).$$

Lemma 1. *Let c be any positive number.*

(a) *If α_j ($j = 1, 2, \ldots$) are the positive roots of the equation*

$$J_0(\alpha c) = 0,$$

then

$$\| J_0(\alpha_j x) \|^2 = \frac{c^2}{2} [J_1(\alpha_j c)]^2 \qquad\qquad (j = 1, 2, \ldots).$$

(b) *If α_j ($j = 1, 2, \ldots$) are the positive roots of the equation*

$$h J_0(\alpha c) + (\alpha c) J_0'(\alpha c) = 0 \qquad\qquad (h > 0),$$

then

$$\| J_0(\alpha_j x) \|^2 = \frac{(\alpha_j c)^2 + h^2}{2\alpha_j^2} [J_0(\alpha_j c)]^2 \qquad\qquad (j = 1, 2, \ldots).$$

(c) *If $\alpha_1 = 0$ and α_j ($j = 2, 3, \ldots$) are the positive roots of the equation*

$$J_0'(\alpha c) = 0,$$

then

$$\| J_0(\alpha_1 x) \|^2 = \frac{c^2}{2} \quad and \quad \| J_0(\alpha_j x) \|^2 = \frac{c^2}{2} [J_0(\alpha_j c)]^2 \quad (j = 2, 3, \ldots).$$

The cases (a), (b), and (c) in this lemma correspond to the cases (a), (b), and (c) in Theorem 1 of Sec. 88. Note how we are able to write the eigenfunction $X_1 = 1$ in case (c) of that theorem as $X_1 = J_0(\alpha_1 x)$ in case (c) here since

$$J_0(\alpha_1 x) = J_0(0) = 1$$

when $\alpha_1 = 0$. This allows us to express its norm in a way similar to the way in which the norms occurring when $j = 2, 3, \ldots$ are expressed. The three cases in Lemma 2 just below correspond, of course, to the three cases in Theorem 2 of Sec. 88.

Lemma 2. *Let c be any positive number and n a positive integer ($n = 1, 2, \ldots$).*

(a) *If α_j ($j = 1, 2, \ldots$) are the positive roots of the equation*

$$J_n(\alpha c) = 0,$$

then

$$\|J_n(\alpha_j x)\|^2 = \frac{c^2}{2} [J_{n+1}(\alpha_j c)]^2 \qquad (j = 1, 2, \ldots).$$

(b) *If* α_j $(j = 1, 2, \ldots)$ *are the positive roots of the equation*

$$hJ_n(\alpha c) + (\alpha c)J_n'(\alpha c) = 0 \qquad (h > 0),$$

then

$$\|J_n(\alpha_j x)\|^2 = \frac{(\alpha_j c)^2 - n^2 + h^2}{2\alpha_j^2} [J_n(\alpha_j c)]^2 \qquad (j = 1, 2, \ldots).$$

(c) *If* α_j $(j = 1, 2, \ldots)$ *are the positive roots of the equation*

$$J_n'(\alpha c) = 0,$$

then

$$\|J_n(\alpha_j x)\|^2 = \frac{(\alpha_j c)^2 - n^2}{2\alpha_j^2} [J_n(\alpha_j c)]^2 \qquad (j = 1, 2, \ldots).$$

Although these two lemmas are stated separately, it is convenient to prove them together. So, unless otherwise stated, n may have any one of the values $n = 0, 1, 2, \ldots$. We start with the fact (Problem 8, Sec. 82) that if α is a nonzero constant, the function

(2) $$X(x) = J_n(\alpha x)$$

satisfies the differential equation

$$x^2 X'' + x X' + (\alpha^2 x^2 - n^2) X = 0,$$

or

(3) $$(xX')' + \left(\alpha^2 x - \frac{n^2}{x}\right) X = 0.$$

Next, we multiply each side of equation (3) by $2x X'$ and write

$$\frac{d}{dx}(xX')^2 + (\alpha^2 x^2 - n^2) \frac{d}{dx}(X^2) = 0.$$

After integrating both terms here and using integration by parts in the second term, we find that

$$[(xX')^2 + (\alpha^2 x^2 - n^2) X^2]_0^c - 2\alpha^2 \int_0^c x X^2 \, dx = 0,$$

where c is any positive number. When $n = 0$, the quantity inside the brackets clearly vanishes at $x = 0$; and the same is true when $n = 1, 2, \ldots$, because then $X(0) = J_n(0) = 0$. Consequently,

$$2\alpha^2 \int_0^c x[X(x)]^2 \, dx = [cX'(c)]^2 + (\alpha^2 c^2 - n^2)[X(c)]^2.$$

Because $X(x) = J_n(\alpha x)$ and $X'(x) = \alpha J_n'(\alpha x)$, it follows that

$$(4) \qquad 2\alpha^2 \int_0^c x[J_n(\alpha x)]^2 \, dx = (\alpha c)^2[J_n'(\alpha c)]^2 + [(\alpha c)^2 - n^2][J_n(\alpha c)]^2.$$

We shall now use equation (4) to find all but one of the norms in Lemmas 1 and 2.

As for case (a) in these two lemmas, since $J_n(\alpha_j c) = 0$, equation (4) tells us that

$$2 \int_0^c x[J_n(\alpha_j x)]^2 \, dx = c^2[J_n'(\alpha_j c)]^2.$$

The integral here is the square of the norm of $J_n(\alpha_j x)$ on the interval $0 < x < c$, with weight function x. Also (Sec. 83)

$$x J_n'(x) = n J_n(x) - x J_{n+1}(x),$$

and it follows that $J_n'(\alpha_j c) = -J_{n+1}(\alpha_j c)$. Hence,

$$2\| J_n(\alpha_j x) \|^2 = c^2[J_{n+1}(\alpha_j c)]^2.$$

This is in agreement with the expressions for the squares of the norms stated in case (a) of Lemmas 1 and 2.

Turning to case (b) in the lemmas, where

$$h J_n(\alpha_j c) + (\alpha_j c) J_n'(\alpha_j c) = 0 \qquad\qquad (h > 0),$$

we see that since

$$(\alpha_j c)^2[J_n'(\alpha_j c)]^2 = h^2[J_n(\alpha_j c)]^2,$$

it follows from equation (4) that

$$2\alpha_j^2 \int_0^c x[J_n(\alpha_j x)]^2 \, dx = [(\alpha_j c)^2 - n^2 + h^2][J_n(\alpha_j c)]^2.$$

This gives us the norms in case (b) of the lemmas.

Finally, we treat case (c) in Lemma 1 differently from case (c) in Lemma 2. Since $J_0(\alpha_1 x) = 1$ in case (c) of Lemma 1,

$$\| J_0(\alpha_1 x) \|^2 = \int_0^c x \, dx = \frac{c^2}{2}.$$

Expressions for $\| J_0(\alpha_j c) \|^2$ $(j = 2, 3, \ldots)$ are obtained by writing $n = 0$ and $\alpha = \alpha_j$ in equation (4). Because $J_0'(\alpha_j c) = 0$, that gives

$$2 \int_0^c x[J_0(\alpha_j x)]^2 \, dx = c^2[J_0(\alpha_j c)]^2,$$

which is the same as the expression for $\| J_0(\alpha_1 x) \|^2$ $(j = 2, 3, \ldots)$ in case (c) of Lemma 1.

Note that in case (b) of Lemma 2 the constant h used in the equation defining the α_j can actually be zero. By canceling out the factor (αc) in the equation

$$(\alpha c) J_n'(\alpha c) = 0$$

that follows when $h = 0$, we have the defining equation for the α_j in case (c) of Lemma 2. The norm in case (c) is, moreover, the norm in case (b) with $h = 0$.

This completes the proof of Lemmas 1 and 2. We are now prepared to find the generalized Fourier series involving the orthonormal sets (1).

91. FOURIER-BESSEL SERIES

Let f be any piecewise continuous function defined on an interval $0 < x < c$, and let $J_n(\alpha_j x)$ $(j = 1, 2, \ldots)$ be an orthogonal set of eigenfunctions arising from Theorem 1 in Sec. 88 when $n = 0$ or Theorem 2 in that section when n has one of the values $n = 1, 2, \ldots$. The *normalized* eigenfunctions are, of course,

$$
(1) \qquad \phi_j(x) = \frac{J_n(\alpha_j x)}{\|J_n(\alpha_j x)\|} \qquad (j = 1, 2, \ldots),
$$

and the Fourier constants c_j (Sec. 62) in the correspondence

$$
(2) \qquad f(x) \sim \sum_{j=1}^{\infty} c_j \, \phi_j(x) = \sum_{j=1}^{\infty} \frac{c_j}{\|J_n(\alpha_j x)\|} J_n(\alpha_j x) \qquad (0 < x < c)
$$

are the numbers

$$
(3) \qquad c_j = (f, \phi_j) = \int_0^c x f(x) \phi_j(x)\, dx = \frac{1}{\|J_n(\alpha_j x)\|} \int_0^c x f(x) J_n(\alpha_j x)\, dx
$$
$$
(j = 1, 2, \ldots).
$$

The norms found in each of the three cases (a), (b), and (c) in the lemmas of Sec. 90 will now be combined with the generalized Fourier series (2) and its coefficients (3) to obtain two theorems involving what are known as *Fourier-Bessel series*. We continue to present our theorems separately when $n = 0$ and when $n = 1, 2, \ldots$. Indeed, these theorems will follow from Lemmas 1 and 2, respectively, in Sec. 90.

Theorem 1. *Suppose that a function f is piecewise continuous on an interval $0 < x < c$.*

(a) *If α_j $(j = 1, 2, \ldots)$ are the positive roots of the equation*

$$
J_0(\alpha c) = 0,
$$

then

$$
f(x) \sim \sum_{j=1}^{\infty} A_j J_0(\alpha_j x) \qquad (0 < x < c)
$$

where

$$
A_j = \frac{2}{c^2 [J_1(\alpha_j c)]^2} \int_0^c x f(x) J_0(\alpha_j x)\, dx \qquad (j = 1, 2, \ldots).
$$

(b) *If α_j $(j = 1, 2, \ldots)$ are the positive roots of the equation*

$$
h J_0(\alpha c) + (\alpha c) J_0'(\alpha c) = 0 \qquad (h > 0),
$$

then

$$
f(x) \sim \sum_{j=1}^{\infty} A_j J_0(\alpha_j x) \qquad (0 < x < c)
$$

where

$$A_j = \frac{2\alpha_j^2}{[(\alpha_j c)^2 + h^2][J_0(\alpha_j c)]^2} \int_0^c x f(x) J_0(\alpha_j x) \, dx \qquad (j = 1, 2, \ldots).$$

(c) *If α_j ($j = 2, 3, \ldots$) are the positive roots of the equation*

$$J_0'(\alpha c) = 0,$$

then

$$f(x) \sim A_1 + \sum_{j=2}^{\infty} A_j J_0(\alpha_j x) \qquad (0 < x < c)$$

where

$$A_1 = \frac{2}{c^2} \int_0^c x f(x) \, dx$$

and

$$A_j = \frac{2}{c^2 [J_0(\alpha_j c)]^2} \int_0^c x f(x) J_0(\alpha_j x) \, dx \qquad (j = 2, 3, \ldots).$$

Note that the equations used to define the numbers α_j in parts (b) and (c) can also be written

$$h J_0(\alpha c) - (\alpha c) J_1(\alpha c) = 0 \qquad \text{and} \qquad J_1(\alpha c) = 0,$$

respectively. (See the remarks immediately following the statement of Theorem 1 in Sec. 88.) Also, the number $\alpha_1 = 0$ in case (c) of Lemma 1 in Sec. 90 does not appear in case (c) of Theorem 1 here since $J_0(\alpha_1 x) = 1$.

Theorem 2. *Let A_j ($j = 1, 2, \ldots$) be the coefficients in the correspondence*

$$f(x) \sim \sum_{j=1}^{\infty} A_j J_n(\alpha_j x) \qquad (0 < x < c),$$

where f is piecewise continuous and n is a positive integer ($n = 1, 2, \ldots$).

(a) *If α_j ($j = 1, 2, \ldots$) are the positive roots of the equation*

$$J_n(\alpha c) = 0,$$

then

$$A_j = \frac{2}{c^2 [J_{n+1}(\alpha_j c)]^2} \int_0^c x f(x) J_n(\alpha_j x) \, dx \qquad (j = 1, 2, \ldots).$$

(b) *If α_j ($j = 1, 2, \ldots$) are the positive roots of the equation*

$$h J_n(\alpha c) + (\alpha c) J_n'(\alpha c) = 0 \qquad (h > 0),$$

then

$$A_j = \frac{2\alpha_j^2}{[(\alpha_j c)^2 - n^2 + h^2][J_n(\alpha_j c)]^2} \int_0^c x f(x) J_n(\alpha_j x) \, dx \qquad (j = 1, 2, \ldots).$$

(c) *If α_j ($j = 1, 2, \ldots$) are the positive roots of the equation*

$$J'_n(\alpha c) = 0,$$

   then

$$A_j = \frac{2\alpha_j^2}{[(\alpha_j c)^2 - n^2][J_n(\alpha_j c)]^2} \int_0^c x f(x) J_n(\alpha_j x)\, dx \qquad (j = 1, 2, \ldots).$$

Recalling a remark just after the statement of Theorem 2 in Sec. 88, we note that the equations used to define the α_j in cases (b) and (c) here can also be written

$$(h + n) J_n(\alpha c) - (\alpha c) J_{n+1}(\alpha c) = 0 \qquad \text{and} \qquad n J_n(\alpha c) - (\alpha c) J_{n+1}(\alpha c) = 0,$$

respectively.

To verify the two theorems in this section, let n have any one of the values $n = 0, 1, 2, \ldots$. Then observe how it follows from correspondence (2) and expression (3) that

$$(4) \qquad\qquad f(x) \sim \sum_{j=1}^{\infty} A_j J_n(\alpha_j x) \qquad\qquad (0 < x < c),$$

where

$$(5) \qquad\qquad A_j = \frac{1}{\|J_n(\alpha_j x)\|^2} \int_0^c x f(x) J_n(\alpha_j x)\, dx \qquad (j = 1, 2, \ldots).$$

The norms in the lemmas in Sec. 90 can now be used in this equation to obtain the expressions for the A_j in the theorems here.

Proofs that correspondence (4) is actually an equality, under conditions similar to those used in Sec. 15 to ensure the representation of a function by its Fourier series, usually involve the theory of functions of a complex variable. We state, without proof, one form of such a representation theorem and refer the reader to the Bibliography.[†]

Theorem 3. *Let f denote a function that is piecewise smooth on an interval $0 < x < c$, and suppose that $f(x)$ at each point of discontinuity of f in that interval is defined as the mean value of the one-sided limits $f(x+)$ and $f(x-)$. Then all of the correspondences in Theorems 1 and 2 are, in fact, equalities when the appropriate coefficients A_j are used.*

92. EXAMPLES

We now illustrate, before turning to physical applications, the use of Theorems 1 and 2 in Sec. 91. The functions in this section and in the problems to follow all satisfy the conditions in Theorem 3 of Sec. 91, and so convergence to those functions will not be in doubt.

[†]This theorem is proved in the book by Watson (1995). Also, see the work by Titchmarsh (1962), as well as the books by Gray and Mathews (1966) and Bowman (1958). These are all listed in the Bibliography.

EXAMPLE 1. Let us expand the function $f(x) = 1 \ (0 < x < c)$ into a series of the type

$$\sum_{j=1}^{\infty} A_j J_0(\alpha_j x),$$

where $\alpha_j \ (j = 1, 2, \ldots)$ are the positive roots of the equation $J_0(\alpha c) = 0$. Case (a) in Theorem 1 of Sec. 91 is evidently applicable here. It tells us that

$$A_j = \frac{2}{c^2 [J_1(\alpha_j c)]^2} \int_0^c x J_0(\alpha_j x) \, dx \qquad (j = 1, 2, \ldots).$$

This integral is readily evaluated by substituting $s = \alpha_j x$ and using the integration formula (Sec. 83)

$$\int_0^x s J_0(s) \, ds = x J_1(x).$$

To be specific,

$$(1) \qquad \int_0^c x J_0(\alpha_j x) \, dx = \frac{1}{\alpha_j^2} \int_0^{\alpha_j c} s J_0(s) \, ds = \frac{1}{\alpha_j^2} \alpha_j c J_1(\alpha_j c) = \frac{c J_1(\alpha_j c)}{\alpha_j}.$$

Consequently,

$$A_j = \frac{2}{c^2 [J_1(\alpha_j c)]^2} \cdot \frac{c J_1(\alpha_j c)}{\alpha_j} = \frac{2}{c} \cdot \frac{1}{\alpha_j J_1(\alpha_j c)};$$

and we arrive at the expansion

$$(2) \qquad 1 = \frac{2}{c} \sum_{j=1}^{\infty} \frac{J_0(\alpha_j x)}{\alpha_j J_1(\alpha_j c)} \qquad (0 < x < c),$$

where $J_0(\alpha_j c) = 0 \ (\alpha_j > 0)$.

EXAMPLE 2. Here we expand the same function $f(x) = 1 \, (0 < x < c)$ as in Example 1 into a Fourier-Bessel series

$$\sum_{j=1}^{\infty} A_j J_0(\alpha_j x),$$

where α_j are the positive roots of the equation

$$(3) \qquad h J_0(\alpha c) + (\alpha c) J_0'(\alpha c) = 0 \qquad (h > 0).$$

We need to refer to case (b) of Theorem 1 in Sec. 91 rather than case (a), which was used in Example 1. Case (b) of the theorem tells us that

$$(4) \qquad A_j = \frac{2 \alpha_j^2}{[(\alpha_j c)^2 + h^2][J_0(\alpha_j c)]^2} \int_0^c x J_0(\alpha_j x) \, dx \qquad (j = 1, 2, \ldots).$$

Even though the α_j in expression (1) are different from the ones here, we can nonetheless use that expression to write

$$A_j = \frac{2\,\alpha_j^2}{[(\alpha_j c)^2 + h^2][J_0(\alpha_j c)]^2} \cdot \frac{c\,J_1(\alpha_j c)}{\alpha_j} = 2c\frac{\alpha_j J_1(\alpha_j c)}{[(\alpha_j c)^2 + h^2][J_0(\alpha_j c)]^2}.$$

Hence,

$$(5) \qquad 1 = 2c\sum_{j=1}^{\infty} \frac{\alpha_j J_1(\alpha_j c)\,J_0(\alpha_j x)}{[(\alpha_j c)^2 + h^2][J_0(\alpha_j c)]^2} \qquad (0 < x < c).$$

Finally, it is interesting to see how expansion (5) can be written in a form that does not involve h. To do this, we need only observe how it follows from equation (3) and the identity $J_0'(\alpha c) = -J_1(\alpha c)$ that

$$h\,J_0(\alpha_j c) = -(\alpha_j c)J_0'(\alpha_j c) = (\alpha_j c)J_1(\alpha_j c).$$

This enables us to write

$$1 = 2c\sum_{j=1}^{\infty} \frac{\alpha_j\,J_1(\alpha_j c)J_0(\alpha_j x)}{(\alpha_j c)^2[J_0(\alpha_j c)]^2 + (\alpha_j c)^2[J_1(\alpha_j c)]^2},$$

or

$$(6) \qquad 1 = \frac{2}{c}\sum_{j=1}^{\infty} \frac{1}{\alpha_j} \cdot \frac{J_1(\alpha_j c)J_0(\alpha_j x)}{[J_0(\alpha_j c)]^2 + [J_1(\alpha_j c)]^2} \qquad (0 < x < c).$$

EXAMPLE 3. To represent the function $f(x) = x\ (0 < x < 1)$ in a series of the form

$$A_1 + \sum_{j=2}^{\infty} A_j J_0(\alpha_j x),$$

where $\alpha_j\ (j = 2, 3, \ldots)$ are the positive roots of the equation $J_1(\alpha) = 0$, we refer to case (c) in Theorem 1 of Sec. 91. Evidently,

$$A_1 = 2\int_0^1 x^2\,dx = \frac{2}{3}$$

and

$$A_j = \frac{2}{[J_0(\alpha_j)]^2}\int_0^1 x^2 J_0(\alpha_j x)\,dx \qquad (j = 2, 3, \ldots).$$

This last integral can be evaluated by referring to the reduction formula (see Sec. 83 and the footnote there)

$$\int_0^x s^2 J_0(s)\,ds = x^2 J_1(x) + x J_0(x) - \int_0^x J_0(s)\,ds$$

and recalling that $J_1(\alpha_j) = 0$:

$$\int_0^1 x^2 J_0(\alpha_j x)\,dx = \frac{1}{\alpha_j^3}\int_0^{\alpha_j} s^2 J_0(s)\,ds = \frac{1}{\alpha_j^3}\left[\alpha_j J_0(\alpha_j) - \int_0^{\alpha_j} J_0(s)\,ds\right].$$

Finally, then,

$$(7) \qquad x = \frac{2}{3} + 2 \sum_{j=2}^{\infty} \left[\alpha_j J_0(\alpha_j) - \int_0^{\alpha_j} J_0(s)\, ds \right] \frac{J_0(\alpha_j x)}{\alpha_j^3 [J_0(\alpha_j)]^2} \qquad (0 < x < 1),$$

where $J_1(\alpha_j) = 0 \ (\alpha_j > 0)$.

EXAMPLE 4. Consider a function f that is defined on the interval $0 < x < 2$ by means of the equations

$$f(x) = \begin{cases} x^4 & \text{when } 0 < x < 1, \\ 0 & \text{when } 1 < x < 2, \end{cases}$$

and $f(1) = 1/2$. To show that

$$(8) \qquad f(x) = \frac{1}{2} \sum_{j=1}^{\infty} \frac{\alpha_j J_5(\alpha_j) J_4(\alpha_j x)}{(\alpha_j^2 - 4)[J_4(2\alpha_j)]^2} \qquad (0 < x < 2),$$

where α_j are the positive roots of the equation $J_4'(2\alpha) = 0$, we refer to case (c) in Theorem 2 of Sec. 91 and write

$$(9) \qquad A_j = \frac{\alpha_j^2}{2(\alpha_j^2 - 4)[J_4(2\alpha_j)]^2} \int_0^2 x f(x) J_4(\alpha_j x)\, dx \qquad (j = 1, 2, \ldots).$$

Keeping in mind that $f(x) = 0$ when $1 < x < 2$ and using the integration formula (see Sec. 83)

$$\int_0^x s^5 J_4(s)\, ds = x^5 J_5(x),$$

we find that the integral in expression (9) reduces to

$$\int_0^1 x^5 J_4(\alpha_j x)\, dx = \frac{1}{\alpha_j^6} \int_0^{\alpha_j} s^5 J_4(s)\, ds = \frac{1}{\alpha_j} J_5(\alpha_j).$$

Hence,

$$A_j = \frac{1}{2} \cdot \frac{\alpha_j J_5(\alpha_j)}{(\alpha_j^2 - 4)[J_4(2\alpha_j)]^2},$$

and expansion (8) is established.

PROBLEMS

1. Show that

$$x = 2 \sum_{j=1}^{\infty} \left[1 - \frac{1}{\alpha_j^2 J_1(\alpha_j)} \int_0^{\alpha_j} J_0(s)\, ds \right] \frac{J_0(\alpha_j x)}{\alpha_j J_1(\alpha_j)} \qquad (0 < x < 1),$$

where $\alpha_j \ (j = 1, 2, \ldots)$ are the positive roots of the equation $J_0(\alpha) = 0$.

2. Derive the representation

$$x^2 = \frac{c^2}{2} + 4 \sum_{j=2}^{\infty} \frac{J_0(\alpha_j x)}{\alpha_j^2 J_0(\alpha_j c)} \qquad (0 < x < c),$$

where $\alpha_j \ (j = 2, 3, \ldots)$ are the positive roots of the equation $J_1(\alpha c) = 0$.

3. Let α_j $(j = 1, 2, \ldots)$ denote the positive roots of the equation $J_0(\alpha c) = 0$, where c is a fixed positive number.

 (a) Derive the expansion

$$x^2 = \frac{2}{c} \sum_{j=1}^{\infty} \frac{(\alpha_j c)^2 - 4}{\alpha_j^3 J_1(\alpha_j c)} J_0(\alpha_j x) \qquad (0 < x < c).$$

 (b) Combine expansion (2) in Example 1, Sec. 92, with the one in part (a) here to show that

$$c^2 - x^2 = \frac{8}{c} \sum_{j=1}^{\infty} \frac{J_0(\alpha_j x)}{\alpha_j^3 J_1(\alpha_j c)} \qquad (0 < x < c).$$

4. Find the coefficients A_j $(j = 1, 2, \ldots)$ in the expansion

$$1 = A_1 + \sum_{j=2}^{\infty} A_j J_0(\alpha_j x) \qquad (0 < x < c)$$

when α_j $(j = 2, 3, \ldots)$ are the positive roots of the equation $J_0'(\alpha c) = 0$.

 Answer: $A_1 = 1$, $A_j = 0$ $(j = 2, 3, \ldots)$.

5. Show that if

$$f(x) = \begin{cases} x & \text{when } 0 < x < 1, \\ 0 & \text{when } 1 < x < 2, \end{cases}$$

and $f(1) = 1/2$, then

$$f(x) = 2 \sum_{j=1}^{\infty} \frac{\alpha_j J_2(\alpha_j) J_1(\alpha_j x)}{(4\alpha_j^2 - 1)[J_1(2\alpha_j)]^2} \qquad (0 < x < 2),$$

where α_j $(j = 1, 2, \ldots)$ are the positive roots of the equation $J_1'(2\alpha) = 0$.

6. Let n have any one of the positive values $n = 1, 2, \ldots$. Show that

$$x^n = 2 \sum_{j=1}^{\infty} \frac{\alpha_j J_{n+1}(\alpha_j) J_n(\alpha_j x)}{(\alpha_j^2 - n^2)[J_n(\alpha_j)]^2} \qquad (0 < x < 1),$$

where α_j $(j = 1, 2, \ldots)$ are the positive roots of the equation $J_n'(\alpha) = 0$.

7. Point out why the eigenvalues of the singular Sturm-Liouville problem

$$x^2 X'' + x X' + (\lambda x^2 - 1) X = 0, \qquad X(1) = 0,$$

on the interval $0 \le x \le 1$ are the numbers $\lambda_j = \alpha_j^2$ $(j = 1, 2, \ldots)$, where α_j are the positive roots of the equation $J_1(\alpha) = 0$, and why the corresponding eigenfunctions are $X_j = J_1(\alpha_j x)$ $(j = 1, 2, \ldots)$. Then obtain the representation

$$x = 2 \sum_{j=1}^{\infty} \frac{J_1(\alpha_j x)}{\alpha_j J_2(\alpha_j)} \qquad (0 < x < 1)$$

in terms of those eigenfunctions.

8. There exist conditions on f under which Fourier-Bessel series representations are valid when n is replaced by ν $(\nu > -1/2)$, where ν is not necessarily an integer. In particular,

suppose that

$$f(x) = \sum_{j=1}^{\infty} A_j J_{1/2}(\alpha_j x) \qquad (0 < x < c),$$

where $\sqrt{x}\, f(x)$ is piecewise smooth, where α_j are the positive roots of the equation $J_{1/2}(\alpha c) = 0$, and where [compare with case (a) in Theorem 2 of Sec. 91]

$$A_j = \frac{2}{c^2 [J_{3/2}(\alpha_j c)]^2} \int_0^c x f(x) J_{1/2}(\alpha_j x)\, dx \qquad (j = 1, 2, \ldots).$$

Using the expressions [Problems 6(a), Sec. 82, and 3, Sec. 83]

$$J_{1/2}(x) = \sqrt{\frac{2}{\pi x}} \sin x \quad \text{and} \quad J_{3/2}(x) = \sqrt{\frac{2}{\pi x}} \left(\frac{\sin x}{x} - \cos x \right)$$

to substitute for the Bessel functions involved, show that this Fourier-Bessel series representation is actually the Fourier sine series representation for $\sqrt{x}\, f(x)$ on the interval $0 < x < c$.

93. TEMPERATURES IN A LONG CYLINDER

In the following two examples, we shall use Bessel functions to find temperatures in an infinitely long circular cylinder $\rho \le c$ whose lateral surface $\rho = c$ is subject to simple thermal conditions. Those conditions and others will be such that the temperatures will depend only on the space variable ρ, which is the distance from the axis of the cylinder, and time t. We assume that the material of the solid is homogeneous.

EXAMPLE 1. When the cylinder is as shown in Fig. 72 and the initial temperatures vary only with ρ, the temperatures $u = u(\rho, t)$ in the cylinder satisfy the special case (Sec. 24)

(1) $$u_t = k \left(u_{\rho\rho} + \frac{1}{\rho} u_\rho \right) \qquad (0 < \rho < c, \, t > 0)$$

FIGURE 72

of the heat equation in cylindrical coordinates and the boundary conditions

(2) $u(c, t) = 0$ $(t > 0)$,

(3) $u(\rho, 0) = f(\rho)$ $(0 < \rho < c)$.

Also, when $t > 0$, the function u and its derivatives must be continuous throughout the cylinder and, in particular, on the axis $\rho = 0$. In solving this problem, we assume that f is piecewise smooth on the interval $0 < \rho < c$ and, for convenience, that f is defined as the mean value of its one-sided limits at each point in that interval where it is discontinuous.

Any solutions of the homogeneous equations (1) and (2) that are of the type $u = R(\rho)T(t)$ must satisfy the conditions

$$RT' = kT\left(R'' + \frac{1}{\rho}R'\right), \qquad R(c)T(t) = 0.$$

Separating variables in the first equation here, we have

$$\frac{T'}{kT} = \frac{1}{R}\left(R'' + \frac{1}{\rho}R'\right) = -\lambda,$$

where $-\lambda$ is a separation constant. Thus,

(4) $\rho R''(\rho) + R'(\rho) + \lambda \rho R(\rho) = 0, \qquad R(c) = 0$ $(0 < \rho < c)$

and

(5) $T'(t) + \lambda k T(t) = 0$ $(t > 0)$.

Problem (4), together with continuity conditions on R and R' in the interval $0 \leq \rho \leq c$, is the singular Sturm-Liouville problem in Theorem 1 of Sec. 88 when the boundary condition (4) there is taken. According to case (a) in that theorem, the eigenvalues and corresponding eigenfunctions of problem (4) here are

$$\lambda_j = \alpha_j^2, \qquad R_j = J_0(\alpha_j \rho) \qquad (j = 1, 2, \ldots),$$

where α_j are the positive roots of the equation $J_0(\alpha c) = 0$.

When $\lambda = \lambda_j$ for any given λ_j, the solutions of equation (5) are constant multiples of $T_j = \exp(-\alpha_j^2 kt)$. So the desired products are

$$u_j = R_j(\rho)T_j(t) = J_0(\alpha_j \rho)\exp(-\alpha_j^2 kt) \qquad (j = 1, 2, \ldots),$$

and their generalized linear combination,

(6) $u(\rho, t) = \sum_{j=1}^{\infty} A_j J_0(\alpha_j \rho)\exp(-\alpha_j^2 kt)$

formally satisfies the homogeneous conditions (1) and (2) in our boundary value problem. It also satisfies the nonhomogeneous initial condition (3) when the coefficients A_j are such that

$$f(\rho) = \sum_{j=1}^{\infty} A_j J_0(\alpha_j \rho) \qquad (0 < \rho < c).$$

This is a valid Fourier-Bessel series representation, according to Theorem 3, Sec. 91, if the coefficients have the values

$$(7) \qquad A_j = \frac{2}{c^2 [J_1(\alpha_j c)]^2} \int_0^c \rho f(\rho) J_0(\alpha_j \rho) \, d\rho \qquad (j = 1, 2, \ldots),$$

obtained from case (a) of Theorem 1 in Sec. 91.

The formal solution of the boundary value problem (1)–(3) is, therefore, given by equation (6) with the coefficients (7), where $J_0(\alpha_j c) = 0 \ (\alpha_j > 0)$. Our temperature function can also be written

$$(8) \qquad u(\rho, t) = \frac{2}{c^2} \sum_{j=1}^{\infty} \frac{J_0(\alpha_j \rho)}{[J_1(\alpha_j c)]^2} \exp(-\alpha_j^2 kt) \int_0^c s f(s) J_0(\alpha_j s) \, ds.$$

EXAMPLE 2. Let us replace the condition that the surface of the infinite cylinder in Example 1 be at temperature zero by the condition that it be insulated. The boundary value problem for the temperature function $u(\rho, t)$ is now

$$(9) \qquad u_t = k \left(u_{\rho\rho} + \frac{1}{\rho} u_\rho \right) \qquad (0 < \rho < c, \, t > 0),$$

$$(10) \qquad u_\rho(c, t) = 0 \qquad (t > 0),$$

$$(11) \qquad u(\rho, 0) = f(\rho) \qquad (0 < \rho < c).$$

When $u = R(\rho)T(t)$, separation of variables produces the eigenvalue problem

$$(12) \qquad \rho R''(\rho) + R'(\rho) + \lambda \rho R(\rho) = 0, \qquad R'(c) = 0 \qquad (0 < \rho < c).$$

Case (c) of Theorem 1 in Sec. 88 tells us that the eigenvalues and corresponding eigenfunctions are

$$\lambda_1 = 0, \quad R_1 = 1 \quad \text{and} \quad \lambda_j = \alpha_j^2, \quad R_j = J_0(\alpha_j \rho) \qquad (j = 2, 3, \ldots),$$

where $\alpha_j \ (j = 2, 3, \ldots)$ are the positive roots of the equation $J_0'(\alpha c) = 0$. Since

$$T'(t) + \lambda kT(t) = 0 \qquad (t > 0),$$

the corresponding functions of t are constant multiples of

$$T_1 = 1 \quad \text{and} \quad T_j = \exp(-\alpha_j^2 kt) \qquad (j = 2, 3, \ldots).$$

Hence,

$$u_1 = R_1(\rho)T_1(t) = 1$$

and

$$u_j = R_j(\rho)T_j(t) = J_0(\alpha_j \rho) \exp(-\alpha_j^2 kt) \qquad (j = 2, 3, \ldots).$$

The desired solution of our boundary value problem is, therefore,

$$(13) \qquad u(\rho, t) = A_1 + \sum_{j=2}^{\infty} A_j J_0(\alpha_j \rho) \exp(-\alpha_j^2 kt)$$

where the coefficients A_1 and A_j ($j = 2, 3, \ldots$) are obtained by writing $t = 0$ and referring to the nonhomogeneous condition (11). More precisely,

$$f(\rho) = A_1 + \sum_{j=2}^{\infty} A_j J_0(\alpha_j \rho) \qquad (0 < \rho < c);$$

and case (c) of Theorem 1 in Sec. 91 reveals that

(14)
$$A_1 = \frac{2}{c^2} \int_0^c \rho f(\rho) \, d\rho$$

and

(15)
$$A_j = \frac{2}{c^2 [J_0(\alpha_j c)]^2} \int_0^c \rho f(\rho) J_0(\alpha_j \rho) \, d\rho \qquad (j = 2, 3, \ldots).$$

In some of the problems to follow, there will be surface heat transfer across a cylindrical surface into surroundings at temperature zero in accordance with Newton's law of cooling (Sec. 26). If, for example, that surface is $\rho = c$, the temperature function $u(\rho, t)$ will satisfy the condition

$$K u_\rho(c, t) = -H u(c, t) \qquad (K > 0, \ H > 0);$$

and we shall find it convenient to use it in the form

(16)
$$c u_\rho(c, t) = -h u(c, t) \qquad \left(h = \frac{cH}{K} > 0 \right).$$

There will also be a number of *steady-state* temperature problems in cylindrical coordinates giving rise to Bessel functions. In such problems, the temperatures will continue to be independent of ϕ. The function $u = u(\rho, z)$ will, then, be harmonic and satisfy Laplace's equation $\nabla^2 u = 0$, where (see Sec. 34)

(17)
$$\nabla^2 u = u_{\rho\rho} + \frac{1}{\rho} u_\rho + u_{zz}.$$

PROBLEMS

1. Let $u(\rho, t)$ denote the solution found in Example 1, Sec. 93, when $c = 1$ and $f(\rho) = u_0$, where u_0 is a constant. With the aid of the table in Sec. 86, show that the first three terms in the series for $u(\rho, t)$ are, approximately, as follows:

$$u(\rho, t) = 2u_0 \left[0.80 \, J_0(2.4\rho) \, e^{-5.8kt} - 0.53 \, J_0(5.5\rho) \, e^{-30kt} + 0.43 \, J_0(8.7\rho) \, e^{-76kt} - \cdots \right].$$

2. Suppose that the surface $\rho = c$ of the infinite cylinder in Sec. 93 is such that heat transfer takes place there into surroundings at temperature zero according to Newton's law of cooling, written in the form (16), Sec. 93:

$$c u_\rho(c, t) = -h u(c, t) \qquad (h > 0).$$

Use this condition, instead of condition (2) or (10) in Sec. 93, to find the temperatures $u(\rho, t)$ in the cylinder.

Answer: $u(\rho, t) = \sum\limits_{j=1}^{\infty} A_j J_0(\alpha_j \rho) \exp(-\alpha_j^2 kt),$

where α_j are the positive roots of the equation $hJ_0(\alpha c) + (\alpha c)J_0'(\alpha c) = 0$ and

$$A_j = \frac{2\alpha_j^2}{[(\alpha_j c)^2 + h^2][J_0(\alpha_j c)]^2} \int_0^c \rho f(\rho) J_0(\alpha_j \rho)\, d\rho \qquad (j = 1, 2, \ldots).$$

3. Derive an expression for the steady temperatures $u(\rho, z)$ in the solid cylinder formed by the three surfaces $\rho = 1$, $z = 0$, and $z = 1$ when $u = 0$ on the side, the bottom is insulated, and $u = 1$ on the top.

Answer: $u(\rho, z) = 2\sum\limits_{j=1}^{\infty} \dfrac{J_0(\alpha_j \rho)}{\alpha_j J_1(\alpha_j)} \cdot \dfrac{\cosh \alpha_j z}{\cosh \alpha_j}$,   where $J_0(\alpha_j) = 0$ $(\alpha_j > 0)$.

4. Find the bounded steady temperatures $u(\rho, z)$ in the semi-infinite cylinder $\rho \leq 1, z \geq 0$ when $u = 1$ on the base and there is heat transfer into surroundings at temperature zero, according to Newton's law of cooling (see Problem 2), on the side.

Answer: $u(\rho, z) = 2h \sum\limits_{j=1}^{\infty} \dfrac{J_0(\alpha_j \rho) \exp(-\alpha_j z)}{J_0(\alpha_j)(\alpha_j^2 + h^2)}$,

where $hJ_0(\alpha_j) + \alpha_j J_0'(\alpha_j) = 0$ $(\alpha_j > 0)$.

5. (*a*) A solid cylinder is formed by the three surfaces $\rho = 1, z = 0$, and $z = b$ $(b > 0)$. The side is insulated, the bottom is kept at temperature zero, and the top is kept at temperatures $f(\rho)$. Derive this expression for the steady temperatures $u(\rho, z)$ in the cylinder:

$$u(\rho, z) = \frac{2z}{b} \int_0^1 sf(s)\, ds + 2\sum_{j=2}^{\infty} \frac{J_0(\alpha_j \rho)}{[J_0(\alpha_j)]^2} \cdot \frac{\sinh \alpha_j z}{\sinh \alpha_j b} \int_0^1 sf(s) J_0(\alpha_j s)\, ds,$$

where $\alpha_2, \alpha_3, \ldots$ are the positive roots of the equation $J_1(\alpha) = 0$.

(*b*) Show that when $f(\rho) = 1$ $(0 < \rho < 1)$ in part (*a*), the solution there reduces to

$$u(\rho, z) = \frac{z}{b}.$$

6. A function $u(\rho, z)$ is harmonic interior to the cylinder formed by the three surfaces $\rho = c, z = 0$, and $z = b$ $(b > 0)$. Assuming that $u = 0$ on the first two of those surfaces and that $u(\rho, b) = f(\rho)$ $(0 < \rho < c)$, derive the expression

$$u(\rho, z) = \sum_{j=1}^{\infty} A_j J_0(\alpha_j \rho) \frac{\sinh \alpha_j z}{\sinh \alpha_j b},$$

where α_j are the positive roots of the equation $J_0(\alpha c) = 0$ and the coefficients A_j are given by equation (7), Sec. 93.

7. Solve this Dirichlet problem (Sec. 31) for $u(\rho, z)$:

$$\nabla^2 u = 0 \qquad\qquad (0 < \rho < 1, z > 0),$$
$$u(1, z) = 0, \qquad u(\rho, 0) = 1,$$

and u is to be bounded in the domain $\rho < 1, z > 0$.

Answer: $u(\rho, z) = 2\sum\limits_{j=1}^{\infty} \dfrac{J_0(\alpha_j \rho)}{\alpha_j J_1(\alpha_j)} \exp(-\alpha_j z)$, where $J_0(\alpha_j) = 0$ $(\alpha_j > 0)$.

8. Solve the following problem for temperatures $u(\rho, t)$ in a thin circular plate with heat transfer from its faces into surroundings at temperature zero:

$$u_t = u_{\rho\rho} + \frac{1}{\rho} u_\rho - bu \qquad\qquad (0 < \rho < 1, t > 0),$$
$$u(1, t) = 0, \qquad u(\rho, 0) = 1,$$

where b is a positive constant.

$$\text{Answer: } u(\rho, t) = 2 \exp(-bt) \sum_{j=1}^{\infty} \frac{J_0(\alpha_j \rho)}{\alpha_j J_1(\alpha_j)} \exp\left(-\alpha_j^2 t\right),$$

where $J_0(\alpha_j) = 0 \, (\alpha_j > 0)$.

9. Solve Problem 8 after replacing the condition $u(1, t) = 0$ by this heat-transfer condition at the edge:

$$u_\rho(1, t) = -hu(1, t) \qquad\qquad (h > 0).$$

10. Interpret this boundary value problem as a temperature problem in a solid cylinder:

$$u_{\rho\rho} + \frac{1}{\rho} u_\rho + u_{zz} = 0 \qquad\qquad (0 < \rho < 1, \ 0 < z < b),$$

$$u_\rho(1, z) = -hu(1, z) \qquad\qquad (0 < z < b),$$

$$u_z(\rho, 0) = hu(\rho, 0), \qquad u(\rho, b) = 1 \qquad\qquad (0 < \rho < 1),$$

where h is a positive constant. Then, with the aid of the expansion (5) appearing in Example 2, Sec. 92, derive the solution

$$u(\rho, z) = 2 \sum_{j=1}^{\infty} \frac{(\alpha_j + h)e^{\alpha_j z} + (\alpha_j - h)e^{-\alpha_j z}}{(\alpha_j + h)e^{\alpha_j b} + (\alpha_j - h)e^{-\alpha_j b}} \cdot \frac{\alpha_j J_1(\alpha_j) J_0(\alpha_j \rho)}{(\alpha_j^2 + h^2)[J_0(\alpha_j)]^2},$$

where $h J_0(\alpha_j) + \alpha_j J_0'(\alpha_j) = 0 \, (\alpha_j > 0)$.

Suggestion: Use the conditions

$$Z''(z) - \alpha_j^2 Z(z) = 0, \qquad Z'(0) = h Z(0)$$

to obtain the expression $Z(z) = C_1 e^{\alpha_j z} + C_2 e^{-\alpha_j z}$, where C_1 is an arbitrary constant and

$$C_2 = \frac{\alpha_j - h}{\alpha_j + h} C_1.$$

Then use the value $C_1 = \alpha_j + h$.

11. Solve this boundary value problem for $u(x, t)$:

$$x u_t = (x u_x)_x - \frac{n^2}{x} u \qquad\qquad (0 < x < c, t > 0),$$

$$u(c, t) = 0, \qquad u(x, 0) = f(x),$$

where u is continuous for $0 \le x \le c, t > 0$ and where n is a positive integer.

$$\text{Answer: } u(x, t) = \sum_{j=1}^{\infty} A_j J_n(\alpha_j x) \exp\left(-\alpha_j^2 t\right), \text{ where } \alpha_j \text{ and } A_j \text{ are the constants}$$

in case (a) of Theorem 2 in Sec. 91.

12. Let $u(\rho, z)$ denote a function that is harmonic interior to the cylinder formed by the three surfaces $\rho = c, z = 0$, and $z = b \, (b > 0)$. Given that $u = 0$ on both the top and bottom of the cylinder and that $u(c, z) = f(z) \, (0 < z < b)$, derive the expression

$$u(\rho, z) = \sum_{n=1}^{\infty} B_n \frac{I_0(n\pi\rho/b)}{I_0(n\pi c/b)} \sin\frac{n\pi z}{b},$$

where

$$B_n = \frac{2}{b} \int_0^b f(z) \sin \frac{n\pi z}{b} \, dz.$$

[See Problem 9, Sec. 82, as well as the comments immediately following equation (14), Sec. 89, regarding the solutions of the modified Bessel equation.]

13. Let the steady temperatures $u(\rho, z)$ in a semi-infinite cylinder $\rho \leq 1, z \geq 0$, whose base is insulated, be such that $u(1, z) = f(z)$ where

$$f(z) = \begin{cases} 1 & \text{when } 0 < z < 1, \\ 0 & \text{when } z > 1. \end{cases}$$

With the aid of the Fourier cosine integral formula (Sec. 54), derive the expression

$$u(\rho, z) = \frac{2}{\pi} \int_0^\infty \frac{I_0(\alpha\rho)}{\alpha I_0(\alpha)} \cos \alpha z \, \sin \alpha \, d\alpha$$

for those temperatures. (See the remarks at the end of Problem 12.)

14. Given a function $f(z)$ that is represented by its Fourier integral formula (Sec. 50) for all real z, derive the following expression for the harmonic function $u(\rho, z)$ inside the infinite cylinder $\rho \leq c, -\infty < z < \infty$ such that $u(c, z) = f(z)$ $(-\infty < z < \infty)$:

$$u(\rho, z) = \frac{1}{\pi} \int_0^\infty \frac{I_0(\alpha\rho)}{I_0(\alpha c)} \int_{-\infty}^\infty f(s) \cos \alpha(s - z) \, ds \, d\alpha.$$

(See the remarks at the end of Problem 12.)

15. Let $u(\rho, z, t)$ denote temperatures in a solid cylinder $\rho \leq 1, \; 0 \leq z \leq \pi$ whose entire surface is kept at temperature zero and whose initial temperature is unity throughout. That is,

$$u_t = k \left(u_{\rho\rho} + \frac{1}{\rho} u_\rho + u_{zz} \right) \qquad (0 < \rho < 1, \; 0 < z < \pi, \; t > 0),$$

$$u(1, z, t) = 0, \qquad u(\rho, 0, t) = 0, \qquad u(\rho, \pi, t) = 0,$$

$$u(\rho, z, 0) = 1.$$

(a) Show that $u(\rho, z, t) = v(\rho, t) w(z, t)$ where $v(\rho, t)$ denotes temperatures in an infinite cylinder $\rho \leq 1$ and $w(z, t)$ represents temperatures in an infinite slab $0 \leq z \leq \pi$ when both the cylinder and the slab have zero boundary temperatures and initial temperatures unity.

(b) Using results in Example 1, Sec. 93, and Example 1, Sec. 39, show that the functions $v(\rho, t)$ and $w(z, t)$ in part (a) are

$$v(\rho, t) = 2 \sum_{j=1}^\infty \frac{J_0(\alpha_j \rho)}{\alpha_j J_1(\alpha_j)} \exp\left(-\alpha_j^2 kt\right),$$

where $J_0(\alpha_j) = 0 \; (\alpha_j > 0)$, and

$$w(z, t) = \frac{4}{\pi} \sum_{n=1}^\infty \frac{\sin(2n-1)z}{2n-1} \exp[-(2n-1)^2 kt].$$

Suggestion: Start the proof in part (a) by assuming that if $u(\rho, z, t)$ is a product of any two functions $v(\rho, t)$ and $w(z, t)$, then

$$u_t - k \left(u_{\rho\rho} + \frac{1}{\rho} u_\rho + u_{zz} \right)$$

becomes

$$v\left(w_t - kw_{zz}\right) + w\left[v_t - k\left(v_{\rho\rho} + \frac{1}{\rho}v_\rho\right)\right]$$

whenever these expressions exist.

94.   A TEMPERATURE PROBLEM IN SHRUNKEN FITTINGS

We consider here a temperature problem in shrunken fittings involving a solid cylinder $\rho \leq 1$ at uniform initial temperature A. A long hollow cylinder $1 \leq \rho \leq 2$ of the same material and at uniform initial temperature B is tightly fitted over the solid cylinder. The outer surface $\rho = 2$ of the second cylinder is then kept at temperature B. (See Fig. 73, where a cross section of the two cylinders is shown.)

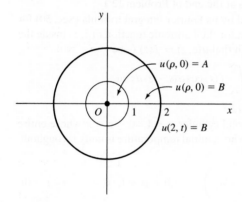

FIGURE 73

The temperatures $u(\rho, t)$ throughout the solid cylinder of radius 2 that is formed must satisfy this boundary value problem:

(1) $$u_t = k\left(u_{\rho\rho} + \frac{1}{\rho}u_\rho\right) \qquad\qquad (0 < \rho < 2,\ t > 0),$$

(2) $$u(2, t) = B \qquad\qquad (t > 0),$$

(3) $$u(\rho, 0) = \begin{cases} A & \text{when } 0 < \rho < 1, \\ B & \text{when } 1 < \rho < 2. \end{cases}$$

The usual continuity conditions on $u(\rho, t)$ and its derivatives are to be satisfied. In particular, $u(\rho, t)$ is to be continuous on the axis $\rho = 0$.

The fact that the boundary condition at $\rho = 2$ is nonhomogeneous reminds us how a substitution similar to

(4) $$u(\rho, t) = U(\rho, t) + \Phi(\rho)$$

was first used in Example 2, Sec. 39, where the rectangular coordinate x, rather than the polar coordinate ρ, was used. Substituting expression (4) into the boundary value problem (1)–(3), we have

$$(5) \qquad U_t = k\left(U_{\rho\rho} + \frac{1}{\rho}\,U_\rho\right) + k\left(\Phi'' + \frac{1}{\rho}\Phi'\right) \qquad (0 < \rho < 2,\ t > 0),$$

and

$$(6) \qquad U(2, t) + \Phi(2) = B \qquad (t > 0),$$

$$(7) \qquad U(\rho, 0) + \Phi(\rho) = \begin{cases} A & \text{when } 0 < \rho < 1, \\ B & \text{when } 1 < \rho < 2. \end{cases}$$

Hence, if

$$(8) \qquad \Phi'' + \frac{1}{\rho}\Phi' = 0 \quad \text{and} \quad \Phi(2) = B,$$

we have the new boundary value problem

$$(9) \qquad U_t = k\left(U_{\rho\rho} + \frac{1}{\rho}\,U_\rho\right) \qquad (0 < \rho < 2,\ t > 0),$$

$$(10) \qquad U(2, t) = 0 \qquad (t > 0),$$

$$(11) \qquad U(\rho, 0) = \begin{cases} A - \Phi(\rho) & \text{when } 0 < \rho < 1, \\ B - \Phi(\rho) & \text{when } 1 < \rho < 2, \end{cases}$$

whose solution can be obtained by referring to Example 1 in Sec. 93, once the function $\phi(\rho)$ satisfying conditions (8) is found.

The first of conditions (8) can be solved by writing it as the Cauchy-Euler differential equation

$$\rho^2\Phi'' + \rho\Phi' + 0\Phi = 0$$

and making the substitution $\rho = \exp s$ (see Problem 1, Sec. 44), which gives us

$$(12) \qquad \frac{d^2\Phi}{ds^2} = 0.$$

The general solution of equation (12) is, of course, $\Phi = C_1 s + C_2$; and, since $s = \ln\rho$, we find that

$$\Phi(\rho) = C_1 \ln\rho + C_2.$$

Because $\Phi(\rho)$ must be bounded when $0 < \rho < 2$, the constant C_1 must be zero. Hence, $\Phi(\rho) = C_2$. By applying the second of conditions (8), we arrive at the expression $\Phi(\rho) = B$.

Now, according to Example 1 in Sec. 93,

$$(13) \qquad U(\rho, t) = \sum_{j=1}^{\infty} A_j J_0(\alpha_j \rho) \exp(-\alpha_j^2 kt)$$

where $J_0(2\,\alpha_j) = 0(\alpha_j > 0)$ and where the constants A_j are yet to be determined.

Because $\Phi(\rho) = B$, condition (11) becomes

$$U(\rho, 0) = \begin{cases} A - B & \text{when } 0 < \rho < 1, \\ 0 & \text{when } 1 < \rho < 2; \end{cases}$$

and, according to expression (7), Sec. 93,

$$(14) \qquad A_j = \frac{A - B}{2\,[J_1(2\,\alpha_j)]^2} \int_0^1 \rho\, J_0(\alpha_j \rho)\, d\rho \qquad\qquad (j = 1, 2, \ldots).$$

The integral here is readily evaluated by making the substitution $s = \alpha_j \rho$ and using the integration formula (Sec. 83)

$$\int_0^x J_0(s)\, ds = x\, J_1(x).$$

More precisely,

$$\int_0^1 \rho\, J_0(\alpha_j \rho)\, d\rho = \frac{1}{\alpha_j^2} \int_0^{\alpha_j} s\, J_0(s)\, ds = \frac{J_1(\alpha_j)}{\alpha_j}.$$

Expression (14) then becomes

$$(15) \qquad A_j = \frac{A - B}{2} \cdot \frac{J_1(\alpha_j)}{\alpha_j[J_1(2\,\alpha_j)]^2} \qquad\qquad (j = 1, 2, \ldots).$$

Substituting these values of A_j into series (13) and then recalling equation (4), we arrive at the solution of the original boundary value problem:

$$(16) \qquad u(\rho, t) = B + \frac{A - B}{2} \sum_{j=1}^{\infty} \frac{J_1(\alpha_j) J_0(\alpha_j \rho)}{\alpha_j [J_1(2\,\alpha_j)]^2}\, \exp(-\alpha_j^2 k t),$$

where $J_0(2\alpha_j) = 0 (\alpha_j > 0)$.

95. INTERNALLY GENERATED HEAT

When the Fourier method cannot be directly applied to obtain solutions involving Bessel functions, modifications of the method learned in earlier chapters can be used, as in Sec. 94. The following example illustrates another modification that we have already seen.

EXAMPLE. We suppose now that heat is generated at a constant rate per unit volume in the cylinder in Sec. 93 and that the surface and initial temperatures are both zero. The temperatures $u = u(\rho, t)$ must, therefore, satisfy the conditions

$$(1) \qquad u_t = k\left(u_{\rho\rho} + \frac{1}{\rho}\,u_\rho\right) + q_0 \qquad\qquad (0 < \rho < c, t > 0),$$

where q_0 is a positive constant (Sec. 23), and

$$(2) \qquad u(c, t) = 0, \qquad u(\rho, 0) = 0.$$

The function u is, of course, required to be continuous in the cylinder.

The differential equation (1) is nonhomogeneous because of the constant term q_0, and this suggests that we apply the method of variation of parameters, first used in Sec. 42. To be specific, we know from Example 1, Sec. 93, that without the term q_0, the eigenfunctions

$$R_j = J_0(\alpha_j \rho) \qquad (j = 1, 2, \ldots),$$

where $J_0(\alpha_j c) = 0 \ (\alpha_j > 0)$, arise. So we seek a solution of the present boundary value problem having the form

$$(3) \qquad u(\rho, t) = \sum_{j=1}^{\infty} A_j(t) J_0(\alpha_j \rho),$$

where the α_j are as just stated.

Substituting this series into equation (1) and noting how the representation

$$q_0 = \frac{2 q_0}{c} \sum_{j=1}^{\infty} \frac{J_0(\alpha_j \rho)}{\alpha_j J_1(\alpha_j c)} \qquad (0 < \rho < c)$$

follows immediately from the one obtained in Example 1, Sec. 92, we find that if series (3) is to satisfy equation (1), then

$$\sum_{j=1}^{\infty} A_j'(t) J_0(\alpha_j \rho) = k \sum_{j=1}^{\infty} A_j(t) \left[\frac{d^2}{d\rho^2} J_0(\alpha_j \rho) + \frac{1}{\rho} \frac{d}{d\rho} J_0(\alpha_j \rho) \right]$$

$$+ \sum_{j=1}^{\infty} \frac{2 q_0 J_0(\alpha_j \rho)}{c \alpha_j J_1(\alpha_j c)}.$$

But, according to Problem 8, Sec. 82,

$$\frac{d^2}{d\rho^2} J_0(\alpha_j \rho) + \frac{1}{\rho} \frac{d}{d\rho} J_0(\alpha_j \rho) = -\alpha_j^2 J_0(\alpha_j \rho).$$

Thus,

$$\sum_{j=1}^{\infty} \left[A_j'(t) + \alpha_j^2 k A_j(t) \right] J_0(\alpha_j \rho) = \sum_{j=1}^{\infty} \frac{2 q_0}{c \alpha_j J_1(\alpha_j c)} J_0(\alpha_j \rho);$$

and by equating coefficients on each side of this equation, we arrive at the differential equation

$$(4) \qquad A_j'(t) + \alpha_j^2 k A_j(t) = \frac{2 q_0}{c \alpha_j J_1(\alpha_j c)} \qquad (j = 1, 2, \ldots).$$

Furthermore, in view of the second of conditions (2),

$$\sum_{j=1}^{\infty} A_j(0) J_0(\alpha_j \rho) = 0 \qquad (0 < \rho < c).$$

Consequently,

$$(5) \qquad A_j(0) = 0 \qquad (j = 1, 2, \ldots).$$

To solve the linear differential equation (4), we multiply each side by the integrating factor

$$\exp\left(\int \alpha_j^2 k\, dt\right) = \exp(\alpha_j^2 kt).$$

This enables us to write the differential equation as

$$\frac{d}{dt}\left[e^{\alpha_j^2 kt} A_j(t)\right] = \frac{2q_0}{c\alpha_j J_1(\alpha_j c)} e^{\alpha_j^2 kt}.$$

After replacing t by τ here, we then integrate each side from $\tau = 0$ to $\tau = t$ and recall condition (5). The result is

$$e^{\alpha_j^2 kt} A_j(t) = \frac{2q_0}{ck\alpha_j^3 J_1(\alpha_j c)}\left(e^{\alpha_j^2 kt} - 1\right),$$

or

(6)
$$A_j(t) = \frac{2q_0}{ck} \cdot \frac{1 - \exp(-\alpha_j^2 kt)}{\alpha_j^3 J_1(\alpha_j c)} \qquad (j = 1, 2, \ldots).$$

Finally, by substituting this expression for the coefficients $A_j(t)$ into series (3), we arrive at the desired temperature formula:

(7)
$$u(\rho, t) = \frac{2q_0}{ck} \sum_{j=1}^{\infty} \frac{1 - \exp(-\alpha_j^2 kt)}{\alpha_j^3 J_1(\alpha_j c)} J_0(\alpha_j \rho),$$

where $J_0(\alpha_j c) = 0$ $(\alpha_j > 0)$. Note how the summation formula

$$\sum_{j=1}^{\infty} \frac{J_0(\alpha_j \rho)}{\alpha_j^3 J_1(\alpha_j c)} = \frac{c}{8}(c^2 - \rho^2) \qquad (0 < \rho < c)$$

[see Problem 3(b), Sec. 92] enables us to put solution (7) in the form

(8)
$$u(\rho, t) = \frac{q_0}{4k}\left[c^2 - \rho^2 - \frac{8}{c} \sum_{j=1}^{\infty} \frac{J_0(\alpha_j \rho) \exp(-\alpha_j^2 kt)}{\alpha_j^3 J_1(\alpha_j c)}\right],$$

which can be more useful when t is large. [Compare with the last paragraph in Example 2, Sec. 39.]

PROBLEMS

1. In the example in Sec. 95, suppose that the rate per unit volume at which heat is internally generated is $q(t)$, rather than simply q_0. Derive the following generalization of the solution (7) found in that example:

$$u(\rho, t) = \frac{2}{c} \sum_{j=1}^{\infty} \frac{J_0(\alpha_j \rho)}{\alpha_j J_1(\alpha_j c)} \int_0^t q(\tau) \exp\left[-\alpha_j^2 k(t - \tau)\right] d\tau,$$

where $J_0(\alpha_j c) = 0$ $(\alpha_j > 0)$.

2. Solve the temperature problem arising when the boundary conditions (2) and (3) in Example 1, Sec. 93, are replaced by

$$u(c, t) = 1, \qquad u(\rho, 0) = 0.$$

Do this by making the substitution $u(\rho, t) = U(\rho, t) + \Phi(\rho)$, where $\Phi(\rho)$ is continuous at $\rho = 0$, and referring to solution (6), with coefficients (7), in that earlier example. Expansion (1) in Example 2, Sec. 92, will also be useful.

$$\text{Answer: } u(\rho, t) = 1 - \frac{2}{c} \sum_{j=1}^{\infty} \frac{J_0(\alpha_j \rho)}{\alpha_j J_1(\alpha_j c)} \exp\left(-\alpha_j^2 kt\right),$$

where $J_0(\alpha_j c) = 0 \ (\alpha_j > 0)$.

3. Use the special case of Duhamel's principle in Sec. 27 and the solution obtained in Problem 2 to solve the temperature problem arising when the boundary condition $u(c, t) = 1$ in that problem is replaced by $u(c, t) = F(t)$, where $F(0) = 0$ and $F(t)$ is continuous and differentiable when $t \geq 0$.

$$\text{Answer: } u(\rho, t) = \frac{2k}{c} \sum_{j=1}^{\infty} \frac{\alpha_j J_0(\alpha_j \rho)}{J_1(\alpha_j c)} \int_0^t F(\tau) \exp\left[-\alpha_j^2 k(t - \tau)\right] d\tau,$$

where $J_0(\alpha_j c) = 0 \ (\alpha_j > 0)$.

4. Give a physical interpretation of the following boundary value problem for a function $u(\rho, t)$ (see the example in Sec. 95):

$$u_t = u_{\rho\rho} + \frac{1}{\rho} u_\rho + q_0 \qquad\qquad (0 < \rho < 1, t > 0),$$

$$u_\rho(1, t) = 0, \qquad u(\rho, 0) = a\rho^2,$$

where q_0 and a are positive constants. Then, after pointing out why it is reasonable to seek a solution of the form

$$u(\rho, t) = A_1(t) + \sum_{j=2}^{\infty} A_j(t) J_0(\alpha_j \rho),$$

where $\alpha_j (j = 2, 3, \ldots)$ are the positive roots of the equation $J_1(\alpha_j) = 0$, use the method of variation of parameters to actually find that solution.

$$\text{Answer: } u(\rho, t) = \frac{a}{2} + q_0 t + 4a \sum_{j=2}^{\infty} \frac{J_0(\alpha_j \rho) \exp\left(-\alpha_j^2 t\right)}{\alpha_j^2 J_0(\alpha_j)},$$

where the α_j are as stated above.

5. Interpret this boundary value problem as a temperature problem in a cylinder (see Sec. 26):

$$u_t = u_{\rho\rho} + \frac{1}{\rho} u_\rho \qquad\qquad (0 < \rho < 1, t > 0),$$

$$u_\rho(1, t) = B, \qquad u(\rho, 0) = 0,$$

where B is a positive constant. Then, after making the substitution

$$u(\rho, t) = U(\rho, t) + \frac{B}{2} \rho^2$$

to obtain a boundary value problem for $U(\rho, t)$, refer to the solution in Problem 4 to derive the temperature formula

$$u(\rho, t) = \frac{B}{4} \left[2\rho^2 + 8t - 1 - 8 \sum_{j=2}^{\infty} \frac{J_0(\alpha_j \rho) \exp\left(-\alpha_j^2 t\right)}{\alpha_j^2 J_0(\alpha_j)} \right],$$

where $\alpha_j \ (j = 2, 3, \ldots)$ are the positive roots of the equation $J_1(\alpha) = 0$. [Note that the substitution for $u(\rho, t)$ made here is suggested by the fact that $U_\rho(1, t) = 0$.]

6. Solve the boundary value problem

$$u_{\rho\rho} + \frac{1}{\rho} u_\rho - \frac{n^2}{\rho^2} u + u_{zz} = 0 \qquad (0 < \rho < 1, z > 0),$$

$$u(1, z) = 0, \qquad u(\rho, 0) = \rho^n,$$

where $u(\rho, z)$ is bounded and continuous for $0 \le \rho < 1, z > 0$ and where n is a positive integer. (When $n = 0$, this problem becomes the Dirichlet problem that was solved in Problem 7, Sec. 93.)

$$\textit{Answer:}\ u(\rho, z) = 2\sum_{j=1}^{\infty} \frac{J_n(\alpha_j \rho)}{\alpha_j J_{n+1}(\alpha_j)} \exp(-\alpha_j z),\ \text{where}\ J_n(\alpha_j) = 0\ (\alpha_j > 0).$$

7. Let the function $u(\rho, \phi, z)$ satisfy Poisson's equation (Sec. 23) $\nabla^2 u + ay = 0$, where a is a constant, inside a semi-infinite half-cylinder $0 \le \rho \le 1, 0 \le \phi \le \pi, z \ge 0$, and suppose that $u = 0$ on the entire surface. The function u, which is assumed to be bounded and continuous for $0 \le \rho < 1, 0 < \phi < \pi, z > 0$, thus satisfies the boundary value problem

$$u_{\rho\rho} + \frac{1}{\rho} u_\rho + \frac{1}{\rho^2} u_{\phi\phi} + u_{zz} + a\rho \sin\phi = 0 \qquad (0 < \rho < 1, 0 < \phi < \pi, z > 0),$$

$$u(1, \phi, z) = 0, \qquad u(\rho, \phi, 0) = 0, \qquad u(\rho, 0, z) = u(\rho, \pi, z) = 0.$$

Use the following method to solve it.

(a) By writing $u(\rho, \phi, z) = a \sin\phi\, v(\rho, z)$, reduce the stated problem to the one

$$v_{\rho\rho} + \frac{1}{\rho} v_\rho - \frac{1}{\rho^2} v + v_{zz} + \rho = 0 \qquad (0 < \rho < 1, z > 0),$$

$$v(1, z) = 0, \qquad v(\rho, 0) = 0$$

in $v(\rho, z)$, where v is bounded and continuous for $0 \le \rho < 1, z > 0$.

(b) Note that when $n = 1$, the solution in Problem 6 suggests that the method of variation of parameters (see the example in Sec. 95) be used to seek a solution of the form

$$v(\rho, z) = \sum_{j=1}^{\infty} A_j(z)\, J_1(\alpha_j \rho),$$

where $J_1(\alpha_j) = 0\ (\alpha_j > 0)$, for the problem in part (a). Apply that method to obtain the initial value problem

$$A_j''(z) - \alpha_j^2 A_j(z) = -\frac{2}{\alpha_j J_2(\alpha_j)}, \qquad A_j(0) = 0$$

in ordinary differential equations. Then, by adding a particular solution of this differential equation, which is a constant that is readily found by inspection, to the general solution of the complementary equation $A_j''(z) - \alpha_j^2 A_j(z) = 0$ (compare with Problem 2, Sec. 46), find $v(\rho, z)$. Thus obtain the solution

$$u(\rho, \phi, z) = 2a \sin\phi \sum_{j=1}^{\infty} \frac{1 - \exp(-\alpha_j z)}{\alpha_j^3 J_2(\alpha_j)} J_1(\alpha_j \rho),$$

where $J_1(\alpha_j) = 0\ (\alpha_j > 0)$, of the original problem.

Suggestion: In obtaining the ordinary differential equation for $A_j(z)$ in part (b), one can write the needed Fourier-Bessel expansion for ρ by simply referring to the expansion already found in Problem 7, Sec. 92. Also, it is necessary to observe how the identity

$$\frac{d^2}{d\rho^2} J_1(\alpha_j \rho) + \frac{1}{\rho} \frac{d}{d\rho} J_1(\alpha_j \rho) - \frac{1}{\rho^2} J_1(\alpha_j \rho) = -\alpha_j^2 J_1(\alpha_j \rho)$$

follows immediately from the differential equation in that problem.

96. TEMPERATURES IN A LONG CYLINDRICAL WEDGE

As illustrated in Problem 1, Sec. 48, some temperature problems have solutions involving double Fourier series. In this section, we consider a temperature problem whose solution involves two series, one of which is a Fourier sine series and the other a Fourier-Bessel series.

EXAMPLE. Using cylindrical coordinates, we derive here an expression for temperatures $u(\rho, \phi, t)$ in the long right-angled cylindrical wedge formed by the surface $\rho = 1$ and the planes $\phi = 0$ and $\phi = \pi/2$ when $u = 0$ on its entire surface and $u = f(\rho, \phi)$ at time $t = 0$. By referring to expression (2), Sec. 24, for the laplacian $\nabla^2 u$ and writing $u_{zz} = 0$ in that expression, we have the heat equation

$$(1) \qquad u_t = k\left(u_{\rho\rho} + \frac{1}{\rho}u_\rho + \frac{1}{\rho^2}u_{\phi\phi}\right) \qquad \left(0 < \rho < 1, 0 < \phi < \frac{\pi}{2}, t > 0\right).$$

The boundary conditions are, of course,

$$(2) \qquad u(1, \phi, t) = 0,$$

$$(3) \qquad u(\rho, 0, t) = 0, u(\rho, \pi/2, t) = 0,$$

$$(4) \qquad u(\rho, \phi, 0) = f(\rho, \phi),$$

where it is understood that $u(\rho, \phi, t)$ is to be continuous throughout.

Upon substituting the product $u = R(\rho)\,\Phi(\phi)\,T(t)$ into equation (1), we see that

$$(5) \qquad \frac{T'}{kT} = \frac{R''}{R} + \frac{R'}{\rho R} + \frac{\Phi''}{\rho^2 \Phi} = -\lambda,$$

where $-\lambda$ is a separation constant. Separation of variables in the second of equations (5) now tells us that

$$\frac{\Phi''}{\Phi} = -\left(\frac{\rho^2 R''}{R} + \frac{\rho R'}{R} + \lambda\rho^2\right) = -\mu,$$

where $-\mu$ is another separation constant. It now follows that if $u = R\Phi T$ satisfies all of the homogeneous conditions (1)–(3), the following conditions must be satisfied:

$$(6) \qquad \rho^2 R''(\rho) + \rho R'(\rho) + (\lambda\rho^2 - \mu)R(\rho) = 0, \qquad R(1) = 0,$$

$$(7) \qquad \Phi''(\phi) + \mu\,\Phi(\phi) = 0, \qquad \Phi(0) = 0, \qquad \Phi(\pi/2) = 0.$$

Equations (5) tell us, moreover, that

(8) $$T'(t) + \lambda k T(t) = 0.$$

According to Sec. 35, conditions (7) make up a Sturm-Liouville problem whose solutions are

$$\mu_n = (2n)^2, \qquad \Phi_n(\rho) = \sin 2n\phi \qquad\qquad (n = 1, 2, \ldots).$$

Conditions (6) then become the singular Sturm-Liouville problem

$$\rho^2 R''(\rho) + \rho R'(\rho) + [\lambda \rho^2 - (2n)^2] R(\rho) = 0, \qquad R(1) = 0;$$

and case (a) of Theorem 2 in Sec. 88 tells us that for each positive integer n,

$$\lambda_{nj} = \alpha_{nj}^2, \qquad R_{nj}(\rho) = J_{2n}(\alpha_{nj}\rho) \qquad\qquad (j = 1, 2, \ldots),$$

where α_{nj} are the positive roots of the equation $J_{2n}(\alpha) = 0$. When $\lambda = \lambda_{nj}$, equation (8) becomes

$$T'(t) + \alpha_{nj}^2 k T(t) = 0;$$

and, except for constant factors,

$$T_{nj} = \exp(-\alpha_{nj}^2 k t).$$

Then

$$R_{nj}\Phi_n T_{nj} = J_{2n}(\alpha_{nj}\rho) \sin 2n\phi \exp(-\alpha_{nj}^2 k t),$$

and the principle of superposition enables us to write

(9) $$u(\rho, \phi, t) = \sum_{n=1}^{\infty} \sum_{j=1}^{\infty} B_{nj} J_{2n}(\alpha_{nj}\rho) \sin 2n\phi \exp(-\alpha_{nj}^2 k t).$$

Now the nonhomogeneous condition (4) requires that

$$f(\rho, \phi) = \sum_{n=1}^{\infty} \sum_{j=1}^{\infty} B_{nj} J_{2n}(\alpha_{nj}\rho) \sin 2n\phi,$$

or

(10) $$f(\rho, \phi) = \sum_{n=1}^{\infty} \left[\sum_{j=1}^{\infty} B_{nj} J_{2n}(\alpha_{nj}\rho) \right] \sin 2n\phi \qquad \left(0 < \phi < \frac{\pi}{2}\right).$$

When ρ is fixed, series (10) is a Fourier sine series on $0 < \phi < \pi/2$, with coefficients

$$\sum_{j=1}^{\infty} B_{nj} J_{2n}(\alpha_{nj}\rho) = \frac{4}{\pi} \int_0^{\pi/2} f(\rho, \phi) \sin 2n\phi \, d\phi.$$

Inasmuch as the series on the left here is a Fourier-Bessel series, we need only refer to case (a) of Theorem 2 in Sec. 91 to see that

$$B_{nj} = \frac{2}{[J_{2n+1}(\alpha_{nj})]^2} \int_0^1 \rho \left[\frac{4}{\pi} \int_0^{\pi/2} f(\rho, \phi) \sin 2n\phi \, d\phi \right] J_{2n}(\alpha_{nj}\rho) \, d\rho.$$

That is,

$$(11) \qquad B_{nj} = \frac{8}{\pi [J_{2n+1}(\alpha_{nj})]^2} \int_0^1 \rho\, J_{2n}(\alpha_{nj}\rho) \int_0^{\pi/2} f(\rho,\phi) \sin 2n\phi \, d\phi \, d\rho.$$

The formal solution of our boundary value problem is, therefore, series (9) with coefficients (11), where, for each positive integer n, the numbers α_{nj} ($j = 1, 2, \ldots$) are the positive roots of the equation $J_{2n}(\alpha) = 0$.

97. VIBRATION OF A CIRCULAR MEMBRANE

Fourier-Bessel series and double series involving them can arise in vibration problems, as illustrated in the following example.

EXAMPLE. A membrane, stretched over a fixed circular frame $\rho = c$ in the plane $z = 0$, is given an initial displacement $z = f(\rho, \phi)$ and released at rest from that position. The transverse displacements $z(\rho, \phi, t)$, where ρ, ϕ, and z are cylindrical coordinates, satisfy this boundary value problem:

$$(1) \qquad z_{tt} = a^2 \left(z_{\rho\rho} + \frac{1}{\rho} z_\rho + \frac{1}{\rho^2} z_{\phi\phi} \right),$$

$$(2) \qquad z(c, \phi, t) = 0 \qquad\qquad\qquad (-\pi \le \phi \le \pi, t \ge 0),$$

$$(3) \qquad z(\rho, \phi, 0) = f(\rho, \phi), \qquad z_t(\rho, \phi, 0) = 0 \qquad (0 \le \rho \le c, -\pi \le \phi \le \pi),$$

where $z(\rho, \phi, t)$ is periodic with period 2π in the variable ϕ and is also continuous.

A function $z = R(\rho)\Phi(\phi)T(t)$ satisfies equation (1) if

$$(4) \qquad \frac{T''}{a^2 T} = \frac{R''}{R} + \frac{R'}{\rho R} + \frac{\Phi''}{\rho^2 \Phi} = -\lambda,$$

where $-\lambda$ is a separation constant. We separate variables again, this time in the second of equations (4), and write

$$\frac{\Phi''}{\Phi} = - \left(\frac{\rho^2 R''}{R} + \frac{\rho R'}{R} + \lambda \rho^2 \right) = -\mu,$$

where $-\mu$ is another separation constant. Evidently, then, the product $R\Phi T$ satisfies the homogeneous conditions in our boundary value problem and has the necessary periodicity with respect to ϕ if R and Φ are eigenfunctions of the Sturm-Liouville problems

$$(5) \qquad \rho^2 R''(\rho) + \rho R'(\rho) + (\lambda \rho^2 - \mu) R(\rho) = 0, \qquad R(c) = 0,$$

$$(6) \qquad \Phi''(\phi) + \mu \Phi(\phi) = 0, \qquad \Phi(-\pi) = \Phi(\pi), \qquad \Phi'(-\pi) = \Phi'(\pi)$$

and T is such that

$$(7) \qquad T''(t) + \lambda a^2 T(t) = 0, \qquad T'(0) = 0.$$

We know from Sec. 49 that problem (6) has eigenvalues

$$\mu_0 = 0, \qquad \mu_n = n^2 \qquad\qquad\qquad (n = 1, 2, \ldots)$$

and corresponding eigenfunctions

$$\Phi_0(\phi) = 1, \qquad \Phi_n(\phi) = A_n \cos n\phi + B_n \sin n\phi \qquad (n = 1, 2, \ldots),$$

where A_n and B_n are arbitrary constants. After noting that problem (5) reduces to

$$\rho R''(\rho) + R'(\rho) + \lambda \rho R(\rho) = 0, \qquad R(c) = 0$$

when $\mu = \mu_0 = 0$ and that case (a) in Theorem 1, Sec. 88, can be combined with case (a) in Theorem 2 of that section, we find that the eigenvalues of problem (5) are

$$\lambda_{0j} = \alpha_{0j}^2, \qquad \lambda_{nj} = \alpha_{nj}^2 \qquad (j = 1, 2, \ldots)$$

for each positive integer n, where α_{nj} are the positive roots of the equations

$$J_n(\alpha c) = 0 \qquad (n = 0, 1, 2, \ldots).$$

The corresponding eigenfunctions are

$$R_{0j} = J_0(\alpha_{0j}\rho), \qquad R_{nj} = J_0(\alpha_{nj}\rho) \qquad (j = 1, 2, \ldots).$$

Also,

$$T_{0j}(t) = 1 \qquad \text{and} \qquad T_{nj}(t) = \cos \alpha_{nj} at.$$

The products $R\Phi T$ are now seen to be

$$R_{0j}\Phi_0 T_{0j} = J_0(\alpha_{0j}\rho) \cos \alpha_{0j} at \qquad (j = 1, 2, \ldots)$$

and, when $n = 1, 2, \ldots,$

$$R_{nj}\Phi_n T_{nj} = J_n(\alpha_{nj}\rho)(A_n \cos n\phi + B_n \sin n\phi) \cos \alpha_{nj} at \qquad (j = 1, 2, \ldots).$$

The generalized linear combination

$$(8) \qquad z(\rho, \phi, t) = \sum_{j=1}^{\infty} A_{0j} J_0(\alpha_{0j}\rho) \cos \alpha_{0j} at$$

$$+ \sum_{n=1}^{\infty} \sum_{j=1}^{\infty} J_n(\alpha_{nj}\rho)(A_{nj} \cos n\phi + B_{nj} \sin n\phi) \cos \alpha_{nj} at$$

of these products formally satisfies all of the homogeneous conditions. Observe that when $n = 1, 2, \ldots$ and the products $R_{nj}\Phi_n T_{nj}$ are multiplied by arbitrary constants, those constants are absorbed into the A_n and B_n but that the resulting constants involve the index j. [Compare with the remark immediately following equation (11) in Sec. 49.] Expression (8) also satisfies the nonhomogeneous condition, which is the first of conditions (3), if the constants A_{0j}, A_{nj}, and B_{nj} are such that

$$(9) \qquad f(\rho, \phi) = \frac{1}{2}\left[\sum_{j=1}^{\infty} 2A_{0j} J_0(\alpha_{0j}\rho)\right]$$

$$+ \sum_{n=1}^{\infty}\left\{\left[\sum_{j=1}^{\infty} A_{nj} J_n(\alpha_{nj}\rho)\right]\cos n\phi + \left[\sum_{j=1}^{\infty} B_{nj} J_n(\alpha_{nj}\rho)\right]\sin n\phi\right\}$$

when $0 \le \rho \le c$, $-\pi \le \phi \le \pi$.

For each fixed value of ρ, series (9) is the Fourier series for $f(\rho, \phi)$ on the interval $-\pi \le \phi \le \pi$ if

$$\sum_{j=1}^{\infty} 2 A_{0j} J_0(\alpha_{0j}\rho) = \frac{1}{\pi} \int_{-\pi}^{\pi} f(\rho, \phi) \, d\phi$$

and

$$\sum_{j=1}^{\infty} A_{nj} J_n(\alpha_{nj}\rho) = \frac{1}{\pi} \int_{-\pi}^{\pi} f(\rho, \phi) \cos n\phi \, d\phi \qquad (n = 1, 2, \ldots),$$

$$\sum_{j=1}^{\infty} B_{nj} J_n(\alpha_{nj}\rho) = \frac{1}{\pi} \int_{-\pi}^{\pi} f(\rho, \phi) \sin n\phi \, d\phi \qquad (n = 1, 2, \ldots).$$

The series on the left-hand side of each of these three equations is the Fourier-Bessel series representation, on the interval $0 < \rho < c$, of the corresponding function of ρ on the right-hand side. Specifically, case (a) in Theorems 1 and 2 in Sec. 91 tells us that

$$(10) \qquad A_{0j} = \frac{1}{\pi c^2 [J_1(\alpha_{0j}c)]^2} \int_0^c \rho J_0(\alpha_{0j}\rho) \int_{-\pi}^{\pi} f(\rho, \phi) \, d\phi \, d\rho$$

and

$$(11) \qquad A_{nj} = \frac{2}{\pi c^2 [J_{n+1}(\alpha_{nj}c)]^2} \int_0^c \rho J_n(\alpha_{nj}\rho) \int_{-\pi}^{\pi} f(\rho, \phi) \cos n\phi \, d\phi \, d\rho,$$

$$(12) \qquad B_{nj} = \frac{2}{\pi c^2 [J_{n+1}(\alpha_{nj}c)]^2} \int_0^c \rho J_n(\alpha_{nj}\rho) \int_{-\pi}^{\pi} f(\rho, \phi) \sin n\phi \, d\phi \, d\rho$$

when $n = 1, 2, \ldots$.

The displacements $z(\rho, \phi, t)$ are, then, given by equation (8) when the coefficients have the values (10), (11), and (12). We assume, of course, that the function f is such that the series in expression (8) has adequate properties of convergence and differentiability.

PROBLEMS

1. The iterated integral (11) in Sec. 96 can be written with the order of integration reversed as

$$B_{nj} = \frac{8}{\pi [J_{2n+1}(\alpha_{nj})]^2} \int_0^{\pi/2} \sin 2n\phi \int_0^1 \rho f(\rho, \phi) J_{2n}(\alpha_{nj}\rho) \, d\rho \, d\phi.$$

Obtain this expression for B_{nj} by writing equation (10), Sec. 96, as

$$f(\rho, \phi) = \sum_{j=1}^{\infty} \left[\sum_{n=1}^{\infty} B_{nj} \sin 2n\phi \right] J_{2n}(\alpha_{nj}\rho) \qquad (0 < \rho < 1)$$

and using case (a) of Theorem 2 in Sec. 91 first.

2. Solve the boundary value problem in the example in Sec. 96 when the entire surface of the wedge is insulated, instead of being kept at temperature zero.

3. Derive the following expression for the temperatures $u(\rho, \phi, t)$ in an infinite cylinder $\rho \leq 1$ when $u = 0$ on the surface $\rho = 1$ and $u = f(\rho, \phi)$ at time $t = 0$:

$$u(\rho, \phi, t) = \sum_{j=1}^{\infty} A_{0j} J_0(\alpha_{0j}\rho) \exp\left(-\alpha_{0j}^2 kt\right)$$

$$+ \sum_{n=1}^{\infty} \sum_{j=1}^{\infty} J_n(\alpha_{nj}\rho)(A_{nj} \cos n\phi + B_{nj} \sin n\phi) \exp\left(-\alpha_{nj}^2 kt\right),$$

where $\alpha_{nj} (j = 1, 2, \ldots)$ are the positive roots of the equations

$$J_n(\alpha) = 0 \qquad\qquad (n = 0, 1, 2, \ldots)$$

and

$$A_{0j} = \frac{1}{\pi [J_1(\alpha_{0j})]^2} \int_0^1 \rho J_0(\alpha_{0j}\rho) \int_{-\pi}^{\pi} f(\rho, \phi) \, d\phi \, d\rho,$$

$$A_{nj} = \frac{2}{\pi [J_{n+1}(\alpha_{nj})]^2} \int_0^1 \rho J_n(\alpha_{nj}\rho) \int_{-\pi}^{\pi} f(\rho, \phi) \cos n\phi \, d\phi \, d\rho \qquad (n = 1, 2, \ldots),$$

$$B_{nj} = \frac{2}{\pi [J_{n+1}(\alpha_{nj})]^2} \int_0^1 \rho J_n(\alpha_{nj}\rho) \int_{-\pi}^{\pi} f(\rho, \phi) \sin n\phi \, d\phi \, d\rho \qquad (n = 1, 2, \ldots).$$

These iterated integrals can, of course, be written with the order of integration reversed. (See Problem 1.)

4. Show that if the plane $\phi = \pi/2$ in the example in Sec. 96 is replaced by a plane $\phi = \phi_0$, the expression for the temperatures in the wedge will, in general, involve Bessel functions J_ν of *nonintegral* orders.

5. Suppose that in Sec. 97 the initial displacement function $f(\rho, \phi)$ is a linear combination of a finite number of the functions

$$J_0(\alpha_{0j}\rho) \qquad \text{and} \qquad J_n(\alpha_{nj}\rho) \cos n\phi, \quad J_n(\alpha_{nj}\rho) \sin n\phi \qquad (n = 1, 2, \ldots).$$

Point out why the iterated series in expression (8) of that section then contains only a finite number of terms and represents a rigorous solution of the boundary value problem.

6. Let the initial displacement of the membrane in Sec. 97 be $f(\rho)$, a function of ρ only, and derive this expression for the displacements when $t > 0$:

$$z(\rho, t) = \frac{2}{c^2} \sum_{j=1}^{\infty} \frac{J_0(\alpha_j\rho) \cos \alpha_j at}{[J_1(\alpha_j c)]^2} \int_0^c s f(s) J_0(\alpha_j s) \, ds,$$

where α_j are the positive roots of the equation $J_0(\alpha c) = 0$.

7. Show that if the initial displacement of the membrane in Sec. 97 is $A J_0(\alpha_k\rho)$, where A is a constant and α_k is some positive root of the equation $J_0(\alpha c) = 0$, then the subsequent displacements are simply

$$z(\rho, t) = A J_0(\alpha_k\rho) \cos \alpha_k at.$$

Observe that these displacements are all periodic in t with a common period; thus the membrane gives a musical note.

8. Replace the initial conditions (3), Sec. 97, by the conditions that $z = 0$ and $z_t = 1$ when $t = 0$. This is the case if the membrane and its frame are moving with unit velocity

in the z direction and the frame is brought to rest at the instant $t = 0$. Derive the expression

$$z(\rho, t) = \frac{2}{ac} \sum_{j=1}^{\infty} \frac{\sin \alpha_j a t}{\alpha_j^2 J_1(\alpha_j c)} J_0(\alpha_j \rho),$$

where α_j are the positive roots of the equation $J_0(\alpha c) = 0$, for the displacements when $t > 0$.

9. Suppose that the *damped* transverse displacements $z(\rho, t)$ in a membrane, stretched over a circular frame, satisfy the conditions

$$z_{tt} = z_{\rho\rho} + \frac{1}{\rho} z_\rho - 2b z_t \qquad (0 < \rho < 1, t > 0),$$

$$z(1, t) = 0, \qquad z(\rho, 0) = 0, \qquad z_t(\rho, 0) = v_0.$$

The constant coefficient of damping $2b$ is such that $0 < b < \alpha_1$, where α_1 is the smallest of the positive zeros of $J_0(\alpha)$. Derive the solution

$$z(\rho, t) = 2 v_0 e^{-bt} \sum_{j=1}^{\infty} \frac{J_0(\alpha_j \rho)}{\alpha_j J_1(\alpha_j)} \cdot \frac{\sin \left(t \sqrt{\alpha_j^2 - b^2} \right)}{\sqrt{\alpha_j^2 - b^2}},$$

where $J_0(\alpha_j) = 0$ $(\alpha_j > 0)$, of this boundary value problem.

CHAPTER

10

LEGENDRE
POLYNOMIALS
AND
APPLICATIONS

As we shall see later in this chapter (Secs. 107 and 108), an application of the method of separation of variables to Laplace's equation in the spherical coordinates r and θ leads, after the substitution $x = \cos\theta$ is made, to *Legendre's equation*

$$(1) \qquad [(1 - x^2)y'(x)]' + \lambda y(x) = 0,$$

where λ is a separation constant. The points $x = 1$ and $x = -1$ correspond to $\theta = 0$ and $\theta = \pi$, respectively, and we begin the chapter by using series to discover solutions of equation (1).

98. SOLUTIONS OF LEGENDRE'S EQUATION

To solve Legendre's equation, we write it as

$$(1) \qquad (1 - x^2)y''(x) - 2xy'(x) + \lambda y(x) = 0$$

and observe that, in standard form, it is a special case of

$$y''(x) + P(x)y'(x) + Q(x)y(x) = 0,$$

where each of the functions

$$P(x) = \frac{-2x}{1 - x^2} \qquad \text{and} \qquad Q(x) = \frac{\lambda}{1 - x^2}$$

has a Maclaurin series representation with positive radius of convergence. Thus $x = 0$ is an *ordinary point* of the differential equation (1), and we seek a solution
326

of the form†

$$(2) \qquad\qquad\qquad y = \sum_{j=0}^{\infty} a_j x^j,$$

where the series is assumed to be differentiable.

Writing

$$y' = \sum_{j=0}^{\infty} j a_j x^{j-1} \quad \text{and} \quad y'' = \sum_{j=0}^{\infty} j(j-1) a_j x^{j-2}$$

and then substituting series (2) and these two derivatives into equation (1), we have

$$\sum_{j=0}^{\infty} j(j-1) a_j x^{j-2} - \sum_{j=0}^{\infty} j(j-1) a_j x^{j} - \sum_{j=0}^{\infty} 2 j a_j x^{j} + \sum_{j=0}^{\infty} \lambda a_j x^{j} = 0,$$

which is the same as

$$\sum_{j=0}^{\infty} j(j-1) a_j x^{j-2} - \sum_{j=0}^{\infty} [j(j-1) + 2j - \lambda] a_j x^{j} = 0.$$

Since the first two terms in the first series here are actually zero and since

$$j(j-1) + 2j = j(j+1)$$

in the second series, we may write

$$\sum_{j=2}^{\infty} j(j-1) a_j x^{j-2} - \sum_{j=0}^{\infty} [j(j+1) - \lambda] a_j x^{j} = 0.$$

Finally, by putting the second of these two series in the form

$$\sum_{j=2}^{\infty} [(j-2)(j-1) - \lambda] a_{j-2} x^{j-2},$$

we arrive at the equation

$$(3) \qquad\qquad \sum_{j=2}^{\infty} \{ j(j-1) a_j - [(j-2)(j-1) - \lambda] a_{j-2} \} x^{j-2} = 0,$$

involving a single series.

Equation (3) is an identity in x if the coefficients a_j satisfy the recurrence relation

$$(4) \qquad\qquad a_j = \frac{(j-2)(j-1) - \lambda}{j(j-1)} a_{j-2} \qquad\qquad (j = 2, 3, \ldots).$$

The power series (2) thus represents a solution of Legendre's equation within its interval of convergence if its coefficients satisfy relation (4). This leaves a_0 and a_1 as arbitrary constants.

---

†For a discussion of ordinary points and a justification for this, see, for example, the books referred to in the footnote Sec. 81.

If $a_1 = 0$, it follows from relation (4) that $a_3 = a_5 = \cdots = 0$. Thus, one nontrivial solution of Legendre's equation, containing only even powers of x, is

$$
(5) \qquad y_1 = a_0 + \sum_{k=1}^{\infty} a_{2k} x^{2k} \qquad (a_0 \neq 0),
$$

where a_0 is an arbitrary nonzero constant and where the remaining coefficients $a_2, a_4, \ldots$ are expressed in terms of a_0 by successive applications of relation (4). (See Problem 4, Sec. 99.) Another solution, containing only odd powers of x, is obtained by writing $a_0 = 0$ and letting a_1 be arbitrary. More precisely, the series

$$
(6) \qquad y_2 = a_1 x + \sum_{k=1}^{\infty} a_{2k+1} x^{2k+1} \qquad (a_1 \neq 0)
$$

satisfies Legendre's equation for any nonzero value of a_1 when $a_3, a_5, \ldots$ are written in terms of a_1 in accordance with relation (4). These two solutions are, of course, linearly independent since they are not constant multiples of each other.

From relation (4), it is clear that the value of λ affects the values of all but the first coefficients in series (5) and (6). As we shall see in Sec. 99, there are certain values of λ that cause series (5) and (6) to terminate and become polynomials. Assuming for the moment that series (5) does not terminate, we note from relation (4), with $j = 2k$, that

$$
\lim_{k \to \infty} \left| \frac{a_{2(k+1)} x^{2(k+1)}}{a_{2k} x^{2k}} \right| = \lim_{k \to \infty} \left| \frac{2k(2k+1) - \lambda}{(2k+2)(2k+1)} x^2 \right| = x^2.
$$

So, according to the ratio and absolute convergence tests, series (5) converges when $x^2 < 1$ and diverges when $x^2 > 1$. Although it is somewhat more difficult to show, series (5) diverges when $x = \pm 1$.[†]

Similar arguments apply to series (6). In summary, then, *if λ is such that either of the series (5) or (6) does not terminate and become a polynomial, that series converges only when $-1 < x < 1$.*

99. LEGENDRE POLYNOMIALS

When Legendre's equation

$$
(1 - x^2) y''(x) - 2x y'(x) + \lambda y(x) = 0
$$

arises in the applications, it will be necessary to have a solution which, along with its derivative, is continuous on the closed interval $-1 \leq x \leq 1$. But we know from Sec. 98 that unless it terminates, neither of the series solutions

$$
(1) \qquad y_1 = a_0 + \sum_{k=1}^{\infty} a_{2k} x^{2k} \qquad (a_0 \neq 0),
$$

$$
(2) \qquad y_2 = a_1 x + \sum_{k=1}^{\infty} a_{2k+1} x^{2k+1} \qquad (a_1 \neq 0)
$$

obtained there satisfies those continuity conditions.

[†]See, for instance, the book by Bell (2004), listed in the Bibliography.

Suppose now that the parameter λ in Legendre's equation has one of the integral values

$$
(3) \qquad\qquad \lambda = n(n+1) \qquad\qquad (n = 0, 1, 2, \ldots),
$$

and then rewrite the recurrence relation (4) in Sec. 98 as

$$
(4) \qquad\qquad a_{j+2} = \frac{j(j+1) - n(n+1)}{(j+2)(j+1)}\, a_j \qquad (j = 0, 1, 2, \ldots).
$$

Note how it follows from relation (4) here that

$$
a_{n+2} = a_{n+4} = a_{n+6} = \cdots = 0.
$$

Consequently, *one of the solutions* (1) *and* (2) *is actually a polynomial,* when λ has one of the values (3).

We now examine that polynomial, first when n is even and then when n is odd.

(i) *n is even*
If $n = 0$, relation (4) tells us that

$$
a_2 = a_4 = a_6 = \cdots = 0;
$$

and series (1) becomes simply $y_1 = a_0$. Moreover, if n is any one of the even integers $2, 4, 6, \ldots$, that series is evidently a polynomial of degree n:

$$
(5) \qquad\qquad y_1 = a_0 + a_2 x^2 + \cdots + a_n x^n \qquad\qquad (a_n \neq 0).
$$

Observe that series (2) remains an infinite series when n is even.

If n is even, it is customary to assign a value to a_0 such that when the coefficients $a_2, \ldots, a_n$ in expression (5) are determined by means of relation (4), the final coefficient a_n has the value

$$
(6) \qquad\qquad a_n = \frac{(2n)!}{2^n (n!)^2}.
$$

The reason for this requirement is that the polynomial (5) will then have the value unity when $x = 1$, as will be shown in Sec. 101. The precise value of a_0 that is needed is not important to us here. Using the convention that $0! = 1$, we note that $a_0 = 1$ if $n = 0$. In that case, $y_1 = 1$.

(ii) *n is odd*
If $n = 1$, we find from relation (4) that $y_2 = a_1 x$, since

$$
a_3 = a_5 = a_7 = \cdots = 0;
$$

and if n is any one of the odd integers $3, 5, 7, \ldots$, series (2) becomes

$$
(7) \qquad\qquad y_2 = a_1 x + a_3 x^3 + \cdots + a_n x^n \qquad\qquad (a_n \neq 0).
$$

Observe that when n is odd, series (1) continues to be an infinite series.

When n is odd, we choose a_1 so that the final coefficient in expression (7) is also given by equation (6). The reason for this choice is similar to the one above regarding the value assigned to a_0. Note that $y_2 = x$ if $n = 1$, since $a_1 = 1$ for that value of n.

When $n = 2, 3, \ldots$, relation (4) can be used to write all of the coefficients that precede a_n in expressions (5) and (7) in terms of a_n. To accomplish this, we first observe that the numerator on the right-hand side of relation (4) can be written

$$j(j+1) - n(n+1) = -[(n^2 - j^2) + (n-j)] = -(n-j)(n+j+1).$$

We then solve for a_j. The result is

$$(8) \qquad a_j = -\frac{(j+2)(j+1)}{(n-j)(n+j+1)} a_{j+2}.$$

To express a_{n-2k} in terms of a_n, we now use relation (8) to write the following k equations:

$$a_{n-2} = -\frac{(n)(n-1)}{(2)(2n-1)} a_n,$$

$$a_{n-4} = -\frac{(n-2)(n-3)}{(4)(2n-3)} a_{n-2},$$

$$\vdots$$

$$a_{n-2k} = -\frac{(n-2k+2)(n-2k+1)}{(2k)(2n-2k+1)} a_{n-2k+2}.$$

Equating the product of the left-hand sides of these equations to the product of their right-hand sides and then canceling the common factors

$$a_{n-2}, a_{n-4}, \ldots, a_{n-2k+2}$$

on each side of the resulting equation, we find that

$$(9) \qquad a_{n-2k} = \frac{(-1)^k}{2^k k!} \cdot \frac{n(n-1) \cdots (n-2k+1)}{(2n-1)(2n-3) \cdots (2n-2k+1)} a_n.$$

Then, upon substituting expression (6) for a_n into equation (9) and combining various terms into the appropriate factorials (see Problem 1), we arrive at the desired expression:

$$(10) \qquad a_{n-2k} = \frac{1}{2^n} \cdot \frac{(-1)^k}{k!} \cdot \frac{(2n-2k)!}{(n-2k)!(n-k)!}.$$

As usual, $0! = 1$.

In view of equation (10), the polynomials (5) and (7), when the nonzero constants a_0 and a_1 are such that a_n has the values (6), can be written

$$(11) \qquad P_n(x) = \frac{1}{2^n} \sum_{k=0}^{m} \frac{(-1)^k}{k!} \cdot \frac{(2n-2k)!}{(n-2k)!(n-k)!} x^{n-2k} \qquad (n = 0, 1, 2, \ldots),$$

where

$$m = \begin{cases} n/2 & \text{if } n \text{ is even,} \\ (n-1)/2 & \text{if } n \text{ is odd.} \end{cases}$$

Another expression for $P_n(x)$ will be given in Sec. 101. Note that since $P_n(x)$ is a polynomial containing only even powers of x if n is even and only odd powers if n is odd, it is an even or an odd function, depending on whether n is even or odd; that is,

(12) $$P_n(-x) = (-1)^n P_n(x) \qquad (n = 0, 1, 2, \ldots).$$

The polynomial $P_n(x)$ is called the *Legendre polynomial of degree n*. For the first several values of n, expression (11) becomes (see Fig. 74)

$$P_0(x) = 1, \qquad\qquad\qquad P_1(x) = x,$$

$$P_2(x) = \frac{1}{2}(3x^2 - 1), \qquad\qquad P_3(x) = \frac{1}{2}(5x^3 - 3x),$$

$$P_4(x) = \frac{1}{8}(35x^4 - 30x^2 + 3), \qquad P_5(x) = \frac{1}{8}(63x^5 - 70x^3 + 15x).$$

Observe that the value of each of these six polynomials is unity when $x = 1$, as anticipated. Also, the polynomials $P_0(x)$, $P_2(x)$, and $P_4(x)$ contain only even powers of x, while $P_1(x)$, $P_3(x)$, and $P_5(x)$ contain only odd powers.

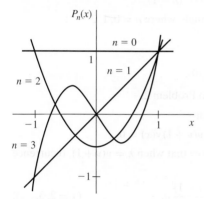

FIGURE 74

We have just seen that Legendre's equation

(13) $$(1 - x^2)y''(x) - 2xy'(x) + n(n+1)y(x) = 0 \qquad (n = 0, 1, 2, \ldots)$$

always has the polynomial solution $y = P_n(x)$, which is solution (5) (n even) or solution (7) (n odd) when appropriate values are assigned to the arbitrary constants a_0 and a_1 in those solutions. Details regarding the standard form of the accompanying series solution, which is denoted by $Q_n(x)$ and is called a *Legendre function of the second kind,* are left to the problems. We, of course, know from the statement in italics at the end of Sec. 98 that the series representing $Q_n(x)$ is convergent only when $-1 < x < 1$. It will, however, be sufficient for us to know that $Q_n(x)$ and $Q_n'(x)$ fail to be a pair of continuous functions on the *closed* interval $-1 \le x \le 1$ (Problem 12, Sec. 105). Since $P_n(x)$ and $Q_n(x)$ are linearly independent, the general solution of equation (13) is

(14) $$y = C_1 P_n(x) + C_2 Q_n(x),$$

where C_1 and C_2 are arbitrary constants.

PROBLEMS

1. Give details showing how expression (10) in Sec. 99 for the coefficients a_{n-2k} in the Legendre polynomials is obtained from equations (6) and (9) there.

  Suggestion: Observe that the factorials in equation (6), Sec. 99, can be written

$$(2n)! = (2n)(2n-1)(2n-2)\cdots(2n-2k+1)(2n-2k)!,$$
$$n! = n(n-1)\cdots(n-2k+1)(n-2k)!,$$
$$n! = n(n-1)\cdots(n-k+1)(n-k)!.$$

2. With the aid of expression (11), Sec. 99, for $P_n(x)$, show that when $n = 2, 3, \ldots$, the constants a_0 and a_1 in equations (5) and (7) in that section must have the following values in order for the final constant a_n to have the value specified in equation (6) there:

$$a_0 = (-1)^{n/2}\, \frac{(1)(3)(5)\cdots(n-1)}{(2)(4)(6)\cdots(n)} \qquad (n = 2, 4, \ldots),$$

$$a_1 = (-1)^{(n-1)/2}\, \frac{(1)(3)(5)\cdots(n)}{(2)(4)(6)\cdots(n-1)} \qquad (n = 3, 5, \ldots).$$

3. Establish these properties of Legendre polynomials, where $n = 0, 1, 2, \ldots$:

 (a) $P_{2n}(0) = (-1)^n \dfrac{(2n)!}{2^{2n}(n!)^2}$;   (b) $P'_{2n}(0) = 0$;

 (c) $P_{2n+1}(0) = 0$;   (d) $P'_{2n+1}(0) = (2n+1)P_{2n}(0)$.

  Suggestion: For parts (a) and (d), refer to Problem 2.

4. Legendre's equation (1), Sec. 98, is often written

$$(1 - x^2)y''(x) - 2xy'(x) + \nu(\nu+1)y(x) = 0,$$

where ν is an unrestricted complex number. Show that when $\lambda = \nu(\nu+1)$, recurrence relation (4), Sec. 98, can be put in the form

$$a_j = -\frac{(\nu - j + 2)(\nu + j - 1)}{j(j-1)}\, a_{j-2} \qquad (j = 2, 3, \ldots).$$

Then, by proceeding as we did in solving Bessel's equation (Sec. 81), use this relation to obtain the following linearly independent solutions of Legendre's equation:

$$y_1 = a_0 \left\{ 1 + \sum_{k=1}^{\infty} (-1)^k \right.$$

$$\left. \cdot \frac{[\nu(\nu-2)\cdots(\nu-2k+2)][(\nu+1)(\nu+3)\cdots(\nu+2k-1)]}{(2k)!} x^{2k} \right\},$$

$$y_2 = a_1 \left\{ x + \sum_{k=1}^{\infty} (-1)^k \right.$$

$$\left. \cdot \frac{[(\nu-1)(\nu-3)\cdots(\nu-2k+1)][(\nu+2)(\nu+4)\cdots(\nu+2k)]}{(2k+1)!} x^{2k+1} \right\},$$

where a_0 and a_1 are arbitrary nonzero constants. (These two series converge when $-1 < x < 1$, according to Sec. 98.)

5. Show that if ν is the complex number

$$\nu = -\frac{1}{2} + i\alpha \qquad (\alpha > 0),$$

Legendre's equation in Problem 4 becomes

$$(1 - x^2)y''(x) - 2xy'(x) - \left(\frac{1}{4} + \alpha^2\right)y(x) = 0.$$

Then show how it follows from the solutions obtained in Problem 4 that the functions

$$p_\alpha(x) = 1 + \sum_{k=1}^{\infty}\left[\alpha^2 + \left(\frac{1}{2}\right)^2\right]\left[\alpha^2 + \left(\frac{5}{2}\right)^2\right]\cdots\left[\alpha^2 + \left(\frac{4k-3}{2}\right)^2\right]\frac{x^{2k}}{(2k)!},$$

$$q_\alpha(x) = x + \sum_{k=1}^{\infty}\left[\alpha^2 + \left(\frac{3}{2}\right)^2\right]\left[\alpha^2 + \left(\frac{7}{2}\right)^2\right]\cdots\left[\alpha^2 + \left(\frac{4k-1}{2}\right)^2\right]\frac{x^{2k+1}}{(2k+1)!}$$

are linearly independent solutions of this differential equation, valid on the interval $-1 < x < 1$. These particular Legendre functions arise in certain boundary value problems in regions bounded by cones.

6. Note that the solutions y_1 and y_2 obtained in Problem 4 are solutions (5) and (6) in Sec. 98 when $\lambda = \nu(\nu + 1)$. They remain infinite series when $\nu = n = 1, 3, 5, \ldots$ and $\nu = n = 0, 2, 4, \ldots$, respectively. When $\nu = n = 2m\,(m = 0, 1, 2, \ldots)$, the Legendre function Q_n of the second kind is defined as y_2, where

$$a_1 = \frac{(-1)^m\, 2^{2m}\, (m!)^2}{(2m)!};$$

and when $\nu = n = 2m + 1\ (m = 0, 1, 2, \ldots)$, Q_n is defined as y_1, where

$$a_0 = -\frac{(-1)^m\, 2^{2m}\, (m!)^2}{(2m+1)!}.$$

Using the fact that

$$\ln\frac{1+x}{1-x} = 2\sum_{k=0}^{\infty}\frac{x^{2k+1}}{2k+1}\qquad (-1 < x < 1),$$

show that

$$Q_0(x) = \frac{1}{2}\ln\frac{1+x}{1-x}\qquad \text{and}\qquad Q_1(x) = \frac{x}{2}\ln\frac{1+x}{1-x} - 1 = xQ_0(x) - 1.$$

100. RODRIGUES' FORMULA

Expression (11), Sec. 99, tells us that

$$P_n(x) = \frac{1}{2^n}\sum_{k=0}^{m}\frac{(-1)^k}{k!}\cdot\frac{(2n-2k)!}{(n-2k)!(n-k)!}x^{n-2k}\qquad (n = 0, 1, 2, \ldots),$$

where

$$m = \begin{cases} n/2 & \text{if } n \text{ is even,}\\ (n-1)/2 & \text{if } n \text{ is odd.} \end{cases}$$

That is,

$$(1)\qquad P_n(x) = \frac{1}{2^n n!}\sum_{k=0}^{m}(-1)^k\frac{n!}{(n-k)!k!}\cdot\frac{(2n-2k)!}{(n-2k)!}x^{n-2k}\qquad (n = 0, 1, 2, \ldots).$$

Since

$$\frac{d^n}{dx^n} x^{2n-2k} = \frac{(2n-2k)!}{(n-2k)!} x^{n-2k} \qquad (0 \le k \le m)$$

and because of the linearity of the differential operator d^n/dx^n, expression (1) can be written

(2) $$P_n(x) = \frac{1}{2^n n!} \frac{d^n}{dx^n} \left[\sum_{k=0}^{m} \frac{n!}{(n-k)!k!} \left(x^2\right)^{n-k} (-1)^k \right].$$

The powers of x in the sum here evidently decrease in steps of 2 as the index k increases; and the lowest power is $2n - 2m$, which is n if n is even and $n + 1$ if n is odd. The sum can actually be extended so that k ranges from 0 to n. This is because the additional polynomial that is introduced is of degree less than n, and its nth derivative is, therefore, zero. Since the resulting sum is the binomial expansion of $(x^2 - 1)^n$, it follows from equation (2) that

(3) $$P_n(x) = \frac{1}{2^n n!} \frac{d^n}{dx^n} (x^2 - 1)^n \qquad (n = 0, 1, 2, \ldots).$$

This is *Rodrigues' formula* for the Legendre polynomials.

Various useful properties of Legendre polynomials are readily obtained from Rodrigues' formula with the aid of *Leibnitz' rule* for the nth derivative of the product of two functions (Problem 2, Sec. 102):

(4) $$D^n(fg) = \sum_{k=0}^{n} \frac{n!}{(n-k)!k!} (D^{n-k} f)(D^k g),$$

where it is understood that all of the required derivatives exist and that the zero-order derivative of a function is the function itself.

EXAMPLE 1. If we write $u = x^2 - 1$, so that

$$u^n = (x^2 - 1)^n = (x - 1)^n (x + 1)^n,$$

it follows from Leibnitz' rule that

$$D^n u^n = \sum_{k=0}^{n} \frac{n!}{(n-k)!k!} [D^{n-k}(x-1)^n][D^k(x+1)^n].$$

Now the first term in this sum is

$$[D^n(x-1)^n][D^0(x+1)^n] = n!(x+1)^n,$$

and the remaining terms all contain the factor $(x - 1)$ to some positive power. Hence the value of the sum when $x = 1$ is $n!2^n$, and it follows from Rodrigues' formula (3) that

(5) $$P_n(1) = 1 \qquad (n = 0, 1, 2, \ldots).$$

Observe how it follows from this and the relation

$$P_n(-x) = (-1)^n P_n(x) \qquad (n = 0, 1, 2, \ldots),$$

obtained in Sec. 99, that

(6) $$P_n(-1) = (-1)^n \qquad\qquad (n = 0, 1, 2, \ldots).$$

EXAMPLE 2. We turn now to the derivation of an important recurrence relation,

(7) $$(n+1)P_{n+1}(x) + nP_{n-1}(x) = (2n+1)xP_n(x) \qquad (n = 1, 2, \ldots),$$

which is to be used in Sec. 104.

Our derivation is based on the following two identities, where $u = x^2 - 1$:

(8) $$Du^{n+1} = D(x^2 - 1)^{n+1} = 2(n+1)xu^n \qquad (n = 0, 1, 2, \ldots),$$

(9) $$D^2 u^{n+1} = 2(n+1)[(2n+1)u^n + 2nu^{n-1}] \qquad (n = 0, 1, 2, \ldots).$$

Identity (8) is obvious and enables us to write

$$\begin{aligned} D(Du^{n+1}) &= 2(n+1)(u^n + x\,Du^n) \\ &= 2(n+1)(u^n + 2nx^2 u^{n-1}) \\ &= 2(n+1)[u^n + 2n(x^2 - 1)u^{n-1} + 2nu^{n-1}], \end{aligned}$$

which is the same as identity (9).

We start by using Rodrigues' formula (3) to write

$$P_{n+1}(x) = \frac{D^{n-1}(D^2 u^{n+1})}{2^{n+1}(n+1)!}.$$

In view or expression (9), this tells us that

$$P_{n+1}(x) = \frac{(2n+1)D^{n-1}u^n + 2nD^{n-1}u^{n-1}}{2^n n!}.$$

Referring to Rodrigues' formula once again, we have

$$D^{n-1}u^{n-1} = 2^{n-1}(n-1)!\,P_{n-1}(x);$$

and so it follows that

$$P_{n+1}(x) = \frac{(2n+1)D^{n-1}u^n + 2^n n!\,P_{n-1}(x)}{2^n n!}.$$

That is,

(10) $$\frac{P_{n+1}(x) - P_{n-1}(x)}{2n+1} = \frac{D^{n-1}u^n}{2^n n!}.$$

On the other hand, we see from Rodrigues' formula (3) and expression (8) that

$$P_{n+1}(x) = \frac{D^n(Du^{n+1})}{2^{n+1}(n+1)!} = \frac{D^n(xu^n)}{2^n n!} = \frac{D^n(u^n x)}{2^n n!}.$$

Inasmuch as the first two terms of Leibnitz' rule (4) are

$$D^n(fg) = (D^n f)g + n(D^{n-1}f)(Dg) + \cdots,$$

this yields

$$P_{n+1}(x) = \frac{x D^n u^n + n D^{n-1} u^n}{2^n n!}.$$

Because

(11) $$D^n u^n = 2^n n! \, P_n(x),$$

then,

(12) $$\frac{P_{n+1}(x) - x P_n(x)}{n} = \frac{D^{n-1} u^n}{2^n n!}.$$

Finally, by equating the left-hand sides of equations (10) and (12), we arrive at recurrence relation (7). Note, too, that the relation

(13) $$P'_{n+1}(x) - P'_{n-1}(x) = (2n+1) P_n(x) \qquad\qquad (n = 1, 2, \ldots)$$

is an immediate consequence of equations (10) and (11).

101.   LAPLACE'S INTEGRAL FORM

We recall having a useful integral form for Bessel functions $J_n(x)$ in Sec. 84 that gave us an upper bound for $|J_n(x)|$. We turn here to a well known integral form for Legendre polynomials and obtain similar upper bounds for $|P_n(x)|$. We state the main result as a theorem and preface it with the following lemma.

Lemma.   *Every polynomial*

(1) $$q(x) = \sum_{k=0}^{n} a_k x^k$$

satisfies the identity

(2) $$q(x) = \frac{1}{2\pi} \int_{-\pi}^{\pi} q(x + y e^{i\phi}) \, d\phi,$$

where x and y are independent of ϕ.

Our proof begins with the integral

(3) $$\int_{-\pi}^{\pi} e^{im\phi} \, d\phi = \begin{cases} 2\pi & \text{when } m = 0, \\ 0 & \text{when } m = 1, 2, \ldots. \end{cases}$$

The value of this integral is obvious when $m = 0$. When $m = 1, 2, \ldots$, Euler's formula enables us to write[†]

$$\int_{-\pi}^{\pi} e^{im\phi} \, d\phi = \int_{-\pi}^{\pi} (\cos m\phi + i \sin m\phi) \, d\phi = \int_{-\pi}^{\pi} \cos m\phi \, d\phi + i \int_{-\pi}^{\pi} \sin m\phi \, d\phi = 0.$$

[†]For a careful treatment of the evaluation of integrals of complex-valued functions of a real variable, see, for example, Sec. 38 of the authors' book (2009) that is listed in the Bibliography.

Now, the binomial formula tells us that

$$(x + ye^{i\phi})^k = x^k + kx^{k-1}(ye^{i\phi}) + \cdots + (ye^{i\phi})^k;$$

and, since each term on the right here, including x^k, has a factor of the form

$$e^{im\phi} \qquad\qquad (m = 0, 1, 2, \ldots, k),$$

it follows from integral (3) that

$$\frac{1}{2\pi} \int_{-\pi}^{\pi} (x + ye^{i\phi})^k \, d\phi = x^k \qquad\qquad (k = 0, 1, 2, \ldots, n).$$

Expression (1) thus becomes

$$q(x) = \sum_{k=0}^{n} a_k \frac{1}{2\pi} \int_{-\pi}^{\pi} (x + ye^{i\phi})^k \, d\phi = \frac{1}{2\pi} \int_{-\pi}^{\pi} \sum_{k=0}^{n} a_k (x + ye^{i\phi})^k \, d\phi.$$

This result is the same as expression (2), and the lemma is proved.

We are now ready to prove the following theorem, which expresses each $P_n(x)$ in a form known as *Laplace's integral form*.

Theorem. *Each Legendre polynomial has the integral representation*

$$(4) \qquad P_n(x) = \frac{1}{\pi} \int_{0}^{\pi} (x + \sqrt{x^2 - 1} \cos \phi)^n \, d\phi \qquad\qquad (n = 0, 1, 2, \ldots).$$

To prove this theorem, we write $q(x) = P_n(x)$ in equation (2):

$$(5) \qquad P_n(x) = \frac{1}{2\pi} \int_{-\pi}^{\pi} P_n(x + ye^{i\phi}) \, d\phi.$$

But we know from Rodrigues' formula (Sec. 100)

$$P_n(x) = \frac{d^n}{dx^n} \left[\frac{1}{2^n n!} (x^2 - 1)^n \right]$$

that

$$P_n(x) = p^{(n)}(x) \qquad\qquad (n = 0, 1, 2, \ldots)$$

where

$$(6) \qquad p(x) = \frac{1}{2^n n!} (x^2 - 1)^n$$

and $p^{(n)}(x)$ denotes the nth derivative of $p(x)$. Consequently, equation (5) can be written

$$(7) \qquad P_n(x) = \frac{1}{2\pi} \int_{-\pi}^{\pi} p^{(n)}(x + ye^{i\phi}) \, d\phi.$$

As usual, we agree that $0! = 1$ and $p^{(0)}(x) = p(x)$.

Now it is readily shown (Problem 5, Sec. 102) that

$$(8) \qquad \int_{-\pi}^{\pi} e^{-ik\phi} p^{(n-k)}(x + ye^{i\phi}) \, d\phi = \frac{k+1}{y} \int_{-\pi}^{\pi} e^{-i(k+1)\phi} p^{(n-k-1)}(x + ye^{i\phi}) \, d\phi,$$

where, in addition to x and y ($y \neq 0$) being independent of ϕ, the integer k is such that $0 \leq k \leq n - 1$. Successive applications of this reduction formula enable us to write equation (7) as

$$(9) \qquad P_n(x) = \frac{n!}{2\pi y^n} \int_{-\pi}^{\pi} e^{-in\phi} p(x + ye^{i\phi}) \, d\phi.$$

Finally, if we require that $x \neq \pm 1$, write $y = \sqrt{x^2 - 1}$, and then use the fact (Problem 6, Sec. 102) that

$$(10) \qquad \frac{n!}{y^n} e^{-in\phi} p(x + ye^{i\phi}) = (x + \sqrt{x^2 - 1} \cos \phi)^n,$$

we can see how expression (9) becomes

$$P_n(x) = \frac{1}{2\pi} \int_{-\pi}^{\pi} (x + \sqrt{x^2 - 1} \cos \phi)^n \, d\phi,$$

which is the same as expression (4) in the statement of the theorem. Note that since $P_n(1) = 1$ and $P_n(-1) = (-1)^n$ (Sec. 100), expression (4) is also valid when $x = \pm 1$. Hence it is valid for all x, and the proof of the theorem is complete.

102. SOME CONSEQUENCES OF THE INTEGRAL FORM

In this section we establish two upper bounds for $|P_n(x)|$ that follow from Laplace's integral form

$$(1) \qquad P_n(x) = \frac{1}{\pi} \int_{0}^{\pi} (x + \sqrt{x^2 - 1} \cos \phi)^n \, d\phi \qquad (n = 0, 1, 2, \ldots),$$

obtained in Sec. 101.

Suppose that $-1 < x < 1$. Since $x = \cos \theta$ for some value of θ between 0 and π inclusive, expression (1) can be written

$$(2) \qquad P_n(\cos \theta) = \frac{1}{\pi} \int_{0}^{\pi} (\cos \theta + i \sin \theta \cos \phi)^n \, d\phi \qquad (0 < \theta < \pi).$$

Furthermore, since $\cos^2 \theta = 1 - \sin^2 \theta$ and $\cos^2 \phi = 1 - \sin^2 \phi$,

$$|\cos \theta + i \sin \theta \cos \phi| = (\cos^2 \theta + \sin^2 \theta \cos^2 \phi)^{1/2} = (1 - \sin^2 \theta \sin^2 \phi)^{1/2};$$

and this means that

$$|P_n(\cos \theta)| \leq \frac{1}{\pi} \int_{0}^{\pi} |\cos \theta + i \sin \theta \cos \phi|^n \, d\phi = \frac{1}{\pi} \int_{0}^{\pi} (1 - \sin^2 \theta \sin^2 \phi)^{n/2} \, d\phi.$$

Moreover, since $\sin(\pi - \phi) = \sin \phi$, we see that

$$(3) \qquad |P_n(\cos \theta)| \leq \frac{2}{\pi} \int_{0}^{\pi/2} (1 - \sin^2 \theta \sin^2 \phi)^{n/2} \, d\phi.$$

Finally, since $0 \leq 1 - \sin^2 \theta \sin^2 \phi \leq 1$ for all values of θ and ϕ, it follows from inequality (3) that $|P_n(\cos \theta)| \leq 1$, or that

$$(4) \qquad |P_n(x)| \leq 1 \quad \text{when} \quad -1 \leq x \leq 1,$$

where $n = 0, 1, 2, \ldots$.

To obtain another important consequence of inequality (3), we assume that

$$0 < \theta < \pi \quad \text{and} \quad 0 < \phi < \frac{\pi}{2}.$$

It is evident from the graphs of

$$y = \sin \phi \quad \text{and} \quad y = \frac{2}{\pi}\phi$$

that

$$\sin \phi > \frac{2}{\pi}\phi \quad \text{and} \quad 0 < \phi < \frac{\pi}{2}.$$

So if

$$u = \left(\frac{2\sin\theta}{\pi}\phi\right)^2,$$

it is straightforward to show that

$$1 - \sin^2\theta \sin^2\phi < 1 - u.$$

Also, $1 - u < e^{-u} (u > 0)$, as can be seen graphically or from the Maclaurin series for e^{-u}. According to inequality (3), then,

$$(5) \qquad |P_n(\cos\theta)| < \frac{2}{\pi}\int_0^{\pi/2} \exp\left(-\frac{2n\sin^2\theta}{\pi^2}\phi^2\right) d\phi \qquad (0 < \theta < \pi)$$

where $n = 1, 2, \ldots$.

Changing the variable of integration in this last integral by means of the substitution (Problem 7)

$$(6) \qquad s = \frac{\sqrt{2n}\sin\theta}{\pi}\phi$$

and noting that because the integrand is always positive, the resulting upper limit of integration can be replaced by ∞, we find that

$$(7) \qquad |P_n(\cos\theta)| < \sqrt{\frac{2}{n}} \cdot \frac{1}{\sin\theta}\int_0^{\infty} \exp(-s^2)\, ds \qquad (0 < \theta < \pi),$$

where $n = 1, 2, \ldots$.

Finally, since the value of this improper integral is $\sqrt{\pi}/2$ (Problem 9, Sec. 58) and since

$$\sin\theta = \sqrt{1 - \cos^2\theta} = \sqrt{1 - x^2}$$

when $x = \cos\theta$, we arrive at the inequality

$$(8) \qquad |P_n(x)| < \sqrt{\frac{\pi}{2n(1-x^2)}} \qquad (-1 < x < 1),$$

where $n = 1, 2, \ldots$. Thus, for each fixed x in the interval $-1 < x < 1$,

$$(9) \qquad |P_n(x)| < \frac{M}{\sqrt{n}} \qquad (n = 1, 2, \ldots),$$

where the value of M depends only on the choice of x.

PROBLEMS

1. From recurrence relation (13), Sec. 100, obtain the integration formula

$$\int_a^1 P_n(x)\,dx = \frac{1}{2n+1}\left[P_{n-1}(a) - P_{n+1}(a)\right] \qquad (n = 1, 2, \ldots).$$

2. Use mathematical induction on the integer n to verify Leibnitz' rule (4), Sec. 100.

3. Write

$$F(x, t) = (1 - 2xt + t^2)^{-1/2},$$

where $|x| \leq 1$ and t is as yet unrestricted.

(a) Note that $x = \cos\theta$ for some uniquely determined value of θ ($0 \leq \theta \leq \pi$), and show that

$$F(x, t) = (1 - e^{i\theta}t)^{-1/2}(1 - e^{-i\theta}t)^{-1/2}.$$

Then, using the fact that $(1 - z)^{-1/2}$ has a valid Maclaurin series expansion when $|z| < 1$, point out why the factors $(1 - e^{i\theta}t)^{-1/2}$ and $(1 - e^{-i\theta}t)^{-1/2}$, considered as functions of t, can be represented by Maclaurin series that are valid when $|t| < 1$. It follows that the product $F(x, t)$ also has such a representation when $|t| < 1.$[†] That is, there are functions $f_n(x)$ ($n = 0, 1, 2, \ldots$) such that

$$F(x, t) = \sum_{n=0}^{\infty} f_n(x)\,t^n \qquad (|t| < 1).$$

(b) Show that the function $F(x, t)$ satisfies the identity

$$(1 - 2xt + t^2)\frac{\partial F}{\partial t} = (x - t)F,$$

and use this result to show that the functions $f_n(x)$ in part (a) satisfy the recurrence relation

$$(n + 1)f_{n+1}(x) + nf_{n-1}(x) = (2n + 1)xf_n(x) \qquad (n = 1, 2, \ldots).$$

(c) Show that the first two functions $f_0(x)$ and $f_1(x)$ in part (a) are 1 and x, respectively, and notice that the recurrence relation obtained in part (b) can then be used to determine $f_n(x)$ when $n = 2, 3, \ldots$. Compare that relation with relation (7), Sec. 100, and conclude that the functions $f_n(x)$ are, in fact, the Legendre polynomials $P_n(x)$; that is, show that

$$(1 - 2xt + t^2)^{-1/2} = \sum_{n=0}^{\infty} P_n(x)\,t^n \qquad (|x| \leq 1, |t| < 1).$$

The function F is, therefore, a *generating function* for the Legendre polynomials.

4. Give an alternative proof of the property (Sec. 100) $P_n(1) = 1$ ($n = 0, 1, 2, \ldots$), using
(a) recurrence relation (7), Sec. 100, and mathematical induction;
(b) the generating function obtained in Problem 3(c).

5. Use integration by parts to obtain the reduction formula (8) in Sec. 101.
  Suggestion: Start by writing the left-hand side of the formula as

$$\int_{-\pi}^{\pi} e^{-i(k+1)\phi}\,\frac{d}{d\phi}\left[\frac{1}{iy}p^{(n-k-1)}(x + ye^{i\phi})\right]\,d\phi,$$

[†] For a discussion of this point, see, for example, the authors' book (2009, pp. 222–223), listed in the Bibliography.

so that

$$u = e^{-i(k+1)\phi} \quad \text{and} \quad dv = \frac{d}{d\phi}\left[\frac{1}{iy}p^{(n-k-1)}(x + ye^{i\phi})\right] d\phi.$$

6. Derive identity (10), Sec. 101, where $x \neq \pm 1$ and $y = \sqrt{x^2 - 1}$.
   Suggestion: The expression

$$\cos\phi = \frac{e^{i\phi} + e^{-i\phi}}{2},$$

   which follows from Euler's formula $e^{i\phi} = \cos\phi + i\sin\phi$, is needed here.

7. In Sec. 102, give details showing how the substitution (6) transforms inequality (5) into inequality (7).

103.   ORTHOGONALITY OF LEGENDRE POLYNOMIALS

Let $X(x)$ denote the dependent variable in Legendre's equation, with arbitrary λ:

$$(1 - x^2)X''(x) - 2xX'(x) + \lambda X(x) = 0.$$

Writing this equation in the form

$$(1) \qquad\qquad [(1 - x^2)X'(x)]' + \lambda X(x) = 0,$$

we see that we have a special case of the Sturm-Liouville differential equation

$$(2) \qquad\qquad [r(x)X'(x)]' + [q(x) + \lambda p(x)]X(x) = 0,$$

where

$$p(x) = 1, \quad q(x) = 0, \quad \text{and} \quad r(x) = 1 - x^2.$$

The function $r(x)$ vanishes at $x = \pm 1$; thus, as already pointed out in Example 2, Sec. 68, equation (1), without boundary conditions, is a singular Sturm-Liouville problem on the closed interval $-1 \leq x \leq 1$, where X and X' are required to be continuous on that interval.

   The following theorem provides us with all the solutions of problem (1).

   Theorem. *The eigenvalues and corresponding eigenfunctions of the singular Sturm-Liouville problem*

$$(3) \qquad\qquad [(1 - x^2)X'(x)]' + \lambda X(x) = 0 \qquad\qquad (-1 < x < 1)$$

are

$$(4) \qquad\qquad \lambda_n = n(n + 1), \qquad X_n = P_n(x) \qquad (n = 0, 1, 2, \ldots),$$

where $P_n(x)$ are the Legendre polynomials. The set $\{P_n(x)\}$ $(n = 0, 1, 2, \ldots)$ is, moreover, orthogonal on the interval $-1 < x < 1$, with weight function unity.

   We start the proof by recalling from Sec. 99 that $P_n(x)$ and $Q_n(x)$ are linearly independent solutions of equation (3) when λ has any one of the values

$$\lambda_n = n(n + 1) \qquad\qquad (n = 0, 1, 2, \ldots).$$

Since the polynomial $P_n(x)$ and its derivative are continuous on the entire interval $-1 \le x \le 1$ and since this is not true of the Legendre function $Q_n(x)$, it is clear that the continuity requirements on X and X' are met only when X is a constant multiple of $P_n(x)$. Hence the λ_n and X_n in the statement of the theorem are, in fact, eigenvalues and eigenfunctions. It remains to show that there are no other eigenvalues.

To accomplish this, we first observe that since the eigenfunctions just noted all correspond to different eigenvalues, the set $\{P_n(x)\}$ $(n = 0, 1, 2, \ldots)$ is, in fact, orthogonal on the interval $-1 < x < 1$, with weight function $p(x) = 1$. (See Theorem 1 in Sec. 69.) That is,

$$(5) \qquad \int_{-1}^{1} P_m(x) P_n(x) \, dx = 0 \qquad (m \ne n).$$

In the notation used for inner products, property (5) reads $(P_m, P_n) = 0$ $(m \ne n)$. Later (Sec. 105) there will be a theorem telling us that if a function f is piecewise smooth on the interval $-1 < x < 1$, then the generalized Fourier series for f with respect to the orthonormal set of functions

$$(6) \qquad \phi_n(x) = \frac{P_n(x)}{\|P_n\|} \qquad (n = 0, 1, 2, \ldots)$$

converges to $f(x)$ at all but possibly a finite number of points in the interval $-1 < x < 1$. The set $\{\phi_n(x)\}$ is, therefore, closed (Sec. 62) in the function space $C_p'(-1, 1)$, defined in Sec. 9. That is, there is no function in $C_p'(-1, 1)$, with positive norm, that is orthogonal to each of the functions (6).

Suppose now that λ is another eigenvalue, different from those listed in the statement of the theorem, and let X denote an eigenfunction corresponding to λ. Because of the orthogonality of eigenfunctions corresponding to distinct eigenvalues, $(X, \phi_n) = 0$ $(n = 0, 1, 2, \ldots)$ where the functions ϕ_n are those in equation (6). But the fact that $\{\phi_n(x)\}$ is closed requires that X, which is continuous on the entire interval $-1 \le x \le 1$, have value zero for each x in that interval. Consequently, since an eigenfunction cannot be identically equal to zero, X is not an eigenfunction. In view of this contradiction, there are no other eigenvalues; and the proof of the theorem is finished.

If the interval $0 \le x \le 1$, rather than $-1 \le x \le 1$, is used, the differential equation (1) along with either one of the boundary conditions $X'(0) = 0$, $X(0) = 0$ is also a singular Sturm-Liouville problem (Sec. 68).

Corollary. *The eigenvalues and corresponding eigenfunctions of the singular Sturm-Liouville problem consisting of the differential equation*

$$(7) \qquad [(1 - x^2) X'(x)]' + \lambda X(x) = 0 \qquad (0 < x < 1)$$

and the boundary condition $X'(0) = 0$ are

$$(8) \qquad \lambda_n = 2n(2n + 1), \qquad X_n = P_{2n}(x) \qquad (n = 0, 1, 2, \ldots).$$

If the condition $X(0) = 0$ is used instead, the eigenvalues and eigenfunctions are

$$(9) \qquad \lambda_n = (2n + 1)(2n + 2), \qquad X_n = P_{2n+1}(x) \qquad (n = 0, 1, 2, \ldots).$$

The sets $\{P_{2n}(x)\}$ $(n = 0, 1, 2, \ldots)$ and $\{P_{2n+1}(x)\}$ $(n = 0, 1, 2, \ldots)$ are, in addition, orthogonal on the interval $0 < x < 1$, with weight function unity.

To see how these solutions arise, we consider first the solutions in the theorem when the condition $X'(0) = 0$ is imposed on them. Since $P_n'(0) = 0$ only when n is even (Problem 3, Sec. 99), it follows that the polynomials $P_{2n+1}(x)$ ($n = 0, 1, 2, \ldots$) must be eliminated. This leaves the eigenvalues and eigenfunctions (8). If, on the other hand, the condition $X(0) = 0$ is imposed, the fact that $P_n(0) = 0$ only when n is an odd integer leads us to the eigenvalues and eigenfunctions (9).

Theorem 1 in Sec. 69, regarding the orthogonality of eigenfunctions, ensures the orthogonality stated in the above corollary:

$$(10) \qquad \int_0^1 P_{2m}(x)P_{2n}(x)\,dx = 0 \qquad\qquad (m \neq n)$$

and

$$(11) \qquad \int_0^1 P_{2m+1}(x)P_{2n+1}(x)\,dx = 0 \qquad\qquad (m \neq n),$$

where $m = 0, 1, 2, \ldots$ and $n = 0, 1, 2, \ldots$. Valid representations of piecewise smooth functions on the interval $0 < x < 1$ will follow (Sec. 105) from representations on the interval $-1 < x < 1$ in terms of the set $\{P_n(x)\}$ ($n = 0, 1, 2, \ldots$), just as Fourier cosine and sine series follow from Fourier series involving both cosines and sines. Hence the same argument, involving closed sets, that was used in the proof of the theorem above can be used to show that there are no other eigenvalues of the Sturm-Liouville problems in the corollary.

104. NORMALIZED LEGENDRE POLYNOMIALS

We saw in Sec. 103 that the set $P_n(x)$ ($n = 0, 1, 2, \ldots$) of Legendre polynomials is orthogonal on the interval $-1 < x < 1$ with weight function unity. We also saw that the sets $P_{2n}(x)$ ($n = 0, 1, 2, \ldots$) and $P_{2n+1}(x)$ ($n = 0, 1, 2, \ldots$) are orthogonal on the interval $0 < x < 1$ with that same weight function. In this section, we shall normalize (Sec. 60) these polynomials and present the results as a theorem. This will enable us to find the coefficients in various series expansions involving Legendre polynomials.

Theorem. *In each of the following cases, the weight function is unity.*

(a) *The set*

$$\phi_n(x) = \sqrt{\frac{2n+1}{2}}\,P_n(x) \qquad\qquad (n = 0, 1, 2, \ldots)$$

is orthonormal on the interval $-1 < x < 1$.

(b) *The set*

$$\phi_n(x) = \sqrt{4n+1}\,P_{2n}(x) \qquad\qquad (n = 0, 1, 2, \ldots)$$

is orthonormal on the interval $0 < x < 1$.

(c) *The set*

$$\phi_n(x) = \sqrt{4n+3}\,P_{2n+1}(x) \qquad\qquad (n = 0, 1, 2, \ldots)$$

is orthonormal on the interval $0 < x < 1$.

In order to verify statement (a) in the theorem, we need to find the norms

$$\|P_n\| = (P_n, P_n)^{1/2} = \left\{ \int_{-1}^{1} [P_n(x)]^2 \, dx \right\}^{1/2} \qquad (n = 0, 1, 2, \ldots).$$

We do this with the aid of the recurrence relations

(1) $$(n+1)P_{n+1}(x) + nP_{n-1}(x) = (2n+1)xP_n(x) \qquad (n = 1, 2, \ldots).$$

obtained in Example 2, Sec. 101, and

(2) $$nP_n(x) + (n-1)P_{n-2}(x) = (2n-1)xP_{n-1}(x) \qquad (n = 2, 3, \ldots),$$

which is found by replacing n by $n-1$ in relation (1). Because

$$(P_{n+1}, P_{n-1}) = 0 \qquad \text{and} \qquad (P_{n-2}, P_n) = 0.$$

it follows from relations (1) and (2) that

(3) $$\frac{n(P_{n-1}, P_{n-1})}{(2n+1)} = (xP_n, P_{n-1})$$

and

(4) $$\frac{n(P_n, P_n)}{(2n-1)} = (xP_{n-1}, P_n).$$

The integrals representing (xP_n, P_{n-1}) and (xP_{n-1}, P_n) are identical, and we need only equate the left-hand sides equations (3) and (4) to see that

$$(2n+1)(P_n, P_n) = (2n-1)(P_{n-1}, P_{n-1}),$$

or

(5) $$(2n+1)\|P_n\|^2 = (2n-1)\|P_{n-1}\|^2 \qquad (n = 2, 3, \ldots).$$

It is easy to verify directly that equation (5) is also valid in the case $n = 1$, involving $P_1(x) = x$ and $P_0(x) = 1$.

Next, we let n be any fixed positive integer and use equation (5) to write the following n equations:

$$(2n+1)\|P_n\|^2 = (2n-1)\|P_{n-1}\|^2,$$
$$(2n-1)\|P_{n-1}\|^2 = (2n-3)\|P_{n-2}\|^2,$$
$$\vdots$$
$$(5)\|P_2\|^2 = (3)\|P_1\|^2,$$
$$(3)\|P_1\|^2 = (1)\|P_0\|^2.$$

Setting the product of the left-hand sides of these equations equal to the product of their right-hand sides and then canceling appropriately, we arrive at the result

$$(2n+1)\|P_n\|^2 = \|P_0\|^2 \qquad (n = 1, 2, \ldots).$$

Since $\|P_0\|^2 = 2$, this means that

(6) $$\|P_n\| = \sqrt{\frac{2}{2n+1}} \qquad (n = 0, 1, 2, \ldots).$$

The set of polynomials

$$(7) \qquad \phi_n(x) = \frac{P_n(x)}{\|P_n\|} = \sqrt{\frac{2n+1}{2}} \, P_n(x) \qquad (n = 0, 1, 2, \ldots)$$

is, therefore, orthonormal on the interval $-1 < x < 1$, as stated in part (a) of the theorem.

As for part (b), we need to evaluate

$$\|P_{2n}\|^2 = \int_0^1 [P_{2n}(x)]^2 \, dx = \frac{1}{2} \int_{-1}^1 [P_{2n}(x)]^2 \, dx.$$

Since this last integral represents the square of a norm in part (a), the norm (6) tells us that

$$\|P_{2n}\|^2 = \frac{1}{2} \cdot \frac{2}{4n+1} = \frac{1}{4n+1};$$

and the orthonormal set is

$$(8) \qquad \phi_n(x) = \frac{P_{2n}(x)}{\|P_{2n}\|} = \sqrt{4n+1} \, P_{2n}(x). \qquad (n = 0, 1, 2, \ldots).$$

Finally, in part (c) we must find

$$\|P_{2n+1}\|^2 = \int_0^1 [P_{2n+1}(x)]^2 \, dx = \frac{1}{2} \int_{-1}^1 [P_{2n+1}(x)]^2 \, dx.$$

Since this last integral also represents the square of a norm in part (a), we know from the norm (6) that

$$\|P_{2n+1}\|^2 = \frac{1}{2} \cdot \frac{2}{4n+3} = \frac{1}{4n+3}.$$

So

$$(9) \qquad \phi_n(x) = \frac{P_{2n+1}(x)}{\|P_{2n+1}\|} = \sqrt{4n+3} \, P_{2n+1}(x) \qquad (n = 0, 1, 2, \ldots),$$

and the proof of the theorem is complete.

105. LEGENDRE SERIES

The theorem in Sec. 104 gave us three different orthonormal sets involving Legendre polynomials. In this section, we apply the theory of generalized Fourier series to those sets and arrive at three different types of *Legendre series* that will be useful in the applications. We recall from Sec. 62 that for a given function f and orthonormal set $\phi_n(x)$ $(n = 0, 1, 2, \ldots)$, defined on an interval $a < x < b$ and with weight function unity, the coefficients c_n in a generalized Fourier series correspondence

$$(1) \qquad f(x) \sim \sum_{n=0}^{\infty} c_n \, \phi_n(x) \qquad (a < x < b)$$

are

$$(2) \qquad c_n = (f, \phi_n) = \int_a^b f(x) \phi_n(x) \, dx \qquad (n = 0, 1, 2, \ldots).$$

The three cases (a), (b), and (c) in the following theorem use the three cases (a), (b), and (c), respectively, in the theorem of Sec. 104.

Theorem 1. *Let f be piecewise continuous on the indicated interval.*

(a) If A_n ($n = 0, 1, 2, \ldots$) are the coefficients in the correspondence

$$f(x) \sim \sum_{n=0}^{\infty} A_n P_n(x) \qquad (-1 < x < 1),$$

then

$$A_n = \frac{2n+1}{2} \int_{-1}^{1} f(x) P_n(x) \, dx \qquad (n = 0, 1, 2, \ldots).$$

(b) If A_{2n} ($n = 0, 1, 2, \ldots$) are the coefficients in the correspondence

$$f(x) \sim \sum_{n=0}^{\infty} A_{2n} P_{2n}(x) \qquad (0 < x < 1),$$

then

$$A_{2n} = (4n + 1) \int_{0}^{1} f(x) P_{2n}(x) \, dx \qquad (n = 0, 1, 2, \ldots).$$

(c) If A_{2n+1} ($n = 0, 1, 2, \ldots$) are the coefficients in the correspondence

$$f(x) \sim \sum_{n=0}^{\infty} A_{2n+1} P_{2n+1}(x) \qquad (0 < x < 1),$$

then

$$A_{2n+1} = (4n + 3) \int_{0}^{1} f(x) P_{2n+1}(x) \, dx \qquad (n = 0, 1, 2, \ldots).$$

To prove part (*a*) of this theorem, we recall from the theorem in Sec. 104 that the set

$$\phi_n(x) = \sqrt{\frac{2n+1}{2}}\, P_n(x) \qquad (n = 0, 1, 2, \ldots)$$

is orthonormal on the interval $-1 < x < 1$ and then use expressions (1) and (2) to write

$$f(x) \sim \sum_{n=0}^{\infty} c_n \sqrt{\frac{2n+1}{2}}\, P_n(x) \qquad (-1 < x < 1)$$

where

$$c_n = \sqrt{\frac{2n+1}{2}} \int_{-1}^{1} f(x) P_n(x) \, dx \qquad (n = 0, 1, 2, \ldots).$$

Part (*a*) here now follows by writing

$$A_n = c_n \sqrt{\frac{2n+1}{2}} \qquad (n = 0, 1, 2, \ldots).$$

The result in part (*b*) also follows from the theorem in Sec. 104, which tells us that the set

$$\phi_n(x) = \sqrt{4n+1}\, P_{2n}(x) \qquad (n = 0, 1, 2, \ldots)$$

is orthonormal on the interval $0 < x < 1$. Thus

$$f(x) \sim \sum_{n=0}^{\infty} C_n \sqrt{4n+1}\, P_{2n}(x) \qquad (0 < x < 1),$$

where

$$C_n = \sqrt{4n+1} \int_0^1 f(x) P_{2n}(x)\, dx.$$

Putting $A_{2n} = C_n \sqrt{4n+1}$ $(n = 0, 1, 2, \ldots)$, we arrive at the result in part (b) here.

Part (c) of this theorem can be verified in a similar way, and details are left to the problems.

We state here, without proof, a representation theorem involving Legendre series that is applicable to piecewise smooth functions.[†]

Theorem 2. *Let f denote a function that is piecewise smooth on the interval $-1 < x < 1$, and suppose that $f(x)$ at each point of discontinuity of f in that interval is defined as the mean value of the one-sided limits $f(x+)$ and $f(x-)$. Then*

$$(3) \qquad\qquad f(x) = \sum_{n=0}^{\infty} A_n P_n(x) \qquad (-1 < x < 1),$$

where the coefficients A_n are given in part (a) of Theorem 1.

Obvious adaptations of this theorem to the series in parts (b) and (c) of Theorem 1 can also be made when f is piecewise smooth on the interval $0 < x < 1$.

EXAMPLE. Let us expand the function $f(x) = 1$ $(0 < x < 1)$ in a series of Legendre polynomials of odd degree. According to part (c) of Theorem 1,

$$1 = \sum_{n=0}^{\infty} A_{2n+1} P_{2n+1}(x) \qquad (0 < x < 1)$$

where

$$A_{2n+1} = (4n+3) \int_0^1 P_{2n+1}(x)\, dx \qquad (n = 0, 1, 2, \ldots).$$

The integral here is readily evaluated with the aid of the integration formula (Problem 1, Sec. 102)

$$\int_a^1 P_n(x)\, dx = \frac{1}{2n+1} [P_{n-1}(a) - P_{n+1}(a)] \qquad (n = 1, 2, \ldots),$$

which tells us that

$$(4) \qquad\qquad A_{2n+1} = P_{2n}(0) - P_{2n+2}(0).$$

[†]The proof, which is rather lengthy, can be found in, for example, the book by Kreider, Kuller, Ostberg, and Perkins (1966, pp. 425–432), listed in the Bibliography. A simplified proof of a special case of the theorem appears in the book by Rainville (1972, pp. 177–179), also listed there.

Thus,

$$1 = \sum_{n=0}^{\infty} \left[P_{2n}(0) - P_{2n+2}(0) \right] P_{2n+1}(x) \qquad (5) \qquad (0 < x < 1).$$

Since [Problem 3(a), Sec. 99]

$$P_{2n}(0) = (-1)^n \frac{(2n)!}{2^{2n}(n!)^2} \qquad (n = 0, 1, 2, \ldots),$$

the coefficients (4) can also be written

$$A_{2n+1} = (-1)^n \frac{4n+3}{n+1} \cdot \frac{(2n)!}{2^{2n+1}(n!)^2}. \qquad (6)$$

This alternative form of representation (5) is then obtained:

$$1 = \sum_{n=0}^{\infty} (-1)^n \frac{4n+3}{n+1} \cdot \frac{(2n)!}{2^{2n+1}(n!)^2} P_{2n+1}(x) \qquad (0 < x < 1).$$

PROBLEMS

1. From the orthogonality of the set $\{P_n(x)\}$, state why

(a) $\int_{-1}^{1} P_n(x)\, dx = 0 \ (n = 1, 2, \ldots)$;

(b) $\int_{-1}^{1} (Ax + B) P_n(x)\, dx = 0 \ (n = 2, 3, \ldots)$, where A and B are constants.

2. Verify directly that the Legendre polynomials

$$P_0(x) = 1, \qquad P_1(x) = x, \qquad P_2(x) = \frac{1}{2}(3x^2 - 1), \qquad P_3(x) = \frac{1}{2}(5x^3 - 3x)$$

form an orthogonal set with weight function unity on the interval $-1 < x < 1$. Show that their graphs are as indicated in Fig. 74 (Sec. 99).

3. Let F denote the odd extension of the function $f(x) = 1 \ (0 < x < 1)$ to the interval $-1 < x < 1$, where $F(0) = 0$. Also, let g be the function defined by means of the equations

$$g(x) = \begin{cases} 0 & \text{when } -1 < x < 0, \\ 1 & \text{when } \ \ 0 < x < 1, \end{cases}$$

and $g(0) = 1/2$. Then, by observing that

$$g(x) = \frac{1}{2} + \frac{1}{2} F(x) \qquad (-1 < x < 1)$$

and referring to expansion (5), Sec. 105, show that

$$g(x) = \frac{1}{2} P_0(x) + \frac{1}{2} \sum_{n=0}^{\infty} \left[P_{2n}(0) - P_{2n+2}(0) \right] P_{2n+1}(x) \qquad (-1 < x < 1).$$

4. Let f denote the function defined by means of the equations

$$f(x) = \begin{cases} 0 & \text{when } -1 < x \le 0, \\ x & \text{when } \ \ 0 < x < 1. \end{cases}$$

(a) State why $f(x)$ is represented by its Legendre series (3), Sec. 105, at each point of the interval $-1 < x < 1$.

(b) Show that $A_{2n+1} = 0$ $(n = 1, 2, \ldots)$ in the series in part (a).

(c) Find the first four nonzero terms of the series in part (a) to show that

$$f(x) = \frac{1}{4}P_0(x) + \frac{1}{2}P_1(x) + \frac{5}{16}P_2(x) - \frac{3}{32}P_4(x) + \cdots \qquad (-1 < x < 1).$$

5. Show that for all x,

(a) $x^2 = \dfrac{1}{3}P_0(x) + \dfrac{2}{3}P_2(x);$ (b) $x^3 = \dfrac{3}{5}P_1(x) + \dfrac{2}{5}P_3(x).$

6. Obtain the first three nonzero terms in the series of Legendre polynomials of even degree representing the function $f(x) = x$ $(0 < x < 1)$ to show that

$$x = \frac{1}{2}P_0(x) + \frac{5}{8}P_2(x) - \frac{3}{16}P_4(x) + \cdots \qquad (0 < x < 1).$$

Point out why this expansion remains valid when $x = 0$, and state what function the series represents on the interval $-1 < x < 1$.

7. Give details showing how part (c) of Theorem 1 in Sec. 105 follows from part (c) of the theorem in Sec. 104.

8. Let f be piecewise continuous on the interval $-1 < x < 1$. Show that

(a) if f is even, so that $f(-x) = f(x)$, the Legendre series in part (a) of Theorem 1 in Sec. 105 becomes the series in part (b) of that theorem;

(b) if f is odd, so that $f(-x) = -f(x)$, the Legendre series in part (a) of the same theorem in Sec. 105 becomes the series in part (c) of that theorem.

      Suggestion: Recall from Sec. 99 that each $P_{2n}(x)$ is even and that each $P_{2n+1}(x)$ is odd.

9. By applying Theorem 1 in Sec. 65 to the Fourier constants used in proving part (a) of Theorem 1 in Sec. 105, state why

$$\lim_{n \to \infty} \sqrt{2n+1} \int_{-1}^{1} f(x) P_n(x)\, dx = 0$$

when f is piecewise continuous on the interval $-1 < x < 1$.

10. (a) By recalling that $P_m(x)$ is a polynomial of degree m containing only the powers $x^m, x^{m-2}, x^{m-4}, \ldots$ of x (Sec. 99), state why

$$x^m = c\,P_m(x) + c_{m-2}x^{m-2} + c_{m-4}x^{m-4} + \cdots,$$

where the coefficients are constants. Apply the same argument to x^{m-2}, etc., to conclude that x^m is a finite linear combination of the polynomials

$$P_m(x),\ P_{m-2}(x),\ P_{m-4}(x), \ldots.$$

(b) With the aid of the result in part (a), point out why

$$\int_{-1}^{1} P_n(x) p(x)\, dx = 0,$$

where $P_n(x)$ is a Legendre polynomial of degree n $(n = 1, 2, \ldots)$ and $p(x)$ is any polynomial whose degree is less than n.

11. Let n have any one of the values $n = 1, 2, \ldots$.

(a) By recalling the result in Problem 1(a), state why $P_n(x)$ must change sign at least once in the open interval $-1 < x < 1$. Then let $x_1, x_2, \ldots, x_k$ denote the totality of distinct points in that interval at which $P_n(x)$ changes sign. Since any polynomial of degree n has at most n distinct zeros, we know that $1 \le k \le n$.

(b) Assume that the number of points $x_1, x_2, \ldots, x_k$ in part (a) is such that $k < n$, and consider the polynomial

$$p(x) = (x - x_1)(x - x_2) \cdots (x - x_k).$$

Use the result in Problem 10(b) to show that the integral

$$\int_{-1}^{1} P_n(x) p(x) \, dx$$

has value zero. Then, after noting that $P_n(x)$ and $p(x)$ change sign at precisely the same points in the interval $-1 < x < 1$, state why the value of the integral cannot be zero. Having reached this contradiction, conclude that $k = n$ and hence that *the zeros of a Legendre polynomial $P_n(x)$ are all real and distinct and lie in the open interval $-1 < x < 1$.*

12. Show in the following way that for each value of n $(n = 0, 1, 2, \ldots)$, the Legendre function of the second kind $Q_n(x)$ (Sec. 99) and its derivative $Q_n'(x)$ fail to be a pair of continuous functions on the closed interval $-1 \le x \le 1$. Suppose that there is an integer N such that $Q_N(x)$ and $Q_N'(x)$ are continuous on that interval. The functions $Q_N(x)$ and $P_n(x)$ $(n \ne N)$ are then eigenfunctions corresponding to different eigenvalues of the singular Sturm-Liouville problem (1), Sec. 103. Point out how it follows that

$$\int_{-1}^{1} Q_N(x) P_n(x) \, dx = 0 \qquad\qquad (n \ne N),$$

and then use Theorem 2 in Sec. 105 to show that $Q_N(x) = A_N P_N(x)$, where A_N is some constant. This is, however, impossible since $P_N(x)$ and $Q_N(x)$ are linearly independent.

106.   THE EIGENFUNCTIONS $P_n(\cos\theta)$

The boundary value problems to be treated in Secs. 107 and 108 will involve singular Sturm-Liouville problems whose eigenfunctions are

$$P_n(\cos\theta) \qquad\qquad (n = 0, 1, 2, \ldots).$$

In this section, we give some modifications of earlier results involving

$$P_n(x) \qquad\qquad (n = 0, 1, 2, \ldots)$$

that will apply to those trigonometric eigenfunctions.

Theorem 1. *Let*

(1)
$$\frac{d}{d\theta}\left(\sin\theta \, \frac{d\Theta}{d\theta} \right) + \lambda \sin\theta \, \Theta = 0$$

be the differential equation in the singular Sturm-Liouville problem involving one of the three cases below. The eigenvalues λ_n and corresponding eigenfunctions Θ_n are as follows:

(a)   *when the interval is $0 \le \theta \le \pi$ and no boundary condition is used,*

$$\lambda_n = n(n+1), \qquad \Theta_n = P_n(\cos\theta) \qquad\qquad (n = 0, 1, 2, \ldots);$$

(b)   when the interval is $0 \leq \theta \leq \pi/2$ and the boundary condition $\Theta'(\pi/2) = 0$ is used,

$$\lambda_n = 2n(2n+1), \qquad \Theta_n = P_{2n}(\cos\theta) \qquad\qquad (n = 0, 1, 2, \ldots);$$

(c)   when the interval is $0 \leq \theta \leq \pi/2$ and the boundary condition $\Theta(\pi/2)=0$ is used,

$$\lambda_n = (2n+1)(2n+2), \qquad \Theta_n = P_{2n+1}(\cos\theta) \qquad\qquad (n = 0, 1, 2, \ldots).$$

The fact that the problem in each of the three cases in this theorem actually involves a singular Sturm-Liouville problem, where Θ and Θ' are required to be continuous on the stated interval, is readily established by referring to Sec. 68.

As for the proof of the theorem, the relation $x = \cos\theta$ enables us to write

$$\frac{d\Theta}{d\theta} = \frac{d\Theta}{dx}\frac{dx}{d\theta} = -\frac{d\Theta}{dx}\sin\theta,$$

or

$$\frac{1}{\sin\theta}\frac{d\Theta}{d\theta} = -\frac{d\Theta}{dx}.$$

Consequently,

$$\sin\theta\,\frac{d\Theta}{d\theta} = (1 - \cos^2\theta)\left(\frac{1}{\sin\theta}\frac{d\Theta}{d\theta}\right) = -(1 - x^2)\frac{d\Theta}{dx};$$

and so

$$\frac{1}{\sin\theta}\frac{d}{d\theta}\left(\sin\theta\,\frac{d\Theta}{d\theta}\right) = \frac{1}{\sin\theta}\frac{d}{dx}\left[-(1 - x^2)\frac{d\Theta}{dx}\right]\frac{dx}{d\theta} = \frac{d}{dx}\left[(1 - x^2)\frac{d\Theta}{dx}\right].$$

Equation (1) thus becomes

$$(2) \qquad\qquad \frac{d}{dx}\left[(1 - x^2)\frac{d\Theta}{dx}\right] + \lambda\Theta = 0,$$

which, except for notation, is Legendre's equation (1) in Sec. 103. It is now evident that under the transformation $x = \cos\theta$, the above theorem is simply an alternative form of the theorem and its corollary in Sec. 103.

The next theorem is just a restatement of Theorem 1 in Sec. 105 regarding Legendre series.

Theorem 2. *Let F be piecewise continuous on the interval stated in each part below.*

(a)   *If A_n $(n = 0, 1, 2, \ldots)$ are the coefficients in the correspondence*

$$F(\theta) \sim \sum_{n=0}^{\infty} A_n P_n(\cos\theta) \qquad\qquad (0 < \theta < \pi),$$

then

$$A_n = \frac{2n+1}{2}\int_0^\pi F(\theta)\,P_n(\cos\theta)\sin\theta\,d\theta \qquad\qquad (n = 0, 1, 2, \ldots).$$

(b) If A_{2n} $(n = 0, 1, 2, \ldots)$ are the coefficients in the correspondence

$$F(\theta) \sim \sum_{n=0}^{\infty} A_{2n} P_{2n}(\cos \theta) \qquad \left(0 < \theta < \frac{\pi}{2}\right),$$

then

$$A_{2n} = (4n + 1) \int_0^{\pi/2} F(\theta) P_{2n}(\cos \theta) \sin \theta \, d\theta \qquad (n = 0, 1, 2, \ldots).$$

(c) If A_{2n+1} $(n = 0, 1, 2, \ldots)$ are the coefficients in the correspondence

$$F(\theta) \sim \sum_{n=0}^{\infty} A_{2n+1} P_{2n+1}(\cos \theta) \qquad \left(0 < \theta < \frac{\pi}{2}\right),$$

then

$$A_{2n+1} = (4n + 3) \int_0^{\pi/2} F(\theta) P_{2n+1}(\cos \theta) \sin \theta \, d\theta \qquad (n = 0, 1, 2, \ldots).$$

To verify this theorem, one need only write $x = \cos \theta$ and define the function

(3)
$$f(x) = F(\cos^{-1} x),$$

where the principal values of the inverse cosine function are to be taken. When this $f(x)$ is used in Theorem 1 of Sec. 105, that theorem becomes Theorem 2 here. If F is piecewise smooth on the stated interval, the correspondence is, of course, an equality for each point θ at which F is continuous.

107. DIRICHLET PROBLEMS IN SPHERICAL REGIONS

For our first application of Legendre series, we shall determine the harmonic function u in the region $r < c$ such that u assumes prescribed values $F(\theta)$ on the spherical surface $r = c$. Here r, ϕ, and θ are spherical coordinates, and u is independent of ϕ. Thus $u = u(r, \theta)$ satisfies Laplace's equation (Sec. 24)

(1)
$$r \frac{\partial^2}{\partial r^2} (ru) + \frac{1}{\sin \theta} \frac{\partial}{\partial \theta} \left(\sin \theta \frac{\partial u}{\partial \theta} \right) = 0 \qquad (r < c, 0 < \theta < \pi)$$

and the condition (Fig. 75)

(2)
$$u(c, \theta) = F(\theta) \qquad (0 < \theta < \pi).$$

The function u and its partial derivatives of the first and second order are to be continuous throughout the interior $0 \le r < c, 0 \le \theta \le \pi$ of the sphere.

Physically, the function u may denote steady temperatures in a solid sphere $r \le c$ whose surface temperatures depend only on θ; that is, the surface temperatures are uniform over each circle $r = c, \theta = \theta_0$. Also, u represents electrostatic potential in the space $r < c$, which is free of charges, when $u = F(\theta)$ on the boundary $r = c$.

We start by seeking a product solution $u = R(r)\Theta(\theta)$ of the homogeneous equation (1) that satisfies the stated continuity requirements. Separation of

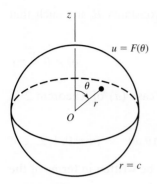

FIGURE 75

variables shows that for some constant λ,

$$\frac{1}{\sin\theta\,\Theta}\frac{d}{d\theta}\left(\sin\theta\,\frac{d\Theta}{d\theta}\right)=-\frac{r}{R}\frac{d^2}{dr^2}(rR)=-\lambda.$$

Consequently, R must satisfy the ordinary differential equation

$$(3)\qquad\qquad\qquad r\frac{d^2}{dr^2}(rR)-\lambda R=0\qquad\qquad\qquad (r<c)$$

and be continuous when $0\le r<c$. Also, for the same constant λ, the function Θ satisfies the equation

$$(4)\qquad\qquad\frac{d}{d\theta}\left(\sin\theta\,\frac{d\Theta}{d\theta}\right)+\lambda\sin\theta\,\Theta=0\qquad\qquad (0<\theta<\pi),$$

where Θ and Θ' are to be continuous on the closed interval $0\le\theta\le\pi$.

Case (a) of Theorem 1 in Sec. 106 tells us that equation (4) is a singular Sturm-Liouville problem whose eigenvalues and corresponding eigenfunctions are

$$(5)\qquad\qquad \lambda_n=n(n+1),\qquad \Theta_n=P_n(\cos\theta)\qquad (n=0,1,2,\ldots).$$

Writing equation (3) in the form

$$r^2R''+2rR'-\lambda R=0,$$

we see that it is a Cauchy-Euler equation, which reduces to a differential equation with constant coefficients after the substitution $r=\exp s$ is made (see Problem 1, Sec. 44). When $\lambda=n(n+1)$, its general solution is

$$(6)\qquad\qquad R(r)=C_1 r^n+C_2 r^{-n-1}=C_1 r^n+\frac{C_2}{r^{n+1}}\qquad (0<r<c),$$

as is easily verified. The continuity of R at $r=0$ requires that $C_2=0$, and so the desired functions of r are $R_n(r)=r^n$ $(n=0,1,2,\ldots)$.

The functions $u_n=r^n P_n(\cos\theta)$ $(n=0,1,2,\ldots)$, therefore, satisfy Laplace's equation (1) and the continuity conditions accompanying it. Formally, their generalized linear combination

$$(7)\qquad\qquad u(r,\theta)=\sum_{n=0}^{\infty}B_n r^n P_n(\cos\theta)$$

is a solution of our boundary value problem if the constants B_n are such that $u(c, \theta) = F(\theta)$, or

$$(8) \qquad\qquad F(\theta) = \sum_{n=0}^{\infty} B_n c^n P_n(\cos \theta) \qquad\qquad (0 < \theta < \pi).$$

To find these constants, we need only refer to case (a) of Theorem 2 in Sec. 106. Evidently, $B_n c^n = A_n$ where

$$(9) \qquad\qquad A_n = \frac{2n+1}{2} \int_0^{\pi} F(\theta) P_n(\cos \theta) \sin \theta \, d\theta \qquad (n = 0, 1, 2, \ldots);$$

and the formal solution of our Dirichlet problem can be written in terms of the constants (9) as

$$(10) \qquad\qquad u(r, \theta) = \sum_{n=0}^{\infty} A_n \left(\frac{r}{c}\right)^n P_n(\cos \theta) \qquad\qquad (r \le c).$$

Note that *the harmonic function u in the unbounded region $r > c$*, exterior to the spherical surface $r = c$, which assumes the values $F(\theta)$ on that surface and is bounded as $r \to \infty$ can be found in like manner. Here $C_1 = 0$ in our solution (6) of equation (3) if R is to remain bounded as $r \to \infty$; and the solutions of equation (1) are

$$u_n = \frac{1}{r^{n+1}} P_n(\cos \theta) \qquad\qquad (n = 0, 1, 2, \ldots).$$

Thus,

$$(11) \qquad\qquad u(r, \theta) = \sum_{n=0}^{\infty} \frac{B_n}{r^{n+1}} P_n(\cos \theta) \qquad\qquad (r \ge c),$$

where the B_n are this time related to the constants (9) by means of the equation $A_n = B_n/c^{n+1}$. That is,

$$(12) \qquad\qquad u(r, \theta) = \sum_{n=0}^{\infty} A_n \left(\frac{c}{r}\right)^{n+1} P_n(\cos \theta) \qquad\qquad (r \ge c).$$

PROBLEMS

1. Suppose that u is harmonic throughout the regions $r < c$ and $r > c$, that $u \to 0$ as $r \to \infty$, and that $u = 1$ on the spherical surface $r = c$. Show from results found in Sec. 107 that $u = 1$ when $r \le c$ and $u = c/r$ when $r > c$.

2. Suppose that for all ϕ, the steady temperatures $u(r, \theta)$ in a solid sphere $r \le 1$ are such that $u(1, \theta) = F(\theta)$ where

$$F(\theta) = \begin{cases} 1 & \text{when } 0 < \theta < \dfrac{\pi}{2}, \\ 0 & \text{when } \dfrac{\pi}{2} < \theta < \pi. \end{cases}$$

Derive the expression

$$u(r, \theta) = \frac{1}{2} + \frac{1}{2} \sum_{n=0}^{\infty} [P_{2n}(0) - P_{2n+2}(0)] r^{2n+1} P_{2n+1}(\cos \theta)$$

for those temperatures.

3. Let $u(r, \theta)$ denote steady temperatures in a hollow sphere $a \leq r \leq b$ when

$$u(a, \theta) = F(\theta) \quad \text{and} \quad u(b, \theta) = 0 \qquad (0 < \theta < \pi).$$

Derive the expression

$$u(r, \theta) = \sum_{n=0}^{\infty} A_n \frac{b^{2n+1} - r^{2n+1}}{b^{2n+1} - a^{2n+1}} \left(\frac{a}{r}\right)^{n+1} P_n(\cos \theta),$$

where

$$A_n = \frac{2n+1}{2} \int_0^\pi F(\theta) P_n(\cos \theta) \sin \theta \, d\theta \qquad (n = 0, 1, 2 \ldots).$$

4. Let $u(x, t)$ represent the temperatures in a nonhomogeneous insulated bar $-1 \leq x \leq 1$ along the x axis, and suppose that the thermal conductivity is proportional to $1 - x^2$. The heat equation takes the form

$$\frac{\partial u}{\partial t} = b \frac{\partial}{\partial x}\left[(1 - x^2)\frac{\partial u}{\partial x}\right] \qquad (b > 0).$$

Here b is constant since we assume that the product of the physical constants σ and δ used in Sec. 22 and in Problem 2, Sec. 23, is constant. Note that the ends $x = \pm 1$ are insulated because the conductivity vanishes there. Assuming that

$$u(x, 0) = f(x) \qquad (-1 < x < 1),$$

derive the expression

$$u(x, t) = \sum_{n=0}^{\infty} A_n \exp\left[-n(n + 1)bt\right] P_n(x),$$

where

$$A_n = \frac{2n+1}{2} \int_{-1}^1 f(x) P_n(x) \, dx \qquad (n = 0, 1, 2 \ldots).$$

5. Show that if $f(x) = x^2$ $(-1 < x < 1)$ in Problem 4, then

$$u(x, t) = \frac{1}{3} + \left(x^2 - \frac{1}{3}\right) \exp(-6bt).$$

6. Give a physical interpretation of the following boundary value problem in spherical coordinates for a harmonic function $u(r, \theta)$:

$$r \frac{\partial^2}{\partial r^2}(ru) + \frac{1}{\sin \theta} \frac{\partial}{\partial \theta}\left(\sin \theta \frac{\partial u}{\partial \theta}\right) = 0 \qquad (1 < r < b, \theta_1 < \theta < \theta_2),$$

$$u(1, \theta) = 0, \qquad u(b, \theta) = 0,$$
$$u(r, \theta_1) = f(r), \qquad u(r, \theta_2) = 0,$$

where $0 < \theta_1 < \theta_2 < \pi$. Then, using the normalized eigenfunctions found in Problem 11(b), Sec. 72, and the functions p_α and q_α in Problem 5, Sec. 99, derive the expression

$$u(r, \theta) = \frac{1}{\sqrt{r}} \sum_{n=1}^{\infty} B_n \frac{F_n(\theta)}{F_n(\theta_1)} \sin(\alpha_n \ln r),$$

where

$$\alpha_n = \frac{n\pi}{\ln b}, \qquad B_n = \frac{2}{\ln b} \int_1^b \frac{f(r)}{\sqrt{r}} \sin(\alpha_n \ln r) \, dr,$$

and

$$F_n(\theta) = p_{\alpha_n}(\cos \theta) \, q_{\alpha_n}(\cos \theta_2) - p_{\alpha_n}(\cos \theta_2) \, q_{\alpha_n}(\cos \theta).$$

108.   STEADY TEMPERATURES IN A HEMISPHERE

In this section, we consider two steady temperature problems for a solid hemisphere $r \le 1, 0 \le \theta \le \pi/2$ of radius unity. They will illustrate the use of cases (b) and (c) in Theorems 1 and 2 in Sec. 106. In each problem, the temperatures $u(r, \theta)$ will satisfy Laplace's equation

$$(1) \qquad r \frac{\partial^2}{\partial r^2}(ru) + \frac{1}{\sin \theta} \frac{\partial}{\partial \theta} \left(\sin \theta \frac{\partial u}{\partial \theta} \right) = 0 \qquad \left(r < 1, 0 < \theta < \frac{\pi}{2} \right),$$

which leads to the ordinary differential equations

$$(2) \qquad r \frac{d^2}{dr^2}(r R) - \lambda R = 0 \qquad\qquad (r < 1)$$

and

$$(3) \qquad \frac{d}{d\theta} \left(\sin \theta \frac{d\Theta}{d\theta} \right) + \lambda \sin \theta \Theta = 0 \qquad \left(0 < \theta < \frac{\pi}{2} \right)$$

when $u = R(r)\Theta(\theta)$ and λ is a separation constant.

EXAMPLE 1. Suppose that the base $r < 1, \theta = \pi/2$ of the hemisphere is kept at temperature $u = 0$ and that the hemispherical surface $r = 1, 0 < \theta < \pi/2$ is maintained at temperature $u = 1$ (Fig. 76). In order to solve this boundary value problem, we need the boundary condition

$$(4) \qquad\qquad u\left(r, \frac{\pi}{2}\right) = 0 \qquad\qquad (0 < r < 1)$$

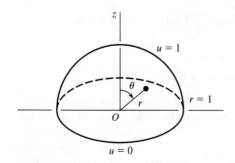

FIGURE 76

and

(5) $$u(1, \theta) = 1 \qquad \left(0 < \theta < \frac{\pi}{2}\right).$$

The homogeneous condition (4) tells us that

(6) $$\Theta\left(\frac{\pi}{2}\right) = 0.$$

When case (c) of Theorem 1 in Sec. 106 is applied to equations (3) and (6), we have the eigenvalues and eigenfunctions

$$\lambda_n = (2n + 1)(2n + 2), \qquad \Theta_n = P_{2n+1}(\cos\theta) \qquad (n = 0, 1, 2, \ldots).$$

Next, let us substitute λ_n into equation (2) and write the result as

$$r^2 R'' + 2r R' - (2n + 1)(2n + 2) R = 0.$$

The general solution of this Cauchy-Euler equation is

$$R(r) = C_1 r^{2n+1} + \frac{C_2}{r^{2n+2}} \qquad (0 < r < 1),$$

and $C_2 = 0$ since $R(r)$ is to be continuous at $r = 0$. Hence, one can write

$$R_n = r^{2n+1} \qquad (n = 0, 1, 2, \ldots)$$

and then, by the principle of superposition,

(7) $$u(r, \theta) = \sum_{n=0}^{\infty} A_{2n+1} r^{2n+1} P_{2n+1}(\cos\theta).$$

Finally we set $r = 1$ in series (7) and use boundary condition (5):

(8) $$1 = \sum_{n=0}^{\infty} A_{2n+1} P_{2n+1}(\cos\theta) \qquad \left(0 < \theta < \frac{\pi}{2}\right).$$

Although we could refer to case (c) in Theorem 2 in Sec. 106, we can at this point simply refer to the example in Sec. 105, where we saw that

$$1 = \sum_{n=0}^{\infty}(-1)^n \frac{4n + 3}{n + 1} \cdot \frac{(2n)!}{2^{2n+1}(n!)^2} P_{2n+1}(x) \qquad (0 < x < 1).$$

If we put $x = \cos\theta$ here, we find that the coefficients in series (8) are

$$A_{2n+1} = (-1)^n \frac{4n + 3}{n + 1} \cdot \frac{(2n)!}{2^{2n+1}(n!)^2} \qquad (n = 0, 1, 2, \ldots).$$

The formal solution of our boundary value problem is, therefore,

(9) $$u(r, \theta) = \sum_{n=0}^{\infty}(-1)^n \frac{4n + 3}{n + 1} \cdot \frac{(2n)!}{2^{2n+1}(n!)^2} r^{2n+1} P_{2n+1}(\cos\theta).$$

EXAMPLE 2. Here the base of the hemisphere is insulated, and the flux of heat inward through the hemispherical surface $r = 1, 0 < \theta < \pi/2$ is kept at prescribed values $F(\theta)$. The boundary value problem for steady temperatures $u(r, \theta)$ in the hemisphere consists of Laplace's equation (1) and the condition of

FIGURE 77

insulation (see Problem 8, Sec. 27)

$$(10) \qquad\qquad u_\theta\left(r, \frac{\pi}{2}\right) = 0 \qquad\qquad (0 < r < 1)$$

at the base, part of which is shown in Fig. 77, and the flux condition (see Sec. 26)

$$(11) \qquad\qquad K u_r(1, \theta) = F(\theta) \qquad\qquad \left(0 < \theta < \frac{\pi}{2}\right),$$

where K is thermal conductivity. In order that temperatures be steady, we assume that the values $F(\theta)$ are such that the resultant rate of flow through the hemispherical surface is zero. That is,

$$(12) \qquad\qquad \int_0^{\pi/2} F(\theta)\, 2\pi \sin\theta\, d\theta = 0.$$

Also, we assume that F is piecewise smooth on the interval $0 < \theta < \pi/2$ and that u satisfies the usual continuity conditions when $0 \le r < 1$ and $0 \le \theta \le \pi/2$.

Writing $u = R(r)\Theta(\theta)$ and separating variables in equation (1), we obtain equation (2), where R must be continuous when $0 \le r < 1$, and equation (3), where Θ and Θ' are to be continuous when $0 \le \theta \le \pi/2$. Also, it follows from condition (10) that

$$(13) \qquad\qquad \Theta'\left(\frac{\pi}{2}\right) = 0.$$

From case (b) in Theorem 1, Sec. 106, we know that the singular Sturm Liouville problem consisting of equations (3) and (13) has eigenvalues and corresponding eigenfunctions

$$\lambda_n = 2n(2n + 1), \qquad \Theta_n = P_{2n}(\cos\theta) \qquad (n = 0, 1, 2, \ldots).$$

When $\lambda = \lambda_n$, equation (5) is the Cauchy-Euler equation

$$r^2 R'' + 2r R' - 2n(2n + 1)R = 0,$$

whose solutions that are continous at $r = 0$ are constant multiples of $R_n = r^{2n}$.

Formally, then,

$$u(r, \theta) = \sum_{n=0}^{\infty} B_n \, r^{2n} \, P_{2n}(\cos \theta)$$

if the constants B_n are such that condition (11) is satisfied. That condition requires that

$$(14) \qquad F(\theta) = \sum_{n=1}^{\infty} (2nK B_n) \, P_{2n}(\cos \theta) \qquad \left(0 < \theta < \frac{\pi}{2} \right).$$

Case (b) of Theorem 2 in Sec. 106 tells us that this is a valid Legendre series representation if $2nK B_n = A_{2n}$, where

$$(15) \qquad A_{2n} = (4n + 1) \int_0^{\pi/2} F(\theta) P_{2n}(\cos \theta) \sin \theta \, d\theta \qquad (n = 1, 2, \ldots),$$

and if F is such that the condition $A_0 = 0$, which is the same as condition (12), is satisfied. Thus B_0 *is left arbitrary*, and

$$(16) \qquad u(r, \theta) = B_0 + \frac{1}{2K} \sum_{n=1}^{\infty} \frac{1}{n} A_{2n} \, r^{2n} \, P_{2n}(\cos \theta) \qquad \left(r \leq 1, 0 \leq \theta \leq \frac{\pi}{2} \right)$$

where the coefficients A_{2n} have the values (15).

The constant B_0 is the temperature at the origin $r = 0$. Solutions of such problems with just Neumann conditions (Sec. 31) are determined only up to such an arbitrary additive constant because all the boundary conditions prescribe only values of derivatives of the harmonic functions.

PROBLEMS

1. The base $r < c, \theta = \pi/2$ of a solid hemisphere $r \leq c, 0 \leq \theta \leq \pi/2$ is insulated. The temperature distribution on the hemispherical surface is $u = F(\theta)$. Derive the expression

$$u(r, \theta) = \sum_{n=0}^{\infty} A_{2n} \left(\frac{r}{c} \right)^{2n} P_{2n}(\cos \theta),$$

   where

$$A_{2n} = (4n + 1) \int_0^{\pi/2} F(\theta) P_{2n}(\cos \theta) \sin \theta \, d\theta \qquad (n = 0, 1, 2, \ldots),$$

   for the steady temperatures in the solid. Also, show that $u(r, \theta) = 1$ when $F(\theta) = 1$.

2. A function u is harmonic and bounded in the unbounded region $r > c, 0 \leq \theta < \pi/2$. Also, $u = 0$ everywhere on the flat boundary surface $r > c, \theta = \pi/2$; and $u = F(\theta)$ on the hemispherical boundary surface $r = c, 0 < \theta < \pi/2$. Derive the expression

$$u(r, \theta) = \sum_{n=0}^{\infty} A_{2n+1} \left(\frac{c}{r} \right)^{2n+2} P_{2n+1}(\cos \theta),$$

   where

$$A_{2n+1} = (4n + 3) \int_0^{\pi/2} F(\theta) P_{2n+1}(\cos \theta) \sin \theta \, d\theta \qquad (n = 0, 1, 2, \ldots).$$

3. The flux of heat $Ku_r(1, \theta)$ into a solid sphere at its surface $r = 1$ is a prescribed function $F(\theta)$, where F is such that the net time rate of flow of heat into the solid is zero. Thus, (see Example 2 in Sec. 108)

$$\int_0^\pi F(\theta)\, 2\pi \sin \theta \, d\theta = 0.$$

Assuming that $u = 0$ at the center $r = 0$, derive the expression

$$u(r, \theta) = \frac{1}{K} \sum_{n=1}^\infty \frac{1}{n} A_n\, r^n\, P_n(\cos \theta),$$

where

$$A_n = \frac{2n+1}{2} \int_0^\pi F(\theta)\, P_n(\cos \theta) \sin \theta \, d\theta \qquad (n = 0, 1, 2, \ldots),$$

for the steady temperatures throughout the entire sphere $0 \le r \le 1$.

4. Heat is generated at a steady and uniform rate throughout the interior of a solid hemisphere $0 \le r \le 1, 0 \le \theta \le \pi/2$, and the entire surface is kept at temperature zero. Thus the steady temperatures $u = u(r, \theta)$ satisfy the nonhomogeneous differential equation

$$\frac{1}{r}\frac{\partial^2}{\partial r^2}(ru) + \frac{1}{r^2 \sin \theta}\frac{\partial}{\partial \theta}\left(\sin \theta \frac{\partial u}{\partial \theta}\right) + q_0 = 0 \qquad \left(0 < r < 1, 0 < \theta < \frac{\pi}{2}\right)$$

and the boundary conditions

$$u(1, \theta) = 0, \qquad u\left(r, \frac{\pi}{2}\right) = 0.$$

Also, $u(r, \theta)$ is continuous at $r = 0$. Point out how Example 1 in Sec. 108 suggests seeking a solution of the form

$$u(r, \theta) = \sum_{n=0}^\infty B_n(r)\, P_{2n+1}(\cos \theta)$$

and applying the method of variation of parameters, which was first used in Sec. 42. Follow the steps below to find the solution by that method.

(a) Observe how it follows immediately from case (c) in Theorem 1, Sec. 106, that

$$\frac{1}{\sin \theta}\frac{d}{d\theta}\left[\sin \theta \frac{d}{d\theta} P_{2n+1}(\cos \theta)\right] = -(2n+1)(2n+2)\, P_{2n+1}(\cos \theta)$$

$$(n = 0, 1, 2, \ldots).$$

Then, with the aid of this identity and expansion (5), Sec. 105, obtain the initial value problem

$$r^2 B_n''(r) + 2r B_n'(r) - (2n+1)(2n+2)B_n(r) = -q_0 A_{2n+1}\, r^2, \qquad B_n(1) = 0$$

$$(n = 0, 1, 2, \ldots),$$

where $A_{2n+1} = P_{2n}(0) - P_{2n+2}(0)$ and where $B_n(r)$ is to be continuous on the interval $0 \le r \le 1$.

(b) Solve the differential equation in part (a) by adding a particular solution of it to the general solution of the complementary equation (compare with Problem 2, Sec. 46). Then apply the required conditions on $B_n(r)$, stated in part (a), to complete the solution of the initial value problem in ordinary differential equations there. Thus arrive at the desired temperature function:

$$u(r, \theta) = \frac{q_0}{2} \sum_{n=0}^{\infty} \frac{P_{2n}(0) - P_{2n+2}(0)}{(2n-1)(n+2)} (r^2 - r^{2n+1}) \, P_{2n+1}(\cos\theta).$$

Suggestion: Observe that the differential equation in part (*a*) has a particular solution of the form $B_n(r) = ar^2$, where a is a constant. Also, note that the complementary equation in part (*b*) is of Cauchy-Euler type, and solve it by the method described in Problem 1, Sec. 44.

5. Verify expression (12) in Sec. 108, regarding the resultant rate of flow through the hemispherical surface $r = 1, 0 < \theta < \pi/2$ in Example 2 in that section.

   Suggestion: Use the fact that the horizontal distance from the z axis to a point on the hemispherical surface is $\sin\theta$, as shown in Fig. 77.

CHAPTER
11

VERIFICATION
OF SOLUTIONS
AND UNIQUENESS

In this chapter, we examine in some detail the question of verifying solutions of boundary value problems. Careful verifications of the solutions of the two boundary value problems solved in Chap. 4, where the Fourier method was introduced, will be made. More precisely, the solutions found for the temperature problem in Sec. 36 and the vibrating string problem in Sec. 37 will be verified.

We shall also consider the question of establishing that a solution of a given problem is the only possible solution. A multiplicity of solutions may actually arise when the statement of the problem does not demand adequate continuity or boundedness of a solution and its derivatives. This was illustrated in Problem 7, Sec. 58.

We begin the chapter with an important theorem that enables us to establish uniform convergence of solutions obtained in the form of series and is often useful in both verifying such a solution and proving that it is unique.

109. ABEL'S TEST FOR UNIFORM CONVERGENCE

We start here with some needed background on uniform convergence. Let $s_n(x)$ denote the sum of the first n terms of a series

$$(1) \qquad \sum_{i=1}^{\infty} X_i(x)$$

of functions $X_i(x)$ that converges to a sum $s(x)$:

$$(2) \qquad s_n(x) = \sum_{i=1}^{n} X_i(x), \qquad s(x) = \lim_{n \to \infty} s_n(x).$$

Suppose that the series converges *uniformly* with respect to x for all x in some set. Then (see Sec. 17), for each positive number ε, there exists a positive integer n_ε, independent of x, such that

(3) $$|s(x) - s_n(x)| < \varepsilon \qquad\qquad \text{whenever } n > n_\varepsilon$$

for every x in the set. The following lemma, known as the *Cauchy criterion*, provides us with an alternative characterization of uniform convergence.

Lemma. *A necessary and sufficient condition for the uniform convergence of series* (1) *on a given set is that for each positive number ε, there exists a positive integer n_ε, independent of x, such that for all points x in the set and all positive integers j,*

(4) $$|s_{n+j}(x) - s_n(x)| < \varepsilon \qquad\qquad \text{whenever } n > n_\varepsilon.$$

To verify the necessity of condition (4), we assume that condition (3) is satisfied and let j denote any positive integer. Since

$$|s_{n+j} - s_n| = |(s_{n+j} - s) + (s - s_n)| \le |s - s_{n+j}| + |s - s_n|,$$

we find that

$$|s_{n+j} - s_n| < 2\varepsilon \qquad\qquad \text{whenever } n > n_\varepsilon;$$

and since ε is an arbitrary positive number, this is the same as statement (4).

To show that condition (4) is also sufficient for uniform convergence, we assume that condition (4) holds and recall from calculus that it is sufficient for the pointwise convergence of series (1). Hence it implies that the sum $s(x)$, defined by means of the second of equations (2), exists. Keeping n fixed in inequality (4) and letting j tend to infinity, we now have the inequality

$$|s(x) - s_n(x)| \le \varepsilon \qquad\qquad \text{whenever } n > n_\varepsilon$$

if x is in the set. That is, since ε is arbitrary, series (1) converges uniformly.

Note that x here may equally well denote elements $(x_1, x_2, \ldots, x_N)$ of some set in N-dimensional space. The uniform convergence is then with respect to all N variables $x_1, x_2, \ldots, x_N$ together.

We now derive a test for the uniform convergence of infinite series whose terms are products of certain types of functions. Its application in verifying formal solutions of boundary value problems will be illustrated in Sec. 110. The test, known as *Abel's test*,[†] involves functions in a sequence $T_i(t)$ $(i = 1, 2, \ldots)$ which is *uniformly bounded* for all points t in an interval. That is, there exists a positive constant M, independent of i, such that

(5) $$|T_i(t)| < M \qquad\qquad (i = 1, 2, \ldots)$$

for all t in the interval. The sequence is, moreover, *monotonic with respect to i*. Thus, for every t in the interval, either

(6) $$T_{i+1}(t) \le T_i(t) \qquad\qquad (i = 1, 2, \ldots)$$

[†]Niels Henrik Abel (1802–1829), Norwegian, pronounced *ah-bel'*.

or

(7) $$T_{i+1}(t) \geq T_i(t) \qquad\qquad (i = 1, 2, \ldots).$$

We state the test as a theorem which shows that when the terms of a uniformly convergent series are multiplied by functions $T_i(t)$ of the type just described, the new series is also uniformly convergent.

Theorem. *The series*

(8) $$\sum_{i=1}^{\infty} X_i(x) T_i(t)$$

converges uniformly with respect to the two variables x and t together in a region R of the xt plane if the following two conditions are satisfied:

(i) *the series*

$$\sum_{i=1}^{\infty} X_i(x)$$

converges uniformly with respect to x for all x such that (x, t) is in R;

(ii) *the functions $T_i(t)$ are uniformly bounded and monotonic with respect to i $(i = 1, 2, \ldots)$ for all t such that (x, t) is in R.*

To start the proof, we let S_n denote partial sums of series (8):

$$S_n(x, t) = \sum_{i=1}^{n} X_i(x) T_i(t).$$

In view of the lemma above, the uniform convergence of that series will be established if we prove that to each positive number ε there corresponds a positive integer n_ε, independent of x and t, such that

$$|S_m(x, t) - S_n(x, t)| < \varepsilon \qquad\qquad \text{whenever } n > n_\varepsilon,$$

for all integers $m = n + 1, n + 2, \ldots$ and for all points (x, t) in R.

We write the partial sum

$$s_n(x) = X_1(x) + X_2(x) + \cdots + X_n(x).$$

Then, for each pair of integers m and n $(m > n)$,

$$
\begin{aligned}
S_m - S_n &= X_{n+1} T_{n+1} + X_{n+2} T_{n+2} + \cdots + X_m T_m \\
&= (s_{n+1} - s_n) T_{n+1} + (s_{n+2} - s_{n+1}) T_{n+2} + \cdots + (s_m - s_{m-1}) T_m \\
&= (s_{n+1} - s_n) T_{n+1} + (s_{n+2} - s_n) T_{n+2} - (s_{n+1} - s_n) T_{n+2} \\
&\quad + \cdots + (s_m - s_n) T_m - (s_{m-1} - s_n) T_m.
\end{aligned}
$$

By pairing alternate terms here, we find that

(9) $$
\begin{aligned}
S_m - S_n &= (s_{n+1} - s_n)(T_{n+1} - T_{n+2}) + (s_{n+2} - s_n)(T_{n+2} - T_{n+3}) \\
&\quad + \cdots + (s_{m-1} - s_n)(T_{m-1} - T_m) + (s_m - s_n) T_m.
\end{aligned}
$$

Suppose now that the functions T_i are nonincreasing with respect to i, so that they satisfy condition (6), and that they also satisfy the uniform boundedness condition (5). Then the factors $T_{n+1} - T_{n+2}, T_{n+2} - T_{n+3}$, etc., in equation (9) are nonnegative, and $|T_i(t)| < M$. Since the series with terms $X_i(x)$ converges uniformly, an integer n_ε exists such that

$$|s_{n+j}(x) - s_n(x)| < \frac{\varepsilon}{3M} \qquad\qquad \text{whenever } n > n_\varepsilon,$$

for all positive integers j, where ε is any given positive number and n_ε is independent of x. Then if $n > n_\varepsilon$ and $m > n$, it follows from equation (9) that

$$|S_m - S_n| < \frac{\varepsilon}{3M} \left[(T_{n+1} - T_{n+2}) + (T_{n+2} - T_{n+3}) + \cdots + |T_m| \right]$$

$$= \frac{\varepsilon}{3M} (T_{n+1} - T_m + |T_m|) \leq \frac{\varepsilon}{3M} (|T_{n+1}| + 2|T_m|).$$

Hence,

$$|S_m(x, t) - S_n(x, t)| < \varepsilon \qquad\qquad \text{whenever } m > n > n_\varepsilon;$$

and the uniform convergence of series (8) is established.

The proof is similar when the functions T_i are nondecreasing with respect to i.

When x is kept fixed, the series with terms X_i is a series of constants; and the only requirement placed on it is that it be convergent. Then the theorem shows that when T_i are bounded and monotonic, the series of terms $X_i T_i(t)$ is uniformly convergent with respect to t.

Extensions of the theorem to cases in which X_i are functions of x and t, or both X_i and T_i are functions of several variables, become evident when it is observed that our proof rests on the uniform convergence of the series of terms X_i and the bounded monotonic nature of the functions T_i.

110. VERIFICATION OF SOLUTION OF TEMPERATURE PROBLEM

We turn now to the full verification of the solution of the temperature problem

$$(1) \qquad\qquad u_t(x, t) = ku_{xx}(x, t) \qquad\qquad (0 < x < c, t > 0),$$

$$(2) \qquad\qquad u_x(0, t) = 0, \qquad u_x(c, t) = 0 \qquad\qquad (t > 0),$$

$$(3) \qquad\qquad u(x, 0) = f(x) \qquad\qquad (0 < x < c)$$

that was obtained in Sec. 36. We recall from Example 1 in Sec. 34 that the continuous functions

$$(4) \qquad u_0 = 1, \qquad u_n = \exp\left(-\frac{n^2\pi^2 k}{c^2} t \right) \cos \frac{n\pi x}{c} \qquad (n = 1, 2, \ldots)$$

satisfy the homogeneous conditions (1) and (2). In that example, the superposition theorem in Sec. 33 was, moreover, used to show how the generalized linear combination

$$(5) \qquad u = A_0 u_0 + \sum_{n=1}^{\infty} A_n u_n$$

formally satisfies conditions (1) and (2). Expression (5), when written as

$$(6) \qquad u(x, t) = A_0 + \sum_{n=1}^{\infty} A_n \exp\left(-\frac{n^2\pi^2 k}{c^2} t\right) \cos\frac{n\pi x}{c},$$

then gave us the formal solution of the boundary value problem when its coefficients were assigned the values (see Sec. 36)

$$(7) \qquad A_0 = \frac{1}{c} \int_0^c f(x)\, dx, \qquad A_n = \frac{2}{c} \int_0^c f(x) \cos\frac{n\pi x}{c}\, dx \qquad (n = 1, 2, \ldots).$$

We assume here that f is piecewise smooth (Sec. 9) on $0 < x < c$. Also, at a point of discontinuity of f in that interval, we define $f(x)$ as the mean value of the one-sided limits $f(x+)$ and $f(x-)$. Note how it follows from expressions (7) that

$$|A_0| \leq \frac{1}{c} \int_0^c |f(x)|\, dx, \qquad |A_n| \leq \frac{2}{c} \int_0^c |f(x)|\, dx \qquad (n = 1, 2, \ldots)$$

and hence that there is a positive constant M, independent of n, such that

$$(8) \qquad |A_n| \leq M \qquad (n = 0, 1, 2, \ldots).$$

We begin our verification by showing that series (5), with coefficients (7), actually converges in the region $0 \leq x \leq c, t > 0$ of the xt plane and that it satisfies the homogeneous conditions (1) and (2). To accomplish this, we first note from expressions (4) and inequalities (8) that if t_0 is a fixed positive number,

$$(9) \qquad |A_n u_n| \leq M \exp\left(-\frac{n^2\pi^2 k}{c^2} t_0\right) \qquad (n = 0, 1, 2, \ldots)$$

whenever $0 \leq x \leq c$ and $t \geq t_0$ (Fig. 78). An application of the ratio test shows that the series

$$(10) \qquad \sum_{n=0}^{\infty} n^i \exp\left(-\frac{n^2\pi^2 k}{c^2} t_0\right)$$

of constants converges when i is any nonnegative integer and, in particular, when $i = 0$. So we know from the comparison and absolute convergence tests that the series (5) converges when $0 \leq x \leq c, t \geq t_0$. One can use series (10) and the Weierstrass M-test (Sec. 17) to show that the series

$$(11) \qquad \sum_{n=0}^{\infty} (A_n u_n)_x, \qquad \sum_{n=0}^{\infty} (A_n u_n)_{xx}$$

FIGURE 78

of derivatives converge uniformly on the interval $0 \leq x \leq c$ for any fixed t ($t \geq t_0$). Likewise, the series

$$(12) \qquad \sum_{n=0}^{\infty} (A_n u_n)_t$$

converges uniformly on the semi-infinite interval $t \geq t_0$ for any fixed x ($0 \leq x \leq c$).

The uniformity of the convergence of these series ensures that series (5) is differentiable twice with respect to x and once with respect to t, provided that $0 \leq x \leq c, t \geq t_0$. Consequently, if we write

$$L = k \frac{\partial^2}{\partial x^2} - \frac{\partial}{\partial t}$$

and note that $Lu_n = 0$ ($n = 0, 1, 2, \ldots$), it follows from the superposition theorem in Sec. 33 that $Lu = 0$ when $0 \leq x \leq c, t \geq t_0$. Thus series (5) converges and satisfies the heat equation (1) in the domain $0 < x < c, t > 0$ since the positive number t_0 can be chosen arbitrarily small.

Writing $L = \partial/\partial x$ and again using the theorem in Sec. 33, we see that series (5) also satisfies boundary conditions (2). Observe that since the first of series (11) is uniformly convergent on the interval $0 \leq x \leq c$ for any fixed t ($t \geq t_0$), the derivative $u_x(x, t)$ of series (5) is *continuous* in x on that interval. Hence the one-sided limits

$$u_x(0+, t) = \lim_{\substack{x \to 0 \\ x > 0}} u_x(x, t), \qquad u_x(c-, t) = \lim_{\substack{x \to c \\ x < c}} u_x(x, t)$$

at the endpoints of the interval $0 \leq x \leq c$ ($t \geq t_0$) exist and have the values $u_x(0, t)$ and $u_x(c, t)$, respectively. Since conditions (2) are satisfied and since t_0 can be chosen arbitrarily small, then,

$$(13) \qquad u_x(0+, t) = 0, \qquad u_x(c-, t) = 0 \qquad (t > 0).$$

In seeking solutions of boundary value problems, we tacitly require that those solutions satisfy such continuity conditions at boundary points. Thus, when conditions (2) are part of a boundary value problem, it is understood that conditions (13) must also be satisfied. As we have just seen, series (5) has that property.

The nonhomogeneous condition (3) is clearly satisfied by our solution since series (6) reduces to the Fourier cosine series

$$(14) \qquad A_0 + \sum_{n=1}^{\infty} A_n \cos \frac{n\pi x}{c} \qquad (0 < x < c)$$

for f when $t = 0$; and Theorem 2 in Sec. 15 ensures that series (14) converges to $f(x)$ when $0 < x < c$.

It remains to show that

$$(15) \qquad u(x, 0+) = f(x) \qquad (0 < x < c).$$

This is a continuity requirement that must be satisfied when $t = 0$, just as conditions (13) must hold on the faces $x = 0$ and $x = c$. One can show that solution (6) has this property by appealing to Abel's test in Sec. 109. According to that test, the series formed by multiplying the terms of a convergent series of constants, such as series (14) with x fixed, by corresponding terms of a bounded sequence of functions of t whose values never increase with n, such as

$$\exp\left(-\frac{n^2\pi^2 k}{c^2} t\right) \qquad (n = 0, 1, 2, \ldots),$$

is uniformly convergent with respect to t. So, for any fixed x $(0 < x < c)$, the series in expression (6) converges uniformly with respect to t when $t \geq 0$ and thus represents a function that is continuous in t $(t \geq 0)$. This shows that our solution $u(x, t)$ is continuous in t when $t \geq 0$, in particular when $t = 0$. That is,

$$\lim_{\substack{t \to 0 \\ t > 0}} u(x, t) = u(x, 0),$$

or $u(x, 0+) = u(x, 0)$, for each fixed x $(0 < x < c)$. Property (15) now follows from the fact that $u(x, 0) = f(x)$ $(0 < x < c)$. This completes the verification that the function (6), with coefficients (7), is a solution of the boundary value problem (1)–(3).

111. UNIQUENESS OF SOLUTIONS OF THE HEAT EQUATION

Let D denote the domain consisting of all points interior to a closed surface S; and let $\bar{D}$ be the *closure* of that domain, consisting of all points in D and all points on S. We assume always that the closed surface S is *piecewise smooth*. That is, it is a continuous surface consisting of a finite number of parts over each of which the outward unit normal vector exists and varies continuously from point to point. Then if U is a function of x, y, and z which is continuous in $\bar{D}$, together with its partial derivatives of the first and second order, a special case of Green's identity that we shall need here states that

$$(1) \qquad \iint_S U \frac{dU}{dn}\, dA = \iiint_D (U \nabla^2 U + U_x^2 + U_y^2 + U_z^2)\, dV.$$

Here dA is the area element on S, the symbol dV represents $dx\,dy\,dz$, and dU/dn is the derivative in the direction of the outward unit vector normal to S.[†]

Consider a homogeneous solid whose interior is the domain D and whose temperatures at time t are denoted by $u(x, y, z, t)$. A fairly general problem in heat conduction is the following:

$$(2) \qquad u_t = k\nabla^2 u + q(x, y, z, t) \qquad\qquad [(x, y, z) \text{ in } D, t > 0],$$

$$(3) \qquad u(x, y, z, 0) = f(x, y, z) \qquad\qquad [(x, y, z) \text{ in } \overline{D}],$$

$$(4) \qquad u = g(x, y, z, t) \qquad\qquad [(x, y, z) \text{ on } S, t \geq 0].$$

This is the problem of determining temperatures in a body, with prescribed initial temperatures $f(x, y, z)$ and surface temperatures $g(x, y, z, t)$, interior to which heat may be generated continuously at a rate per unit volume proportional to $q(x, y, z, t)$.

Suppose that the problem has two solutions

$$u = u_1(x, y, z, t), \qquad u = u_2(x, y, z, t)$$

where both u_1 and u_2 are continuous functions in the closed region $\overline{D}$ when $t \geq 0$, while their derivatives of the first order with respect to t and of the first and second order with respect to x, y, and z are continuous in $\overline{D}$ when $t > 0$. Since u_1 and u_2 satisfy the linear equations (2), (3), and (4), their difference

$$U(x, y, z, t) = u_1(x, y, z, t) - u_2(x, y, z, t)$$

satisfies the homogeneous problem

$$(5) \qquad\qquad U_t = k\nabla^2 U \qquad\qquad [(x, y, z) \text{ in } D, t > 0],$$

$$(6) \qquad\qquad U(x, y, z, 0) = 0 \qquad\qquad [(x, y, z) \text{ in } \overline{D}],$$

$$(7) \qquad\qquad U = 0 \qquad\qquad [(x, y, z) \text{ on } S, t \geq 0].$$

Moreover, U and its derivatives have the continuity properties of u_1 and u_2 assumed above.

We shall now show that $U = 0$ in D when $t > 0$, so that the two solutions u_1 and u_2 are identical. That is, not more than one solution of the boundary value problem in u can exist if the solution is required to satisfy the stated continuity conditions.

The continuity of U with respect to x, y, z, and t together in the closed region $\overline{D}$ when $t \geq 0$ implies that the integral

$$(8) \qquad\qquad I(t) = \frac{1}{2} \iiint_D [U(x, y, z, t)]^2 \, dV$$

[†]Identity (1) is found by applying Gauss's divergence theorem to the vector field $U \operatorname{grad} U$. See the book by Taylor and Mann (1983, pp. 492–493), listed in the Bibliography.

is a continuous function of t when $t \geq 0$; and, according to equation (6), $I(0) = 0$. Also, in view of the continuity of U_t when $t > 0$, we may use equation (5) to write

$$I'(t) = \iiint_D U U_t \, dV = k \iiint_D U \nabla^2 U \, dV \qquad (t > 0).$$

Identity (1) applies to the last integral here because of the continuity of the derivatives of U when $t > 0$. Thus,

$$(9) \qquad \iiint_D U \nabla^2 U \, dV = \iint_S U \frac{du}{dn} \, dA - \iiint_D \left(U_x^2 + U_y^2 + U_z^2 \right) dV$$

when $t > 0$. But $U = 0$ on S, and $k > 0$; consequently,

$$I'(t) = -k \iiint_D \left(U_x^2 + U_y^2 + U_z^2 \right) dV \leq 0.$$

The mean value theorem for derivatives applies to $I(t)$. That is, for each positive t, a number t_1 $(0 < t_1 < t)$ exists such that

$$I(t) - I(0) = t I'(t_1);$$

and since $I(0) = 0$ and $I'(t_1) \leq 0$, it follows that $I(t) \leq 0$. However, definition (8) of the integral shows that $I(t) \geq 0$. Therefore,

$$I(t) = 0 \qquad\qquad (t \geq 0);$$

and so the nonnegative integrand U^2 cannot have a positive value at any point in D. For if it did, the continuity of U^2 would require that U^2 be positive throughout some neighborhood of the point, and that would mean $I(t) > 0$. Consequently,

$$U(x, y, z, t) = 0 \qquad\qquad [(x, y, z) \text{ in } \overline{D}, t \geq 0];$$

and we arrive at the following theorem on uniqueness.

Theorem 1. *Let a function $u = u(x, y, z, t)$ satisfy these conditions of regularity:*

(i)   *it is a continuous function of the variables x, y, z, and t together when the point (x, y, z) is in the closure $\overline{D}$ of a given domain D and $t \geq 0$;*

(ii)   *the derivatives of u appearing in the heat equation (2) are continuous in the same sense when $t > 0$.*

If u is a solution of the boundary value problem (2)–(4), it is the only possible solution satisfying conditions (i) and (ii).

When conditions (i) and (ii) in Theorem 1 are added to the requirement that u is to satisfy the heat equation and the boundary conditions, our boundary value problem is completely stated; and u will be the only possible solution if it exists.

The condition that u be continuous in $\overline{D}$ when $t = 0$ restricts the usefulness of our theorem. It is clearly not satisfied if the initial temperature function f in condition (3) fails to be continuous throughout $\overline{D}$, or if at some point on S the initial value $g(x, y, z, 0)$ of the prescribed surface temperature differs from the value $f(x, y, z)$. The continuity requirement at $t = 0$ can be relaxed in some cases.[†]

The proof of Theorem 1 required that the integral

$$\iint_S U \frac{dU}{dn} \, dA$$

in equation (9) either vanish or have a negative value. It vanished because $U = 0$ on S. Note that it is never positive if condition (4) is replaced by the boundary condition

$$(10) \qquad\qquad \frac{du}{dn} + hu = g(x, y, z, t) \qquad\qquad [(x, y, z) \text{ on } S, t > 0]$$

where $h \geq 0$, since in that case $dU/dn = -hU$ and $U dU/dn \leq 0$ on S. Thus, our theorem can be modified as follows.

Theorem 2. *The conclusion in Theorem 1 is true if boundary condition (4) is replaced by condition (10) or if condition (4) is satisfied on part of the surface S and condition (10) is satisfied on the rest.*

EXAMPLE. In the problem of temperature distribution throughout a slab with insulated faces $x = 0$ and $x = c$ and initial temperatures $f(x)$ (Sec. 110), write $c = \pi$ and assume that f is continuous and f' is piecewise continuous on the interval $0 \leq x \leq \pi$. Then the Fourier cosine series for f converges uniformly to $f(x)$ on that interval (Sec. 17). Let $u(x, t)$ denote the sum of the series

$$(11) \qquad\qquad A_0 + \sum_{n=1}^{\infty} A_n e^{-n^2 kt} \cos nx \qquad\qquad (0 \leq x \leq \pi, t \geq 0),$$

which is the formal solution (6), Sec. 110, of the boundary value problem when $c = \pi$, the constants $2A_0$ and A_n $(n = 1, 2, \ldots)$ being the coefficients in the Fourier cosine series for f on $0 < x < \pi$.

One can see from Abel's test (Sec. 109) that series (11) converges uniformly with respect to x and t together in the region $0 \leq x \leq \pi, t \geq 0$ of the xt plane; and so u is continuous there. When $t \geq t_0$, where t_0 is any positive number, the series obtained by differentiating series (11) term by term any number of times with respect to x to t is uniformly convergent, according to the Weierstrass M-test (Sec. 17). Consequently, we now know that u satisfies all of the equations in the boundary value problem (compare with Sec. 110) and also that u_t, u_x, and u_{xx} are continuous functions in the region $0 \leq x \leq \pi, t > 0$. Thus u satisfies the regularity conditions (*i*) and (*ii*) stated in Theorem 1, and Theorem 2 applies to show that the sum $u(x, t)$ of series (11) is the only solution that satisfies those conditions.

[†]Integral transforms can sometimes be used to prove uniqueness of solutions of certain types of boundary value problems. This is illustrated in the book by Churchill (1972, Sec. 79), listed in the Bibliography.

112.   VERIFICATION OF SOLUTION OF VIBRATING STRING PROBLEM

In this section, we shall verify the formal solution that we found in Sec. 37 for the boundary value problem

$$(1) \qquad\qquad y_{tt}(x, t) = a^2 y_{xx}(x, t) \qquad\qquad (0 < x < c, t > 0),$$

$$(2) \qquad\qquad y(0, t) = 0, \qquad y(c, t) = 0,$$

$$(3) \qquad\qquad y(x, 0) = f(x), \qquad y_t(x, 0) = 0.$$

The given function f was assumed to be continuous on the interval $0 \le x \le c$; also, $f(0) = f(c) = 0$. Assuming further that f' is *at least piecewise continuous,* we know (Sec. 15) that $f(x)$ is represented by its Fourier sine series when $0 \le x \le c$. The coefficients

$$(4) \qquad\qquad B_n = \frac{2}{c} \int_0^c f(x) \sin \frac{n\pi x}{c} \, dx \qquad\qquad (n = 1, 2, \dots)$$

in that series are the ones in the series solution

$$(5) \qquad\qquad y(x, t) = \sum_{n=1}^{\infty} B_n \sin \frac{n\pi x}{c} \cos \frac{n\pi a t}{c}$$

that we obtained. So when $t = 0$, the series in expression (5) converges to $f(x)$; that is, $y(x, 0) = f(x)$ when $0 \le x \le c$.

The nature of the problem calls for a solution $y(x, t)$ that is continuous in x and t when $0 \le x \le c$ and $t \ge 0$ and is such that $y_t(x, t)$ is continuous in t at $t = 0$. Hence the prescribed boundary values in conditions (2) and (3) are also limiting values on the boundary of the domain $0 < x < c, t > 0$:

$$y(0+, t) = 0, \qquad y(c-, t) = 0 \qquad\qquad (t \ge 0),$$

$$y(x, 0+) = f(x), \qquad y_t(x, 0+) = 0 \qquad\qquad (0 \le x \le c).$$

In order to verify that series (5) represents a solution, we must prove that it converges to a continuous function $y(x, t)$ satisfying the wave equation (1) and all of the boundary conditions. But series (5), with coefficients (4), can fail to be twice differentiable with respect to x and t even when it has a sum that satisfies the wave equation. This is, in fact, the case with the solution in the example in Sec. 37, where the coefficients B_n were found to be

$$B_n = \frac{8h}{n^2 \pi^2} \sin \frac{n\pi}{2} \qquad\qquad (n = 1, 2, \dots).$$

After series (5) is differentiated twice with respect to x or t when those values of B_n are used, it is apparent that the resulting series cannot converge since its nth term does not tend to zero. The closed form of series (5) that was obtained in Sec. 45 will, however, enable us to verify our solution. That closed form was

$$(6) \qquad\qquad y(x, t) = \frac{1}{2} [F(x + at) + F(x - at)],$$

where F is the odd periodic extension of f, with period $2c$:

(7) $$F(x) = f(x) \qquad\qquad \text{when } 0 \leq x \leq c$$

and

(8) $$F(-x) = -F(x), \qquad F(x + 2c) = F(x) \qquad\qquad \text{for all } x.$$

We turn now to the verification of our solution in the form (6). From our assumption that f is continuous when $0 \leq x \leq c$ and that $f(0) = f(c) = 0$, we see that the odd periodic extension F is continuous for all x (Fig. 79). Let us also *assume that f' and f'' are continuous when $0 \leq x \leq c$ and that*

$$f''(0) = f''(c) = 0.$$

FIGURE 79

It is then easy to show that the derivatives F' and F'' are continuous everywhere. For, by recalling that $F(x) = -F(-x)$ and then applying the chain rule, one can write

$$F'(x) = -\frac{d}{dx}F(-x) = F'(-x),$$

where $F'(-x)$ denotes the derivative of F evaluated at $-x$. Thus F' is an *even* periodic function; likewise, F'' is an *odd* periodic function. Consequently, F' and F'' are continuous, as indicated in Fig. 80.

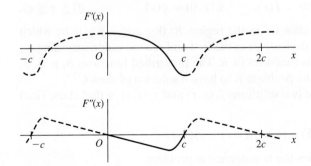

FIGURE 80

In order to show that the function (6) satisfies the wave equation (1), we need only refer to Sec. 30. It was shown there that the general solution of equation (1) has the form

$$y(x, t) = \phi(x + at) + \psi(x - at),$$

where the arbitrary functions $\phi(u)$ and $\psi(v)$ are twice differentiable. The function (6) evidently has that form. Furthermore, because F is continuous for all x, the function (6) is continuous for all x and t, in particular when $0 \le x \le c$ and $t \ge 0$.

While it is evident from series (5) that our solution $y(x, t)$ satisfies the conditions $y(0, t) = y(c, t) = 0$ and $y(x, 0) = f(x)$, expression (6) can also be used to verify this. For example, when $x = c$ in expression (6), one can write

$$F(c - at) = -F(-c + at) = -F(-c + at + 2c) = -F(c + at).$$

Therefore,

$$y(c, t) = \frac{1}{2}[F(c + at) - F(c + at)] = 0.$$

As for the final boundary condition $y_t(x, 0) = 0$, we observe that

$$y_t(x, t) = \frac{a}{2}[F'(x + at) - F'(x - at)].$$

Hence $y_t(x, 0) = 0$, and the continuity of F' ensures that $y_t(x, t)$ is continuous. The function (6) is now fully verified as a solution of the boundary value problem (1)–(3). In Sec. 113, we shall show why it is the only possible solution which, together with its derivatives of the first and second order, is continuous throughout the region $0 \le x \le c, t \ge 0$ of the xt plane.

113.   UNIQUENESS OF SOLUTIONS OF THE WAVE EQUATION

Consider the following generalization of the problem verified in Sec. 112 for the transverse displacements in a stretched string:

(1) $$y_{tt}(x, t) = a^2 y_{xx}(x, t) + \phi(x, t) \qquad (0 < x < c, t > 0),$$

(2) $$y(0, t) = p(t), \qquad y(c, t) = q(t) \qquad (t \ge 0),$$

(3) $$y(x, 0) = f(x), \qquad y_t(x, 0) = g(x) \qquad (0 \le x \le c).$$

Here we require y to be of class C^2 in the region $R: 0 \le x \le c, t \ge 0$, by which we shall mean that y and its derivatives of the first and second order, including y_{xt} and y_{tx}, are to be continuous functions in R. The prescribed functions ϕ, p, q, f, and g must be restricted if the problem is to have a solution of class C^2.

Suppose that there are two solutions $y_1(x, t)$ and $y_2(x, t)$ in that class. Then the difference

$$Y(x, t) = y_1(x, t) - y_2(x, t)$$

is of class C^2 in R and satisfies the homogeneous problem

(4) $$Y_{tt}(x, t) = a^2 Y_{xx}(x, t) \qquad (0 < x < c, t > 0),$$

(5) $$Y(0, t) = 0, \qquad Y(c, t) = 0 \qquad (t \ge 0),$$

(6) $$Y(x, 0) = 0, \qquad Y_t(x, 0) = 0 \qquad (0 \le x \le c).$$

We shall prove that $Y = 0$ throughout R; thus $y_1 = y_2$, as stated in the following theorem.

Theorem. *The boundary value problem* (1)–(3) *cannot have more than one solution of class* C^2 *in* R.

To start the proof, we note that the integrand of the integral

(7)
$$I(t) = \frac{1}{2} \int_0^c \left(Y_x^2 + \frac{1}{a^2} Y_t^2 \right) dx \qquad (t \geq 0)$$

satisfies conditions such that

(8)
$$I'(t) = \int_0^c \left(Y_x Y_{xt} + \frac{1}{a^2} Y_t Y_{tt} \right) dx.$$

Since $Y_{tt} = a^2 Y_{xx}$ and $Y_{xt} = Y_{tx}$, the integrand here can be written

$$Y_x Y_{tx} + Y_t Y_{xx} = \frac{\partial}{\partial x} (Y_x Y_t).$$

So in view of equations (5), from which it follows that

$$Y_t(0, t) = 0, \qquad Y_t(c, t) = 0,$$

one can write

(9)
$$I'(t) = Y_x(c, t) Y_t(c, t) - Y_x(0, t) Y_t(0, t) = 0.$$

Hence $I(t)$ is a constant. But equation (7) shows that $I(0) = 0$ because $Y(x, 0) = 0$, and so $Y_x(x, 0) = 0$; also, $Y_t(x, 0) = 0$. Thus $I(t) = 0$. The nonnegative continuous integrand of that integral must, therefore, vanish; that is,

$$Y_x(x, t) = Y_t(x, t) = 0 \qquad (0 \leq x \leq c, t \geq 0).$$

So Y is constant. In fact, $Y(x, t) = 0$ since $Y(x, 0) = 0$; and the proof of the theorem is complete.

If y_x, instead of y, is prescribed at the endpoint in either or both of conditions (2), the proof of uniqueness is still valid because condition (9) is again satisfied.

The requirement of continuity on derivatives of y is severe. Solutions of many simple problems involving a wave equation have discontinuities in their derivatives.

APPENDIX 1

BIBLIOGRAPHY

The following list of books and articles for supplementary study of the various topics that have been introduced is far from exhaustive. Further references are given in the ones mentioned here.

Abramowitz, M., and I. A. Stegun (Eds.): *Handbook of Mathematical Functions with Formulas, Graphs, and Mathematical Tables*, Dover Publications, Inc., New York, 1972.

Apostol, T. M.: *Mathematical Analysis* (5th ed.), Addison-Wesley Publishing Company, Inc., Reading, MA, 1981.

Arpaci, V. S.: *Conduction Heat Transfer*, Addison-Wesley Publishing Co., Inc., Reading, MA, 1966.

Articolo, G. A.: *Partial Differential Equations and Boundary Value Problems with Maple*, 2d ed., Elsevier Science & Technology Books, San Diego, CA, 2009.

Bartels, R. C. F., and R. V. Churchill: Resolution of Boundary Problems by the Use of a Generalized Convolution, *Bull. Amer. Math. Soc.*, vol. 48, pp. 276–282, 1942.

Bartle, R. G.: *The Elements of Real Analysis*, 2d ed., John Wiley & Sons, Inc., New York, 1976.

Bell, W. W.: *Special Functions for Scientists and Engineers*, Dover Publications, Inc., New York, 2004.

Berg, P. W., and J. L. McGregor: *Elementary Partial Differential Equations*, The McGraw-Hill Companies, New York, 1988.

Birkhoff, G., and G.-C. Rota: *Introduction to Ordinary Differential Equations* (4th ed.), John Wiley & Sons, Inc., New York, 1989.

Bowman, F.: *Introduction to Bessel Functions*, Dover Publications, Inc., New York, 1958.

Boyce, W. E., and R. C. DiPrima: *Elementary Differential Equations* (9th ed.), John Wiley & Sons, Inc., Hoboken, NJ, 2009.

Broman, A.: *Introduction to Partial Differential Equations*, Dover Publications, Inc., New York, 1989.

Brown, J. W., and R. V. Churchill: *Complex Variables and Applications* (8th ed.), McGraw-Hill Higher Education, Boston, 2009.

—— and F. Farris: On the Laplacian, *Math. Mag.*, vol. 59, no. 4, pp. 227–229, 1986.

Buck, R. C.: *Advanced Calculus* (3d ed.), Waveland Press, Inc., Long Grove, IL, 2004.

Budak, B. M., A. A. Samarskii, and A. N. Tikhonov: *A Collection of Problems on Mathematical Physics*, Dover Publications, Inc, New York, 1988.

Byerly, W. E.: *Fourier's Series and Spherical Harmonics*, Dover Publications, Inc., New York, 2003.

Cannon, J. T., and S. Dostrovsky: *The Evolution of Dynamics, Vibration Theory from 1687 to 1742*, Springer-Verlag, New York, 1981.

377

Carslaw, H. S.: *Introduction to the Theory of Fourier's Series and Integrals* (3d ed.), Dover Publications, Inc., New York, 1952.

—— and J. C. Jaeger: *Conduction of Heat in Solids* (2d ed.), Oxford University Press, New York, 1986 (reprinted 1990).

Churchill, R. V.: *Operational Mathematics* (3d ed.), The McGraw-Hill Companies, New York, 1972.

Coddington, E. A.: *An Introduction to Ordinary Differential Equations*, Dover Publications, Inc., New York, 1989.

—— and N. Levinson: *Theory of Ordinary Differential Equations*, Krieger Publishing Co., Inc., Melbourne, FL, 1984.

Courant, R., and D. Hilbert: *Methods of Mathematical Physics*, vols. 1 and 2, John Wiley & Sons, Inc., New York, 1996.

Davis, H. F.: *Fourier Series and Orthogonal Functions*, Dover Publications, Inc., New York, 1990.

Derrick, W. R., and S. I. Grossman: *Elementary Differential Equations* (4th ed.), Addison-Wesley Educational Publishers, Inc., Reading, MA, 1997.

Erdélyi, A. (Ed.): *Higher Transcendental Functions*, vols 1–3, Krieger Publishing Co., Inc., Melbourne, FL, 1981.

Farrell, O. J., and B. Ross: *Solved Problems in Analysis as Applied to Gamma, Beta, Legendre, and Bessel Functions*, Dover Publications, Inc., New York, 1971.

Folland, G. B.: *Fourier Analysis and Its Applications*, Wadsworth, Inc., Belmont, CA, 1992.

Fourier, J.: *The Analytical Theory of Heat*, translated by A. Freeman, Dover Publications, Inc., New York, 2003.

Franklin, P.: *A Treatise on Advanced Calculus*, Dover Publications, Inc., New York, 1964.

Grattan-Guinness, I.: *Joseph Fourier, 1768–1830*, The MIT Press, Cambridge, MA, and London, 1972.

Gray, Alfred, and M. A. Pinsky: Gibbs' Phenomenon for Fourier-Bessel Series, *Expo. Math.*, vol. 11, pp. 123–135, 1993.

Gray, Andrew, and G. B. Mathews: *A Treatise on Bessel Functions and Their Applications to Physics* (2d ed.), with T. M. MacRobert, Dover Publications, Inc., New York, 1966.

Haberman, R.: *Applied Partial Differential Equations with Fourier Series and Boundary Value Problems* (4th ed.), Prentice-Hall, Inc., Upper Saddle River, NJ, 2003.

Hanna, J. R., and J. H. Rowland: *Fourier Series, Transforms, and Boundary Value Problems* (2d ed.), Dover Publications, Inc., New York, 2008.

Hayt, W. H., Jr., and J. A. Buck: *Engineering Electomagnetics* (7th ed.), McGraw-Hill Higher Education, Burr Ridge, IL, 2005.

Herivel, J.: *Joseph Fourier: The Man and the Physicist*, Oxford University Press, London, 1975.

Hewitt, E., and R. E. Hewitt: The Gibbs-Wilbraham Phenomenon: An Episode in Fourier Analysis, *Arch. Hist. Exact Sci.*, vol. 21, pp. 129–160, 1979.

Hildebrand, F. B.: *Advanced Calculus for Applications* (2d ed.), Prentice-Hall, Inc., 1976.

Hobson, E. W.: *The Theory of Spherical and Ellipsoidal Harmonics* (2d printing), Chelsea Publishing Company, Inc., New York, 1965.

Hochstadt, H.: *The Functions of Mathematical Physics*, Dover Publications, Inc., New York, 1987.

Ince, E. L.: *Ordinary Differential Equations*, Dover Publications, Inc., New York, 1956.

Jackson, D.: *Fourier Series and Orthogonal Polynomials*, Dover Publications, Inc., New York, 2004.

Jahnke, E., F. Emde, and F. Lösch: *Tables of Higher Functions* (6th ed.), The McGraw-Hill Companies, New York, 1960.

Kaplan, W.: *Advanced Calculus* (5th ed.), Addison-Wesley Publishing Company, Inc., Reading, MA, 2003.

——: *Advanced Mathematics for Engineers*, Addison-Wesley Publishing Company, Inc., Reading, MA, 1981.

——, and D. J. Lewis: *Calculus and Linear Algebra* (combined ed.), John Wiley & Sons, New York, 1971.

Kellogg, O. D.: *Foundations of Potential Theory*, Dover Publications, Inc., New York, 1974.

Kevorkian, J.: *Partial Differential Equations: Analytical Solution Techniques* (2d ed.), Springer-Verlag, New York, 1999.

Körner, T. W.: *Fourier Analysis*, Cambridge University Press, Cambridge, England, 1990.

Kreider, D. L., R. G. Kuller, D. R. Ostberg, and F. W. Perkins: *An Introduction to Linear Analysis*, Addison-Wesley Publishing Company, Inc., Reading, MA, 1966.

Lanczos, C.: *Discourse on Fourier Series*, Hafner Publishing Company, New York, 1966.

Langer, R. E.: Fourier's Series: The Genesis and Evolution of a Theory, Slaught Memorial Papers, no. 1, *Am. Math. Monthly*, vol. 54, no. 7, part 2, pp. 1–86, 1947.

Lebedev, N. N.: *Special Functions and Their Applications*, Dover Publications, Inc., New York, 1972.

——, I. P. Skalskaya, and Y. S. Uflyand: *Worked Problems in Applied Mathematics*, Dover Publications, Inc., New York, 1979.

Luke, Y. L.: *Integrals of Bessel Functions*, The McGraw-Hill Companies, New York, 1962.

McLachlan, N. W.: *Bessel Functions for Engineers* (2d ed., with corrections), Oxford University Press, London, 1961.

MacRobert, T. M.: *Spherical Harmonics* (3d ed.), with I. N. Sneddon, Pergamon Press, Ltd., Oxford, England, 1967.

Magnus, W., F. Oberhettinger, and R. P. Soni: *Formulas and Theorems for the Special Functions of Mathematical Physics* (3d ed.), Springer-Verlag, New York, 1966.

Oberhettinger, F.: *Fourier Expansions: A Collection of Formulas*, Academic Press, New York and London, 1973.

Olver, F. W. J., D. W. Lozier, R. F. Boisvert, and C. W. Clark: NIST *Handbook of Mathematical Functions*, Cambridge University Press, Cambridge, England, 2010.

Özişik, M. N.: *Boundary Value Problems of Heat Conduction*, Dover Publications, Inc., New York, 2003.

Papp, F. J.: Two Equivalent Properties for Orthonormal Sets of Functions in Complete Spaces, *Int. J. Math. Educ. Sci. Technol.*, vol. 22, pp. 147–149, 1991.

Pinsky, M. A.: *Partial Differential Equations and Boundary-Value Problems with Applications* (3d ed.), Waveland Press, Inc., Long Grove, IL, 2003.

Powers, D. L.: *Boundary Value Problems and Partial Differential Equations* (6th ed.), Elsevier Science & Technology Books, San Diego, CA, 2010.

Rainville, E. D.: *Special Functions*, Chelsea Publishing Company, Inc., New York, 1972.

——, P. E. Bedient, and R. E. Bedient: *Elementary Differential Equations* (8th ed.), Prentice-Hall, Inc., Upper Saddle River, NJ, 1997.

Rogosinski, W.: *Fourier Series* (2d ed.), Chelsea Publishing Company, Inc., New York, 1959.

Sagan, H.: *Boundary and Eigenvalue Problems in Mathematical Physics*, Dover Publications, Inc., New York, 1989.

Sansone, G., and A. H. Diamond: *Orthogonal Functions* (rev. ed.), Dover Publications, Inc., New York, 1991.

Seeley, R. T.: *An Introduction to Fourier Series and Integrals*, Dover Publications, Inc., New York, 2006.

Smirnov, V. I.: *Complex Variables-Special Functions*, Addison-Wesley Publishing Company, Inc., Reading, MA, 1964.

Sneddon, I. N.: *Elements of Partial Differential Equations*, Dover Publications, Inc., New York, 2006.

——: *Fourier Transforms*, Dover Publications, Inc., New York, 1995.

——: *Special Functions of Mathematical Physics and Chemistry* (3d ed.), Longman, New York, 1980.

——: *The Use of Integral Transforms*, The McGraw-Hill Companies, New York, 1972.

Snider, A. D.: *Partial Differential Equations*, Prentice-Hall, Inc., Upper Saddle River, NJ, 1999.

Stakgold, I.: *Boundary Value Problems of Mathematical Physics*, Society for Industrial and Applied Mathematics, Philadelphia, 2000.

——: *Green's Functions and Boundary Value Problems* (2d ed.), John Wiley & Sons, Inc., New York, 1998.

Streeter, V. L., E. B. Wylie, and K. W. Bedford: *Fluid Mechanics* (9th ed.), The McGraw-Hill Companies, New York, 1998.

Stubhaug, A.: *Niels Henrik Abel and His Times*, Springer-Verlag, Berlin, 2000.

Taylor, A. E., and W. R. Mann: *Advanced Calculus* (3d ed.), John Wiley & Sons, Inc., New York, 1983.

Temme, N. M.: *Special Functions: An Introduction to the Classical Functions of Mathematical Physics*, John Wiley & Sons, Inc., New York, 1996.

Timoshenko, S. P., and J. N. Goodier: *Theory of Elasticity* (3d ed.), The McGraw-Hill Companies, New York, 1970.

Titchmarsh, E. C.: *Eigenfunction Expansions Associated with Second-Order Differential Equations*, Oxford University Press, London, part I (2d ed.) 1962; part II, 1958.

——: *Introduction to the Theory of Fourier Integrals* (3d ed.), Chelsea Publishing Company, Inc., New York, 1986.

Tolstov, G. P.: *Fourier Series*, Dover Publications, Inc., New York, 1976.

Tranter, C. J.: *Bessel Functions with Some Physical Applications*, Hart Publishing Company, Inc., New York, 1969.

Trim, D. W.: *Applied Partial Differential Equations*, PWS-KENT Publishing Company, Boston, 1990.

Van Vleck, E. B.: The Influence of Fourier's Series upon the Development of Mathematics, *Science*, vol. 39, pp. 113–124, 1914.

Watson, G. N.: *A Treatise on the Theory of Bessel Functions* (2d ed.), Cambridge University Press, Cambridge, England, 1995.

Weinberger, H. F.: *A First Course in Partial Differential Equations with Complex Variables and Transform Methods*, Dover Publications, Inc., New York, 1995.

Whittaker, E. T., and G. N. Watson: *A Course of Modern Analysis* (4th ed.), Cambridge University Press, Cambridge, England, 1996.

Zygmund, A.: *Trigonometic Series* (2d ed.), vols. I and II, Cambridge University Press, Cambridge, England, 1988.

SOME FOURIER SERIES EXPANSIONS

Some of the Fourier series expansions found in this book are listed on this and the following page.

Fourier Cosine Series

$$x = \frac{\pi}{2} - \frac{4}{\pi} \sum_{n=1}^{\infty} \frac{\cos(2n-1)x}{(2n-1)^2} \qquad (0 < x < \pi)$$

$$\pi - x = \frac{\pi}{2} + \frac{4}{\pi} \sum_{n=1}^{\infty} \frac{\cos(2n-1)x}{(2n-1)^2} \qquad (0 < x < \pi)$$

$$x^2 = \frac{c^2}{3} + \frac{4c^2}{\pi^2} \sum_{n=1}^{\infty} \frac{(-1)^n}{n^2} \cos \frac{n\pi x}{c} \qquad (0 < x < c)$$

$$x^4 = \frac{\pi^4}{5} + 8 \sum_{n=1}^{\infty} (-1)^n \frac{(n\pi)^2 - 6}{n^4} \cos nx \qquad (0 < x < \pi)$$

$$\cos ax = \frac{2a \sin a\pi}{\pi} \left[\frac{1}{2a^2} + \sum_{n=1}^{\infty} \frac{(-1)^{n+1}}{n^2 - a^2} \cos nx \right] \qquad (0 < x < \pi),$$

where $a \neq 0, \pm 1, \pm 2, \ldots$

$$\cosh ax = \frac{\sinh a\pi}{a\pi} \left[1 + 2a^2 \sum_{n=1}^{\infty} \frac{(-1)^n}{a^2 + n^2} \cos nx \right] \qquad (0 < x < \pi),$$

where $a \neq 0$

$$\sin x = \frac{2}{\pi} - \frac{4}{\pi} \sum_{n=1}^{\infty} \frac{\cos 2nx}{4n^2 - 1} \qquad (0 < x < \pi)$$

Fourier Sine Series

$$1 = \frac{4}{\pi} \sum_{n=1}^{\infty} \frac{\sin(2n-1)x}{2n-1} \qquad (0 < x < \pi)$$

$$x = 2 \sum_{n=1}^{\infty} \frac{(-1)^{n+1}}{n} \sin nx \qquad (0 < x < \pi)$$

$$\pi - x = 2 \sum_{n=1}^{\infty} \frac{\sin nx}{n} \qquad (0 < x < \pi)$$

$$x^2 = 2c^2 \sum_{n=1}^{\infty} \left[\frac{(-1)^{n+1}}{n\pi} - 2 \frac{1-(-1)^n}{(n\pi)^3} \right] \sin \frac{n\pi x}{c} \qquad (0 < x < c)$$

$$x(2c - x) = \frac{32 \, c^2}{\pi^3} \sum_{n=1}^{\infty} \frac{1}{(2n-1)^3} \sin \frac{(2n-1)\pi x}{2c} \qquad (0 < x < 2c)$$

$$x^3 = 2 \sum_{n=1}^{\infty} (-1)^{n+1} \frac{(n\pi)^2 - 6}{n^3} \sin nx \qquad (0 < x < \pi)$$

$$x(\pi^2 - x^2) = 12 \sum_{n=1}^{\infty} \frac{(-1)^{n+1}}{n^3} \sin nx \qquad (0 < x < \pi)$$

$$x(1 - x^2) = \frac{12}{\pi^3} \sum_{n=1}^{\infty} \frac{(-1)^{n+1}}{n^3} \sin n\pi x \qquad (0 < x < 1)$$

$$x(x - 1)(x - 2) = \frac{12}{\pi^3} \sum_{n=1}^{\infty} \frac{\sin n\pi x}{n^3} \qquad (0 < x < 1)$$

$$\cos \pi x = \frac{8}{\pi} \sum_{n=1}^{\infty} \frac{n}{4n^2 - 1} \sin 2n\pi x \qquad (0 < x < 1)$$

$$\sinh ax = \frac{2 \sinh a\pi}{\pi} \sum_{n=1}^{\infty} (-1)^{n+1} \frac{n}{a^2 + n^2} \sin nx \qquad (0 < x < \pi)$$

Fourier Series

$$e^{ax} = \frac{\sinh a\pi}{a\pi} + \frac{2 \sinh a\pi}{\pi} \sum_{n=1}^{\infty} \frac{(-1)^n}{a^2 + n^2} (a \cos nx - n \sin nx) \qquad (-\pi < x < \pi),$$

where $a \neq 0$

$$e^x = \frac{\sinh c}{c} + 2 \sinh c \sum_{n=1}^{\infty} \frac{(-1)^n}{c^2 + (n\pi)^2} \left(c \cos \frac{n\pi x}{c} - n\pi \sin \frac{n\pi x}{c} \right) \qquad (-c < x < c)$$

SOLUTIONS OF SOME REGULAR STURM-LIOUVILLE PROBLEMS

The eigenvalues and normalized eigenfunctions, together with weight functions, of some of the regular Sturm-Liouville problems solved in this book are listed in appendix.

1. $X'' + \lambda X = 0,$ $\qquad X'(0) = 0,$ $\qquad hX(c) + X'(c) = 0$ $\qquad (h > 0).$

 Solutions: Weight function $p(x) = 1$;

$$\lambda_n = \alpha_n^2, \qquad \phi_n(x) = \sqrt{\frac{2h}{hc + \sin^2 \alpha_n c}} \cos \alpha_n x \qquad (n = 1, 2, \ldots),$$

where $\qquad\qquad\qquad\qquad \tan \alpha_n c = \dfrac{h}{\alpha_n}$ $\qquad (\alpha_n > 0).$

2. $X'' + \lambda X = 0,$ $\qquad X(0) = 0,$ $\qquad hX(1) + X'(1) = 0$ $\qquad (h > 0).$

 Solutions: Weight function $p(x) = 1$;

$$\lambda_n = \alpha_n^2, \qquad \phi_n(x) = \sqrt{\frac{2h}{h + \cos^2 \alpha_n}} \sin \alpha_n x \qquad (n = 1, 2, \ldots),$$

where $\qquad\qquad\qquad\qquad \tan \alpha_n = -\dfrac{\alpha_n}{h}$ $\qquad (\alpha_n > 0).$

3. $(xX')' + \dfrac{\lambda}{x} X = 0,$ $\qquad X'(1) = 0,$ $\qquad X(b) = 0.$

 Solutions: Weight function $p(x) = \dfrac{1}{x}$;

$$\lambda_n = \alpha_n^2, \qquad \phi_n(x) = \sqrt{\frac{2}{\ln b}} \cos(\alpha_n \ln x) \qquad (n = 1, 2, \ldots),$$

where $\qquad\qquad\qquad\qquad \alpha_n = \dfrac{(2n - 1)\pi}{2 \ln b}.$

4. $(xX')' + \dfrac{\lambda}{x}X = 0,$ $X(1) = 0,$ $X(b) = 0.$

   Solutions: Weight function $p(x) = \dfrac{1}{x}$;

$$\lambda_n = \alpha_n^2, \quad \phi_n(x) = \sqrt{\dfrac{2}{\ln b}}\sin(\alpha_n \ln x) \quad (n = 1, 2, \ldots),$$

   where

$$\alpha_n = \dfrac{n\pi}{\ln b}.$$

5. $(xX')' + \dfrac{\lambda}{x}X = 0,$ $X'(1) = 0,$ $hX(b) + X'(b) = 0$ $(h > 0).$

   Solutions: Weight function $p(x) = \dfrac{1}{x}$;

$$\lambda_n = \alpha_n^2, \quad \phi_n(x) = \sqrt{\dfrac{2hb}{hb\ln b + \sin^2(\alpha_n \ln b)}}\cos(\alpha_n \ln x) \quad (n = 1, 2, \ldots),$$

   where

$$\tan(\alpha_n \ln b) = \dfrac{hb}{\alpha_n} \quad (\alpha_n > 0).$$

6. $X'' + \lambda X = 0,$ $X'(0) = 0,$ $X(c) = 0.$

   Solutions: Weight function $p(x) = 1$;

$$\lambda_n = \alpha_n^2, \quad \phi_n(x) = \sqrt{\dfrac{2}{c}}\cos\alpha_n x \quad (n = 1, 2, \ldots),$$

   where

$$\alpha_n = \dfrac{(2n-1)\pi}{2c}.$$

7. $X'' + \lambda X = 0,$ $X(0) = 0,$ $X'(c) = 0.$

   Solutions: Weight function $p(x) = 1$;

$$\lambda_n = \alpha_n^2, \quad \phi_n(x) = \sqrt{\dfrac{2}{c}}\sin\alpha_n x \quad (n = 1, 2, \ldots),$$

   where

$$\alpha_n = \dfrac{(2n-1)\pi}{2c}.$$

8. $X'' + \lambda X = 0,$ $X(0) = 0,$ $X(1) - X'(1) = 0.$

   Solutions: Weight function $p(x) = 1$;

$$\lambda_0 = 0, \quad \lambda_n = \alpha_n^2 \quad (n = 1, 2, \ldots),$$

$$\phi_0(x) = \sqrt{3}\,x, \quad \phi_n(x) = \dfrac{\sqrt{2(\alpha_n^2 + 1)}}{\alpha_n}\sin\alpha_n x \quad (n = 1, 2, \ldots),$$

   where

$$\tan\alpha_n = \alpha_n \quad (\alpha_n > 0).$$

9. $X'' + \lambda X = 0,$ $hX(0) - X'(0) = 0$ $(h > 0),$ $X(1) = 0.$

    Solutions: Weight function $p(x) = 1$;

$$\lambda_n = \alpha_n^2, \qquad \phi_n(x) = \sqrt{\frac{2h}{h + \cos^2 \alpha_n}} \, \sin \alpha_n (1 - x) \qquad (n = 1, 2, \ldots),$$

where

$$\tan \alpha_n = -\frac{\alpha_n}{h} \qquad (\alpha_n > 0).$$

10. $(x^2 X')' + \lambda X = 0,$ $X(1) = 0,$ $X(b) = 0.$

    Solutions: Weight function $p(x) = 1$;

$$\lambda_n = \frac{1}{4} + \alpha_n^2, \qquad \phi_n(x) = \sqrt{\frac{2}{x \ln b}} \, \sin(\alpha_n \ln x) \qquad (n = 1, 2, \ldots),$$

where

$$\alpha_n = \frac{n\pi}{\ln b}.$$

SOME FOURIER-BESSEL SERIES EXPANSIONS

Some of the Fourier-Bessel series expansions found in this book are listed in this appendix.

1. $1 = \dfrac{2}{c} \displaystyle\sum_{j=1}^{\infty} \dfrac{J_0(\alpha_j x)}{\alpha_j J_1(\alpha_j c)}$ $(0 < x < c)$,

where $J_0(\alpha_j c) = 0$ $(\alpha_j > 0)$.

2. $x = \dfrac{2}{3} + 2 \displaystyle\sum_{j=2}^{\infty} \left[\alpha_j J_0(\alpha_j) - \int_0^{\alpha_j} J_0(s)\, ds \right] \dfrac{J_0(\alpha_j x)}{\alpha_j^3 [J_0(\alpha_j)]^2}$ $(0 < x < 1)$,

where $J_1(\alpha_j) = 0$ $(\alpha_j > 0)$.

3. $f(x) = \begin{cases} x^4 & \text{when} \quad 0 < x < 1, \\ 0 & \text{when} \quad 1 < x < 2, \end{cases}$ and $f(1) = \dfrac{1}{2}$.

$$f(x) = \dfrac{1}{2} \sum_{j=1}^{\infty} \dfrac{\alpha_j J_5(\alpha_j)\, J_4(\alpha_j x)}{(\alpha_j^2 - 4)\, [J_4(2\alpha_j)]^2} \qquad (0 < x < 2),$$

where $J_4'(2\alpha_j) = 0$ $(\alpha_j > 0)$.

4. $x = 2 \displaystyle\sum_{j=1}^{\infty} \left[1 - \dfrac{1}{\alpha_j^2 J_1(\alpha_j)} \int_0^{\alpha_j} J_0(s)\, ds \right] \dfrac{J_0(\alpha_j x)}{\alpha_j J_1(\alpha_j)}$ $(0 < x < 1)$,

where $J_0(\alpha_j) = 0$ $(\alpha_j > 0)$.

5. $x^2 = \dfrac{c^2}{2} + 4 \displaystyle\sum_{j=2}^{\infty} \dfrac{J_0(\alpha_j x)}{\alpha_j^2 J_0(\alpha_j c)}$ $(0 < x < c)$,

where $J_1(\alpha_j c) = 0$ $(\alpha_j > 0)$.

6. $f(x) = \begin{cases} 1 & \text{when} \quad 0 < x < 1, \\ 0 & \text{when} \quad 1 < x < 2, \end{cases}$ and $f(1) = \dfrac{1}{2}$.

$$f(x) = \dfrac{1}{2} \sum_{j=1}^{\infty} \dfrac{J_1(\alpha_j)\, J_0(\alpha_j x)}{\alpha_j\, [J_1(2\alpha_j)]^2} \qquad (0 < x < 2),$$

where $J_0(2\alpha_j) = 0$ $(\alpha_j > 0)$.

7. $x^2 = \dfrac{2}{c} \displaystyle\sum_{j=1}^{\infty} \dfrac{(\alpha_j c)^2 - 4}{\alpha_j^3 J_1(\alpha_j c)} J_0(\alpha_j x) \qquad (0 < x < c),$

where $\qquad\qquad\qquad J_0(\alpha_j c) = 0 \qquad (\alpha_j > 0).$

8. $c^2 - x^2 = \dfrac{8}{c} \displaystyle\sum_{j=1}^{\infty} \dfrac{J_0(\alpha_j x)}{\alpha_j^3 J_1(\alpha_j c)} \qquad (0 < x < c),$

where $\qquad\qquad\qquad J_0(\alpha_j c) = 0 \qquad (\alpha_j > 0).$

9. $1 = \dfrac{2}{c} \displaystyle\sum_{j=1}^{\infty} \dfrac{1}{\alpha_j} \cdot \dfrac{J_1(\alpha_j c) J_0(\alpha_j x)}{[J_0(\alpha_j c)]^2 + [J_1(\alpha_j c)]^2} \qquad (0 < x < c),$

where $\qquad h J_0(\alpha_j c) + (\alpha_j c) J_0'(\alpha_j c) = 0 \qquad (h > 0, \ \alpha_j > 0).$

10. $f(x) = \begin{cases} x & \text{when} \ \ 0 < x < 1, \\ 0 & \text{when} \ \ 1 < x < 2, \end{cases} \qquad \text{and} \quad f(1) = \dfrac{1}{2}.$

$$f(x) = 2 \sum_{j=1}^{\infty} \frac{\alpha_j J_2(\alpha_j) J_1(\alpha_j x)}{(4\alpha_j^2 - 1) [J_1(2\alpha_j)]^2} \qquad (0 < x < 2),$$

where $\qquad\qquad\qquad J_1'(2\alpha_j) = 0 \qquad (\alpha_j > 0).$

11. $x^n = 2 \displaystyle\sum_{j=1}^{\infty} \dfrac{\alpha_j J_{n+1}(\alpha_j) J_n(\alpha_j x)}{(\alpha_j^2 - n^2)[J_n(\alpha_j)]^2} \qquad (n = 1, 2, \ldots; \ 0 < x < 1),$

where $\qquad\qquad\qquad J_n'(\alpha_j) = 0 \qquad (\alpha_j > 0).$

12. $x = 2 \displaystyle\sum_{j=1}^{\infty} \dfrac{J_1(\alpha_j x)}{\alpha_j J_2(\alpha_j)} \qquad (0 < x < 1),$

where $\qquad\qquad\qquad J_1(\alpha_j) = 0 \qquad (\alpha_j > 0).$

INDEX

Note: Page numbers followed by *n* refer to footnotes.